Fodor's

Central Islip Public Library
33 Hawthorne Avenue
Central Islip, NY 11722

ESSENTIAL
SOUTH AFRICA

D1127370

Welcome to South Africa

Lions freely roam vast game reserves such as Kruger National Park, vineyards stretch across the Cape Winelands, and mountains cascade into the sea along miles of beaches. In addition to dream safaris and romantic honeymoons, South Africa offers modern cities with thriving arts and dining scenes. South Africans are welcoming, and the country's emergence from a turbulent past provides a dramatic history lesson and the promise of something new every time you visit. As you plan your travels, please confirm that places are still open and let us know when we need to make updates by writing to us at editors@fodors.com.

TOP REASONS TO GO

★ **Wildlife:** The "Big Five"—lion, elephant, rhino, leopard, Cape buffalo—and many more.

★ **Scenery:** From the soaring Drakensberg Range to the endless Kalahari Desert.

★ **Cities:** Cape Town, Johannesburg, and Durban are vibrant cultural centers.

★ **Wine:** World-renowned viticulture, beautiful Cape Dutch architecture, and charming hotels.

★ **Beaches:** Surf, sand, endangered penguins, and abundant whale-watching from the shore.

★ **African Culture:** A diverse population (Zulu and Xhosa predominate) speaks 11 languages.

Contents

MAPS

Chapter 1

EXPERIENCE
SOUTH AFRICA

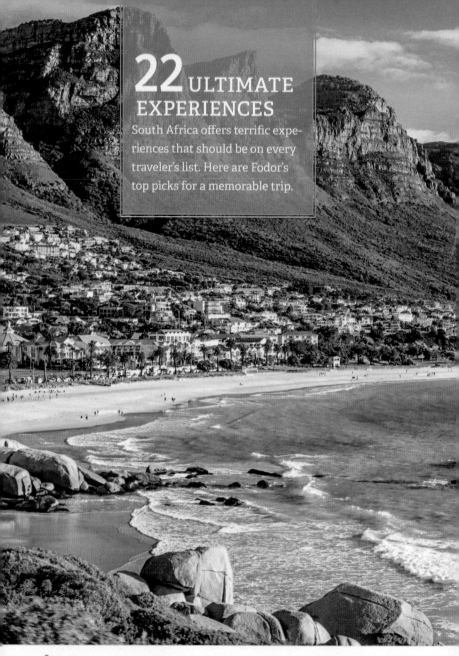

22 ULTIMATE EXPERIENCES

South Africa offers terrific experiences that should be on every traveler's list. Here are Fodor's top picks for a memorable trip.

1 Enjoy Cape Town

South Africa's "Mother City" spreads magnificently around Table Mountain. Its popular V&A Waterfront is a vibrant setting for many of the city's top hotels and restaurants. *(Ch. 3)*

2 Get to Know Nelson Mandela

See his grave in the Eastern Cape, the cell where he was imprisoned for 18 years on Robben Island, and the house where he lived in Soweto until 1961. *(Ch. 3, 8, 10)*

3 Wine Tasting in the Cape Winelands

Known for Pinotage and Chenin Blanc varietals, as well as Cape Dutch architecture, South Africa's famous wineries are near Stellenbosch, Franschoek, and Paarl. *(Ch. 5)*

4 Discover the Cradle of Humankind

The bones of our ancestors have been found in the complex of limestone caves that comprise this impressive World Heritage Site northwest of Johannesburg. *(Ch. 10)*

5 Drive Along the Scenic Garden Route

The 130-mile stretch of coast from Mossel Bay to Storms River has spectacular scenery and quaint towns, and it's one of the country's top draws for driving and hiking. *(Ch. 7)*

6 Unearth the Secrets of the Kalahari Desert

The Northern Cape, the country's least populated province, is home to the native San people and a vast, semi-arid savannah that stretches into Namibia and Botswana. *(Ch. 6)*

7 Go Whale-Watching from the Shore

Hermanus harbors some of the world's best shoreside whale-watching. Southern right whales arrive here on their annual migration between June and November. *(Ch. 5)*

8 Hike the Drakensberg Mountains

The Zulu call this World Heritage Site the uKhahlambra ("Barrier of Spears"). It offers some of the most dramatic landscapes and best hiking in South Africa. *(Ch. 9)*

9 Spot the Big Five at Kruger National Park

Seeing lions, elephants, rhinos, leopards, and buffalo in their natural habitat is a breathtaking and humbling experience. *(Ch. 11)*

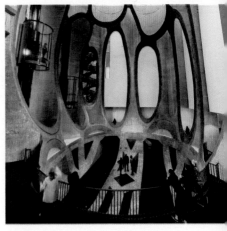

10 Explore Africa's Southernmost Point

Just over 40 miles south of Cape Town, near the southernmost point of Africa, you can look out to the sea where the waters of the Atlantic meet the Indian Ocean. *(Ch. 4)*

11 See the Zeitz Museum of Contemporary Art

With cutting-edge architecture and a focus on telling the stories of African art in insightful new ways, the Zeitz MOCAA in Cape Town is one of the world's most influential art museums. *(Ch. 3)*

12 Ascend Table Mountain

Whether you hike or climb aboard the cable car, a trip atop Cape Town's Table Mountain, especially at sunset, is a must-do activity. *(Ch. 3)*

13 Penguins! Penguins! Penguins!

Boulders Beach in False Bay is home to a colony of African Penguins. It's actually the only place in the world where you can get close to these adorable creatures. *(Ch. 4)*

14 Delve into Zulu History

Visit the battlefields of Blood River and Isandlwana in KwaZulu-Natal Province, where the Zulus fought for their longtime homeland against the invading Boers and British. *(Ch. 9)*

15 Attend a Braai

The South African BBQ is a feast of meat (steak, lamb chops, chicken, boerewors), seafood, and vegetables served with plenty of beer and wine.

16 Sunbathe on Durban's Golden Mile

With more than 320 sunny days a year, this beachy playground on the Indian Ocean offers miles and miles of glistening sands, warm waters, and robust waves. *(Ch. 9)*

17 Trace Young Gandhi's Footsteps

Sites in Durban and Johannesburg honor the great political and spiritual leader, who took his first steps toward antiviolent resistance while living in South Africa. *(Ch. 7, 8)*

18 Kayak in KwaZulu-Natal

The waterways of iSimangaliso Wetland Park teem with hippos and Nile crocs. Keep an eye out for yellow-billed storks, flamingos, and other colorful birds. Boat tours are offered, too. *(Ch. 9)*

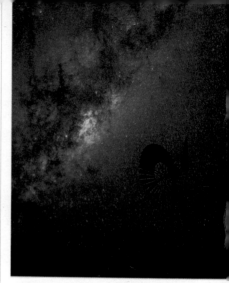

19 Find the Southern Cross in the Karoo Sky

Karoo's skies are among the clearest on Earth, where the stars seem so close you can reach out and touch them. *(Ch. 7)*

20 Learn from the Horrors of Apartheid

The ugliness of apartheid and the hope of reconciliation are revealed at Jo'burg's Apartheid Museum, Cape Town's District Six Museum, and the Nelson Mandela Museum in Mthatha. *(Ch. 3, 8)*

21 Explore a Rejuvenating Johannesburg

Trendy places in this sprawling metropolis are on the rise, including Maboneng Precinct's quirky food joints, Melville's 7th Street with the eclectic 44 Stanley nearby, and Park Corner's funky galleries. *(Ch. 10)*

22 See Seas of Wildflowers

Never-ending carpets of wildflowers—more than 3,500 species, including the celebrated African daisy—explode every spring in Namaqualand, in the Northern Cape. *(Ch. 6)*

WHAT'S WHERE

1 Cape Town.
Overlooking magnificent Table Bay, South Africa's oldest, thoroughly cosmo, multicultural city flourishes with arts, dining, and nightlife.

2 Cape Peninsula.
This rocky, 32-mile outcrop extends from Cape Town into the icy Atlantic at the Cape of Good Hope, offering beaches, penguins, whale-watching, and dramatic scenery.

3 Western Cape and Winelands. This province has tranquil farms, popular beach resorts, and stellar wine regions. Whale-watching is guaranteed along the southern Cape coast.

4 Northern Cape. This emerging tourist region offers seriously off-the-beaten-track adventures, including the spectacular Kgalagadi National Park, as well as the must-see spring flowers in Namaqualand.

5 Garden Route and the Little Karoo. The aptly named Garden Route is more than 100 miles of forested mountains, waterways, and beaches. The Little Karoo, through which threads the awesome R62, is separated from the coast by the

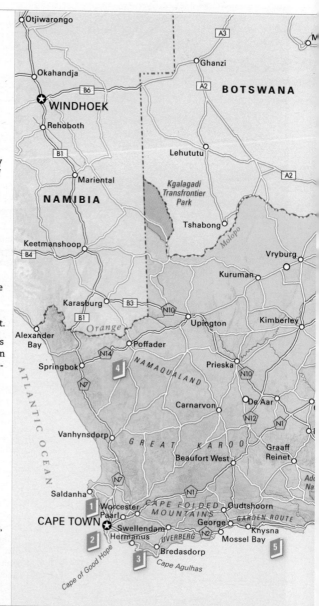

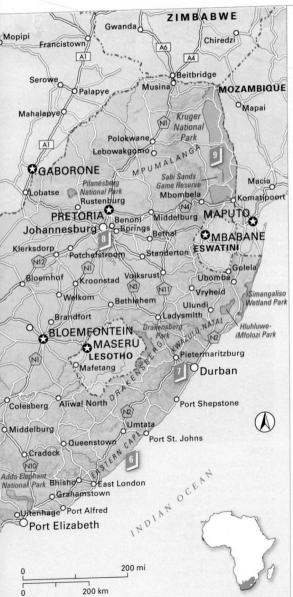

Outeniqua Mountains, famous for their ostrich farms and the hugely impressive Cango Caves.

6 Eastern Cape. Birthplace of Nelson Mandela, this province of rolling green hills offers seaside family getaways on the Wild Coast, the country's lesser-publicized but fascinating battlefields, and the nation's premier elephant reserve, Addo Elephant National Park.

7 Durban and KwaZulu-Natal. Durban's a bustling tropical port city, but inland there are battlefields where Boers, Britons, and Zulu fought to control the country. There's also the dramatic Drakensberg mountains and wildlife viewing that rivals Kruger.

8 Johannesburg. This historic gold town orbited by the capital of Pretoria and the Soweto township is also an urban African powerhouse. Do not miss the sobering but excellent Apartheid Museum, and see some of the world's oldest human fossils at the nearby Cradle of Humankind.

9 Mpumalanga and Kruger National Park. South Africa's premier wildlife destination is packed with epic battle and gold-rush history, and all the animals you wish to see.

Wildlife

SPRINGBOK
South Africa's national symbol, this small antelope is named from the Afrikaans words for "jump" and "antelope," for its penchant to leap repeatedly in the air. Some herds still roam free, and they are commonly spotted in national, provincial, and private reserves.

ELEPHANT
South Africa is home to the African Bush Elephant, aka the savanna elephant, the world's largest land mammal. One of the Big Five, you can see them at Kruger and Addo Elephant Park, among other parks and reserves.

AFRICAN BUFFALO
Many consider this horned bovine, often called the Cape buffalo, to be the most dangerous of the Big Five because of its unpredictability and speed. Kruger has the largest number, with smaller populations found in KwaZulu-Natal and Eastern Cape provinces.

HIPPO
Though they may be comical looking, hippos are actually one of Africa's most dangerous animals. Part of the Big Five, they live in parks and reserves throughout the country, including Kruger, but the best experience is at iSimangaliso Wetland Park.

LION
Africa's largest predator inhabits diverse habitats, from woodland to savannah to desert. They're mainly active at night, sleeping through the day. You'll find these regal cats—one of the Big Five—in many game reserves and parks, including Kruger, Gondwana, Aquila, and Shamwari.

LEOPARD
Leopards can vary in appearance, their coat ranging from a light tawny hue in dry areas to darker shades in the forest. One of the Big Five, they're found throughout South Africa except the Little Karoo.

PENGUIN
Some 80% of the world's endangered African penguin population resides in the Western and Eastern Capes, with the easiest colony to access located at Boulders Beach near Simon's Town. More intrepid penguin seekers should also check out Betty's Bay and Robben Island.

RHINO
Two species of these massive primeval-looking animals are found in South Africa: the black, or hook-lipped rhino, and the white, or square-lipped rhino. The best places to see them are Kruger, Hluhluwe-Imfolozi, and Pongola.

WARTHOG
Scouring for food in family groups, this member of the domestic pig family, with four large tusks emerging from the sides of its snout, is ubiquitous in South Africa's parks. They run with their long, spindly, tufted tails high in the air.

GIRAFFE
The biggest ruminant and tallest living animal, giraffes are social creatures residing in loose herds that can spread out over half a mile. Giraffes either walk or gallop and are ubiquitous in most of South Africa's parks and reserves.

South Africa's Unusual Accommodations

TURBINE HOTEL & SPA, THESEN ISLAND
The old workings of a wood-fired turbine power station were incorporated into the industrial-chic design of this five-star hotel on the Garden Route's Thesen Island. Sunny suites, lagoon views, and an awesome sun deck are included. *(Ch. 7)*

SPEEKHOUT TREE AND COTTAGE, EASTERN CAPE
A one-of-a-kind treehouse perched in a wild karee tree in the Baviaanskloof has an outdoor shower, retractable star-gazing roof, and 360-degree views. Hiking trails wander through the surrounding veld, a wildlife and birder haven. *(Ch. 8)*

SATYAGRAHA HOUSE, JOHANNESBURG
Mohandas Gandhi's house in Johannesburg, where he stayed in a minimalist attic room, is now a relaxing, retreat-like guesthouse in a serene garden; a museum explores the civil rights leader's life and legacy. *(Ch. 10)*

THE SILO, CAPE TOWN
High above Cape Town's V&A Waterfront, the luxurious Silo converts a historic grain elevator into a mod-industrial showcase, each guestroom outfitted with custom furniture and polished finishes. The city's modern art museum occupies the floors below. *(Ch. 3)*

THE TREEHOUSES AT LIONS SANDS, SABI SANDS GAME RESERVE
Watch the sunset over the African bush, enjoy a picnic dinner, then fall asleep at one of Lion Sands' three luxe treehouses with the stars twinkling above and wildlife roaming below. Perched in a leadwood tree, the Chalkley Treehouse was the property's first; it pays homage to the camp's founder, Guy Aubrey Chalkley, who legend has it also set up camp in a tree. The Kingston and Tinyeleti treehouses are just as spectacular. *(Ch. 11)*

RAWDONS COUNTRY HOTEL, THE MIDLANDS
In the heart of the lush KwaZulu-Natal Midlands, an English cottage-style haven on a lake offers lawn tennis, walking trails, a distillery, and a brewery, with beers best enjoyed at the Boars Head Pub. *(Ch. 9)*

The glass-walled Kruger Shalati is a great place to watch game.

PROTEA BREAKWATER LODGE, CAPE TOWN

An old British prison on the V&A Waterfront is the venue for this luxury hotel in Cape Town, with breathtaking views over Table Mountain and Table Bay. Markets, restaurants, and boat rides await just outside the door. *(Ch. 3)*

HOUSEBOAT MYRTLE, KNYSNA

Be the captain of your own adventure aboard a wood-trimmed, two-deck houseboat on the Knysna Lagoon. Fishing and swimming add to the fun. *(Ch. 7)*

SWELL ECO LODGE, TRANSKEI

Thatched-roofed, eco-friendly huts designed after Xhosa rondavels may look traditional outside, but inside await all the conveniences of modern life. The crashing waves of the Indian Ocean, frolicking whales, and roaming cattle create a true Wild Coast experience. *(Ch. 8)*

KRUGER SHALATI, KRUGER NATIONAL PARK

A stationary, glass-walled train sits on a historic bridge in Kruger National Park, harking back to when the park's first train visitors in the 1920s parked overnight on this precise spot. Luxurious rooms, sweeping wildlife views, and a rooftop deck pool promise an unforgettable stay. *(Ch. 11)*

KAGGA KAMMA, KAGGA KAMMA NATURE RESERVE

Who thought sleeping in a rock cave could be luxurious? Located in the Swartruggens area of the Cederberg, Kagga Kamma offers well-appointed suites carved out of an unworldly red-sandstone outcrop. Rock-art tours, nature drives, and mountain biking await nearby. *(Ch. 5)*

What to Eat and Drink in South Africa

FRIKKADELS

These beef, lamb, or chicken meatballs, served hot or cold, alone or with a sauce, are occasionally wrapped in cabbage leaves and flavored with nutmeg, reminiscent of Eastern European stuffed cabbage dishes.

POTJIE

A *potjie* (poy-kee) is a three-legged cast-iron pot as well as the name of the traditional Afrikaner stew typically prepared in it. Meat on the bone is layered with vegetables (potatoes, onions, garlic, dried beans) and cooked over low coals for hours.

ROTIS

This soft-griddled flatbread, pronounced *root*-ee , is called a salomi (sah- *low*-me) when filled with curry-mince.

MALVA PUDDING

Apricot-jam-and-vinegar sauce poured over sponge cake is the recipe for this sweet-and-sour pudding, pronounced *muhl*-vah.

ROOIBOS

Pronounced *roy*-boss, this unique South African red bush tea is full of antioxidants. "Red espresso" is a wonderfully intense version of rooibos.

SUNDOWNERS

With G&Ts long being a favored sundowner across Africa, it perhaps comes as no surprise that artisanal gin has become a craze in Cape Town. Local gins like Inverroche, Musgrave, and Bloedlemoen are all wonderful, distilling their brews with combinations of classic and local botanicals.

MELKTERT

The extremely popular *melktert* (melk-tet) is a thick custard with a flaky crust, typically dusted with cinnamon or nutmeg. It originated among 17th-century Dutch Cape migrants.

BRAAI

South Africans love to *braai* (rhymes with rye)—that is, barbecue—at any opportunity. *Boerewors* (pronounced boorah-vors; beef-and-pork sausages with heady doses of coriander seed), lamb chops, and chicken pieces are all *braai* staples . *Sosaties* (so-*sah*-teez), skewers of meat with fruit or vegetables, are also popular. Potatoes and sweet potatoes often are wrapped in foil and cooked among the coals. Another braai favorite, *rooster brood* (roosta-brewat) are sandwiches (typically white bread, cheese, onion, and tomato) cooked on the fire to the perfect consistency: crisp on the outside, moist on the inside.

SAMOOSAS

A deep-fried, triangular-shaped pastry (pronounced sah- *moo*-sah here), filled with a vegetarian or spicy meat filling, is found at nearly every corner café.

PINOTAGE

Pinotage, a cross between Pinot Noir and Cinsault, is a native cultivar and widely available.

WATERBLOMMETJIE-BREDIE

This Western Cape specialty, literally "flower stew" in Afrikaans, is made from the blooms

Potjie is a traditional Afrikaner meat stew.

of an indigenous flower that's stewed with lamb or mutton, pepper, and onions.

MOSBOLLETJIES
During the grape harvest (March and April), this soft, sweet bread (pronounced *mohss*-ball-eh-keys) is made from the grape must; it's especially irresistible when purchased fresh from the oven.

PAP
Pap (pronounced pup; also known as *samp*) is made from maize meal and cooked to varying consistencies—*krummel* (*kruh*-muhl) is dry and crumbly, whereas *stywe* (*stay*-ver) is like a stiff porridge. The texture is like couscous, and the flavor of this African staple is mild enough that it goes with everything; it's traditionally served alongside stewed vegetables or meats.

KOEKSISTERS
A braided sweet dough boiled in cinnamon-spiced syrup; finger-shaped coconut doughnuts available at Cape Malay restaurants or at carnivals are also called koeksisters (pronounced cook-sis-ter).

MALAY CUISINE
The cuisine of Cape Town's Malay community is not Malaysian, but instead mixes the flavors, spices, and preparations of Indonesia, India, Africa, and Europe. Among the favorite dishes are tomato *bredie*, a piquant stew; *biryani*, or mixed rice; and *bobotie*, curried, chopped beef with raisins, topped with a savory custard mixture—it most closely resembles English shepherd's pie, with a kick. Masala, a mix of spices, is a popular flavoring.

THE GATSBY
The Gatsby is a long hero roll packed with lettuce, tomatoes, French fries, and melted cheese; meat (usually sausage or steak) is added, and the whole thing topped with anything from mayonnaise to peri-peri (fiery Mozambican-style tomato-and-chili sauce).

BUNNY CHOW
Made famous in Durban by indentured Asian laborers who couldn't sit down to eat, this is a half or quarter white-bread loaf that's hollowed out, filled with biryani, and capped by the leftover bread.

BILTONG
This popular snack, comprising air-cured meat flavored with vinegar and spices, is found just about everywhere from roadside stands to high-end markets. Types range from beef and ostrich to game (kudu is a favorite). "Wet" biltong is a moist version.

Unique Things to Bring Home From South Africa

BEADWORK CRAFTS
Indigenous women began using glass beads imported from Europe in the 19th and 20th centuries to create handmade beaded crafts. These items are now found throughout South Africa, from street corners to souvenir shops to fine-art galleries. Animals are popular—penguins, birds, elephants, giraffes—as are candle holders, flowers, and more.

SPORTS JERSEYS
South Africans love their rugby, and you'll find official jerseys for all their teams—Blue Bulls, Springboks, or Golden Lions—throughout South Africa.

WIRE ART
This functional and decorative artwork—including bowls, vases, sculptures, and sought-after model cars—uses discarded metal and telephone wire.

HANDMADE TRADITIONAL BASKETS
Xhosa, Zulu, and other groups of women make beautifully woven, highly sought-after traditional baskets, bowls, trays, planters, and more, using ilala palm fronds, mountain grasses, sometimes combined with recycled plastic strapping, and other natural materials.

SPICES
One of the secrets to South Africa's cuisine is its melting pot of spices, from masalas for cooking curries to *aromat*, a seasoning salt used on eggs and meat, to Kalahari salt. Atlas Trading in the Bo-Kaap neighborhood of Cape Town is famed for its array of spices.

ROOIBOS TEA
This high antioxidant, flavorful tea is grown only in South Africa, typically in the mountainous Cederberg region. It's similar to hibiscus tea in taste and color. You can also find rooibos (*roy-boss*) beauty products such as hand lotion and face masks.

XHOSA SHWESHWE FABRIC
This brightly patterned, traditional cotton fabric is fashioned into vibrant clothing, tablecloths, handbags, pillowcases, and more. You can buy shweshwe fabric at most craft outlets throughout South Africa. It's also known as *isishweshwe* and *shoeshoe*.

Once used in battle, Zulu shields are now mainly used for traditional ceremonies.

ZULU SHIELD, KNIFE, OR JEWELRY

Decorative shields crafted from Nguni cow hide, spears (some with beaded handles), masks, and beaded jewelry represent the Zulu tradition, South Africa's largest ethnic group and nation, largely found in KwaZulu-Natal province. The shields were used in battle for hundreds of years, dating back to King Shaka Zulu, though these days they're brought out only for traditional ceremonies such as weddings and funerals.

ARDMORE CERAMIC ART

Founded in 1985, this quirky ceramic studio supports local artists who make exquisitely painted ceramic bowls, patterns, vases, statues, tea sets, and more. The studio can be visited in the Midlands, where you can view the artists at work, though artworks also are sold in high-end shops and galleries throughout South Africa. The artists draw on Zulu traditions and folklore, flora and fauna, history, and their own lives for inspiration.

SOUTH AFRICAN ART

The country is poised to become the art and design capital of the continent, so the purchase of a unique work of art may also be a smart investment decision. It's also a one-of-a-kind memento of your trip. You'll find beautiful artwork everywhere you go, but Cape Town, Durban, and Johannesburg have vibrant galleries. The opening of the Zeitz Museum of Contemporary Art in 2017 has contributed to Cape Town's—and the country's—artistic surge.

What's New in South Africa

SAFARIS ARE THE HOT TICKET

Safaris are always popular, but now, with travelers wary of big groups and indoor activities, many are deciding it's the perfect time to experience South Africa's wildlife bounty—amid luxurious lodgings. You can enjoy game drives in private vehicles and have exclusive-use villas (such as Phinda Homestead and Cottar's Bush Village) all to yourself, including private rangers, tracker, butler, and chef. Multigenerational families in particular are taking over entire camps for exclusivity and peace of mind. Another development is the number of activities being offered during downtime. In between game drives, you generally have six or seven hours of free time, often used for napping and lounging about. Some companies are offering a variety of in-between activities, including tennis, mountain biking, kayaking, wildlife courses, photo workshops, and more. Londolozi Founders Camp at Sabi Sands Game Reserve, for example, has baking experiences, sling-shot competitions, sandcastle building in the riverbed, and a dung-spitting contest.

SLOW-PACED, IMMERSIVE TRAVEL IS IN

With the pandemic still on people's minds, visitors are looking for ways to slow down the pace of life and enjoy the beauty along the way. Luxury train rides, such as on the famous Blue Train, hark back to a bygone era of romantic train travel. Everything is taken care of for you, including meals and activities, so all you need to do is sit back and enjoy the scenery. Hiking trails with luxury huts, such as the Dolphin Trail along the Garden Route, provide a chance to truly smell the flowers (and watch for seals and whales in the surf). Slow safaris are a recent development in which guests spend no less than four or five nights at the same lodge, allowing for an intimate view and a better understanding of the wildlife and their various ecosystems.

A REDISCOVERED LOVE OF WIDE, OPEN SPACES

With its vast landscapes and unconfined spaces, South Africa is being viewed as a prime destination for post-pandemic international travel. In fact, it's been surveyed as one of the world's most popular post-Covid escapes expressly because of its great outdoors—of which there are many. The less-traveled Northern Cape, South Africa's largest and least-populated province, is a big draw, with its striking scenery of rocky, semi-desert plains, the Kalahari Desert's red dunes, and the Atlantic Ocean's striking coastline. Highlights here include the Tswalu private game reserve in the Green Kalahari, with only two camps and a maximum of 28 people. And Namaqualand's flower season is always popular, with plenty of room for everyone to hike and camp. The Wild Coast in the Eastern Cape has miles and miles of lonely, surf-crashed beaches, while the Karoo, with its empty landscapes, has sublime star-gazing (see if you can spot the celestial "big five")—and color-saturated, sky-filling sunsets. Top all of this off with more than 20 national parks, including the world-famous Kruger and Kgalagadi, as well as many parks under provincial authority.

HOTELS MAKING A DIFFERENCE

South Africa has long been committed to conservation, and hotels are joining the fight with innovative approaches that provide life-changing experiences for visitors. The Homestead, for example, is slated to launch in 2022 on Nambiti Private Game Reserve, which is one of the country's most ambitious conservation initiatives. The eco-luxury lodge interweaves customized excursions into a stay, in which guests can hike through diverse habitats, learn about anti-poaching, and partake in other opportunities to gain a better understanding of their role in the world. And Ellerman House, a luxurious boutique hotel in Cape Town, is just one of South Africa's many hotels that donate to good causes; their ArtAngels benefit raises funds for children's education causes. And a more prosaic note, Cape Town experienced a severe water shortage in 2017, to the point of nearly running out of water, and visitors should expect provisions being made especially in hotels to minimize water usage. Cape Town is at the forefront of sustainability, finding innovative ways to manage water.

A NEW NATIONAL PARK
NE Cape Grasslands National Park, in the mountains of the Eastern Cape, will be a new high-altitude park that encompasses stunning Naude's Nek pass, South Africa's highest lying road at over 8,200 feet. The park will focus on protecting the region's rich biodiversity and endemic species, as well as water security. With plans to open within the next five years, it's also dedicated to creating jobs in the area.

A GROUNDBREAKING ARTS AND DESIGN SCENE
Spearheaded by the 2017 opening of Cape Town's world-class Zeitz Museum of Contemporary Art Africa, South Africa is fast becoming the continent's leader in art and design. The country has had to play catchup, suffering from a global boycott of its economy and culture during apartheid coupled with art capitals like Dakar and Lagos having the advantage of proximity to Europe. But more and more commercial art galleries are popping up, and museums and collectors are increasingly acquiring South African works. Among the most notable galleries is Southern Guild in Cape Town's revitalizing Silo District,

which has pioneered the continent's limited collectible design category with works that are locally made and globally important. Adding to this, the annual FNB Art Joburg in Johannesburg, the continent's most important contemporary African art exhibition, is changing the face of galleries (traditionally white, elitist, and discriminatory) with an increasing number of diverse artists and audiences. It's a convergence of art happenings that promise South Africa an important place on the world's artistic stage.

CAPE TOWN'S GIN CRAZE
Boutique gin distilleries, brands, and bars are taking Cape Town by storm. What sets this gin apart is the local, home-grown ingredients, including fynbos, the fine-leafed shrubs endemic to the region; rooibos, a local red bush tea full of antioxidants; and Karoo botanicals. Among eight craft gin distilleries in the Mother City are Hope on Hopkins in Salt River, Triple Three, and New Harbour Distillery (which is carbon neutral). The Gin Bar, showcasing an open-air Mediterranean-style courtyard accessed through a chocolate shop and offering more than 140 gins are on the menu, is credited with kicking off the craft gin revolution in Cape Town. The revolution, however, is extending beyond Cape Town, with over 50 distilleries throughout South Africa, and new ones emerging all the time. Particular bars worth stopping by to get a pulse on the craze are Royal Hotel in Riebeek Kasteel; Gin Gallery Pop UP Bar in Durban; and Social on Main in Johannesburg.

South Africa's History

THE FIRST KNOWN INHABITANTS

Two-million-year-old hominid fossils of the earliest known prehuman ancestors were found at the Sterkfontein Caves near Johannesburg, in the area now known as the Cradle of Humankind. Meanwhile, the 2015 discovery of a previously unknown human relative, *Homo Naledi,* has changed the way scientists view human evolution.

Among the descendants of these prehistoric Africans were the San, Stone Age hunter-gatherers. From AD 200 to 400, people speaking various Bantu/Nguni languages moved into the area that is now South Africa's Eastern Cape and KwaZulu-Natal provinces, bringing with them Iron Age culture. Between AD 500 and the 1300s, the Khoikhoi—pastoralists and nomadic cattle herders—moved south and interacted, as well as clashed, with the San, as did a later group of farmers from the north. As the population increased, powerful kingdoms developed.

EUROPEAN COLONIZATION

The Portuguese landed in the Cape—in 1487—when pioneering a sea route to India, but it was the Dutch who set up a refreshment station in 1652. Station commander Jan van Riebeeck later established a permanent settlement and imported a large number of enslaved people, mostly from the East Indies. The Cape Colony expanded outward, and the Khoikhoi, who lived in the Cape, were no match for European weaponry. The colonial drive caused the Khoikhoi to lose most of their livestock, grazing areas, and population, and those who remained became marginalized servants.

Over the next 100 years, the Dutch pushed farther inland, often clashing with indigenous inhabitants. Official control seesawed between the Dutch and the British until the region was formally recognized by the 1815 Congress of Vienna as a British colony.

THE GREAT TREK

The British government subsequently annexed the Cape Colony and outlawed slavery in 1834. The Boers, or Afrikaners, fled inland, setting up new communities and drawing up constitutions explicitly prohibiting racial equality in church and state.

Also known as the Voortrekkers (or pioneers), the Boers traveled into lands occupied by Bantu-speaking peoples, including the Zulu kingdom. Ruled by Shaka, the Zulus evolved during the 1820s into the most powerful Black African kingdom in southern Africa and occupied most of present-day KwaZulu-Natal.

Between 1837 and 1838, Afrikaner farmer and businessman Piet Retief attempted to negotiate a land agreement with the Zulu king, Dingane. Deceit entered the frame, and the Zulus killed Retief and more than 500 Voortrekkers.

In retaliation, a Boer raiding party defeated the Zulus at the Battle of Blood River in 1838, establishing the short-lived Republic of Natalia. Also around that time, two Boer republics were established: the South African Republic (now Mpumalanga, North West, and Limpopo provinces) and the Orange Free State (now Free State).

PROSPERITY AND CONFLICT

After the discovery of diamonds in Kimberley in 1867 and gold in 1886 outside Johannesburg, the economic center moved from the British-controlled Cape to the Boer republics, and an agricultural society was transformed into an urbanized, industrial one.

Mining companies required a great deal of labor, supplied almost exclusively by poorly treated Black, male migrant workers. The British wanted to control the entire country and thus its mineral wealth. To this end, they took over Natalia and invaded Zulu territory. They next turned their attention to the two Boer republics.

To preempt an invasion by the British, the Boers declared war in 1899. The Anglo-Boer war (now called the South African War, as it involved all races) lasted until 1902. Britain's "scorched earth" policy meant farms were burned and women and children were placed in concentration camps. The Boers eventually surrendered, but bitterness toward the British remained. By 1910 the former British colonies were united as the Union of South Africa, and Afrikaners were appointed to government positions in an attempt to reconcile English and Afrikaans speakers.

APARTHEID

In 1913, the Natives Land Act divided the country into black and white areas. Given less than 10% of land, many Blacks were forced to become migrant workers on white-owned farms and mines. Black political leaders established the South African Native National Congress in 1912, a forerunner to the African National Congress (ANC).

During World War I, South Africa, as part of the British Empire, was at war with Germany, and invaded German South West Africa (later Namibia). White Afrikaners tried to exploit this opportunity to win back their country but failed. Between the World Wars, the country was ruled by an Afrikaner-dominated government. The ANC continued to peacefully protest, with little success.

Once World War II began, the Union voted to support the British by a small majority; many Afrikaners openly supported Nazi Germany. The National Party won the 1948 election on the platform of pro-apartheid policies, the cornerstone of which—the 1950 Population Registration Act—classified all South Africans according to race, and established the segregation of schools, universities, residential areas, and public facilities.

OPPOSITION TO APARTHEID

The government introduced severe penalties for opposition to apartheid, and banned the ANC and Pan Africanist Congress (PAC)—a faction of the ANC, which went underground or into exile.

ANC leaders, Nelson Mandela among them, were arrested in 1952 and, after a lengthy detention and trial, sentenced to life imprisonment on Robben Island in 1964.

By the mid-1970s the antiapartheid struggle was revived, aided by condemnation from other countries. In 1976 several thousand Black African school children marched through the township of Soweto to protest Afrikaans becoming the language of instruction. During what became known as the Soweto Uprising, police opened fire on the crowds, killing between 200 and 500 people and injuring thousands. After this, the government was increasingly forced to rely on force to crush resistance and impose order; it never fully regained control.

By the 1980s, international condemnation of, and reaction to, apartheid had reached a fever pitch. Despite this, the government continued to arrest South African journalists, students, and other opponents, detaining them without trial. However, sanctions, boycotts, strikes, and campaigns by the liberation organizations were damaging the economy, and business began to be badly affected.

THE DAWN OF DEMOCRACY

W. de Klerk became president of South Africa in December 1989, and in his first speech to Parliament two months after his election, he made the unexpected and astonishing announcement: Mandela and other political prisoners were to be released and the ANC and PAC were to be unbanned. Talks began between the government and the liberation movements, although racial tensions remained. In 1994, South Africa had its first democratic election, and Mandela became president. South Africa rejoined the rest of the world on the political stage, resuming full participation in the United Nations and the Commonwealth, and sending its first racially integrated team to the Olympics.

A government-appointed panel called the Truth and Reconciliation Commission, headed by Anglican archbishop Desmond Tutu, began public hearings to probe human-rights violations during the apartheid years. People could talk about their experiences, and the full extent of apartheid atrocities came to light; many considered this to be an important healing process.

Mandela was succeeded in 1999 by Thabo Mbeki, a Sussex (U.K.) university–educated intellectual who continued to guide the transformation process from a white-dominated, apartheid government to a democratic one.

In 2008, the populist Jacob Zuma became leader of the ANC, succeeding Mbeki as president in 2009. Although South Africans hoped that Zuma's populist leanings would translate into action to improve the lives of the South African people, his administration was hounded by scandal and corruption.

THE PRESENT

Cyril Ramaphosa of the ANC replaced Zuma in 2018, and Zuma was imprisoned for contempt of court when he refused to testify at the Zondo Commission, which explored corruption allegations during his presidency. Civil unrest erupted in KwaZulu-Natal and Gauteng provinces in July 2021, the country's worst violence since apartheid's end.

Like the rest of the world, South Africa suffered immensely during the global Covid pandemic, with more than 90,000 deaths and a national lockdown causing dramatic economic loss, including a plummeting stock market, unemployment, and food insecurity. Major events were postponed or canceled, including sports seasons, musical performances, and annual festivals. It will take time to recover.

What to Watch and Read

JOCK OF THE BUSHVELD BY SIR JAMES PERCY FITZPATRICK
To get a sense of South Africa of colonial yore, *Jock of the Bushveld*, by Sir James Percy Fitzpatrick, was published in 1907. It's the tale of a man and his dog exploring the present-day Transvaal in the 1880s.

COCONUT
This 2007 film by Kopano Matlwa tells the story of two Black girls—one whose family is wealthy and the other who lives in poverty and abuse—and how they both struggle with identity in white suburban neighborhoods.

SHAKA ZULU
As far as movies go, this 1986 film showcases the life of Zulu King Shaka, while *Zulu* (1964) provides insight into the battle at Rorke's Drift between Zulu warriors and British soldiers.

CRY FREEDOM
Released in 1987, this movie tells the story of South African journalist Donald Woods, played by Kevin Kline, who flees the country after investigating the death of his friend, the Black activist Steve Biko, played by Denzel Washington.

INVICTUS
The 2009 film starring Morgan Freeman and Matt Damon and directed by Clint Eastwood, showcases the true tale of Nelson Mandela using rugby to unite a race-divided nation.

BLOOD DIAMOND
Featuring Leonardo DiCaprio, Djimon Hounsou, and Jennifer Connelly, this 2006 film delves into the adventure world of a priceless diamond coveted by a fisherman, a smuggler, and a syndicate of businessmen.

BLOOD AND WATER
Available on Netflix, this popular South African TV show follows a young woman searching for her missing sister who was kidnapped at birth by human traffickers. Also available on Netflix, *Tjovitjo* (2017) is a dance drama centering on an impoverished community that strives to do better through dance.

MADE IN SOUTH AFRICA
Netflix has curated a collection of over 80 South African films, series, documentaries, and reality shows that showcase some of the country's most prodigious talent.

HISTORY OF SOUTH AFRICA
This podcast deep-dives into the country's history, while "Lesser Known Somebodies" features conversations with fascinating South Africans. Both can be found at the iPhones Podcasts app.

BOOKS ON APARTHEID
A slew of books provides insight into the long and twisty road of apartheid. Alan Paton's *Cry, the Beloved Country* (1948) is the compelling and lyrical story of a Black man's country under white man's law in pre-apartheid South Africa. There have also been two film adaptations. Trevor Noah's *Born a Crime* recounts the author's childhood under apartheid. His crime? Being biracial. And *Long Walk to Freedom* (1995) is Nelson Mandela's moving autobiography detailing his extraordinary life fighting against racism.

Did You Know?

The constant presence of the "Cape Doctor" (the strong Southeasterly wind) has made beach towns near Cape Town a destination for kitesurfing.

Chapter 2

TRAVEL SMART

2

Updated by
Barbara Noe Kennedy

✈ **AIRPORTS:**
CPT, DUR, JNB

★ **CAPITAL:**
Pretoria, Cape Town,
Bloemfontein

👫 **POPULATION:**
60,266,150

$ **CURRENCY:**
Rand (ZAR)

☎ **COUNTRY CODE:**
27

⚠ **EMERGENCIES:**
10111; 10177; 112 (cell phone
emergency)

🚘 **DRIVING:**
On the left

🕑 **TIME:**
GMT +2 (7 hours ahead of
New York, 6 hours during
daylight saving time)

🚗 **MAJOR MOBILE
COMPANIES:**
Cell C, MTN, Telkom,
Vodacom

🌐 **WEB RESOURCES:**
www.southafrica.net,
www.tourism.gov.za,
www.sa-venues.com

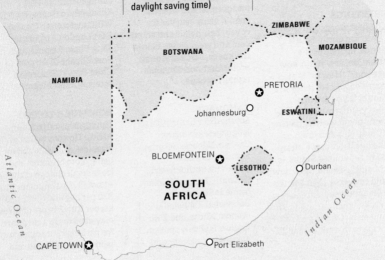

Know Before You Go

Do you need a visa to visit? What immunizations are required? Can you drink water from the tap? How about money? Are there ATMs? Should you tip in restaurants and if so, how much? What languages are spoken? We've got answers and a few tips to help you make the most of your visit to South Africa.

CAPE TOWN ADDRESSES
Street signs in Cape Town alternate between English and Afrikaans. For example, *Wale* is English and *Waal* is Afrikaans, but they mean the same thing. In Afrikaans you don't put a space between the name and the street. So an address could be Orange Street or Oranjestraat. Kaapstad is Afrikaans for Cape Town. Increasingly, streets are renamed after heroes of the struggle or use African-language names.

GREETINGS
The first words you should say to anyone in South Africa, no matter the situation, are "Hello, how are you?" "Howzit" is also commonly used. It doesn't matter if you are in a hurry—African conversations begin with a greeting. To skip this and jump to the question, as we often do in the United States, is considered rude. Slow down and converse, then ask for what you need. After a few weeks, you'll get used to it and miss it when you return home to instant demands.

CASUAL DRESS
South Africa, unlike the rest of the continent, is relatively casual. Aside from top-end restaurants, you can dress fairly casually in shorts and sandals. In national parks and by the beach, rules are even more flexible, and many people stroll into cafés right off the beach, wearing only cover-ups. *See the What to Pack feature for a more detailed packing list.*

If you're visiting a house of worship, dress modestly. This is especially true at mosques, where women should bring scarves to cover their heads and shoulders and wear skirts below the knees. Some mosques prefer that non-Muslims remain outside.

LANGUAGE
South Africa has 11 official languages: Afrikaans, English, Ndebele, Sesotho, Sesotho sa Leboa (Northern Sotho), Swazi (SiSwati), Tsonga, Tswana (same as Setswana in Botswana), Tshivenda (Venda), Xhosa, and Zulu. English is widely spoken, although road signs and other important markers often alternate between English and Afrikaans.

"Coloured" is a term commonly used in South Africa to define people of mixed ethnic origin, with ancestry from Europe or Asia, as well as with the indigenous Khoikhoi, San, and Xhosa. It also refers to a specific group of people in Cape Town, the Cape Malays or "Cape Coloureds." There are increasing calls to abolish this term and replace it with a more inclusive word.

PLACE-NAMES
Countless cities, towns, streets, parks, and more have gotten or will get new monikers, both to rid the country of names that recall the apartheid era and colonial past and to honor the previously unsung. The names in this book were accurate at the time of writing but may still change. Some notable changes include Port Elizabeth to Gqeberha; King Williamstown to Qonce; East London Airport to King Phalo Airport; and Port Elizabeth Airport to Chief Dawid Stuurman International Airport.

HOW MUCH TO TIP?
Tipping is usual in South Africa. Tip your waiter at least 10%, with 15% and up being more common, and leave small change at the bar. At hotels, tip the porter R10–R20 per bag and the housekeeper R10–R15 per day. You may need to tip a car guard for parking spots outside of paid parking garages and

lots, R5–R10 on average. Petrol attendants receive R5–R20. Pay your taxi driver 10%–20% of your fare.

Tour guides receive R20–R50 per person per day for a group tour and R100 and up per day for a private tour.

Safari staff should receive R100–R250 per couple per night. You'll need to tip your game ranger R200–R300 per day, and your tracker R100–R200 per day, though it up be higher at luxury lodges. Safari lodges generally leave three separate envelopes for tips.

IS THE WATER SAFE TO DRINK?

South Africa's tap water is among the cleanest in the world. It's perfectly safe to drink from the tap. Be sure to bring along a reusable water bottle that you can fill up and bring with you during the day.

Because of droughts, there have often been water restrictions throughout the country in recent years. The situation has improved, but please don't waste water, even if it seems plentiful.

IS SOUTH AFRICA SAFE?

South Africa is generally safe, though some areas experience a high level of crime, including pickpocketings, muggings, armed assaults, carjackings, and robberies. "Snatch and grabs," in which car windows are broken and valuables taken while cars are stopped at intersections, are common as well. Keep your car doors locked at all times.

As always, it's imperative to use common sense and be aware of your surroundings. Don't wear jewelry or display any other signs of affluence. Do not carry your wallet in your back pocket. Store your passports and other valuables in the safety deposit box at your hotel. Avoid demonstrations and large gatherings.

Know where you're headed, especially at night. If you believe you are being followed, go directly to a police station. At night avoid the areas of Berea, Hillbrow, and Yeoville in Johannesburg, Sunnyside in Pretoria, and the beachfront and wharf in Durban. In Cape Town, avoid walking from downtown hotels to the waterfront.

Wildlife viewing can also pose risks; pay attention to your guides and tour operators. Be wary of aggressive monkeys and baboons. Shark attacks have been reported in several areas, including in KwaZulu-Natal and Western Cape. Swim where shark nets are in place.

DO YOU NEED A VISA?

You may need a visa to enter South Africa, depending on your nationality. Citizens of 48 countries, including Canada, the United States, Australia, Ireland, and the UK, who are visiting South Africa for 90 days or less for tourism do not need visas.

If a visa is not required, you can stay for up to 90 days with a valid passport; passports must be valid at least 30 days after the intended date of departure and must have at least two blank pages. Children under 18 must carry a birth certificate.

DO YOU NEED IMMUNIZATIONS?

No vaccinations are required to visit South Africa, but the CDC recommends several, including hepatitis A, hepatitis B, typhoid, and measles. A proof of yellow fever vaccination is required on arrival if you're traveling from a country with yellow fever transmission. A rabies shot is also recommended (or just stay away from animals, especially stray dogs). If you are visiting a malaria region, you should take prescription medicine starting several days before your trip.

As this went to press, all international travelers arriving in South Africa are required to provide a negative Covid-19 test. Visitors are expected to follow the Covid rules set out by the government, including social distancing, washing and sanitizing hands, and compulsory wearing of masks. This situation is fluid, so be sure to double-check before you go.

HOW ABOUT MONEY?

South Africa's currency is the rand (R), with 100 cents (¢) equaling R1. Bills come in R10, R20, R50, R100, and R200 denominations, which are differentiated by color (beware of the similar color of the R50 and R200 notes). Coins are minted in 5¢, 10¢, 20¢, 50¢, R1, R2, and R5 denominations. At this writing, the rand is trading at about R15.3 to $1. You're almost always better off getting foreign currency at an ATM or exchanging money at a bank.

Getting Here

Countless cities, towns, streets, parks, and more have gotten or will get new monikers, both to rid the country of names that recall the apartheid era and to honor the previously unsung. The names in this book were accurate at time of writing but may still change.

Air

If you're arriving from abroad, you'll probably touch down at Johannesburg's OR Tambo International Airport. From here you can catch flights to other major cities and to many far-flung destinations like game lodges.

There are fairly long distances between gates and terminals at the airport, particularly between the international and domestic terminals, so clear security before stopping for a snack or shopping, as you don't want to scramble for your flight. ■ TIP→ **Allow 10–15 minutes' walking time between international and domestic terminals.**

If you're visiting a game lodge deep in the bush, you will be arriving on a small plane and will be restricted in how much you can bring. Excess luggage can usually be stored with the operator until your return. Don't just gloss over this: charter operators take weight very seriously, and some will charge you for an extra ticket if you insist on bringing excess baggage. *(see Charter Flights)*

Airfares with budget airlines, such as Lift, FlySafair, Mango, or Kulula, are more expensive than bus fares, but traveling by plane is much more efficient and comfortable, because the distances in South Africa can be vast. Be sure to book as far in advance as you can if you are going to fly or go by bus, as tickets can get more expensive as you approach the date of travel, and during peak holiday times (especially over Easter in April and December/January) tickets can sell out.

AIRPORTS

Johannesburg's OR Tambo International Airport (JNB), sometimes abbreviated O.R.T.I.A. by safari companies, is 19 km (12 miles) from the city. The airport has a tourist information desk, a V.A.T. refund office, several ATMs, and a computerized accommodations service. Porters, who wear a bright-orange-and-navy-blue uniform, work exclusively for tips of about R5 or R10 a bag. The international terminal (Terminal A) and the domestic terminal (Terminal B) are connected by a busy and fairly long walkway.

The country's other major airports are in Cape Town and Durban, but international flights departing from Cape Town often stop in Johannesburg. Cape Town International (CPT) is 19 km (12 miles) southeast of the city, and Durban's King Shaka International Airport (DUR) is 35 km (22 miles) north of the city.

If you are traveling to or from the airport at Johannesburg or Cape Town (and, to a lesser extent, Durban) be aware of the time of day. Traffic can be horrendous between 7 and 9 in the morning and between about 3:30 and 6 in the evening.

Just 40 km (25 miles) outside Johannesburg's city center in the northern suburbs, Lanseria International Airport (HLA) handles domestic scheduled flights to and from Cape Town and some charter flights to safari camps. It has a 24-hour customs and immigration counter, a café, and a high-end flight store. It's a popular alternative for visiting VIPs.

The other major cities are served by small airports that are easy to navigate. Chief David Stuurman (Gqeberha/Port Elizabeth) and King Phalo (East London) are the main airports for the Eastern

Cape, and Goringhaikona (George) serves the Garden Route. Skukuza is the only airport located in Kruger National Park and is serviced by scheduled daily non-stop flights from Johannesburg and Cape Town. The next closest airports to Kruger National Park are Kruger Mpumalanga International Airport in Mbombela (Nelspruit) and the small airports at Hoedspruit and Phalaborwa. Most airports are managed by the Airports Company of South Africa.

For more information about airports and ground transportation, see Getting Here and Around in each chapter.

INTERNATIONAL FLIGHTS

South Africa's international airline is South African Airways (SAA). It offers nonstop service between Johannesburg and New York–JFK (JFK) and Washington–Dulles (IAD), though some flights from Dulles make a stopover in Dakar, Senegal. Delta also offers nonstop service from the U.S. to South Africa.

European airlines serving South Africa include Austrian Airlines, Air France, British Airways, KLM, Lufthansa, Swiss, Turkish Airlines, and Virgin Atlantic,

Some South Africa–bound flights from U.S. cities have refueling stops en route, and sometimes those stops can be delayed. Don't plan anything on the ground right after arriving; leave yourself a cushion for a connecting flight to a game lodge.

If you are returning home with souvenirs, leave time for a V.A.T. (Value-Added Tax) inspection before you check in for your international flight check-in. And it's always a good idea to check what items you can and cannot carry onto the plane.

DOMESTIC FLIGHTS

Two major domestic airlines have flights connecting South Africa's principal airports. SA Airlink is a subsidiary of SAA, and Comair is a subsidiary of British Airways. Both airlines serve Livingstone, Zambia (for Victoria Falls); SAA serves Victoria Falls airport in Zimbabwe.

Recent years have seen an explosion of low-cost carriers serving popular domestic routes in South Africa with regularly scheduled flights. Kulula.com (owned by Comair) and Mango provide reasonably priced domestic air tickets if you book in advance.

In the summer peak season (December to February) and during school holidays, give yourself at least an extra half hour at the airport for domestic flights, as the check-in lines can be endless.

CHARTER FLIGHTS

Charter companies are a common mode of transportation when getting to safari lodges and remote destinations throughout southern Africa. These aircraft are well maintained and are almost always booked by your lodge or travel agent.

The major charter companies run daily shuttles from OR Tambo to popular tourism destinations like Kruger National Park. Keep in mind that you probably won't get to choose the charter company you fly with. The aircraft you get depends on the number of passengers flying and can vary from very small (you will sit in the copilot's seat) to a much more comfortable commuter plane.

Because of the limited space and size of the aircraft, charter carriers observe strict luggage regulations: luggage must be soft-sided and weigh no more than 44 pounds and often less; on many charter flights the weight cannot exceed 33 pounds.

Getting Here

Based at Johannesburg's OR Tambo International Airport, Federal Air (Fedair) is the largest charter air company in South Africa. Its efficient terminal has a gift shop and a unique, thatched-roof outdoor lounge. It also has hubs in Durban and Kruger Mpumalanga International Airport in Mbombela (Nelspruit). Wilderness Air is a Botswana-based charter company that will take you anywhere there's a landing strip from its base in Johannesburg's Lanseria Airport.

 ## Bus

Intercape Mainliner and Translux operate extensive bus networks that serve all major cities. The buses are comfortable, sometimes show videos, and serve tea and coffee on board. Departures are usually pretty punctual. Opt for first class if possible.

Travel times can be long. For example, Cape Town to Johannesburg takes 19 hours. The Garden Route from Cape Town to Gqeberha (Port Elizabeth) takes 12 hours. Intercape buses can be booked directly or through Computicket.

Approximate one-way prices for both major bus lines from Cape Town to Tshwane (Pretoria) are from R550; from Cape Town to Springbok from R560; Cape Town to Goringhaikona (George) from R480; Cape Town to Gqeberha (Port Elizabeth) from R500; Johannesburg to Durban from R300; and Cape Town to Durban from R670.

Car

South Africa has a superb network of highways, so driving can be a pleasure. Distances are vast, so guard against fatigue, which is an even bigger killer

than alcohol. Wildlife is also a concern, so it's best not to drive at night. Toll roads, scattered among the main routes, charge anywhere from R10 to R80. Although some accept credit card payment, it's advisable to have some rand on hand.

South Africa's Automobile Association publishes a range of maps, atlases, and travel guides, available online and at all major bookstores in South Africa.

In South African parlance, traffic lights are known as "robots," and what people refer to as the "pavement" is actually the sidewalk. Gas is referred to as petrol, and gas stations are petrol stations.

GASOLINE

Service stations that operate 24 hours are positioned at regular intervals along all major highways in South Africa. Tip the attendant R5 (more if you've filled the tank). South Africa has a choice of unleaded or leaded gasoline, and many vehicles operate on diesel—be sure you get the right fuel. Gasoline is measured in liters, and the cost is higher than in the U.S. When driving long distances, check your routes carefully, as the distances between towns—and hence gas stations—can be more than 100 miles.

PARKING

You will almost certainly need to pay for parking in cities, and it will probably run you about R10 per hour. Many towns have an official attendant (who should be wearing a vest of some sort) who will log the number of the spot you park in. You're asked to pay up front for the amount of time you expect to park. If the guard is unofficial, acknowledge them on arrival, ask them to look after your car, and pay a few rand when you return.

At pay-and-display parking lots you pay in advance; other garages expect payment at the exit. Many (such as those at shopping malls and airports) require

Driving From	To	Rte./ Distance
Cape Town	Gqeberha (Port Elizabeth)	769 km (478 miles)
Cape Town	Johannesburg	1,402 km (871 miles)
Johannesburg	Durban	583 km (361 miles)
Johannesburg	Kruger National Park	355 km (220 miles)
Kruger National Park	Victoria Falls, Zimbabwe	1,090 km (677 miles)
Johannesburg	Pretoria	65 km (40 miles)

that you pay for your parking at kiosks located near the exits. Your receipt allows you to exit.

ROAD CONDITIONS

South African roads are excellent. It's dangerous to drive at night in some rural areas because animals often stray onto the roadway. In very remote areas only the main roads are paved, while many secondary roads are made of high-quality gravel. Traffic is often light in these areas, so be sure to bring extra water and carry a spare, a jack, and a tire iron (your rental car should come with these).

South Africans tend to be aggressive drivers, thinking nothing of tailgating at high speeds and passing on blind rises. If it's safe to do so, it's expected that slower vehicles will move over onto the shoulder to let faster ones pass. Impatient drivers will flash their lights at you if you don't. When there are two lanes in each direction, the right-hand lane is for passing. In towns and cities, stay alert for minibus taxis swerving in and out of traffic without warning to pick up customers.

■ TIP→ **Always lock your car doors. Carjackings occur so frequently that certain high-risk areas are marked by permanent carjacking signs.**

RULES OF THE ROAD

South Africans drive on the left-hand side of the road, British-style. That may be confusing at first, but having the steering wheel on the right helps to remind you that the driver should be closer to the middle of the road.

Throughout the country, the speed limit is 100 kph (60 mph) or 120 kph (about 75 mph) on the open road and usually 60 kph (35 mph) or 80 kph (about 50 mph) in towns. Of course, many people drive far faster than that. Wearing seat belts is required by law, and drunk driving is taken very seriously. It is illegal to talk on a handheld mobile phone while driving.

Many cities have mini-traffic circles instead of four-way stops. These can be dangerous, particularly if you're not used to them. In theory, the first vehicle to the circle has the right-of-way; otherwise yield to the right. In practice, keep your wits about you at all times. In most cities, traffic lights are on poles at the side of the street. In Johannesburg, the lights are at the far side of each intersection.

RENTAL CARS

Renting a car gives you the freedom to roam freely and set your own timetable. Most of Cape Town's most popular destinations are an easy drive from the City Bowl. Many people enjoy the slow pace of exploring South Africa's Garden Route by car, or a few days meandering through the Winelands on their own.

Rental car rates are similar to those in the United States. Some companies charge more on weekends, so it's best to get a range of quotes before booking your car. Request car seats and extras such as GPS when you book, and ask

2

Travel Smart South Africa **GETTING HERE**

Getting Here

for details on what to do if you have a breakdown or other emergency.

When comparing prices, make sure you're getting the same thing. Some companies quote prices without insurance, some include 80% or 90% coverage, and some quote with 100% protection. Get all terms in writing before you leave on your trip.

Most major international companies have offices in cities and at international airports. The range of vehicles is the same as you'd find at home. There's no need to rent a four-wheel-drive vehicle, as all roads are paved, including those in Kruger National Park, but for the best game-viewing, an SUV or 4x4 gives you a higher outlook.

Maui Motorhome Rentals offers fully equipped motor homes, camper vans, and 4x4 vehicles, many of which come totally equipped for a bush sojourn. Prices start at around R1,500 per day in low season (January–August), not including insurance.

You can often save some money by booking a car through a broker, who will access the car from one of the main agencies. Smaller, local agencies often give a much better price, but the car must be returned in the same city. This is popular in Cape Town but not so much in other centers.

You can drive in South Africa for up to six months on any English-language license. To rent a car you need to be 18 years or older and have held a driver's license for a year or more (requirements vary by company, car category, and location). International drivers under 25 can rent from some companies but will pay a premium. You need to get special permission to take rental cars into neighboring countries (including Lesotho and eSwatini/Swaziland). Do this when you book rather than when you arrive at the rental office. Most companies allow additional drivers, but some charge extra.

In South Africa it's necessary to buy special insurance if you plan to cross the border into neighboring countries. CDW and TDW (collision damage waiver and theft-damage waiver) are optional on domestic rentals.

Leave ample time to return your car when your trip is over. You shouldn't feel rushed when settling your bill. Be sure to get a copy of your receipt.

🚆 Train

Shosholoza Meyl operates an extensive system of passenger trains along eight routes that connect all major cities and many small towns in South Africa. Departures are usually limited to three per week. Distances are vast, so many journeys require overnight travel.

The service is good and the trains are safe and well maintained, but this is far from a luxury option. The exception is Premier Classe, the luxury service that runs between Johannesburg and Cape Town. There will soon be a Cape Town–Oudtshoorn route; and a Cape Town–Durban–Johannesburg route. In Premier Classe, sleeping compartments accommodate up to four travelers. Compartments include air-conditioning, bedding, and limited room service.

Tourist Class (the old First Class) has two-sleeper and four-sleeper compartments. Don't expect air-conditioning, heat, or a shower. Bathrooms are shared and bedding can be purchased. The dining car serves pretty ordinary food, but it's inexpensive. We do not recommend Economy Class, which is also known as "sitter class," because you spend up to 25 hours on a hard seat with up to 71 other people in the car.

The Johannesburg routes to Cape Town, Durban, and Gqeberha (Port Elizabeth) have compartments for vehicles (including 4x4s). Rates start at about R360 per person Johannesburg to Durban.

Reserve tickets in Premier Classe and Tourist Class. You can book up to 12 months in advance online, by telephone, with travel agents, and at railway stations.

A fun way to see the country is on the Shongololo Express. The train is as basic as the Shosholoza Meyl trains, but each day you pile into tour buses and explore the surroundings. Trips include the Dune Express (to the dunes of Namibia), the Good Hope (Cape Hope attractions), and the Southern Cross (four African countries). By the way, a *shongololo* is a millipede.

LUXURY TRAINS

South Africa's leisurely and divine luxury trains come complete with gold-and-brass-plated fixtures, oak paneling, and full silver service for every meal. The elegant Blue Train travels several routes, but the most popular one is between Cape Town and Tshwane (Pretoria). It departs once a week in each direction, takes 31 hours, and starts at R31,915 per person. The fare includes all meals (extravagant three-course affairs), drinks (a great selection of South African wines), and excursions (usually a two-hour stop in Kimberley). Only caviar and French Champagne are excluded. The Blue Train also goes to Kruger National Park for R42,145 per person.

Rovos Rail's *Pride of Africa* runs from Cape Town to Tshwane. Fares are R24,250 for the three-day trip in Pullman Class; fancier suites cost up to R48,900. It includes all excursions, sumptuous meals, all drinks (except French Champagne), and excellent butler service. The *Pride of Africa* creates an atmosphere of Victorian colonial charm (no cell phones or laptops in public spaces), and is the only luxury train in the world in which you can open the windows.

Rovos also has a nine-day Namibia Safari, including a visit to a cheetah conservation project, starting at R125,000 for the Pullman Suite. There's also a 15-day epic Cape Town–Dar es Salaam adventure offered in February, July, September, and October. Prices can reach R119,700 for the Royal Suite on the six-night, seven-day trip from Cape Town to Victoria Falls.

Essentials

🌐 Customs and Duties

Visitors may bring in new or used gifts and souvenirs up to a total value of R5,000 duty-free. Duty-free allowances of tobacco and alcoholic beverages are also limited.

The United States is a signatory to CITES, a wildlife protection treaty, and therefore does not allow the importation of living or dead endangered animals or their body parts, such as rhino horns or ivory. Check to determine whether you need a permit to bring in zebra skins or other tourist products.

🍽 Dining

South Africa's cities and towns are full of dining options, from chain restaurants like the popular Nando's to chic cafés and fine-dining restaurants. Children are welcome in all restaurants, but don't expect toys and games as in American restaurants.

Indian food and Cape Malay dishes are regional favorites in Cape Town, and traditional smoked meats and sausages are available countrywide. If you love seafood, you should make a point of visiting one of the casual West Coast beach restaurants in the Western Cape, where you sit on the beach in a makeshift structure and eat course after course of seafood cooked on an open fire.

The restaurants we list are the cream of the crop in each price category. Price categories are based on the average cost of a main course at dinner (or at lunch if that is the only option). For food-related health issues, see Health.

MEALS AND MEALTIMES

In South Africa dinner is eaten at night and lunch at noon. Breakfast generally consists of something hot and eggy, but many people are moving over to muesli and fruit. South Africans may eat muffins for breakfast, but don't expect too many other morning sweets. Restaurants serve breakfast until about 11:30; a few serve breakfast all day.

If you're staying at a game lodge, your mealtimes will revolve around the game drives—usually coffee and rusks (similar to biscotti) early in the morning, more coffee and probably muffins on the first game drive, a huge brunch in the late morning, no lunch, tea and something sweet in the late afternoon before the evening game drive, cocktails and snacks on the drive, and a substantial supper, or dinner, at about 8 or 8:30.

Unless otherwise noted, the restaurants listed in this guide are open daily for lunch and dinner.

PAYING

Many restaurants accustomed to serving tourists accept credit cards, usually Visa and American Express, with MasterCard increasingly accepted. *For guidelines on tipping, see Tipping.*

RESERVATIONS AND DRESS

Most restaurants welcome casual dress, including jeans and sneakers. Very expensive restaurants and old-fashioned hotel restaurants (where colonial traditions die hard) may welcome nicer dress, but few require a jacket and tie.

WINES, BEER, AND SPIRITS

You can buy wine in supermarkets and many convenience stores. Beer is available only in bottle shops licensed to sell spirits. Most restaurants stock wine and beer, and many also offer spirits. From Saturday evening through Sunday, you can buy alcohol only in restaurants and bars. You may not take alcohol onto beaches, and it's illegal to walk down the street with an open container. You can, however, drink with a picnic or enjoy sun-downers (cocktails at sunset) in almost any public place, such as Table Mountain or Kirstenbosch. The beach rule is also somewhat relaxed at sundowner time, but be careful.

Electricity

The standard electrical current is 230 volts, 50 cycles alternating current. Wall outlets in most of the region take 15-amp plugs with three round prongs. Some take the European two narrow prongs, and a few take the straight-edged three-prong plugs, also 15 amps.

If your appliances are dual voltage—meaning they operate equally well on 110 and 220 volts—you'll need only an adapter. Most laptops and mobile phone chargers are dual voltage. Don't use 110-volt outlets marked "for shavers only" for high-wattage appliances such as hair dryers.

In remote areas (and even in some lodges) power may be solar or from a generator. This means that delivery is erratic both in voltage and supply. In even the remotest places, however, lodge staff will find a way to charge video and camera batteries, but you will receive little sympathy if you insist on using a hair dryer or electric razor.

Health

South Africa is a modern country, but Africa still poses certain health risks even in the most developed areas.

These days everyone is sun sensitive (and sun can be a big issue in South Africa), so pack plenty of your favorite sunblock and use it generously. Drink plenty of water to avoid dehydration.

The drinking water in South Africa is treated and, except in rural areas, is absolutely safe to drink. You can eat fresh fruits and salads and have ice in your drinks.

It is always wise for travelers to have medical insurance that includes emergency evacuation. Most safari operators require emergency evacuation coverage and may ask you to pay for it along with your tour. If you don't want general travel insurance, many companies offer medical-only policies.

COVID-19

COVID-19 brought travel to a virtual standstill from 2020 to 2022, but vaccinations have made travel possible again. However, each destination may have its own requirements. Travelers may have to wear a mask in some places and obey any other rules. Given how abruptly travel was curtailed at the onset of the pandemic, it's smart to purchase a travel insurance policy that will reimburse you for cancellations related to COVID-19. Not all travel insurance policies protect against pandemic-related cancellations, so always read the fine print.

MALARIA

In South Africa, the most serious health problem facing travelers is malaria, which is present in the prime game-viewing areas of Mpumalanga, Limpopo Province, and northern KwaZulu-Natal. The risk is moderate at the height of the summer and very low in winter. All travelers heading into malaria-prone regions should consult a healthcare professional at least a month before departure for advice. Malaria seems to be able to develop a resistance to new drugs pretty quickly, so the best prevention is to avoid being

Essentials

bitten by mosquitoes in the first place. After sunset, wear loose, light-colored, long-sleeve shirts, long pants, and shoes and socks. Apply mosquito repellent generously. Always sleep in a mosquito-proof room or tent, and, if possible, keep a fan going in your room. If you are pregnant or trying to conceive, avoid malaria areas entirely.

Generally speaking, the risk is much lower in the dry season (May–October) and peaks immediately after the first rains, which should be in November, but El Niño has made that a lot less predictable.

BILHARZIA

Many lakes and streams, particularly east of the watershed divide, are infected with *bilharzia* (schistosomiasis), a disease carried by parasitic worms. The microscopic fluke enters through the skin and lays eggs in blood vessels. Fast-moving water is considered safe, but still or slow-moving water is hazardous. If you've been wading or swimming in doubtful water, dry yourself off vigorously with a towel immediately upon exiting the water, as this may help to dislodge any flukes before they can burrow into your skin. If you have been exposed, purchase a course of treatment from a pharmacy. Have a checkup once you get home. Bilharzia is easily diagnosed, and it's also easily treated in the early stages.

HIV

Be aware of the dangers of becoming infected with HIV (a big problem in Africa) or hepatitis. Make sure you use a condom during a sexual encounter. They're sold in supermarkets, pharmacies, and most convenience stores. If you feel there's a possibility you've been exposed to the virus, you can get antiretroviral treatment (called post-exposure prophylaxis or PEP) from private hospitals, but you must do so within 48 hours of exposure.

RABIES

Rabies is extremely rare in domesticated animals in South Africa, but is more common in wild animals. If you are bitten by a monkey or other wild animal, seek medical attention immediately. The chance of contracting rabies is extremely small, but the consequences are so horrible that you really don't want to gamble on this one.

INSECTS AND OTHER PESTS

In the summer ticks may be a problem, even in open areas close to cities. If you intend to walk or hike anywhere, use a suitable insect repellent. After your walk, examine your body and clothes for ticks, looking carefully for pepper ticks, which are tiny but may cause tick-bite fever. If you find a tick has bitten you, do not pull it off. If you do, you may pull the body off but leave the head embedded in your skin, causing an infection. Smother the area with petroleum jelly and the tick will eventually let go, as it will be unable to breathe. You can then scrape it off with a fingernail. If you are bitten, don't panic. Most people who are bitten by ticks suffer no more than an itchy bump. If the tick was infected, the bite will swell, itch, and develop a black center. This is a sign of tick-bite fever, which usually hits after about 8 to 12 days. Symptoms may be mild or severe, depending on the patient. This disease is not usually life-threatening in healthy adults, but it's unpleasant.

As always, avoid mosquitoes. Even in nonmalarial areas they are extremely irritating. When walking anywhere in the bush, keep a lookout for snakes. Most will slither away when they feel you coming, but keep your eyes peeled. If you see one, give it a wide berth and you should be fine. Snakes usually bite only when they are taken by surprise, so you don't want to step on a napping puff adder.

TIP→ When camping, check your boots and shake out your clothes for spiders and other crawlies before getting dressed.

OVER-THE-COUNTER REMEDIES

You can buy over-the-counter medication in pharmacies and supermarkets, and you will find more general remedies in chain stores selling beauty products. Your body may not react the same way to the South African version of a product, even something as simple as a headache tablet. Bring your own supply and rely on pharmacies for emergency medication.

SHOTS AND MEDICATIONS

South Africa does not require any inoculations for entry. Travelers arriving within six days of leaving a country infected with yellow fever require a vaccination certificate. The U.S. Centers for Disease Control and Prevention (CDC) recommends that you be vaccinated against hepatitis A and B if you intend to travel to more isolated areas. Discuss cholera vaccines with your doctor.

If you are coming to South Africa for a safari, chances are you are heading to a malarial area. Only a handful of game reserves are nonmalarial. Millions of travelers take oral prophylactic drugs before, during, and after their safaris. If you're pregnant or traveling with small children, consider a nonmalarial region for your safari.

The CDC provides up-to-date information on health risks and recommended vaccinations and medications for travelers to southern Africa. In most of South Africa you need not worry about any of these, but if you plan to visit remote regions, check with the CDC's traveler's health line.

MEDICAL CARE IN SOUTH AFRICA

South African doctors are generally excellent. The equipment and training in private clinics rivals the best in the world, but public hospitals tend to suffer from overcrowding and underfunding. If you need medical treatment, ask your hotel or safari operator to recommend a hospital. In South Africa, foreigners are expected to pay in full for any medical services, so check your existing health plan to see whether you're covered while abroad, and supplement it if necessary.

On returning home, if you experience any unusual symptoms—including fever, painful eyes, backache, diarrhea, severe headache, general lassitude, or blood in urine or stool—be sure to tell your doctor where you have been. These symptoms may indicate malaria, tick-bite fever, bilharzia, or—if you've been traveling north of South Africa's borders—some other tropical malady.

 Lodging

The Tourism Grading Council of South Africa is the official accreditation and grading body for accommodations in South Africa. However, you may still find some establishments clinging to other grading systems. Hotels, bed-and-breakfasts, guesthouses, and game lodges are graded on a star rating from one to five. Grading is not compulsory, and there are many excellent establishments that are not graded. Those that are given a grade are revisited annually; however, these marks are purely subjective and reflect the comfort level and quality of the surroundings.

Essentials

Be warned that in southern Africa, words do not necessarily mean what you think they do. The term *lodge* is a particularly tricky one. A guest lodge or a game lodge is almost always an upmarket facility with loads of extra amenities. But when applied to city hotels, the term often indicates a minimum-service hotel. A backpacker lodge, however, is essentially a hostel.

There are a couple of terms you might not have heard before. A *rondavel* can be a small cabin, often in a rounded shape, and its cousin, the *banda,* can be anything from a basic stand-alone structure to a Quonset hut. Think very rustic.

Be sure you understand the hotel's cancellation policy. Some places allow you to cancel without any kind of penalty—even if you prepaid to secure a discounted rate—at least 24 hours in advance. Others require you to cancel a week in advance or penalize you the cost of one night. Small inns and B&Bs are most likely to require you to cancel far in advance. Always have written confirmation of your booking when you check in.

In South Africa, most accommodations include a hearty English breakfast in the rate. Most game lodges include all meals, or they may be all-inclusive (including alcohol as well). *All hotels listed have private bath unless otherwise noted.*

BED-AND-BREAKFASTS
B&Bs are ubiquitous in South Africa. Many are very small and have personal service. For more information, contact the Bed and Breakfast Association of South Africa. The Portfolio Collection represents more than 700 lodging options in South Africa.

FARM STAYS
The Farm Stay website lists a range of farms with self-catering or bed-and-breakfast accommodations in rural areas. Activities on offer include game-viewing, bird-watching, hiking, biking, and horse riding.

GAME LODGES
Game lodges in South Africa are often designed to fulfill your wildest wildlife fantasy. Top designers have created magical worlds. At the highest end, you can enjoy dinner under the stars on your own deck, or swap stories around the boma (outdoor eating area) at night. For some people the first glimpse of their accommodations is a thrill to rival the best game-viewing.

GUESTHOUSES
In South Africa, guesthouses are a cross between an inn and a B&B. Usually located in residential neighborhoods, they offer an intimate experience that benefits from the proprietor's tastes and interests. For example, a guesthouse manager might make special arrangements to drive you to a local attraction. Long-term visitors tend to choose guesthouses where they can meet other like-minded travelers who are interested in experiencing the country, not just checking off sites.

HOTELS
For hotels in South Africa, peak season mean peak prices. There are many international chains represented in South Africa, so check with your frequent-stay program to see if you can get a better room or better rate. It might be more fun, though, to experience a local establishment.

Most hotel rates will include breakfast in the hotel's dining room, and in South Africa that means a full array of meats, cheeses, and eggs cooked to order—a little bonus that makes it easier to ease into your touring day.

💲 Money

Because of inflation and currency fluctuations, it's difficult to give exact exchange rates. It's safe to say, though, that the region is a good value, with high-quality accommodations and food at about two-thirds or half the cost they would be at home.

A bottle of good South African wine costs about the equivalent of $9 (double or triple in a restaurant), and a meal at a prestigious restaurant won't set you back more than $50 per person. An average restaurant, with wine, might be about $40 for two. Double rooms in the country's finest hotels may cost $400 a night, but $200 is more than enough to secure high-quality lodging in most cities, and charming, spotless B&Bs or guesthouses with full breakfasts can be less than $80 in many areas.

Not everything in South Africa is cheap, especially the exclusive private game lodges in Mpumalanga, Limpopo Province, or KwaZulu-Natal. Expect to pay from $2,000 and $3,000 per couple per night, which could include a flight charter. Flights to South Africa are expensive, but the crowd of new low-cost carriers makes popular domestic routes less expensive, with most trips less than $150 one way. Taxis are uncharacteristically expensive, compared with other vacation needs.

Prices throughout this guide are given for adults. Substantially reduced fees are sometimes available for children, students, and senior citizens.

ATMS AND BANKS

South Africa has a modern banking system, with branches throughout the country and ubiquitous ATMs, especially at tourist attractions, in gas stations, and in shopping malls. Banks open at 9 in the morning weekdays and close at 3:30 in the afternoon; on Saturday they close at 11 in the morning (sometimes up to 12 or 1). Many banks can perform foreign-exchange services or international electronic transfers, but you will always get a better exchange rate from an ATM. The major South African banks are ABSA, FirstRand, Nedbank, and Standard.

If your card gets swallowed, *stay at the ATM* and call the help line number displayed. If possible, withdraw money during the day and choose ATMs with security guards present or those inside stores.

CREDIT CARDS

MasterCard and Visa are accepted almost everywhere (American Express less widely), but Diners Club and Discover are not.

It's a good idea to inform your credit-card company before you travel, especially if you're going abroad and don't travel internationally very often. Otherwise, the credit-card company might put a hold on your card owing to unusual activity—not a good thing halfway through your trip. Record all your credit-card numbers—as well as the phone numbers to call if your cards are lost or stolen—in a safe place, so you're prepared should something go wrong. MasterCard, Visa, and American Express all have general numbers you can call collect if you're abroad.

Essentials

If you plan to use your credit card for cash advances, you'll need to apply for a PIN at least two weeks before your trip. Although it's usually cheaper (and safer) to use a credit card abroad for large purchases (so you can cancel payments or be reimbursed if there's a problem), note that some credit-card companies *and* the banks that issue them add substantial percentages to all foreign transactions, whether they're in a foreign currency or not. Check on these fees before leaving home so there won't be any surprises when you get the bill.

CURRENCY AND EXCHANGE

The unit of currency in South Africa is the rand (R), with 100 cents (¢) equaling R1. Bills come in R10, R20, R50, R100, and R200 denominations, which are differentiated by color. (Beware of the similar color of the R50 and R200 notes.) Coins are minted in 5¢, 10¢, 20¢, 50¢, R1, R2, and R5 denominations.

At this writing, the rand is trading at about R15.3 to $1. It's a good bargain given the quality of lodgings, which cost probably two-thirds the price of comparable facilities in the United States.

To avoid administrative hassles, keep all foreign-exchange receipts until you leave the region, as you may need them as proof when changing any unspent local currency back into your own currency. You may not take more than R25,000 or US$10,000 in cash in or out of South Africa.

■ TIP→ **Even if a currency-exchange booth has a sign promising no commission, rest assured that there's some kind of huge, hidden fee. And as for rates, you're almost always better off getting foreign currency at an ATM or exchanging money at a bank.**

Item	Average Cost
Cup of coffee	$2
Glass of beer	$1.70–$2
Half of roasted chicken with salad and drink at a fast-food restaurant	$5–$7
Room-service sandwich in a hotel	$5–$7
2-km (1-mile) taxi ride	$6–$8

🌐 Passports

American citizens, including infants, need only a valid passport to enter South Africa for visits of up to 90 days. If your passport will expire within six months of your return date you need to renew it in advance, as South Africa won't let you enter with a soon-to-expire passport. You also need to have two blank facing pages in your passport.

Before your trip, make two copies of your passport's data page (one for someone at home and another for you to carry separately). Or scan the page and email it to yourself.

➕ Safety

South Africa is a country in transition, and as a result experiences growing pains that reveal themselves in economic inequities. This results in high crime rates. Although the majority of visitors experience a crime-free trip to South Africa, it's essential to practice vigilance and extreme care.

Crime is a problem in the whole region, particularly in large cities, and all visitors should take precautions to protect themselves. Do not walk alone at night, and exercise caution even during the day.

Avoid wearing jewelry (even costume jewelry), don't invite attention by wearing an expensive camera around your neck, and don't flash a large wad of cash. If you are toting a handbag, wear the strap across your body; even better, wear a money belt, preferably hidden from view under your clothing. When sitting at airports or at restaurants, especially outdoor cafés, make sure to keep your bag on your lap or between your legs—otherwise it may just quietly "walk off" when you're not looking. Even better, loop the strap around your leg, or clip the strap around the table or chair.

Carjacking is another problem, with armed bandits often forcing drivers out of their vehicles at traffic lights, in driveways, or during fake accidents. Always drive with your windows closed and doors locked, don't stop for hitchhikers, and park in well-lighted places. At traffic lights, leave enough space between you and the vehicle in front so you can pull into another lane if necessary. In the unlikely event you are carjacked, don't argue, and don't look at the carjacker's face. Just get out of the car, or ask to be let out of the car. Do not try to keep any of your belongings—they are all replaceable, even that laptop with all that data on it. If you aren't given the opportunity to leave the car, try to stay calm, ostentatiously look away from the hijackers so they can be sure you can't identify them, and follow all instructions. Ask again, calmly, to be let out of the car.

Many places that are unsafe in South Africa don't look like it. Make sure you know exactly where you're going. Purchase a good map and obtain comprehensive directions from your hotel, rental-car agent, or a trusted local. Taking the wrong exit off a highway into a township could lead you straight to disaster. Many cities are ringed by "no-go" areas. Learn from your hotel or the locals which areas to avoid. If you sense you have taken a wrong turn, drive toward a public area, such as a gas station, or building with an armed guard, before attempting to correct your mistake, which could just compound the problem. When parking, don't leave anything visible in the car; stow it all in the trunk—this includes clothing or shoes. As an added measure, leave the glove box open, to show there's nothing of value inside.

Before setting out on foot, ask a local, such as your hotel concierge or a shopkeeper, which route to take and how far you can safely go. Walk with a purposeful stride so you look like you know where you're going, and duck into a shop or café if you need to check a map, speak on your mobile phone, or recheck the directions you've been given.

Lone women travelers need to be particularly vigilant about walking alone and locking their rooms. South Africa has one of the world's highest rates of rape. If you do attract someone who won't take a firm but polite *no* for an answer, appeal immediately to the hotel manager, bartender, or someone else who seems to be in charge. If you have to walk a short distance alone at night, such as from the hotel reception to your room in a dark motel compound or back from a café along a main street, have a plan, carry a whistle, and know what you'll do if you are grabbed.

$ Taxes

All South African hotels pay a bed tax, which is included in quoted prices. In South Africa, the Value-Added Tax (V.A.T.), which at this writing is 15%, is included in the price of most goods and services, including hotel accommodations

Essentials

and food. To get a V.A.T. refund, foreign visitors must present their receipts (minimum of R250) at the airport and be carrying any purchased items with them or in their luggage. You must fill out Form V.A.T. 255, available at the airport V.A.T. refund office. Whatever you buy, make sure that your receipt is an original tax invoice, containing the vendor's name and address, V.A.T. registration number, and the words "tax invoice." Refunds are paid by check, which can be cashed immediately at an airport bank or refunded directly onto your credit card, with a small transaction fee. Be sure you visit the V.A.T. refund desk in the departures hall before you go through check-in procedures, and try to organize your receipts as you go, to make for easy viewing. Officials will go through your receipts and randomly ask to view your purchases.

 Tipping

Tipping is an integral part of South African life, and it's expected that you'll tip for services that you might take for granted at home. Most notable among these is getting gas at full-service stations. If the attendant simply fills your tank, tip R5; if he or she offers to clean your windshield, checks your tires, oil, or water and is generally helpful, tip R5 to R10. In restaurants, the size of the tip should depend on the quality of service, but 10% to 20% is standard unless a service charge has already been added to the bill. Give the same percentage to bartenders, taxi drivers, and tour guides.

At the end of your stay at a game lodge, you're expected to tip the ranger, the tracker, and the general staff. Different lodgings handle it differently, and

checking with the management is one way to make sure you tip properly. However, a good model to follow is to factor 10% of your total room bill. Fifty percent of this figure should go to your ranger/tracker, and 50% should go to the general staff. If you have a personal butler, factor an additional 10% (of your total tip figure). If you have your laundry done, leave R5–R10 for the laundress in a special envelope. Envelopes are usually provided in safari rooms for tipping, but it's a nice touch to bring your own note cards to write a personal message.

Informal parking attendants operate in the major cities in South Africa and even in some tourist areas. Although they often look a bit seedy, they do provide a good service, so tip them RR5 if your car is still in one piece when you return to it.

When to Go

High Season: November through February is often considered the best time to visit. Though the bush is very hot in the southern hemisphere's summer season, it's the best time to see young animals.

Low Season: May through August has unpredictable weather. The southern hemisphere winter is the best time to go on safari—vegetation is sparse and water is scarce, so it's easier to spot game congregating around water holes.

Value Season: Cape Town's best weather is between February and March, and September and October are still great months to go on safari.

What to Pack

In South Africa it's possible to experience muggy heat, bone-chilling cold, torrential thunderstorms, and scorching sun all within a couple of days. The secret is to pack lightweight clothes that you can wear in layers, and at least one lightweight fleece pullover or sweater.

Take along a warm jacket, hat, and scarf, too, especially if you're going to a private game lodge. It can get mighty cold sitting in an open Land Rover at night or on an early-morning game drive. It really and truly does get very cold in almost every part of South Africa, so don't fall into the it's-Africa-so-it-must-always-be-hot trap.

It's easy to get fried in the strong sun, especially in mile-high Johannesburg or windy Cape Town, where the air can feel deceptively cool. Pack plenty of sunscreen (SPF 30 or higher), sunglasses, and a hat. An umbrella comes in handy during those late-afternoon thunderstorms but is almost useless in Cape Town in the winter, as it will get blown inside out. Bring a raincoat or windbreaker.

Dress standards have become less rigid and more interesting since the late Nelson Mandela redefined the concept of sartorial elegance with his Madiba shirts. You can go almost anywhere in neat, casual clothes, but you can still get dolled up to go to the theater or to a nice restaurant.

It's always a good idea to have at least a couple of tissues in your bag, and moist towelettes, because there may not be a restroom (or toilet paper) when you need it. And, if you're in a safari vehicle, even on a dry day, you can get covered in dust.

Bring enough prescription medicines and a copy of your prescription if you anticipate needing a refill. South Africa's pharmacies and grocery stores are very similar to those in the States, but the brand names may be different.

Make copies of all your important documents. Leave one set in one bag, another at home, and try to save them online in a PDF file, which may be the fastest way to access data if you need to replace anything. Consider carrying a small card with emergency contact numbers on it, such as the local U.S. embassy, in case things go terribly wrong.

PACKING LIST FOR SOUTH AFRICA

- Waterproof, lightweight jacket, windbreaker, or poncho

- Sweater for cool nights and early mornings

- Quick-drying shirts and socks

- A pair of lightweight pants

- One wrinkle-free dress-up outfit

- Hiking boots or shoes that can get muddy and wet

- Waterproof sport sandals for the beach

- Swimsuit and coverup

- Insect repellent with DEET

- Day pack for game drives

- Flashlight with spare batteries

- Sunscreen with a minimum SPF 30

- Large, portable water bottle

- Hat with a brim

- Binoculars with carrying strap

- Imodium, Pepto-Bismol, and any prescriptions

- Swiss Army knife

- Zip-style plastic bags

- Toilet paper and wipes

Great Itineraries

South Africa in 7 Days

With only one week, you can still enjoy the best of South Africa, including Johannesburg and Cape Town highlights, as well as a short safari.

DAYS 1 TO 3: KRUGER NATIONAL PARK

Spend your first afternoon recovering from your long international flight by lazing around at your luxury lodge. Depending on where you stay, you may be able to arrange a massage or spa treatment during this time (it helps with the jet lag). If there's an afternoon or evening game drive, don't miss it. Meals are all arranged, and bedtime is early.

Experience your first full safari on Day 2. Have a quick jolt of caffeine before sunrise, then set out on a game drive in the wildness. Return to the lodge for lunch and a rest during the midday heat. After a proper afternoon tea of sweet and savory options, you're off in the vehicle again. Having sundowner drinks at sunset is an experience you'll never forget. After the evening drive, it's back to the lodge for drinks and dinner, where guests and guides share tales from the day.

You'll be able to fit in a morning game drive before departing the camp on Day 3. As you head back to Johannesburg, take in the sites along the Mpumalanga Panorama Route and Blyde River Canyon's breathtaking scenery. You'll arrive in Johannesburg late in the day. Turn in your rental car and take a taxi to your lodging. Shoppers might select a small B&B or guesthouse in the Melville, Parkhurst, or Maboneng neighborhoods. Rosebank's shopping malls will be short drive away. To experience life outside the cloistered environment and walk down a street or sit at a café, Melville is the bohemian choice.

Logistics: To make the most of your time, take a direct flight from OR Tambo Airport to a safari lodge in Kruger National Park. International flights usually arrive in the early morning, making it easy to board a mid-morning flight to an airfield servicing one of the private reserves like Timbavati and Sabi Sands. Rent a car for your return trip.

DAY 4: JOHANNESBURG

Take a tour of Soweto to learn about the roots of apartheid and the way entrepreneurs are changing lives within the community. A tour of Alexandra township will be just as informative but off the beaten track. Be sure to stop at the Apartheid Museum for an excellent, if sobering, taste of the country's history. Catch a late-afternoon or early-evening flight to Cape Town, where you'll spend the next two nights.

Logistics: Arrange a township tour before your trip. Choose a company that offers a pickup at your hotel so you don't have to drive.

DAY 5: CAPE TOWN

A stay at the Victoria & Alfred Waterfront puts you within strolling distance of its many attractions, but if you prefer something more authentically Cape Town, try one of the excellent guesthouses or boutique hotels in the CBD/Gardens/Tamboerskloof areas. Whichever you choose, dinner will feature Table Mountain as a backdrop.

On the following morning, take the first boat to Robben Island to see where Nelson Mandela spent decades and inhale that bracing sea air. When you return, grab a taxi to the base of Table Mountain and ride up the cable car for magnificent views. Walk a few miles on one of the trails to stretch your legs and enjoy the gorgeous fynbos plants. If you're a shopper, you could easily spend the rest of the afternoon browsing the shops in town. (The area between Wale, Bree, Hout, and St

Georges Mall is ideal.) Grab a snack in one of the numerous cafés in the same zone. The Cape Quarter in De Waterkant offers more chic shopping and cafés. Alternatively, you could rent a car to visit Kirstenbosch National Botanical Gardens to see magnificent protea plants, the national flower. In summer there are concerts on the lawn. You may even have time to dip into some nearby wine-tasting rooms before heading to Camps Bay for sunset cocktails and a stroll along the beach before heading back to town for dinner.

Logistics: Your day in Cape Town will be busy, so plan out your route ahead of time. If possible, book a guided tour to maximize your time.

DAY 6: CAPE WINELANDS
Strike out early to the university town of Stellenbosch, less than an hour from Cape Town. Check out the historic downtown's Cape Dutch architecture before settling into a typical South African B&B. (La Petit Ferme in Franschhoek has standout views.) Consider booking some spa time wherever you stay. Stop for some wine tastings at the excellent estates by Helshoogte Pass or Annandale Road, both of which areas also have wonderful lunching options. We love Tokara and Overture, depending on which area you choose.

Tips

■ Think how many times you will visit South Africa: it's probably worth splurging on a luxury fly-in camp in Kruger.

■ In Cape Town, always prepare for sudden weather changes, especially on Table Mountain. An extra layer is a good idea, even in summer.

Logistics: You don't have to rent a car to do this trip, nor do you have to spend a night in the Winelands. There are plenty of companies that offer tours that will allow you to taste wines with impunity.

DAY 7: CAPE PENINSULA
Get an early start on your last morning. Take in False Bay village gems like Kalk Bay (for its harbor) and Simon's Town (for the fantastic penguins at Boulders). Visit Cape Point before finishing up at Cape Town's airport for a flight home that evening.

Logistics: You can do all of this exploring on a guided tour if you don't want to drive yourself.

Great Itineraries

South Africa in 10 Days

With 10 days to explore, you can spend the majority of your time on safari and finish up with highlights of the Cape.

DAYS 1 AND 2: JOHANNESBURG

Start your journey in the City of Gold. A variety of excellent accommodations and activities are a highlight in this place colloquially known as "Jozi" or "Jo'burg." Many new developments within the central business district, such as the Maboneng Precinct and Braamfontein, offer a great variety of local eateries and opportunities to stroll the city streets, discovering the history and evolution of this South African icon. The museums and outdoor educational tours on offer— from paleo-anthropological interests to South Africa's more modern heritage, including the evolving Soweto and Alexandra townships—are captured in this city. On Day 2, a trip to the Cradle of Humankind would be worthwhile.

Logistics: Don't drive in Johannesburg. You can do all your local exploring on guided tours, which will maximize your time and your safety. But do rent a car and drive to Madikwe. It's only three hours on good roads; alternatively, you can arrange a transfer.

DAYS 3 AND 4: MADIKWE GAME RESERVE

Madikwe Game Reserve, on the border of Botswana, is a little more compact than Kruger National Park. It was one of the largest relocation projects in South Africa's conservation history, so it offers a slightly different safari experience. Although this is still Big Five country, you'll also see a wider variety of birdlife. Spend the early afternoon visiting a community program just outside the reserve's gates, then head to your resort and enjoy the still air of the middle of the day from your own private balcony or plunge pool. Night drives may bring out the elusive leopards or lions feasting on a kill.

Go on a morning safari on your second day before heading to Kruger National Park in the afternoon. Stay overnight along the way in Dullstroom, which is in misty-morning highland trout country. It has plenty of excellent accommodations. The early part of the drive will give you views of contemporary African villages in the country's platinum-mining belt, as well as the distant Waterberg and Pilanesberg ranges, which add awesome vistas to the drive.

Logistics: It's a long trip to Kruger from Madikwe, so you may prefer to return to Jo'burg and fly to Kruger so you can have three nights there.

DAYS 5 TO 7: KRUGER NATIONAL PARK

Rise early on Day 5 so you can meander through the scenic Blyde River Canyon and take in the views of the distant eastern Drakensberg Range. Consider visiting the Three Rondavels and God's Window, a lookout where you can see all the way to Mozambique. Stop for lunch in quaint Pilgrim's Rest, a former mining town. Enter Kruger National Park's gates long before sundown so that you have time to settle in (and avoid the fines for driving after dark). There are hundreds of accommodations in the area, and many of them offer spas, walking safaris, and local community visits in addition to game drives. Reservations should be made far in advance.

On your first full day in Kruger, take an organized guided trip at a rest camp to get your bearings and learn how to spot game. Book a dinner at a *boma* under the stars or a stargazing safari for an only-in-Africa experience. Your final day should be spent exploring the park in detail, viewing your favorite animals for as long as you wish.

Logistics: From Madikwe, it's a seven-hour drive to Mbombela. It's only about two hours from Mbombela to Pilgrim's Rest, but leave plenty of time to take in the scenery. It's a long trip back to Jo'burg by car. Consider dropping off your rental in Mbombela and flying back.

DAYS 8 TO 10: CAPE TOWN

After arriving in Cape Town and dropping your bags, you should have enough time for a stroll along the promenade at Mouille Point. Take in the V&A Waterfront and browse at the excellent market, where you'll find great local buys. Afterward, enjoy a sundowner or a sunset cruise. If you choose sightseeing, book dinner at any excellent city restaurant.

Head out early the next morning to see the highlights outside of town. Stop to shop or eat in charming Kalk Bay before seeing the penguins at Boulders Beach. At Cape Point, hike down to Old Lighthouse or check out wild Diaz Beach. (Please don't feed the baboons—it makes them aggressive and can end badly.) Head back via the Atlantic side, possibly stopping in Noordhoek Farm Village for a bite to eat before heading over Chapman's Peak Drive. Finish your long day with a sundowner at Camps Bay or dinner at one of the many establishments across the way.

Tips

■ Three nights inside a park or reserve allows you much more flexibility to relax and take in the experience. If you stay two nights at a game lodge, you'll have at most four drives.

■ You can split your stay between more than one lodge in Kruger, but the best plan is to base yourself in one place and visit others during the day.

On your final day, plan to visit both Table Mountain and Robben Island. If the wind gets in the way, head to Kirstenbosch National Botanical Garden. Either way, lace up your hiking shoes and fit in enough walking before your long flight home. There's no better place to do it.

Logistics: Whether driving or flying, make sure you get back to Johannesburg in time for an early-afternoon flight to Cape Town. For convenience, base yourself at a V&A Waterfront hotel in Cape Town or, if you want a more relaxing experience, a hotel in Gardens or Camps Bay. If you don't want to rent a car in Cape Town, there are plenty of tour companies that are eager to show you the Cape Peninsula.

Great Itineraries

Most flights to the U.S. leave in the early evening, so you can have a full day of sightseeing before your departure.

South Africa in Two Weeks

Depending on where your inbound flight lands, you can begin or end at Cape Town. Most long-haul flights allow you to start and end wherever you wish.

DAYS 1 TO 4: CAPE TOWN AND ENVIRONS

In four days, you can enjoy Cape Town's attractions at a leisurely pace. Take two days to explore the city's outdoor spaces and fabulous markets. Live music and laid-back days are enjoyed in most open spaces in summer—including the almost legendary Kirstenbosch National Botanical Garden on the backside of Table Mountain, and the Company's Garden in the city center—surrounded by museums and the antiapartheid political landmark, St George's Cathedral.

On Day 3, get an early start and set out on a day-pack hike, allowing you to take in the scenery of Table Mountain. Lions Head is a good option if time is tight. Either way, you'll be treated to spectacular views. Lunch could be a relaxing picnic on the lawn of the Roundhouse in the Glen, right below Lions Head, overlooking Camps Bay. Then hit a restaurant along trendy Bree Street for dinner.

Use Day 4 to make a full loop of the Cape Peninsula, heading out of town through Hout Bay. Make sure to drive over Chapman's Peak Drive, one of the world's most spectacular routes, then take a stroll among the penguins at Boulders Beach. Be sure to stop at Cape Point for a walk around Cape Peninsula National Park. As you loop back up the False Bay coast, consider stopping for dinner at the Harbour House in charming Kalk Bay.

Logistics: If you don't want to drive yourself around Cape Town, then tours can get you to all the same places. For a longer stay, pick a more relaxing location for your hotel than the V&A Waterfront. There are plenty of inviting guesthouses and B&Bs.

DAYS 5 TO 7: THE GARDEN ROUTE VIA THE CAPE WINELANDS

Heading out early from Cape Town on Day 5, you'll have plenty of time to linger over culinary wonders in Stellenbosch, dine on gourmet French food in Franschhoek, and stroll down the main street of Paarl to enjoy its mix of Cape Dutch, Edwardian, Victorian, and Art Deco architecture. With so many excellent guesthouses to choose from, part of the fun is deciding which fantasy accommodation suits you best—tranquil lakeside cottages to mountain retreats to historic cottages in Stellenbosch, Paarl, or Franschhoek.

Begin Day 6 with a drive to Hermanus for lunch, where you can watch whales from the shore or if you're brave, try a little shark-cage diving in Gansbaai. Spend the night in remarkable accommodations at the gorgeous Grootbos Private Nature Reserve.

The next day, head for Africa's southernmost point at Cape Agulhas. It's also called the Cape of Storms for its many shipwrecks. Nearby is Stilbaai, with 30 km (19 miles) of sandy beaches, gentle surf, and delicious seafood. Spend the night in Knysna or Plettenberg Bay. The former is packed with history, standout golf courses,

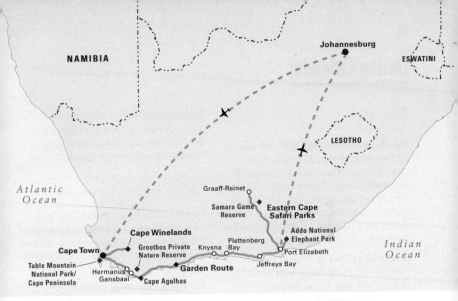

and water sports; the latter has some of the best swimming beaches in the country, framed by rugged mountain ranges.

Logistics: Rent a car in Cape Town for the remainder of your trip. You could accomplish everything with guided tours, but it's nicer to go at your own pace.

DAYS 8 TO 12: EASTERN CAPE SAFARI PARKS

An early start from your accommodation will see you cruise past the turnoff to the surfing mecca of Jeffreys Bay as you make your way to the outskirts of Gqeberha (Port Elizabeth). The remaining time is for winding down in sublime surroundings. Spend them between the Addo Elephant National Park, where you will overnight and are bound to see some of the best elephant activity on offer, and Samara Private Game Reserve, a little more than two hours inland outside the beautiful historic Karoo town of Graaff-Reinet. Samara is a remarkable reserve that has reclaimed old farming land and been restocked with indigenous game.

It has a standout cheetah-monitoring program and a resident population of rhinos. The accommodations here are as good as it gets.

Logistics: Spend two nights in Gorah Elephant Camp in Addo and two more nights in Samara Private Game Reserve.

DAYS 13 AND 14: JOHANNESBURG

After your Eastern Cape safari, you'll be relaxed and ready to head to Johannesburg, Africa's shopping mecca, for two final days of exploring. Visit the Maboneng Precinct, see the city's exciting rejuvenation, watch some theater, and take a quad bike through Soweto or art tour through Alexandra. It's a fine way to complete a fantastic trip to South Africa.

Logistics: It's a two-hour drive back to Gqeberha (Port Elizabeth), where you board a flight to Johannesburg for two final nights. There, you can see everything on guided tours.

On the Calendar

January

Cape Town Minstrels Carnival. Also known as Kaapse Klopse and Tweede Nuwe Jaar, the Cape Malay celebration sees thousands of minstrels in colorful outfits, with lots of singing and dancing to banjo beats, take to the streets of Cape Town during the first week of January. ⊕ *www. facebook.com/capetownminstrelca.*

South African Open. In mid- to late January (sometimes December), South Africa's best golfers take to the greens on one of the country's top courses. ⊕ *www. suninternational.com.*

February

Sangoma Khekhekhe's First Fruits and Snake Dance. Zulus gather in February for the "first fruits ceremony," dating back to early Zulu kings and involving traditional healers (sangoma), pythons, and cattle slaughtering. The celebration is held at private residences and some tourists are lucky enough to visit.

March

AFI Cape Town Fashion Week. The best of local and continental designers are celebrated over three days at this popular fashion festival. ⊕ *www.africanfashioninternational.com.*

Cape Town International Jazz Festival. One of the world's largest jazz festivals showcases international jazz and African music legends and discoveries alike. ⊕ *www. capetownjazzfest.com.*

Spier Light Art Festival. Creative light installations in Stellenbosch draw thousands of visitors through April. ⊕ *www. spier.co.za/events/spier-light-art.*

April

Kucheza Afrika Dance Festival. Formerly Dance Umbrella, the best contemporary choreography and dance is performed at the State Theatre in Pretoria. ⊕ *statetheatre.co.za.*

Two Oceans Marathon. Some 20,000 runners take to a scenic 56-km (35-mile) route through the Cape Peninsula on Easter Saturday. ⊕ *www.twooceansmarathon.org.za.*

Splashy Fen. South Africa's longest-running music festival (since 1990), held in KwaZulu-Natal, is a three-day musical extravaganza featuring more than 100 international acts, along with arts, crafts, food, and drink. ⊕ *splashyfen.co.za.*

May

The Sardine Run. From May through July, millions of sardines, chased by hungry predators, swim from the Atlantic's cold waters to the Indian Ocean's subtropical temperatures along the Wild Coast in the planet's greatest dive show. ⊕ *thesardinerun-info.africa-media.org.*

June

National Arts Festival. The 11-day festival anchored in Makhanda, Eastern Cape, features performances from cutting-edge to classical. It's South Africa's oldest, and largest, festival of its kind. ⊕ *nationalartsfestival.co.za.*

July

Knysna Oyster Festival. The popular 10-day festival not only celebrates the oyster, but raises money for charity. ⊕ *www.knysnaoysterfestival.co.za.*

Hollywoodbets Durban July. Horse racing and extravagant fashions converge at this internationally acclaimed event. ⊕ *www.hollywoodbetsdurbanjuly.co.za.*

September

Heritage Day. South Africa's diverse culture and heritage is celebrated on September 24 throughout the country, oftentimes with a braai (barbecue). ⊕ *www.gov.za/heritage-day.*

Macufe. Bloemfontein's Mangaung African Cultural Festival showcases African and international music, theater, dance, fine art, and crafts over 10 days in late September and early October. ⊕ *www.facebook.com/OfficialMacufe.*

Soweto Wine and Lifestyle Festival. South African wine, food, and fashion are enjoyed over three days in Soweto. ⊕ *www.facebook.com/SowetoWineFestival.*

October

Franschhoek Uncorked Festival. Special events and wine tastings highlight this mid-October wine festival showcasing Franschhoek's wine industry. ⊕ *www.franschhoekuncorked.co.za.*

Turbine Art Fair. Known as TAF, this art fair features contemporary South African art, live music, entertainment, and food for the entire family. ⊕ *turbineartfair.co.za.*

November

FNB Art Joburg. The continent's best contemporary artists convene at South Africa's first 100% Black-owned art fair, at the Sandton Convention Center. ⊕ *art-joburg.com.*

December

The Ballito Pro. One of the world's great surfing events takes place on the Durban beachfront in mid-December. ⊕ *theballitopro.com/.*

Reconciliation Day. This public holiday, on December 16, promotes national unity and reconciliation between different racial groups with parades and various festivities throughout the country. ⊕ *www.gov.za/events/reconciliation-day.*

Contacts

Air

AIRPORT INFORMATION
Airports Company of South Africa. ☎ *086/727–7888 flight information* ⊕ *www. acsa.co.za.*

CHARTER COMPANIES Federal Airlines. ☎ *011/395–9000* ⊕ *www.fedair.com.* **Wilderness Air.** ⊕ *www. wilderness-air.com.*

DOMESTIC AIRLINES
Comair. ☎ *011/921–0222 in South Africa, 800/247–9297 in U.S.* ⊕ *www. britishairways.com.* **Kulula.** ☎ *086/158–5852 in South Africa* ⊕ *www.kulula.com.* **Mango.** ☎ *011/086–6100 in Johannesburg, 021/815–4100 in Cape Town, 086/101–0002 toll-free in South Africa* ⊕ *www. flymango.com.* **SA Airlink.** ☎ *011/451–7300 in South Africa* ⊕ *www.flyairlink. com.*

INTERNATIONAL AIRPORTS Cape Town International Airport. (*CPT*). ✉ *Matroosfontein, Cape Town* ☎ *021/937–1200* ⊕ *www.capetown-airport. com.* **King Shaka International Airport.** (*DUR*). ✉ *King Shaka Dr., La Mercy* ☎ *032/436–6000* ⊕ *www.kingshakainternational.co.za.* **Lanseria International Airport.** (*HLA*). ✉ *Airport Rd., Lanseria,*

Johannesburg ☎ *011/367–0300* ⊕ *www.lanseria. co.za.* **OR Tambo International Airport.** (*JNB*). ✉ *OR Tambo Airport Rd., Johannesburg* ☎ *011/921–6262* ⊕ *www.acsa.co.za.*

Bus

BUS COMPANIES
Computicket. ☎ *0861/915–8000* ⊕ *www.tickets.computicket.com.* **Intercape Mainliner.** ☎ *021/380–4400* ⊕ *www.intercape.co.za.* **Translux.** ☎ *0861/589–282* ⊕ *www.translux.co.za.*

🚗 Car

EMERGENCY SERVICES
Emergency numbers. ☎ *112 from mobile phone, 10111 from landline, 107 in Cape Town.*

LOCAL RENTAL AGENCIES
Maui Motorhome Rentals. ☎ *011/230–5200* ⊕ *www. maui.co.za.*

🏳 Embassy

U.S. Consulate, Cape Town. ✉ *2 Reddam Ave., Westlake* ☎ *021/702–7300 in Cape Town, 703/439–2301 in U.S.* ⊕ *za.usembassy. gov.* **U.S. Embassy to South Africa.** ✉ *877 Pretorius St., Pretoria* ☎ *012/431–4000.*

Train

PASSENGER SERVICE
Premier Classe. ☎ *011/774–4555.* **Shongololo Express.** ☎ *012/315–8242* ⊕ *www. shongololo.com.* **Shosholoza Meyl.** ☎ *086/000–8888* ⊕ *www.shosholozameyl. co.za.*

LUXURY SERVICE Blue Train. ☎ *012/334–8459 in Pretoria, 021/449–2672 in Cape Town, 973/832–4384 in U.S.* ⊕ *www. bluetrain.co.za.* **Rovos Rail.** ☎ *012/315–8242* ⊕ *www. rovos.com.*

📍 Visitor Information

Cape Town Tourism. ⊕ *www.capetown.travel.* **South Africa National Parks.** ⊕ *www.sanparks.org.* **South African Tourism.** ⊕ *www.southafrica.net.* **SouthAfrica.info.** ⊕ *www. southafrica.info.* **V.A.T. Refund Office.** ☎ *011/979–0055* ⊕ *www.taxrefunds. co.za.*

Chapter 3

CAPE TOWN

3

Updated by
Mary Fawzy

⊙ Sights	🍴 Restaurants	🛏 Hotels	🛍 Shopping	🍸 Nightlife
★★★★★	★★★★★	★★★★★	★★★★★	★★★★☆

WELCOME TO CAPE TOWN

TOP REASONS TO GO

★ **City Sophistication:** This cosmopolitan city with a long historical significance has trendy shops and restaurants, and cutting-edge art and design.

★ **Table Mountain:** Towering over Cape Town, exploring the mountain is a must; take the cable car to the top or hike up various routes.

★ **Nature's Playground:** Capetonians make the most of their city's breathtaking natures-capes and the mountains and beaches, no matter the season.

★ **Markets Galore:** Cape Town's markets are informal, creative, and funky, with a good selection of food, fashion, and trinkets.

★ **Historical Heritage:** Stand in Nelson Mandela's old cell at Robben Island. Learn about apartheid's destruction of one of the country's most vibrant inner-city neighborhoods at the District Six Museum. Visit the Castle of Good Hope, South Africa's oldest building, to hear about the beginning of colonial rule in the region.

Cape Town's dynamism lies in how different neighborhoods and areas possess a unique character. Depending on what type of experience and environment you're looking for, you'll likely find a place (or many) you'll love.

1 **Cape Town City Centre.**

2 **Bo-Kaap.**

3 **Woodstock.**

4 **Observatory.**

5 **Gardens.**

6 **Tamboerskloof.**

7 **Oranjezicht.**

8 **V&A Waterfront.**

9 **Green Point.**

10 **Mouille Point.**

11 **Sea Point.**

12 **Clifton.**

13 **Camps Bay.**

14 **Table Mountain National Park.**

15 **Constantia.**

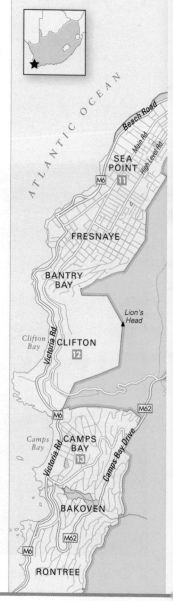

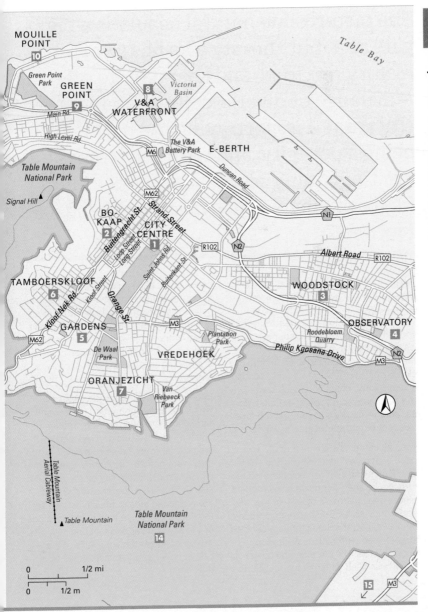

With its breathtaking mountains, lush forests, and inviting beaches, Cape Town is so much more than its good looks. The picturesque natural beauty is a big part of it, but the city also has so much history, art, food, and character to offer. A melange of diverse cultures makes the city what it is, portraying the nature of being a port city; and with that comes an exciting dining scene, another defining factor of why you'll love the so-called Mother City.

Table Mountain is vital to Cape Town's identity. It dominates the city in a way that's difficult to comprehend until you visit. Many Cape Town residents say if you get lost, "look for the mountain;" it's a great way to orientate yourself. In the afternoon, when creeping fingers of clouds spill over Table Mountain, creating a "tablecloth" effect and reach toward the city, the whole town seems to hold its breath—because in summer it brings frequent strong southeasterly winds.

The city center is a contrast of old and new; with many historic buildings still in use, Dutch and Victorian colonial architecture can be seen alongside shiny modern offices and apartment blocks. In the predominantly Malay Bo-Kaap neighborhood, the call to prayer echoes through cobbled streets lined with houses painted in bright pastels. The city's central business hub is also filled with restaurants, clubs, cafes, urban parks, galleries, shops, and imposing British monuments. Flower sellers, newspaper hawkers, and numerous markets keep street life pulsing, and every lamppost advertises another festival, concert, or cultural happening. This is a relaxed city, packed with occasions and events.

Interestingly, a lot of the city center was historically submerged underwater. Strand and Waterkant streets (meaning "beach" and "waterside," respectively) are now far from the sea; however, when they were named, they were right on the beach. Almost all the city on the seaward side of Strand and Waterkant is part of the reclaimed area of the city known as the Foreshore. If you look at old paintings of the city, you will see that originally waves lapped at the very walls of the castle, now more than half a mile from the ocean.

Unfortunately, the legacy of its terrible colonial and apartheid history is still clearly visible in the city, and there is deep inequality, with mansions on the beach on one side, and extreme poverty in informal settlements on the outskirts, known as townships. This reality is not easy to ignore, although apartheid's urban planning really tried to make it so. Alongside the strife, you can witness a rising tide of people telling their own stories and owning their resistance in many ways, through leading walking tours, organizing storytelling events, and through the art, music, and poetry that permeates the city's corners. Keeping this reality in mind can help make sense of the place, and discover the deep authenticity of the people of Cape Town, who will likely let you in with open arms if you're open to it. These community engagements make the city the dynamic and wonderful place it is.

Planning

Cape Town lies at the northern end of the Cape Peninsula, a 75-km (47-mile) tail of mountains that ends at the Cape of Good Hope. Drive 15 minutes out of town, and you'll find yourself immersed in the colonial remnants of the 18th-century Cape Dutch manors, historic wineries, and white-sand beaches backed by sheer mountains.

Everyone uses Table Mountain for orientation. Cape Town's aptly named heart, the City Bowl, fills the basin between the lower northern slopes of the mountain and the rim of a busy harbor. Though it's called interchangeably "City Centre" or "Cape Town Central," the City Bowl actually encompasses Cape Town Central as well as adjacent neighborhoods of Gardens and Bo-Kaap. Cape Town is compact, and neighborhood boundaries can be fluid, but navigation is generally not a problem.

Getting Here and Around

AIR

Cape Town International Airport (CPT) is about 19 km (12 miles) from the city center. It should take about 20 minutes to get from the airport to the city; during rush hour plan to double that. Private airport-transfer operators abound, and there is now public bus service (MyCiti) to and from the airport. All major car-rental companies have counters at the airport, and driving to the City Bowl or V&A Waterfront is straightforward in daylight. If your flight arrives after dark, consider prearranging transportation through your hotel. There is a main tourist information desk as you approach the exit from either the domestic or international terminal. Ubers are also always available around the airport and can usually be a more affordable option.

For information about airlines that fly to Cape Town, see Air in Travel Smart.

CONTACTS Cape Town International Airport. ✉ *Matroosfontein, Cape Town* ☎ *021/937–1200, 086/727–7888 flight information* ⊕ *capetown-airport.co.za.*

AIRPORT TRANSFERS

Metered taxis and shuttle services (usually minivans) are based inside the domestic baggage hall and outside the international and domestic terminals and can also be phoned for airport drop-offs. Rates vary depending on the operator, number of passengers, destination, and time of arrival. The fare for one person to the city center is R350 in a metered taxi; a group of up to four will usually pay the same rate. A surcharge of up to R50 is sometimes levied from 10 pm until early morning, and some services charge more for arrivals than for departures to cover waiting time. MyCiti, a public bus, also serves the airport, and for R90.50 it's the cheapest way to or from the airport and City Centre. ■TIP→ **Reports of over-charging are common, so discuss the fare before entering any taxi.**

BUS

Within Cape Town, MyCiti bus service now serves the entire city, including the Cape Flats. Buses run at regular 10-minute intervals during the morning rush (5 am to 9 am) and at 20-minute intervals for the rest of the day. The service is perfect for tourists because you can catch a bus into town—a short ride—and from there walk the entire city. Or you can catch a connecting bus almost anywhere, including Hout Bay, the Waterfront, and Blouberg Beach. Only prepaid cards are accepted for MyCiti (get these at kiosks in every station and at some retailers). Timetables are found at each stop and can be scanned for easy reference. These buses run until 9 or 9:30 pm. The Backpacker Bus is also an economical way to get to or from the airport or Stellenbosch winelands.

To visit other Western Cape destinations from Cape Town, Intercape Mainliner is the main option; Translux/City-to-City also provides service. Common routes from Cape Town include Johannesburg and Tshwane, Springbok, Windhoek, George, Gqeberha (Port Elizabeth), and Durban. All the main bus companies operate from the bus terminal alongside the central train station on Adderley Street, and most have their offices there.

See Bus Travel in Travel Smart for details on intercity bus companies.

CONTACTS Backpacker Bus. ✉ *Cape Town* ☎ *082/809–9185* ⊕ *www.backpackerbus. co.za.* **MyCiti.** ✉ *Cape Town* ☎ *080/065–6463* ⊕ *myciti.org.za.*

CAR

Although many locals drive, tourists may find Uber, public transportation (MyCiti buses), or taxis a better option; save the rental car for when you are getting out of town. Cape Town's roads are excellent, but getting around can be a bit confusing. Signage is inconsistent, switching between Afrikaans and English, between different names for the same road (especially highways), and between different destinations on the same route. Sometimes the signs simply vanish. ■TIP→ **Cape Town is also littered with signs indicating "Cape Town" instead of "City Centre," as well as "Kaapstad," which is Afrikaans for Cape Town.**

A good one-page map is essential and available from car-rental agencies and tourism information desks. The city is well updated on navigation apps, so using Google Maps or a GPS is another great option. Things to look out for while driving are pedestrians running across highways, speeding vehicles, and minibus taxis, which would be given the right of way. Roadblocks for document and DWI checks are also becoming more frequent.

Parking in the City Center is a nightmare. There are simply not enough parking garages, longer-stay parking spaces are scarce, and most hotels charge a small fortune for parking. There are numerous pay-and-display (i.e., put a ticket in your windshield) and pay-on-exit parking lots around the city, but parking is strictly enforced. Prices range from R8 to R12 per half hour. For central attractions like Greenmarket Square, the Company's Garden, the South African National Gallery, and the Castle of Good Hope, look for a lot around the Grand Parade on Darling Street. Picbel Parking Garage on Strand Street and the Sanlam Golden Acre Parking Garage on Adderley Street offer covered parking, and Queen Victoria Street alongside the South African Museum (and Company's Garden) sometimes has a few spaces.

The main arteries leading out of the city are the N1, which bypasses the city's Northern Suburbs en route to Franschhoek and Paarl and, ultimately, Johannesburg; and the N2, which heads out past Khayelitsha and through Somerset

West to the Overberg and the Garden Route before continuing on through the Eastern Cape to Durban and beyond. Branching off the N1, the N7 goes to Namibia. The M3 splits off from the N2 near Observatory, leading to the False Bay side of the peninsula via Claremont and Constantia; it's the main and quickest route to the beaches of Muizenberg, Kalk Bay, St James, and Simon's Town. Rush hour sees bumper-to-bumper traffic on all major arteries into the city from 6 to 9 am, and out of the city from 4 to 6:30 pm.

MOTORCYCLE AND SCOOTER

Renting a scooter or motorbike (motorcycle license and deposit required) is a good option within the city if you have a motorcycle license. Scooters can be rented from Scoot Dr. for R300 to R500 per day, and at far cheaper rates the longer you keep it.

CONTACTS Scoot Dr. ✉ *Castle Mews, 16 Newmarket St., Foreshore* ☎ *021/418–5995* ⊕ *www.scootdr.com.*

TAXI

Until the arrival of Uber, Cape Town taxis were expensive and not necessarily easily hailed. This is still the case, so if you are going old-school, don't expect to see the throngs of cabs you find in London or New York. Know that you are unlikely to hail a cab in the street, and taxis rarely have roof lights to indicate availability. If you do flag an occupied cab, the driver may radio another car for you. Your best bet is to summon a taxi by phone or head to one of the major taxi stands, such as those at the V&A Waterfront, Greenmarket Square, or either end of Adderley Street (near the Slave Lodge and outside the train station). Expect to pay R60–R70 for a trip from the city center to the Waterfront (far less if using Uber or Bolt).

In addition to the companies listed here, ask your hotel or guesthouse which company it recommends. Lodging establishments often have a relationship with particular companies and/or drivers, and this way you will be assured of safe, reliable service. If you have the app and a smartphone with data, Uber or Bolt (formerly Taxify) rides are almost always the fastest, cheapest, and best option.

CONTACTS Citi Hopper. ✉ *Cape Town* ☎ *021/936–3460* ⊕ *www.citihopper. co.za.* **Excite Taxis.** ✉ *Cape Town* ☎ *021/448–4444* ⊕ *www.excitetaxis. co.za.* **Unicab.** ✉ *Cape Town* ☎ *021/486–1600* ⊕ *www.unicab.co.za.*

TRAIN

Cape Town's train station is on Adderley Street, in City Centre, surrounded by lively rows of street vendors and a taxi stand. The station building received a complete revamp as part of the general infrastructure upgrade in 2010. The station services local, interprovincial, and the odd luxury lines (Blue Train and Rovos Rail).

Metrorail, Cape Town's commuter line, offers regular service but has issues with safety and is not recommended for most tourists.

National carrier Shosholoza Meyl runs the Trans-Karoo most days to Johannesburg. Shongololo Express runs multiday journey-tours, with its Good Hope train traveling from Cape Town through the Karoo, the Garden Route, Durban, the Drakensberg mountains and Kruger Park to Johannesburg over 15 days. And the luxurious Blue Train and Rovos Rail's *Pride of Africa* both have several departures per week for Tswhane.

For more information on all these services, see Train in Travel Smart.

Beaches

With panoramic views of mountains tumbling to the ocean, the stunning white beaches of the Cape Peninsula are a major draw for Capetonians and visitors alike.

For more information about the Cape Peninsula's Beaches, see Cape Peninsula.

Hotels

Finding lodging in Cape Town can be a nightmare during peak travel season (December through January), as many of the more reasonable accommodations are booked up. It's worth traveling between April and August, if you can, to take advantage of the "secret season" discounts that are sometimes half the high-season rate. Other reduced rates can be scored by booking directly online, checking the "Best Available Rate" at large hotels, or simply asking if any specials or discounts are available. If you arrive in Cape Town without a reservation, head for any branch of the Tourism office, which has a helpful accommodations desk.

First-time, short-term, or business visitors will want to locate themselves centrally. The historic city center is a vibrant and pedestrian-friendly place by day, but at night can feel a bit deserted and edgy, depending on where you are. Night owls may prefer to stay amid the nonstop action of Long Street or Kloof Street, or at the V&A Waterfront, with its plethora of pedestrian-friendly shopping and dining options. Boutique hotels and bed-and-breakfasts in the more residential Gardens, Tamboerskloof, and Higgovale areas are often within walking distance of attractions and dining but will be quieter and often enjoy lovely views. Options along the Atlantic Seaboard (from Mouille Point to Camps Bay) are also relatively close to the action and

(mostly) pedestrian-friendly, with the added advantage of sea and sunset views. Staying farther out on the Cape Peninsula, whether the False Bay or Atlantic side, provides the closest thing in Cape Town to a beach-vacation atmosphere despite the cold ocean waters. The Southern Suburbs, especially around Constantia, Tokai, or Newlands can make a good base from which to explore the area's wine estates as well as the peninsula, but are truly suburban, meaning you'll need a car for everything, and should plan on 25 to 45 minutes to get into town.

Most international flights arrive in the late morning, and return flights depart in the evening. Because most hotels have an 11 am checkout and 2 pm check-in, you may find yourself with a lodging gap on travel days. All hotels will hold your luggage, and most will try to accommodate you (some of the larger hotels have lounges where you can spend the hours before your flight), but in peak season you may need to organize a backup plan. Also note that many small, luxury accommodations either do not permit children or have minimum-age restrictions. Always inquire in advance if traveling with kids. Cape Town also follows the global trend of not smoking in public places. All hotels will have no-smoking rooms, and most are entirely smoke-free.

LODGING ALTERNATIVES

When South Africans travel, they often stay in guesthouses or B&Bs, which are numerous in Cape Town and range from simple and "homey" lodgings to some of the most elegant and professionally run establishments available; the latter will offer everything a hotel does but on a smaller, more personal scale. If you prefer more anonymity or want to save money, consider renting a fully furnished apartment or even a room in a shared space, especially if you're staying two or more weeks. **Airbnb** has hundreds of listings in Cape Town, and several agencies can help you make bookings.

Cape Stay offers a huge selection of accommodations to suit different needs, from very simple and affordable apartments to luxurious villas to special rates at well-known hotels, covering both Cape Town, the Cape Peninsula, and other popular Western Cape destinations.

CAPSOL has more than 2,000 high-quality, furnished, fully stocked luxury villas and apartments along the Atlantic seaboard from Cape Town to Bakoven, including Clifton, Bantry Bay, and Camps Bay. Apartments range from R3,000 to R40,000 per night, most with a minimum three-night stay depending on the season.

CONTACTS CAPSOL Luxury Villas & Apartments. ✉ *The Penthouse, 13 Totnes Ave., Camps Bay* ☎ *21/438–9644* ⊕ *www.capsol.co.za.*

Nightlife

There's plenty to do in Cape Town after dark. The city's nightlife is concentrated in a number of areas, so you can explore a different one each night or move from one hub to another. Unfortunately walking isn't always advisable, as some parts of the city are completely deserted and unsafe. Anyone who isn't very street savvy should avoid walking alone or even in pairs (especially for women) at night.

One of the safest places after dark is the V&A Waterfront, where you can choose from movies, restaurants, bars, and pubs and walk between them quite happily, as there are plenty of security guards and other people walking around. The top end of Long Street is probably the city's best-known young nightlife area. Here you'll find several blocks of bars, restaurants, and backpacker lodges that are open till the wee hours. The area bounded by Loop, Long, Wale, and Orange streets is the best place to get a feeling for Cape Town's always-changing nightclub scene, but the district known as the

Fringe—around Roeland, Harrington, and de Villiers streets—is increasingly where the club set hang out. Lower Main Road in the eclectic Observatory comes alive at night, with live music venues, bars, and restaurants buzzing with students and artsy folk. De Waterkant in Green Point is also very busy at night and is home to many of Cape Town's gay venues; if you're in the area, you can take in the Green Point strip, where restaurants and bars open out onto the streets. On weekends these bars are packed, and you'll get a good idea of how Capetonians let down their hair. Heritage Square, in Cape Town Central, hosts an ever-changing mix of bars and restaurants generally catering to a more discerning (think wine bars and microbrewery) crowd. Mouille Point's Platinum Mile and Granger Bay are also good for evening cocktails with breathtaking views over the Atlantic and onto Robben Island. Be prepared to line up to get into places, especially on a Friday night.

The weekly entertainment roundup for Cape Town is called *48 Hours* and is available all over town. Websites like ⊕ *www. capetownmagazine.com* and ⊕ *www. insideguide.co.za* are great resources, as is the "Top of the Times" in Friday's *Cape Times*, along with the *Argus* newspaper's "Tonight" section.

Cape Town is a relatively gay-friendly city. Geared toward gay (and to a far lesser extent lesbian) travelers, the site ⊕ *www. gaycapetown4u.com* provides information on events and venues in Cape Town.

Restaurants

The city's dining establishments always dominate the country's "best of" lists, while food trucks, smaller takeaway shops, and family-owned restaurants offer food that is as delicious as it is affordable—eating out in Cape Town is notoriously cheap by global standards.

This city offers a global culinary experience; French and Italian fare has long been available, but with Thai, Japanese, and Pan-Asian influences flooding in, accents of lemongrass, miso, and yuzu have become de rigueur in fine-dining kitchens. Middle Eastern cuisine is finally making some headway, and a growing interest in local and African foods is also starting to cement its presence. American foods have also been popular and easy to find, with plenty of burgers and ribs, and even chicken and waffles popping up on menus these days, not to mention a few South American and passable Mexican eateries. Sushi is also easily found, though largely limited to tuna and salmon, and often prepared with lots of drizzled mayo and sauces.

WINE

Wine lists at many restaurants reflect the enormous expansion and resurgence of the Cape wine industry, with some establishments compiling exciting selections of lesser-known gems. More and more restaurants employ a sommelier to offer guidance on wine, but diners, even in modest establishments, can expect staff to be well versed about both wine lists and menus. Wines are expensive in restaurants (often three times what you'd pay in a wineshop), and connoisseurs may be irritated by corkage charges (around R40), but only a handful of restaurants will refuse to open a bottle you bring.

TIMING AND WHAT TO WEAR

During summer months restaurants in trendier areas are geared up for late-night dining but will accept dinner orders as early as 6. In winter locals tend to dine earlier and kitchens can often close by 9:30 if customers aren't waiting. That said, there are venues that stay open late year-round, particularly at the V&A Waterfront and the Camps Bay beachfront along the Atlantic seaboard. Other areas that are meccas for food lovers include Kloof Street and Bree Street in the City Bowl up through Gardens. Many restaurants are crowded in high season, so it's best to book in advance whenever possible; top-rated restaurants can be fully booked months in advance. With the exception of a very few high-end restaurants—where a jacket is suggested but never required—the dress code in Cape Town is very casual.

Restaurant reviews have been shortened. For full information, visit Fodors.com.

RESTAURANT AND HOTEL PRICES

Restaurant prices in the reviews are the average cost of a main course at dinner, or if dinner is not served, at lunch. Hotel prices in the reviews are the lowest cost of a standard double room in high season.

What it Costs in South African rand			
$	$$	$$$	$$$$
RESTAURANTS			
under R100	R100–R150	R151–R200	over R200
HOTELS			
under R1,500	R1,500–R2,500	R2,501–R3,500	over R3,500

Safety

Cape Town is a safe city to enjoy, as long as you make certain adjustments and are careful and knowledgeable about your surroundings.

Women and couples are strongly advised not to walk in isolated places after dark. If you want to walk somewhere in the evening, make sure you do so in a large group. Keep flashy jewelry and expensive cameras hidden or don't take them with you, much as you would in any unfamiliar city. Street-based people are wrongly blamed for much of the petty crime in the city, but are usually just asking for some change or food. If you are approached for some, please respond humanely.

If you're renting a car, don't leave anything visible on the seats as windows can be smashed to snatch cell phones or bags.

At busy transportation hubs and on trains, mind your belongings and pockets. It's better to sit in a crowded car; if you suddenly find yourself alone, move to another one. Public transportation collapses after dark and is not always safe to use so it's best to use Ubers or metered taxis.

Trendy nightlife areas like Long Street and Kloof Street (which leads on via a dogleg from Long Street), and the predominantly gay nightlife scene around Greenpoint, are frequented by both teens and adults. These areas are safe, but one should always be vigilant at night, i.e., stay in busier areas, don't flash expensive items, and mind your pockets.

Despite thousands of safe visits every year, Lion's Head—the peak below Table Mountain—and the running trails around Newlands Forest have been the sites of some knife-point robberies which occurred around sunrise or sunset. Be sure to hike in a group or on the popular paths during busier times of the day. And even though Table Mountain is in the middle of a major city, a hike to the top should be taken seriously: follow the paths, always bring water, sunscreen, and a warm layer—it's another world up there.

Visiting townships can be an important part of getting to know the real lives of the majority of the people of Cape Town. If you do plan a visit, make sure it's with a resident, or as part of an organized tour. However, keep in mind that township tours are quite controversial with some residents, as they would not like their lives to be considered tourism. Opt for a small and more intimate tour that supports local residents, their dignity, and their stories.

Shopping

When it comes to shopping, Cape Town has something for everyone—from sophisticated malls to trendy markets and street vendors. Although African art and curios are obvious choices (and you will find some gems), South Africans have woken up to their own sense of style and creativity; the results are fantastic, and Cape Town is the epicenter of the South African design explosion. In a single morning, you could bag some sophisticated tableware, a funky wire-art ornament from a street vendor, and a beautifully designed handbag made by HIV-positive women working as part of a community development program.

Cape Town also has great malls selling well-known international brands. The V&A Waterfront is an excellent place to start by virtue of its location at the harbor and its mix of international labels with the fantastic Watershed Market, where you can also find unique local goods. But it's beyond the malls that you're most likely to have a shopping experience that can give you greater insight into the soul of the city and its people.

Shopping malls usually have extended shopping hours beyond the normal 9–5 on weekdays and 9–1 on Saturday. Most shops outside of malls (except for small grocery stores) are closed on Sunday.

Tours

Countless companies offer guided tours of the city center, the peninsula, the Winelands, and any place else in the Cape (or beyond) that you might wish to visit. They differ in type of transportation used, focus, size, and guide quality. For comprehensive information on touring companies, head to one of the Cape Town Tourism offices or ask for recommendations at your hotel. Listings here are limited to more specialized tours.

ART TOURS
Juma Art Tours
GUIDED TOURS | Each tour is led by a local artist who wants to promote ethical tourism by offering you the choice to get your hands dirty and contribute something to the community like painting or gardening. Juma, the owner, and the other guides are passionate about art and how it can engage and uplift communities so a tour with Juma means you'll be taken on a creative journey of discovery and engagement, and ultimately be able to be involved in a project that is improving people's lives. ✉ *Woodstock* ☎ *073/400–4064* ⊕ *www.jumaarttours.co.za* ✉ *From R250; prices vary depending on tour duration.*

BIRD-WATCHING TOURS
Birding Africa Tours
SPECIAL-INTEREST TOURS | FAMILY | One of the top five bird-tour companies in the world according to *Birdwatch*, a British monthly magazine, these are the go-to guides in Cape Town. They organize customized birding trips of any length, and can also take you far beyond the Mother City. ■ **TIP→ All of their guides are great, but consider asking for Callan Cohen.** ✉ *Hilltop St., Cape Town* ☎ *083/959–5174* ⊕ *www.birdingafrica.com* ✉ *From R80000 for an all-inclusive 2 week excursion.*

BOAT TOURS
Boat tours are very popular, but the only ones that actually land on Robben Island are the ferries operated by the museum there.

Tigger 2 Charters
CRUISE EXCURSIONS | This Waterfront-based luxury operation offers corporate, sunset, and lunch cruises along one of the world's most dramatic and famous coastlines, including trips to Clifton 4th Beach. ✉ *V&A Waterfront, Cape Town* ☎ *021/418–0241* ⊕ *www.tigger2.co.za* ✉ *1½ hour Champagne Sunset Cruise R440 pp.*

Waterfront Charters
BOAT TOURS | FAMILY | This operation seems to offer everything that's connected to having fun on Table Bay and the eastern seaboard, with trips on a range of boats, from yachts to large motor cruisers. A 1½-hour sunset cruise from the V&A Waterfront costs about R360 and includes a glass of bubbly. Cruise & Dine Packages cost R660 for dinner, R375 for lunch. Jet boat rides are R880 per hour. ✉ *Shop 5, Quay 5, V&A Waterfront* ☎ *021/418–3168* ⊕ *www.waterfrontcharters.co.za* ✉ *From R360.*

BUS TOURS
Art Route Cape Town
SPECIAL-INTEREST TOURS | Owned and operated by artist and art historian Talita Swart, Art Routes creates bespoke tours of Cape Town's exploding art scene for groups of any size (all in the comfort of a Mercedes with free Wi-Fi onboard). From art galleries to artists' studios to the archives of national arts institutions, Art Routes guides provide you with a fascinating and inspiring insider overview of whichever aspect of local art interests you. ✉ *Cape Town* ☎ *082/091–0859* ⊕ *www.artroute.capetown* ✉ *From R900 for half day; R1,200 for full day.*

Cape Sidecar Adventures
SPECIAL-INTEREST TOURS | FAMILY | Unique for Cape Town, this operator uses vintage Chinese military motorcycles dating back to the early 1960s to show off the Mother City. Great for children, too, the cycles chug stylishly and safely around some of the most beautiful roads and views on the planet in their designer gear—you actually get kitted out rather stylishly. There's a nice little coffee bar in the shop afterward that offers an awesome collection of helmets (Batman's included) for sale. ✉ *1 Dickens Rd., Salt River* ☎ *021/434–9855* ⊕ *www.sidecars.co.za* ✉ *2 hour tour R2400, full-day R4800 (rates are 1 or 2 passengers).*

City Sightseeing Bus Cape Town

BUS TOURS | FAMILY | This "hop on–hop off" bus tour is a great way to familiarize yourself with Cape Town, especially early on in your trip. It's accessible at various points around the city while hitting all the major landmarks and attractions, including Table Mountain, the V&A Waterfront, Camps Bay, and more. You can choose when to get off and spend some time, skip what you're not interested in, or stay on the bus and see the whole city in a day. Wherever you get off, you'll be able to return back to your starting point. They offer various languages on audio, as well as other tour options that may include walking tours, canal cruises at the waterfront, and trips around the Winelands and peninsula. Tickets are available at the Waterfront outside the aquarium or on the bus. ☎ 021/511–6000 ⊕ www.citysightseeing.co.za ✉ R225, R130 for children.

Coffeebeans Routes

SPECIAL-INTEREST TOURS | If authenticity is what you're looking for, a tour with Coffeebeans Routes is where it's at. The company offers specialized tours like the famous Jazz Safari ($130), which takes small groups to meet key musicians of Cape Town's jazz scene in their homes for dinner, followed by a visit to non-touristy jazz clubs in the Cape Flats. There's also the Revolution Route, Cape Town Cuisine Route, or Theatre in the Backyard experiences, which are infused with an authentic element of storytelling. ✉ Cape Town ☎ 079/495–8782 ⊕ www.coffeebeansroutes.com ✉ From R4000 per person depending on group number.

Hylton Ross Tours

GUIDED TOURS | FAMILY | This massive and fairly generic tour operator offers half-day and full-day tours of Cape Town—and pretty much the whole country. They also offer custom private tours according to your wants, the smaller and more personalized the tour, the higher the price. ✉ Cape Town ☎ 021/506–2575 ⊕ www.hyltonross.co.za ✉ From R590 per person for a half-day trip, R1440 for a full-day cultural and Robben Island tour.

Kiff Kombi Tours

DRIVING TOURS | An alternative way to see the sights, this company uses VW vans (known locally as kombi) to take you on tours that can be scenic or aimed at culture, including things like craft beer tastings, local foods, and graffiti art stops. ✉ 8 Kloof St., Cape Town ☎ 021/213–3888 ⊕ www.kiffkombitours.co.za ✉ From R990–R1900 per person depending on group size and activity (slightly higher for food and drink tours).

Maboneng Township Arts Experience

SPECIAL-INTEREST TOURS | This is a creative and intimate way to visit and learn about Langa, the oldest township in Cape Town. These art tours take you into the gallery homes of artists where you can see (and sometimes purchase) vibrant artwork, share a local meal, and learn about the history of the area, after which you will visit other important public art and architecture spots. ✉ Langa, Cape Town ☎ 068/023–5048 ⊕ www.maboneng.com ✉ From R1200–R3000 depending on the duration of tour and activity.

FISHING TOURS

Hooked on Africa

BOAT TOURS | FAMILY | Based in Hout Bay harbor, this operation is in one of the richest fishing grounds left in the world today. If you're keen to take to the open ocean for some deep-sea fishing, you'll have plenty of choices, as South Africa has excellent game fish, such as dorado, yellowfin tuna, and broadbill swordfish. The company offers private, full-boat charters of a 32-foot catamaran for a full day of deep-sea fishing. Call to inquire about current rates and to see if there are any organized trips you could join in lieu of a full-boat charter. ☎ 021/790–5332 ⊕ www.hookedonafrica.co.za ✉ From R10,000.

Inkwazi Fly-Fishing Safaris

SPECIAL-INTEREST TOURS | Inkwazi offers guided and tutorial fly fishing excursions on the streams of the Limietberg nature reserve, just an hour or so away from Cape Town. The streams contain a healthy number of self-populating wild rainbow trout and the fishing can be exceptionally good with crystal clear water. Equipment is supplied, as is plenty of good advice. Regulations allow them to guide no more than two anglers, and trips are frequently just one person. Booking in advance is essential. Rates are inclusive of transport to and from Cape Town, permits, tackle, flies and consumables, lunch, and refreshments. ⊠ *Cape Town* ☎ *083/626–0467* ⊕ *www. inkwaziflyfishing.co.za* 🎫 *R3900 for single angler with guide, R4900 for two anglers with guide.*

WALKING TOURS

Pamphlets for a self-guided walking tour of city-center attractions can be picked up at Cape Town Tourism.

Cape Town Free Walking Tours

WALKING TOURS | FAMILY | Join these daily walking tours along several routes through the city with a knowledgeable and passionate guide. Options include the Historic City Walking Tour, Bo-Kaap Walking Tour, and the Apartheid to Freedom Tour. Tours are free, although tips/donations are appreciated, and don't require bookings (unless you are more than 10 people); private tours tailored to your interests can also be organized for a fee. Tours happen every day, 365 days a year, rain or shine and depart at 11 am and 2 pm. ⊠ *Mandela Rhodes Pl., Cape Town Central* ☎ *076/636–9007* ⊕ *free-walkingtourscapetown.co.za.*

Eat Like a Local Cape Town Tour

FOOD AND DRINK TOURS | Experience Cape Town's exciting and delicious food culture on foot with passionate food expert Rupesh, who takes you away from tourist traps and brings you to local favorites and niche food and drink spots in Cape Town

City Bowl and Bo-Kaap. You'll discover how much of a foodie haven Cape Town is while learning about its culinary culture and social scene. You'll also get some pointers for where to go on other days. Plant-based tours are also available. ⊠ *Wale St., Cape Town* ☎ *082/469–8088* ⊕ *www.eatlikealocal.co.za* 🎫 *Tour (including alcohol) R1380; tour (excluding alcohol) R1200.*

Wanderlust Audio Walking Tours

WALKING TOURS | These audio tours, based on Ursula Stevens's comprehensive books written on Cape Town, are full of interesting historical information. You can do a self-guided exploration following the VoiceMap audio tours that Ursula created in English and German. These tours are ideal for visitors with less time on their hands and those who wish to be independent of groups. You can purchase a guide on the VoiceMap App. ⊠ *Cape Town, Cape Town* ⊕ *www.wanderlust. co.za* 🎫 *From R40.*

Visitor Information

Cape Town Tourism Information has many branches. The office in City Centre is open weekdays from 9 to 5. The branch at the Waterfront is open daily 9 to 6, and the airport branch is open 8 to 5 on weekdays and 9 to 1 on weekends.

CONTACTS Cape Town Tourism. ⊠ *33 Martin Hammerschlag Way, Cape Town Central* ☎ *021/487–6800* ⊕ *www.cape-town.travel.*

When to Go

Whatever activities you hope to accomplish in Cape Town, head up Table Mountain as soon as the wind isn't blowing. Cape Town wind is notorious, and the cable car can be closed for days on end when the gales blow. Summer (October–March) is the windiest time of the year, and from December to April winds

Cape Town Itineraries

3 Days: With three days you can manage to see many of the city's major sights—including Company's Garden, District Six Museum, and the Bo-Kaap—on your own or with a tour. Weather permitting, try to work in a Robben Island tour—which will take a morning—and lunch at one of the outdoor restaurants at the V&A Waterfront, where you can eat while watching working tugboats maneuver past the occasional sleek million-dollar yacht. The cable-car ride to the summit of Table Mountain is a must; go in the morning, and in the afternoon, drive out to Camps Bay, and kick off your shoes for a sandy stroll before finding a sophisticated sea-facing bar for a sundowner. Head back to town for dinner at any of the dozens of great Bree Street eateries. On another evening, discover the sounds of the city by heading to The Crypt Jazz Club. Or for more traditional African food and music, go to Gold Restaurant in Green Point. If you've still got time, spend a few hours meandering the gorgeous Kirstenbosch gardens.

5 or More Days: With at least five days, you can enjoy all the sights listed here as well as a trip to the Winelands in Constantia, Stellenbosch, Franschhoek, or Paarl. Spend an afternoon checking out the magnificent and profound artworks at Zeitz MocAA, Africa's first museum of contemporary art. Seeking something more outdoorsy? Take a hike up Lion's Head and get prepared to sweat. It's a steep uphill walk but has an easy trail for novice hikers. The views from there are breathtaking. However you spend your time, on your last night in Cape Town have a drink somewhere on the water—The Willaston Bar or (if weather permits) the rooftop bar at the Silo Hotel (near the V&A Waterfront) offers a cozy and modern setting with magnificent views of both the harbor and the Table Mountain skyline. You won't want to leave.

can reach 60 km (37 miles) an hour. The winter months are not immune from wind, either—though it is much less of a problem. If you're planning to visit Robben Island during peak season, it's also wise to book well in advance. One of the best months to visit is April, when the heat and wind have abated and the Cape is bathed in warm autumnal hues. Winter rains can put off visitors, but this time of the year holds its own surprises: the countryside is a brilliant green, and without fail the best sunny and temperate days come between the rainy spells.

FESTIVALS AND EVENTS

Cape Town Carnival. Held in March along Green Point's pedestrian "Fan Walk," this parade of fantastical costumes, live music, and street party revelry celebrates creativity and the diverse communities making up the city. ⊕ *www.capetowncarnival.com.*

Cape Town Cycle Tour. The largest timed cycle tour in the world (even Lance Armstrong has taken part in it) usually brings Cape Town to stand still. This event, also known as "the Argus" takes place every March and has been for the past 44 years. Cyclists from all over the world take part in this most scenic race, while non-cyclists have a day out, usually crowding the promenade, picnicking, and cheering them on. ⊕ *www.capetowncycletour.com.*

3

Cape Town PLANNING

Cape Town International Jazz Festival.
Music, especially jazz and African music, was an extremely potent instrument for social change during the oppressive apartheid regime. South Africans remain passionate about music, and they celebrate their love of jazz with this festival, the biggest in Africa. Usually held in late March or early April, the event is on the scale and popularity of the Montreal and New Orleans Jazz Festivals. There's an even mix of local and international stars, and past festivals have included the likes of Randy Crawford; Abdullah Ibrahim; Hugh Masekela; Ismael Lo; Chaka Khan; Earth, Wind & Fire; and Ladysmith Black Mambazo. ⊕ *www.capetownjazzfest. com.*

Cape Town Pride Festival. A parade and festival take place around the end of February every year to celebrate and raise awareness for the LGBTQIA+ community in Cape Town and around the world. The parade marks the end of a whole host of parties and events. ⊕ *capetownpride.org.*

Design Indaba Festival. World Design Capital winner in 2014, Cape Town is the epicenter of all things design in South Africa. As such, this conference and festival held in February or March and sporting the tagline "a better world through creativity," is a great opportunity to hear and see how South African and African designers and artists approach the world of objects, in some cases to improve the world, and in others to simply make it more beautiful. A host of music and film events runs simultaneously. ⊕ *www. designindaba.com.*

Encounters Documentary Film Festival.
This small but well-curated festival held in June or July showcases an always fascinating array of documentary films by a mix of acclaimed South African, African, and international filmmakers. ⊕ *www. encounters.co.za.*

First Thursdays. Following a similar initiative in other cities around the world, on the first Thursday of every month, a number of art galleries and museums open up for free and Cape Town city center becomes alive with people, music, art, and restaurant specials. Many restaurants host musicians and performers, opening out their spaces onto the streets, many streets close and become for pedestrian use only. A great night out, but use Uber or a taxi service as parking is a nightmare. ⊕ *first-thursdays.co.za.*

Kirstenbosch Summer Sunset Concerts.
From late November to early April, enjoy the best in South African music, from pop to classical to house, at the outdoor concerts on Sundays at Kirstenbosch Summer Sunset Concerts. It's a Cape Town summer institution, not to be missed. ⊕ *www.sanbi.org.*

MCQP. A key annual event on Cape Town's party calendar is December's MCQP, hosted by the Mother City's Queer Project. This huge themed bash started in 1994 to celebrate the birth of South Africa's new constitution and its inclusion of gay rights. It's part Mardi Gras, part Gay Pride, and all enormous fancy-dress party. All are welcome! ⊕ *www.mcqp. co.za.*

2 Oceans Marathon. Africa's biggest running event usually takes place on Easter Friday and has become a national institution for runners and walkers from around the country and the rest of the world. Known as the "world's most beautiful marathon" the spectacular route runs through some of the most scenic parts of the Cape Peninsula. A popular family day, this event sees people of all ages, backgrounds, and abilities take place, and like the Argus, a whole crowd of people cheering them on, volunteering, and setting up stalls of food and drink. ⊕ *www. twooceansmarathon.org.za.*

Built between 1666 and 1679, the Castle of Good Hope is the country's oldest existing colonial building.

Tweede Nuwe Jaar Parade. Also known as the "Second New Year" or the "Klaapse Klopse Parade," this is one of the oldest celebrations in Cape Town. Usually held on January 2nd, the origins of this festival date to the early colonial period, when this was the one day of the year that enslaved people were given the day off, and they used it to celebrate. The tradition continued even after the emancipation of slaves, and today is celebrated by thousands of people in vibrant sequined get up, to sing and dance, accompanied by marching bands. The celebration lasts one or two days, but many communities around the cape spend the entire year preparing for this celebration.

Cape Town City Centre

Bounded by Buitenkant Street to the east, Buitengracht Street to the west, the Company's Garden to the south, and the Foreshore to the north, Cape Town's City Center—also referred to as the CBD, the City Bowl, and sometimes just Cape Town or Kaapstad (Afrikaans name)—is where you'll find moderately sized glass-and-steel office blocks that soar over street vendors selling everything from seasonal fruit and flowers to clothes and cigarettes. Sandwiched in between these modern high-rises are historic buildings dating to the 1600s. There's an impressive collection of art deco buildings, and there is always something undergoing restoration. Don't try to navigate the center of Cape Town by car. It's small enough to walk, and on foot you can explore the many galleries, coffee shops, and markets that appear on every corner. If your feet have had it, the MyCiti bus is a treat if you have a card.

TIMING AND PRECAUTIONS
If you are pressed for time, you can explore the city in a day, getting the lay of the land and a feel for the people of Cape Town while visiting or skipping sights as your interests dictate. However, if you'd like to linger in various museums and galleries, you could easily fill two or three days. Start at about 9, when most

workers have finished their commute, and then stop for a long, leisurely lunch, finishing the tour in the late afternoon. If you have to head out of town on either the N1 or N2, be sure to depart before 4, when rush-hour congestion takes over.

Except for the top end of Long Street, Kloof Street, Bree Street, and around Heritage Square where there are lots of bars and cafés, the city center is very quiet at night, and you are advised not to wander the streets after dark. The last commuters leave around 6 (note that the city center can also be deserted on weekends). The biggest threat is being mugged for your cell phone, jewelry, or money. However, if you walk around during the weekday and leave flashy items at home, you'll have a wonderful and safe time in the city center.

Sights

Adderley Street

STREET | Originally named Heerengracht after a canal that once ran the length of the avenue, this street has always been Cape Town's principal thoroughfare. Although there are a couple of historical buildings dating to the early 1900s, and the beautiful Adderley Street Flower Market—one of the city's oldest markets, located in Trafalgar Place between Strand and Darling streets—has hung on, Adderley Street in recent years has become mostly a commercial hub for office buildings and franchise stores. The sidewalks are packed with street vendors selling everything from fruits and vegetables to cell phone covers and tea towels, serving people going to and from work. This is the place to experience the busy hustle and bustle of everyday Cape Town. ⊠ *Adderley St., Cape Town Central.*

Castle of Good Hope

CASTLE/PALACE | Despite its name, the castle isn't the fairy-tale fantasy type but rather a squat fortress that hunkers down as if to avoid shellfire. Built between

1665 and 1676 by the Dutch East India Company (VOC) to replace an earthen fort constructed in 1652 by Jan van Riebeeck, the Dutch commander who settled Cape Town, it's the oldest building in the country. Its pentagonal plan, with a diamond-shaped bastion at each corner, is typical of the Old Netherlands defense system adopted in the early 17th century. The design was intended to allow covering fire for every portion of the castle. As an added protection, the whole fortification was surrounded by a moat, and back in the day, the sea nearly washed up against its walls. The castle served as both the VOC headquarters and the official governor's residence and still houses the regional headquarters of the National Defence Force. Despite the bellicose origins of the castle, no shot has ever been fired from its ramparts, except ceremonially.

You can wander around on your own or join one of the highly informative guided tours at no extra cost. ⊠ *1 Buitenkant St., Cape Town Central* ☎ *021/787–1249* ⊕ *www.castleofgoodhope.co.za* ⊠ *R50.*

City Hall

GOVERNMENT BUILDING | From a balcony in this building overlooking Darling Street, Nelson Mandela gave the historic speech upon his release from prison in 1990. This Edwardian building constructed in 1905 is gradually being spruced up and is still a commanding presence overlooking the Grand Parade. What was the seat of local administration is now home to the Cape Town Philharmonic Orchestra (the acoustics in the main hall are phenomenal) and a traffic department. Some of the building's stone was imported from Bath, England, and the clock is a scaled-down replica of Big Ben. ⊠ *Darling St., Cape Town Central* ⊠ *Free.*

Company's Garden

GARDEN | FAMILY | One of Cape Town's best-kept secrets is also a great place to seek relief from a sweltering summer day if the beach is packed. These lush,

A visit to the District Six Museum is a must to learn about one of the city's most vibrant multicultural neighborhoods and its destruction under the apartheid government.

landscaped gardens are all that remain of a 43-acre tract laid out by Jan van Riebeeck in April 1652 to supply fresh vegetables to ships on their way to the Dutch East Indies. By 1700 free burghers (Dutch-speaking colonists no longer indebted to the Dutch East India Company) were cultivating plenty of crops on their own land, and in time the VOC vegetable patch was transformed into a botanic garden. It remains a delightful haven in the city center, graced by fountains, exotic trees, rose gardens, and a pleasant outdoor café. At the bottom of the gardens, close to Government Avenue, look for an old well that used to provide water for the town's residents and the garden. The old water pump, engraved with the maker's name and the date 1842, has been overtaken by an oak tree and now juts out of the tree's trunk some 6 feet above the ground. A huge statue of the colonist Cecil Rhodes, and Cape's prime minister in the late 19th century, looms over the path that runs through the center of the gardens. He points to the north, and an inscription reads, "your hinterland is there," a reference to Rhodes's dream of extending the British Empire from the Cape to Cairo. A self-guided walking brochure (R20) with detailed historical information about the gardens and nearby sights is sold at the shop next door to the small but informative visitors center, which are both by the restaurant. ⊠ Between Government Ave. and Queen Victoria St., Cape Town Central ☎ 021/426–2157 ⌖ Free ⊙ Visitors center closed weekends.

District Six Museum

HISTORY MUSEUM | Housed in the Buitenkant Methodist Church, this small museum preserves the memory of one of Cape Town's most vibrant multicultural neighborhoods and of the district's destruction in one of the cruelest acts of the apartheid-era Nationalist government. District Six was proclaimed a white area in 1966, and existing residents were evicted from their homes, which were razed to make way for a white suburb. The people were forced to resettle in bleak outlying areas on the Cape Flats,

E-BERTH

KEY

- **1** *Exploring Sights*
- **1** *Restaurants*
- **1** *Quick Bites*
- **1** *Hotels*

Sights ▼

1 Adderley Street **E5**
2 Castle of Good Hope ... **G6**
3 City Hall **E6**
4 Company's Garden **C6**
5 District Six Museum..... **E7**
6 Greenmarket Square... **D5**
7 Iziko Bo-Kaap
  Museum **B4**
8 Iziko Slave Lodge **D6**
9 Long Street **D4**
10 St George's
  Cathedral **D5**
11 St. George's Mall......... **E4**

Restaurants ▼

1 Allium **E5**
2 Biesmiellah
  Restaurant.............. **B4**
3 Bombay Brasserie...... **D5**
4 Butter **D4**
5 Chef's Warehouse
  Pinchos & Wine Bar..... **C4**
6 Clarke's Bar &
  Dining Room.............. **C5**
7 Dias Tavern.............. **F7**
8 Hemelhuijs............... **D3**
9 Little Ethiopia............ **D4**
10 Madame Taitou **D4**
11 Mazza **C4**
12 The Meeting Point...... **D4**
13 mulberry & prince **B5**
14 SeaBreeze
  Fish and Shell **B6**
15 South China
  Dim Sum Bar **B6**
16 Tjing Tjing Tori........... **D5**

Quick Bites ▼

1 Against The Grain **B4**
2 The Company's Garden
  Restaurant................ **C6**
3 Moro Gelato.............. **C5**
4 New York Bagels **E7**
5 Truth Coffee **E7**

Hotels ▼

1 Cape Heritage Hotel.....**C4**
2 Daddy Long Legs
  Boutique Hotel **C5**
3 Long Street
  Boutique Hotel **B6**
4 Rouge On Rose............**C3**
5 Taj Cape Town........... **D5**
6 The Westin
  Cape Town................ **F2**

and by the 1970s all the buildings here, except churches and mosques, had been demolished. Huge controversy accompanied the proposed redevelopment of the area, and only a small housing component, Zonnebloem, and the campus of the Cape Technicon have been built, leaving much of the ground still bare—a grim reminder of the past. The museum consists of street signs, photographs, life stories of the people who lived there, and a huge map, where former residents can identify the sites of their homes and record their names. This map is being used to help sort out land claims. You can arrange in advance for a two-hour walking tour of the district with a former resident for a nominal fee. ⊠ *25 Buitenkant St., Cape Town Central* ☎ *021/466–7200* ⊕ *www.districtsix.co.za* ⊠ *Self-guided visit R45; tour with former resident/guide R60.*

Greenmarket Square

PLAZA/SQUARE | For more than a century this cobbled square served as a forum for public announcements, including the 1834 declaration abolishing slavery, which was read from the balcony of the Old Town House, overlooking the square. In the 19th century the square became a vegetable market as well as a popular watering hole, and you can still enjoy a drink at an open-air restaurant or hotel veranda while watching the crowds go by. Today the square has been re-cobbled, and the outdoor market sells predominantly African crafts from around the continent. It is also flanked by some of the best examples of art-deco architecture in South Africa. ⊠ *Greenmarket Sq., Burg St., between Longmarket and Hout Sts., Cape Town Central.*

Iziko Slave Lodge

HISTORIC SIGHT | Built in 1679 by the Dutch East India Company to house the enslaved people they'd brought to the Cape for labor, it also housed the supreme court from 1815 to 1914. The lodge now holds a museum with a fascinating and sobering account of slavery in the Cape, as well as excellent and evocative temporary exhibits that generally examine more contemporary views on apartheid and human rights. The somewhat randomly curated upper galleries house exhibits and artifacts from the various groups populating the Cape, as well as ceramics and an Egyptology collection. ⊠ *49 Wale St., Cape Town Central* ☎ *021/467–7229* ⊕ *www.iziko.org.za/museums/slave-lodge* ⊠ *R30* ⊘ *Closed Sun.*

Long Street

STREET | The section of Long between Orange and Strand streets is lined with magnificently restored Georgian and Victorian buildings. Wrought-iron balconies and fancy curlicues on these colorful houses evoke the French Quarter in New Orleans. Today antique dealers, backpackers' lodges, the Pan-African Market, funky clothing outlets, and a plethora of cafes, bars, and restaurants make this one of the best browsing streets in the city; by night, it can live up to some of its older reputation—a place for debauchery. At the mountain end is the Long Street Baths, an indoor swimming pool, and an old Turkish *hammam* (steam bath). ⊠ *Long St., between Orange and Strand Sts., Cape Town Central.*

St. George's Cathedral

CHURCH | This stunning cathedral was once the religious seat of one of the most recognizable faces—and voices—in the fight against apartheid, Archbishop Desmond Tutu. In his position as the first Black archbishop of Cape Town (he was elected in 1986), he vociferously denounced apartheid and relentlessly pressed for a democratic government. It was from these steps that he led a demonstration of more than 30,000 people and coined the phrase the Rainbow People to describe South Africans in all their glorious diversity. The cathedral continues in its active monitoring role today, holding marches and the new government to account. The Anglican cathedral was designed by Sir Herbert Baker in the Gothic Revival style; construction began in 1901, using sandstone from Table Mountain. The structure contains the largest stained-glass window in the country, some beautiful examples of late-Victorian stained glass, and a 1,000-year-old Coptic cross. If you want to hear the magnificent organ, go to the choral evensong at 6 on Sunday evening. ✉ *5 Wale St., Cape Town Central* ☎ *021/424–7360* 🌐 *www.sgcathedral.co.za* 🎫 *Free.*

St. George's Mall

PEDESTRIAN MALL | This pedestrian-only promenade stretches about five blocks from St. George's Cathedral through the city center (passing Greenmarket Square) to the financial district. Shops and cafés line the mall, and street vendors sell everything from T-shirts to African arts and crafts. Street performers and dancers gather daily to entertain crowds of locals and visitors, who rub shoulders on their way to and from work or while sightseeing. The very good "Earthfair" food market is held on the Cathedral end of the mall every Thursday from 11 to 3. ✉ *Between Burg and Adderley Sts. from Wale St. to Thibault Sq., Cape Town Central.*

🍴 Restaurants

Hardly a month goes by without a new café or restaurant opening in the city center. Many are housed in historic buildings, and most are open only for lunch and breakfast, as "town" tends to get quiet after hours. However, the areas of Heritage Square and Long and Bree streets are an exception, and you'll find some fantastic dinner choices listed here.

★ Allium

$$$$ | **KOREAN** | This elegant and inviting Korean restaurant in the heart of the City Center serves meals that mix the traditional with the innovative. The small team brings the finest ingredients to life; wine pairings are available and as are numerous other house brews of teas and other beverages. **Known for:** Korean fusion; delicate dishes; friendly service. [$] *Average main: R490* ✉ *37 Parliament St., Cape Town Central* ☎ *087/702–4505* 🌐 *www.alliumcapetown.com* ⏲ *Closed Sat.–Thurs. No lunch.*

Bombay Brasserie

$$$$ | **INDIAN** | Turning the old Reserve Bank Building into a scene of fantastical opulence with ornate, handblown glass chandeliers, lots of dark wood, and luxurious fabrics, the Taj Hotel's Indian fine-dining restaurant does not disappoint when it comes to either ambience or flavor. Choose between the five-course chef's menu, or order à la carte from a menu that is filled with new takes on authentic Indian classics. **Known for:** fabulous renditions of classic Indian dishes; luxurious ambience; excellent service. [$] *Average main: R210* ✉ *Taj Cape Town, Wale St., Cape Town Central* ☎ *021/819–2000* ⏲ *No lunch.*

Butter

$ | **CAFÉ** | An all-day breakfast bistro and bar, this bright little cafe in the heart of Cape Town serves yummy breakfasts and lunches like pancakes, eggs Benedict, wraps, and burgers. As the name implies, buttery goodness and comfort foods are on offer, but the menu is large and includes lots of fresh salads and vegetable-filled options as well as all-day cocktails and great coffee. **Known for:** delicious healthy food in smallish portions; laptop-friendly; good smoothies, teas, and fresh juices. [$] *Average main: R90* ✉ *70 Loop St., Cape Town Central* ☎ *082/853–1939* 🌐 *www.butterallday.com* ⏲ *Closed Mon. No dinner.*

Chef's Warehouse Pinchos and Wine Bar

$$$$ | SPANISH | Part of the Chef's Warehouse chain of Liam Tomlin's famous restaurants, this tapas and wine bar provides a sophisticated and romantic meal for two, or a lively and delicious group outing. Come early, or expect to wait for a table as this popular restaurant is small and doesn't take reservations, but the food and drink pairings are worth it. **Known for:** always changing menu; great wine list; reservations not accepted. $ *Average main: R400* ⊠ *213 Bree St., Cape Town Central* ☎ *021/422–0128* ⊕ *www.chefswarehouse.co.za/pinchos* ⊘ *Closed Sun.*

Clarke's Bar & Dining Room

$ | AMERICAN | A Bree Street institution beloved by the young and hip, Clarke's is known for many things, among them its burgers (with their famously butter-fried brioche buns), drinks (from smoothies and fresh juices to excellent cocktails and everything else you'd expect from a place with the word "bar" in its name), and delicious breakfasts (the huevos rancheros are yummy if not strictly authentic). As day turns to night, this light and bright restaurant (seating options range from a few tables on the sidewalk, to a designer-diner interior, to a small plant-filled courtyard) morphs from a child-friendly brunch spot to a casual coffee and burger joint, to a vibey nighttime bar, where DJs and parties are not unusual. **Known for:** fun drinks spot; burgers and other American-style comfort food; good breakfasts. $ *Average main: R75* ⊠ *133 Bree St., Cape Town Central* ☎ *087/470–0165* ⊕ *www.clarkesdining.co.za* ⊘ *No dinner Sat.–Mon.*

Dias Tavern

$$ | PORTUGUESE | This Portuguese taverna in District Six is Cape Town's answer to a dive-bar-meets-diner. Serving classic South African Portuguese fare—think spicy *trinchado* (braised beef), *prego* rolls (rump steak fried in wine and garlic with a fried egg), spicy peri-peri chicken livers, and grilled sardines—for lunch and dinner, Dias Tavern is an institution. **Known for:** cheap, cheerful fun (don't be surprised if there's a 60th birthday and a bachelor party at the same time; Portuguese South African fare—heavy on the garlic and spice. $ *Average main: R110* ⊠ *15 Caledon St., District Six, Cape Town Central* ☎ *021/465–7547* ⊕ *www.diastavern.co.za* ⊘ *Closed Sun.*

★ Hemelhuijs

$$ | ECLECTIC | Super-stylish Hemelhuijs is both a showcase for a range of exquisite and fanciful ceramicware, and a centrally located restaurant serving equally fanciful and exquisite food. Though a little pricey for lunch, the owner-chef's inventive seasonal dishes burst with freshness and flavor (think pear-and-celeriac salad with hazelnuts and trout, or a crispy panfried veal of sublime flavor and texture) are well worth it. **Known for:** intimate friendly service; supercreative and seasonal menu; constantly evolving designer interior. $ *Average main: R140* ⊠ *71 Waterkant St., Cape Town Central* ☎ *021/418–2042* ⊕ *www.hemelhuijs.co.za* ⊘ *Closed Sun. No dinner.*

Little Ethiopia

$$$ | ETHIOPIAN | At this unassuming hole-in-the-wall restaurant, chef and owner Yeshi Mekonnen has a deep love for her cuisine which is evident in the traditional and fresh Ethiopian food she prepares from scratch. Meals are served on large sharing platters or individual plates and come with the traditional injera (naturally gluten-free flatbread); meat and vegan options are available. **Known for:** vegetarian friendly; intimate setting; homemade Ethiopian dishes. $ *Average main: R180* ⊠ *76 Shortmarket St., Cape Town Central* ☎ *021/424–8254* ⊕ *littleethiopia.co.za* ⊘ *Closed Sun.*

★ Madame Taitou

$$ | ETHIOPIAN | Get ready to eat with your hands at this otherwordly Ethiopian restaurant that's covered head-to-toe in obscure trinkets, plants, and trees.

There's always a delightful smell of cooked spices, and the food is delicious, with meat and vegan options, all served with tangy and spongy injera (naturally gluten-free flatbread). **Known for:** flavorful Ethiopian food; funky decor; Ethiopian coffee ceremony. $ *Average main: R120* ⊠ *77 Long St., Cape Town Central* ☎ *021/426–6969* ⊕ *madamtaitou.simdif.com.*

Mazza
$$$$ | MIDDLE EASTERN | The newest restaurant from chef Liam Tomlin, this Middle Eastern fusion restaurant has an open kitchen that gives diners a glimpse of the busy chefs. You can order a set menu, dishes to share, or individual plates (although sharing is what's intended). **Known for:** reservations not accepted; lively vibe; Middle Eastern fusion sharing plates. $ *Average main: R230* ⊠ *Heritage Square, Cape Town Central* ☎ *021/422–0128* ⊕ *www.localheritage.co.za/eatdrink/mazza* ⊙ *Closed Sun.*

The Meeting Point
$ | AFRICAN | A cozy and friendly little Tanzanian restaurant in the bustling CBD, the Meeting Point aims to bring people together, hence the inspiration for the name. The menu features all sorts of tasty poultry, meat, fish, and vegetarian East African classics, but you must try the mandazi, a Tanzanian donut that's crispy, spiced, and not too sweet. **Known for:** Tanzanian and East African food; vegan options; warm hospitality. $ *Average main: R90* ⊠ *67 Strand St., Cape Town Central* ☎ *087/378–1498* ⊕ *www.facebook.com/meetingpointtanzaniancuisine.*

★ mulberry & prince
$$ | CONTEMPORARY | Exceptionally delicious things—think classics like eggs Benedict, French toast, American-style pancakes, and chicken and waffles with creative, tasty spins—are happening in this designer space of exposed brick, funky lighting, and leather seats. With a constantly changing menu, expect some exciting new dishes in this trendy space, a favorite among locals for upmarket sweet and savory breakfasts and late brunches. **Known for:** Instagram-worthy decadent comfort foods; great coffee; understated designer interior. $ *Average main: R150* ⊠ *12 Pepper St., Cape Town Central* ⊕ *www.mulberryandprince.co.za* ⊙ *Closed Mon. and Tues. No dinner* ☞ *Bookings via Dineplan (on website) only.*

SeaBreeze Fish and Shell
$$$ | SEAFOOD | Serving locally and sustainably caught seafood, SeeBreeze has become the go-to spot on Bree Street for oysters, cocktails, and a well-made light dishes. Bringing a contemporary take to traditional seafood dishes, expect to find things like fish and chips, prawn linguine, creamy mussels, and grilled whole fish. **Known for:** boozy lunches; fresh oysters and seafood; trendy but relaxed vibe. $ *Average main: R189* ⊠ *213 Bree St., Cape Town Central* ☎ *074/793–9349* ⊕ *www.seabreezecapetown.co.za/* ⊙ *No lunch Mon. and Tues.*

★ South China Dim Sum Bar
$$ | ASIAN FUSION | This quaint little dim sum bar on the top of Long Street is often packed in the evenings. The menu is always changing with available options written on a little chalkboard, but flavorful and delicate dim sum is always on offer, as is a warm brothy soup. **Known for:** small menu; delicious dim sum; local favorite. $ *Average main: R170* ⊠ *289 Long St., Cape Town Central* ☎ *078/846–3656* ⊙ *Closed Sun. and Mon.*

Tjing Tjing Tori
$$$ | JAPANESE | Tjing Tjing House is a four-venue Japanese cuisine marvel that shares skilled chefs and bartenders, great design style, and a 200-year-old heritage building in the heart of Cape Town. On the ground floor you have Torii, serving meals and snacks comprised of crowd-pleasing Japanese bar food—think deep-fried sushi rice, excellent tempura, baos, hot-dogs, and karaage chicken;

Cape Town's City Centre, reminiscent of New Orleans, has numerous shops and restaurants worth visiting.

there's also a rooftop bar and the excellent and more high-end Momiji, which serves refined tasting style menus on the middle floor. **Known for:** romantic atmosphere; friendly and efficient service; fantastic cocktails. ⓢ *Average main: R160* ✉ *165 Longmarket St., Cape Town Central* ☎ *021/422–4374* ⊕ *www.tjingtjing. co.za/torii* ⊗ *Closed Sun. and Mon.*

☕ Coffee and Quick Bites

The Company's Garden Restaurant
$ | CAFÉ | FAMILY | Located in the leafy green of the Company's Gardens, this restaurant serves a wide range of light meals, teatime favorites, and South African fare from morning to late afternoon. It's a gorgeous place to sit and watch the buzz of Cape Town's foot traffic passing you by, and also great for kids. **Known for:** beautiful garden setting; hearty brunch options; family and animal friendly. ⓢ *Average main: R70* ✉ *15 Queen Victoria St., Cape Town Central* ☎ *021/423–2919* ⊕ *thecompanysgarden.com* ⊗ *No dinner.*

★ Moro Gelato
$ | ICE CREAM | FAMILY | This small, stylish gelateria has some of the best Italian gelato in Cape Town with traditional flavors like stracciatella, pistachio, and chocolate, as well as locally-inspired flavors like rooibos, milk tart, and whatever produce is in season. The cafe also serves decadent hot chocolate and thick, creamy milkshakes, and there are many dairy-free and vegan options. **Known for:** seasonal flavors using local ingredients; traditional gelato; decadent milkshakes. ⓢ *Average main: R56* ✉ *165 Long St., Cape Town Central* ⊕ *morogelato.co.za.*

New York Bagels
$ | CAFÉ | A four-generation family-run business, this fuss-free bagel shop and deli specializes in traditional boiled and baked New York–style bagels that are made fresh daily, with a number of delicious toppings—go with a simple schmear of cream cheese on a poppy-seed bagel or try the brisket, smoked salmon, or pastrami. They also serve great coffee, pastries, and an amazing

New York cheesecake. **Known for:** traditional bagels; very busy during the breakfast and lunch rush; the place for a good NY cheesecake. [$] *Average main: R90* ✉ *44 Harrington St., Cape Town Central* ☎ *066/005–0320* 🌐 *www.facebook.com/NYBCT* 🕒 *Closed Mon. No dinner.*

Truth Coffee

$$ | **CAFÉ** | With its steampunk design, full bar, and live performances on many nights, this spot captures the happening atmosphere in Cape Town's creative area that was once part of District Six. A great coffee shop with a variety of coffees and teas, the fun usually spills out onto the pavement so come prepared to have fun. **Known for:** tasty pastries and light meals; coffee lover's haven; open every day. [$] *Average main: R120* ✉ *36 Buitenkant St., Cape Town Central* ☎ *021/201–7000* 🌐 *www.truthcoffee.com.*

🛏 Hotels

Cape Heritage Hotel

$$$ | **HOTEL** | Built as a private home in 1771, this centrally located boutique hotel's spacious rooms are individually decorated, melding the best of South Africa's dynamic contemporary art scene with its historic architecture, and making the most of the building's teak-beamed ceilings, foot-wide yellowwood floorboards, and numerous other details that recall its gracious past. **Pros:** great location in Cape Town's historic district; excellent eateries in adjoining Heritage Square and Bree Street; beautiful old building and quirky style. **Cons:** lighting in some rooms is too dark; parking isn't free; bordered by one busy road. [$] *Rooms from: R3135* ✉ *90 Bree St., Cape Town Central* ☎ *021/424–4646* 🌐 *www.capeheritage.co.za* 🔑 *20 rooms* 🍴 *Free Breakfast.*

Daddy Long Legs Boutique Hotel

$ | **B&B/INN** | Independent travelers with artistic streaks love this place, which was built to represent the creative community of Cape Town, and the location is great if you are looking for nearby nightlife. **Pros:** friendly, helpful service; lots of dash for the cash; central location for party animals. **Cons:** breakfast not included; Long Street is noisy until late into the night; small rooms. [$] *Rooms from: R1450* ✉ *134 Long St., Cape Town Central* ☎ *021/422–3074* 🌐 *www.daddylonglegs.co.za* 🔑 *13 rooms* 🍴 *No Meals.*

Long Street Boutique Hotel

$$ | **B&B/INN** | The upper floors of a beautifully restored Victorian building on trendy Long Street house this incredibly good-value boutique hotel made up of 12 luxurious rooms. **Pros:** in the heart of Cape Town's nightlife; surprisingly opulent for the price; free unlimited Wi-Fi and air-conditioning. **Cons:** must pay for parking (R100 per night); not a tranquil neighborhood; no elevator. [$] *Rooms from: R1500* ✉ *230 Long St., Cape Town Central* ☎ *021/426–4309* 🌐 *www.longstreethotel.com* 🔑 *12 rooms* 🍴 *No Meals.*

Rouge on Rose

$$ | **HOTEL** | This owner-managed boutique hotel in the colorful and very central Bo-Kaap neighborhood offers spacious and comfortable suites with a surprising number of amenities—think espresso makers, slippers and robes, and super-fast Wi-Fi—for the price. **Pros:** tasty hot breakfast choices; great location in walking distance to city center attractions and restaurants; personalized, friendly service from owners. **Cons:** three-story building with no elevator; a few quiet blocks adjacent to Rose Street prevent complete confidence in walking at night; off-street parking is limited (but free). [$] *Rooms from: R2300* ✉ *25 Rose St., Bo-Kaap* ☎ *021/426–0298* 🌐 *www.capetownboutiquehotel.co.za* 🔑 *9 rooms* 🍴 *Free Breakfast.*

★ **Taj Cape Town**

$$$$ | **HOTEL** | With an amazing location in the heart of historic Cape Town, the Taj sits in the grand former headquarters of the South African Reserve Bank and

provides the professional and luxurious hospitality that one would expect from this brand. **Pros:** fantastic spa; one of the few five-star hotels that attracts a truly multicultural clientele; excellent Indian fine-dining restaurant and gorgeous Twankey bar. **Cons:** despite warm service, it lacks the intimacy of a smaller hotel; breakfast is not great; can have a bit of business feel. [$] *Rooms from: R5100* ✉ *1 Wale St., Cape Town Central* ☎ *021/819–2000* 🌐 *www.tajhotels.com/en-in/taj/taj-cape-town* 🛏 *176 rooms* 🍴 *Free Breakfast.*

The Westin Cape Town

$$$ | HOTEL | Conveniently linked to the Cape Town International Convention Centre, this sophisticated business hotel still caters to vacationers with features like an excellent spa with killer views, indoor and outdoor pools, and a stop for the water taxi that plies the canals to the V&A Waterfront. **Pros:** excellent and varied conference and business facilities; stellar views over the harbor and Signal Hill on one side and city and Table Mountain on the other from the top-floor restaurant; fantastic spa, gym, and infinity pool. **Cons:** restaurants not particularly good for a hotel at this price point; not much within immediate walking distance in this part of the city, referred to as the Foreshore; busy corporate hotel. [$] *Rooms from: R3200* ✉ *Convention Sq., 1 Lower Long St., Cape Town Central* ☎ *021/412–9999* 🌐 *www.westincapetown.com* 🛏 *483 rooms* 🍴 *Free Breakfast.*

Nightlife

BARS AND PUBS

The Athletic Club and Social

BARS | An upmarket, vintage, 3 story bar and restaurant in the city center overlooking Signal Hill, each floor of the Athletic Club has a distinct feel and decor, while sports memorabilia is littered throughout the venue. Enjoy some tapas in the restaurant before heading upstairs for drinks—the cocktail menu offers both the traditional and more avant-garde cocktails, with a good selection of wine, beer, and whiskey. There's occasional live music. ✉ *35 Buitengracht St., Cape Town Central* ☎ *084/087–5566* 🕒 *Closed Sun.*

Beerhouse

BARS | Cape Town has jumped on the craft-beer bandwagon, and with 25 taps and 99 of the best local and international beers available, this is the place to come see what the fuss is all about. ✉ *223 Long St., Cape Town Central* ☎ *079/360–8990* 🌐 *www.beerhouse.co.za.*

Harrington's Cocktail Lounge

COCKTAIL LOUNGES | A snazzy cocktail lounge, frequented by young professionals, Harrington's has comfortable velvet booths and a large selection of drinks, with a small food menu, including tapas. ✉ *61 Harrington St., Cape Town Central* ☎ *078/916–7903* 🌐 *harringtonstreet.co.za* 🕒 *Closed Mon.*

The Perseverance Tavern

BARS | Known locally as Percy's, South Africa's oldest pub is traditional and recommendable, with decent food and pizza, craft beers, and even an inviting outdoor area. Plus, you'll find plenty of TV screens to watch football. ✉ *83 Buitenkant St., Cape Town Central* ☎ *087/821–7995* 🌐 *www.perseverancetavern.co.za* 🕒 *Closed Mon.*

The Waiting Room

BARS | Find this old bar, club, and live music venue on top of Royale Eatery by climbing the narrow staircase. The grungy, yet hip, bar has a small dancefloor and a great balcony overlooking Long Street. Many nights have guest DJs playing themed music like 90s hip hop, 2000s, etc. It's also a queer-friendly venue. ✉ *273 Long St., Cape Town Central* ☎ *082/425–7732* 🕒 *Closed Sun.–Tues.*

The Village Idiot

BARS | Styled with large leather benches and dark wooden tables, this vintage bar is laid back and jovial. A pool table, music, and a menu full of comfort foods draw crowds on the weekends. ✉ *32 Loop St., Cape Town Central* ☎ *021/418–1548* ⊕ *thefirmct.co.za/the-village-idiot* ⊘ *Closed Sun.–Tues.*

Yobo Wine and Whiskey Bar

BARS | A laid-back, but sophisticated bar, offering a good selection of cocktails, wines and whiskeys. Small eats are sometimes available. ✉ *86 Shortmarket St., Cape Town Central* ☎ *064/752–0555* ⊘ *Closed Sun.–Tues.*

LIVE MUSIC

District

LIVE MUSIC | District is the live music component of a three-part nighttime venue in the space formerly known as The Assembly. Catering to live-music and electronica, this space features everything from South African indie-rock to Afro-Brazilian electronica. The crowd is typically pretty young, with plenty of guests in their late teens, and smoking is allowed. Adjacent sister venues Harringtons Cocktail Lounge and SurfaRosa are an upscale drinks and punk-styled outdoor patio bar, respectively. ✉ *61 Harrington St., District 6, Cape Town Central* ☎ *021/461–2276* ⊕ *thefirmct.co.za/district.*

Selective Live

LIVE MUSIC | Unassuming from the outside, this new gem is a magical world of music, drinks, and food. Owned by the recording company Selective Hearing, this venue brings to life the live music scene that has been slowly fading away in recent years, and which took a major blow during the pandemic. They feature intimate performances by artists from all corners of Cape Town's music scene. It's also an option for laid-back sundowners with a beautiful view of the mountain and city center. ✉ *189 Buitengracht St., Cape Town Central* ☎ *061/588–8388* ⊕ *selectivehearing.co.za.*

🎭 Performing Arts

Artscape Theatre Centre

OPERA | Cape Town's premier performing arts venue is where you come for opera, dance, and bigger theater productions. Opened in 1971, it includes an opera house that seats more than 1,400, a theater auditorium seating more than 500, and a second smaller theater space seating more than 100. ✉ *D.F. Malan St., Foreshore* ☎ *021/410–9800* ⊕ *www.artscape.co.za.*

★ First Thursdays Cape Town

CULTURAL FESTIVALS | On the first Thursday of every month, art galleries in Cape Town's center stay open until 9 pm or later. With them, some retail shops (mostly design-oriented) extend their hours, and often other cultural events and openings are held in the area's hotels (The Taj) and restaurants. The main axes are Bree and Church streets. It is one of the few times the city feels truly pedestrian-friendly after dark, and you can expect a crowd. In summer, food trucks gather in parking lots to add to the festivity. ■**TIP→ Don't even think about driving—parking will be impossible and you will want to save your strolling for the gallery-crawl.** ✉ *Bree St., Cape Town Central* ⊕ *www.first-thursdays.co.za* 🎟 *Free.*

🛍 Shopping

The center of Cape Town's art and antique business, this pleasant block of Church Street is a pedestrian mall filled with art galleries, antique dealers, small cafés, and a few excellent boutiques. Among the art galleries worth visiting are AVA (✉ *35 Church St.*), World Art (✉ *54 Church St.*), and The Cape Gallery (✉ *60 Church St.*). A daily antiques and flea market is also held here. ■**TIP→ Note that Church Street is (somewhat confusingly) not located directly off of Church Square and Groote Kerk (the church for which the street is named), but across Adderley Street.**

ARTS AND CRAFTS

A number of stores in Cape Town sell African art and crafts, much of which come from various African countries, or neighboring provinces in South Africa. Street vendors, particularly on St. George's Mall and Greenmarket Square, often sell the same curios for half the price of a shop. Pick up the excellent Arts & Crafts Map at Cape Town Tourism for listings of excellent and cutting-edge galleries, boutiques, and designers.

African Image

CRAFTS | Look here for contemporary and funky African art and township crafts, colorful cloth from Nigeria and Ghana, plus West African masks, Malian blankets, and beaded designs from southern African tribes. Local and international collectors, as well as local institutions such as the South African National Gallery and the Standard Bank Collection of African Art, buy goods here. It's a top-notch place offering fair-trade pricing. They also have a branch at the Watershed Market in the V&A Waterfront. ✉ *Burg St. at Church St., Cape Town Central* ☎ *021/423–8385* ⊕ *www. african-image.co.za* ☽ *Closed Sun.*

BOOKS

The Book Lounge

BOOKS | Cape Town's best independent bookstore has a fantastic selection of titles, with many classics and contemporary must-haves on all things African. It also frequently hosts readings and book launches and has a nice café downstairs where you can enjoy a cappuccino while browsing. ✉ *71 Roeland St., Cape Town Central* ☎ *021/462–2425* ⊕ *www.book-lounge.co.za.*

★ Clarke's Bookshop

BOOKS | Open since 1957, Clarke's specializes in African literature and non-fiction works, with a specific focus on Southern Africa. There are new and second books to browse including contemporary current affairs and historical rare finds. ✉ *199 Long St., Cape Town Central* ☎ *021/423–5739* ⊕ *clarkesbooks.co.za* ☽ *Closed Sun.*

MARKETS

Greenmarket Square

MARKET | Visit this historic square to find a plethora of African jewelry, art, crafts, and fabrics, as well as good buys on clothing (especially T-shirts), and locally made leather shoes and sandals. It's one of the best places in town to purchase souvenirs and gifts, but it's lively and fun whether or not you buy anything. More than half the stalls are owned by people from other parts of Africa, and if you stop to chat, you'll find political and economic refugees from Ethiopia, Eritrea, Zimbabwe, and the Democratic Republic of Congo trying to eke out a living. Bargain, but do so with a conscience. ✉ *Longmarket, Burg, and Shortmarket Sts., Cape Town Central* ☎ ☽ *Closed Sun.*

The Long Street Antique Arcade

ANTIQUES & COLLECTIBLES | At this row of antique stores in the heart of Long Street, you'll find all sorts of collectibles, artifacts, furniture, and jewelry. It's a treasure trove with friendly owners who are knowledgeable and always up for a chat. ✉ *127 Long St., Cape Town Central* ☎ *078/545–7934* ☽ *Closed Sun.*

Bo-Kaap

Bo-Kaap is the historic home of the city's Muslim population, brought from the East as slaves in the late 17th and early 18th century. The Auwal Mosque, the oldest mosque in South Africa, built in 1798, is also here. You'll know you're in the Bo-Kaap (Afrikaans for "on top of the Cape") when you hear the call of the muezzin from one of the many mosques in the area. You might even have to sidestep lights, cameras, and film stars, since the district is an oft-used setting for movies and magazine shoots—the brightly colored houses make a stunning backdrop. With a threat of the ever-growing gentrification of the neighborhood, residents are holding on to one of the last remaining areas that didn't get

A visit to Bo-Kaap's brightly painted houses should be on everyone's must-do list.

forcefully removed during Apartheid. Today the area remains proudly Muslim and Malay, and it's fascinating to wander the narrow, cobbled lanes past mosques and the largest collection of pre-1840 architecture in South Africa. The Bo-Kaap is also known as the Malay quarter, even though its inhabitants originated from all over, including the Indonesian archipelago, India, Turkey, and Madagascar.

TIMING AND PRECAUTIONS
There have been a few muggings in the Bo-Kaap, so to experience all that the area has to offer we recommend that you take a guided tour, or walk during the mid-morning in the busier streets like Wale, Dorp, and Shortmarket streets. *(See Walking Tours, in Planning, at the beginning of the chapter.)*

Sights

★ Iziko Bo-Kaap Museum
HISTORIC HOME | Most guided tours of the Malay quarter include a visit to this 18th-century home, which originally belonged to well-known Turkish scholar and prominent local Muslim leader, Abu Bakr Effendi. The museum showcases local Islamic heritage and culture, with highlights including "Who Built Cape Town?," "Mapping Bo-Kaap: History, memories and spaces," and the documentary "Viewing Bo-Kaap." ⊠ *71 Wale St., Bo-Kaap* ☎ *021/481–3938* ⊕ *www. iziko.org.za/museums/bo-kaap-museum* 🎫 *R20* 🕐 *Closed Sun.*

🍽 Restaurants

Biesmiellah Restaurant
$$ | **SOUTH AFRICAN** | **FAMILY** | A much-loved cultural Cape Town and Bo-Kaap landmark, diners flock to this no-frills restaurant to eat traditional Cape Malay cuisine, like *bredies* (a thick slow-cooked stew, usually tomato-based and made with spices, meatballs, mutton, or lentils and vegetables), *denning vleis* (usually made with lamb or mutton, this traditional dish is cooked with tamarind and has a sweet and sour flavor), curries, and of course beloved snacks like samoosas,

Cape History at a Glance

It's said that Cape Town owes its current existence to Table Mountain. The freshwater streams running off its slopes were what first prompted early colonists to anchor here. In 1652, Dutch settlers established the first European toehold in South Africa—a refreshment station for the Dutch East India Company (VOC); it's still called the Mother City.

The indigenous Khoekhoen and San lived on the land before the Dutch arrived, but much of their lives, history, culture, and way of being were wiped out by the Dutch when they decided to settle and take the land, bringing with them European diseases that are known to have killed up to 90% of the population. A small group of descendants is still fighting to reclaim their culture, language, and land.

In 1910, when the Union of South Africa was created, Cape Town was named the legislative capital, and it remains so today. The wounds of colonialism continued through its new form, apartheid. Although apartheid ended in the 1990s, its legacy of under-development remains, and Cape Town still remains divided along racial, economic, and physical lines. As you drive into town along the N2 from the airport, you can't miss the shacks built on shifting dunes as far as the eye can see—a sobering contrast to the first-world luxury of the city center on the other side of Table Mountain.

Khayelitsha is the main Black township with well over 2 million people, most of whom originated in the Eastern Cape province, where the main language spoken is Xhosa. Cape Town has a massive Xhosa-speaking population, with Afrikaans and English following. While Afrikaans spoken by South Africa's Coloured (an official racial category created during apartheid but still used today) population is often looked down on compared to the so-called "suiwer" Afrikaans (i.e., the term that white Afrikaaners call "pure" or "proper" Afrikaans), Afrikaans is actually incorrectly considered to be a white language, as it originated in the Cape among the enslaved people who created a creole of Dutch, Malay, Indonesian, Portuguese and Khoekhoe, and San languages. In fact, the first written script of Afrikaans was the Quran, written in Arabic. Much of the Afrikaans spoken in the Cape has a unique dialect and is named by some as "Afrikaaps" or "Kaaps" and being proudly reclaimed.

Much of South Africa's rich and fascinating history is reflected in Cape Town. The District Six Museum tells the heartbreaking story of the apartheid-era demolition of one of Cape Town's most vibrant multi-cultural neighborhoods, and the Bo-Kaap Museum tells the story of the city's Muslim community, who settled here after the abolition of slavery. The Castle of Good Hope, the former seat of the British and Dutch governments, is still the city's military headquarters. Mandela's tiny jail cell has been preserved on Robben Island, and you can learn about his banishment there as well as about the ecological significance of the island. Visit Kirstenbosch National Botanical Garden to learn about the Cape's amazing variety of indigenous plants—it's one of the world's most biodiverse and endemic regions.

half-moons (savory breadcrumb covered, fried dough bites filled with meat or vegetables) and chili bites (a spicy deep-fried snack, usually chickpea flour-based, made with onion, spices, and herbs). The menu though is not limited to Cape Malay cuisine but includes Indian dishes and light meals like toasties (toasted sandwiches like grilled cheese) and wraps. **Known for:** a Bo-Kaap institution; delicious traditional Cape Malay cuisine; a casual, family restaurant. $ *Average main: R120* ✉ *2 Wale St., Bo-Kaap* ☎ *021/423–0850* ⊕ *www.biesmiellah. co.za* ⊗ *Closed Sun.*

☕ Coffee and Quick Bites

Against the Grain
$ | **SOUTH AFRICAN** | A new offering in Bo-Kaap for delicious bagels with a Cape Malay twist, Against the Grain has great coffee and their famous *koeksisters* (traditional spiced donuts). With elegant, ornate decor, this little cafe is a love-ly place to stop for coffee or lunch in town. **Known for:** coffee and koeksisters; delicious bagels with a Cape Malay twist. $ *Average main: R80* ✉ *142 Buitengracht St., Bo-Kaap* ☎ *081/015–6185* ⊗ *No dinner.*

🛍 Shopping

Atlas Trading Company
FOOD | Located in Cape Town's Bo-Kaap neighborhood, Atlas Trading is famed for its array of spices, as well as rice and hard-to-find international products. Estab-lished in 1946, the family-run business ships anywhere in the world, and can assist guests with items to bring home. ✉ *104 Wale St., Bo-Kaap* ☎ *021/423–4361* ⊕ *www.atlastradingcompany.co.za* ⊗ *Closed Sun.*

Woodstock

Once a working-class neighborhood, Woodstock is just a stone's throw north-east of City Center. The area continues to be the recipient of massive, if sometimes controversial, regeneration efforts, and it's now home to numerous galleries, shops, restaurants, and the famous Old Biscuit Mill Saturday market.

Most of Cape Town's best-known gal-leries are clustered along a few blocks of Sir Lowry Road (✉ *Main Road*) and a slightly longer stretch of Albert Road (✉ *Lower Main Rd.*) in Woodstock. Along with the renovation of The Old Biscuit Mill (✉ *375 Albert Rd.*) and its celebrated Saturday market, came the relocation of galleries like Stevenson (✉ *160 Sir Low-ry Rd.*) and The Goodman Cape Town (✉ *176 Sir Lowry Rd.*) from the CBD. While wandering from gallery to gallery (Whatiftheworld, blank projects, and Art It Is are also worthwhile), art lovers can also enjoy the plethora of cafés and boutiques that have sprung up on Sir Lowry Road, and on the stretch of Albert Road between The Biscuit Mill and The Woodstock Exchange (✉ *66 Albert Rd.*). While in the area keep an eye out for the remarkable street art—mostly in the form of graffiti murals—much of which predates the gallery invasion. To fully appreciate the latter, take a tour like those offered by Juma Art Tours *(see Tours at the beginning of the chapter).*

👁 Sights

Greek Orthodox Cathedral of St George
CHURCH | Though it's not as well-known as the St George's on Wale Street, this unassuming Greek Orthodox cathedral is a sight to behold. Painted all white on the outside, it's easy to miss, but once you enter, the flood of bright colors, light blue domed ceilings, and hand-painted murals on the walls are breathtaking. Built in 1904, but painted in the 1990s by Father

You'll feel like a local as you explore Woodstock's Neighbourgoods Market, also known as the Old Biscuit Mill, looking for a bite to eat or a piece of art to bring home.

Nikolai (the serving priest), it's a must-see. Call ahead to arrange a viewing, or attend the Sunday service; it's in Greek, but the deacons and choir chant beautifully. ✉ *75 Mountain Rd., Woodstock* ☎ *021/551–0788* ⊕ *www.goarch.co.za/our-churches/cape-town*.

🍴 Restaurants

Andalousse Moroccan Restaurant
$$ | MOROCCAN | This unassuming little restaurant on the busy Main Road has become a beloved gem in Woodstock. Tastefully decorated with Moroccan decor, the food packs a punch in terms of flavor and generosity; be sure to try the tajines, couscous, or the mixed grills. **Known for:** generous portions; warm hospitality; fresh and flavor-packed Moroccan food. $ *Average main: R150* ✉ *148 Victoria Rd., Woodstock* ☎ *021/447–1708.*

The GrillFather
$$ | STEAKHOUSE | What started as a grill house in Mitchell's Plain has expanded to include this Woodstock location that has a cult following. Plan to go hungry to this burger and steak house, as portions of comfort food favorites like chicken wings, jalapeño poppers, and a footlong boerewors roll (the South African equivalent of the hot dog) are generous. **Known for:** friendly service; comfort food; great burgers with a local twist. $ *Average main: R110* ✉ *135 Albert Rd., Woodstock* ☎ *061/945–3643* 🕙 *Closed Sun. and Mon.*

★ Pahari African Restaurant
$ | AFRICAN | Try a taste of Zimbabwean cuisine at this cozy restaurant in Salt River that serves fresh traditional meals like *millet pap* (a type of starch made from millet grains) or *kapenta* (a traditional dried fish) in peanut butter, or go for a more hearty oxtail stew or tilapia fish in curry. Food is generous, so plan to order a main meal with a starch of your choice, a platter to share, or an individual plate. **Known for:** delicious Zimbabwean food; warm service; sharing plates. $ *Average main: R90* ✉ *121 Cecil Rd., Woodstock* ☎ *078/107–1541* ⊕ *pahari.co.za.*

★ **The Pot Luck Club**

$$$$ | ECLECTIC | A meal at this playful and inventive tapas-style venture from Cape Town star-chef Luke Dale Roberts always promises fabulous fun. With great harbor and mountain views from its position on the sixth floor of a renovated silo, this hip eatery serves an eclectic but clearly Asian-influenced array of fine-dining nibbles. **Known for:** two seatings for dinner—don't expect to linger if you choose the early one; super-creative and umami-packed dishes with distinct Asian flair; simultaneously hip, elegant, and casual ambience. [$] *Average main: R300* ✉ *Old Biscuit Mill, 375 Albert Rd., Silo top fl., Woodstock* ☎ *021/447–0804* 🌐 *www.thepotluckclub.co.za* 🕑 *No dinner Sun.*

Coffee and Quick Bites

Buns Bakery

$ | BAKERY | This cute cafe at the Old Biscuit Mill bakes fresh and decadent cakes, cookies, brownies, brioche buns, donuts, and more, as well as select savories like pies, tarts, and quiches. You can order ahead or go early to get some treats before they sell out, as they tend to. **Known for:** cakes, pies and donuts; pretty and delicious baked goods; everything is handmade. [$] *Average main: R50* ✉ *Old Biscuit Mill, Woodstock* ☎ *068/237–2548* 🌐 *bunsbakery.co.za* 🕑 *Closed Sun.–Tues.*

Shopping

ARTS AND CRAFTS

Streetwires

CRAFTS | You'll see streetwire art everywhere in Cape Town, but this shop is a trove of the form, which uses a combination of wire, beads, and other recycled materials to create bowls, lights, mobiles, and expressive sculptures. ✉ *Maxton Center, 1st fl., 354 Albert Rd., Woodstock* ☎ *021/426–2475* 🌐 *www.streetwires.co.za* 🕑 *Closed Sun.*

MARKETS

The Neighbourgoods Market

MARKET | Known as the Biscuit Mill, this market is partially responsible for putting ever-gentrifying Woodstock on the map with Cape Town's hip, organic types who scoot in on their Vespas looking for artisan breads, pesto, home-cured olives, and fancy cheeses. It gets frantically busy by 10 am, but if you want to rub shoulders with trendy design types and eat fabulous artisanal everything, this is the place to be. The prepared foods are wonderful, and many of Cape Town's most beloved eateries got their start here and most still maintain a presence. When you're done browsing the food market, check out the crafts section with its lovely handmade leather goods, designer clothing, and jewelry, or carry on to the great stores in the same complex. Get there before 9:30 (or after 1:30) or be crushed by the crowds. Music events are not uncommon, and craft beer and boutique wines are also for sale. ✉ *373–375 Albert Rd. (Lower Main Rd.), Woodstock* 🌐 *www.neighbourgoodsmarket.co.za.*

Observatory

Observatory is an old but eclectic neighborhood where artists, intellectuals, and musicians tend to live and gather. It also has a major student and immigrant population, which makes for an interesting mix of lively and homey. This is where you'll find great cafes, vintage thrifting, live music, and vinyl stores. While the majority of "Obs," as it's more popularly referred to, is residential, Lower Main Road is where you'll find it all happening. Unfortunately, the area is experiencing rapid gentrification, but there is still much of the original charm of the neighborhood that hasn't yet changed.

Woodstock and Observatory

KEY
- 1 Exploring Sights
- 1 Restaurants
- 1 Quick Bites

Table Mountain National Park

Sights ▼
1 Cape Town Science Centre **H6**
2 Greek Orthodox Cathedral of
  St George............................**C4**

Restaurants ▼
1 A Touch of Madness **J6**
2 The African Box.....................**J6**
3 Andalousse Moroccan
  Restaurant...........................**C3**
4 Ferdinando's Pizza..................**I5**
5 The GrillFather **B2**
6 Pahari African Restaurant........**G4**
7 The Pot Luck Club **F2**
8 Timbuktu Café.......................**J8**

Quick Bites ▼
1 Buns Bakery..........................**F2**
2 Tapi Tapi **J6**

Voortrekker Road

R102

Malta Road

M57

Chatham Road

SALT
RIVER

Tennyson Street

Milton Road

Lower Main Road

Coleridge Road

Burns Road

Dryden Street

Lenton Road

Goldsmith Road

Kingston Road

Cecil Road

Shelley Road

Kipling Street

Rochester Road

Polo Road

Campbell Street

Scott Road

Arnold Street

Howe Street

Bishop Road

Bedford St.

Blake St.

Seymour St.

OBSERVATORY

Station Road

Nuttall Road

Trill Road

Eden Rd.

Main Road

Bowden Road

Wrensch Road

Sussex Road

Cranko Road

Dane Street

Penzance Rd.

Victoria Road

Falmouth Road

George Street

N2

M3

M3

Table Mountain
National Park

0 _____ 1,000 ft
0 _____ 200 m

Sights

Cape Town Science Centre

SCIENCE MUSEUM | FAMILY | This is a non-profit science center that's part of a wide range of non-classroom initiatives aiming at improving the understanding of science in the country. While the building may look a little rundown from the outside, this science center is full of cool things to see and do and is a huge hit with children. ✉ *370B Main Rd., Observatory* ☎ *021/300–3200* 🌐 *www.ctsc.org.za* 🎟 *R80.*

Restaurants

The African Box

$$ | AFRICAN | This cozy little restaurant is run by folks who are passionate about African food and share the pride, deliciousness, and generosity of African cuisine, with an emphasis on Southern African cuisine. Enjoy a small but well-made menu, in an open and light setting covered in artwork. **Known for:** friendly service; delicious Southern African cuisine. [$] *Average main: R140* ✉ *76 Lower Main Rd., Observatory* ☎ *078/830–2243* 🌐 *the-african-box.business.site* 🕓 *Closed Mon.*

Ferdinando's Pizza

$$ | PIZZA | FAMILY | Another quirky Observatory restaurant, this unassuming pizza place makes amazing pizzas and has become a favorite among locals over many years. There's a casual and colorful setting, with warm service and a touch of humor. **Known for:** vegan options; quirky and warm vibe; great pizza. [$] *Average main: R128* ✉ *205 Lower Main Rd., Observatory* ☎ *084/771–0485* 🌐 *www.ferdinandospizza.com.*

Timbuktu Café

$$ | ETHIOPIAN | As one of the first Ethiopian restaurants in Cape Town (although originally in Long Street), Timbuktu has been a local favorite for close to two decades; it was also one of Cape Town's first racially integrated restaurants. The decor is eclectic vintage, meets plant heaven—it's something you just have to see to understand—and the fare is exquisite Ethiopian food. **Known for:** eclectic decor; delicious and affordable Ethiopian food. [$] *Average main: R120* ✉ *16 Lower Main Rd., Observatory* ☎ *072/378–9697.*

A Touch of Madness

$ | CAFÉ | This quaint but quirky restaurant serves up a gastro-pub style menu with items like spare ribs, burgers, fried calamari, pasta, and salads. Located in an old Observatory home with a garden, the spot has a cozy and party atmosphere at the same time—people come for the music and stay to eat and socialize in a relaxed setting. **Known for:** relaxed environment made lively with music; friendly service; small, but good menu. [$] *Average main: R95* ✉ *12 Nuttall Rd., Observatory* ☎ *021/447–4650* 🌐 *atouchofmadness.co.za.*

Coffee and Quick Bites

★ Tapi Tapi

$ | ICE CREAM | This ice cream cafe has become an Obs and Cape Town institution and is a must-visit as Tapiwa, ice cream maker and founder of Tapi Tapi, makes delicious and daring handcrafted African ice creams. This cafe is small but packs a punch, and the ice cream will give you an education and not just a frozen dessert. **Known for:** Tapiwa, the ice-cream maker, is wonderful to chat to; handcrafted African ice-cream; exciting flavors that change weekly. [$] *Average main: R35* ✉ *76 Lower Main Rd., Observatory* ☎ *076/914–5614* 🌐 *www.tapitapi.co.za* 🕓 *Closed Mon.*

Shopping

Bang Bang Vintage Market

MIXED CLOTHING | If you love thrifting and finding unique vintage or alternative clothing items, this is the store for you. With a large collection of one-of-a-kind

The Best View of Cape Town

Make the 25-km (16-mile), 40-minute trip north from the city to the other side of Table Bay, and you'll be rewarded with an exceptional (and the most famous) view of Cape Town and Table Mountain as well as a good, albeit windy, beach that is known for kite surfing and also kite flying. The Kite Shop in Victoria Wharf at the V&A Waterfront has many colorful, high-tech kites for sale, and there is a kite shop in the new shopping development next to the beach. The lawns of the Blue Peter Hotel are a favorite sunset cocktail spot, especially with tired kite- and windsurfers. The thatched restaurant Ons Huisie (an internationally recognized heritage site) is a winner for fish-and-chips and has a children's jungle gym area attached. If you want to come from the city for the sunset—possibly the best in Cape Town—leave Cape Town Central before 4 pm to avoid the horrible rush-hour traffic.

3

Cape Town GARDENS

pieces, you'll love going through the store and finding hidden gems. Once you're done browsing, head out to explore the numerous vintage clothing stores all along Lower Main Road. ⊠ *65 Lower Main Rd., Observatory* ☎ *072/264–1246* ⊕ *www.facebook.com/ BangBangVintageMarkets* ⊗ *Closed Sun.*

Better Half

WOMEN'S CLOTHING | A small store that has lovely locally designed women's clothing and trinkets, Better Half offers one-of-a-kind vintage pieces as well as their own small selection of clothing. The in-house design is of impeccable quality, with a small line of pieces done in different colors or fabrics. ⊠ *114 Lower Main Rd., Observatory* ☎ *067/263–6697* ⊕ *www. betterhalf.co.za.*

Gardens

This affluent city neighborhood begins at the southern end of the Company's Garden, stretching south toward the base of Table Mountain and Lion's Head. Populated largely by young professionals, it has numerous restaurants, cafés, hotels, and shops, as well as many beautiful homes. Main thoroughfares like Kloof Street are packed with funky boutiques and are pleasant to stroll and explore. It's a popular place both to stay and explore, day or night.

TIMING AND PRECAUTIONS

Unlike Cape Town Central, Gardens' commercial zone remains relatively lively into the evening. From where Kloof Street begins (at the end of Long Street) until it intersects with Camp Street, restaurants, cafés, and Cape Town's art-house cinema make the area lively and safe for walking until about 10 pm. In other areas take the usual precautions.

Sights

Cape Town Holocaust Centre
HISTORY MUSEUM | The center is both a memorial to the 6 million Jews and other victims who were killed during the Holocaust and an education center whose aim is to create a caring and just society in which human rights and diversity are valued. The permanent exhibit is excellent and very moving. A multimedia display, comprising photo panels, text, film footage, and music, creates a chilling reminder of the dangers of prejudice, racism, and discrimination. The center is next to the South African

Sights ▼

1 Cape Town Holocaust Centre **H3**

2 Iziko South African
   Museum & Planetarium **G2**

3 South African
   Jewish Museum **H3**

4 South African National Gallery... **H2**

Restaurants ▼

1 Aubergine **H4**

2 Black Sheep Restaurant........... **E4**

3 Kloof Street House **F2**

4 Kyoto Sushi Garden **E3**

5 Maria's Greek Cafe **H3**

6 Miller's Thumb **E3**

7 Saigon.............................. **E4**

8 Societi Bistro..................... **G2**

9 Yindee's **E4**

Quick Bites ▼

1 Afternoon Tea at
   Mount Nelson..................... **G3**

2 Deluxe Coffeeworks
   Kloof Street....................... **G2**

3 Grumpy and Runt **H3**

4 SCHOON Kloof Street Village **G2**

Hotels ▼

1 Cactusberry Lodge **H6**

2 Cape Cadogan Boutique
   Hotel & More Quarters............ **E4**

3 Cape Milner Hotel **E2**

4 Derwent House **D4**

5 Kensington Place.................. **D7**

6 La Grenadine Petit Hotel........... **F2**

7 Mount Nelson Hotel................ **F4**

8 Protea Fire & Ice!
   by Marriott......................... **F1**

9 Three Boutique Hotel **H6**

10 Welgelegen Boutique
    Hotel................................ **E5**

3

Cape Town GARDENS

Jewish Museum. ⊠ *88 Hatfield St., Gardens* ☎ *021/462–5553* ⊕ *www.holocaust. org.za* ✉ *Free* ☉ *Closed Sat. and Jewish holidays.*

Iziko South African Museum & Planetarium
OBSERVATORY | FAMILY | Founded in 1825, this natural history museum houses more than 1.5 million scientific specimens, but is most popular for its "Whale Well," where life-size casts of enormous marine mammals are suspended over a multi-storied chamber, which leads to displays of marine and terrestrial animals in the old diorama style. International photography exhibits are often on display upstairs, and there is an interesting if creepy section on the fossil remains of prehistoric "mammal-like" reptiles. In the adjoining planetarium, visitors can experience the thrills of a 360-degree multisensory, full-dome theater, where a variety of shows for children and adults play throughout the week. ⊠ *25 Queen Victoria St., Gardens* ☎ *021/481–3800* ⊕ *www.iziko.org.za/museums/south-african-museum* ✉ *Museum R30* ☉ *Closed May 1 and Dec. 25.*

South African Jewish Museum
HISTORY MUSEUM | FAMILY | Housed in the Old Synagogue—South Africa's first synagogue, built in 1863—this museum sits in the same complex as the Cape Town Holocaust Centre and spans 150 years of South African Jewry. The themes of Memories (immigrant experiences), Reality (integration into South Africa), and Dreams (visions for the future) are conveyed with high-tech multimedia and interactive displays, models, and artifacts. The complex also includes the Great Synagogue (built in 1905), an active place of worship, a temporary gallery for changing exhibits, an auditorium, and a museum restaurant and shop. The museum also exhibits the extraordinary Isaac Kaplan collection of Japanese netsuke, considered among the world's

finest. ⊠ *88 Hatfield St., Gardens* ☎ *021/465–1546* ⊕ *www.sajewishmuseum.co.za* ✉ *R60* ☉ *Closed Sat. and Jewish holidays.*

South African National Gallery
ART GALLERY | This museum houses a good collection of 19th- and 20th-century European art, but its most interesting exhibits are the South African works, many of which reflect the country's traumatic history. The gallery owns an enormous body of work, so exhibitions change regularly, but there's always something provocative—whether it's documentary photographs or a multimedia exhibit chronicling efforts to "disrupt" traditional boundaries. The museum would like to position itself as a leader of contemporary and traditional African art. Free guided tours on Tuesday and Thursday take about an hour. ⊠ *Government Ave., Gardens* ☎ *021/481–3970* ⊕ *www. iziko.org.za/museums/south-african-national-gallery* ✉ *R30.*

🍴 Restaurants

Aubergine
$$$$ | EUROPEAN | In this warm space of yellowwood tables, sash windows, and reed ceilings, chef-owner Harald Bresselschmidt has served classic European-with-a-twist cuisine since 1996 at one of the city's oldest fine-dining establishments. Using the freshest South African produce prepared with classical European methods, the chef cooks with wine in mind, and Aubergine's cellar and pairings are unsurprisingly superb. **Known for:** old-school approach and feel; consistency of the classic European cuisine; warmly elegant and unpretentious dining room has great acoustics. $ *Average main: R245* ⊠ *39 Barnet St., Gardens* ☎ *021/465–0000* ⊕ *www.aubergine.co.za* ☉ *Closed Sun. and Mon. No lunch Tues., Wed., and Sat.*

★ Black Sheep Restaurant

$$$ | **SOUTH AFRICAN** | A cozy yet elegant restaurant with a select seasonal menu posted on a chalkboard, Black Sheep features food inspired by all of the Cape's culinary influences: indigenous, North African, Asian, Middle Eastern, and more. Ingredients are locally and ethically sourced, and the restaurant has a nose-to-tail food philosophy. **Known for:** hearty fare won't leave you hungry; lively, busy vibe; locally and ethically sourced ingredients. [$] *Average main: R175* ✉ *104 Kloof St., Gardens* ☎ *021/426–2661* 🌐 *blacksheeprestaurant.co.za* 🕑 *Closed Sun.*

Kloof Street House

$$$ | **MEDITERRANEAN** | An upmarket gem in the lower end of Kloof Street, this eclectic restaurant in an old Victorian house has a simple but great French-inspired menu, with meat, fish, and vegetarian dishes, and impressive cocktails. The decor is vintage opulence meets modern accents, with different seating areas, including outdoors for warmer days. **Known for:** excellent cocktails; Moroccan-spiced lamb rump; festive atmosphere. [$] *Average main: R195* ✉ *30 Kloof St., Gardens* ☎ *021/423–4413* 🌐 *www.kloofstreethouse.co.za* 🕑 *No lunch Mon.*

★ Maria's Greek Cafe

$$ | **GREEK** | **FAMILY** | Located in the vibey Dunkley Square, this lovely Greek restaurant serves all kinds of Greek mezzes which can be ordered as a platter, or traditional dishes like moussaka, calamari, and lamb chops. This local favorite also serves pitas, souvlaki, and burgers, as well as good vegetarian options. **Known for:** beautiful outdoor dining (weather permitting); mezze platters and sharing plates; lots of vegan options. [$] *Average main: R145* ✉ *31 Barnet St., Gardens* ☎ *021/461–3333* 🌐 *www.facebook.com/MariasGreekCafe.*

Saigon

$$ | **VIETNAMESE** | An upmarket and modern Vietnamese restaurant, Saigon has a superb and extensive menu with dishes that include spicy beef basil with chili sauce and Saigon ginger fish. Views of Table Mountain and an inviting atmosphere, have made this a popular spot so make sure you book ahead. **Known for:** sophisticated dining; delicious and wide variety of Vietnamese dishes; views of the city. [$] *Average main: R149* ✉ *Corner of Kamp and Kloof sts, Gardens* ☎ *021/424–7670* 🌐 *facebook.com/SaigonCapeTown* 🕑 *Closed Mon.*

Societi Bistro

$$$ | **BISTRO** | This much-loved neighborhood bistro offers a reliable and seasonal menu of French- and Italian-style classics. In a renovated 19th-century Georgian-style home just off Kloof Street, the dining room is all exposed brick and wooden floors, with roaring fires in the winter and a large, lovely garden in the summer. **Known for:** convivial atmosphere; roasted chicken with crispy potatoes; excellent wine list. [$] *Average main: R161* ✉ *50 Orange St., Gardens* ☎ *021/424–2100* 🌐 *www.societi.co.za* 🕑 *Closed Sun.*

★ Yindee's

$$$ | **THAI** | **FAMILY** | Located near the top of Kloof Street, this Thai restaurant has an extensive menu full of flavorful grills, curries, and salads. Whether you sit on the romantic side where guests can dine at low tables while sitting on cushions on the floor, or at a table on the side with elegant traditional decor, you're bound to have a delicious meal and warm service. **Known for:** romantic ambience; extensive Thai menu; beautiful ornate decor. [$] *Average main: R170* ✉ *22 Kamp St., Gardens* ☎ *021/422–1012* 🌐 *yindees.com* 🕑 *Closed Mon.*

Coffee and Quick Bites

Afternoon Tea at Mount Nelson

$$$$ | **CAFÉ** | Don't miss Mount Nelson's legendary high tea, which has been offered since the hotel was erected in 1899 to welcome the Prince of Wales on his visit to the Cape. Served from 2:30 to 5:30, afternoon tea offers a pastry selection that can tempt even the most jaded palate, with savory treats that make for a scrumptious meal, and more than 40 tea varieties, which an expertly-trained tea sommelier can guide you through. **Known for:** delicate pastries and cakes; sophisticated and elegant setting; traditional tea ceremony. [$] *Average main: R395* ✉ *Mount Nelson Hotel, 76 Orange St., Gardens* ☎ *021/483–1000* 🌐 *www.mount-nelson.co.za* 🕓 *Closed Mon. and Tues.*

Deluxe Coffeeworks Kloof Street

$ | **CAFÉ** | A treat for coffee lovers, the talented baristas at this unassuming little cafe have built a loyal following over the years. Come for quality coffee and espresso to go and grab some beans as well ... you'll thank us. **Known for:** unassuming coffee roastery with quality, barista brewed coffee; fast service; loyal regulars. [$] *Average main: R25* ✉ *8 Kloof St., Gardens* ☎ *060/871–6561* 🌐 *www.deluxecoffeeworks.co.za* 🕓 *Closed Sun.*

★ **Grumpy and Runt**

$ | **BAKERY** | This unassuming little bakery and deli in Dunkley Square makes the most scrumptious donuts in the city. Women-owned and all vegan, all sorts of sandwiches, bagels, subs, coffees, and treats are also on offer. **Known for:** best donuts in town; vegan deli; woman-owned and run. [$] *Average main: R85* ✉ *22 Dunkley St., Gardens* ☎ *060/365–4917* 🌐 *www.grumpyandrunt.com* 🕓 *Closed Mon. and Tues.*

SCHOON Kloof Street Village

$ | **BAKERY** | Originally a well-loved Stellenbosch bakery, Schoon expanded to Cape Town where it continues to offer freshly baked bread and pastries of all kinds. The plethora of freshly baked bread also ensures great sandwiches served on rye, sourdough, and baguettes, as well as pizzas, croissants, and other hearty breakfast and lunch options. **Known for:** fresh baked goods; great coffee; shares a space with other eateries. [$] *Average main: R75* ✉ *Kloof Street Village, Corner of Kloof St. and Rheede St., Gardens* ☎ *087/106–3314* 🌐 *schoon.co.za.*

Hotels

Cape Cadogan Boutique Hotel & More Quarters

$$$$ | **HOTEL** | **FAMILY** | The lovely and well-located Georgian and Victorian Cape Cadogan boutique hotel dates back to the beginning of the 19th century, and boasts a style that successfully blends contemporary and antique furnishings. **Pros:** walking distance to great restaurants, bars, and shops; free shuttle within 6-km (4-mile) radius; unique apartment-hotel concept at More Quarters gives best of both worlds. **Cons:** not accessible; rooms can be quite uneven in size at Cadogan; traffic noise from nearby intersection can be a problem. [$] *Rooms from: R7400* ✉ *5 Upper Union St., Gardens* ☎ *021/480–8080* 🌐 *www.capecadogan.co.za* 🛏 *33 rooms* 🍴 *Free Breakfast.*

Kensington Place

$$$$ | **B&B/INN** | A beautiful garden entrance leads you into this stylish oasis of a guesthouse where you can expect an atmosphere of luxurious privacy and attentive concierge service from on-site management. **Pros:** fantastic staff and service; gorgeous peaceful location that is still walking distance to upper Kloof Street attractions; great breakfast and other meals available from on-site kitchen. **Cons:** lots of stairs make it wheelchair-unfriendly; no kids under 12; steep hill might dissuade walking back from town. [$] *Rooms from: R6700* ✉ *38 Kensington Crescent, Higgovale, Gardens* ☎ *021/424–4744* 🌐 *www.kensington-place.co.za* 🛏 *9 rooms* 🍴 *Free Breakfast.*

★ La Grenadine Petit Hotel

$$ | B&B/INN | FAMILY | Built around a verdant courtyard shaded by pomegranate, guava, and avocado trees, the five gorgeous rooms at this well-located and good-value hotel are all Gallic-charm-meets-South-African-vintage-hipster: hand-embroidered bed linens, badminton paddles repurposed as mirrors, and art deco light fittings. **Pros:** wonderful fusion of French and South African vintage style; great bustling location in walking distance to dozens of restaurants and attractions; excellent Continental breakfast filled with homemade treats. **Cons:** some rooms have bathrooms that are not fully closed off; limited off-street parking; no TVs in rooms and Wi-Fi can be slow. $ Rooms from: R2500 ⊠ 15 Park Rd., Gardens ☎ 021/424–1358 ⊕ www. lagrenadine.co.za ⌑ 10 rooms ⦿ Free Breakfast.

★ Mount Nelson Hotel

$$$$ | HOTEL | FAMILY | An icon of Cape Town since it opened its doors in 1899, this superbly located landmark sits on 9 beautifully landscaped acres and retains a charm and gentility unusual even in the world of luxury hotels. **Pros:** the "Nellie's" lavish high tea is an institution, and the glam Planet Bar an ideal place for a cocktail; decor achieves the perfect balance between colonial elegance and contemporary style; great location in walking distance to Company's Garden and downtown, or Kloof Street attractions. **Cons:** spread out across multiple buildings, each with its own style, so you must be sure to state your preferences; may be booked out during high season as much as a year in advance; breakfast restaurant Oasis lacks the charm of the rest of the hotel. $ Rooms from: R13800 ⊠ 76 Orange St., Gardens ☎ 021/483–1000 ⊕ www.belmond.com/mount-nelson-hotel-cape-town ⌑ 198 rooms ⦿ Free Breakfast.

Protea Fire & Ice! by Marriott

$ | HOTEL | Initially built around somewhat kitschy themes—think interior elements like elevators kitted out as a shark cage underwater or a Table Mountain cable car mid-journey—this large hotel (one of the few in the area) will appeal to those who value a vibey social atmosphere and proximity to Cape Town's nightlife. **Pros:** friendly and helpful staff; proximity to restaurants and other activities on foot; brilliant views of Table Mountain from rooms above the fifth floor. **Cons:** rooms are small; zany decoration won't suit all tastes. $ Rooms from: R1200 ⊠ 64 New Church St., Gardens ☎ 021/488–2555 ⊕ www.marriott.com/hotels/travel/cptcf-protea-hotel-fire-and-ice-cape-town ⌑ 201 rooms ⦿ No Meals.

Welgelegen Boutique Hotel

$$$ | B&B/INN | FAMILY | In Dutch, welgelegen means "well situated," and this charming boutique hotel in two beautifully restored Victorian mansions is just that: nestled under Table Mountain in a quiet street just minutes away from city attractions. **Pros:** great staff make guests feel like part of the family; walking distance to Kloof Street cafés; one of the few boutique hotels that welcomes children of all ages. **Cons:** it's an old building, so the occasional creaky floorboard is to be expected; Wi-Fi can be slow; breakfast dining room is a bit dark. $ Rooms from: R2880 ⊠ 6 Stephen St., Gardens ☎ 021/426–2373 ⊕ www.welgelegen.co.za ⌑ 13 rooms ⦿ Free Breakfast.

Tamboerskloof

Like Gardens, this lovely area along the lower slopes of Table Mountain, from Lion's Head toward Signal Hill and extending to Kloof Street, has grown in popularity as a place where eateries and bars frequented by the young professionals who reside here are thriving. It's also home to numerous bed-and-breakfasts and small guesthouses, most on quiet residential streets, but still within walking distance of numerous options on trendy Kloof Street.

 Restaurants

★ Kyoto Sushi Garden

$$$$ | JAPANESE | Elegant and tranquil, this small oasis near the Kloof Street drag serves pricey but beautifully executed Japanese fare. Sourcing as much as possible from Japan, the owner verges on obsessive in his effort to maintain a high standard of both ingredients and technique, evidenced in the lightness of the tempura and the freshness and variety of seafood. **Known for:** amazing Japanese whiskey and sake selections; most authentic Japanese food in Cape Town. $ *Average main: R280* ✉ *11 Lower Kloofnek Rd., Tamboerskloof* ☎ *021/422–2001* ⊕ *www.kyotogardensushict.com* ⊗ *Closed Sun.*

Miller's Thumb

$$$ | SEAFOOD | FAMILY | This cozy home-style seafood restaurant is a neighborhood classic, owned by a husband-and-wife team who are very friendly and knowledgeable. With a small menu, you can expect simple but consistently good fresh fish dishes inspired by Cape flavors, but the meat and vegetarian options are also great. **Known for:** homestyle restaurant; friendly service; great seafood dishes. $ *Average main: R190* ✉ *10B Kloof Nek Rd., Tamboerskloof* ☎ *021/424–3838* ⊕ *millersthumb.co.za* ⊗ *Closed Sun. No lunch Mon.*

 Hotels

Cape Milner Hotel

$$$ | HOTEL | The only midsize hotel in the lovely Tamboerskloof area, the clean and comfortable Milner makes a convenient location from which to explore trendy nearby Kloof Street and beyond. **Pros:** great views of Table Mountain from pool; great location minutes from city; good dining options within walking distance. **Cons:** Table Mountain views from rooms

that have them are partially obscured by strange window awnings; overlooks a road that's busy (and loud) at peak times; one-way roads make it tricky to access. $ *Rooms from: R3463* ✉ *2 Milner Rd., Tamboerskloof* ☎ *021/426–1101* ⊕ *www.capemilner.com* ⮌ *57 rooms* ¶○¶ *Free Breakfast.*

Derwent House

$$$ | B&B/INN | The nine rooms comprising this beautiful Victorian house in a very central Tamboerskloof location make for a stylish and convenient base while exploring Cape Town. **Pros:** gracious management by owners with decades in the hospitality industry; super-convenient location to Kloof Street eateries and attractions; well-stocked honor bar and complimentary afternoon cake and treats. **Cons:** only two rooms have unobstructed mountain views; can hear creaks and noises on occasion; some rooms a bit small. $ *Rooms from: R3300* ✉ *14 Derwent Rd., Tamboerskloof* ☎ *021/422–2763* ⊕ *www.derwenthouse.co.za* ⮌ *9 rooms* ¶○¶ *Free Breakfast.*

 Nightlife

Publik Wine Bar

WINE BARS | Perhaps the best place in Cape Town to acquaint yourself with lesser-known, boutique, and very special vintages. ✉ *11D Kloofnek Rd., Tamboerskloof* ⊕ *www.publik.co.za* ⊗ *Closed Sun.*

Oranjezicht

The heavily residential area above Gardens and just below Table Mountain, upscale Oranjezicht is home to a few excellent B&Bs and gorgeous boutique guesthouses, and is generally a quiet and tranquil place to base yourself. You'll be more likely to want wheels to get around, especially at night, but that's what taxis are for.

Hotels

Cactusberry Lodge

$$ | **B&B/INN** | This great-value guesthouse in an appealing shade of cinnamon terra cotta (aka cactusberry) is in a quiet neighborhood that is still within walking distance of many attractions and restaurants. **Pros:** great breakfast; personalized concierge service from the owner; homey, friendly place to meet other travelers. **Cons:** no TV in rooms; creaky floors if downstairs; rooms on the small side. [$] *Rooms from: R1800* ✉ *30 Breda St., Oranjezicht* ☎ *021/461–9787* 🌐 *www.cactusberrylodge.com* 🛏 *6 rooms* 🍴 *Free Breakfast.*

Three Boutique Hotel

$$$$ | **HOTEL** | A tranquil four-star boutique hotel on the slopes of Table Mountain, the Three is located in the quiet neighborhood of Oranjezicht just a few minutes walk to cafes and restaurants. **Pros:** great breakfast; beautiful location and views; private location. **Cons:** largely residential area (not much to do nearby); some may find it too quiet and intimate; located in quite a windy area. [$] *Rooms from: R3514* ✉ *3 Flower St., Oranjezicht* ☎ *021/465–7517* 🌐 *www.thethree.co.za* 🛏 *18 rooms* 🍴 *Free Breakfast.*

V&A Waterfront

The V&A (Victoria & Alfred) Waterfront is the culmination of a long-term project undertaken to breathe new life into the city's historical dockland. Although some Capetonians deem the area too "mallish," the Waterfront remains Cape Town's most popular attraction—probably because of the ease and safety of being a pedestrian here, coupled with favorable currency exchange rates for North American and European visitors, and the ever-increasing number of truly worthwhile attractions and activities on offer. Hundreds of shops, movie theaters, restaurants, and bars share quarters in restored warehouses and dock buildings, all connected by pedestrian plazas and promenades. Newer developments like the excellent Watershed craft market and two fantastic food markets have made the V&A more appealing to locals, and the much-anticipated Zeitz Museum of Contemporary Art—Africa's first such institution—adds even more to look forward to within one area.

TIMING AND PRECAUTIONS

You could see the area's major sights in a day, but that won't give you much time for shopping, coffee stops, or lunch, or for all that the worthwhile aquarium has to offer. A more leisurely approach would be to set aside a whole day, at the end of which you could find a waterside restaurant or bar to enjoy a cold glass of wine or a cocktail. With its crowds of people, security cameras, and guards, this is one of the safest places to shop and hang out in the city. That said, you should still keep an eye on your belongings and be aware of pickpockets.

Sights

Cape Town Diamond Museum

HISTORY MUSEUM | This small museum attached to the Shimansky boutique tells the fascinating history of the little stones that played such a big role in South Africa's history. The 45-minute tour covers a time line of 3 billion years, mostly focusing on how the local industry developed in the 19th and early 20th centuries, and ending in a showroom where polishers are busy "brillianteering" stones that are available for purchase. ✉ *Level, The Clocktower Waterfront, V&A Waterfront* ☎ *021/421–2488* 🌐 *www.capetowndiamondmuseum.org* 🎟 *R50.*

Chavonnes Battery Museum

MILITARY SIGHT | An archaeological sight housing the remains of Cape Town's oldest cannon battery, this museum, which opened in 2008, reconstructs the outer battlements and underground rooms

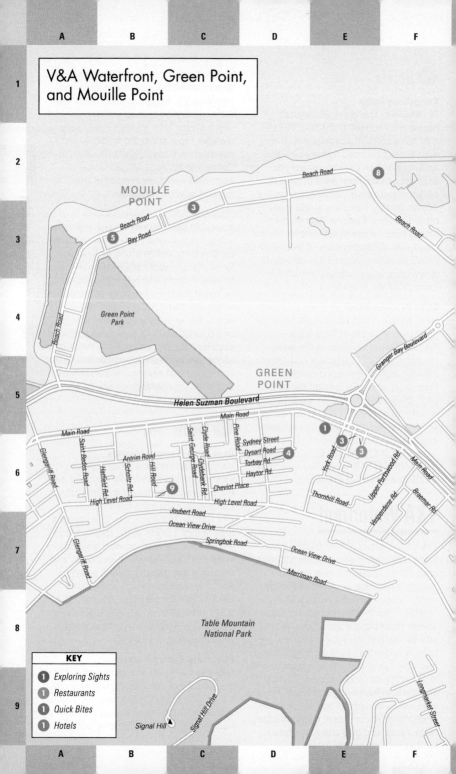

V&A Waterfront, Green Point, and Mouille Point

MOUILLE POINT

GREEN POINT

Beach Road

Beach Road

Bay Road

Beach Road

Beach Road

Green Point Park

Granger Bay Boulevard

Helen Suzman Boulevard

Main Road

Main Road

Sydney Street

Pine Road

Clyde Road

Saint George Road

Clytebank Rd.

Dysart Road

Torbay Rd.

Haytor Rd.

Cheviot Place

High Level Road

Antrim Road

Saint Bedes Road

Scholtz Rd.

Hill Road

Hatfield Rd.

High Level Road

Glengariff Road

Hort Road

Thornhill Road

Upper Portswood Rd.

Vesperdene Rd.

Braemar Rd.

Main Road

Joubert Road

Ocean View Drive

Springbok Road

Ocean View Drive

Merriman Road

Glengariff Road

Table Mountain National Park

Longmarket Street

Signal Hill

Signal Hill Drive

KEY

1 *Exploring Sights*

1 *Restaurants*

1 *Quick Bites*

1 *Hotels*

Sights ▼

1	Cape Town Diamond Museum....	I5
2	Chavonnes Battery Museum......	I5
3	Robben Island.....................	H1
4	South African Maritime Centre	H4
5	Two Oceans Aquarium............	G5
6	V&A Waterfront Amphitheatre......................	H4
7	Zeitz Museum of Contemporary Art Africa...........	I5

Restaurants ▼

1	Baía Seafood Restaurant..........	I4
2	Den Anker	I5
3	El Burro	E6
4	Emazulwini Restaurant............	J6
5	Gold Restaurant....................	H7
6	Harbour House V&A	H4
7	Nobu	G6
8	Pigalle..............................	G7
9	SIBA The Restaurant..............	I3
10	Willoughby & Co.	I3

Quick Bites ▼

1	Giovanni's Deli	E5
2	Grand Africa Café & Beach	G3
3	Jason Bakery	E6
4	Maker's Landing	J6
5	V&A Food Market.................	H5

Hotels ▼

1	Cape Grace Hotel..................	H6
2	The Dock House Boutique Hotel..................................	H4
3	Dolphin Inn	C3
4	Dysart Boutique Hotel.............	D6
5	La Splendida Hotel	B3
6	One&Only Cape Town.............	G6
7	Protea Hotel Cape Town Waterfront Breakwater Lodge.................	G5
8	Radisson Blu Hotel Waterfront..........................	E2
9	Romney Park Hotel & Spa	B6
10	The Silo Hotel	I5
11	Table Bay Hotel	I3
12	Victoria & Alfred Hotel............	H5

that formed one of the major defense outposts on the Cape. Detailed miniature replicas of the cannons and the different types of projectiles are fascinating, as are interpretative materials about the Cape's natural heritage at the time that the battery was in use. In addition, the museum always has an international photo exhibit on, including the Underwater Photographer of the Year. History buffs will also enjoy the surprisingly good walking tour of the Waterfront given by guides dressed in period costumes, which departs from the museum twice daily; reservations are recommended. ✉ *Clock Tower Precinct, V&A Waterfront* ☏ *021/416–6230* ⊕ *www.chavonnesbattery.co.za* ✍ *R35.*

★ **Robben Island**

ISLAND | Made famous by its most illustrious inhabitant, Nelson Mandela, this island, whose name is Dutch for "seals," has a long and sad history. At various times a prison, leper colony, mental institution, and military base, it is finally filling a positive, enlightening, and empowering role in its latest incarnation as a museum.

Declared a World Heritage site on December 1, 1997, Robben Island has become a symbol of the triumph of the human spirit. In 1997 around 90,000 made the pilgrimage; in 2006 more than 300,000 crossed the water to see where some of the most prominent struggle leaders in South Africa spent decades of their lives. Visiting the island is a sobering experience. The approximately four-hour tour begins at the Nelson Mandela Gateway to Robben Island, an impressive embarkation center that doubles as a conference center. Changing exhibits display historic photos of prisoners and prison life. Next make the 45-minute journey across the water, remembering to watch Table Mountain recede in the distance and imagine what it must have been like to have just received a 20-year jail sentence. Boats leave three or four times a day, depending on season and weather.

Tours are organized by the Robben Island Museum (other operators that advertise Robben Island tours only take visitors on a boat trip *around* the island.) Most guides are former political prisoners, and during the two-hour tour, they will take you through the prison where you will see the cells where Mandela and other leaders were imprisoned. The tour also takes you to the lime quarry, Robert Sobukwe's place of confinement, and the leper church. Due to increased demand for tickets during peak season (December and January), make reservations at least three weeks in advance. Take sunglasses and a hat in summer. ■**TIP→ You are advised to tip your guide only if you feel that the tour has been informative.** ✉ *Nelson Mandela Gateway, V&A Waterfront* ☏ *021/413–4200* ⊕ *www.robben-island.org.za* ✍ *R600.*

South African Maritime Centre

HISTORY MUSEUM | Inside the Union-Castle House, this museum explains the Cape's long history with the sea, in particular documenting the history of the Union-Castle shipping line. Before World War II many English-speaking South Africans looked upon England as home, even if they had never been there. The emotional link between the two countries was symbolized most strongly by the mail steamers, carrying both mail and passengers that sailed weekly between South Africa and England. Models of ships are accompanied by memorabilia such as a collection of postcards sold from the ships between 1910 and 1960. A fascinating re-creation of Cape Town harbor as it appeared in 1885, which was built by convicts, is on permanent display, as is a chilling exhibit about the SS *Mendi,* a cargo vessel turned troopship that was carrying the South African Native Labour Contingent to help with the war effort in France during World War I. She was accidentally rammed by a British cargo ship, resulting in the deaths of 607 Black troops. ✉ *Union-Castle Bldg., Dock Rd., Quay 4, V&A Waterfront*

☎ 021/405–2884 ⊕ www.iziko.org.
za/museums/maritime-centre ☞ R25
⊗ Closed May 1 and Dec. 25.

★ Two Oceans Aquarium

AQUARIUM | FAMILY | This aquarium is
widely considered one of the finest
in the world. Stunning displays reveal
the regional marine life of the warmer
Indian Ocean and the icy Atlantic. It's
a hands-on place, with a touch pool for
children, opportunities to interact with
penguins, and (for certified divers only)
to dive in the vast, five-story ocean
exhibit with shoals of fish, huge turtles,
and stingrays, or the new shark exhibit,
where you might share the water with
large ragged-tooth sharks (Carcharias
taurus) and enjoy a legal adrenaline rush
(for an additional fee, of course). If you
don't fancy getting wet, you can still
watch daily feedings in either the ocean,
penguin, or shark exhibits. But there's
more to the aquarium than just snapping
jaws. Look for the trippy jellyfish display,
the Knysna seahorses, and the alien-like
spider crabs. ⊠ Dock Rd., V&A Waterfront ☎ 021/418–3823 ⊕ www.aquarium.
co.za ☞ R210.

V&A Waterfront Amphitheatre

OTHER ATTRACTION | If the scattered
benches looking out at the harbor activity
are full, this open-air space is a good spot
to eat your take-away lunch—if there's
no performance on. This popular outdoor
space mounts performances ranging
from concerts by the Cape Town Philhar-
monic Orchestra to gigs by jazz and rock
bands and even variety performances.
(Check the Waterfront's website or its
branch of the tourism office for a schedule of events.) The amphitheater stands
on the site where, in 1860, a teenage
Prince Alfred inaugurated the construction of a breakwater to protect ships in
the harbor from devastating northwest-
erly winds. ⊠ Near Market Sq., Victoria
and Alfred Waterfront, V&A Waterfront
☎ 021/408–7600 for schedule ⊕ www.
waterfront.co.za.

★ Zeitz Museum of Contemporary Art Africa

ART MUSEUM | Opened in September 2017,
the Zeitz is the first major museum dedicated to contemporary art from Africa
and its diaspora. Inhabiting the massively
renovated historic Grain Silo in what is
now called the Silo District of the V&A
Waterfront, the museum itself is a work
of art, reimagined by designer Thomas
Heatherwick. Give yourself half a day
to go through and look at the provoc-
ative and thought-provoking art on the
exhibit. ⊠ Silo District, S Arm Rd., V&A
Waterfront ☎ 087/350–4777 ⊕ www.
zeitzmocaa.museum ☞ R210 ⊗ Closed
Mon.–Wed.

🍴 Restaurants

Generally speaking, restaurants here
tend to cater to tourists (i.e., they have
no need to gain diners' loyalty). There are,
however, some very good exceptions
(though you'll pay for them), as well as
plenty of cheap fast-food options.

Baía Seafood Restaurant

$$$$ | PORTUGUESE | This chic upmarket
Portuguese restaurant has held a popular
position for many years in a prime part of
the Waterfront, with great views of the
harbor; closed in with high glass walls,
you can have an outdoor feel even in
winter. Seafood is the star of the menu,
although the meat and vegetarian options
are just as good. Known for: amazing
views of the harbor; seafood platters; a
great spot for celebration meals. 💲 Average main: R451 ⊠ 19 Breakwater Blvd.
☎ 021/421–0935 ⊕ baiarestaurant.co.za
⊗ No lunch Mon.–Thurs.

Den Anker

$$$$ | BELGIAN | Take a break from your
Waterfront wanderings at this Bel-
gian-style eatery, where you can enjoy
great views while also savoring an
impressive range of Belgian beers and
as good a pot of mussels with frites
as you're likely to find anywhere in
Cape Town. With its focus on meat and

seafood, expect other dishes like fillet béarnaise, rabbit simmered in Belgian beer, or Norwegian salmon in a beurre blanc. **Known for:** mussels, seafood, and Wagyu burger; wide range of imported Belgian beers, with six served on tap; attractive glassed-in space with harbor and mountain views. $ *Average main: R245* ✉ *Victoria and Alfred Waterfront* ☎ *021/419–0249* ⊕ *www.denanker.co.za.*

★ Emazulwini Restaurant

$$$$ | SOUTH AFRICAN | This highly acclaimed new offering at Maker's Landing sees chef Mmabatho Molefe putting the spotlight on modern Zulu cuisine and celebrating African ingredients with an innovative tasting menu that pushes the boundaries for South African cuisine. Emazulwini means "the heavens" and the name is befitting the delicious heights that the food will send you to. **Known for:** African ingredients; modern Zulu cuisine inspired by traditional foods; innovative South African dishes. $ *Average main: R350* ✉ *Makers Landing, The Cruise Terminal, V&A Waterfront* ☎ *073/292–7441* ⊕ *linktr.ee/emazulwini. restaurant* ⊗ *Closed Mon.–Wed. No dinner Sun.*

Harbour House V&A

$$$$ | SEAFOOD | Sister restaurant to the original Harbour House in Kalk Bay, the V&A location serves the same reliably fresh and tasty seafood menu from an enviable spot overlooking the harbor. As with the Kalk Bay location, the fresh fish of the day is always a good bet, and desserts are excellent. **Known for:** sushi bar upstairs is a great cocktail spot in summer; great location with beautiful harbor and mountain views; reliable fresh seafood. $ *Average main: R245* ✉ *Quay 4, V&A Waterfront, V&A Waterfront* ☎ *021/418–4744* ⊕ *www. harbourhouse.co.za.*

Nobu

$$$$ | JAPANESE FUSION | If you've always wanted to try Nobuyuki "Nobu" Matsuhisa's famous Japanese cuisine, but were put off by the potential bill in New York or London, Nobu Cape Town offers a chance to sample what may not constitute exactly the same level of cuisine, but will nonetheless make for a highly enjoyable experience. A vast modern space in the Waterfront's One&Only resort provides a fitting backdrop for the splurge of the Omakase multicourse tasting menu, which will likely include dishes such as the signature Alaskan black cod with miso. **Known for:** glitzy, bold atmosphere; branch of the famous Nobu chain. $ *Average main: R475* ✉ *One&Only Cape Town, Dock Rd., V&A Waterfront* ☎ *021/431–4511* ⊕ *www.oneandonlyresorts.com* ⊗ *No lunch.*

SIBA The Restaurant

$$$$ | AFRICAN | FAMILY | Brought to you by celebrity South African chef Siba Mtongana, this new upmarket restaurant at the Table Bay Hotel offers fine-dining global cuisine with an African flair. The restaurant is warm and inviting, especially on Sunday when the lunch menu is served family-style and features many South African favorites like roast leg of lamb and peppermint crisp tart. **Known for:** South African classics; long Sunday lunches. $ *Average main: R245* ✉ *6 W Quay Rd., V&A Waterfront* ☎ *021/406–5762* ⊕ *www.suninternational.com/table-bay* ⊗ *Closed Mon. and Tues. No lunch Wed.–Sat. No dinner Sun.*

★ Willoughby & Co.

$$$ | JAPANESE | Though unfortunately inside the mall, this buzzing hive of activity consistently churns out what many say is the city's best sushi along with a surprisingly good array of other Japanese dishes as well as seafood favorites like English fish-and-chips and a prawn pasta. It is probably fair to say that South African

sushi was defined by Willoughby & Co., with its fanciful and decadent signature rolls, such as the creamy rock-shrimp maki (a tuna-style roll graced with large chunks of tempura-fried crayfish in a spicy mayo-based sauce) and the rainbow nation roll (salmon, avocado, and tuna topped with caviar and a few squizzles of delicious sesame-oil and sweet chili sauces). **Known for:** long lines during dinner, alleviated by free wine samples; excellent and decadent sushi rolls; great seafood. [$] *Average main: R245* ✉ *19 Dock Rd., Shop 6132, V&A Waterfront* ☎ *021/418–6115* 🌐 *www.willoughbyandco.co.za.*

Coffee and Quick Bites

Grand Africa Café & Beach

$$$$ | **EUROPEAN** | In a restored warehouse, this trendy operation has made good use of what was once a derelict piece of land between the V&A Waterfront and the harbor. It's now a place for locals to be seen, with a private beach, several bars, and comfortable covered seating scattered about—everything is overpriced, but the view and toes-in-the-sand vibe may merit a drink or two. **Known for:** boozy lunches; summer hangouts for families and large groups; mussels and cocktails. [$] *Average main: R220* ✉ *Granger Bay Rd., off Beach Rd., V&A Waterfront* ☎ *021/425–0551* 🌐 *grandafrica.com.*

★ **Maker's Landing**

$ | **SOUTH AFRICAN** | This new food market at the cruise terminal near the Waterfront showcases some of the best local foods that Cape Town has to offer. Try some killer wings from Sidewing, or a beloved traditional Koesister (a Cape Malay spiced donut) from Fuzzy's Food and grab a good cup of coffee from Coffee by Moses. **Known for:** Cape Town's favorite foods; celebrating South African cuisine in all its forms. [$] *Average main: R80* ✉ *The Cruise Terminal* ☎ *021/408–7529* 🌐 *www.makerslanding.co.za* 🕒 *Closed Mon.–Thurs.*

V&A Food Market

$ | **FUSION** | **FAMILY** | Located in the Old Power Station, the Food Market is a great place to stop for a quick bite to eat while exploring the Waterfront. There are more than 40 vendors to choose from including Truth Coffee (🌐 *za.truth.coffee*), Kynsa Oyster Company (🌐 *oystersonline.co.za*), and the Bar Upstairs and the Bar Downstairs. **Known for:** wide variety of local and global cuisine; delis and bakeries; craft beer. [$] *Average main: R70* ✉ *The Old Power Station, Dock Rd., Building 19, Pier Head, V&A Waterfront* ✣ *across from Noble Square and the Victoria Alfred Hotel* ☎ *021/418–1605* 🌐 *waterfrontfoodmarket.com.*

Hotels

Cape Grace Hotel

$$$$ | **HOTEL** | **FAMILY** | Enjoying a stellar location in the working harbor section of the Waterfront—and rightfully renowned for its excellent service—the discreetly refined Cape Grace is popular with American celebrities, including the likes of Bill and Hillary Clinton. **Pros:** mountain or harbor views from all rooms; excellent, personalized service; extremely family-friendly for such a posh hotel. **Cons:** unconventional decor may not suit all tastes; spa is great, but facilities like sauna and steam room are coed; some rooms a bit dark. [$] *Rooms from: R14,343* ✉ *Quay Rd.* ☎ *021/410–7100* 🌐 *www.capegrace.com* 🛏 *120 rooms* 🍴 *Free Breakfast.*

The Dock House Boutique Hotel

$$$$ | **HOTEL** | Victorian splendor meets modern glam at this small and intimate boutique hotel perched over Cape Town's trendy and ever-popular V&A Waterfront. **Pros:** can walk to all the V&A Waterfront's restaurants, shops, and entertainment options; elegant, stylish oasis that feels amazingly private given location; great service. **Cons:** no kids under 12; those wishing to socialize with other guests should look elsewhere;

guests have to walk outside to reach the gym and spa. [$] *Rooms from: R5752* ✉ *5 Portswood Rd., V&A Waterfront* ☎ *021/418–1466* 🌐 *www.dockhouse.co.za* 🛏 *6 rooms* 🍴 *Free Breakfast.*

One&Only Cape Town
$$$$ | **RESORT** | **FAMILY** | In the spirit of founding investor Sol Kerzner's "go big or go home" philosophy, the One&Only Cape Town is a splendid tribute to excess with its four-story glass window views onto Table Mountain from the aptly named Vista Bar and decadent island spa surrounded by a moat. **Pros:** conveniently located in the heart of the Waterfront; oceans of space and great views from all rooms; great kids' programs. **Cons:** Marina Rise guests must walk through the lounge in their swimsuit/robe to reach the pool or spa; lacks the intimacy of a smaller hotel. [$] *Rooms from: R22000* ✉ *Dock Rd., V&A Waterfront* ☎ *021/431–5888* 🌐 *www.oneandonlyresorts.com* 🛏 *131 rooms* 🍴 *Free Breakfast.*

Protea Hotel Cape Town Waterfront Breakwater Lodge
$$ | **HOTEL** | Housed in an old British prison, this luxury hotel has breathtaking views over Table Mountain and Table Bay. Markets, restaurants, and boat rides await just outside the door. **Pros:** guest rooms have a/c; within walking distance of dining and shopping; free Wi-Fi throughout hotel. **Cons:** central location can be noisy and busy; fee for onsite parking. [$] *Rooms from: R2445* ✉ *Portswood Rd., V&A Waterfront* ☎ *021/406–1911* 🌐 *www.marriott.com* 🛏 *191 rooms* 🍴 *No Meals.*

Radisson Blu Hotel Waterfront
$$$$ | **HOTEL** | **FAMILY** | When it comes to great locations, this hotel is one of Cape Town's front-runners, perched on the edge of the Atlantic Ocean, at one end of the popular pedestrian seafront promenade, and less than 10 minutes' walk to the popular V&A Waterfront. **Pros:** amazing location with sunset and sunrise views and proximity to promenade and Waterfront; sound of the water crashing against the breakwater; friendly, warm service. **Cons:** "tray charge" every time you order room service; very close but not in the V&A Waterfront; standard rooms without a view may not warrant cost. [$] *Rooms from: R5,675* ✉ *100 Beach Rd., V&A Waterfront* ☎ *021/441–3000* 🌐 *www.radissonblu.com* 🛏 *177 rooms* 🍴 *No Meals.*

The Silo Hotel
$$$$ | **HOTEL** | Brilliantly melding industrial grit and sumptuous glamour, Cape Town's hottest luxury hotel rises out of the old grain silo in the working harbor section of the Waterfront. **Pros:** incredible views from rooftop bar; surprisingly child-friendly; mind-blowing decor and artwork. **Cons:** extremely pricey; starting category rooms are small; policy towards nonresidents still being worked out, resulting in guests potentially being treated as strangers. [$] *Rooms from: R23400* ✉ *Silo Square, Victoria and Alfred Waterfornt, V&A Waterfront* ☎ *021/670–0500* 🌐 *www.theroyalportfolio.com/the-silo/overview* 🛏 *28 rooms* 🍴 *Free Breakfast.*

Table Bay Hotel
$$$$ | **HOTEL** | This glitzy hotel that is part of the Sun International group sits in a prime spot at the tip of the V&A Waterfront, enjoying fabulous views from all sides. **Pros:** incredibly convenient location with direct access to the V&A Waterfront mall; wonderful high tea and public lounge spaces; all rooms have sea/harbor or mountain views. **Cons:** lacks the intimacy and personality of a smaller hotel; breakfast quality doesn't quite meet expectations based on its grand presentation; service is friendly but sometimes a bit slow. [$] *Rooms from: R12365* ✉ *6 W Quay Rd., V&A Waterfront* ☎ *021/406–5000* 🌐 *www.suninternational.com* 🛏 *329 rooms* 🍴 *Free Breakfast.*

Victoria & Alfred Hotel
$$$$ | **HOTEL** | Smack in the middle of the Waterfront and surrounded by shops, bars, and restaurants, 94 luxurious

Worthwhile Waterfront Markets [🛍]

Featuring more than 150 vendors selling the best of local design, arts, and crafts, the extremely worthwhile Watershed Market (🌐 *www.waterfront.co.za/shop/markets*) is located in a huge warehouse by the aquarium. Next door is the V&A Food Market (🌐 *waterfrontfoodmarket.com*), where you can find everything from sushi to biltong to curry, craft beer to gelato to handmade organic chocolate. Another must-visit is the Oranjezicht City Farm Market (🌐 *www.ozcf.co.za/market-day*), which showcases the Cape's bounty in the form of organic produce, wonderfully prepared foods, and scrumptious take-away treats (think dried meats, artisanal cheeses, fantastic pastries, and the like), all with a great view of the sea every Saturday from 9 to 2. The newest market on the docks, located by the cruise terminal, Maker's Landing (🌐 *www.makerslanding.co.za*) brings together small food businesses from all over Cape Town under one roof to celebrate African food and South Africa's food heritage. There's also a fascinating museum of South African food on the top floor.

rooms occupy the three floors that once served as a warehouse for cargo from the ships visiting what was once a purely working harbor. **Pros:** great service from restaurant and hotel staff; best value at the Waterfront; excellent breakfasts with great views include healthy and diabetic options. **Cons:** pool and gym located at nearby sister property are an effort to find; buskers in the piazza can be loud; economical loft rooms are very small. $ *Rooms from: R6500* ✉ *On the Waterfront Pierhead, Dock Rd., V&A Waterfront* ☎ *021/419–6677* 🌐 *www.newmarkhotels.com* 🛏 *94 rooms* 🍴 *Free Breakfast.*

🍸 Nightlife

BARS AND PUBS

Mitchell's Scottish Ale House

PUBS | A traditional Scottish Pub outside the main mall, you can kick back and have a beer or two from a wide selection of brews. There's also a small food menu of burgers, pizza and other pub food. Occasional karaoke nights take place. ✉ *Dock Rd., V&A Waterfront* ☎ *021/419–5074* 🌐 *mitchellsalehouse.co.za.*

Ukhamba Beerworx Brewery

BREWPUBS | A proudly Southern African craft beer brewery, this venue has great beer, music, food, and vibes. Inspired by the history of African beer, the Ukhamba husband-and-wife team wanted to create a beer brand that celebrates that heritage. There's occasional live music, DJs, and events. ✉ *Maker's Landing, The cruise terminal* ☎ *078/417–0567* 🕓 *Closed Mon.–Thurs.*

🛍 Shopping

BOOKS

Exclusive Books Waterfront

BOOKS | The biggest bookstore chain in the country, this well-stocked branch carries a wide selection of local and international periodicals and books, all the best sellers making literary waves around the world, an extensive magazine selection, and also has a nice coffee shop. You'll find branches at all the big malls and the airports. ✉ *Victoria and Alfred Waterfront, Shop 6160, Cape Town* ☎ *021/419–0905* 🌐 *www.exclusivebooks.co.za.*

The Oranjezicht City Farm Market is held every Saturday at the Granger Bay part of the V&A Waterfront.

MARKETS

Oranjezicht City Farm Market Day

MARKET | FAMILY | Held every Saturday from 9 till 2 at the Granger Bay part of the V&A Waterfront, the OZCF Market Day is a community farmers'-style market for independent local farmers and artisanal food producers where you can buy everything from fresh organic veggies to unique artisanal products (meats, cheeses, chocolates, etc.). The prepared foods are also fabulous (everything from shakshuka to eggs Benedict on a rosti to Korean fried chicken) and can be enjoyed at the big tables set up with sea views. Some lovely crafts and fashion vendors also trade here. Great for the whole family. ⊠ *Granger Bay, Beach Rd., V&A Waterfront* ⊕ *Parking available adjacent to market* ☎ *083/628–3426* ⊕ *www.ozcf. co.za/market-day*.

The V&A Waterfront Watershed

MARKET | This market brings together the best of local arts and crafts with 150 vendors selling more than 365 brands of jewelry, fashion, and accessories, pottery and home decor, and artwork, all of which are made in South Africa and the majority of which is of extremely high quality. The market is open every day until 6 pm. ⊠ *Dock Rd., next to the aquarium, V&A Waterfront* ☎ *021/408–7600* ⊕ *www.waterfront.co.za/shop/markets*.

Maker's Landing

FOOD | FAMILY | A new market on the cruise terminal, Maker's hosts numerous vendors showcasing some of the most delicious food businesses in Cape Town. With its incubator program, Maker's Landing gives neighborhood favorites a place to launch their business successfully and aims to promote pride in African foods. Here you'll find intriguing bites, drinks, and views of docks. ⊠ *The Cruise Terminal* ☎ *021/408–7529* ⊕ *www.mak-erslanding.co.za* ⊙ *Closed Sun.–Thurs.*

Green Point

Inland from the soccer stadium, this mixed residential and business area is home to numerous dining options, most of which are on Main Road (aka Somerset West) and tend to cater to locals. Numerous guesthouses and B&Bs at many price points make it a convenient base for independent travelers. The Green Point Park surrounding the stadium has become a wonderful spot to bring a picnic or go for a stroll, and its playground equipment is the best you'll find in Cape Town.

 Restaurants

El Burro

$$ | MEXICAN | In the heart of Greenpoint, this fun and funky Mexican joint serves great margaritas and very reasonable Mexican food that may fall short of "auténtico," but will certainly scratch the itch for most of us. The ceviche is a winner, as are the tacos, which come with the choice of corn or flour tortillas, and which you assemble yourself with a mass of nice fixings. **Known for:** a South African take on Mexican, but still delicious; great margaritas; festive ambience, but unfortunate acoustics can make it hard to hear. $ *Average main: R150* ⊠ *79 Main Rd., Green Point* ☎ *021/433–2364* ⊕ *www.elburro.co.za* ⊗ *Closed Sun.*

Gold Restaurant

$$$$ | AFRICAN | FAMILY | In a huge brick warehouse space decorated with African artifacts and artworks, like giant Malian puppets, beautiful beadwork, and wooden carvings, Gold instantly prepares you for the touristy but thoroughly enjoyable meal and show to come. Your 14-course pan-African "taste safari" may include dishes from Cape Malay curry to Moroccan tagine; the food is fine but not the sole reason you are here. **Known for:** lively dinner entertainment experience; great way to experience a variety of African cuisines; fantastic puppets and great dancing and drumming show. $ *Average main: R355* ⊠ *15 Bennett St., Green Point* ☎ *021/421–4653* ⊕ *www.goldrestaurant.co.za* ⊗ *No lunch.*

Pigalle

$$$$ | PORTUGUESE | This stylish restaurant is one of the only dinner and dance venues in Cape Town; expect a big menu with well-made meat, seafood, and vegetarian dishes with a Portuguese flair. A lively band performs all sorts of classical tunes from Frank Sinatra to George Michael, and there are lots of sing-alongs, but more importantly, music to dance to, which diners do in between courses. **Known for:** dinner and dancing; Portuguese inspired menu; elegant setting. $ *Average main: R270* ⊠ *51A Somerset Rd., Green Point* ☎ *021/421–4848* ⊕ *pigalle.capetown* ⊗ *Closed Sun. No lunch Mon.–Fri.*

☕ Coffee and Quick Bites

Giovanni's Deli

$ | CAFÉ | With floor-to-ceiling shelves stacked with everything delicious from French Champagne to truffle oil, Giovanni's is a classic Italian deli with many extra global ingredients, making it a great place to stock up for a gourmet picnic or enjoy a bite to eat at the counter. There's always a wide selection of hams and cold cuts as well as fantastic cheeses, and the fridges have fresh pasta dishes and greens, but the deli section and espresso bar are where most customers congregate. **Known for:** fantastic prepared meals for takeaway; excellent stock of Italian deli meats and cheeses; great vibe at the always-busy espresso counter. $ *Average main: R75* ⊠ *103 Main Rd., Green Point* ☎ *021/434–6893* ⊕ *giovannisdeli.co.za.*

★ **Jason Bakery**

$ | **CAFÉ** | This well-loved bakery and cafe is where locals meet for coffee, breakfast, or to buy their freshly baked bread and pastries. The cafe menu serves classics like eggs Benedict and Reuben sandwiches, and on Saturdays, they sell their famous "doughssants" (donut meets croissant) which tend to sell out by mid-morning, so go early, it's worth trying! **Known for:** great breakfasts, sandwiches, and coffee; freshly baked breads and pastries; "doughssants" on Saturdays. [$] *Average main: R80* ✉ *83 Somerset Rd., Green Point* ☎ *021/433–0538* 🌐 *jasonbakery.com* 🕒 *Closed Mon. No dinner.*

Hotels

Dysart Boutique Hotel

$$$ | **B&B/INN** | This small and stylish boutique hotel in Green Point is perfect for those who appreciate a minimalist-artsy decor, seeking a quiet stay in a convenient location. **Pros:** quiet and peaceful; minimalist style with small contemporary art collection; nice views from pool and common areas. **Cons:** no phone in room; light switches for bedside annoyingly located by doorway/entrance; located between Green Point and Sea Point, it's a (little) bit of a walk to restaurants, etc. [$] *Rooms from: R3280* ✉ *17 Dysart Rd., Green Point* ☎ *021/439–2832* 🌐 *www.dysart.de* 🛏 *8 rooms* 🍴 *Free Breakfast.*

Romney Park Hotel & Spa

$$$$ | **HOTEL** | In upper Green Point, this converted apartment block incorporates adjoining houses to provide luxury sea-facing suites, all with balconies and fully fitted kitchens. **Pros:** nice spa; rooms are spacious with updated decor and balconies; quiet location. **Cons:** some rooms' views obstructed by new eyesore of a building; no gym; secure parking is not free. [$] *Rooms from: R3990* ✉ *Romney Rd., at Hill Rd., Green Point* ☎ *021/439–4555* 🌐 *www.romneypark.co.za* 🛏 *30 rooms* 🍴 *Free Breakfast.*

Mouille Point

Just a few kilometers from the Waterfront, this lovely seafront area is mostly residential, and a convenient place to stay, though it lacks a critical mass of dining options within immediate walking distance. Families with small children will appreciate the large, enclosed kids' park complete with a mini train to ride and blow-up jumping castle.

Hotels

Dolphin Inn

$$ | **B&B/INN** | An excellent value-for-money location on Mouille Point's sought-after strip, this simple inn's rooms are basic but neat and comfortable, a few even enjoying sea views. **Pros:** lovely, friendly service; great location; good value for money. **Cons:** restaurant serves breakfast only; sea-facing rooms are noisy, located by the entrance and over the road; basic amenities might leave you wanting more. [$] *Rooms from: R1700* ✉ *75 Beach Rd., Mouille Point* ☎ *021/434–3175* 🌐 *www.dolphin-inn.co.za* 🛏 *11 rooms* 🍴 *Free Breakfast.*

La Splendida Hotel

$$ | **HOTEL** | This good-value chic hotel enjoys a great location between the popular seafront promenade and Green Point park, and is also just a 15-minute walk from the V&A Waterfront. **Pros:** friendly staff; expansive views from sea-facing rooms; very reasonably priced for location and room size. **Cons:** horn from nearby lighthouse can ruin one's sleep on a foggy morning; limited off-street parking; noise from restaurant downstairs and the road from some rooms. [$] *Rooms from: R1900* ✉ *121 Beach Rd., Mouille Point* ☎ *021/439–5119* 🌐 *www.lasplendida.co.za* 🛏 *24 suites* 🍴 *Free Breakfast.*

Sea Point

Defined largely by The Prom, an incredibly popular pedestrian promenade that stretches from Sea Point's southern edge and carries on to Mouille Point and Granger Bay in the Waterfront, this is one of the few middle-income residential areas in Cape Town that is actually on the sea. Previously considered a dead zone dining-wise, this has changed in recent years, and the area is home to numerous inexpensive (though largely unremarkable) options, as well as a few real winners, and the fantastic **Mojo Market**, where you can find literally dozens of great dining and drinking options, as well as some fabulous boutiquey shopping.

Sights

Sea Point Pavilion

POOL | FAMILY | This may be the world's most stunningly located public swimming pool. Surrounded by views of Lion's Head and the Atlantic Ocean, the only downside to this amazing saltwater pool is that it isn't heated (and it can get very busy during school holidays). ⊠ *Lower Beach Rd., Sea Point* ☎ *021/434–3341.*

The Sea Point Promenade

PROMENADE | FAMILY | About 10 km (6 miles) long, The Prom, as its locally known, starts at Mouille Point near the V&A Waterfront, and continues through to Sea Point. It's populated by a constant slew of walkers, runners, dog walkers, and cyclists. To one side of the promenade, grassy lawns buffer pedestrians from the street, making them a popular spot for picnics, pick-up soccer games, and people-watching. To the other side, a few city beaches (none recommended for swimming) offer stunning urban views of the wild Atlantic Ocean. ⊠ *Sea Point Promenade, Sea Point.*

Restaurants

Dahlia on Regent

$$ | ASIAN FUSION | Owner and chef Damian Dafel serves up Asian street food-inspired dishes made with locally sourced, organic ingredients at this small restaurant. The decor is simple, yet chic with modern-meets-vintage Asian accents. **Known for:** great food, bursting with flavor; Biang Biang noodles (wide hand-pulled wheat flour noodles); a small, seasonal menu. Ⓢ *Average main: R115* ⊠ *77 Regent Rd., Sea Point* ☎ *087/470–0296* ⊕ *dahliaonregent.co.za* ⊗ *Closed Mon. and Tues.*

Hesheng Chinese Restaurant

$$ | CHINESE | FAMILY | A no-frills, local favorite for Chinese food, the large menu includes dim sum (the soup dumplings are great), salads, stir-fries, delicious beef rolls, and scallion pancakes, as well as Sichuan classics. It gets really busy in peak times, but the food is consistently good with fast service. **Known for:** casual and no-frills restaurant; family-style dining; soup dumplings and Sichuan beef. Ⓢ *Average main: R130* ⊠ *269 Main Rd., Sea Point* ☎ *021/433–0739* ⊗ *Closed Tues.*

★ Kleinsky's Delicatessen

$ | JEWISH DELI | FAMILY | A popular Sea Point institution since 2014, this New York–style deli blends traditional Jewish recipes with the best local ingredients to bring freshly baked bagels and an assortment of schmears, toppings, and homemade sauces. Be sure to grab other delicious pastries like babka and rugelach when not sold out. **Known for:** traditional Jewish deli items; quick service; freshly baked, New York–style bagels. Ⓢ *Average main: R70* ⊠ *92 Regent Rd., Sea Point* ☎ *021/433–2871* ⊕ *kleinskys.co.za* ⊗ *No dinner Sun. and Mon.*

La Boheme Wine Bar & Bistro

$$ | MEDITERRANEAN | Serving hearty unpretentious Mediterranean fare and tapas at reasonable prices, this

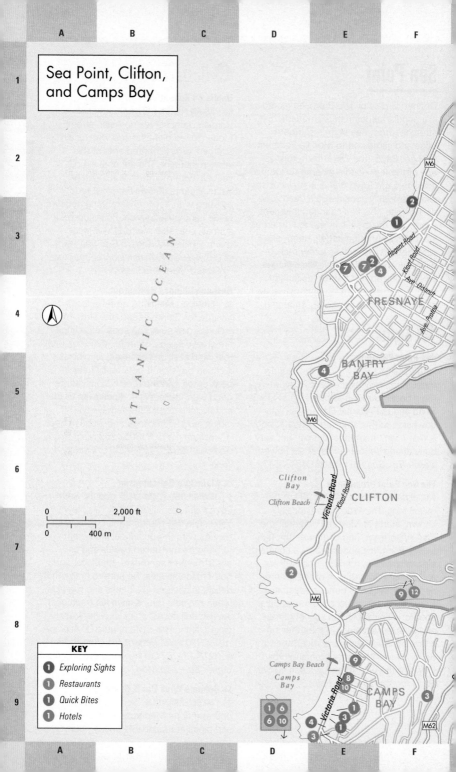

Sea Point, Clifton, and Camps Bay

ATLANTIC OCEAN

Regent Road

Kloof Road

Ave. Disandt

Ave. Pretus

FRESNAYE

BANTRY BAY

M6

Clifton Bay

Clifton Beach

Victoria Road

Kloof Road

CLIFTON

0   2,000 ft

0   400 m

M6

Camps Bay Beach

Camps Bay

Victoria Road

CAMPS BAY

M62

KEY

- ● Exploring Sights
- ● Restaurants
- ● Quick Bites
- ● Hotels

Sights ▼

1 Sea Point Pavilion F3
2 The Sea Point Promenade......... F3

Restaurants ▼

1 Azure................................ D9
2 Bungalow........................... D7
3 The Codfather...................... E9
4 Dahlia on Regent E3
5 Hesheng Chinese Restaurant.... G1
6 Hussar Grill D9
7 Kleinsky's Delicatessen............ E3
8 La Boheme
  Wine Bar & Bistro G2
9 The Lawns at the Roundhouse.... F7
10 Mantra Cafe........................ E9
11 Mykonos Taverna.................. G2
12 Salsify at the Roundhouse......... F7
13 Syriana............................. G2

Quick Bites ▼

1 Gelato Mania....................... E9
2 Jarryd's
  Espresso Bar + Eatery E3
3 La Belle Bistro & Patisserie E9
4 Plant Cafe.......................... E9

Hotels ▼

1 The Bay Hotel E9
2 Blackheath Lodge H1
3 Boutique @10...................... F9
4 Ellerman House E5
5 The Glen Boutique
  Hotel & Spa........................ G2
6 Ocean View House D9
7 Peninsula All-Suite Hotel E3
8 Place on the Bay................... E9
9 POD................................ E8
10 Twelve Apostles Hotel & Spa D9
11 Winchester Boutique Hotel G1

unassuming wine bar and bistro on Sea Point's Main Road is often packed. The menu changes frequently, but focuses on Mediterranean-inspired dishes like ostrich meatballs and tagliatelle in a spicy Neapolitan sauce, sesame-crusted fish cakes with a chunky Greek salad, and a good selection of classically Spanish-style tapas. **Known for:** tasty tapas; reasonably priced and hearty prix-fixe menus; great wine by the glass selection. Ⓢ *Average main: R165* ✉ *341 Main Rd., Sea Point* ☎ *021/434–8797* ⊕ *www.labohemebistro.co.za* ⊗ *Closed Sun.*

Mykonos Taverna

$$ | **GREEK** | **FAMILY** | This Greek taverna has been a Sea Point classic since the '80s, although it has been refurbished with modern Greek decor and bright white interiors, and it's a great place to watch the comings and goings on the busy Main Road. The large menu features mezzes, souvlaki, and hearty main dishes like moussaka and kleftiko (slow-cooked) lamb. **Known for:** occasional Greek parties with plate breaking; great Greek food; family friendly. Ⓢ *Average main: R130* ✉ *343 Main Rd., Sea Point* ☎ *021/439–2106* ⊕ *www.mykonostaverna.co.za.*

Syriana

$$ | **MIDDLE EASTERN** | **FAMILY** | This new Middle Eastern restaurant has quickly become a popular hotspot for Syrian food, delicious desserts, and hookah. With simple, but stylish decor and artwork, this cozy restaurant has a large menu of grills, salads, man'ouches, and flavor-packed mezzes. **Known for:** flavorful mezze platters; Zaatar Man'ouche (flatbread with herbs); popular hookah hangout. Ⓢ *Average main: R125* ✉ *45 Bellevue Rd., Sea Point* ☎ *064/509–2823.*

☕ Coffee and Quick Bites

★ Jarryd's Espresso Bar + Eatery

$$ | **CAFÉ** | This trendy cafe serves breakfast and brunch classics with a modern twist like brioche French toast with white chocolate and cornflake crunch, Reuben eggs benedict, smoothie bowls, and a large section of toasts (think avocado). The space can get packed but the service is efficient and friendly, and there's great coffee to boot. **Known for:** trendy decor and dishes; decadent and creative breakfasts; great coffee. Ⓢ *Average main: R125* ✉ *90 Regent Rd., Sea Point* ☎ *074/076–0474* ⊗ *No dinner.*

Hotels

★ Blackheath Lodge

$$$$ | **B&B/INN** | Conveniently located on a quiet street in upper Sea Point, this small good-value hotel in a beautiful Victorian-era home boasts concierge-level owner-rendered service and gorgeous quirky style in spades. **Pros:** gorgeous style; excellent 24-hour service; complimentary treats throughout the day. **Cons:** no kids under 10; no gym; only three rooms have bathtubs. Ⓢ *Rooms from: R4750* ✉ *6 Blackheath Rd., Sea Point* ☎ *021/439–2541* ⊕ *www.blackheathlodge.com* 🛏 *16 rooms* ⦿ *Free Breakfast.*

★ Ellerman House

$$$$ | **HOTEL** | Built in 1906 for shipping magnate Sir John Ellerman, what may be Cape Town's finest hotel sits high on a hill up from Sea Point in Bantry Bay, graced with stupendous views of the sea, and an art collection that puts the National Gallery to shame. **Pros:** fully stocked complimentary guest pantry available 24 hours; amazing sense of intimacy and privacy to enjoy this spectacular environment; lovely treats like canapés and cocktails at sunset. **Cons:** often booked a year in advance; Kloof Road is busy (though noise not audible from hotel). Ⓢ *Rooms from: R14500* ✉ *180 Kloof Rd., Bantry Bay, Sea Point* ☎ *021/430–3200* ⊕ *www.ellerman.co.za* 🛏 *15 rooms* ⦿ *Free Breakfast.*

The Glen Boutique Hotel & Spa

$$$$ | **HOTEL** | This midsize boutique hotel on a quiet street in Sea Point is one part

playful, Ibiza-inspired style—think orchids and a bright Greek Isle palette of white and turquoise—and one part elegant African touches. **Pros:** full-service restaurant with an elegant ambience; great dual pool area with seaside vibey atmosphere; very close to Sea Point promenade. **Cons:** decor in the two sections is very different—be sure to state preference; no kids under 16; a bit clubby for some tastes. $ *Rooms from: R4995* ⊠ *3 The Glen, Sea Point* ☎ *021/439–0086* ⊕ *www.glenhotel. co.za* 🛏 *24 rooms* ⊚⫯ *Free Breakfast.*

Peninsula All-Suite Hotel

$$$ | **APARTMENT** | **FAMILY** | In an 11-story building across the street from the popular Sea Point pedestrian promenade, this friendly, apartment-style accommodation with a view is great for families or groups. **Pros:** convenient preorder grocery and delivery service; good dining and self-catering options within walking distance; high-tech room with family-friendly gaming options. **Cons:** bookings (especially over holidays) can fill up far in advance; popular business conferencing venue, can feel overly busy; outside noise can be a bit obtrusive. $ *Rooms from: R3250* ⊠ *313 Beach Rd., Sea Point* ☎ *021/430–7777* ⊕ *www.peninsula.co.za* 🛏 *110 suites* ⊚⫯ *Free Breakfast.*

Winchester Boutique Hotel

$$$$ | **HOTEL** | Built in the 1920s, this old-school hotel enjoys a wonderful position overlooking the beautiful Sea Point promenade, with an elegant sea-facing terrace that is deservedly popular for tea and afternoon drinks. **Pros:** recently renovated; great location with lots of dining options within walking distance; some rooms have nice sea views. **Cons:** otherwise nice hotel bar allows smoking inside; overall style is quite old-fashioned. $ *Rooms from: R5680* ⊠ *221 Beach Rd., Sea Point* ☎ *021/434–2351* ⊕ *www. winchester.co.za* 🛏 *76 rooms* ⊚⫯ *Free Breakfast.*

🛍 Shopping

MARKETS

Mojo Market

MARKET | **FAMILY** | This fantastic seven-day-a-week food-and-lifestyle market in Sea Point boasts 45 designer retail stalls selling everything from fashion to home decor to funky local souvenirs, as well as 25 food vendors representing some of Cape Town's favorite city restaurants and craft wine and beer makers. Large tables enjoying views of the Sea Point promenade and free weekend events like live music encourage hanging out as much as shopping. ⊠ *30 Regent Rd., Sea Point* ☎ *021/422–4888* ⊕ *www.mojomarket. co.za.*

Clifton

Much of the city's most expensive housing sits above the four beaches that make up Clifton. During holidays it is almost a 24/7 madhouse, and your chances of finding parking at these times are nil. If you plan to visit the beaches in midsummer—which you really should do, they are wonderful despite the freezing water—consider renting a scooter or motorcycle instead of a car, taking a taxi from your hotel, or going early in the morning, when people are still sleeping off their Champagne from the night before. The Clifton beaches are also deservedly beloved as summer evening picnic spots—just remember that alcohol is not officially allowed on any public beach. Note that you're going to need to go down some stairs to get to the beaches.

🏖 Beaches

★ Clifton Beach

BEACH | **FAMILY** | Almost always wind-free, these fantastic white-sand beaches are primarily enjoyed by locals, with certain sections known to attract certain crowds.

Clifton's wind-free, white-sand beaches are divided into four segments—-First, Second, Third, and Fourth beaches.

Granite outcroppings divide the beach into four segments, unimaginatively known as First, Second, Third, and Fourth beaches. Fourth Beach is popular with families and teens, whereas the others support a strong social and singles' scene. Dogs are technically allowed only on First. Swimming is reasonably safe, although the undertow is strong and the water, again, freezing. Lifeguards are on duty on weekends and in peak season. Clifton is also a favorite for drinks and sunset picnics, but take care with containers, as alcohol is officially prohibited. Fairly steep staircases provide access to all four beaches, but once you arrive, you will find vendors with drinks, ice cream, and beach loungers for rent in summer. Some of the Cape's most desirable houses cling to the slopes above Clifton, and elegant yachts often anchor in the calm water beyond the breakers. **Amenities:** food and drink; lifeguards; parking; showers; toilets. **Best for:** partiers; sunset; surfing; walking. ■ **TIP→ Parking can be a nightmare in season; rather take an Uber or the MyCiti bus, which has convenient stops here.** ✉ *Off Victoria Rd., Clifton.*

🍴 Restaurants

Bungalow

$$$$ | **FRENCH FUSION** | A trendy Clifton restaurant with a prime location for views of the Atlantic Ocean and the Twelve Apostles Mountains, Bungalow has plenty of outdoor seating that makes this the place to go on a warm sunny day. The menu is large, offering many classic meat, seafood, and vegetarian dishes, as well as salads and sushi. **Known for:** ocean-view dining; large French and Italian inspired menu; great cocktails. [$] *Average main: R225* ✉ *3 Victoria Rd., Clifton* ☎ *021/438–2018* 🌐 *www.thebungalow.co.za.*

Camps Bay

Known as the beach where the beautiful people come to play, the gorgeous Camps Bay main drag (aka Victoria Road, aka "The Strip") is lined with cafés, bars, and restaurants, most of which exist solely for their views. Admittedly, these views are fantastic and these spots are oddly among the very few places in Cape Town where you can gaze at the surf while imbibing fluids or solids—but don't get your culinary hopes too high. However, for those in search of a good meal, there are a few reliable options.

Beaches

Camps Bay Beach

BEACH | The spectacular western edge of Table Mountain, known as the Twelve Apostles, provides the backdrop for this long, sandy beach that slopes gently to the very cold water from a grassy verge. Playing Frisbee or volleyball is very popular on this beach. The surf is powerful, but sunbathers can cool off in a tidal pool on the west end of the beach or under the outdoor showers. Camps Bay's ubertrendy, popular bar-and-restaurant strip lies yards away across Victoria Road. The wind can blow hard here—or not. The strip is alternately a refreshment break for groups of cyclists training for the annual Cape Argus; a watering hole for movie stars, models, and the wannabe rich and famous; and a tourist trap. As such, it tends toward the pretentious on weekends. **Amenities:** food and drink; parking; showers. **Best for:** partiers; surfing; walking. ✉ *Victoria Rd., Camps Bay* [M] *Hout Bay bus from OK Bazaars on Adderley St.*

Restaurants

The Codfather

$$$$ | **SEAFOOD** | The Codfather serves an excellent array of fresh seafood in a casual yet buzzing environment by way of a slightly unorthodox system. Rather than ordering from a menu, you instead head to a display of fresh seafood on ice, where, with the help of your waiter, you select everything from fish to shellfish in the quantities and style of your choice (you're charged by weight, as in Greece). **Known for:** order your seafood Greek-style, from a display; excellent fresh seafood; unadorned cooking style (most seafood is grilled, no fancy sauces, etc.). [$] *Average main: R350* ✉ *37 The Drive, Camps Bay* ☎ *021/438–0782, 021/438–0783* 🌐 *www.codfather.co.za.*

Hussar Grill

$$$ | **STEAKHOUSE** | **FAMILY** | This branch of one of the Cape's favorite steak houses offers an unpretentious and friendly place to enjoy excellent and reasonably priced steaks and ribs in an area where restaurants tend to focus more on views than food. A few minutes' drive away from Camps Bay's main beach drag, the interior here is more Boston than Miami—all leather booths and historic photographs, well suited to the carnivorous feast that awaits. **Known for:** friendly, efficient service; excellent steaks and game meat; unpretentious old-school vibe. [$] *Average main: R165* ✉ *108 Camps Bay Dr., Shop 2, Camps Bay* ☎ *021/438–0151* 🌐 *www.hussargrill.co.za* ⏲ *No lunch Mon.–Sat.*

The Lawns at the Roundhouse

$$$ | **BRASSERIE** | A more casual offering at the old Roundhouse, the Lawns has the same beautiful views and greenery, and there's lovely outdoor seating perfect for summer cocktails, lunch, or snacks. While food isn't the main draw, you can order decent pizzas, salads, pastas,

burgers, fish and chips, and lovely desserts. **Known for:** treacherous parking; perfect spot for outdoor summer lunches and drinks; great views of Camps Bay. $ *Average main: R195* ⊠ *Round House Rd., Camps Bay* ☎ *021/438–4347* ⊕ *thelawnsct.com* ⊙ *Closed Mon. and Tues.*

Mantra Cafe

$$$ | CAFÉ | Delivering great and unfussy café food from a gorgeously casual space, Mantra's second-floor vantage provides sweeping views of the beach and sea while also lifting you above the street-level irritations of cars and hawkers. The scones and smoothies are fantastic at breakfast (it's quickly become a favorite local breakfast joint), while tapas, salads, pizzas, and heartier mains from mussels to burgers to pork ribs are available from 11:30 till closing. **Known for:** nice small gift shop attached with some lovely local goods; caters to locals in both price and quality, an anomaly in touristy Camps Bay; a full bar and cocktail menu makes this a great sundowner spot, occasionally with live music. $ *Average main: R195* ⊠ *43 Victoria Rd., Camps Bay* ☎ *021/437–0206* ⊕ *www.mantracafe.co.za.*

★ **Salsify at the Roundhouse**

$$$$ | FRENCH FUSION | Away from the Camps Bay "strip" and higher up on the mountains in the historical Roundhouse building, an opulent culinary experience awaits you at Salsify. Be prepared for fine-dining excellence with French-inspired takes on local ingredients served as a 6 or 7 course-course tasting menu where you may choose a dish for some courses and wine pairings are optional. **Known for:** exquisite, seasonal tasting menu; world-class service; immaculate views and service. $ *Average main: R740* ⊠ *Round House Rd., Camps Bay* ☎ *021/010–6444* ⊕ *salsify.co.za* ⊙ *Closed Mon.*

☕ Coffee and Quick Bites

Gelato Mania

$ | ICE CREAM | Everyone fancies some gelato on beach days and this is the place to get some in Camps Bay. With several franchises in Cape Town, this family-run gelateria offers traditional flavors as well as sorbet and vegan and diabetic options. **Known for:** extensive gelato flavors; good selection of dairy-free gelatos; decadent waffles. $ *Average main: R35* ⊠ *11 Victoria Rd., Camps Bay* ☎ *078/696–5055* ⊕ *gelatomania.co.za.*

La Belle Bistro & Patisserie

$$ | CAFÉ | This cozy cafe has a prime spot on the promenade, where you can enjoy freshly baked pastries, great breakfasts, or a heartier meal with beautiful views of the beach. French toast, eggs Benedict, and buttermilk pancakes are crowd favorites, as are the smoothies, freshly pressed juices, and good selection of teas. **Known for:** freshly bakes cakes and pastries; breakfast and brunch; friendly service. $ *Average main: R135* ⊠ *Promenade, Victoria Rd., Shop 120, Clifton* ☎ *021/437–1278* ⊕ *www.labellecamps-bay.co.za.*

Plant Cafe

$ | CAFÉ | What started in Bo-Kaap as Cape Town's first vegan cafe, can now be enjoyed with views of Camps Bay. This tiny but bright cafe is perfect for breakfast or a takeaway to enjoy as a beach picnic; everything is freshly prepared and they guarantee 15 minutes to make your order. **Known for:** casual ocean-view cafe; fast service; freshly prepared vegan food. $ *Average main: R80* ⊠ *87 Victoria Rd., Camps Bay* ☎ *076/296–1665* ⊕ *www.plantcafe.co.za.*

Hotels

The Bay Hotel
$$$$ | **HOTEL** | The only large hotel in glitzy Camps Bay, this luxurious yet beachy property—vintage motorcycles and surfboards serve as decor—sits directly across the street from a famously beautiful stretch of white sand and is backed by the towering cliffs of the Twelve Apostles. **Pros:** intimate old-school hotel bar "Caamil's"; very popular beach a few steps away; at the epicenter of high-season social life. **Cons:** commercial feel with things like posters advertising classic car rentals in your room; extra small charges like using the Nespresso pods in your room can be irritating; road between hotel and beach is often busy and sometimes gridlocked. [$] *Rooms from: R4160* ✉ *69 Victoria Rd., Camps Bay* ☎ *021/430–4444 host manager, 021/430–4013 bookings* 🌐 *www.thebayhotel.com* 🛏 *78 rooms* 🍴 *Free Breakfast.*

Boutique @10
$$$$ | **B&B/INN** | Up against the mountainside right in the middle of Camps Bay, this small, intimate guesthouse enjoys stunning views over the popular seaside neighborhood below and across the ocean beyond. **Pros:** nice touches like complimentary wine tastings; amazing views; owner-managed. **Cons:** lots of stairs; decor in some rooms tending toward a 1970s vibe, in need of small updates; no fridges in rooms (except one). [$] *Rooms from: R4195* ✉ *10 Medburn Rd., Camps Bay* ☎ *021/438–1234* 🌐 *www.boutique10.co.za* 🛏 *4 rooms* 🍴 *Free Breakfast.*

Ocean View House
$$$$ | **B&B/INN** | **FAMILY** | Located in huge garden filled with indigenous succulents, ancient milkwood trees, and koi-filled water features, this good value family-owned and-managed B&B also enjoys gorgeous views of both the Atlantic Ocean and the majestic Twelve Apostles. **Pros:** gorgeous indigenous garden and natural stream running through property; amazing location with great views and just a few minutes' walk to Bakoven Beach; friendly, warm service. **Cons:** Wi-Fi can be a bit slow; not all rooms have full sea views; decor in some of the older rooms needs a bit of an update. [$] *Rooms from: R3900* ✉ *33 Victoria Rd., Camps Bay* ☎ *021/438–1982* 🌐 *www.oceanview-house.com* 🛏 *24 rooms* 🍴 *Free Breakfast.*

Place on the Bay
$$$$ | **APARTMENT** | Also incorporating the Fairways Hotel, these self-catering apartments on the beachfront in Camps Bay are within easy walking distance of a host of restaurants and bars. **Pros:** great location; management responds seriously to concerns and complaints. **Cons:** traffic noise from Victoria Road; Wi-Fi not free in rooms; limited parking. [$] *Rooms from: R4038* ✉ *35 Victoria Rd., Camps Bay* ☎ *021/437–8500* 🌐 *www.placeonthebay.co.za* 🛏 *27 apartments* 🍴 *No Meals.*

POD
$$$$ | **HOTEL** | This compact designer boutique hotel that blends modern sleekness with accents of stone, rough wood, and slate to create a sexy Zen ambience enjoys a great location on a quiet corner just a block from Camps Bay's main drag. **Pros:** eco-friendly additions like door sensor to switch air-conditioning off and tree planting for guests of three nights or more; excellent breakfast; wellness room with shower for use by late check-outs. **Cons:** eyesore apartment block across the street from some rooms; no on-site restaurant after breakfast; classic rooms are small, and open-plan bathrooms might be too much sharing. [$] *Rooms from: R7720* ✉ *3 Argyle St., Camps Bay* ☎ *021/438–8550* 🌐 *www.pod.co.za* 🛏 *17 rooms* 🍴 *Free Breakfast.*

If you have limited time, the Table Mountain Aerial Cableway is the easiest, and quickest, way to get to the top of the mountain.

Table Mountain National Park

Nowhere else in the world does an area of such spectacular beauty and rich biodiversity exist almost entirely within a metropolitan area. Large swaths of the Cape Peninsula are devoted to this spectacular 220-square-km (85-square-mile) park, which is home to countless hiking trails and gorgeous beaches, as well as two world-renowned landmarks: the eponymous Table Mountain and the legendary Cape of Good Hope. Although several parts of the park are within the boundaries of Cape Town, others are in the Cape Peninsula *(see Cape Peninsula)*. The park requires entrance payments only at three points: the Cape Point nature reserve, Boulders Beach, and Silvermine Nature Reserve. The rest of the park is open and free for all to enjoy.

TIMING AND PRECAUTIONS

It would be easy for nature lovers to spend days in the park. Most visitors spend about three hours going up Table Mountain—hiking takes longer than the cable car—and another half-day visiting Cape Point. For the fit, hiking up Table Mountain (and taking the cable car down) is a far more rewarding way to experience the mountain, but requires decent weather and at least half a day. To experience the wild beauty of Cape Point, a full day is recommended to visit the point lighthouse (either walking or by funicular), walk to the Cape of Good Hope, and explore the gorgeous empty beaches around Olifantsbos or Platboom. Within Cape Point, the main safety issue is baboons: they are dangerous and should not be messed with. Do not feed them. In other parts of the park (e.g., hiking trails around the city bowl, Camps Bay, Hout Bay, the Southern Suburbs, Muizenberg, and Silvermine Nature Reserve) remember that much of the park is bordered by city neighborhoods, and muggings can occur in isolated areas.

Don't walk alone, and don't carry valuables if you can avoid it. When hiking on Table Mountain, be aware that dramatic weather changes can (and probably will) occur, so regardless of conditions when you set out, always carry extra layers of clothing, water, a hat, and sunscreen. Finally, don't underestimate the mountain because of its popularity—it is a massive mountain and can be treacherous, for your own safety, stick to one of the many hiking trails of various difficulties.

◉ Sights

★ Hoerikwaggo Trail

TRAIL | A great way to get acquainted with Table Mountain and all its moods is to hike part of the Hoerikwaggo Trail, which opened in 2006. The trail follows the spine of the mountains that run the length of the peninsula; there are four camps though only Slangkop and Smitswinkel are currently open and parts of the trail are closed due to fire damage and land disputes. Multiple-day, guided hikes can be arranged with an operator like Walks in Africa (⊕ *www.walksinafrica.co.uk/hoerikwaggo-trail/*). ⊠ *Table Mountain National Park* ☎ *021/422–1601* ⊕ *www.sanparks.org/parks/table_mountain* ⊠ *R2945 per person.*

★ Kirstenbosch National Botanical Garden

GARDEN | **FAMILY** | Spectacular in each season, this renowned botanical garden was established in 1913, and was the first in the world to conserve and showcase a country's indigenous flora. With its magnificent setting extending up the eastern slopes of Table Mountain and overlooking the city and distant Hottentots Holland Mountains, these gardens are truly a national treasure. In addition to thousands of out-of-town visitors, Capetonians flock here on weekends to laze on the grassy lawns, picnicking and reading newspapers while the kids run riot. Walking trails meander through the plantings, which are limited to species indigenous to Southern Africa. Naturally the fynbos

biome—the hardy, thin-leaved plants that proliferate in the Cape—is heavily featured, and you will find plenty of proteas, ericas, and restios (reeds). Garden highlights include the Tree Canopy Walkway, a large cycad garden, the Bird Bath (a beautiful stone pool built around a crystal-clear spring), the fragrance garden (which is wheelchair-friendly and has a tapping rail), and the Sculpture Garden. Free 90-minute guided tours take place daily except Sunday. Those who have difficulty walking can enjoy a comprehensive tour lasting one hour (R70, hourly 9–3) in seven-person (excluding the driver) golf carts. Concerts featuring the best of South African entertainment—from classical music to township jazz to indie rock—are held on summer Sundays at 5 (be sure to arrive early to get a spot), and the Galileo Outdoor Cinema screens movies on Wednesdays an hour after sunset. A visitor center by the nursery houses a restaurant, bookstore, and coffee shop. There are also several trails taking you to the top of Table Mountain, from which point you can hike to the cable car station. Unfortunately, muggings have become increasingly more common in the gardens' isolated areas, and women are advised not to walk alone in the upper reaches of the park far from general activity. ⊠ *Rhodes Dr., Newlands* ☎ *021/799–8783* ⊕ *www.sanbi.org* ⊠ *R75.*

Lion's Head and Signal Hill

MOUNTAIN | The prominent peak to the right of Table Mountain is Lion's Head, a favorite hiking spot for locals. The hike takes about 1½ hours (each way), with 360-degree views of the city unfolding as you spiral up the "lion" as well as from the top. The trail is gorgeous and well marked; unfortunately its charms have made it so popular that on nice days you can find yourself in a hiker-jam. That said, it's a great hike, and though easier than climbing Table Mountain, the last quarter will earn you a post-hike beer or *malva* pudding (a baked sponge cake sauced

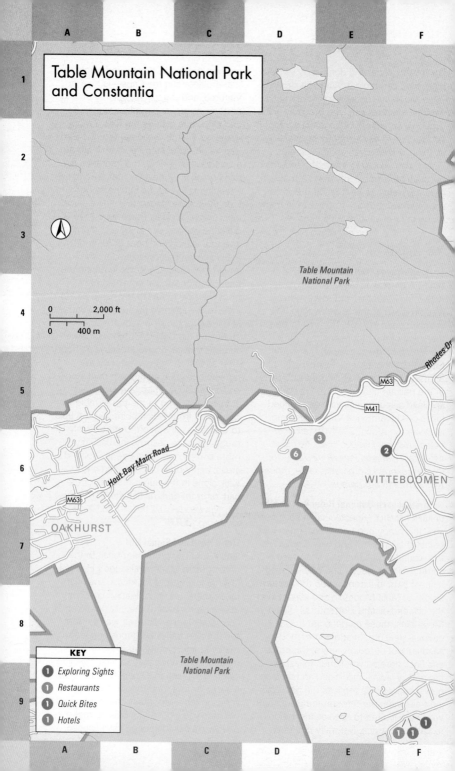

Table Mountain National Park and Constantia

Table Mountain National Park

Rhodes Dr

M63

M41

③

⑥

②

WITTEBOOMEN

Hout Bay Main Road

M63

OAKHURST

Table Mountain National Park

0   2,000 ft
0   400 m

①

①   ①

KEY

① *Exploring Sights*

① *Restaurants*

① *Quick Bites*

① *Hotels*

3

Cape Town TABLE MOUNTAIN NATIONAL PARK

The Wilds of Table Mountain

Despite being virtually surrounded by the city, Table Mountain is a remarkably unspoiled wilderness. Most of the Cape Peninsula's 2,200 species of flora—about as many plant species as there are in all of North America and Europe combined—are found on the mountain. This includes magnificent examples of Cape Town's wild indigenous flowers known as *fynbos*, Afrikaans for "fine bush," a reference to the tiny leaves characteristic of these heathlike plants. The best time to see the mountain in bloom is between September and March, although you're sure to find all kinds of flowers throughout the year.

Long gone are the days when Cape lions, zebras, and hyenas roamed the mountain, but you can still glimpse *grysbokke* (small antelopes), baboons, and the rabbitlike *dassie* (rhymes with fussy). Although these creatures, also called rock hyraxes, look like oversize guinea pigs, this is where the similarities end; the dassie's closest relative is the elephant. They congregate in large numbers near the Upper Cable Station, where they've learned to beg for food. Over the years a diet of junk food has seriously compromised their health. ■TIP→ Do not feed the dassies, no matter how endearing they look.

with orange juice, apricot jam, and vinegar). As always, don't hike alone, and keep alert, especially as sunset approaches. For those less inclined to sweat, Signal Hill is the smaller flat-topped hill extending from the northern lower slopes of Lion's Head, also sometimes called the "Lion's Rump." Once the location for signal flags communicating weather warnings to ships visiting the bay, Signal Hill is also the home of the Noon Gun, still operated by the South African Navy and South African Astronomical Observatory. Both Lion's Head and Signal Hill are accessed by Signal Hill Road, which ends at the Signal Hill parking lot. The lot has spectacular views of Sea Point and Table Bay. ⚠ Be careful especially after hours and/or if it's deserted. There have been incidents of violent crime. ✉ *Signal Hill Rd., Table Mountain National Park.*

★ **Table Mountain**

FOREST | Table Mountain truly is one of Southern Africa's most beautiful and impressive natural wonders. The views from its summit are awe-inspiring. The mountain rises more than 3,500 feet above the city, and its distinctive flat top

is visible to sailors 65 km (40 miles) out to sea. Climbing up the step-like Plattekloof Gorge—the most popular route up—will take two to three hours, depending on your fitness level. There is no water along the route; you *must* take at least 2 liters (½ gallon) of water per person. Table Mountain can be dangerous if you're not familiar with the terrain. Many paths that look like good routes down the mountain end in treacherous cliffs. ⚠ Do not underestimate this mountain: every year local and foreign visitors to the mountain get lost, some falling off ledges, with fatal consequences.

It may be in the middle of a city, but it is not a genteel town park. Because of occasional muggings near the Rhodes Memorial east of the mountain, it's unwise to walk alone on that side. It's recommended that you travel in a group or, better yet, with a guide. If you want to do the climb on your own, wear sturdy shoes or hiking boots; always take warm clothes, including a windbreaker or fleece; travel with a mobile phone; and let someone know of your plans. Consult the staff at a Cape Town Tourism office for more guidelines. Another (much easier) way to reach the summit is to take the cable car, which affords fantastic views. Cable cars (R135 one way) depart from the Lower Cable Station, which lies on the slope of Table Mountain near its western end; the station is a long way from the city on foot, so save your hiking energy for the mountain, and take a taxi or the MyCiti bus to get here. ✉ *Tafelberg Rd., Table Mountain National Park* ☎ *021/712–0527* ⊕ *www.sanparks.org/parks/table_mountain.*

Table Mountain Aerial Cableway

MOUNTAIN | This is a slick operation. Two large, wheelchair-friendly revolving cars that provide spectacular views take three to five minutes to reach the summit. The Lower Cable Station lies on the slope of Table Mountain near its western end. Save your walking energy for the mountain, and take a taxi or MyCiti bus to get to the station.

Operating times vary from month to month according to season, daylight hours, and weather. To avoid disappointment, phone ahead for exact times. In the ever-expanding peak season (December–April), if you arrive at 10 am you could wait for an hour, so it's best to book online beforehand. Several tour operators also include a trip up the mountain in their schedules. ■TIP→ **Lines to purchase tickets for the cable car can be crazy in peak/high season, so book online to speed things up.**

⚠ **The cable car stops operating in strong wind conditions (common in summer), so be sure to factor in that possibility, especially if relying on it to get back down after a tiring hike up and take note of the last one down's time (changes but can be as early as 4 pm).** ✉ *Tafelberg Rd., Table Mountain National Park* ☎ *021/424–8181* ⊕ *www.tablemountain.net* ☑ *R380 round-trip.*

🍴 Restaurants

Azure

$$$$ | ECLECTIC | Although Azure's blue-and-white nautical-theme decor may feel a bit outdated to some, the restaurant's jaw-dropping sea and mountain views are reason enough to experience the mostly inspired menu. Signature dishes like the crayfish-and-prawn cocktail, beef Stroganoff, and rice pudding have a classic old-school bent and are divinely comforting, while more contemporary dishes like the prawn dhal in a coriander yogurt with pineapple salsa, or nouvelle mushrooms on watercress panna cotta are also true winners. **Known for:** fantastic breakfast buffet that includes fresh oysters and sparkling wine; founder Bea Tollman's classically delicious comfort food; amazing ocean views from nautically themed dining room. $ *Average main: R225* ✉ *Twelve Apostles Hotel & Spa, Victoria Rd., Camps Bay* ☎ *021/437–9029* ⊕ *www.12apostleshotel.com.*

☕ Coffee and Quick Bites

Table Mountain Cafe

$ | CAFÉ | During the warm summer months—and on the many good winter days—Capetonians are fond of taking picnic baskets up the mountain; the best time to picnic is after 5, as some say sipping a glass of chilled Cape wine while watching the sunset from Table Mountain is one of life's great joys. If you fail to bring your own provisions, this large self-service restaurant at the top of Table Mountain serves reasonable hot breakfasts, sandwiches, buffet-style meals, and local wine. **Known for:** offers hot meals and picnic food options; great views of Cape Town; self-service canteen-style cafe. $ *Average main: R75* ✉ *Table Mountain Aerial Cableway, Tafelberg Rd., Table Mountain National Park* ☎ *021/424–0015* ⊕ *www.tablemountain.net.*

Hotels

★ Twelve Apostles Hotel & Spa

$$$$ | **HOTEL** | If you fancy taking a helicopter to the airport or lazing in a bubble bath while looking out floor-to-ceiling windows at breathtaking sea and mountain views, then this award-winning, luxurious hotel and spa that is the only such property within Table Mountain National Park may be for you. **Pros:** great breakfast in Azure restaurant with insane sea views; wonderfully attentive staff; stunning and unique location in Table Mountain National Park. **Cons:** views and room size are extremely varied; nearest off-site restaurant is at least 10 minutes by car; overlooks a road that gets busy. [$] *Rooms from: R9820* ✉ *Victoria Rd., Camps Bay* ☎ *021/437–9000* 🌐 *www.12apostleshotel.com* 🛏 *70 rooms* 🍴 *Free Breakfast.*

Constantia

The most upmarket of the so-called Southern Suburbs, this primarily residential zone is home to several of the Cape's oldest wine estates, as well as some of the city's best dining options. It's about a half-hour drive from Cape Town Central, so you'll need wheels to get around. The forests that line the roads are a sight in themselves, beautiful greenery and landscapes are plentiful here. If you don't have time for the Cape Winelands but still want to experience the Cape's stellar wines, Constantia's many excellent estates are a lovely substitute- and also a perfect choice in winter days where you can still enjoy views of the winery, inside in chic lounges and restaurants.

Sights

Buitenverwachting

WINERY | Once part of Dutch governor Simon van der Stel's original Constantia farm, Buitenverwachting (meaning "beyond expectation" and roughly pronounced "Bait-in-fur-VAGH-ting") boasts one of the most gorgeous bucolic settings imaginable. An oak-lined avenue leads past fields of horses and over a small stream until passing the Cape Dutch homestead and eventually arriving at the small modern cellar. Acres of vines spread up hillsides flanked by more towering oaks and the rocky crags of Constantiaberg Mountain. Buitenverwachting's wine is just as good as the view. The biggest seller is the flagship red, "Christine," a Bordeaux-style blend of mostly Cabernet Franc and Merlot. The winery's eponymous restaurant is also excellent and enjoys fabulous views of the vineyards. ✉ *Off Klein Constantia Rd., Constantia* ☎ *021/794–5190* 🌐 *www.buitenverwachting.com* 🎟 *R50* 🕒 *Closed Sun.*

Constantia Glen

WINERY | Yet another award-winning wine estate, this one enjoys sweeping open views of the Constantia winelands just below the Constantia Nek roundabout. A huge "tasting room" spread across four different areas including a beautiful covered veranda, glassed-in conservatory space, and cozy lounge space offers wine tastings with a small menu of delicious light fare, cheese platters, and the like. A wine-and-chocolate pairing is also available. ✉ *Constantia Main Rd., Constantia* ☎ *021/795–5639* 🌐 *www.constantiaglen.com* 🎟 *R50.*

Groot Constantia

WINERY | The town of Constantia takes its name from the wine estate established here in 1685 by Simon van der Stel, one of the first Dutch colonial governors of the Cape. This site was one of the largest owners of enslaved people who must be acknowledged as the actual builders and growers of this establishment—and often get overlooked because of the terrible history of this property. After van der Stel's death in 1712, the land was subdivided, with the heart of the estate preserved at Groot Constantia. The enormous complex, which enjoys the status of a national monument, is by far the most commercial and touristy of the wineries (the tasting room includes a shop, small gallery, free Wi-Fi, and branch of Constantia Valley Tourism). Van der Stel's magnificent homestead, the oldest in the Cape, lies at the center of Groot Constantia. It's built in traditional Cape Dutch style, with thick, whitewashed walls, a thatch roof, small-paned windows, and ornate gables. The house is a museum furnished with exquisite period pieces. The old "Cloete" wine cellar sits behind the manor house and serves as an additional tasting room. Built in 1791, it is most famous for its own ornate gable, which contains a sculpture designed by Anton Anreith. The sculpture, depicting fertility, is regarded as one of the most important in the country.

In the 19th century the sweet wines of Groot Constantia were highly regarded in Europe, but today Groot Constantia is known for its award-winning Chardonnay (voted best in the world in 2013) and splendid red wines. The best of the latter is the excellent Bordeaux-style Gouverneurs Reserve, made mostly from Cabernet Sauvignon grapes with smaller amounts of Merlot and Cabernet Franc. The Pinotage is consistently good, too, reaching its velvety prime in about five years. The estate operates two restaurants: the homey Jonkershuis and Simon's, which serve both sophisticated meals as well as deli-style offerings and picnics, which you can enjoy on the surrounding lawns. ✉ *Off Constantia Rd., Constantia* ☎ *021/794–5128 winery, 021/795–5149 museum, 021/794–6255 Jonkershuis, 021/794–1143 Simon's* 🌐 *www.grootconstantia.co.za* 🎫 *Museum R30; tasting R75; museum, wine tour, and tasting R95.*

★ **Norval Foundation**

ARTS CENTER | FAMILY | A relatively new establishment, the Norval Foundation is a center for art and cultural expression, holding numerous prolific art exhibitions and events. Along with the gallery and museum are an incredible sculpture garden, a children's playground, a research library, and the Skotnes Restaurant, which is worth visiting for creative South African fine dining. The views of the mountain are spectacular and there is a large paid car park. ✉ *4 Steenberg Rd., Tokai* ☎ *087/654–5900* 🌐 *www.norvalfoundation.org* 🎫 *R180* 🕒 *Closed Tues.*

🍴 Restaurants

beyond Restaurant at Buitenverwachting

$$$$ | EUROPEAN | A relatively new offering on this historic wine estate in Constantia, this fine-dining restaurant serves excellent fare from an original Cape Dutch building with charming views of the vineyards. The elegant but unpretentious tasting menu is available for lunch or dinner, and the service is attentive and gracious. ■ **TIP→ Request a table on the balcony in warm weather to enjoy the wonderful vineyard views. Known for:** hushed, attentive service; beautiful views of one of the Cape's oldest wine estates; a menu that includes both "rustic" and "haute" cuisine. [$] *Average main: R650* ✉ *Klein Constantia Rd., Constantia* ☎ *021/794–0306* 🌐 *www.buitenverwachting.com* 🕒 *Closed Sun.*

Blanko

$$$ | ITALIAN | FAMILY | Located in a historic manor house, this restaurant serves tasty and hearty Italian fare from multiple dining rooms whose white walls are adorned with an impressive collection of contemporary South African art. Classics like white anchovies in a shallot-and-olive-oil dressing, escalopes of veal, and fresh ravioli are all pleasing, filling, and reasonably priced, if not culinary events.

Known for: location in historic manor house; edgy South African art collection; unpretentious and tasty Italian fare. $ *Average main: R195* ✉ *Alphen Boutique Hotel, Alphen Dr., Constantia* ☎ *021/795–6300* ⊕ *www.blanko.co.za.*

★ Chef's Warehouse at Beau Constantia

$$$$ | **ECLECTIC** | Enjoy soaring views of the Constantia winelands from this coolly elegant space of carved wood and huge glass windows, where a fantastic and well-priced "tapas for two" menu reminds you why long lunches were invented. Eight dishes—all marked by freshness of ingredients and a globe-trotting host of inspiration—served in three courses are available for lunch and dinner, and change with the seasons or chef's inspiration. **Known for:** sister restaurant to the beloved Chef's Warehouse in Cape Town Central; fantastic "tapas for two" menu that delightfully takes the decision making out of your hands; amazing views and beautiful interior space. $ *Average main: R600* ✉ *Beau Constantia Wine Estate, Constantia Main Rd., Constantia* ☎ *021/794–8632* ⊕ *www.beauconstantia.com/eat* ☾ *No dinner Sun.*

The Conservatory at The Cellars Hohenort

$$$$ | **SOUTH AFRICAN** | Discover the wonders of South African haute cuisine in this modern, glassed-in conservatory overlooking the beautiful gardens of the historic Cellars-Hohenort Hotel. The cuisine is playful but high-end, with a medley of multicultural techniques and flavors being used to great effect on local ingredients, resulting in dishes like a springbok (local venison) loin served with tempura shiitake mushrooms, karoo lamb with pumpkin mousse and fynbos honey, or Atlantic tuna with kimchee and apple. **Known for:** stylish dining room with garden views; inventive and playful South African modern cuisine; an exquisite high tea is served daily. $ *Average main: R225* ✉ *Cellars-Hohenort Hotel, 93 Brommersvlei Rd., Constantia*

☎ *021/794–2137* ⊕ *www.thecellars-hohenorthotel.com.*

★ Foxcroft Restaurant & Bakery

$$$$ | **ECLECTIC** | Serving a range of exquisitely prepared international fusion cuisine in a casually elegant-industrial setting, this restaurant and bakery in the heart of leafy Constantia is a true gem. The extremely seasonal menu changes often, but includes about a dozen mind-blowing tapas options—incorporating flavors from harissa to ponzu to smoked garlic—as well as a half dozen more traditional mains, such as chalmar beef with duck fat fries and café au lait sauce, or pan-seared line fish with mussel chowder. **Known for:** surprisingly affordable for such high-quality cuisine; casual but elegant ambience that captures Capetonian style; amazing attached bakery serving breakfast. $ *Average main: R395* ✉ *High Constantia Centre, Constantia Main Rd. at Groot Constantia Rd., Constantia* ☎ *021/202–3304* ⊕ *www.foxcroft.co.za.*

★ La Colombe

$$$$ | **ECLECTIC** | Rightfully known as one of South Africa's most lauded fine-dining establishments and listed in the world's top 100 restaurants, La Colombe's sublime French-Asian inspired tasting menus are served in a delightful minimalist setting overlooking the bucolic green of the Constantia wine valley. The menu changes regularly, but the best option is to order the full eight-course gourmand menu, as there is not a false note to be found. **Known for:** fantastic wine pairings; stellar French-Asian fusion haute cuisine; excellent, knowledgeable service. $ *Average main: R995* ✉ *Silvermist Wine Estate, Main Rd., Constantia Nek, Constantia* ☎ *021/794–2390* ⊕ *www.lacolombe.co.za.*

Coffee and Quick Bites

Coffee BloC

$$ | **CAFÉ** | **FAMILY** | This delightful coffee shop serves excellent freshly baked pastries and cakes, as well as very good breakfasts and light lunches. Coffee is roasted on-site, and numerous seating options inside and out mean you can find a cozy, shady, or sunny nook depending on mood and whim. **Known for:** coffee roasted on-site; delicious fresh baked goods;. [$] *Average main: R140* ✉ *Buitenverwachting Wine Estate, off Klein Constantia Rd., Constantia* ☎ *021/794–5190* 🌐 *www.buitenverwachting.com/coffee_bloc.html* 🕒 *Closed Sun.*

La Belle Constantia

$$ | **CAFÉ** | A charming cafe in the Alphen Boutique Hotel, La Belle Constantia has fresh bakes, salads, and more filling lunches, though they are known for their cakes and pastries—be sure to try the lemon meringue or the berry frangipane. In warmer weather take advantage of the delightful outside seating. **Known for:** great breakfasts; delicious cakes and pastries. [$] *Average main: R150* ✉ *Alphen Boutique Hotel, Alphen Dr., Constantia* ☎ *021/795–6336* 🌐 *www.labellecampsbay.co.za.*

Hotels

Alphen Boutique Hotel

$$$$ | **HOTEL** | Situated on 11 acres of gardens in leafy Constantia, this glamorous and avant-garde boutique hotel was originally an 18th-century Cape Dutch manor house and working farm. **Pros:** spacious rooms with bold voluptuous style; convenient beautiful location for exploring Constantia winelands; great pool area (although unheated). **Cons:** need a car; no elevator; no gym. [$] *Rooms from: R6900* ✉ *Alphen Dr., Constantia* ☎ *021/795–6300* 🌐 *www.alphen.co.za* 🛏 *19 rooms* 🍴 *Free Breakfast.*

Cellars-Hohenort Hotel & Spa

$$$$ | **HOTEL** | With acres of gardens and spectacular views across the Constantia Valley, this idyllic old-school getaway in two historic buildings makes the world beyond disappear. **Pros:** fantastic breakfast in lovely Conservatory Restaurant; beautiful gardens; two pools (one for children). **Cons:** a lot of stairs to access best rooms; more modern rooms on Cellars side are starting to feel old-fashioned; need a car to get around. [$] *Rooms from: R8706* ✉ *93 Brommersvlei Rd., Constantia* ☎ *021/794–2137* 🌐 *www.collectionmcgrath.com/hotels/the-cellars-hohenort* 🛏 *53 rooms* 🍴 *Free Breakfast.*

The Last Word Constantia

$$$$ | **HOTEL** | A great base for exploring the Constantia winelands, this peaceful boutique hotel with a lovely garden and incredibly spacious rooms successfully combines elegance with homey intimacy. **Pros:** convenient location in the heart of Constantia; incredibly spacious rooms; beautiful gardens and lovely pool. **Cons:** no gym; a car is needed to do anything; music from restaurant next door can be loud some evenings. [$] *Rooms from: R7250* ✉ *34 Spaanschemat River Rd., Constantia* ☎ *021/794–7657* 🌐 *www.thelastword.co.za* 🛏 *9 rooms* 🍴 *Free Breakfast.*

Activities

Cape Town is the unofficial adventure capital of the universe. Whatever you want to do—dive, paddle, fly, jump, run, slide, fin, walk, or clamber—this is the city to do it, and there is always somebody to help make it happen.

For spectator sports, it's easy to get tickets for ordinary club matches and interprovincial games. Getting tickets to an international test match is more of a challenge.

Biking

Bike & Saddle

BIKING | Offering city bike tours, trips from the "sip and cycle" tour through the winelands to a day around the Cape Peninsula or even a cycle safari, this "eco-active" outfit has all your cycling needs covered. They also organize multiday journeys that combine cycling, hiking, and paddling (or whatever combination thereof appeals). ✉ *32 Jamieson St., Gardens* ☎ *021/813–6433* ⊕ *www.bikeandsaddle.com.*

Up Cycles

BIKING | Cape Town's first drop-and-go bike rental company has a network of stations around the city, making two wheels the most fun and easy way to get around town on a gorgeous day. Their main location in town also has a lovely café where you can enjoy a coffee or juice and free Wi-Fi while you rent or return a bike, or even get your own wheels serviced. Helmets and locks are inclusive, and child seats can be rented. ✉ *Waterkant St., Cape Town Central* ☎ *074/100–9161, 076/135–2223* ⊕ *www.upcycles.co.za* 🎫 *From R90 per hr.*

Climbing

Cape Town has hundreds of bolted sport routes around the city and peninsula, ranging from an easy 10 to a hectic 30. To give you some idea of difficulty, a route graded a 10 in South Africa would be equivalent to a 5.5 climb in the United States. A grade 20 climb would register around 5.10c, and the hardest you'll find in South Africa is probably a 35, which American climbers would know as a 5.14c. The toughest climb up Table Mountain rates about 32, which is a 5.14a. Both Table Mountain sandstone and Cape granite are excellent hard rocks.

There's a wide range of traditional, as well as sport climbing and bouldering

areas scattered throughout the peninsula: a few favorite climbing areas include Table Mountain (from various angles), Lion's Head, Silvermine, and Muizenberg Peak. There are trad and sport climbing route guides that cover all the major climbing areas, plus a number of friendly climbing schools in Cape Town. The climbing forum is a great source (⊕ *www.climbing.co.za*), as are books by Tony Lournes.

Hiking and Canyoning

Cape Town and the surrounding areas offer some of the finest hiking in the world. "Kloofing," known as canyoning in the United States, is the practice of following a mountain stream through its gorge, canyon, or kloof by swimming, rock hopping, and jumping over waterfalls or cliffs into deep pools, so it's definitely more hard-core than simple hiking. There are some exceptional kloofing venues in the Cape.

For more information on the Hoerikwaggo Trail, see the Table Mountain section, above.

Hike Table Mountain

HIKING & WALKING | This fully South African, owner-operated mountain guiding service specializes in hikes and climbs (mountaineering) on Table Mountain and the Cape Peninsula. Guides, many of whom seem to practically live on the mountain, are passionate and knowledgeable. ☎ *060/539–9340* ⊕ *www.hiketablemountain.co.za* 🎫 *From R950.*

Mother City Hikers

HIKING & WALKING | Originally from Chicago, Lauren Medcalf came to Cape Town on an extended vacation in 2006 and has never left. With Table Mountain standing tall over the city and surrounded by the southern oceans, it has become her home away from home. Mother City Hikers uses qualified and accredited mountain guides, who have fulfilled the requirements for Adventure Guiding/ Mountaineering and are also qualified to offer mountain walking and overnight trips. All guides are also certified in first aid and CPR with the National First Aid Academy in South Africa. Prices include pickup at your hotel and transportation to the hiking site. ☎ *072/530–3464* ⊕ *mothercityhikers.co.za* ✉ *From R1100.*

RidgwayRamblers
HIKING & WALKING | Binny Ridgway is one of the most experienced Table Mountain guides. If you want to get the most out of this iconic rock, it's best to learn a little about the area and its flora and fauna while getting some exercise and not having to think too hard for yourself. Hikes may go from Skeleton Gorge to Maclears Beacon (on the mountain) or to the Twelve Apostles (above Camps Bay). Binny also runs overnight hikes on Table Mountain, and other hikes around the Western Cape. ⊠ *Tafelberg Rd.* ☎ *082/522–6056* ⊕ *www.ridgwayramblers.co.za* ✉ *From R950.*

Kayaking

Kaskazi Kayaks & Adventures
KAYAKING | You don't have to be a pro to discover Cape Town by kayak. Kaskazi has regular sunset and sunrise paddles off Sea Point, no experience necessary. The delightful two-hour paddles are reasonably priced and popular for good reason. ⊠ *179 Beach Rd., Mouille Point* ☎ *067/927–7158* ⊕ *kaskazi.co.za* ✉ *From R500.*

Rappelling

Abseil Africa
ROCK CLIMBING | Abseil Africa offers a 350-foot abseil (rappel) off the top of Table Mountain. Another excursion—the "Kamikaze Kanyon"—takes you abseiling over a waterfall in the Helderberg Mountains (about an hour away), along with a whole lot of hiking and kloofing

(canyoning). Tours include both transportation and lunch. This is a good operation that's been around a long time. ⊠ *297 Long St., Cape Town Central* ☎ *072/065–1520* ⊕ *www.abseilafrica.co.za* ✉ *From R1195.*

Scuba Diving

The diving around the Cape is excellent, with kelp forests, cold-water corals, very brightly colored reef life, and numerous wrecks. An unusual experience is a dive in the Two Oceans Aquarium. CMSA, NAUI, and PADI dive courses are offered by local operators; open-water certification courses begin at about R7500 (all-inclusive).

Ocean Experiences
DIVING & SNORKELING | Ocean Experiences (previously named Adrenalised) can introduce you to some of Cape Town's amazing dive options, from diving with Seven Gill Cow sharks in Simon's Town to scuba diving with Cape Fur Seals in Cape Town, or just exploring wrecks and kelp forests. They also run PADI certification courses, free-diving courses and trips, and snorkeling trips. ⊠ *V&A Waterfront, Shop 8, Quay 5* ☎ *079/711–4755* ⊕ *www.adrenaliseddiving.co.za* ✉ *From R1260 (single dive with equipment).*

Shark Diving

Seeing great white sharks hunting seals around False Bay's Seal Island is one of the most intense natural displays you're likely to witness. And if witnessing it all from a boat is not thrilling enough, you can get in the water (in a cage). *See the Cape Peninsula chapter for more information.*

Spas

Danté Wellness Spa

SPAS | Focusing on facial treatments, this spa founded by two sisters offers personalized service and well-priced facial treatments in the unpretentious setting of a Sea Point shopping center. Specialties include the Dermalogica Deep Cleanse facial and the Environ Facial Treatments. A vertical tanning booth, manicures and pedicures, and a partner "skin renewal" business (with nonsurgical treatments like Botox and laser) complete the scene. Body wraps and massage are also available. ⊠ *Piazza Da Luz, 94 Regent Rd., Shop 12, Sea Point* ☎ *021/434–1011* ⊕ *www.dantewellness.co.za.*

★ Mai Thai Wellness Spa

SPAS | This excellent, reasonably priced, and owner-managed boutique spa is one of the few not associated with a hotel. The highly trained therapists offer an extensive range of Thai-inspired massage therapy, as well as facials, luxury hand and feet treatments, and waxing and tinting services for men and women. Located in a charming building in De Waterkant, the spa also has a bamboo courtyard relaxation room where you can enjoy post-treatment teas and a cool breeze. ⊠ *7 Breda St., Green Point* ☎ *071/611–1886* ⊕ *www.maithaiwellness.com.*

One&Only Spa

SPAS | This artfully designed spa exudes pampered exclusivity of the type intended for the rich and famous: that is, fabulous and pricey. On a private island and part of a swank resort within the V&A Waterfront, its contemporary-minimalist African- and Japanese-influenced treatment rooms look out onto Table Mountain and lush gardens. Clients are handed tea or pure pomegranate juice upon arrival, and the relaxation room is stocked with beverages, dried fruit, and nuts. This spa also offers manicures and pedicures by the famous Bastien Gonzalez. Leave time to enjoy the vitality pool, steam room, sauna (with an ice fountain right outside), and relaxation time in the gardens. ⊠ *One&Only Cape Town, Dock Rd., V&A Waterfront* ☎ *021/431–5810* ⊕ *www.oneandonlyresorts.com.*

Spa at Cape Grace

SPAS | Great service and professionalism are the hallmarks of this intimate spa in the Cape Grace, whose paprika-and-saffron-hued spice-route motif is vibrant yet elegant. Drawing on Khoi-San healing customs, Kalahari treatments use a signature range of products from the Namibian desert, and other facial therapies and body treatments employ either the Comfort Zone or QMS ranges. The relaxation and hot spa area facilities (sauna, steam room, rain showers) are unfortunately coed and a bit cramped, but enjoy lovely views of Table Mountain. ⊠ *Cape Grace, West Quay Rd., V&A Waterfront* ☎ *021/410–7140* ⊕ *www.capegrace.com.*

12 Apostles Spa

SPAS | Given its stunning situation, you'd expect more—as in a view. Thanks to its unique location as the only development past Camps Bay on the pristine fynbos-covered slopes, overlooking the wild Atlantic Ocean, this spa comes in at the top of many lists. Unfortunately, its dark indoor space doesn't profit sufficiently from its gorgeous setting. But as this is really about spa therapy, you can book your massage, manicure, facial, or a romantic Moonlight Treatment for two in a temperature-controlled, glassed-in gazebo 300 feet away for some of the best views on the Cape (request a gazebo when you reserve). Many of the wraps and treatments incorporate natural, locally sourced ingredients (Cape snowbush, Cape lavender, and *buchu,* an indigenous medicinal herb). Indoor hydrotherapy facilities include a brine flotation pool, heated jet pool, cold plunge pool, and sauna. ⊠ *Twelve Apostles Hotel & Spa, Victoria Rd., Camps Bay* ☎ *021/437–9060* ⊕ *www.12apostleshotel.com.*

Chapter 4

CAPE PENINSULA

4

Updated by
Mary Fawzy

 Sights
★★★★★

 Restaurants
★★★★☆

 Hotels
★★★★★

 Shopping
★★★☆☆

 Nightlife
★★☆☆☆

WELCOME TO CAPE PENINSULA

TOP REASONS TO GO

★ **Beautiful Beaches Galore:** The Cape Peninsula has some of the most scenic coastlines in the world, with beautiful mountainous backdrops and white-sandy beaches, each with its own character and communities.

★ **Small Town Charm:** Quaint small towns with cute cafes, shops, and beaches pepper the Peninsula. People are friendly and laid back, which promotes top relaxation.

★ **Unmatched Views:** Between the mountains, cliff edges, beaches, and varying terrain expect views, unlike anything you've seen before. You'll also likely spot some wildlife!

★ **Outdoor Adventures, Sports, and Activities:** Whether it's kite-surfing, hiking, scuba diving, or swimming with sharks—there's bound to be an outdoor adventure for you.

★ **Biodiversity Hotspot:** The Cape Peninsula is one of the world's most biodiverse regions, with hundreds of plants and flowers endemic to the region.

There are plenty of little towns and attractions to discover in the Cape Peninsula, each with its own vibe, community, and beaches.

1 Hout Bay. A large valley enclosed by mountains and ocean, this former fishing village has numerous neighborhoods with its own harbor with a fish market, white sand beaches, quaint shops, and craft stores.

2 Noordhoek. Home to the Cape's more eco-conscious population, expect artisanal bakeries, coffee roasters, large farm-like estates with lakes, horseriding, and country-style living, and a quiet, pristine beach perfect for walks.

3 Kommetjie. A small rustic village known for abundant crayfish fishing, excellent kite-surfing and wind-surfing conditions, and bird watching.

4 Muizenberg. On the eastward curvature of False Bay, Muizenburg is known as "surfer's corner" as it's one of the best places to surf in the peninsula. The town's vibe matches the laid-back surfer personality you'd expect.

5 St James. Famous for its colorful beach huts and large tidal pool, this little seaside town gets really busy during hot days.

6 Kalk Bay. A charming fishing village historically developed by enslaved laborers, you'll find lovely cafes, fresh fish and chips, and boutiques.

7 Fish Hoek. Surrounded by jagged mountains with houses built on them, the sandy beach is one of the Cape Peninsula's safest to swim in and is frequented by families, dog-walkers, and people strolling along its coastal walkway.

8 Simon's Town. Home to the largest South African Naval base, this is an adventure town. The beach is the starting point for many water sports, including scuba diving, shark-cage diving, and the gateway to False Bay's "Marine Big 5," including penguins.

9 Cape of Good Hope Nature Reserve. With dramatic landscapes and beautiful indigenous flora and fauna, Cape Point is a must-visit including a funicular ride to the lighthouse for breathtaking views of the ocean and peninsula.

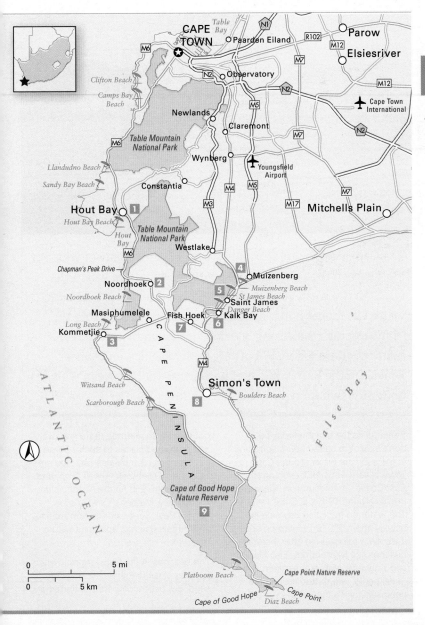

THE CAPE PENINSULA BEACHES

The family-friendly St James beach is known for its colorful Victorian-style bathing boxes and numerous tidal pools.

The Cape Peninsula's stunning white beaches, many of which have earned the prestigious "Blue Flag" status, are worth the visit. On the West, you have the Atlantic Ocean with colder water but longer hours of sunshine and protection from the "Cape Doctor" (the strong Southeasterly wind), which means better conditions for sunbathing, beach picnics, and sunset walks. On the East, you have the warmer Indian Ocean which is better for swimming, surfing, and diving.

Beautiful as the beaches may be, don't expect to spend hours splashing in the surf: the water around Cape Town is very, very cold, even on the East Coast—in midsummer the water hovers around 10°C–15°C (50°F–60°F). The water on the False Bay side is usually about 5°C (9°F) warmer, so if it's swimming you're after, head to beaches like Muizenberg, Fish Hoek, and Boulders. Numerous man-made "tidal pools" are dotted around the peninsula, and although the water is not that much warmer, there are lovely and protected places to swim. Some of our favorites on the False Bay side are St James, Dalebrook (in Kalk Bay), and Miller's Point; and on the Atlantic side: Camps Bay, Maiden's Cove (also in Camps Bay), Soetwater (in Kommetjie), and Buffels Bay (in Cape Point nature reserve).

The beaches in the Cape are renowned for their clean, snow-white, powdery sand, but beachcombers will find every kind of beach to suit them, from intimate boulder-strewn coves to sheltered bays and wild, wide beaches. If you're looking for more tropical water temperatures, head for the warm Indian Ocean waters of KwaZulu-Natal, the Eastern Cape, or the Garden Route.

Every False Bay community has its own beach, but most are not reviewed here. In comparison with Atlantic beaches, most of them are rather small and often crowded, sandwiched between the sea and the commuter rail line, with Fish Hoek being a major exception. South of Simon's Town, the beaches tend to be wilder and less developed, except for the very popular Seaforth and Millers Point beaches.

The major factor that affects any day at a Cape beach is wind. In summer howling southeasters, known as the Cape Doctor, are all too common and can ruin a trip to the beach; during these gales, you're better off at Clifton or Llandudno, as Atlantic beaches remain protected by the mountain from even the worst southeast wind. On the False Bay side, the sheltered but very small St James Beach and sometimes the southern corner of Fish Hoek Beach or one of the pools along Jager's Walk can still be pleasant. Boulders and Seaforth are also relatively sheltered from southeasters.

Sunseekers can take the train to St James beach.

Camps Bay beach is on the Atlantic Ocean.

The peninsula beaches have meticulous shark sighting techniques, so whatever you intend to do at the beach, look out for the shark flag which alerts beachgoers if there's a shark sighting nearby, coupled with an alarm, which means people have to get out of the water.

THINGS TO KNOW

Beaches are free, except those at the Cape of Good Hope Nature Reserve where you pay a park entrance fee.

Toilet facilities can be found at most of the main beaches.

Alcohol is forbidden; at some beaches (especially the protected ones) dogs aren't allowed.

Picnics are welcomed, but it's expected that you bring out what you brought in.

There's usually parking near most beaches, but on weekends and during the festive season (mid-December to early January) parking can be a real nightmare so consider a taxi/Uber.

TIMING AND PRECAUTIONS

The closest Cape Peninsula beaches to Cape Town are St James and Muizenberg, but in summer weekend traffic it can take a frustratingly long time. If you're driving, go early (before 10 am), or rather go on a weekday; traffic doesn't budge on December weekdays either.

4

Cape Peninsula THE CAPE PENINSULA BEACHES

The beach at Fish Hoek is a great place to swim as there are lifeguards and shark spotters.

Expect powerful waves, a strong undertow, and dangerous riptides at many of the beaches. Lifeguards work the main beaches, but only on weekends and during school breaks; other beaches are unpatrolled. Remember that it's risky to wander off on your own in a deserted area. If you want to take a stroll, it's best to stick to more populated beaches.

Southeasters can bring blue bottles (jellyfish-like creatures) near the beaches. If you see them washed up on the shore, it's best to stay out of the water as they can sting.

WHERE TO GO

Wildlife and adventure: Simon's Town is where you'll find Seaforth and Boulder's Beach; the latter is home to the popular penguin beach where you can see and even swim with a large penguin colony. This is also where you can see the rest of the "Marine Big 5," i.e., seals, whales, dolphins, and sharks.

Water sports: Kommetjie is place for kite-surfing and windsurfing. Muizenburg is known as the surfer's corner.

Walks: If you're the active only on land type, walks on Noordhoek and Fish Hoek beach are spectacular.

Swimming and sunbathing: Fish Hoek and Muizenburg are good for swimming given warmer temperatures, less wind, and safety (lifeguards and shark spotters). Both get really busy on weekends, but you'll always find a spot for sunbathing.

Beach town leisure: If exploring a beach town is more you're speed, Kalk Bay and Hout Bay are perfect for that. Kalk Bay has numerous cute cafes and boutiques, as well as artisans selling their crafts right on the coastline. Hout Bay has a lovely harbor market and great harbor views, as well as lively buskers, sleepy seals, and really good fish and chips.

A visit to Cape Town is synonymous with a visit to the peninsula south of the city, and for good reason. With pristine white-sand beaches, hundreds of mountain trails, and numerous activities from surfing to paragliding to mountain biking, the accessibility, variety, and pure beauty of the great outdoors will keep nature lovers and outdoor adventurers occupied for hours, if not days. A week exploring just the city and peninsula is barely enough.

The Cape Peninsula lies at the southern end of Cape Town and ends at the Cape of Good Hope. Just 15 minutes out of Cape Town, you'll begin to see the stunning landscapes of scenic beaches backed by sheer mountains.

The peninsula is a massive treat for any Cape Town visitor, and a round-trip drive that takes in both the False Bay coastline and the Atlantic Ocean may be one of your most memorable experiences. Among the highlights of the False Bay coast are the quaint fishing village of Kalk Bay and the penguins at Boulders Beach; both are must-visits, the former for the great food, bars, and shops in a historic village right on the sea, and the latter for the privilege of walking among the threatened African (jackass) penguins that call the national park's protected beach home.

Cape Point and the Cape of Good Hope nature reserve are 15 minutes farther on at the tip of the peninsula, and few fail to fall in love with the area's windswept beauty. The wilder and more rugged Atlantic coastline is one of the most stunning in the world. Highlights include a drive along the Misty Cliffs between Scarborough and Witsands, and horseback riding down Noordhoek beach. You might even consider spending a night or two in one of the many B&Bs that dot the coast, or even inside the Cape Point nature reserve at one of the cottages on Olifantsbos Beach.

MAJOR REGIONS

The Cape Peninsula, with a landmass of approximately 470 square km (181 square miles), juts out into the Atlantic Ocean at the South-Westernmost part of Africa. It then travels South and all the way around into the Indian Ocean on the east. It can be divided into three major regions.

The **Atlantic Seaboard,** the rocky mountainous land of the Western part of the peninsula, starts in **Hout Bay** and includes **Noordhoek, Kommetjie,** and **Scarborough** where it meets the Cape of Good Hope Nature Reserve.

The **Cape of Good Hope National Reserve**, part of the Table Mountain National Park, is a vast area of natural beauty, renowned for its rich biodiversity. It's largely uninhabited, including a world heritage site, Cape Point, and the Cape of Good Hope nearby.

The **False Bay** part of the peninsula is the Eastern side, starting at **Simon's Town** and reaching towards **Muizenberg**. This area is populated by charming coastal towns and enjoys the warmer water of the Indian Ocean.

Planning

When to Go

Certainly, a visit to the Cape Peninsula is glorious all year round, but there are some time periods to plan around if you want to make the best of certain activities.

To take advantage of the beaches for swimming and sunbathing, the summers are gorgeous and warm weather can be enjoyed from October to March. The beaches will be packed on the weekends during those months, and even more so during the festive season from mid-December to early January, so if you can't stand the crowd, avoid these times at all costs, but if you don't mind them, it's indeed a festive time to enjoy the beaches, with lots of activities and good spirits in the air.

October to March is also the best time for kite-surfing and wind-surfing as the summer's south-easterly winds create the perfect wind conditions.

Peak whale viewing season is from June to December but whales are seen most in False Bay in spring August to late September when wildflowers are also in bloom. The best time to see the great white sharks is between February and September when they tend to gather near False Bay during the winter. The best conditions for shark-cage diving are between February to early May.

While penguins can be seen all year round, their mating season occurs in summer, during December to February, which is perfect for swimming with them in the crystal waters at Boulder's Beach.

Getting Here and Around

Distances on the peninsula are not that great, so it's certainly possible to drive the roughly 120-km (75-mile) loop in a day, visiting a few sights of interest. It's equally possible, and far more rewarding, to spend three days here, either moving slowly around the peninsula and staying in a different guesthouse each night or returning to a central spot in the Southern Suburbs or town at the end of each day. Just remember, however, that during peak season (generally mid-November–late-January) and holidays, traffic—particularly along the M3 getting in or out of Cape Town, and then again between Muizenberg and Kalk Bay—can keep you gridlocked for many frustrating hours. Although touring the peninsula poses no obvious danger, you are advised not to park or walk alone in isolated areas. And watch out for baboons at Cape Point. If you're carrying food, they invite themselves to lunch and can be highly aggressive—the result of human folly.

AIR

Cape Town International Airport (CPT) is the region's major airport. Luckily, it's about a 30-minute drive (28 km [18 miles]) from the airport to the nearest Cape Peninsula beaches on the East Coast (Muizenberg, St James, etc.). It's roughly the same distance from the airport to Hout Bay on the West Coast. The most efficient way to get from the airport to your peninsula destination is to take a taxi/Uber; public transportation is available but renting a car or getting a taxi/Uber is really your best bet.

CONTACTS Cape Town International Airport. (CPT) ✉ Matroosfontein, Cape Town ☎ 021/937–1200 ⊕ www.cape-town-airport.com. **Metrorail.** ✉ Cape Town ☎ 021/449–6478 ⊕ www.metrorail.co.za. **MyCiti.** ✉ Cape Town ☎ 080/065–6463 ⊕ myciti.org.za.

BUS

While you can take the national Golden Arrow bus from Cape Town as far as Simon's Town on the east coast, bus networks within the peninsula are extremely limited.

CONTACTS Golden Arrow Bus. ✉ Cape Town ⊕ www.gabs.co.za.

CAR

Car travel is one of the best ways to explore the peninsula at your own leisure. The roads are well maintained and offer beautiful scenic drives, and it's fairly easy to navigate the main highways and roads. While taxis and Ubers are plentiful in Cape Town, don't expect to find many in the peninsula; if you're not renting a car, it's best to hire a touring company to take you around.

CONTACTS Europcar Rentals South Africa. ✉ Cape Town ☎ 086/113–1000 ⊕ www.europcar.co.za. **Hertz Car Rentals.** ✉ Cape Town ☎ 021/935–4500 ⊕ www.hertz.co.za.

Hotels

The gorgeous but wild Atlantic side of the Cape Peninsula is primarily residential and most accommodations are in the form of self-catering vacation homes, though there are a few lovely, but small hotels, guesthouses, and B&Bs. There is

no public transport to speak of, so you'll need your own car to go anywhere.

The eastern, or False Bay side of the Cape Peninsula includes the popular seaside villages of Muizenberg, St James, Kalk Bay, and Simon's Town. It's a lovely base for those seeking more of a beach-vacation vibe, with some of the Cape's most popular swimming and surfing beaches. There are also some great boutique hotels, guesthouses, and charming B&Bs in this area.

Hotel reviews have been shortened. For full information, visit Fodors.com.

LODGING ALTERNATIVES

The popularity of Airbnb has increased the availability of good apartments and holiday houses in the Cape Peninsula, which are affordable options for larger groups. There are also some lovely holiday villas available on sites like Vrbo.

Cape Stay also offers some good alternatives, ranging from luxurious villas in the area, to more affordable hotel rates, and even camping options, both on the Atlantic seaboard and in False Bay. Safari Now has numerous campsites along the peninsula along with caravan sites.

CONTACTS Safari Now. ✉ Longkloof Studios, Darters Rd, Cape Town ☎ 021/710–5800 ⊕ www.safarinow.com.

Restaurants

Although there are a few refined dining options, restaurants in the Cape Peninsula tend to be more rustic and casual than what you find in Cape Town. Options are more family-friendly, less trendy, but this doesn't mean taste or quality takes any hits; on the contrary, many restaurants offer freshly caught seafood and more attention to detail than the larger Cape Town restaurants. There are plenty of cute cafes and coffee shops serving light meals and bakes, just don't expect to find any of the global takeout chains.

In general, dining starts and ends earlier than in the city, as is expected in more small-town establishments.

Restaurant reviews have been shortened. For full information, visit Fodors.com.

RESTAURANT AND HOTEL PRICES
Restaurant prices in the reviews are the average cost of a main course at dinner, or if dinner is not served, at lunch. Hotel prices in the reviews are the lowest cost of a standard double room in high season.

What it Costs in South African rand			
$	**$$**	**$$$**	**$$$$**
RESTAURANTS			
under R100	R100–R150	R151–R200	over R200
HOTELS			
under R1500	R1500–R2500	R2501–R3500	over R3500

Safety

As with the advice when visiting Cape Town, be aware of your surroundings, don't walk alone, and avoid walks later in the evening.

While the peninsula has larger open spaces of land, you are going to be quite safe if camping, hiking, or driving on the open roads, on the marked paths in the Cape Point Nature Reserve, and in the busy parts of the towns, near the restaurants and shops.

Tours

Booking a private tour bus is one of the best ways to visit the peninsula, and there are plenty of options like the City Sightseeing Bus, which offers a Cape Point and Penguin Explorer Bus tour which takes you to Cape Point and back, stopping at Boulder's Beach and the Cape of Good Hope.

African Peninsula Tours
PRIVATE GUIDES | This scenic full-day excursion takes you on a private tour of the peninsula. It starts along the False Bay coast, through Muizenberg to Simon's Town, stopping for penguin viewing at Boulder's Beach. It then continues on to the Cape Point Nature Reserve, and then back via the Atlantic seaboard. You'll be driven and guided by Neville, a passionate, friendly, and knowledgeable guide. The tour is from 8:30 am to 5:30 pm and the rates do not include park entry fees. ⊠ *V&A Waterfront, Cape Town* ☎ *083/496–6160* ⊕ *www.aptt.co.za* ✉ *R1000 per person.*

Cape Point Route
GUIDED TOURS | **FAMILY** | Owned and run by locals, this Noordhoek-based company custom-designs tours that focus on the peninsula. ⊠ *Noordhoek Farm Village, Noordhoek* ☎ *021/789–0093* ⊕ *www. capepointroute.co.za* ✉ *From R740.*

City Sightseeing Cape Point and Penguin Explorer
BUS TOURS | This 8-hour round trip takes you on a guided tour of the most scenic parts of the peninsula, stopping at Boulder's Beach to see the penguins, at Cape Point, and at the Cape of Good Hope, with enough time "off the bus" to explore these spots. It includes the entry fee for the national park. There are pick-up points for the bus at the V&A Waterfront, Long Street, and sometimes a complimentary pickup service near where you are staying. ⊠ *Tourism Office, 2 Oceans Aquarium, Cape Town* ☎ *021/511–6000* ⊕ *www.citysightseeing. co.za* ✉ *R779.*

Kabura Travel Tours
PRIVATE GUIDES | This full-day private tour around the peninsula caters to your needs. Tours are taken on a luxury minibus with a dedicated tour guide, which allows you to skip the queues at the attractions. Pickup is from your accommodation in the morning, and you are able to choose what time and

how long your tour will be. The price is also inclusive of entrance fees for the sites. ✉ *4 Queen's Park Ave., Cape Town* ☎ *073/847–6425* ⊕ *www.privatetoursca-petown.com* ✆ *From R2600 per person.*

Springbok Atlas Tours

BUS TOURS | FAMILY | This full-day tour takes you around the whole peninsula, starting with a drive through Camps Bay to Hout Bay where you can stop to see the seals, time permitting. Then the tour continues to the breathtaking Cape Point and then back around via Simon's Town where you can visit the penguin colony (not included). The tour includes return transfers from central Cape Town hotels, entrance to Cape Point Nature Reserve, and the Chapmans Peak drive (if open). It excludes lunch and entrance to the penguin colony. ✉ *17 Chiappini St., Cape Town* ☎ *021/460–4700* ⊕ *www.spring-bokatlas.com* ✆ *R1430.*

Visitor Information

CONTACTS Cape Town Tourism Simon's Town. ✉ *543 Portion St., Simon's Town* ☎ *021/786–8440.* **Fish Hoek Tourism.** ✉ *81 Main Rd., Fish Hoek* ☎ *086/111–1950.*

Hout Bay

23 min (19.2 km) south of Cape Town City Centre

About 25-minutes' drive from Cape Town City Centre, this once-quiet fishing village on the Atlantic coast is the gateway to Chapman's Peak Drive. Those basing themselves here will want a car to get around, but proximity to various Atlantic beaches (Hout Bay Beach itself is not great), the Constantia wine estates, the peninsula, and the city—plus relatively good-value accommodations—are the draw. The drive along Chapman's Peak, which winds its way down to Noordhoek, is a must, and Hout Bay's quay-side fish and chips right at the farthest point of

the harbor, and its all-weekend market are good value and worth visiting. If you're getting hungry, head to Snoekies (pronounced like cookies) right on the water, at the southern end of the little harbor. Snoek is a barracuda-like fish that is eaten smoked and given its traditional Malay treatment. Try the more touristy Mariners Wharf if the former is full. Friday to Sunday sees the bustling **Bay Harbour Market**, a weekly social event for locals by night where you can also find lots of gift options for your loved ones back home. You'll also find craft beers, music, and good food. The market is open all day on weekends, but it gets very full.

GETTING HERE AND AROUND
Getting to Hout Bay is best with a car because you'll need it to move around once you get there; it's a 35-minute bus ride from the Cape Town waterfront or the city center. However, the City Sightseeing Bus has a Mini Peninsula Tour bus that stops at Mariner's Wharf, which is near the Harbour Bay Market. You can also take the 109 My Citi bus to Hout Bay from Adderley Street/Sea Point Main Road.

TOURS

Drumbeat Charters

BOAT TOURS | FAMILY | In operation since 1989, Drumbeat Charters is based in the fishing village of Hout Bay, offering daily scenic cruises. Their big attraction is the Seals & the Shipwreck trip, where you'll visit Duiker Island, home of the Cape fur seals, and then travel farther along the Kabonkelberg Mountain range to Moari Bay to view the shipwreck of the *Bos 400*, which ran aground in 1994 during a Cape winter storm. ✉ *60 Harbour Rd., Hout Bay* ☎ *082/658–7055* ⊕ *www. drumbeatcharters.co.za.*

Hooked on Africa

BOAT TOURS | FAMILY | Based in Hout Bay harbor, this operation is in one of the richest fishing grounds left in the world today. If you're keen to take to the open ocean for some deep-sea fishing, you'll have plenty of choices, as South Africa

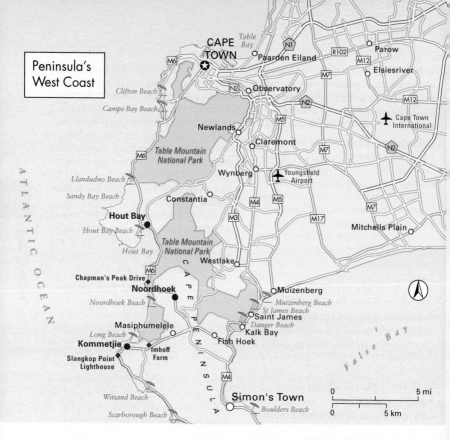

Peninsula's West Coast

ATLANTIC OCEAN

CAPE TOWN

Table Bay

M6

N1

Parow

R102

M12

Paarden Eiland

Elsiesriver

Clifton Beach

N2

Observatory

M7

M12

Camps Bay Beach

N2

Cape Town International

Newlands

M5

Claremont

M7

N2

Table Mountain National Park

M6

Wynberg

Youngsfield Airport

Llandudno Beach

Sandy Bay Beach

Constantia

M4

M5

Hout Bay

M3

M17

M7

Hout Bay Beach

Mitchells Plain

Hout Bay

Table Mountain National Park

Westlake

Chapman's Peak Drive

M6

Muizenberg

Noordhoek

Muizenberg Beach

Noordhoek Beach

C A P E

St James Beach

Saint James

Masiphumelele

Danger Beach

Kalk Bay

Long Beach

Fish Hoek

Kommetjie

Imhoff Farm

Slangkop Point Lighthouse

P E N I N S U L A

M4

False Bay

Witsand Beach

Simon's Town

Boulders Beach

Scarborough Beach

0   5 mi

0   5 km

has excellent game fish, such as dorado, yellowfin tuna, and broadbill swordfish. The company offers private, full-boat charters of a 32-foot catamaran for a full day of deep-sea fishing. Call to inquire about current rates and to see if there are any organized trips you could join in lieu of a full-boat charter. ☎ 021/790–5332 ⊕ www. hookedonafrica.co.za ⊠ From R10,000.

◉ Sights

Chapman's Peak Drive

SCENIC DRIVE | Rock slides and unstable cliff faces mean this fantastically scenic drive can often be closed for maintenance, as it was for the greater part of 2008–2009. Work began on the drive in 1910, when it was considered an impossibility. Charl Marais, a mining surveyor, wasn't deterred by the task and set about surveying a route by sending a worker ahead of him to chop out footholds and create rudimentary platforms for his theodolite. There are stories of him hanging on to the side of the cliff by ropes and nearly losing his life on a number of occasions. With the help of 700 convicts, a road was chipped and blasted out of the rock. Chapman's Peak Drive officially opened in 1922 with views rivaling those of California's Pacific Route 1 to Big Sur. When open, you can access the drive from both Noordhoek and Hout Bay. The toll-gate installed on the drive has been the source of huge local controversy—but you as a tourist won't notice a thing (apart from the fee). Also, this is part of the route for the Cape Argus, the world's largest timed bicycle race—with about 35,000 entries every year from around the globe. ⊠ Hout Bay ⊕ From Hout Bay to Nordhoek ☎ 021/791–8222 ⊕ www.chapmanspeak-drive.co.za ⊠ R54 toll for cars each way.

World of Birds

WILDLIFE REFUGE | FAMILY | Here you can walk through a sanctuary housing more than 400 species of indigenous and exotic birds, including eagles, vultures, penguins, and flamingos. With neither bars nor nets separating you from most of the birds, you can get some pretty good photographs; however, the big raptors are (wisely) kept behind fences. Kids will love the "monkey jungle," where a few dozen highly inquisitive squirrel monkeys roam freely, often lighting on your shoulders or back. There's also a small jungle gym for kids to play on at the end of the park. ⊠ *Valley Rd., Hout Bay* 🕿 *021/790–2730* ⊕ *www.worldofbirds.org.za* 🖺 *R85.*

Beaches

Hout Bay Beach

BEACH | FAMILY | Cradled in a lovely bay of the same name and guarded by a 1,000-foot peak known as the Sentinel, Hout Bay is the center of Cape Town's crayfishing industry (legal and otherwise) and operates several fish-processing plants. It also has knockout views of the mountains, gentle surf, and easy access to the restaurants and bars of Mariner's Wharf. The fact that this is a working harbor, added to the raw sewage of the Inzamo Yethu informal settlement a short walk upstream, means this is, unfortunately, a polluted beach, however beautiful it looks. You are advised not to swim here. **Amenities:** food and drink; parking. **Best for:** solitude; walking. ⊠ *Off M6, Hout Bay.*

Restaurants

Cheyne's & Lucky Bao

$$$$ | ASIAN FUSION | Serving Pacific Rim cuisine from a funky and intimate location in Hout Bay, Cheyne's is the place to go for inventive, pan-Asian small plates. The menu changes entirely each season but is generally divided into the categories of sea, land, earth, poké bowls, and happy endings. **Known for:** vibey graffiti-mural interior; fun and intensely flavored pan-Asian cuisine; biggest rum selection in Hout Bay. 🟕 *Average main: R300* ⊠ *35 Main Rd., Hout Bay* 🕿 *066/412–3289* ⊕ *www.facebook.com/LuckyBaoBar* ☾ *Closed Sun. No lunch Mon.–Wed.*

Clay Café

$$ | CAFÉ | FAMILY | This family-friendly cafe has an extensive menu of pizzas, salads, sandwiches, cake, and coffee, as well as an added surprise—paint your own ceramics. Enjoy a light meal while you paint anything from dishes, bowls, vases, or figurines. **Known for:** paint your own clay creations; kid-friendly with lots of activities; fun cafe for all ages. 🟕 *Average main: R120* ⊠ *4080 Main Rd., Hout Bay* 🕿 *076/810–5120* ⊕ *claycafe.co.za* ☾ *No dinner.*

Massimo's

$$ | ITALIAN | FAMILY | Having begun as a pizza joint, this casual Hout Bay eatery located in an old barn now serves a range of delightfully simple Italian fare from antipasti to pastas, as well as what is still arguably Cape Town's best pizza. The "spuntini" or antipasti include classics like Italian meatballs, Caprese salad, and panfried spinach with toasted pine nuts. **Known for:** frequent specials; excellent Italian-style pizza; friendly, warm service. 🟕 *Average main: R120* ⊠ *Oakhurst Farm Park, Main Rd., Hout Bay* 🕿 *067/324–0261* ⊕ *www.massimos.co.za* ☾ *No lunch Mon.–Thurs.*

Hotels

Cube Guest House

$$ | B&B/INN | This stylish, modern guesthouse high on a hill in residential Hout Bay enjoys stunning bay and mountain views and makes the perfect pampered base from which to explore all the Cape's offerings. **Pros:** free unlimited Wi-Fi; great service; no end-time for breakfast. **Cons:** you'll need a car for most activities; all rooms accessed by stairs; not kid-friendly. 🟕 *Rooms from: R2450* ⊠ *20 Luisa Way, Hout Bay* 🕿 *071/441–8161* ⊕ *www.*

cube-guesthouse.com 🛏 *5 rooms* 🍴 *Free Breakfast.*

Hout Bay Hideaway
$$ | **B&B/INN** | Tranquil and intimate with only four rooms, this owner-managed guesthouse tucked away in a lush neighborhood setting is perfect for those seeking peace and privacy. **Pros:** barbecue grills for guests; lovely private breakfast on your patio; wood-burning fires and underfloor heating. **Cons:** no indoor public lounge space; you'll want to have a car for most activities; smokers aren't welcome. [$] *Rooms from: R2400* ✉ *37 Skaife St., Hout Bay* ☎ *021/790–8040* 🌐 *www.houtbay-hideaway.com* 🛏 *4 rooms* 🍴 *Free Breakfast.*

★ **Tintswalo Atlantic**
$$$$ | **RESORT** | Visitors attracted to the Cape Peninsula for its natural grandeur will think they've died and gone to heaven when arriving at this discreetly luxurious boutique hotel. **Pros:** fantastic breakfast in one of the most beautiful spots imaginable; unique mind-blowing location; attentive service and setup creates a bit of a "safari by the sea" ambience. **Cons:** about a 35- to 40-minute drive from Cape Town Central; building requirements in the national park mean exteriors of buildings have a prefab look; must drive to all activities and sights. [$] *Rooms from: R12550* ✉ *Chapman's Peak Dr., Km 2, Hout Bay* ☎ *021/201–0025* 🌐 *www.tintswalo.com/atlantic* 🛏 *11 rooms* 🍴 *Free Breakfast.*

Shopping

MARKETS

Bay Harbour Market
MARKET | **FAMILY** | This funky market in Hout Bay's working harbor offers more than 100 stalls selling everything from great food and drinks to clothing, crafts, and some truly worthwhile "made in South Africa" memorabilia. With good-quality live music performances, a wide and affordable selection of tasty treats, and a kids' play area, this all-weekend shopping spot is a great place for the whole family to shop, eat, or just hang out—by day or night—in the Hout Bay Harbour area. ✉ *31 Harbour Rd., Hout Bay* ☎ *084/370–5715* 🌐 *www.bayharbour.co.za* 🕒 *Closed Mon.–Thurs.*

Noordhoek

38 km (24 miles) southwest of Cape Town.

This popular beach community has stunning white sands that stretch all the way to Kommetjie along the aptly named Long Beach. The Noordhoek Farm Village is a welcome rest stop with several great restaurants and a few galleries and boutiques showcasing the work of local artists and craftspeople. Long Beach is popular with surfers and runners, and you can walk all the way to Kommetjie. Just don't walk alone or when the beach is deserted, as attacks are not uncommon. Horseback riding along the beach and through the fynbos-covered dunes is a memorable and highly worthwhile excursion.

GETTING HERE AND AROUND

Noordhoek doesn't have any bus lines or train stations nearby, the closest you would get is Muizenberg, so traveling by car is the only way. Uber and taxis are available in the area, although with a bit of wait.

TOURS

Horse-riding Cape Town
SPECIAL-INTEREST TOURS | **FAMILY** | Enjoy horseback riding along Noordhoek's magnificent Long Beach with views of Chapman's Peak and The Sentinel. Rides are 90 minutes and are suitable for novice and experienced riders. ✉ *Crofter's Valley, Noordhoek* ☎ *076/251–8584* 🌐 *horseridingcapetown.com* 🎟 *R620 per person.*

Noordhoek Farm Village has several great eateries and shops showcasing local artists.

◉ Sights

Noordhoek Farm Village

MARKET | This lovely collection of great restaurants, art galleries, and boutiques is a great place to spend a few hours or get a quick bite to eat while passing through. Want to stay awhile? The Noordhoek Village Hotel is on the property as is The Burrow pub. ✉ *Noordhoek Main Rd., Noordhoek ⊹ 25 minutes from Cape Town's City Centre ⊕ thefarmvillage. co.za.*

🍴 Restaurants

Café Roux

$$ | **CAFÉ** | **FAMILY** | Easy eating in a family-friendly atmosphere doesn't get much better than this café, deservedly beloved by the outdoorsy crowd that populates the Cape Peninsula. Sit outside under the oak trees or in, where reed-covered ceilings and a wood-burning stove create a cozy ambience, and enjoy hearty and tasty breakfasts and lunches. **Known for:** super-relaxed and casual setting is great for families; reliable, unfussy food with lots of choice; live music some afternoons and evenings. $ *Average main: R110 ✉ Noordhoek Farm Village, Noordhoek Main Rd., Noordhoek ☎ 021/789–2538 ⊕ www.caferoux.co.za ⊙ No dinner.*

★ The Foodbarn Café and Tapas

$$$$ | **FRENCH FUSION** | Probably the best restaurant on the Cape Peninsula, the aptly named Foodbarn serves delicious, unpretentious French-influenced cuisine in the relaxed setting of a renovated barn near Noordhoek Beach. The chef makes a point of only using sustainable seafood, which he puts to great use in starters like fish tartar with miso cream and a sublime bouillabaisse. **Known for:** the only fine-dining location on the peninsula; extremely well-priced tasting menus for dinner; generous winter and lunch specials. $ *Average main: R205 ✉ Noordhoek Farm Village, Noordhoek Main Rd., Noordhoek ☎ 021/789–1390 ⊕ www. thefoodbarn.co.za ⊙ Closed Jan. 1.*

158

Coffee and Quick Bites

The Food Barn Deli

$ | SANDWICHES | Sister venue to the fabulous Food Barn Restaurant, this casual but excellent deli serves delicious and reasonably priced breakfasts, lunches, and snacks from a cozy book-lined space that invites lingering. Those stocking up for a picnic will also do well here. **Known for:** artisanal food products; evening tapas; friendly service. $ Average main: R80 ⊠ Noordhoek Farm Village, Chapman's Peak Dr., Noordhoek ☎ 021/789–1966 ⊕ www.thefoodbarn. co.za/deli-shop.

Kristen's Kick-Ass Ice Cream

$ | ICE CREAM | FAMILY | A Noordhoek-born business that has started expanding across the Cape, this tiny ice-cream store is the original location. From classic to funky flavors, and colorful kid flavors, this cafe will delight people of all ages and eating preferences as they have a selection of vegan, dairy-free, and sugar-free ice creams. **Known for:** exciting flavors; dairy, non-dairy, vegan and sugar-free ice creams available; handmade and delicious ice creams and cones. $ Average main: R35 ⊠ Noordhoek Farm Village, Village La., Noordhoek ☎ 079/265–5108 ⊕ www.kristenskickass.co.za.

Hotels

Noordhoek Village Hotel

$$ | HOTEL | FAMILY | Situated in the family-friendly Noordhoek Farm Village with its great restaurants and cute shops, this clean and comfortable hotel is a practical option for families exploring the peninsula. **Pros:** great location in the Noordhoek Farm Village, with numerous good restaurants; connecting rooms are suitable for families; one of the few hotels on the Atlantic side of the peninsula. **Cons:** service from management can be inconsistent; no views to speak of, and nearby pub can be noisy at night; a good 35-minute drive to Cape Town. $ Rooms

from: R1500 ⊠ Noordhoek Farm Village, 6 Village La., Noordhoek ☎ 021/789–2760 ⊕ www.noordhoekhotel.co.za ⇨ 20 rooms ⊚| Free Breakfast.

Kommetjie

3 km (1 mile) south of Noordhoek; 41 km (25 miles) southwest of Cape Town.

About halfway down the peninsula's west coast is this pleasant, somewhat isolated, and almost entirely residential neighborhood; the main attraction is its beach. Take the scenic 45-minute walk down Long Beach to the wreck of the Kakapo, a steamship that ran aground on her maiden voyage in 1900. This area is also a surfer's paradise, with some really big waves, a few gentler breaks, and for swimmers, a dangerous undertow. Because of a few muggings on Long Beach a couple of years back, people generally walk here in groups or in couples in the early mornings and at sundown.

GETTING HERE AND AROUND
You need a car to get to and around Kommetjie as virtually no public transport stops here.

Sights

Imhoff Farm

FARM/RANCH | FAMILY | This historic Cape farmstead offers a hodgepodge of shops and activities, including an excellent if small wine shop, a deli-style farm stall, several decent casual eateries and boutiques, and various animal-related attractions that kids will love. The latter include a petting farm, camel and horse rides, and a snake park. ⊠ Imhoff Farm, Kommetjie Rd., Cape Town ☎ 021/783–4545 ⊕ www.imhofffarm.co.za.

Slangkop Point Lighthouse

LIGHTHOUSE | At 111 feet, this is the tallest cast-iron tower on South Africa's coast, and the views are incredible. Located almost exactly midway between Robben

February through early May are the best months for shark-cage diving.

Island and Cape Point, the lighthouse has a 5-million-candlepower light and a range of 30 nautical miles. Since the lamp was officially lit in 1919 it has been capable of producing four flashes every 30 seconds. It's one of the few lighthouses in the world still to be manned by a keeper—known these days as a "lighthouse officer." ■TIP→ **If you're alone or not in a big group, this is a safer place to walk than Long Beach.** ⊠ *45 Lighthouse Rd., Kommetjie* ☎ *021/449–2400* ⊘ *Closed Sat. and Sun.*

Beaches

Long and Noordhoek Beaches
BEACH | A vast expanse of white sand stretching 6½ km (4 miles) from the base of Chapman's Peak (Noordhoek Beach starts here) to Kommetjie (where you find Long Beach), this is one of the wildest and least populated stretches of uninterrupted beach, with fluffy white sand and dunes, behind which sit a lagoon and private nature reserve. Because of the wind and the space, these beaches attract horseback riders and walkers rather than sunbathers, and the surfing is excellent (especially off Long Beach). There are no lifeguards and there is no bus service, and, as at some other beaches, at the wrong times and more isolated spots, there are real safety concerns (particularly the lonely stretch of sand right in the middle). Despite patrollers on horseback and the occasional all-terrain vehicle, crime is an issue here, and women, in particular, should be careful. Tourists always do best not to look like tourists. Hang out with other people, just in case, unless you're part of a group. **Amenities:** parking; toilets (Noordhoek). **Best for:** solitude; sunset; surfing; walking. ⊠ *Off M6, Noordhoek.*

Hotels

★ The Last Word Long Beach
$$$$ | **HOTEL** | All the spacious rooms at this elegant beach-themed boutique hotel—decor is clean and minimalist in shades of white, sand, and pale blue—have balconies with superb sea views

making the most of the fact that you are literally on the beach. **Pros:** friendly staff make you feel like they are there to serve only you; fabulous location right on Kommetjie's Long Beach; the only stellar hotel on this side of the peninsula. **Cons:** Wi-Fi can be slow; very limited dinner options in immediate vicinity; a good 45-minute drive to Cape Town. [$] *Rooms from: R7350* ✉ *1 Kirsten Ave., Kommetjie* ☎ *021/794–6561* 🌐 *www.thelastword.co.za* 🛏 *6 rooms* 🍴 *Free Breakfast.*

Muizenberg

30 km (19 miles) south of Cape Town.

Many of the beautiful art deco beachfront buildings that were fast becoming rundown in this once fashionable resort town have been renovated into upscale apartments or taken over by popular chain restaurants like Knead, Tiger's Milk, and Lucky Fish & Chips. Muizenberg now appeals to families, backpackers, beginner surfers, and stand-up paddleboarders. Surf shops offering lessons, rental boards, and wet suits line the beachfront. A dated but charming pavilion houses a swimming pool, waterslides, toilets, changing rooms, and snack shops.

GETTING HERE AND AROUND

Getting to Muizenberg from Cape Town is possible by car or taxi via the M3 highway; on sunny weekends, expect the Main Road leading into Muizenberg to be packed up with cars. To skip the traffic, and to take a more scenic route, take the Metrorail train from Cape Town to Muizenberg on the Southern Line. It's about a 20-minute train ride and the Muizenberg station is a five-minute walk from the beach.

Beaches

Muizenberg Beach

BEACH | FAMILY | Once the fashionable resort of South African high society, this beach is now the place where locals—from all corners of Cape Town—swim, picnic, and learn to surf. A long, sandy beach with a reliable break, this grand old lady of the city's warm-water beaches is known for the colorful bathing boxes of the type once popular at British resorts. Lifeguards are on duty, and the sea is shallow and reasonably safe—and there is reliable shark spotting. If you're keen on stretching your legs, you can walk along the beach or take the picturesque concrete promenade known as the Catwalk, which connects Muizenberg to St James. **Amenities:** food and drink; lifeguards; parking; showers; toilets; water sports. **Best for:** sunrise; surfing; swimming; walking; windsurfing. ✉ *Off M4, Muizenberg.*

Restaurants

Casa Labia

$$ | ITALIAN | Sitting atop fynbos-covered hills overlooking the magnificent False Bay surf, this Italian-inspired restaurant serves tasty and well-priced meals in the opulent setting—think gold-coffered ceilings, Venetian wallpaper, and marble fireplaces—that once served as home to South Africa's first Italian ambassador, Count Natale Labia. The weekend breakfasts are lovely, with treats like the grilled polenta, or the casa frittata, and the lunch menu features hearty dishes like slow-cooked beef ossobuco and pea risotto and a selection of pasta dishes and many inviting desserts. **Known for:** excellent pianist ups the ambience ante on weekend afternoons and Friday evenings when dinner is served; gorgeous museum-like setting, where children are surprisingly welcome; great Italian-inspired menu. [$] *Average main: R145* ✉ *192 Main Rd., Muizenberg* ☎ *021/180–3119* 🌐 *www.casalabia.co.za* ⏲ *No dinner Mon. and Tues.*

The Commons

$ | **CAFÉ** | This cozy vegan cafe is the perfect beach hangout to relax, listen to vinyl (and sometimes live music), have a bite or a drink, look at books and meet people all while having a perfect view of the ocean. The food is lovingly prepared and delicious, with lots of creative vegan dishes like arancini, kimchi fried rice, Philly cheesesteaks, west African peanut stew, and lots of burgers, pasta, and sandwiches. **Known for:** laid-back collaborative space; delicious and extensive vegan menu; live music and vinyl. $ *Average main: R75* ⊠ *13 York Rd., Muizenberg* ☎ *066/257–9120* ⊕ *thecommons. co.za* ⊗ *Closed Mon.*

Empire Cafe

$ | **CAFÉ** | Overlooking Muizenberg's surfers' beach, Empire is a place to come barefoot with sand still between your toes for unexpectedly good food, though often with less-than-great service. The chalkboard menu changes regularly, but expect items from burgers and wraps to pastas and salads. **Known for:** delicious sweet treats; tasty food in super-casual environment; service can be slow. $ *Average main: R95* ⊠ *11 York Rd., Muizenberg* ☎ *021/788–1250* ⊕ *www.empirecafe.co.za* ⊗ *Closed Mon. No dinner.*

 ## Activities

SURFING

The Cape Peninsula has some great but cold surf, and conditions can be complicated by the winds. Though it's no J-Bay (Jeffreys Bay), Muizenberg is one of the peninsula's most popular surfing spots, and there's always a group of surfers in the water. Surfing schools like Gary's can provide surfing lessons and/or equipment rentals.

Spotting Sharks

Shark spotters are employed at several of Cape Town's False Bay beaches—and on Boyes Drive looking down on the bay—to warn swimmers when great white sharks are out and about. Great whites are usually found close to the shore in the summer months (September–March), and spotters record around 170 sightings per year. A shark flag is raised and an alarm is sounded when sharks are spotted.

Gary's Surf School

SURFING | **FAMILY** | Gary's was the first surf school in South Africa, and it's still going strong, offering surfing lessons to youngsters and the young at heart in the relatively warm and gentle waters at Muizenberg. A basic two-hour lesson includes an hour of instruction and an hour of practice. All lessons are conducted at low tide to make things as safe and simple as possible. Surf boards and wet suits are available to rent. ⊠ *Balmoral Bldg., 34 Beach Rd., Muizenberg* ☎ *021/788–9839* ⊕ *www.garysurf.com* ⊠ *From R450.*

St James

27½ km (17 miles) south of Cape Town.

The tiny village of St James is located on the coastline between Muizenberg and Kalk Bay. Set on the shores of False Bay against a mountain backdrop, this pretty town is a quiet, mostly residential area, with the beach as its focal point. Here you can find the colorful beach huts seen on postcards and a tidal pool towards the south end of the beach where the

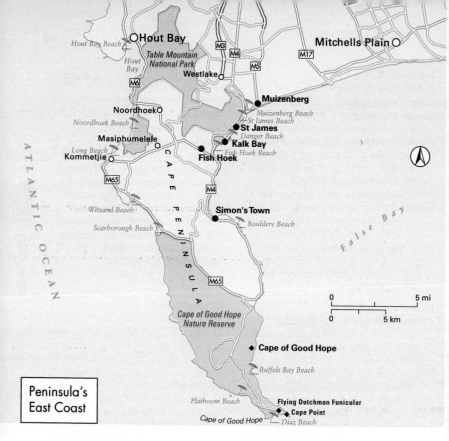

Hout Bay Beach · **Hout Bay** ○ ● **Mitchells Plain** ○

M3 M4

Table Mountain
National Park

M5

Hout
Bay

Westlake ○

M6 M17

● **Muizenberg**

Noordhoek ○
Muizenberg Beach
St James Beach

Noordhoek Beach ● **St James**
Danger Beach

Masiphumelele
● **Kalk Bay**
Fish Hoek Beach

Long Beach ○
Kommetjie ○ ● **Fish Hoek**

C
A
P
E

M65 M4

P
E
N
Witsand Beach I ● **Simon's Town**
N Boulders Beach
Scarborough Beach S

U
L
A

M65

False Bay

ATLANTIC OCEAN

0 _____ 5 mi
0 _____ 5 km

Cape of Good Hope
Nature Reserve

◆ **Cape of Good Hope**

Buffels Bay Beach

**Peninsula's
East Coast**

Platboom Beach **Flying Dutchman Funicular**
◆ **Cape Point**
Cape of Good Hope Diaz Beach

---

water is a bit warmer and calmer. The rock pools are also a favorite for families taking kids out to look for sea creatures. Other than a lovely local cafe, the train station, and the beach, there isn't a lot going on here, but it's a walkable distance to Kalk Bay on the Main Road, which has charming little houses along it. However, there are some wonderful guesthouses here that offer a peaceful and scenic stay.

GETTING HERE AND AROUND

St James is one of the stops on the Southern Line of the Metrorail train from Cape Town. The stop is between Kalk Bay and Muizenberg, easy to miss sometimes between these bigger stations. It's also easy to take the 30-minute drive here on the M3 from Cape Town, but also easy to miss because of how small the town is, so keep an eye out for the St James street sign.

Sights

St James Catholic Church

CHURCH | St James gets its name from this historical church, built in 1858 for the Catholic Filipino fishermen of Kalk Bay, who at the time petitioned the colonial governor of the Cape to build this church instead of the hazardous journey they had to make to Simon's Town each Sunday, by sea or by road. The community built this church themselves and the church steps were documented to have been built from stone taken from the mountain in St James. The church is largely unchanged and still operational with regularly scheduled mass. You can see the times on the website. ⊠ *Main Rd., St. James* ☎ *021/788–1275* ⊕ *saintjames.co.za.*

🔼 Beaches

Danger Beach

BEACH | This beach is a well-known surf spot because of its rip tides and large waves, hence its name. It's recommended that people swim in the tidal pools, farther up the beach for safety. This small strip of beach can be accessed via the subway, underneath the railway. What the beach lacks in amenities it makes up for in peacefulness and good waves for surfing. **Amenities:** none. **Best for:** surfing, windsurfing. ⊠ *Danger Beach, St. James.*

St James Beach

BEACH | FAMILY | Known for its brightly colored Victorian-style bathing boxes, this stretch of sand has tidal pools that are great for exploring with children; the shallow tidal pools make for safer and warmer swimming conditions. A sheltered cove from the wind, and conveniently located near the St James train station makes this beach incredibly popular during summer and can get really busy on weekends. The bathing huts on the beach with a mountain backdrop make for great holiday pictures. Parking can be a nightmare on busy days because only street parking is available. **Amenities:** toilets. **Best for:** swimming, sunbathing. ⊠ *St James Beach, St. James.*

☕ Coffee and Quick Bites

⭐ Folk Cafe

$$ | CAFÉ | FAMILY | This large cafe is a hidden gem in tiny St James, serving excellent coffee and an extensive menu that features various breakfasts, bakes, pizzas, burgers, and other hot meals. Supporting local producers where possible, they source their ingredients with care, using free-range eggs and chicken, and grass-fed beef, as well as having an environmental ethos to their packaging. **Known for:** quality and thoughtful meals; environmentally conscious; welcoming and warm atmosphere. $ *Average main:*

R125 ⊠ *Old Post Office, 54 Main Rd., St. James* ☎ *021/276–3656* ⊕ *www.folkcafe. co.za* ⊗ *No dinner on Mon.*

🏨 Hotels

⭐ St James Guesthouses

$$$$ | HOTEL | FAMILY | For a luxurious and private seaside retreat, a room in this casually elegant guesthouse—or even better, the whole house—is just the ticket. **Pros:** great views and ambience of classic elegance; lots of perks like inclusive beverages; intimacy and privacy. **Cons:** some of the fixtures in the Manor feel in need of an update; not all rooms are equally stunning; noise from the road out front can be irritating. $ *Rooms from: R3675* ⊠ *Main Rd., Peninsula False Bay, St. James* ☎ *021/788–4543* ⊕ *www. stjamesguesthouses.com* 🛏 *3 rooms* ⦿ *Free Breakfast.*

Kalk Bay

30 km (19 miles) south of Cape Town.

This small but fascinating harbor shelters a weathered fishing fleet, and takes its name from the seashells that were once baked in large kilns to produce lime (*kalk* in Afrikaans). Charming cottages and villas cling to the mountain above narrow, cobbled streets. Exploring the town's funky clothing shops, galleries, antique shops, and cozy bistros can fill a whole day of rambling. Here, fisherfolk rub shoulders with artists and surfers. During whale-watching season the gentle giants sometimes enter the harbor, and if you time your visit right, you can almost touch them. You can also walk up any of the steep stairways to Boyes Drive, and from there continue up the mountain on one of many hiking trails. If that's too strenuous, rather head down to the water and relax with a few beers at the Brass Bell, watching local surfers strutting their stuff on Kalk Bay reef. Other possibilities on your to-do list might include dropping your own line off the pier (fishing supplies are available from the small supermarket on the Main Road) or watching the harbor seals lolling around waiting for fishy discards when the boats come in. If you go to haggle for a fresh fish at the harbor, bear in mind that declining fish stocks mean this way of life may soon be a thing of the past.

GETTING HERE AND AROUND

Kalk Bay is a stop on the Southern Line of the Metrorail trail running from Cape Town, through the Southern suburbs. Taking the train is an easy and popular way to get here; granted it's during the day for safety reasons. However, Kalk Bay is also easily accessible by car from the M3, but traffic on weekends can be quite blocked up on Main Road that lines the coast of Kalk Bay.

TOURS

★ Aweh Kaapstad Walking Tour

WALKING TOURS | This is what Traci Kwaai, founder and guide, calls the anti-tour of Kalk Bay. She takes you on a history and story-telling tour of her life, and the lives of real people that still live here today. It's a history of colonialism, enslavement, and apartheid while following the triumphs and heartbreaks of the people that built, developed, and shaped Kalk Bay through history, many of whom came from parts of Asia, like Indonesia and the Philippines. The fascinating stories of this community take you through the last remaining neighborhood of the original inhabitants while meeting some of them along the way, showing you how life continues for many, as the area becomes rapidly gentrified. Traci's personality is infectious and she is incredibly knowledgeable while being warm and familiar. If you're lucky, you'll stop and get some of the best fresh koesisters from an aunty's house on the way. Tours take place on Sundays, but it's essential to book in advance by email, or DM on Instagram at @AwehKaapstad. ✉ *Kalk Bay* ☎ *079/496–2862* 🌐 *awehkaapstad.co.za* 🎫 *R300.*

🍴 Restaurants

Harbour House

$$$$ | **SEAFOOD** | Built on the breakwater of a working harbor, this iconic seafood restaurant has an unbeatable location—waves are known to crash against the huge plate-glass windows at high tide and many tables literally feel perched over the sea. Large, light filled, and orchid adorned, this jaw-droppingly beautiful space of white wood and lots of decking makes the perfect place to enjoy fresh seafood. **Known for:** freshness of the seafood; insane sea views from just about everywhere. [$] *Average main: R245* ✉ *Kalk Bay Harbour, Main Rd., Kalk Bay* ☎ *021/788–4136* 🌐 *www.harbourhouse.co.za.*

☕ Coffee and Quick Bites

Kalky's

$ | **FAST FOOD** | **FAMILY** | Right on the harbor, this cash-only establishment is the first choice for a generous portion of fish and chips. It's a great setting, and watching the waves break over the harbor wall when the sea is pounding (and you are inside) is thrilling, just be aware that the seagulls will fight for your leftovers, as will Robby, the resident seal. **Known for:** on the harbor; popular fried fish and chips; fast and no-frills establishment. [$] *Average main: R70* ✉ *Kalk Bay Harbour, Kalk Bay* ☎ *021/788–1726* 💳 *No credit cards.*

★ Olympia Café

$$ | **CAFÉ** | This tiny Kalk Bay institution with its mismatched tables and open kitchen is much beloved by locals as a super-casual destination for consistently excellent food and a great cup of coffee. The quality of the mostly Mediterranean fare is high, and the servers sassy (some might call it something else). **Known for:** no reservations often means waiting for a table; amazing treats from the café's bakery around the corner; fantastic fresh seafood and unpretentious Mediterranean fare. $ *Average main: R120* ⊠ *134 Main Rd., Kalk Bay* ☎ *021/788–6396* ⊕ *www. olympiacafe.co.za.*

🛏 Hotels

★ Chartfield Guesthouse

$ | **B&B/INN** | **FAMILY** | This surprisingly stylish and great-value guesthouse is within walking distance of all the bohemian pleasures in the charming fishing village of Kalk Bay. Located in a grand old house above the harbor, bright and airy rooms are decorated in a contemporary beach-chic style, and most have sea views. **Pros:** funky and charming decor; great value for the location; within walking distance of numerous restaurants and the train. **Cons:** Wi-Fi is not free; lots of stairs (some very steep); no parking. $ *Rooms from: R950* ⊠ *30 Gatesville Rd., Kalk Bay, Kalk Bay* ☎ *021/788–3793* ⊕ *www. chartfield.co.za* ⇆ *17 rooms* ⍾ *Free Breakfast.*

Inn at Castle Hill

$ | **B&B/INN** | This reasonably priced inn in an Edwardian villa is a pleasant stroll away from charming Kalk Bay's numerous restaurants, antiques shops, and seaside. **Pros:** friendly management; good value at a great location; free bicycles for guest use. **Cons:** two rooms do not have bathrooms; limited on-site parking; location on top of a steep hill. $ *Rooms from: R950* ⊠ *37 Gatesville Rd., Kalk Bay* ☎ *021/788–2554* ⊕ *www. innatcastlehill.co.za* ⇆ *5 rooms (2 with shared bath)* ⍾ *No Meals.*

Fish Hoek

2 km (1 mile) south of Kalk Bay; 43 km (27 miles) south of Cape Town.

With its relatively gentle and semi-protected waters, Fish Hoek Beach is a favorite for retired folks and families alike. Jager's Walk, from the south side of Fish Hoek Beach to Sunny Cove, is a pleasant, scenic, wheelchair-friendly pathway that meanders through the rocks, providing access to some sheltered natural rock pools that are also great for swimming. For coffee or snacks, check out the excellent **C'est La Vie** bakery and coffee shop, located just off the beach on Recreation Road. Otherwise the town itself doesn't have too much going on, though you will find useful facilities like gas stations, fast food, and ATMs. Outside of peak traffic, it takes about 40 minutes to get from Cape Town to Fish Hoek, but over Christmas and New Year's the roads get very congested, so leave early to miss the crowds.

GETTING HERE AND AROUND

Fish Hoek is the last stop on the Southern Line of the Metrorail train from Cape Town, making it a good option of transport to take to this small seaside town. Getting here by car is also a good option especially if you go early enough to avoid the traffic that clogs the M3 and Main Road during the weekends in summer.

🏊 Beaches

Fish Hoek Beach

BEACH | FAMILY | With the southern corner protected from southeasters by Elsie's Peak, this sandy beach attracts retirees and families with young kids, who appreciate the calm, clear water—it may be the safest swimming beach in the Cape, although sharks are sighted fairly regularly in the bay between September and March (though that doesn't stop people from swimming, surfing, and Boogie boarding here); shark spotters are employed to keep an eye out and warn beachgoers. The middle and northern end of the beach are also popular with catamaran sailors and windsurfers, who often stage regattas offshore. The snorkeling is good, and it's a great beach for Boogie boarding. It's also one of the best places to see whales during calving season—approximately August to November—though there have been whale sightings as early as June and as late as January. **Amenities:** food and drink; lifeguards; parking (fee); showers; toilets; water sports. **Best for:** surfing; swimming; walking; windsurfing. ✉ *Beach Rd., Fish Hoek* ✛ *Parking is at southern end of the beach.*

☕ Coffee and Quick Bites

C'est La Vie

$ | CAFÉ | Just off the beach, this excellent French-style bakery and café is an unexpected gem in the otherwise fairly depressing food scene that is Fish Hoek. Serving some of Cape Town's best artisanal loaves, fresh juices, great coffee, and, of course, fantastic sweet treats, this café also serves yummy breakfast and lunch options. **Known for:** popular for their baked goods; casual cafe with friendly service; dog-friendly outdoor seating. 💲 *Average main: R75* ✉ *4 Recreation Rd., Fish Hoek* ☎ *083/676–7430* 🌐 *www.facebook.com/cestlaviebaker* 🕑 *Closed Mon. and Tues. No dinner.*

Simon's Town

10 km (6 miles) south of Kalk Bay; 45 km (28 miles) south of Cape Town.

Picturesque Simon's Town has many lovely old buildings and some of the peninsula's best swimming beaches at Seaforth and Boulders, the latter being a gem that is also home to a large colony of African penguins. The town has a long association with the Royal Navy. British troops landed here in 1795 before defeating the Dutch at the Battle of Muizenberg, and the town served as a base for the Royal Navy from 1814 to 1957 when it was handed over to the South African Navy. Today you are bound to see plenty of men and women decked out in crisp white uniforms.

Jubilee Square, a dockside plaza that serves as the de facto town center, is just off the main road (St. George's Road). Next to the dock wall stands a statue of **Just Nuisance**, a Great Dane adopted as a mascot by the Royal Navy during World War II. Just Nuisance apparently liked his pint of beer and would accompany sailors on the train into Cape Town. He had the endearing habit of leading drunken sailors—and only sailors—that he found in the city back to the station in time to catch the last train. The navy went so far as to induct him into the service as an able seaman attached to the HMS *Afrikander*. He died at the age of seven in April 1944 and was given a military funeral. Just below Jubilee Square is the small but popular Simon's Town Waterfront. Fronted by shops and restaurants, this harbor is the point from which day cruises, deep-sea fishing trips, whale-watching excursions, and kayaking trips depart.

If you're looking to entertain children, the area has several options, including the SAS *Assegaai*, the South African Naval Museum's submarine, which is moored in the harbor with former submariners as guides, a toy museum, and the nearby Scratch Patch.

GETTING HERE AND AROUND

Getting to Simon's Town is possible on the Metrorail Southern Line from Cape Town, but it's advisable to go by car because it's hard to get around the town without one, and Ubers/taxis are not common. By car, it's about a 60-minute drive on the M3.

TOURS

Simon's Town Boat Company

BOAT TOURS | FAMILY | Simon's Town's exclusive whale and dolphin watching tour operator books trips to Seal Island or Cape Point with a friendly, knowledgeable, and professional crew; this company has you covered for False Bay water activities. Wheelchair boarding is available. ⊠ *2 Wharf St., Simon's Town* ☎ *083/257–7760* ⊕ *www.boatcompany. co.za* ✉ *R550.*

Sights

Scratch Patch

FACTORY | FAMILY | At Scratch Patch, a gemstone factory about 1 km (½ mile) north of Simon's Town, you can buy and fill a bag (you pay according to the size of the bag) with gemstones that you pick from a garden filled ankle-deep with semiprecious stones, such as tiger's eye, rose quartz, amethyst, jasper, agates, and crystals. Obviously this is a winner with children, and since 1970, when Scratch Patch opened, the owners claim it has been copied around the world. If you're lucky, you might find the rare Blue Lace Agate, which has a really interesting story linking it to mineral-rich Namibia and South Africa's little town of Springbok. Attached is Mineral World, a store that sells gemstone jewelry. Another branch of both is found at the V&A Waterfront in Cape Town. ⊠ *Dido Valley Rd., Simon's Town* ☎ *021/786–2020* ⊕ *www. scratchpatch.co.za* ✉ *Free; bags of gemstones R10–R95.*

Endangered African Penguins

Populations of the African penguin (*Spheniscus demersus*) have plummeted because of declining anchovy and sardine stocks, as well as predation by a growing seal population. Up to 50,000 of the birds—who call Boulders Beach and Stony Point near Betty's Bay in the Overberg home—were lost in just two years, and the current population hovers around 2,700. Penguins mate for life and have been known to return to the same nesting site for up to 15 years.

Simon's Town Museum

HISTORY MUSEUM | The historical exhibits at this rustic museum can feel like artifacts themselves; however, a section with numerous photographs and memorabilia from former Black residents who were removed to the townships of the Cape Flats in the 1960s makes it worthwhile. The museum is currently by appointment only; email to book. ⊠ *The Residency, Court Rd., Simon's Town* ☎ *021/786– 3046* ✉ *cathy@simonstownmuseum. co.za* ⊕ *www.simonstown.com/museum/stm.htm* ✉ *R10* ⊗ *Closed Sun.*

South African Naval Museum

MILITARY SIGHT | FAMILY | The naval museum is filled with model ships, old navigational equipment, old South African navy divers' equipment, a few real, life-size boats, and, oddly enough, a helicopter. You can also climb to the top of the building's clock tower. The newer "Transformation" section includes a display about the SS *Mendi* and information about how the navy has changed in democratic South Africa. It's staffed by

The Cape of Good Hope covers more than 19,000 acres.

naval personnel and volunteers. ✉ *Naval Dockyard, St. George's St., Simon's Town* ☎ *021/787–4686* ⊕ *sanavymuseum.co.za* 📧 *Free (donations accepted).*

Warrior Toy Museum

OTHER MUSEUM | FAMILY | Dinky Toys, boats, trains, soldiers, airplanes, some 4,000 model cars, and 500 dolls—what's not to like about this toy museum that is equally enjoyable for both kids and adults? It's packed with hundreds of models of all things locomotive: from cars to trains and tanks, these miniature vehicles date from the 1920s to the present. Some are on sale at the attached collectibles shop. ✉ *1067 King George Way, Simon's Town* ☎ *021/786–1395* 📧 *R10.*

🏖 Beaches

★ Boulders Beach

BEACH | FAMILY | This series of small coves lies among giant granite boulders on the southern outskirts of Simon's Town. Part of Table Mountain National Park, the beach is best known for its resident colony of African penguins. You must stay out of the fenced-off breeding beach, but don't be surprised if a wandering bird comes waddling up to your beach blanket to take a look. Penguin-viewing platforms, accessible from either the Boulders Beach or Seaforth side, provide close-up looks at these comical birds. When you've had enough penguin peering, you can stroll back to Boulders Beach for some excellent swimming in the quiet sheltered coves. This beach is great for children because it is so protected, and the sea is warm(ish) and calm. It can get crowded in summer, though, so go early. Without traffic, it takes about 45 minutes to get here from town, less from the Southern Suburbs. **Amenities:** none. **Best for:** walking, swimming. ✉ *Kleintuin Rd., Sea Forth, Simon's Town* ✣ *Follow signs from Bellvue Rd.* ☎ *021/786–2329* 🌐 *www.sanparks.org* 🎫 *R170 adults, R85 children 2–11.*

Coffee and Quick Bites

★ The Lighthouse Cafe

$$ | **CAFÉ** | Arguably Simon's Town's best restaurant, regulars come here for good food and a charming host with a great story: A big-city Jo'burg boy met his girl and came to live by the sea. A friendly place to stop for breakfast (until 11), lunch, or dinner. **Known for:** generous portions; welcoming service; fresh and tasty meals, thoughtfully prepared. [$] *Average main: R100* ✉ *90 St. George's St., Simon's Town* ☎ *021/786–9000* 🌐 *www.thelighthousecafe.co.za* 🕒 *No dinner Sun.–Tues.*

The Sweetest Thing

$ | **BAKERY** | The Sweetest Thing serves Simon's Town's best house-made cakes, pastries, and cookies, as well as breakfast until noon, and light lunch options like savory pies and quiches. It's a must-visit if you're hungry and in town during lunchtime, or looking for a good cup of coffee and treat. **Known for:** house-made cakes and pastries; breakfasts and light lunches; homey atmoshpere. [$] *Average main: R80* ✉ *82 St. George's St., Simon's Town* ☎ *021/786–4200.*

Hotels

aha Simon's Town Quayside Hotel

$$ | **HOTEL** | On Jubilee Square, part of the Simon's Town Waterfront, this hotel is right in the action and has wonderful views over Simon's Town Bay, the harbor, and the yacht club. **Pros:** great views of fishing boats and naval fleet from sea-facing bedrooms; great location at Jubilee Square, the town's epicenter; good breakfast. **Cons:** mountain view rooms look over Main Road, which can be noisy; no nightlife in Simon's Town. [$] *Rooms from: R2100* ✉ *Jubilee Sq., St. George's St., Simon's Town* ☎ *021/786–3838* 🌐 *www.aha.co.za/quayside* 🛏 *26 rooms* 🍴 *Free Breakfast.*

★ Residence William French

$$ | **B&B/INN** | The French-born owner of this gem of a guesthouse just past Boulders Beach takes his vocation seriously, providing a level of engagement and service that truly make you feel like a guest in this gorgeous retreat where edgy, rustic, and super-elegant design features combine to great effect, all bolstered by fantastic views of False Bay. With only five rooms—each styled differently, but all mixing polished concrete surfaces in neutral tones with a few carefully selected ornate pieces of furniture—it's all intimate, quiet relaxation. **Pros:** gorgeous views of False Bay from quiet location just past Boulders Beach; lovely, personalized service from owner; wonderful breakfasts and dinners (the latter by request). **Cons:** location is residential and you'll want a car to get around; lacks facilities of a larger hotel (gym, concierge service, etc.); no children under 14. [$] *Rooms from: R2400* ✉ *44 Dorries Dr., Simon's Town* ☎ *072/403–2463* 🌐 *www.williamfrench.co.za* 🛏 *5 rooms* 🍴 *Free Breakfast.*

Simon's Town Guest House

$$ | **B&B/INN** | This clean and contemporary African-themed guesthouse in a residential area about 3 km (2 miles) outside of Simon's Town offers spacious rooms with magnificent views over False Bay. All five spacious rooms have their own sitting areas with unobstructed views of the ocean and the surrounding mountain. **Pros:** friendly staff; delicious full English and Continental breakfast; amazing views. **Cons:** very steep hill; breakfast ends at 9:30; not actually in Simon's Town. [$] *Rooms from: R1700* ✉ *20 Bennett Close, Simon's Town*

☎ 021/786–5552 ⊕ www.simons-townguesthouse.co.za ⇋ 5 rooms ⫶O⫶ Free Breakfast.

Activities

KAYAKING

Kayak Cape Town

KAYAKING | Join this friendly operator based in Simon's Town for a paddle to see the penguins on Boulders Beach—there is nothing else quite like it. They also run full-moon-rising evening trips. ✉ Simon's Town Jetty, Simon's Town ☎ 065/707–4444 ⊕ www.kayakcape-town.co.za ⫷ R350.

SCUBA DIVING

Apex Shark Expeditions

DIVING & SNORKELING | Run by marine biologists, Apex Shark Expeditions operates small-group trips from Simon's Town during season (February–September). If the great whites aren't around, try the Ocean Predator Trip, in which you cage dive with makos and blues. Co-founder Chris Fallows is a local legend in the shark photography and observation world, and the go-to guy for many international broadcasters. ✉ Wharf St., Simon's Town ☎ 079/051–8558 ⊕ www.apexpredators.com ⫷ R2995.

Scuba Shack Diving

DIVING & SNORKELING | The friendly Scuba Shack is based out of Kommetjie and can organize dives around the peninsula—both the Atlantic and the warmer False Bay, with Simon's Town as the meeting point. Options include diving with cow sharks, traveling through kelp forests, and snorkeling with seals. It's a refreshing experience—and not just the water temperature—but so very different from the more typical vacation diving world of subtropical corals. ✉ Mountain Rd., Kommetjie ☎ 072/603–8630 ⊕ scubashack.co.za ⫷ From R1300.

Cape of Good Hope

60 km (37 miles) southwest of Cape Town.

Once a nature reserve on its own, this section of Table Mountain National Park covers more than 19,000 acres. Much of the park consists of rolling hills covered with fynbos and laced with miles of walking trails, for which maps are available at the park entrance. It also has beautiful deserted beaches (you can swim at some of these beaches, but note that there are no amenities or lifeguards). Eland, baboon, ostrich, and bontebok (a colorful antelope nearly hunted to extinction in the early 20th century) are among the animals that roam the park, but you may also see zebras and other wildlife. A paved road runs 12½ km (8 miles) to the tip of the peninsula, and a turnoff leads to the Cape of Good Hope, a rocky cape that is the southwesternmost point of the continent. A plaque marks the spot—otherwise you would never know the site's significance.

The park has some excellent land-based whale-watching spots. From about June to November, whales return to these waters to calve. You're most likely to see the Southern Right whale in False Bay, but the occasional humpback and Bryde's whale also show up. When the water is calm, you may even be lucky enough to see a school of dolphins looping past. The Rooikrans parking lot is good for whale-watching, but there are a number of lookout points. It's just a matter of driving around until you see the characteristic spray or a shiny black fluke.

GETTING HERE AND AROUND

Getting here is only possible by car or on a booked tour. This scenic drive should take just over an hour and the drive itself is part of the attraction, with incredible views. There are plenty of tour operators

Cape Point Nature Reserve has numerous trails to explore including the Shipwreck Trail; hikers can see upwards of 26 recorded wrecks on a good day.

that can take you from Cape Town to the various points in this national park, including Cape Point and the Cape of Good Hope.

 Sights

★ Cape Point

NATURE PRESERVE | FAMILY | Cape Point is a dramatic knife's edge of rock that slices into the Atlantic. Looking out to sea from the viewing platform, you feel you're at the tip of Africa, even though that honor officially belongs to another dramatic point at Cape Agulhas, about 160 km (100 miles) to the southeast. From Cape Point the views of False Bay and the Hottentots Holland Mountains are astonishing. The walk up to the viewing platform and the old lighthouse is very steep; a funicular makes the run every three or four minutes. Take a jacket or sweater—the wind can be fierce. It took six years, from 1913 to 1919, to build the old lighthouse, 816 feet above the high-water mark. On a clear day the old lighthouse was a great navigational mark, but when the mists rolled in it was useless, so a new and much lower lighthouse (286 feet) was built at Dias Lookout Point. The newer, revolving lighthouse, the most powerful on the South African coast, emits a group of three flashes every 30 seconds. It has prevented a number of ships from ending up on Bellows or Albatross Rock below. You can't go into the lighthouses, but the views from their bases are spectacular.

Stark reminders of the ships that didn't make it are dotted around the Cape. You'll see their rusty remains on some of the beaches. One of the more famous wrecks is the *Thomas T. Tucker*, one of hundreds of Liberty Ships produced by the United States to enable the Allies to move vast amounts of supplies during World War II. It wasn't the German U-boats patrolling the coastline that did the ship in. Rather the fog closed in, and on her maiden voyage in 1942, it ended up on Olifantsbos Point. Fortunately, all on board were saved, but the wreck soon broke up in the rough seas that pound the coast.

The mast you see on the western slopes of Cape Point near the lighthouse belongs to the Global Atmosphere Watch Station (GAW). The South African Weather Bureau, together with the Fraunhofer Institute in Garmisch, Germany, maintains a research laboratory here to monitor long-term changes in the chemistry of the earth's atmosphere, which may impact climate. This is one of 20 GAWs throughout the world, chosen because the air at Cape Point is considered particularly pure most of the time.

During peak season (December–January), visit Cape Point as early in the day as possible to avoid being swamped by an armada of tour buses. There are a few shops and snack kiosks.

The best way to experience the park is to hike on one of the numerous walking trails (favorites include the boardwalk trail to Diaz Beach and the shipwreck trail) and/or enjoy a picnic and dip at the Bordjiesrif or Buffels Bay tidal pools, or on Platboom or Oliphantsbos beaches. A fantastic alternative is to stay overnight in the comfortable basic accommodations, booked through South African National Parks. ⚠ **Do not feed the indigenous resident chacma baboons, which are increasingly under threat.**

Despite the peninsula's population being estimated at only 450 individuals, baboons continue to be shot for raiding homes and stealing food; baboon-feeding tourists are largely responsible for this serious situation, and you should always be wary of them; they can be dangerous if provoked or if they think you have food. ✉ *Off M65 (Plateau Rd.)* ✛ *60 km (37 miles) southwest of Cape Town* ☎ *021/780–9010* ⊕ *capepoint.co.za* ✉ *R360 park entrance.*

The Flying Dutchman Funicular

TRANSPORTATION | If you're short on time, the funicular, named after the legendary Flying Dutchman ghost ship, leaves from the lower station at the Cape Point car park, taking passengers to the upper lighthouse every 3 minutes. It's also known as the Cape Point Funicular. ✉ *Off M65 (Plateau Rd.), Cape of Good Hope* ✛ *60 km (37 miles) southwest of Cape Town* ☎ *021/780–9010* ⊕ *capepoint.co.za* ✉ *R70 one-way, R85 roundtrip.*

Chapter 5

THE WESTERN CAPE AND WINELANDS

Updated by
Lucy Corne

 ⊙ Sights
★★★★★

 🍽 Restaurants
★★★★★

 🛏 Hotels
★★★★★

 🛍 Shopping
★★★★☆

 🍸 Nightlife
★★★☆☆

WELCOME TO THE WESTERN CAPE AND WINELANDS

TOP REASONS TO GO

★ **Land of Divine Wine:** Against this stunning backdrop of mountains rising above vine-covered valleys and 300-year-old homesteads, you can visit scores of wineries and tour their cellars.

★ **Whale of a Time:** From mid-winter to early summer, the icy seas teem with southern right whales, which come here to calve creating some of the world's best land-based whale-watching; you can also take a boat tour.

★ **Flower Power:** Each spring millions of flowers, including yellow, white, and orange daisies, carpet the West Coast hills.

★ **Fabulous Food:** A new generation of chefs is making the most of the area's fabulous fresh produce, and restaurants in Franschhoek and Stellenbosch regularly get voted among the world's best.

★ **The Great Outdoors:** The Western Cape's real charm lies outdoors, from spectacular golf courses to hikes that unveil ancient rock formations.

1 **Somerset West.**

2 **Stellenbosch.**

3 **Franschhoek.**

4 **Paarl.**

5 **Tulbagh.**

6 **Worcester.**

7 **Robertson.**

8 **McGregor.**

9 **Montagu.**

10 **Gordon's Bay.**

11 **Betty's Bay.**

12 **Kleinmond.**

13 **Bot River:**

14 **Hermanus.**

15 **Bredasdorp.**

16 **Arniston.**

17 **Swellendam.**

18 **Greyton.**

19 **Darling.**

20 **Langebaan.**

21 **Paternoster.**

22 **Elands Bay.**

23 **Clanwilliam.**

24 **Citrusdal.**

25 **Riebeek West and Riebeek Kasteel.**

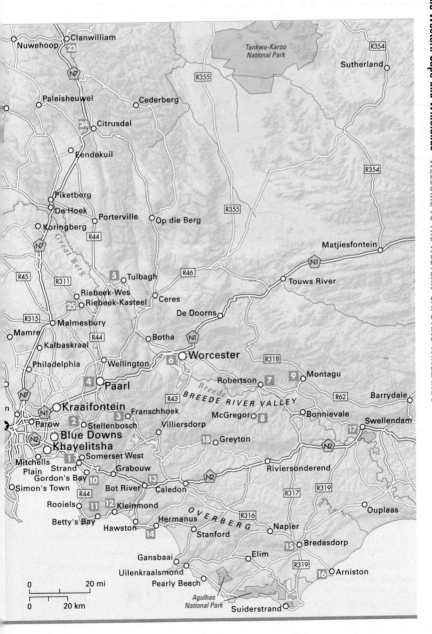

CAPE WINELANDS 101

Founded in 1685, Boschendal Wine Estate is one of the gems of the Cape Winelands. Who could resist sipping wine in this setting?

The South African wine industry is booming. Today there's enormous interest in South African reds and whites. Although South Africa has a reputation for delivering good quality at the bottom end of the market, more and more ultra-premium wines are emerging. Good-quality wines at varied prices are readily available—even in supermarkets.

THE WINES

When it comes to South African terroir, think sun, sea, and soil. Whereas Northern Hemisphere farmers work hard to get as much sunlight onto their grapes as possible, local viticulturists have to deal with soaring summer temperatures (this is why the cooling influence of the two oceans is so welcome). South Africa also has some of the world's oldest soil, and there's a mineral element to its wines. Notable varietals include Chenin Blanc, Sauvignon Blanc, and Bordeaux-style red blends of Cabernet Sauvignon, Merlot, and Cabernet Franc.

Though it legally can't be called Champagne, Cap Classique, South Africa's version of the bubbly, is made in exactly the same way. You'd be unwise to pass on an offer of Graham Beck Cuvée Clive or Villiera Brut Tradition.

■ Great Sauvignon Blancs: Tokara Reserve, Cederberg Private Cellar Ghost Corner, and Cape Point Vineyards Reserve Sauvignon Blanc.

■ Great red blends: Meerlust Rubicon, Vergelegen GVB Red, and Kanonkop Paul Sauer.

■ Great Chenin Blancs: Beaumont Hope Marguerite, Mullineux Granite, and Mulderbosch Single Vineyard Block W.

A SOUTH AFRICAN WINE

In the 1920s, a professor at Stellenbosch University decided to create a truly South African varietal. He crossed Pinot Noir (a tricky grape to grow) with Cinsaut (a vigorous and very hardy grape)—he liked the idea of combining a drama queen with a pragmatic, no-nonsense type—and came up with Pinotage. Though it's had its ups and downs, including being accused by everyone from critics to connoisseurs of being bitter and rubbery, strides are being made to express the grape's character. One example is the coffee Pinotage. It's been on the market since 2001 and became hugely popular because it's a ballsy, bold wine. There's a distinct mocha flavor to it that's a combination of the soil and the wine-making technique. A good example of this is the Diemersfontein. Other Pinotages to keep an eye out for: Stellenzicht Golden Triangle Pinotage, Spier Private Collection Pinotage, and Kanonkop Pinotage. Former Kanonkop cellar master Beyers Truter is known as the Pinotage King in South Africa; be sure to try Beyerskloof Pinotage.

Wine tastings are a must in the Winelands.

The wine cellar at Vergelegen Wine Estate.

WINE ROUTES AND REGIONS

Although the Cape Winelands region is largely thought of as the wine centers of Stellenbosch, Franschhoek, and Paarl, today these areas make up only about 33% of all the land in the Cape under vine. This wine-growing region is now so vast, you can trek to the fringes of the Karoo Desert, in the northeast, and still find a grape. There are around 20 wine routes in the Western Cape, ranging from the Olifants River, in the north, to the coastal mountains of the Overberg and beyond. There's also a well-established Winelands brandy route, and an annual port festival is held in Calitzdorp, in the Little Karoo.

Driving yourself is undoubtedly the best way to appreciate the area. Better still, join a tour of your chosen route. Stellenbosch has a plethora of organized tours, plus the Vine Hopper, which transports you between wine farms but gives you the freedom to stay as long as you like before hopping on another shuttle. In Franschhoek, the Wine Tram is a must. It gives you the luxury of sipping to your heart's content without the rigid structure of a tour.

Each wine route is clearly marked with attractive road signs, and there are complimentary maps available at the tourism bureaus and at most

Vergelegen Wine Estate's traditional thatched Cape Dutch buildings look like something from a fairy tale.

wine farms. Roads are generally good, and even the dirt roads leading up to a couple of the farms are nothing to worry about.

TIME FOR TRANSFORMATION

Many wineries are working at Black empowerment. Thokozani, based at Diemersfontein in Wellington, is part-owned by the farm staff. It's one of the earliest and most successful Black empowerment projects in the wine industry. Another farm that has been dedicated to empowerment and transformation is Bosman Family Vineyard, also in Wellington.

There is also a growing number of Black-owned wine estates and labels including Aslina (Stellenbosch), Seven Sisters (Stellenbosch), Klein Goed-erust (Franschhoek), and Tesserlaasdal (Hemel-en-Aarde).

VISITING WINERIES

The secret to touring the Cape Winelands is not to hurry. Dally over lunch on a vine-shaded verandah at a 300-year-old estate, enjoy an afternoon nap under a spreading oak, or sip wine while savoring the impossible views.

Of the scores of wineries and estates in the Cape Winelands, the ones listed here are chosen for their great wine, their beauty, or their historic signifi-cance. It would be a mistake to try to cover them all in less than a week. You have nothing to gain from hightailing it around the Cape Winelands other than a headache. If your interest is more aesthetic and cultural than wine driven, you would do well to focus on the historic estates of Stellenbosch and Franschhoek. Most Paarl wineries stand out more for the quality of their wine than for their architectural beauty.

Generally speaking, you don't need to book ahead for a tasting, although some smaller wineries only offer tastings by appointment. It's not always essential, but it's a good idea to call or email in advance if you'd like to take a cellar tour or try out one of the many food and wine pairing experiences.

TASTING ROOM FEES

Most wineries charge a small fee for a tasting—usually in the range of R30 to R70—though this is often waived if you end up buying wine. An increasing number of wineries also offer innovative pairing experiences, and you can sample wines alongside anything from cheese and biltong to mini burgers, nougat, or doughnuts. Tipping is not expected at tasting rooms, but a 10% to 15% gratuity is always welcome.

NAME-DROPPING
There are some iconic South African wines you really should try before you leave the country. Of course, the list of such wines varies depending on whom you talk to, but keep an eye out for these:

- Boekenhoutskloof Cabernet Sauvignon
- Boplaas Vintage Reserve Port
- Cape Point Isliedh
- De Toren Fusion V
- Eben Sadie Palladius or Columella
- Hamilton Russell Chardonnay and Pinot Noir
- Jordan Chardonnay
- Kanonkop Pinotage or Paul Sauer
- Klein Constantia Vin de Constance
- Meerlust Rubicon
- Mullineux Granite Syrah
- Springfield Méthode Ancienne Cabernet Sauvignon
- Steenberg Sauvignon Blanc Reserve
- Vergelegen V

TO SHIP OR NOT TO SHIP
You're bound to want to take some great South African wine home with you, but it's not as easy as cramming your hand luggage with your favorite tipple. Travelers to the United States can take only two bottles on board. Any more than that and it will need to be shipped to you by an agent. Each person is allowed two cases (or 24 bottles), but some states won't allow you to import a single bottle without an importer's license, which can end up setting you back thousands of rands. A far easier alternative is to ask the estate if they distribute in the United States—many of them do. The Vineyard Connection (⊕ *www.vineyardconnection.co.za*) is just one of the agents who can help you get your favorite bottle delivered to your destination.

READING MATERIAL
If you're serious about wine, arm yourself with the *Platter's Wine Guide*, an annual publication rating hundreds of wines throughout the Western Cape (and beyond). Also check out ⊕ *www.winemag.co.za* (the digital version of the former *Wine* magazine) for news and reviews. For an in-depth read and fantastic photos, pick up *Wines and Vineyards of South Africa* by Wendy Torein. It's rather out of date now, but is still a great insight into the history of South African wine. *Wines of the New South Africa: Tradition and Revolution* by Tim James is also recommended reading.

Most wineries charge a small fee for tastings.

Anchored by Cape Town in the southwest, the Western Cape is an alluring province, a sweep of endless mountain ranges, empty beaches, and European history dating back more than three centuries. The cultures of the indigenous Khoekhoen and San people—the first inhabitants of this enormous area—also contribute to the region's richness. You can reach most of the province's highlights in less than two hours from Cape Town, making the city an ideal base from which to explore.

The historic Winelands, in the city's backyard, produce fine wine amid the exquisite beauty of rocky mountains, serried vines, and elegant Cape Dutch estates handed down from one generation to another for centuries.

Wildflowers are an extraordinary element of this natural setting. The Western Cape is famous for its fynbos (pronounced *fane*-boss), the hardy, thin-leaf vegetation that gives much of the province its distinctive look. Fynbos composes a major part of the Cape floral kingdom, the smallest and richest of the world's six floral kingdoms. More than 8,500 plant species are found in the province, of which 5,000 grow nowhere else on Earth. The region is dotted with nature reserves where you can hike through this profusion of flora, admiring the majesty of the king protea or the shimmering leaves of the silver tree. When the wind blows and mist trails across the mountainsides, the fynbos-covered landscape takes on the look of a Scottish heath.

Not surprisingly, people have taken full advantage of the Cape's natural bonanza. In the Overberg and along the West Coast, rolling wheat fields extend to the horizon, while farther inland jagged mountain ranges hide fertile valleys of apple orchards, orange groves, and vineyards. At sea, hardy fisherfolk battle icy swells to harvest succulent crayfish (similar to lobster), delicate *perlemoen* (abalone), and line fish, such as the delicious *kabeljou*. Each June though November hundreds of whales return to the Cape shores to calve, and the stretch of coastline that includes Hermanus, now referred to as the Whale Coast, becomes one of the best places for land-based whale-watching in the world.

For untold centuries this fertile region supported the Khoekhoen and San indigenous peoples who lived off the land as pastoralists and hunter-gatherers. With the arrival of European settlers, however, they were chased off, killed, or enslaved. In the remote recesses of the Cederberg Mountains and along the West Coast you can still see the fading rock paintings left by the San, whose few remaining clans have long since retreated into the Kalahari Desert. The population of the Western Cape today is of mixed race and descendants of imported slaves, the San, the Khoekhoen, and European settlers.

MAJOR REGIONS

The Cape Winelands, 45 minutes east of Cape Town, is the Napa Valley of southern Africa. The region boasts some of South Africa's best restaurants and hotels, not to mention incredible wine. The area fans out around three historic towns and their valleys. Founded in 1685, **Stellenbosch's** oak-lined streets, historic architecture, stellar restaurants, interesting galleries, and vibrant university community make it an ideal base for wine travel. **Franschhoek**, enclosed by towering mountains, is the original home of the Cape's French Huguenots, whose descendants have made a conscious effort to reassert their French heritage. **Paarl** lies beneath huge granite domes, its main street running 11 km (7 miles) along the Berg River past some of the country's most elegant historical monuments. **Somerset West,** just 30 minutes southeast of Cape Town, has a few historic estates that are worth visiting, too.

Running in a broad band from northeast to southeast is the beautiful **Breede River Valley**, home to farms, vineyards, and orchards. (So it should come as no surprise that one of the towns in the area is called Ceres, after the Roman goddess of agriculture.) Small-town hospitality, striking mountains, and wide-open spaces are hallmarks of this area. In summer the heat can be overwhelming,

and in winter the mountain peaks are often covered with snow. Here you'll find picturesque **Tulbagh** as well as the farming town of **Robertson**. There are also sleepy little towns like **McGregor** and the area's largest town, **Worcester,** as well as **Montagu** with its hot springs and Cape Victorian architecture.

East of the Cape Winelands and bordering the Atlantic Ocean, the **Overberg** is separated from the city by the Hottentots Holland Mountains. The region is also home to the rocky headland of Cape Agulhas, where the Indian and Atlantic oceans officially meet at the southernmost tip of the continent. The Overberg harbors unspoiled beaches, coastal mountains, and the small towns and villages of **Gordon's Bay, Betty's Bay, Kleinmond, and Hermanus**. Inland, Overberg villages of **Bot River, Bredasdorp, Greyton,** and **Swellendam** embody a bygone age.

North of Cape Town on the **West Coast,** small fishing villages like **Paternoster and Eland's Bay,** and larger towns popular with Cape Town weekenders like **Langebaan, Riebeek West, and Riebeek Kastrel,** sit along the windswept Atlantic coastline. Each spring, the entire region explodes in a spectacular wildflower display that slowly spreads inland to the Cederberg mountains in places like **Darling, Citrusdal, and Clanwilliam**. For nature lovers, the West Coast provides some unique opportunities, including birding at the West Coast National Park and hiking or rock climbing in the remote wilderness areas of the Cederberg.

Planning

Many people come to the Western Cape after getting a big-game fix in Kruger. Although it's possible to explore Cape Town and the Cape Winelands in three or four days—the area is compact enough to allow it—you need six or seven to do it justice. You can get a good sense of either the Overberg or the West Coast on a three- or four-day jaunt, but set aside a week if you plan to tackle more than one or two of the regions in this chapter. For a shorter trip, focus on the splendors of the Overberg's coastal route from Gordon's Bay to Hermanus, and then head north toward Greyton and Swellendam.

Getting Here and Around

BUS

Intercape Mainliner and Translux provide daily bus service throughout most of the Western Cape, stopping at bigger towns such as Worcester and Robertson on their way upcountry. Although each company's timetable varies, most have approximately four trips a day from Cape Town. From Cape Town it takes about 1½ hours to Worcester and about 2 hours to Robertson. A one-way trip to Robertson costs around R650.

Swellendam is a major hub and a good transit point, but to enjoy smaller towns such as Greyton or those along the coast, you'll need your own transportation.

Intercape Mainliner heads from Cape Town daily up the N7, which is the main route up to the Cederberg. The bus stops at Citrusdal and Clanwilliam, but not coastal towns such as Langebaan and Elands Bay. Expect to pay around R550 to Citrusdal and R840 to Clanwilliam. The journey to Clanwilliam from Cape Town takes about four hours.

CAR

The best way to explore the Western Cape is to rent a car and take to the roads, which are generally very good. Although you might have to navigate some dirt roads, they tend to be graded regularly and are in fine condition. Navigating your way around is not difficult. There are three main routes out of the city: the N1, N2, and N7. The N1 and N2 take you to the Cape Winelands of

Stellenbosch, Franschhoek, and Paarl, and the N7 heads up the West Coast. To reach the Overberg, take the N2 out of town and head up over Sir Lowry's Pass. ■TIP→ **Getting lost after taking a wrong turn can take you into unsafe areas, so plan your route before setting out.**

Driving is also the way to go when exploring the Breede River valley, as it will give you the flexibility you need to discover interesting back roads or to linger at a lovely lunch spot. The best way to get to this area is to take the N1 from Cape Town past Paarl. You can either go through the Huguenot toll tunnel (around R45 per vehicle) or over the spectacular Bain's Kloof mountain pass to Worcester. From there take the R60 to Robertson and Montagu.

The Overberg stretches over an enormous area, so you need to decide where you're heading before hitting the road. For the most part, you'll come across gravel roads only around Elim and Napier and from Swellendam to Malgas, and they may be a bit rutted and bumpy. A two-wheel-drive vehicle is fine, but take it easy if it's been raining, as gravel roads can get slippery. You'll need a 4x4 only if you're planning to tackle some of the more remote back roads or want to do a 4x4 route. If you want to enjoy the beauty of the coast, then take the N2 from Cape Town, but, instead of heading up Sir Lowry's Pass, turn off to Gordon's Bay and follow the R44, also known as Clarence Drive, along the scenic route. Just after Kleinmond the road becomes the R41 and turns inland to bypass the Bot River lagoon. It becomes the R43 as it makes its way toward Hermanus. If you want to explore inland, however, take the N2 over Sir Lowry's Pass and past Caledon and Swellendam. To get to the pretty hamlet of Greyton, take the R406 to your left just before Caledon.

To get up the West Coast and to the Cederberg, take the N1 out of Cape Town. Just before Century City shopping center, take Exit 10, which is marked "Goodwood, Malmesbury, Century City Drive, and Sable Road" and leads to the N7, the region's major access road. Though the highway is well marked, get yourself a good map from a bookstore or tourism office and explore some of the smaller roads, which offer surprising vistas or a glimpse into the rural heart of the Western Cape. The Versveld Pass, between Piketberg and the hamlet of Piket-Bo-Berg, at the top of the mountains, has views that stretch for miles.

Health and Safety

If you plan to go hiking in the mountains, come prepared with the right clothing and the correct attitude—each year tourists get lost in the mountains. Cape weather is notoriously changeable, so you need something warm and preferably waterproof. Take at least two liters of water per person and something to eat. If possible, hike with somebody who knows the area well. If you're walking without a guide, be sure to take a cell phone. Let somebody know of your route and when you expect to return, and don't stray from the paths if the mist closes in.

Hotels

The Cape Winelands are compact enough that you can make one hotel your base. Stellenbosch and Paarl, situated close to dozens of wineries and restaurants, offer the most flexibility. Here bed-and-breakfasts and lodges are often less expensive than hotels and provide a better taste of life in the country. Franschhoek is comparatively isolated, which many visitors consider a blessing.

The West Coast, the Cederberg, and the Overberg are much more spread out, so you'll want to stay in one place for a day or two and then move on. During the peak season of December and January, book well in advance and be prepared for mandatory two-night minimum stays on weekends. Although the winter months of June to September are usually a lot quieter, seaside towns get really busy when the whales arrive to calve. The same is true up the West Coast during flower season.

Hotel reviews have been shortened. For full information, visit Fodors.com.

Restaurants

The dining scene in the Western Cape and Winelands ranges from country-style cooking to refined South African cuisine. The most exciting food scene is in the Winelands. Franschhoek restaurants attract some of the country's most innovative chefs, and they aren't afraid to experiment with unusual ingredients or cooking techniques.

The types of food you encounter will change as you travel around the area. Coastal towns in the Western Cape usually concentrate on seafood, often served in open-air restaurants perched on the cliffs or spilling out onto the beach. Farther inland, the cuisine tends to be more down-to-earth and the portions less dainty. While you're in the area, be sure to try some Cape Malay cuisine, characterized by mild, slightly sweet curries and aromatic spices.

Casual wear is acceptable at most restaurants. On the coast, people pull shorts and T-shirts over their swimsuits before tucking into a plate of fish-and-chips. Some upscale restaurants in the Winelands expect their patrons to dress up a bit. Even so, jackets and ties are almost never expected.

If there's someplace you really want to try, reserve ahead. In December and January, popular restaurants book up quickly, and reservations are advised at least a day or two in advance.

For more information on South Africa food, see the What to Eat and Drink feature in the Experience chapter. Restaurant reviews have been shortened. For full information, visit Fodors.com.

RESTAURANT AND HOTEL PRICES
Restaurant prices are the average cost of a main course at dinner or, if dinner is not served, at lunch. Hotel prices are the lowest cost of a standard double room in high season.

What it Costs In South African rand			
$	$$	$$$	$$$$
RESTAURANTS			
under R100	R100– R150	R151– R200	over R200
HOTELS			
under R1,500	R1,500– R2,500	R2,501– R3,500	over R3,500

Tours

Cape Winelands tours are often operated by companies based in Cape Town. Most offer a range of half- or full-day tours. Many include cheese tastings or cellar tours in addition to wine tastings. Expect to pay around R900 for a half day and R1,200 for a full day.

There are some great individual guides operating in Breede River towns. Because the guides are from the area, they provide rare insights about the history and the culture. If you wish to hike in the Montagu Mountain Reserve, where the trails are not well marked, it's a good idea to head out with someone familiar with the area. Your best bet is to ask at local tourism offices.

A number of small companies offer customized tours to the Overberg. There's a wide range of tours available. Some head to regional parks (De Hoop Nature Reserve is popular), others take

you through the spectacular scenery (like heading over Tradouw Pass and through the spectacular Cape Fold Mountains). A few concentrate on the historic towns of Arniston, Bredasdorp, and Elim.

To see the exceptional rock art in the Cederberg, you'll get much more out of the experience with a guide. Ask at Clanwilliam tourism for a list of local operators.

African Eagle Day Tours
GUIDED TOURS | Great half- and full-day Winelands tours are offered by African Eagle. On the full-day tour (about R1,180), you'll be whisked through Stellenbosch, Paarl, and Franschhoek to walk around the towns, tour cellars, and taste wines. The half-day tour—you can choose morning or afternoon—is all about Stellenbosch. This tour costs R880. ⊠ 4 Malta Rd., Salt River ☎ 021/464–4266 ⊕ www.daytours.co.za ⊠ From R880.

Cape Fusion Tours
SPECIAL-INTEREST TOURS | Foodie Pam McOnie from Cape Fusion Tours has an eye for what's unique. She and her team focus on small- to medium-sized vineyards producing one-of-a-kind wines. She has the inside scoop on what's new in the Winelands' food-and-wine world. ⊠ Cape Town ☎ 021/461–2437, 083/235–9777 ⊕ www.capefusiontours.com.

Cederberg Heritage Route
SPECIAL-INTEREST TOURS | For something completely out of the ordinary, travel by traditional donkey cart from the top of the Pakhuis Pass down to the tiny hamlet of Heuningvlei in the heart of the Cederberg Wilderness Area. The route is winding and takes you through some spectacular scenery and flora. The company also offers community-based trips along five hiking trails. ⊠ Pakhuis Pass, Clanwilliam ✛ 17 km (10½ miles) outside Clanwilliam ☎ 083/468–8030 ⊕ www.cedheroute.co.za.

Elandsberg Eco Tourism

SPECIAL-INTEREST TOURS | Rooibos tea is a big part of this region's economy, and Elandsberg Eco Tourism takes you to a plantation and a processing plant to see how it is made. The 1½-hours tour costs R210 per person. The outfitter also has tours of the West Coast and Cederberg regions. ✉ Off R364, Graafwater ✛ 22 km (14 miles) outside Clanwilliam ☎ 027/482–2022 ⊕ www.elandsberg. co.za 🖾 From R210.

Gourmet Wine Tours

SPECIAL-INTEREST TOURS | This is an excellent choice for those wanting a tour of the greater Winelands area, including Franschhoek, Paarl, Stellenbosch, Somerset West, and Hermanus. Guide Stephen Flesch is great at selecting the most interesting vineyards and the best restaurants where you can sample their products. Expect to pay around R3400 for the first person and R1700 per additional person for a personalized tour. ✉ 22 Alnwick Rd., Diep River, Cape Town ☎ 021/710–5454, 083/299–3581 ⊕ www. gourmetwinetours.co.za 🖾 From R2,260.

Hylton Ross Tours

GUIDED TOURS | A full-day Winelands tour with this massive outfitter includes commentary from a knowledgable guide and three different wine tastings. A full-day tour costs around R1210 per person. ✉ 94 Voortrekker Rd., Salt River ☎ 021/506–2575 ⊕ www.hyltonross. co.za 🖾 From R860.

Springbok Atlas Tours & Safaris

GUIDED TOURS | This outfitter offers full-day tours of the Winelands that include visits to wine estates in Paarl, Franschhoek, and Stellenbosch. Tours cost R1210 per person, excluding lunch. A shorter afternoon tour includes wine tasting at one or two estates and costs R860 per person. ✉ Chiappini Sq., 17 Chiappini St., Cape Town Central ☎ 021/460–4700 ⊕ www. springbokatlas.com 🖾 From R860.

Thoza Tours

PRIVATE GUIDES | Run by Thomazile Stuurman—affectionately known as "Mr. T"—Thoza Tours offers tailor-made tours of the Western Cape. He also offers full-day tours of the Overberg and the Cape Peninsula. A full-day tour costs approximately R3500 for two people. ☎ 072/203–7806 ⊕ hermanus-tourism. co.za/info/thoza-tours.

Vine Hopper

SELF-GUIDED TOURS | An excellent alternative to a guided tour, the Vine Hopper is a hop-on, hop-off bus tour around the Stellenbosch region. There are three routes to choose from, with up to six wineries on each route. You can opt for a one- or two-day pass. They cover transport only, not wine tasting fees. ✉ 1 Noordwal Wes Rd., Stellenbosch ☎ 021/882–8112 ⊕ www.vinehopper.co.za.

Vineyard Ventures

SPECIAL-INTEREST TOURS | For those serious about wine, Vineyard Ventures is the region's oldest outfitter specializing in wine tours. They really know their stuff, and will customize tours based on your interests. It's around R4,300 for up to three people, and includes transport and refreshments. ✉ Punta Del Mar, Milton Rd., Sea Point ☎ 021/434–8888, 082/920–2825 ⊕ www.vineyardventures. co.za 🖾 From R4,300.

Wellington Wine Walk

SPECIAL-INTEREST TOURS | This woman-run company's three- or four-day walking tours leads you from one upscale guesthouse to the next through vineyards in the picturesque Wellington Valley. Your guides know all about the history and culture of the region, as well as the wines. The walking isn't tough, but you cover around 12 km (8 miles) each day. Your luggage is transferred for you from place to place, so all you have to carry is a light day pack. ✉ Wellington ☎ 083/235–5570 ⊕ www.winewalk.co.za 🖾 Three-day hike R9876.

Winetour

SPECIAL-INTEREST TOURS | This outfitter has a great all-day tour that's very reasonably priced and even includes lunch. You get picked up at Stellenbosch and tour four wine estates in the regions, such as Fairview, Simonsig, and Backsberg. Tours are around R1290. ⊠ *12 Market St., Stellenbosch* ☎ *082/229–8865* ⊕ *www. winetour.co.za* ✉ *From R1290.*

Visitor Information

There are tourist offices in most towns along the West Coast, but Weskus Tourism has information on the entire area as well as the Flowerline, a central hotline that provides details about where the flowers are best seen each day. You can call 24 hours a day July–September.

CONTACTS Weskus Flowerline.
☎ *079/593–9864.* **Weskus Tourism.** ⊠ *65 Long St., Moorreesburg* ☎ *022/433–8505* ⊕ *www.weskustourism.org.*

When to Go

Summer (late November through January) is high season in the Western Cape, and during that time you will seldom visit major places of interest without encountering busloads of fellow visitors. The weather is warm and dry, and although strong southeasterly winds can be a nuisance, they do keep the temperature bearable. ■ **TIP→ The UV index in the Western Cape is exceptionally high in summer, so if you do plan to visit then, make sure you take precautions to avoid severe sunburn.**

If soaking up the sun is not of primary importance and you prefer to tour during quieter times, spring (September and October) and autumn to early winter (late March through May) are ideal. The weather is milder, and the lines are shorter. Spring also brings Southern Right whales close to the shores of the Western Cape to calve, and late August through October are the months to see the wildflowers explode across the West Coast. If the Cape Winelands are high on your list of must-dos, remember that the busiest time in the vineyards and cellars is January through April, when they begin harvesting and wine making.

Somerset West

45 km (28 miles) southeast of Cape Town on the N2.

Nestled at the foot of the Helderberg Mountains, Somerset West is just 30 minutes from the center of Cape Town and close to Gordon's Bay and the Strand beaches. Once an important farming town, its former dairy fields are now covered with cookie cutter town houses and faux Tuscan villas. But a few historic estates still remain and are worth visiting.

Just before you reach the center of town you'll see the turnoff to Lourensford Road, which runs 3 km (2 miles) to Vergelegen and Morgenster. If you're keen to stretch your legs, the Helderberg Nature Reserve overlooks the beautiful False Bay and is home to plenty of fauna and flora.

GETTING HERE AND AROUND

Somerset West is 40 minutes southeast of Cape Town on the N2 and 30 minutes from the airport. Public transportation in these outlying towns leaves a lot to be desired. Your best bet is to rent a car and invest in a good map. Don't be tempted to catch trains out to the Cape Winelands after dark—you run the risk of being mugged.

VISITOR INFORMATION

CONTACTS Cape Town Tourism–Helderberg Branch. ⊠ *186 Main Rd.* ☎ *021/840–1400* ⊕ *www.capetown.travel.*

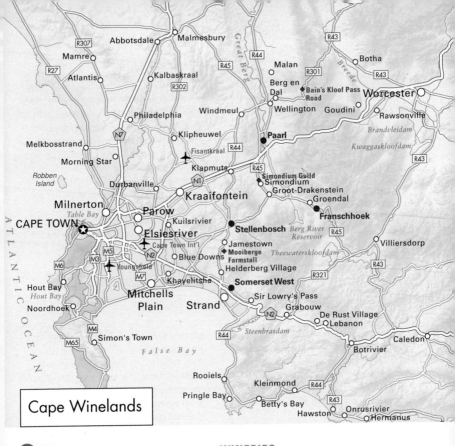

Cape Winelands

Sights

Mooiberge Farmstall

FARM/RANCH | FAMILY | You can't drive down the R44 between Somerset West and Stellenbosch without noticing the remarkable scarecrows at Mooiberge Farmstall. They're riding bicycles, driving tractors, and working in the strawberry fields, where you can spend a morning picking the luscious red fruit. The strawberry season varies from one year to the next but usually begins in October and runs to January. You pay for what you pick, and you can also buy jams, dried fruit, and other refreshments at the farm stall. Look for the interesting display of old farm implements at the side of the building. ⊠ *R44, between Somerset West and Stellenbosch* ☎ *021/881–3222* ⊕ *www.zetler.co.za/mooiberge.html* ⊠ *Free.*

WINERIES
Morgenster

WINERY | A leading producer of excellent extra-virgin olive oils and wines is the historic estate Morgenster (Morning Star), which was part of Cape Governor Willem Adriaan van der Stel's original 17th-century farm. In the mid-1990s the estate was restored to its original splendor, and thousands of olive trees were imported from Italy. It is now producing some of the best olive oils in the country and internationally. Seventeen different olive cultivars on the farm have been carefully selected from all the regions in Italy; these are pressed and stored individually before they're blended. For R55 you can taste the olives, the oil, balsamic vinegar, and the delicious olive paste. It's also worth lingering in the beautiful wine-tasting room, which was designed by acclaimed South African architect Revel

Cape Dutch Architecture

As you travel around the region, the most visible emblems of settler culture you'll encounter are the Cape Dutch–style houses. Here 18th- and 19th-century manor houses share certain characteristics: thick, white-washed walls, thatch roofs curving around elegant gables, and small-pane windows framed by wooden shutters. It's a classic look—a uniquely Cape look—ideally suited to a land that is hot in summer and cold in winter.

The Cape Dutch style developed in the 18th century from traditional long houses: simple rectangular sheds capped by thatch. As farmers became more prosperous, they added the ornate gables and other features. Several estates, most notably Vergelegen (near Somerset West) and Boschendal (on the Franschhoek wine route), have opened their manor houses as museums. The Oude Drostdy Museum just outside of Tulbagh is another fine example of classic Cape Dutch architecture.

Fox. Phone a day ahead if you're traveling in a group bigger than six. Reservations are recommended on weekends. ⊠ *Vergelegen Ave., off Lourensford Rd.* ☎ *021/852–1738* ⊕ *www.morgenster. co.za* 🖃 *Olive tasting R55, wine tasting R95.*

★ Vergelegen

WINERY | Established in 1700 by Willem Adriaan van der Stel, who succeeded his father as governor of the Cape, this traditional thatched Cape Dutch homestead looks like something from a fairy tale. An octagonal walled garden aflame with flowers surrounds it, and huge camphor trees, planted over 300 years ago, stand as gnarled sentinels. The homestead is now a museum, furnished in period style. Other historic buildings include a magnificent library and the old stables, which is now the Stables Restaurant, where you can have breakfast or lunch while looking onto the Hottentots Holland Mountains. You can also purchase a picnic to enjoy in the grounds during the summer months.

Vergelegen's flagship wines include Vergelegen V (a full-bodied Cabernet Sauvignon), and Vergelegen GVB Red, a Bordeaux blend of Cabernet Sauvignon,

Merlot, and Cabernet Franc. Reservations are recommended for the hour-long wine tours, but no children are allowed. Note that there are also 70 steep stairs leading to the cellar. Apart from award-winning wine, there are 18 themed gardens, including the Camellia Garden of Excellence—a collection of more than 1,000 plants which flower during the winter months (June–August). There's also a lovely children's play area adjacent to the restaurant. ⊠ *Lourensford Rd.* ☎ *021/847–2100* ⊕ *www.vergelegen. co.za* 🖃 *Entrance R10, tastings R40, tours R75.*

🍴 Restaurants

96 Winery Road

$$$$ | **INTERNATIONAL** | This relaxed venue is always buzzing with folk from the wine industry, locals from the area, and up-country visitors. The menu changes regularly but tempts with favorites such as Karoo lamb, the "Hollandse" pepper fillet, and the decadent crème brûlée. **Known for:** local favorite; cozy setting; impressive wine list. $ *Average main: R235* ⊠ *Zandberg Farm, Winery Rd., between Somerset West and*

Hugging False Bay, Clarence Drive is one of the most beautiful drives in the Western Cape.

Stellenbosch ☎ *021/842–2020* ⊕ *ww-w.96wineryroad.co.za* ⊗ *No dinner Sun.*

Stellenbosch

15 km (9½ miles) north of Somerset West.

You could easily while away a week in this small, sophisticated town with its abundant sidewalk cafes. South Africa's second-oldest municipality, after Cape Town, Stellenbosch actually *feels* old, unlike so many other historic towns. Wandering the oak-shaded streets, which still have open irrigation furrows (known as the *lei water,* pronounced lay *vaa*-ter), you'll see some of the finest examples of Cape Dutch, Georgian, Victorian, and Regency architecture in the country.

The town was founded in 1679 by Simon van der Stel, first governor of the Cape, who recognized the agricultural potential of this fertile valley. Wheat was the major crop grown by the early settlers, but vine-yards now blanket the surrounding hills. Stellenbosch is considered the center of the Cape Winelands, and many of the older and more established wineries are nearby. Wine routes fan out like spokes of a wheel, making excellent day trips if you're staying in town. The town is also home to the University of Stellenbosch, and the students lend a youthful air to this wonderful old town.

GETTING HERE AND AROUND

The best way to get to this area is by renting a car. Expect to pay around R400 for an entry-level car per day and up to R1200 for a Mercedes C Class. Once you're there, walking around is an excellent way to explore. Parking can be hard to find, so once you've found a spot, leave your rented car while you explore. There is usually a fee, so be sure to find out before venturing off. Avoid public transportation.

Western Cape Itineraries

3 Days: You could devote a couple of days to touring the wineries, spending perhaps one day visiting Stellenbosch-area wineries such as Simonsig and Villiera, and another day around Franschhoek or Paarl. Consider breaking up your wine touring with horseback riding at one of the vineyards and a night in Franschhoek. A third day could be devoted to a long, scenic route back to Cape Town after lunch at one of Franschhoek's many tasty restaurants. Another option is to spend the first day wine tasting, and then drive over Sir Lowry's Pass through Elgin and on to Greyton, where you can wander around the village and visit the Moravian Mission complex in Genadendal. The last morning of your stay could be spent in Greyton before you head back to Cape Town via coastal Clarence Drive, which passes Kleinmond, Betty's Bay, Pringle Bay, and Gordon's Bay.

5 Days: With five days, you can work in time to see the Cape Winelands as well as Clanwilliam, at the edge of the Cederberg. (The drive to the Clanwilliam area will take you through the Swartland and the beginning of the wildflower route, which sees the usually monochrome landscape burst into color in August and September.) If nature beckons, head into the Cederberg, where you can easily spend two nights in some of the country's most spectacular scenery. You can hike, swim in crystal-clear rock pools, and admire ancient San rock art. You could also combine a trip to the Cape Winelands or Cederberg with a visit to the coast's Langebaan and West Coast National Park, where the birding is exceptional.

7 Days: A week would allow you to comfortably visit the Cape Winelands, Cederberg, and the coast. You could spend a few days in the Cederberg and then head through Riebeek Kasteel and Wellington and on to the Cape Winelands towns of Paarl, Stellenbosch, and Franschhoek, where you can linger for the next two or three days. Spend your last days in the beautiful Franschhoek Valley, or take a scenic back route on the R45 and then the R321 into the Overberg. If you haven't tired of wine by this point, sample some of the Overberg wines, particularly the Pinot Noirs of the Hemel-en-Aarde Valley.

TOURS

The historic area of Stellenbosch is so pretty and compact that it's a pity just to drive through. Pull on your walking shoes and stride out with Stellenbosch on Foot for their 1½-hour walking tour.

Stellenbosch on Foot

WALKING TOURS | Take a walking tour with one of the knowledgeable guides from Stellenbosch on Foot. Tours costing R180 per person leave the tourism office twice a day and last around 90 minutes, taking in all the well-known sights. Book ahead on weekends. ⊠ *47 Church St., Stellenbosch* ☎ *084/479–7262* 🖭 *R180.*

VISITOR INFORMATION

CONTACTS Stellenbosch Tourism and Information Bureau. ⊠ *47 Church St., Stellenbosch* ☎ *021/886-4310* ⊕ *www. visitstellenbosch.org.*

◉ Sights

Start your tour of the town at the corner of Dorp Street and the R44, where you first enter Stellenbosch. Look for street names written in yellow on curbs; they're easy to miss, so remember to look down and not up.

Architecture buffs will be happy to know that there are still examples of 19th-century Stellenbosch design around. To check them out, turn left off Market Street onto Herte Street. (Market is Mark in Afrikaans; some maps use the names interchangeably, which can be confusing.) The whitewashed cottages along this street were built by and for freed slaves after the Emancipation Act of 1834. Although they are no longer thatch, the houses on the left-hand side of the road are still evocative of this era.

Die Braak

HISTORIC DISTRICT | Some of Stellenbosch's most historic buildings face the Braak, the grassy town square. St. Mary's Church stands at the north end of the Braak. Built in 1852 as an Anglican church, it reflects the growing influence of the English in Stellenbosch. Across Bloem Street from St. Mary's is the Burgher House, built in 1797. Today it houses the offices of Historical Homes in South Africa but you can view the main rooms during office hours. At the southern end of the Braak is the Rhenish Mission Church, erected by the Missionary Society of Stellenbosch in 1823. ✉ Bordered by Bloem, Alexander, and Bird Sts., Stellenbosch.

Dorp Street

HISTORIC DISTRICT | Stellenbosch's most historic avenue is oak-lined Dorp Street. Almost the entire street is a national monument, flanked by lovely restored homes from every period of the town's history. Look out for **Voorgelegen** at no. 116, a perfectly preserved Georgian home from the 19th century. Perhaps most interesting is **La Gratitude** at no. 95.

This early 18th-century home was built in traditional Cape Dutch town-house style. The all-seeing eye of God molded on its gable was designed as a talisman to watch over the owner's property and keep him and his family safe from harm. ✉ Dorp St. at Papegaai Rd., Stellenbosch.

Oom Samie Se Winkel

STORE/MALL | Redolent of tobacco, dried fish, and spices, this 19th-century-style general store is one of Stellenbosch's most popular landmarks. In addition to the usual Cape kitsch, Oom Samie sells some genuine South African produce, including *witblits* and *mampoer*, both Afrikaner versions of moonshine. The shop has a restaurant, too. ✉ 84 Dorp St., Stellenbosch ☎ 021/887–2372.

Rhenish Complex

NOTABLE BUILDING | One of the most impressive restoration projects ever undertaken in South Africa and a good example of what early Stellenbosch must have been like, this complex consists of an art center, which melds elements of English and Cape architecture; and a two-story building that is typically English. The complex is west of Die Braak, facing a large lawn. The Toy and Miniature Museum houses a collection of scale dollhouses and antique toys, as well as a miniature model of the famous Blue Train. ✉ Bordered by Herte, Market, Bloem, and Dorp Sts., Stellenbosch.

Stellenbosch Museum

HISTORY MUSEUM | This museum includes four dwellings scattered within a two-block radius. Dating from different periods in Stellenbosch's history, the houses have been furnished to reflect changing lifestyles and tastes. The oldest is the very basic Schreuderhuis, built in 1709. The others date from 1789, 1803, and 1850. ✉ 18 Ryneveld St., at Church St., Stellenbosch ☎ 021/887–2937 ⊕ www.stelmus.co.za ⊠ R50 ☉ Closed Sun.

Stellenbosch Wine Route

Along R310

West of Stellenbosch, the R310 (also known locally as Baden Powell Drive) forks to the left, but go straight on the M12 (also known as Polkadraai Road); Asara is first up on your right, followed by **Neethlingshof**. Turn right on Stellenbosch Kloof Road, where **Overgaauw** is a Merlot mainstay. Follow the winding road through pretty vineyards; at the end is **Jordan**, known for its excellent Chardonnay. Double back to Stellenbosch, and at the set of traffic lights, take the R310 to your right to the touristy but fun **Spier**. Next up this road is **Meerlust**, with its superlative reds.

If you drive east on the R310 from Stellenbosch, detour up the Idasvallei Road and follow a narrow lane through cattle pastures and oak groves to **Rustenberg**, which focuses on reds. Then it's up and over the scenic Helshoogte Pass to **Thelema Mountain Vineyards**, which has knockout reds and whites. Its neighbor, **Tokara**, is a great lunch spot, and **Delaire Graff Estate**, over the road, has breathtaking views and an upmarket wine-tasting lounge.

Along R44

Some important wineries are on the R44 north of Stellenbosch. About 8 km (5 miles) north of the town center, turn right on Knorhoek Road to reach low-key **Muratie**, with some good reds. Back on the R44, travel a short way and then turn left on Kromme Rhee Road to visit **Simonsig**, home to wonderful bubbly. On the R44 once more, continue to **Kanonkop**, which has won numerous awards, and **Warwick**, with great red blends and lots of places to picnic. Carry on to Klapmuts and take the Simondium Road to the right to get to Babylonstoren, not to be missed for its gardens and interesting restaurant.

Along R304

This road shoots northwest from Stellenbosch past several wine farms. Cross over Kromme Rhee Road and head for **Villiera**, known for sparkling wine and lush Sauvignon Blanc.

V.O.C. Arsenal

NOTABLE BUILDING | Next to the Burgher House, just across from the Braak on a traffic island in Market Street, stands the V.O.C. Arsenal, often called the **V.O.C. Kruithuis** (*kruithuis* means "powder house"). It took 91 years for the political council to decide that Stellenbosch needed its own magazine, and just six months in 1777 to complete the structure. Today the arsenal contains a wide selection of guns, gunpowder holders, and cannons. If the arsenal is closed, call or pop into the Toy and Miniature Museum and someone will open it up for you.

✉ Market St., Stellenbosch ☎ 021/886–4153 💳 By donation ⏱ Closed Sat., Sun.

WINERIES

Many wine estates are wheelchair friendly, and you'll be able to access the tasting rooms without a problem. Phone ahead so you know what to expect.

Delaire Graff Estate

WINERY | This has to be one of the most spectacular settings of any winery in the country. Sit on the terrace of the tasting room or restaurant and look past a screen of pin oaks to the valley below and the majestic crags of the Groot Drakenstein and Simonsberg Mountains.

It's an ideal place to stop for lunch, and you'll need at least three hours to do your meal and the wines justice. The flagship Delaire Graff Restaurant champions local ingredients, while ultra-high-end Indo-chine celebrates South Africa's historical links to Southeast Asia through Cape Malay dishes and pan-Asian specialties. Although the Botmaskop Red Blend is the farm's flagship wine, do try the Cabernet Franc Rosé, a lovely take on a varietal that usually gets added to the Bordeaux Blend. The Coastal Cuvée Sauvignon Blanc is exceptional and has won numerous awards. ⊠ *Helshoogte Pass Rd., between Stellenbosch and Franschhoek, Stellenbosch* ☎ *021/885–8160* ⊕ *www.delaire.co.za* ⊠ *Tastings R125.*

Jordan

WINERY | At the end of Stellenbosch Kloof Road, this meticulous winery, flanked by the Bottelary hills, overlooks rolling vineyards and jagged mountains. Husband-and-wife team Gary and Kathy Jordan studied at the University of California at Davis and worked at California's Iron Horse Winery. Since the first vintage in 1993, the winery has established a formidable reputation. The Sauvignon Blanc makes for good summer drinking; the dense but fruity Nine Yards Chardonnay is extremely popular and has regulars stocking up on cases at a time. Another wine to try is the Cobblers Hill Bordeaux blend. The wine estate has an excellent restaurant, as well as a bakery where you can enjoy breakfast or a light lunch. Cellar tours are available by appointment; book at least a day ahead. ⊠ *Stellenbosch Kloof Rd., Stellenbosch* ☎ *021/881–3441 cellar, 021/881–3612 restaurant* ⊕ *www.jordanwines.com* ⊠ *Tastings R20.*

★ Kanonkop

WINERY | In the days when the Dutch East India Company stopped in Cape Town en route to the East, a ship would fire a cannon as it entered the harbor to let farmers know provisions were needed. A set of relay cannons on the hilltops would carry the message inland. One such cannon was on this farm, which was then called Kanonkop, Afrikaans for Cannon Hill. The beauty of Kanonkop today is not in its history or its buildings, but in its wine. Paul Sauer, a blend of about 70% Cabernet Sauvignon, 15% Merlot, and 15% Cabernet Franc, rakes in awards both in South Africa and internationally year after year. The Kanonkop Black Label Pinotage is an iconic wine produced in small quantities and sold only from the farm. There are no guided tours, but during harvest you can do a walkabout in the cellar to see the action. An added attraction is the art gallery featuring works from 50 leading South African artists. It's a wonderful selection of the totally traditional to the strikingly modern. ⊠ *R44, between Paarl and Stellenbosch, Stellenbosch* ☎ *021/884–4656* ⊕ *www.kanonkop.co.za* ⊠ *Tastings R75* ⊗ *Closed Sun.*

Meerlust

WINERY | A visit to Meerlust, one of South Africa's most celebrated estates, provides an introduction to Cape history. In the same family for generations, the vineyard was bought by Johannes Albertus Myburgh in 1757. When Nicolaas Myburgh took over the reins in 1959, he began restoring the farm's Cape Dutch buildings. The entire complex was declared a national monument. Nico Myburgh did more than just renovate. In the '70s, conventional wisdom had it that Cabernet Sauvignon was king, but Nico went against the grain and opted for a Bordeaux-style blend, planting both Merlot and Cabernet Franc. The first wine, made in 1980 and released in 1983, was named Rubicon (an allusion to Julius Caesar) to symbolize the crossing of a significant barrier. Rubicon garners awards year after year and is rated as an international best seller. The estate makes only one white, a delicious, full-bodied Chardonnay. Meerlust's other wines—Cabernet Sauvignon, Pinot Noir, and Merlot—are also notably good. The low-key, relaxed tasting offers great value for money ⊠ *Off R310, Stellenbosch* ☎ *021/843–3587* ⊕ *www.meerlust.co.za* 🍷 *Tastings R30* ⊗ *Closed Sun.*

Morgenhof Wine Estate

WINERY | This beautiful Cape Dutch estate, with a history stretching back 300 years, lies in the lee of a steep hill covered with vines and pine trees. In 1993 Morgenhof was acquired by Anne Cointreau of Cognac, France, who spared no expense in making this a showpiece estate with a lovely rose garden on top of the working underground cellar. The estate has a talented winemaker, Andries de Klerk, and some distinguished wines. The Morgenhof Estate Blend 2006 is a complex wine made from a blend of Cabernet Sauvignon, Merlot, Malbec, Petit Verdot, and Cabernet Franc. Look out for black cherries, prunes, hints of chocolate, and spice on your palate. On a hot summer's day (and the temperatures can soar in Stellenbosch) try the 2015 Chardonnay with fresh pear, passion fruit, and pineapple flavors. Morgenhof is an excellent place to stop for lunch while you watch the peacocks roaming around. There's also a coffee shop if you want a snack before heading off to the next farm. Tour reservations are advisable in summer. ⊠ *R44, between Paarl and Stellenbosch, Stellenbosch* ☎ *021/889–2000* ⊕ *www.morgenhof.com* 🍷 *Tastings R55.*

Mulderbosch Vineyards

WINERY | FAMILY | A long and beautiful driveway emerges at Mulderbosch's tasting room and restaurant, both of which overlook a small lake. It's a relaxed and family-friendly spot, with a small jungle gym and unpretentious food like wood-fired pizzas and sliders. On the wine side, try the Single Vineyard Chenin Blanc series; these wines capture all that's good about the underrated Chenin varietal. Look for mango, pineapple, and citrus flavors with crisp acidity, perfect for summer drinking. A huge portion of the farm has been left to indigenous vegetation

and wildlife, and they're attempting to restore endangered native renosterveld and fynbos vegetation. ⊠ *Polkadraai Rd., Stellenbosch* ☎ *021/881–8140* ⊕ *www. mulderbosch.co.za* 🍷 *R50* ⊗ *Closed Mon., Tues., and July.*

Muratie Wine Estate

WINERY | Ancient oaks and a cellar that truly seems to be more concerned with the business of producing wine than with decor make this a refreshing change from the "prettier" wineries. It's a small estate, specializing in rich, earthy reds and full-bodied dessert wines. Muratie's port is an old favorite in the Cape, and the well-balanced Amber Forever is a fortified dessert wine has pleasing citrus notes to counter the sweetness. Worth looking out for are the Pinot Noirs, from some of the oldest vines of this cultivar in the Cape. The farm's flagship wine is the Ansela van der Caab, a red blend of Cabernet Sauvignon, Cabernet Franc, and Merlot, named after the freed slave who married the first owner of the farm, Laurens Campher, and helped set up the vineyards in the early 1700s. The Ronnie Melck Shiraz and Muratie Martin Melck Family Reserve Cabernet Sauvignon also come highly recommended. There are cottages on site and an unfussy restaurant serving steaks, salads and a few South African specialties. ⊠ *Knorhoek Rd., off the R44, between Stellenbosch and Paarl, Stellenbosch* ☎ *021/865–2330* ⊕ *www.muratie.co.za* 🍷 *Tastings R60* ☞ *Tours by appointment only.*

Neethlingshof

WINERY | FAMILY | A long avenue of pines leads to this lovely estate, which traces its origins to 1692. The magnificent 1814 Cape Dutch manor house looks out across formal rose gardens to the Stellenbosch Valley and the Hottentots Holland Mountains. The Gewürztraminer is an off-dry, very elegant wine with rose-petal and spice aromas, and the Maria Noble Late Harvest (named after the feisty woman who built the manor house) is one of the best of its kind, having scooped up almost every local award since 1990. The farm's Owl Post Pinotage is a single-vineyard wine matured in Hungarian oak, which makes it a funkier take on an old South African favorite. Look out for mocha, raspberry, and cherry flavors. Try the food-and-wine pairings, which include five bite-size servings paired with the estate wines—there's even a kids' version available. The restaurant is more casual than most found in wineries, serving salads, steak, burgers, and wood-fired pizza. On Wednesday evenings in summer enjoy live music, food, and wine as the sunsets. ⊠ *Neethlingshof Estate, 7599 Polkadraai Rd., Stellenbosch* ☎ *021/883–8988* ⊕ *www.neethlingshof. co.za* ⊡ *Tastings R65, food-and-wine pairings R150.*

Overgaauw
WINERY | Among the established estates on Stellenbosch Kloof Road, Overgaauw definitely deserves a visit. You can admire the pretty Victorian tasting room while exploring the range of big red wines. David van Velden is the fourth-generation winemaker on the farm. Tradition hasn't stood in the way of innovation, however. In 1982 Overgaauw was the first South African estate to make a Merlot, but it also experiments with other varietals, and you should, too. Try the wonderful Cape Vintage Port made with Portuguese varietals such as *touriga, tintas, souzao,* and *cornifesto.* The result is a richly balanced blend. The Tria Corda, a red blend, sells out faster than it can be released. The spicy, fruity Sylvaner is named for a grape of the same name. To date, Overgaauw is the only Cape estate to grow this varietal, which comes from the Alsace region of France, so it's definitely worth exploring. ⊠ *Stellenbosch Kloof Rd., Vlottenburg* ☎ *021/881–3815* ⊕ *www.overgaauw.co.za* ⊡ *Tastings R50* ☞ *By appointment only.*

Rustenberg
WINERY | This estate may date back to 1682, but it's been brought thoroughly up to date with a state-of-the art winery and underground vaulted maturation rooms. It is known for red wines, particularly its 100% Cabernet Peter Barlow (named after the present owner's father), which is made from grapes from one lovely, well-tended vineyard. The Five Soldiers Chardonnay is delicious and also made from a single vineyard, which gives it its unique character. It's named for the five tall pine trees that stand guard on top of the hill above the Chardonnay grapes. The farm uses screw caps on about half of its wines for quality and environmental reasons. Make time to explore the estate's beautiful gardens and labyrinth. These are open year-round but are best in summer. The lovely manor house gardens are open to the public only once a year over the last weekend of October, alas. Book ahead for tastings. ⊠ *Rustenberg Rd., off Leslie St./R310, Ida's Valley* ☎ *021/809–1200* ⊕ *www.rustenberg.co.za* ⊡ *Tastings R40.*

Rust en Vrede
WINERY | Nestled against the base of Helderberg Mountain, the peaceful Rust en Vrede winery is shaded by giant oaks and looks out over steep slopes of vines and roses. This comparatively small estate specializes entirely in reds and produces some of the very best in South Africa. In fact, Nelson Mandela chose this wine to be served at his Nobel Peace Prize dinner when he was president. Rust en Vrede Estate is the flagship wine, a blend of predominantly Cabernet Sauvignon, Syrah, and Merlot. Enjoy it now, but you can also put it away to mature in the bottle for another 10 years or more. Another weighty wine is the 1694 Classification (named after the year the farm was established). Look out for raspberry, cedar, and pencil shavings on palate and nose. ⊠ *Annandale Rd., off R44, between Somerset West and Stellenbosch, Somerset West* ☎ *021/881–3881* ⊕ *www.rustenvrede. com* ⊡ *Tastings R50–R100.*

Simonsig

WINERY | FAMILY | Sitting in a sea of vines is this estate with tremendous views back toward Stellenbosch and the mountains. Simonsig has more than a dozen white and red wines of impressive range, both in terms of taste and price. But quantity certainly doesn't mean that it has compromised on quality. This family-run farm produces exciting and consistent wines. Kaapse Vonkel was South Africa's first Méthode Cap Classique, and since 1971 this classic blend of Chardonnay, Pinot Noir, and a touch of Pinot Meunier has been among the best. The Pinotage demonstrates how well this varietal fares with no wood aging, but the Red Hill Pinotage, from old bush vines, shows just how much good oaking can improve it. This is a good place for kids, with a small playground, a labyrinth that takes about 10 minutes to walk through, and a small vineyard they can explore. Cuvee restaurant offers seasonal, locally inspired dishes in a relaxed environment. ⊠ *Kromme Rhee Rd., Koelenhof* ☎ *021/888–4900* ⊕ *www.simonsig.co.za* ✉ *Tastings R75–150.*

★ Spier

WINERY | FAMILY | This is one of the oldest farms in the area, established in 1692 on the banks of the Eerste River. The farm produces excellent wines, which go from strength to strength. The flagships are the Frans K. Smit red and white blends, named after the winemaker. Also try the 21 Gables Chenin Blanc and Pinotage—both excellent. The farm's owners value biodiversity and arts and culture: their enormous art collection is displayed across the farm's public spaces, and their farm-grown produce is used in the restaurants. You can order a picnic and enjoy it on the banks of the river. Visit Eagle Encounters, an on-site rehabilitation center for raptors—your kids will never want to leave. And if you just can't drag them away there is a delightful hotel on site complete with kids' club, so you can sip while they play. ⊠ *Lynedoch Rd.,* *Stellenbosch* ☎ *021/809–1100* ⊕ *www. spier.co.za* ✉ *Tastings R50–R70.*

Thelema Mountain Vineyards

WINERY | On the slopes of the Simonsberg, just off the Helshoogte Pass, this is an excellent example of the exciting developments in the Cape Winelands since the early 1980s, when farmers began to eye land that hadn't traditionally been earmarked for vineyards. When Gyles and Barbara Webb started the farm in 1983, there was nothing here but very good soil and old fruit trees. It's a testament to their efforts that the winery has regularly won prizes for both its reds and whites ever since. To cap it all off, the view of the Groot Drakenstein Mountains from the tasting room is unforgettable. Ever the pioneers, the Webbs have also bought Sutherland, an old fruit farm in the Elgin area. The Sutherland wines, which can be tasted at Thelema, are wonderfully fragrant; look out for the Pinot Noir and Chardonnay. The local favorite, however, is Ed's Reserve, a single-vineyard Chardonnay named after the farm's matriarch, the late Edna McLean, Barbara's mother; she originally bought the Thelema farm and was a stalwart in the tasting room. ⊠ *Off R310, between Stellenbosch and Franschhoek, Stellenbosch* ☎ *021/885–1924* ⊕ *www.thelema. co.za* ✉ *Tastings R100* ⊗ *Closed Sun.*

★ Tokara

WINERY | FAMILY | Perched on the crest of the Helshoogte Pass between Stellenbosch and Franschhoek, Tokara is the brainchild of banker G. T. Ferreira. For a city slicker with lots of money, he's done everything right and has scooped up awards. The Chardonnay was once voted one of the top 10 wines from around the world at the Chardonnay-du-Monde Awards. The flagship red, a blend of Cabernet Sauvignon, Merlot, Petit Verdot, and Malbec, is well worth taking home. Be on the lookout for the farm's limited-release Pinotage, taken from one block on the foothills of the Simonsberg.

Tokara also has farms in the cooler Elgin and Hemel-en-Aarde regions, which means it can produce a stunning white wine blend (Sauvignon Blanc and Semillon) with plenty of complexity. The farm also presses its own premium olive oil, which you can buy from the Olive Shed. The restaurant is a foodie's delight, and the Delicatessen is a perfect venue for a breakfast or light lunch. Kids love the free-form jungle gym—as good-looking as any contemporary sculpture—and the weaver's nest they can climb into that hangs in a huge oak. ⊠ *Off R310, between Stellenbosch and Franschhoek, Stellenbosch* ☎ *021/808–5900 vineyard, 021/808–2550 restaurant* ⊕ *www.tokara. com* ⊠ *Tastings R100.*

Villiera
WINERY | Since starting in wine making in 1984, the Grier family has notched numerous successes. As John Platter, one of South Africa's foremost wine writers, once said, "Other winemakers might jog or work out in the gym; Jeff Grier gets all the exercise he needs stepping up to the podium for wine industry awards." The farm is famous for its range of Méthode Cap Classique sparkling wines. Try the Brut Natural, which is 100% Chardonnay and made using wild yeast; it has no added sulfur and no added sugar. The creamy Monro Brut made of Chardonnay and Pinot Noir is a multiple award winner. The barrel-fermented Chenin Blanc is also very popular. Registered as a biodiversity farm, the winery produces chemical-free wines as much as possible; they use ducks to help control the snails and work to attract raptors to scare off the smaller birds that feast on the ripening grapes. You can combine a wine tasting with a drive through the 545-acre wildlife sanctuary (2 hours, R260), where you'll see eland, gemsbok, giraffe, bush pig, and other wild animals. Booking is essential. ⊠ *R101 and R304 (Old Paarl and Stellenbosch Rds.), Koelenhof* ☎ *021/865–2002* ⊕ *www.villiera.com* ⊠ *Tastings R40* ☉ *Closed Sun.*

Tasting Tip

Many wineries will waive the tasting fee if you buy wine, even if it's only a bottle or two. It's not always advertised, but it is always worth asking, assuming you want to take some wine away with you.

★ Warwick
WINERY | FAMILY | This Ratcliffe-family-run farm is all business. Norma Ratcliffe, the grande dame of the estate, spent a couple of years in France perfecting traditional techniques, which have influenced Warwick's reds. The first female winemaker in South Africa, Norma pioneered the way for a new breed of young women who are now making their mark in the industry. Trilogy is a stylish and complex red made with Cabernet Franc, Cabernet Sauvignon, and Merlot. Another great red, the Three Cape Ladies, was named after the indomitable Ratcliffe women, and is a fabulous blend of Cabernet Sauvignon, Cabernet Franc, and Pinotage. The Cabernet Franc is undoubtedly one of the best wines made from this varietal in the Winelands. There are kid-friendly vineyard tours that compare grape varietals to the Big Five animals. Afterward, enjoy a picnic on the lawn. ⊠ *R44, between Stellenbosch and Klapmuts, Elsenburg* ☎ *021/884–4410* ⊕ *www.warwickwine.com* ⊠ *Tastings R50–R100.*

🍴 Restaurants

★ Helena's
$$$ | FRENCH FUSION | In the Coopmanhuijs Boutique Hotel, this small restaurant exudes the elegance of a French bistro with its white tablecloths and pretty wrought iron patio furniture. The menu combines classical French cuisine with uniquely South African ingredients in

dishes like twice-baked cheese and biltong soufflé. **Known for:** tender lamb neck; al fresco dining; decadent desserts. $ *Average main: R195* ⊠ *33 Church St., Stellenbosch* ☎ *021/883–8207* ⊕ *www.helenasrestaurant.co.za.*

Kleine Zalze

$$$$ | **ECLECTIC** | The setting on a golf estate and wine farm is pretty, but it's the excellent food and service that really stand out here. The menu changes regularly to make use of the fresh, local produce such as West Coast mussels, Karoo lamb, and venison, and there are tapas-sized portions as well as main meals. **Known for:** accessible fine dining; delicious hot and cold tapas; locally sourced ingredients. $ *Average main: R220* ⊠ *Kleine Zalze Residential Golf Estate, Strand Rd., between Somerset West and Stellenbosch, Stellenbosch* ☎ *021/880–8167* ⊕ *www.kleinezalze.co.za* ⊗ *No dinner Wed., Thurs., and Sun. Closed Mon. and Tues.*

Overture

$$$$ | **ECLECTIC** | Overture has a constantly changing menu that manifests a pure love of food with distinctly South African dishes featuring local cheese, game meat, and *biltong* (the national snack of dried, spiced meat). The food is very good value for this level of cuisine; the menu can be ordered as a three- or five-course banquet. **Known for:** great value; friendly service; excellent tasting menu. $ *Average main: R515* ⊠ *Hidden Valley Wines, Annandale Rd., Stellenbosch* ☎ *021/880–2721* ⊕ *www.bertusbasson.com* ⊗ *Closed Mon. No dinner Sun.–Wed.*

★ Rust en Vrede

$$$$ | **ECLECTIC** | When you arrive at this gorgeous old Dutch farmhouse, a staffer greets you and suggests a pre-dinner drink on the rose-trellised terrace. Chef Fabio Daniel serves contemporary French cuisine that also draws on his Brazilian and Italian heritage. **Known for:** exquisite service; apératifs of the terrace;

amazing tasting menu. $ *Average main: R790* ⊠ *Annandale Rd., Stellenbosch* ☎ *021/881–3881* ⊕ *www.rustenvrede.com* ⊗ *No lunch. No dinner Sun. and Mon.*

Spek & Bone

$$$$ | **SOUTH AFRICAN** | Hidden in the center of town, Spek and Bone is a cozy restaurant with a lush courtyard whose tables and chairs are set under a canopy of vines. The menu focuses on what they call tapas, although they have an international flair rather than a strong Spanish influence. **Known for:** great wine list; one of South Africa's best-known chefs; Asian influences. $ *Average main: R325* ⊠ *84 Dorp St., Stellenbosch* ☎ *082/569–8958* ⊕ *www.bertusbasson.com* ⊗ *Closed Sun. and Mon.*

★ Tokara

$$$$ | **ECLECTIC** | At the top of the Helshoogte Pass with absolutely amazing views of the valley and mountains, Tokara is a Winelands must-visit. Chef Carolize Coetzee grew up in small-town South Africa and honors local ingredients and cooking methods in her wide range of dishes. **Known for:** striking local art; upmarket farm-style food; South African specialties. $ *Average main: R270* ⊠ *Helshoogte Pass Rd., Stellenbosch* ☎ *021/885–2550* ⊕ *www.tokara.co.za* ⊗ *Closed Mon. and Tues. No dinner Sun.*

 # Hotels

Asara Wine Estate & Hotel

$$$ | **HOTEL** | At this lovely lodging, the contemporary rooms are classically decorated in muted shades of cream, beige, and gray and have balconies overlooking the vineyards or hotel courtyard. **Pros:** restaurants worth staying in for; easy access to both Cape Town and the Winelands; highly rated wines produced on the estate. **Cons:** you'll need deep pockets; location isn't the most inspiring; lacks the gracious charm of some historic wine farms. $ *Rooms from: R3100*

✉ M12 (Polkadraai Rd.), Vlottenburg ☎ 021/888–8000 ⊕ www.asara.co.za ↻ 41 rooms ¶◎¶ Free Breakfast.

★ Delaire Graff Estate Lodges

$$$$ | HOTEL | The gorgeously landscaped grounds at this dramatically located hotel—featuring a mix of indigenous and exotic species that create an opulent yet grounded feel—are scattered with enormous "lodges," each with their own butler's kitchen and private heated pool. **Pros:** stunning natural setting; free shuttles to Stellenbsosch; staff sees to all your needs. **Cons:** this level of luxury doesn't come cheap; guests from other lodgings come to snap pics; you'll be sad to leave. $ Rooms from: R16500 ✉ Helshoogte Pass Rd., between Stellenbosch and Franschhoek, Stellenbosch ☎ 021/885–8160 ⊕ www.delaire.co.za ↻ 10 lodges ¶◎¶ Free Breakfast.

Lanzerac Manor

$$$$ | HOTEL | The sheer beauty of the setting has not changed since this wine estate was founded in 1692. **Pros:** stunning location with views of the Helderberg Mountains; friendly staff; wonderful onsite winery. **Cons:** not within walking distance of Stellenbosch; rooms are at the expensive end of the scale; can feel a little too quiet. $ Rooms from: R8950 ✉ Jonkershoek Valley, Lanzerac Rd., 1 km (½ mile) from Stellenbosch, Stellenbosch ☎ 021/887–1132 ⊕ www.lanzerac.co.za ↻ 48 rooms ¶◎¶ Free Breakfast.

Majeka House

$$$$ | HOTEL | This cluster of vine-covered buildings nestled in gardens overflowing with roses, lavender, frangipani, and jasmine sits in an upmarket residential corner of Stellenbosch. **Pros:** friendly and competent service; a perfect oasis and a great base for exploration; rooms are like modern works of art. **Cons:** on-site restaurant isn't as good as it was; not in the prettiest part of Stellenbosch; you'll need a car to explore the area. $ Rooms

from: R4300 ✉ 26–32 Houtkapper St., Paradyskloof, Stellenbosch ☎ 021/880–1549 ⊕ www.majekahouse.co.za ↻ 23 rooms ¶◎¶ Free Breakfast.

Oude Werf Hotel

$$ | B&B/INN | A national monument, this attractive 1802 hotel is thought to be the oldest continuously running inn in South Africa. **Pros:** perfect location in the heart of Stellenbosch; heated outdoor pool; excellent in-house restaurant. **Cons:** can get a bit noisy in the center of town; entry-level rooms are quite small; some rooms are dark. $ Rooms from: R2500 ✉ 30 Church St., Stellenbosch ☎ 021/887–4608 ⊕ www.oudewerf.co.za ↻ 58 rooms ¶◎¶ Free Breakfast.

Spier Hotel

$$ | HOTEL | FAMILY | Resembling a Mediterranean village—albeit a very luxurious one—this lodging is made up of a collection of two-story buildings with their own swimming pools. **Pros:** very close to the N2; plenty of entertainment on offer; perfect for the whole family. **Cons:** you'll share the vineyard with day visitors; attracts families with young children; can get busy in peak season. $ Rooms from: R2500 ✉ Spier Estate, Lynedoch Rd., Stellenbosch ☎ 021/809–1100 ⊕ www.spier.co.za ↻ 158 rooms ¶◎¶ Free Breakfast.

Nightlife

Wijnhuis

WINE BARS | Take a stroll on and around Church Street, where shops stay open late and bars and cafés spill onto the sidewalks. A good place to start, the Wijnhuis quickly fills up with well-heeled locals wanting to unwind. ✉ Church St. at Andringa St., Stellenbosch ☎ 021/887–5844 ⊕ www.wijnhuis.co.za.

Performing Arts

Oude Libertas Amphitheatre

MUSIC | Each summer, performances ranging from African jazz to opera to ballet are staged at the Oude Libertas Amphitheatre, a delightful open-air venue. ⊠ *Adam Tas St. at Oude Libertas Rd., Stellenbosch* ☎ *021/809–7473* ⊕ *www.oudelibertas.co.za.*

Franschhoek

22 km (14 miles) northeast of Stellenbosch.

Franschhoek—an elegant way to say "French Corner"—takes its name from French Huguenots who fled to the Cape to escape Catholic persecution in France in the late 1600s. By the early 18th century, about 200 Huguenots had settled in the region. Today their descendants—with names like de Villiers, Malan, and Joubert—number in the tens of thousands. With their experience in French vineyards, the early Huguenots were instrumental in nurturing a wine-making culture in South Africa.

Franschhoek is the most spectacular of the three wine centers: a long valley encircled by towering mountain ranges and fed by a single road that runs through town. As spectacular as the valley is today, it must have been even more so in the 17th century, when it teemed with game: In calving season, herds of elephants would migrate to the valley via the precipitous Franschhoek Mountains. The last wild elephant in the valley died in the 1930s. Some leopards still survive high in the mountains, but you won't see them.

What you will see is an increasingly upscale village with beautifully renovated cottages and gorgeous gardens. Although it can get very busy during the summer season, you will always be able to find a quiet spot surrounded by rose bushes and swaths of lavender, which do well here. Franschhoek has developed into a culinary mecca, with some of the country's best restaurants and cafés lining the pretty main street. In May the fabulous Franschhoek Literary Festival features local and international writers. Bastille Day is a huge draw, when the town is decked out in red, white, and blue, and events commemorate the town's French history.

The town is more touristy than agrarian, although you will see the occasional wine farmer steaming into town with his dogs on the back of his *bakkie* (pickup truck), looking for tractor tires or other essentials. It's a great place for lunch or for a couple of days, as there are excellent small hotels and guesthouses to choose from.

GETTING HERE AND AROUND

The best way to explore this area is by renting a car and cruising the Cape's highways and byways. Be aware that drunken walking can be a hazard, so keep a sharp eye out for staggering pedestrians, especially over the weekends.

VISITOR INFORMATION

CONTACTS Franschhoek Wine Valley Tourism. ⊠ *62 Huguenot Rd., Franschhoek* ☎ *021/876–2861* ⊕ *www.franschhoek.org.za.*

 Sights

Franschhoek Wine Tram

TRANSPORTATION | The Wine Tram is the best way to see Franschhoek, allowing you to visit up to six wineries in a day with the freedom to stay for as long as you like at each estate. There are eight different routes to choose from, covering the entire valley. The tram line itself is pretty short, with most routes actually serviced by a trolley bus. A day pass is R270, but all wine tastings are extra. There are also guided tours if you want something more formal. ⊠ *Main Rd. and Cabriere St., Franschhoek*

Franschhoek Wine Route

Along R310

The drive out of Stellenbosch up the Helshoogte Pass is spectacular. In winter you'll more than likely find snow on the mountain peaks; in summer, once you top the pass you enter a verdant valley of fruit trees and ordered vineyards.

Then head to beautiful **Boschendal**, one of the oldest and most established estates in the country.

Along R45

There are more than 40 estates to choose from here, and there's something for everyone—from enormous farms covering hundreds of acres to smaller, boutique vineyards producing just a few hundred bottles each year. If you turn right on R45 from the R310, **L'Ormarins** is one of the first wine farms you'll come to.

Just outside town, **La Motte** is a sister farm to L'Ormarins. Closer to town the estates come thick and fast. Amid this flurry—Môreson (up the aptly named Happy Valley Road), Rickety Bridge, Agusta, Chamonix, and Dieu Donne—is **Mont Rochelle**, a relatively small producer of lovely wines and home to a luxury hotel owned by Richard Branson. Outside town and up the Franschhoek Pass toward Villiersdorp, the fabulous **Haute Cabrière** has an excellent restaurant and wines to match. The final stop is **La Petite Ferme** with its unpretentious restaurant and beautiful setting.

If you turn left on the R45 from the R310, you'll find more outstanding wine farms, including **Plaisir de Merle**, which makes a distinctive Cabernet and Sauvignon Blanc.

☎ *021/300–0338* ⊕ *www.winetram.co.za* 🚋 *R270.*

Huguenot Memorial Museum

HISTORY MUSEUM | To trace the history of the Huguenot community here, visit the Huguenot Memorial Museum. Its main building is modeled after the Saasveld house, built in 1791 by renowned Cape architect Louis Thibault in Cape Town. Wall displays profile some of the early families. Exhibits also focus on other aspects of the region's history, such as the development of Cape Dutch architecture and the relationship of the Huguenots with the Dutch East India Company. Displays in the annex cover the culture and life of the Khoekhoen, or Khoikhoi, once derogatorily known as Hottentots, as well as the role of slaves and local laborers in the development of the Franschhoek Valley. Bring a picnic basket and take advantage of the lovely garden.

Be sure to visit the adjacent Huguenot Memorial. ⊠ *Lambrecht St. at Huguenot St., Franschhoek* ☎ *021/876–2532* ⊕ *www.museum.co.za* 🚋 *R100.*

Huguenot Monument

MONUMENT | At the end of the main road through Franschhoek is the Huguenot Monument, built in 1948 to commemorate the contribution of the Huguenots to South Africa's development. The three arches symbolize the Holy Trinity, the sun and cross reference the Huguenots' emblem, and the female figure in front represents Freedom of Conscience. The nearby graveyard date back 300 years. Most graves are marked with rectangular headstones or obelisks, rather than the symbol associated with the church the Huguenots were so desperate to escape. ⊠ *Lambrecht St. at Huguenot St., Franschhoek* ⊕ *www.museum.co.za.*

WINERIES

It should come as no surprise that the Franschhoek Valley produces excellent wines. After all, the original French settlers brought with them an intimate understanding of viticulture. Some of the country's oldest estates can be found at the base of the spectacular Groot Drakenstein Mountains, and the wine farmers here are constantly producing increasingly spectacular wines.

Allée Bleue

WINERY | FAMILY | Set against the dramatic Drakenstein Mountains and surrounded by vineyards and orchards, Allée Bleue is one of the oldest wine farms in the Cape. This picturesque estate is well known for its fresh and fruity white wines and well-matured, spicy reds. You can taste their award-winning wines on the tree-shaded terrace overlooking the vineyards or by an open fire in the tasting room. Bistro Allée Bleue offers breakfast and light lunches on weekend, or in summer you can buy a picnic basket filled with a selection of salads, breads, nibbles, cheeses, and desserts. There's even a kids' picnic menu, along with a jungle gym, trampoline, sand pit, and jumping castle to keep the little ones occupied. The farm also produces a range of fruit including pears, plums, and nectarines. ⊠ *Intersection of R45 and R310, Franschhoek* ☎ *021/874–1021* ⊕ *www. alleebleue.co.za* ☕ *Tastings R40.*

★ Boschendal

WINERY | With a history that dates back three centuries, this lovely estate is one of the Cape's major attractions. Recent renovations have added polish to an already top-notch estate. Cradled between the Simonsberg and Groot Drakenstein mountains at the base of Helshoogte Pass, Boschendal runs one of the most pleasant wine tastings in the region: on warm days you sit outside at wrought-iron tables under a spreading oak. In 1981, Boschendal was the first to pioneer a Blanc de Noir, a pink wine made in a white-wine style from black grapes. The Boschendal Blanc de Noir remains one of the best-selling wines of this style. The recently renovated Werf Restaurant serves excellent country-style cuisine, and picnic baskets are available to enjoy on the lawns. Hour-long vineyard tours and cellar tours are available; be sure to book ahead. You can also take a horse ride through the vines, and there's a jungle gym and hands-on farm activities for kids. ⊠ *R310 between Franschhoek and Stellenbosch, Groot Drakenstein* ☎ *021/870–4210 winery, 021/870–4274 restaurants* ⊕ *www.boschendal.co.za* ☕ *Tastings R65.*

Haute Cabrière

WINERY | Built in 1994 on the lower slopes of the Franschhoek Mountains, Haute Cabrière was the brainchild of Achim von Arnim, one of the Cape's most colorful winemakers. To avoid scarring the mountain, the complex, which includes the fine Haute Cabrière restaurant and terrace, hunkers into the hillside. Von Arnim's son, Takuan, has taken over as cellarmaster and continues to produce excellent wines. There are three Cap Classique sparkling wines under the Pierre Jordan label, and four Haute Cabrière wines. The fruity, mouth-filling unwooded Pinot Noir is consistently one of the best. Also delicious is the Chardonnay–Pinot Noir blend, an ideal, extremely quaffable wine to enjoy at lunchtime. Cellar tours depart at noon every day. ⊠ *R45 (Franschhoek Pass Rd.), Franschhoek* ☎ *021/876–8500* ⊕ *www. cabriere.co.za* ☕ *Tastings R50–R200.*

La Motte Estate

WINERY | There's a lot happening at this farm: take a guided tour of the estate's the artworks or join a hike along one of the farm's stunning trails. And then there's great wine tasting, food-and-wine pairings, and high tea; the estate's Pierneef à La Motte restaurant is regularly voted one of the country's best. The farm also has a wonderful collection of Jacob

Hendrik Pierneef's art; view his iconic landscapes in the gallery. But don't get too sidetracked—the wine is excellent as well. The Pierneef Collection is the farm's premium range, and the Shiraz Viognier blend is being snapped up for its whiffs of dark chocolate, smoked beef, black cherry, and blackberry. The estate's Sauvignon Blanc is also outstanding. ⊠ R45 (Main Rd.), Franschhoek ☎ 021/876–8000 ⊕ www.la-motte.com ⊠ Tastings R60 ⊗ Closed Mon.

La Petite Ferme

WINERY | True to its name, this is a small estate produces just enough wine for the restaurant and to keep its faithful customers happy. Try the full-bodied, barrel-fermented Chardonnay or the Merlot, which scoops up awards year after year. The Verdict, a Cape-style blend, is also a crowd-pleaser. Recommended is the Vine Orientation, a guided walk through the vineyards followed by a tasting of wine and canapes. Advance bookings are essential. ⊠ R45 (Franschhoek Pass Rd.), Franschhoek ☎ 021/876–3016 ⊕ www.lapetiteferme.co.za ⊠ Tour and tasting R200.

L'Ormarins

WINERY | Dating from 1811, the archetypal Cape Dutch manor house is festooned with flowers and framed by majestic peaks. But instead of remaining in the past, this winery has embraced the future and pumped serious money into a major revamp. L'Ormarins is the main estate and part of the Rupert empire, but there are five labels produced by their various farms dotted around the Western Cape. The farm has three state-of-the-art cellars and two tasting rooms. At the Anthonij Rupert Tasting Room, in the manor house, you can try the Cape of Good Hope and Anthonij Rupert wine ranges. High tea is served here in the afternoon (by reservation only). You can try the other ranges at the Terra Del Capo Tasting Room. There's an antipasto bar below the tasting room, where you can enjoy tasty tapas. The AR Merlot is exceptional: look out for mulberries, blackberries, and hints of fynbos along with fruitcake and cloves. The TDC Sangiovese is a brilliant, light drinking wine, and the Pinot Grigio is always a pleasure. Visit the estate's Franschhoek Motor Museum, home to more than 80 vintage cars in mint condition. ⊠ R45 (Franschhoek Rd.), Groot Drakenstein ☎ 021/874–9041 ⊕ www.lormarinswines.com ⊠ Tastings R30–R125, museum R80 ⊗ Anthonij Rupert Tasting Room closed Sun.; Terra del Capo Tasting Room and antipasto bar closed Mon.

Mont Rochelle

WINERY | This picture-pretty estate has one of the best views in the valley. Mont Rochelle, owned by Sir Richard Branson, boasts more than 90 acres of vineyard, and the wines produced here are excellent. Book ahead to visit the tasting center and sample a variety of Mont Rochelle wines—try the Mont Rochelle Syrah and the signature Miko Chardonnay. For relaxed and formal dining, the hotel has two restaurants: the Country Kitchen, which is the perfect place for a light lunch or relaxed dinner, and Miko, a contemporary gourmet restaurant where you can enjoy a cocktail at sunset or an intimate meal. ⊠ Dassenberg Rd., Franschhoek ☎ 021/876–2770 ⊕ www.montrochelle.co.za ⊠ Tastings R55.

Plaisir de Merle

WINERY | The name means "Pleasure of the Blackbird" and has its origins with the original French owners of the farm. This huge estate is the showpiece of Distell, a big wine and spirit producer. With its innovative architecture and conservation area, it truly feels different from the ubiquitous oak-and-gable wineries that you see all over the Cape. But forget the frills—it really is all about the wine. Don't miss the full-bodied, barrel-fermented Chardonnay, which spends nine months in the barrel developing its lovely rich and layered flavor. The farm's flagship wine is the Grand Plaisir, a complex red blend. When tasting, look out for flavors of ripe plums, oak with hints of tobacco, vanilla, and cedar. There is also a range of pairing experiences on offer, including wine with nougat, fudge, or savory snacks. ✉ *R45, Simondium* ☎ *021/488–9977* 🌐 *www.plaisirdemerle.co.za* 🎫 *Tastings R65 ,cellar tour R130.*

🍴 Restaurants

Epice
$$$$ | ECLECTIC | Headed by former La Colombe chef Charné Sampson, Epice is inspired by a culinary adventure through India. The menu—a 10-course tasting feast—features spices from the subcontinent married with dishes from around the world, such as cumin-infused Welsh rarebit and chili-ginger Wagyu shortrib served with roti. **Known for:** Indian-fusion food; beautifully presented dishes; unpretentious setting. [$] *Average main: R1295* ✉ *Le Quartier Français, Berg and Wilhelmina Sts, Franschhoek* ☎ *021/492–4044* 🌐 *www.epice.restaurant/food* 🕓 *Closed Mon. No lunch Tues.–Thurs.*

Haute Cabrière
$$$$ | ECLECTIC | Try to reserve a window table for views across the vine-clad valley at this restaurant atop a working winery built into the mountainside. The three-course menu is distinctly South African but rooted in French techniques, with dishes like venison loin with Cape Malay jus. **Known for:** smart wine pairings; two- and three-course menus; delicious steak tartare. [$] *Average main: R350* ✉ *Lambrechts Rd., Franschhoek* ☎ *021/876–8500* 🌐 *www.cabriere.co.za* 🕓 *Closed Tues. and Wed.*

★ **La Petite Colombe**
$$$$ | ECLECTIC | Sister restaurant to Cape Town's fêted La Colombe, the food, ambiance, wine selection and service at La Petite Colombe are simply impeccable. The decor is sleek and understated because the true work of art is the food—an 11-course banquet showcasing French cooking techniques and the finest ingredients. **Known for:** vegetarians are well taken care of; elaborate tasting menu; excellent wine list. [$] *Average main: R1595* ✉ *Leeu Estates, Dassenberg Rd, Franschhoek* ☎ *021/202–3395* 🌐 *www.lapetitecolombe.restaurant/food.*

Miko
$$$$ | INTERNATIONAL | Miko is a contemporary fine-dining restaurant with seating indoors and out, both offering spectacular views of the Franschhoek Valley. Many dishes have an Indian influence, such as the pork belly with biryani rice and cauliflower masala purée. **Known for:** inventive desserts; quirky decor; seasonal produce. [$] *Average main: R225* ✉ *Dassenberg Rd., Franschhoek* ☎ *011/876-2770* 🌐 *www.montrochelle.co.za.*

Ou Meul Bakkery
$ | BAKERY | This rustic bakery is best known for its savory pies, but you can also get tasty salads and sandwiches to enjoy in the shady garden. There are now seven locations, with the original in Riviersonderend. **Known for:** savory meat pies; breakfast is a favorite with locals; best coffee in the area. [$] *Average main: R95* ✉ *Tonis Fontyn Farm, R45 (Franschhoek Rd.), Groot Drakenstein Handelshuis, Simondium* ☎ *021/874–1079* 🌐 *www.oumeul.co.za.*

The Restaurant at Grande Provence
$$$$ | ECLECTIC | The chic and industrial decor here is a bold contrast to the old-world charm of Huguenot architecture: high-backed leather chairs, wine-bottle chandeliers, and steel doors that open onto a sculpture garden. The menu is fairly compact and yet impressively varied, featuring venison, beef, seafood, and Franschhoek trout, along with a couple of vegetarian options. **Known for:** striking decor; exceptional service; elaborately creative meals. [$] *Average main: R225* ✉ *Grande Provence Estate, off R45, Franschhoek* ☎ *021/876–8600* 🌐 *www.grandeprovence.co.za* 🕓 *No dinner Sun.–Thurs.*

Reuben's

$$$$ | **ECLECTIC** | Best known as a judge on the local edition of *MasterChef*, Reuben Riffel's flagship restaurant in his hometown of Franschhoek is a wonderful blend of fine dining techniques and unpretentious surroundings. Dishes marry local ingredients with French techniques, and in many cases they have a sprinkling of Asian influence. **Known for:** globally inspired fare; owned by one of the region's top chefs; favorite destination of locals. [$] *Average main: R255* ✉ *2 Daniel Hugo St., Franschhoek* ☎ *021/876–3772* 🌐 *www.reubens.co.za.*

The Werf Restaurant

$$$$ | **SOUTH AFRICAN** | Set in the manor house of one of the country's oldest vineyards, The Werf does an excellent job at serving refined farm-to-table meals. Try to book a table in the conservatory that overlooks the lush vegetable garden. **Known for:** friendly service; al fresco dining option; farm-sourced ingredients. [$] *Average main: R260* ✉ *Boschendal, R310 (Pniel Rd.), Groot Drakenstein, Franschhoek* ☎ *021/870–4274* 🌐 *www.boschendal.com.*

Hotels

★ **Akademie Street Boutique Hotel**

$$$$ | **B&B/INN** | With eight individually designed suites hidden on a leafy street in Franschhoek, this peaceful and modern 19th-century Cape Dutch house is one of the area's best-kept secrets. **Pros:** rooms are unique and beautifully designed; complimentary cake and coffee in the afternoon; friendly staff. **Cons:** decor is a little chintzy; you'll need deep pockets for the suites; you have to book far in advance. [$] *Rooms from: R9500* ✉ *5 Akademie St.* ☎ *082/300–0940* 🌐 *www.aka.co.za* 🛏 *8 rooms* 🍴 *Free Breakfast.*

Le Ballon Rouge

$$ | **B&B/INN** | If you fancy being in the heart of the village, Le Ballon Rouge makes a good base because you're just a five-minute walk from galleries, restaurants, and the general buzz. **Pros:** airport shuttles available; private wine tours and safaris are on offer; personal and attentive service. **Cons:** no children under 12; pricey for solo travelers; the handful of rooms can book up quickly. [$] *Rooms from: R1700* ✉ *7 Reservoir St., Franschhoek* ☎ *021/876–3743* 🌐 *www.leballonrouge.co.za* 🛏 *10 rooms* 🍴 *Free Breakfast.*

★ **Le Quartier Français**

$$$$ | **HOTEL** | Part of the Leeu Collection—which seems to own half the town these days—this classy guesthouse exuding privacy and peace is a Winelands favorite. **Pros:** right in the center of town; focus on comfort; utmost privacy and tranquility. **Cons:** rates can be pricey; spa is a short drive away; hard to snag reservation for restaurants. [$] *Rooms from: R8800* ✉ *Berg and Wilhelmina Sts., Franschhoek* ☎ *021/492–2222* 🌐 *leeucollection.com/SA/le-quartier-francais* 🛏 *13 rooms, 8 suites* 🍴 *Free Breakfast.*

Leeu Estates

$$$$ | **B&B/INN** | The stunning flagship property of the Leeu Collection (which also includes Leeu House), this luxurious and sprawling retreat has stunning views of the mountains and vineyards. **Pros:** excellent restaurant; lovely views of the Franschhoek Valley; glistening swimming pool. **Cons:** not in the center of town; rooms are a little expensive; service can be slow. [$] *Rooms from: R9900* ✉ *Dassenberg Rd., Franschhoek* ☎ *021/492–2222* 🌐 *www.leeucollection.com/leeu-estates* 🛏 *17 rooms* 🍴 *Free Breakfast.*

Leeu House

$$$$ | **B&B/INN** | Although this contemporary guesthouse is located on the main street in the middle of town, it's so tranquil, you'd think it was in the countryside. **Pros:** easy walk to shops and restaurants; intimate setting; rooms are beautifully designed. **Cons:** only a few inexpensive rooms; on-site restaurant isn't as good as others in town; spa and gym are a short drive away. [$] *Rooms from: R8500* ✉ *12 Huguenot Rd.* ☎ *021/492–2221* 🌐 *www.leeucollection.com/leeu-house* 🛏 *12 rooms* 🍴 *Free Breakfast.*

The Owner's Cottage

$$$$ | **B&B/INN** | You know you're in good company at the understated and elegant Owner's Cottage on Grande Provence Wine Estate when the visitors' book includes Jude Law and British royals Sophie and Prince Edward. **Pros:** lovely pool area; you'll be made to feel right at home; close to the action in Franschhoek. **Cons:** so many on-site amenities you may never leave; some people don't like the smell of thatch; unless you rent the whole house, you'll have to share it with other guests. [$] *Rooms from: R6300* ✉ *Grand Provence, off R45, Franschhoek* ☎ *021/876–8600* 🌐 *www.grandeprovence.co.za* 🛏 *6 rooms* 🍴 *Free Breakfast.*

Paarl

30 km (18 miles) northwest of Franschhoek.

Paarl takes its name from the granite domes of Paarl Mountain, which looms above the town—*paarl* is Dutch for "pearl." The first farmers settled here in 1687, two years after the founding of Stellenbosch. The town has its fair share of historic homes and estates, but it lacks the charm of its distinguished neighbors. Main Street, the town's oak-lined thoroughfare, extends some 11 km (7 miles) along the western bank of the Berg River. You can gain a good sense of the town's history on a drive along this lovely street.

GETTING HERE AND AROUND

As in the rest of the area, driving yourself is your best option in and around Paarl. To really get the best out of the area you do need your own wheels.

VISITOR INFORMATION

CONTACTS Paarl Taxis & Tours. ✉ *111 Loop St., Paarl* ☎ *021/872–5671.* **Paarl Visitor Information Center.** ✉ *216 Main St., Paarl* ☎ *021/872–4842* 🌐 *www.paarl-wellington.co.za.*

Sights

Most visitors to Paarl drive down the town's main street, take in the historic buildings, and then head off to the Cape Winelands, golf estates, and restaurants. If you have the time, check out the Afrikaanse Taalmonument (Afrikaans Language Monument) and Jan Phillips Mountain Drive. For some excellent examples of Cape Dutch, Georgian, and Victorian homes, head to Zeederberg Square, a grassy park on Main Street just past the Paarl Tourism Bureau.

Afrikaanse Taalmonument

(*Afrikaans Language Monument*)

MONUMENT | Set high on a hill overlooking Paarl, the towering Afrikaanse Taalmonument is a fascinating step back into the past. It was designed by architect Jan van Wijk and built with Paarl granite and cement. The rising curve of the main pillar represents the growth and potential of Afrikaans. When it was unveiled in 1975, the monument was as much a gesture of political victory as it was a paean to the Afrikaans language. Ironically, the monument—although built during apartheid—gives recognition to all the diverse origins of Afrikaans (from Africa, Europe, and Asia). Afrikaans is one of South Africa's 11 official languages and although it is gradually coming under threat, attempts are being made to ensure that the rich culture isn't lost. The view from the top of the hill is incredible, taking in Table Mountain, False Bay, Paarl Valley, and the various mountain ranges of the Winelands. A short, paved walking trail leads around the hillside past impressive fynbos specimens, particularly proteas. ■TIP→ **You can buy a picnic basket at the monument's restaurant and find a pretty spot to enjoy the wonderful view.** ⊠ *Afrikaanse Taalmonument Rd., Paarl* ☎ *021/863–0543* ⊕ *www.taalmuseum.co.za* ☎ *R40.*

Bain's Kloof Pass Road

SCENIC DRIVE | Built by engineer Andrew Geddes Bain and opened in 1853, Bain's Kloof Pass Road links Wellington to Ceres and Worcester. The road, an extension of the R303, winds north from Wellington and through the Hawekwa Mountains, revealing breathtaking views across the valley below. On a clear day you can see as far as the coast. The road has a good tar surface, but unlike many Western Cape passes, Bain's Kloof has not been widened much since it was built, so take your time and enjoy the views. There are places where you can park and walk down to lovely, refreshing mountain pools—great on a hot summer's day. ⊠ *Bain's Kloof Pass Rd., Paarl.*

Jan Phillips Mountain Drive

SCENIC DRIVE | Halfway down the hill from the Afrikaans Language Monument is a turnoff onto a dirt road and a sign for the Paarl Mountain Nature Reserve. The dirt road is Jan Phillips Mountain Drive, which runs 11 km (7 miles) along the mountainside, offering tremendous views over the valley. Along the way it passes the **Mill Water Wildflower Garden** and the starting points for several trails, including hikes up to the great granite domes of Paarl Mountain. The dirt road rejoins Main Street at the far end of Paarl. ⊠ *Paarl.*

Paarl Museum

OTHER MUSEUM | Coming from the north, Main Road doglegs to the right at Lady Grey Street before continuing its way south. On your left, the Paarl Museum, formerly the Oude Pastorie, occupies

a fine Cape Dutch home built as a parsonage in 1787. The building itself is of more interest than the collection, which includes odds and ends such as silver, glass, and kitchen utensils donated by local families. ⊠ *303 Main St., Paarl* ☎ *021/872–2651* ☎ *R10* ۞ *Closed Sun.*

Simondium Guild

BREWERY | FAMILY | Based in a converted old wine cellar, this complex between Franschhoek and Paarl can occupy a whole family for the afternoon. There's an award-winning craft brewery here, specializing in unique, barrel-aged beers, some fermented with yeast harvested from surrounding fynbos. It's also home to the tasting room of Painted Wolf Wines, best known for their spicy Shiraz, and Stillman Distillery, who make great gin. For kids and artsy types, you can design and paint a glass bowl at Fanglasstic, or just shop for some of their beautifully etched glassware. Papi's Eatery provides sustenance after all the beer, wine, and gin, with hearty burgers, smoked meats, and excellent milkshakes. ⊠ *R45, Paarl* ✢ *1 km north of the Klapmuts Rd. turnoff* ⊕ *www.facebook. com/Simondiumguild.*

WINERIES

Avondale Wine

WINERY | Although the farm was established as early as 1693, current owners Johnny and Ginny Grieve have done some serious reorganizing in the vineyards and built a state-of-the-art cellar that's dug into a dry riverbed. Avondale started producing wines in 1999, making it one of the newer kids on the block. The winery hit the ground running, and its wines win one award after another. The reds are especially good, and the intense Paarl summers result in full-bodied grapes that deliver knockout flavors. Great care is taken to maintain top-quality soil, and no pesticides or herbicides are used. If you're interested in the wine-making process, book an Eco Wine Safari and visit Avondale's state-of-the-art

Paarl Wine Route

Wineries here are spread far apart, so plan carefully to make the most of your time. Start in Paarl, home to the impressive **KWV**, with cellars covering 55 acres and a wide selection of wines as well as brandy.

Along R301/303

On its way to Franschhoek, the R301/303 runs past **Avondale Wine**, a relatively new farm with a state-of-the-art cellar, a gorgeous rose garden, and excellent wines.

Between R44 and R45

On your way from Franschhoek to Paarl, take a detour down the Simondium Road to the wonderful **Babylonstoren**, where you could easily spend a morning. Continue on to **Glen Carlou** for wine tasting or lunch. As you reach the end of the Simondium Road, turn right onto the R44 then right again

onto the R101. Cross over the N1 and follow the goat signs to Suid-Agter-Paarl Road and Fairview.

Along Suid-Agter-Paarl and Noord-Agter-Paarl Roads

Fairview is as famous for its goats and cheese as it is for its wines. Leave yourself plenty of time here and at the neighboring farm, **Spice Route**, with its veritable village of artisans. From Spice Route, turn right onto the Suid-Agter-Paarl Road and make your way to **Landskroon**, known for full-bodied reds. Turn right on the R44 and, after about 10 km (6 miles), right onto the WR8 (Noord-Agter-Paarl Road), and then right again to **Rhebokskloof Private Cellar.** If you continue on the R44 toward Wellington, you'll pass Nelson Wine Estate (aka Nelson's Creek) on your left.

gravity-flow cellar, constructed three stories underground. There are also gentle hikes and a bike track, or if you're looking for something less energetic, book a table at the fabulous Faber restaurant. ✉ Lustigan Rd., off R301, Paarl ☎ 021/863–1976 ⊕ www.avondalewine. co.za ⌖ Tastings R75.

Diemersfontein Winery

WINERY | Diemersfontein is best-known for originating what has become one of the most successful styles South Africa has yet created: coffee Pinotage. Pinotage, a South African grape that is a cross between Pinot Noir and Hermitage, can be bitter and is sometimes described as rubbery. Through careful yeast selection and the addition of toasted oak staves during aging, Diemersfontein's Bertus Fourie brought out prominent coffee and chocolate notes in the wine, creating a new and hugely popular style. The

estate's other brand, Thokozani, is a Black empowerment project, partly owned by the winery staff. ✉ R301 (Jan van Riebeck Dr.), Wellington ☎ 021/864–5050 ⊕ www.diemersfontein.co.za ⌖ Tastings R40.

Fairview

WINERY | **FAMILY** | A visit to Fairview is a treat for the whole family, including kids and adults who aren't fans of wine. Children get a kick out of seeing peacocks roaming the grounds and goats clambering up a spiral staircase into a goat tower. And those goats aren't just for decoration—Fairview produces a superb line of goat cheeses and olive oil, all of which you can sample. Visit the Vineyard Cheesery, the first carbon-neutral cheesery on the African continent, and taste the Roydon Camembert. But don't let Fairview's sideshows color your judgment about the wines. The estate's wines are top-drawer and often surprising. The Fairview Eenzaamheid Shiraz is excellent, as is the La Beryl Blanc. The winery also makes creative use of the farm's many Rhône varieties. Perhaps it's just because the pun was irresistible, but (as claimed by the label) goats are sent into the vineyard to personally select grapes for the Goats-do-Roam, which is indeed like a young Côtes du Rhône (infuriating French winemakers). If you care to linger, you can have a light meal and freshly baked bread at the Goatshed Restaurant. ⊠ WR3, off R101 (Suid-Agter-Paarl Rd.), Paarl ☎ 021/863–2450 ⊕ www.fairview.co.za ⊠ Cheese tastings R25, wine and cheese tastings R50.

Glen Carlou

WINERY | What comes out of Glen Carlou is rather special. The Quartz Stone Chardonnay is exceptional, and the Gravel Quarry Cabernet is also remarkable. A unique feature of the estate is the Zen Fynbos Garden, a great place to relax after you've stocked up on some seriously good wines. You can also enjoy a superb lunch at the restaurant. The menu changes seasonally, but you can look forward to dishes like whipped goat cheese with truffle honey, and lamb shoulder with summer peas and red wine jus. There's also a children's menu. ⊠ WR1 (Simondium Rd.), Klapmuts ✛ Between R44 and R45 ☎ 021/875–5528 ⊕ www.glencarlou.co.za ⊠ Tastings R50.

KWV Emporium

WINERY | Short for Ko-operatieve Wijnbouwers Vereniging (Cooperative Winegrowers' Association), KWV regulated and controlled the local wine industry for decades. This is no longer the case, and KWV is seeking to redefine itself as a top wine and spirit producer. KWV produces an enormous selection of excellent wines, and its cellars are some of the largest in the world, covering around 55 acres. Cellar tours here are very popular; among the highlights is the famous Cathedral Cellar, with a barrel-vaulted ceiling and giant vats carved with scenes from wine-making history. The tour ends with a tasting of two white wines, two red wines, a fortified wine, and a brandy. There is a range of fun pairing experiences on offer too, including bubbly and cheesecake, brandy and chocolate, or wine with savory pies. As well as award-winning wines, KWV produces some of the finest spirits, with the KWV 12-year-old regularly raking in the accolades. ⊠ André du Toit Bldg., Kohler St., Paarl ☎ 021/807–3007 ⊕ www.kwvemporium.co.za ⊠ Tastings R65–R110.

Landskroon

WINERY | With a name meaning "crown of the land" in Afrikaans, this venerable estate, run by the ninth generation of the de Villiers family, produces a Cabernet Sauvignon—with hints of spice and oak—that's up there with the best. Look out for the Paul de Villiers Wine Range. For a little something to sip after a long, leisurely dinner, try the Cape Vintage Port—a dark, fortified wine with aromas of black prunes and tobacco. As well as tastings, there are food and wine pairing options. Bring a picnic to enjoy in the grounds. ⊠ Suid-Agter-Paarl Rd., Suider Paarl ☎ 021/863–1039 ⊕ www.landskroonwines.com ⊠ Tastings R35 ☾ Closed Sun.

Rhebokskloof Private Cellar

WINERY | FAMILY | This winery sits at the head of a shallow valley, backed by hillsides covered with vines and fynbos. It's a lovely place for lunch on a sunny day, and you can explore the estate and beyond on a series of walking, biking, or horseback trails. The restaurant serves à la carte meals and teas on an oak-shaded terrace overlooking the gardens and mountains. There's also a pizzeria, or you can order a picnic basket for two brimming with fresh baguettes, cold meats, salads, delicious cheeses, and a bottle of wine (must be booked in advance). The estate makes an excellent Shiraz, thanks to its unique terroir, which is composed of old decomposed granite soils. Other wines to look out for are the Pinotage, Chardonnay, and Chenin Blanc. ⊠ *WR8, Paarl* ☎ *021/869–8386* ⊕ *www.rheboksk-loof.co.za* ⊜ *Tastings R50.*

★ Spice Route Winery

WINERY | FAMILY | Charles Back, the owner of Fairview, also owns the neighboring farm in Paarl. Spice Route produces deep-flavored wines, using mostly untrellised "bush" vines. This practice, which is uncommon outside of South Africa, leads to fruit with great flavor intensity but lower volumes. Try the Spice Route Chakalaka, a signature Swartland blend, which has clove and savory notes. There is good reason to spend an entire day on the estate: artisan shops include Barley & Biltong Emporium; De Villiers Chocolate, where you can join a tutored chocolate pairing; and the Cape Brewing Company, which offers craft beer tasting. At the Grapperia, you can taste grappa and schnapps made on-site and nibble on pizza and charcuterie. There's ice cream for the kids, plus lovely lawns and two jungle gyms. ⊠ *Suider-Agter-Paarl Rd., Paarl* ☎ *021/863–5200* ⊕ *www.spicer-oute.co.za* ⊜ *Tastings R75.*

Wellington Wines

WINERY | FAMILY | Driving down Bain's Kloof Road, keep an eye out for the tasting room of Wellington Wines on the right. Constructed in 1907 in traditional style, the building itself is not notewor-thy, but it has a vast picture window offering a stupendous view of the undu-lating vineyards beyond. Be sure to try the Centennial Range Shiraz-Mourvèdre blend, which promises great things. With plenty of well-priced, good-quality wines to choose from, you likely won't go away empty-handed. Unusual tasting options include a wine and doughnut pairing and a juice tasting option for the little ones. ⊠ *Bain's Kloof Rd., Welling-ton* ☎ *021/873–1582* ⊕ *www.welling-tonwines.com* ⊜ *Tastings from R55* ⊗ *Closed Sun.*

⊕ Restaurants

★ Babel

$$$$ | ECLECTIC | Set on the grounds of one of the Cape's oldest farms, Babel is a vision in white surrounded by lush fruit and vegetable gardens and a gorgeous backdrop of mountains. Everything about this farm is stylish: the restaurant is in a converted cow shed, and the menu includes inventive dishes influenced by whatever is bountiful in the garden that day. **Known for:** spectacular farm setting; bold flavors and unusual combinations; lots of choices for vegetarians. $ *Aver-age main: R295* ⊠ *Klapmuts Rd., Paarl* ☎ *021/863–3852* ⊕ *www.babylonstoren. com* ⊗ *No lunch Mon. and Tues.*

★ Faber

$$$$ | ECLECTIC | As is the case for Avon-dale, the vineyard where the restaurant is based, Faber places a heavy focus on being sustainable. The menu changes often but always features carefully composed dishes using ethically sourced meat and fish, plus herbs and vegeta-bles harvested from the estate garden. **Known for:** excellent selection of wines; children's menu available; unpreten-tious fine dining. $ *Average main: R220* ⊠ *Avondale Estate, Lustigan Road, Paarl* ☎ *021/202–1219* ⊕ *www.avondalewine. co.za/faber* ⊗ *Closed Mon. and Tues. No dinner Wed. and Sun.*

Noop

$$$$ | ECLECTIC | This long-running place is a local favorite, managing to serve delicious and delightfully plated food while remaining totally unpretentious. The menu is small and eclectic, featuring some Asian-inspired dishes, classics like steak and fries, or pan-fried catch of the day. **Known for:** extensive wine list; in a charming older building with towering windows; guests get a warm welcome. $ *Average main: R240* ⊠ *127 Main Rd, Paarl* ☎ *021/863–3925* ⊕ *www.noop. co.za* ⊗ *Closed Sun.*

★ **Restaurant at Grande Roche Hotel**

$$$$ | ECLECTIC | This restaurant here has big shoes to fill because its predecessor, Bosman's, was highly regarded. Luckily, Chef Kevin Grobler and his team will have no problem continuing to wow guests. **Known for:** award-winning wine list; extraordinary service; decadent tasting menu. $ *Average main: R255* ⊠ *Grande Roche Hotel, Plantasie St., Paarl* ☎ *021/863–5100* ⊕ *www.granderoche.com.*

★ **The Table at De Meye**

$$$$ | SOUTH AFRICAN | Set on the De Meye Wine Estate, between Stellenbosch and Paarl, The Table is run by a husband-and-wife team tirelessly churning out hearty, family-style dishes with what's available from local producers that day. Delicious meals—think slow-cooked grass-fed beef flat rib, garden kale salad, and wood-fired sourdough loaf—are served family-style. **Known for:** children are welcome; three-course menu changes often; outdoor dining in summer. $ *Average main: R450* ⊠ *Old Paarl Rd., Muldersvlei, Stellenbosch* ☎ *072/696–0530* ⊕ *www. thetablerestaurant.co.za* ☽ *No dinner. Closed Mon.*

🛏 Hotels

★ **Babylonstoren**

$$$$ | HOTEL | Set on a 500-acre working farm that is among the oldest on the Cape, Babylonstoren is a bucolic lodging with a dozen lovingly renovated thatched roof-cottages gazing up at the dramatic Drakenstein Mountains. **Pros:** canoes and bicycles for exploring; pick your own produce for the chef to prepare; soothing treatments at the spa. **Cons:** lots of day visitors; some rooms can be pricey; families with young children can't stay in the Farmhouse. $ *Rooms from: R8700* ⊠ *45 Klapmuts Rd., Klapmuts* ☎ *021/863–3852* ⊕ *www.babylonstoren.com* ☞ *22 rooms* ⦿*Free Breakfast.*

★ **Bartholomeus Klip Farmhouse**

$$$$ | B&B/INN | This Victorian guesthouse offers luxurious accommodations and excellent food in the middle of 17,000 acres of rare renosterveld scrubland, home to the endangered geometric tortoise. **Pros:** good wildlife sightings; once you arrive there's no need to leave; very tranquil setting close to vineyards. **Cons:** area can get unbearably hot in summer; no children allowed in the main house; accommodations may be a bit intimate for some. $ *Rooms from: R10,400* ⊠ *Off the R44, near Bo-Hermon, Paarl* ☎ *022/448–1087* ⊕ *www.bartholomeusklip.co.za* ☞ *5 rooms, 1 self-catering house (sleeps 8)* ⦿*Free Breakfast.*

De Leeuwenhof Estate

$ | B&B/INN | This restored Cape Dutch homestead, built in 1698 and situated on 30 acres of farmland, has rustic decor and spacious rooms with all the creature comforts. **Pros:** great for animal lovers; exceptional service with a personal touch; can get deeper insight into wine-making. **Cons:** children over 2 are charged as adults; no dinner available in winter months; television reception is poor in some rooms. $ *Rooms from: R1450* ⊠ *Sonstraal Rd., Paarl* ☎ *021/862–1384* ⊕ *www.deleeuwenhof.co.za* ☞ *16 rooms* ⦿*Free Breakfast.*

Diemersfontein Country Estate

$$ | B&B/INN | The rooms and cottages at this 19th-century farmstead are comfortably furnished and decorated in a relaxed country style with floral throws and fresh flowers. **Pros:** airport shuttle; very peaceful setting; lovely gardens. **Cons:** room decor is a little chintzy; Wi-Fi can be patchy; frequently used as a wedding venue. $ *Rooms from: R1850* ⊠ *Jan van Riebeek Dr. (R301), Wellington* ☎ *021/864–5050* ⊕ *www.diemersfontein. co.za* ☞ *30 rooms* ⦿*Free Breakfast.*

★ Grande Roche

$$$$ | HOTEL | In a gorgeous Cape Dutch manor house that dates from the mid-18th century, the hotel sits amid acres of vines beneath Paarl Rock, overlooking the Drakenstein Mountains. **Pros:** in-room spa treatments; estate was named a national monument; unrivaled service. **Cons:** rarefied atmosphere doesn't suit everybody; gets busy with wedding parties; a long walk to the town's museums. $ Rooms from: R5300 ⊠ 1 Plantasie Str., Paarl ☎ 021/863–5100 ⊕ www.granderoche.com ⇌ 28 suites ⦿ Free Breakfast.

Lemoenkloof Guest House

$ | B&B/INN | This classic guesthouse on the Paarl Wine Route is tastefully decorated in a comfortable and homey style—crisp white linens, wood-frame mirrors, and ornate lampshades highlight each of the guest rooms. **Pros:** 10-minute drive from golf courses; warm and friendly service; reasonable rates and weekend specials. **Cons:** no room service; room sizes vary a lot; can get booked up with conferences. $ Rooms from: R1500 ⊠ 396A Main St., Paarl ☎ 021/872–3782 ⊕ www.lemoenkloof.co.za ⇌ 31 rooms ⦿ Free Breakfast.

 ## Activities

BALLOONING
Wineland Ballooning

BALLOONING | This company makes one-hour hot air balloon flights over the Winelands every morning from about the end of November through April. After the flight there's a Champagne breakfast at the Grand Roche. ⊠ Paarl ☎ 021/863–3192, 083/983–4687 ⊕ www.kapinfo.com ☞ R3,900 per person.

GOLF
Boschenmeer Golf Club

GOLF | This picturesque 18-hole golf course has lovely mountain views. The course is covered with graceful trees and dotted with water hazards. There's a pro shop, driving range, and terrace that looks out over the course. ⊠ 848 Wemmershoek Rd., Paarl ☎ 021/863–1140 ⊕ www.boschenmeergolf.co.za ☞ R695 ⚑ 18 holes, 6368 yards, par 72 ☞ Facilities: driving range, putting green, pitching area, golf carts, caddies, rental clubs, golf academy/lessons, restaurant, bar.

Pearl Valley Signature Golf Estate & Spa

GOLF | In a breathtaking setting in the valley, the course, designed by Jack Nicklaus, has golfers in rapture. There's also a hotel and spa on the premises. ⊠ R301, Paarl ☎ 021/867–8000 ⊕ pearlvalley.co.za ☞ R1970 ⚑ 18 holes, 6654 yards, par 72 ☞ Facilities: driving range, putting green, golf carts, rental clubs, golf academy/lessons, restaurant, bar.

HORSEBACK RIDING
Wine Valley Adventures

HORSEBACK RIDING | Beginners can join an hour-long horseback ride around the Rhebokskloof Wine Estate vineyards while more experienced equestrians can venture into the surrounding Paarl Mountain Nature Reserve. If horses aren't your thing, you can have fun on an all-terrain vehicle. ⊠ Rhebokskloof Wine Estate, WR8, off the R44, Paarl ☎ 083/226–8735 ⊕ www.horsetrails-sa.co.za ☞ R575 per hour.

Tulbagh

60 km (37 miles) north of Paarl.

Founded in 1743, the town of Tulbagh is nestled in a secluded valley bound by the Witzenberg and Groot Winterhoek mountains. A devastating earthquake in September 1969 shook the city and destroyed many of the original facades of the historic town. After this disaster, well-known South African architect Gawie Fagan—together with his wife, Gwen—helped rebuild the community in the style of an 1860s hamlet, and the result is a photographer's paradise. The 32 buildings that make up Church Street were all declared national monuments

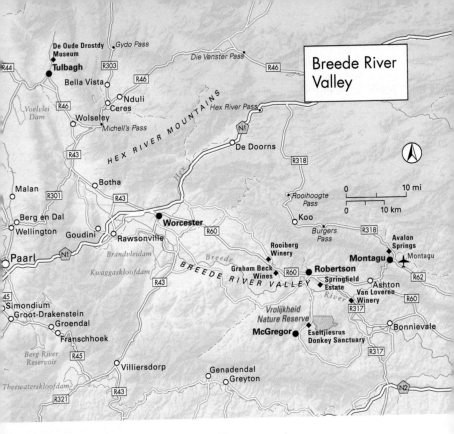

and constitute the largest concentration of national monuments in one street in South Africa. The rest of the town is quite dreary, however.

GETTING HERE AND AROUND

You won't be able to experience the beauty of this area unless you can explore on your own terms, so be sure to rent a car. If you want to travel on the back routes, do some asking around first—you might need a 4x4 in winter after heavy rains, when the gravel roads become very slippery.

VISITOR INFORMATION

CONTACTS Tulbagh Tourism. ⊠ *4 Church St., Tulbagh* ☎ *023/230–1348* ⊕ *www. tulbaghtourism.co.za.*

● Sights

Church Street

HISTORIC DISTRICT | Much of the town is not much to look at, but the real attraction of Tulbagh is Church Street, parallel to the main Van der Stel Street, where each of the 32 buildings is restored to its original form and subsequently declared a national monument. ⊠ *Tulbagh.*

De Oude Drostdy Museum

OTHER MUSEUM | About 4 km (2½ miles) out of town, set on high ground commensurate with its status, is the majestic De Oude Drostdy Museum. Built by architect Louis Thibault in 1804, the structure was badly damaged by fire in 1934 and later by the 1969 earthquake, but it has been carefully restored and is a fine example of neoclassical architecture. The building now houses an impressive collection of antique furniture and artifacts. Look for the gramophone collection and the Dutch grandfather clock that has a painting of Amsterdam harbor painted on its face. There's a small coffee shop inside where you can grab a quick bite. ⊠ *Winterhoek Rd., Tulbagh* ☎ *023/230–0203* ⊠ *Free* ⊗ *Closed Sun.*

Oude Kerk (*Old Church*)

HISTORY MUSEUM | This museum stands at the entrance to Church Street and is the logical departure point for a self-guided tour of the area. The church has been extensively restored and has an interesting collection of artifacts from the area, including carvings made by Boer prisoners of war. A ticket includes admission to two other buildings on Church Street, which operate as annexes of the main museum. These show a practical history of events before, during, and after the quake. The buildings have been painstakingly reconstructed. ⊠ *21 Church St., Tulbagh* ☎ *023/230–1041* ⊠ *R30.*

WINERIES

Twee Jonge Gezellen

WINERY | The House of Krone at Twee Jonge Gezellen specializes in the production of sparkling wine. One of the finest and oldest wineries in the area, it's known for its fantastic Cap Classiques, particularly Krone Borealis Vintage Cuvée Brut. As well as the standard tasting, you can opt for a fascinating vertical tasting of vintage bubblies from 2015 to 2018. ⊠ *Twee Jonge Gezellen Rd., Tulbagh* ☎ *023/230–0680* ⊕ *www.kronecapclassique.co.za* ⊠ *Tastings from R50* ⊗ *Closed Sun.*

 Restaurants

Olive Terrace Bistro & Lounge Bar

$$ | SOUTH AFRICAN | At the Tulbagh Hotel, the Olive Terrace Bistro serves local wines and tasty food on a pretty terrace shaded by white karee tree on summer days. In winter there's a cozy indoor dining area with a roaring fire and a view of the snow-covered mountains. **Known for:** cozy atmosphere; al fresco dining in warm weather; hearty breakfasts. $ *Average main: R125* ⊠ *Tulbagh Hotel, 22 Van der Stel St., Tulbagh* ☎ *023/230–0071* ⊕ *tulbaghhotel.co.za/dining.*

Readers

$$ | ECLECTIC | This cozy eatery's small, seasonal menu changes daily and features innovative fare and simple presentations. If the delicious wildebeest with gooseberry and Amarula sauce is on the menu, do not miss out. **Known for:** South African specialties; delicious game meat; eclectic decor. $ *Average main: R130* ⊠ *12 Church St., Tulbagh* ☎ *023/230–0087, 082/894–0932* ⊕ *www.readersrestaurant.co.za* ⊗ *Closed Tues. and Aug.*

 Hotels

Cape Dutch Quarters

$ | B&B/INN | The rooms here are in various centuries-old houses dotted about historic Church Street. **Pros:** pretty swimming pool; in the heart of Tulbagh; stunning manor house. **Cons:** pool shared among multiple properties; some properties are a short walk from breakfast area; lots of traffic in the main guesthouse. $ *Rooms from: R1200* ⊠ *33 Van Der Stel St., Tulbagh* ☎ *079023/051–2059* ⊕ *www.cdq.co.za* ⊠ *10 rooms* ⊗ *Free Breakfast.*

Rijk's Country House

$$ | B&B/INN | On the outskirts of the village, this rural abode sits on a ridge overlooking a dam where you can enjoy sweeping views of the surrounding mountains. **Pros:** fine dining on your doorstep; tranquil location; great bird-watching. **Cons:** no fences, so you have to keep an eye on kids; not many nearby dining options; quite far from bigger towns. $ *Rooms from: R1650* ⊠ *Van Der Stel Extension, Winterhoek Rd., Tulbagh* ☎ *023/230–1622* ⊕ *www.rijks.co.za* ⊠ *12 rooms* ⊗ *Free Breakfast.*

Worcester

45 km (28 miles) southeast of Tulbagh; 50 km (31 miles) east of Paarl.

You're unlikely to linger in Worcester, by far the largest town in the Breede River valley. Much of the town's burgeoning commerce and industry is connected to agriculture—viticulture, in particular. But the town serves as a pit stop for prettier inland destinations. Pause to visit the Karoo Desert National Botanical Garden or if you're traveling with kids, pop in at the Worcester Museum.

GETTING HERE AND AROUND

Worcester is east of Paarl on the N1, a 90-minute drive from Cape Town. You can get here by bus, but renting a car is preferable since Worcester is more of a stop-gap than a destination.

VISITOR INFORMATION

CONTACTS Worcester Tourism Association.
✉ *Mountain Mill Mall, 13 Mountain Mill Dr., Worcester* ☎ *023/342–6244* ⊕ *www. worcestertourism.com.*

 Sights

Karoo Desert National Botanical Garden

GARDEN | With several hundred species of indigenous flora, including succulents, bulbs, aloes, and trees, the Karoo Desert National Botanical Garden has been billed as one of the most important such collections in the world. If you phone ahead, you can arrange a guided tour through the gardens and the collection houses for around R60 per person. The garden lies on the opposite side of the N1 highway from the town of Worcester, but is easy to find if you follow the signs eastward from the last set of traffic lights on High Street. Follow the road from the entrance to the garden to the main parking area, the starting point of three clearly marked walks. There is also a Braille Garden geared toward the visually impaired. ✉ *Roux Rd., Worcester* ☎ *023/347–0785* ⊕ *www.sanbi.org* 💰 *R35.*

Worcester Museum

MUSEUM VILLAGE | FAMILY | Although it's looking a little worn around the edges, the Worcester Museum makes a welcome change from dusty artifacts in glass cases. It's a collection of original buildings from the area that have been re-erected around a working farmyard. Museum staffers bake bread, twist tobacco, make horseshoes in a smithy, and distill *witblits* (meaning moonshine). There are witblits tastings, but keep in mind that some types have an alcohol content of almost 80%. The museum also has a shop where you can buy produce from the farmyard. ✉ *Kleinplasie Agricultural Showgrounds, Robertson Rd., Worcester* ☎ *023/342–2225* ⊕ *www.worcestermuseum.org.za* 💰 *R15* 🕐 *Closed Sun.*

 Activities

RAFTING AND CANOEING

The Breede River has tiny rapids near Worcester, where it twists and turns between clumps of *palmiet* (river reeds) and overgrown banks.

Felix Unite River Adventures

CANOEING & ROWING | Enjoy a two-night stay at River Camp Round The Bend on the banks of the Breede River and head out each day to navigate some rapids or drift lazily along, depending on the water levels. ✉ *Vans Rd., Cape Winelands* ☎ *087/354–0578* ⊕ *www.felixunite.com* 💰 *R2,100.*

Robertson

48 km (30 miles) southeast of Worcester.

If you're on your way to McGregor or Montagu, don't be in too much of a rush. There are some excellent—and underrated—wine estates in Robertson. The town was founded primarily to service the surrounding farms, and it retains its agricultural and industrial character. The town largely lives up to its mantra of "small town, big heart"—the townsfolk are welcoming and friendly, which makes up for the lack of action.

GETTING HERE AND AROUND
Robertson is less than a 30-minute drive from Worcester. Renting a car is the only way to get around in a reasonable amount of time.

VISITOR INFORMATION
CONTACTS Robertson Tourism Bureau. ⊠ 2 Reitz St., Robertson ☎ 023/626–4437 ⊕ www.robertsonr62.com.

Sights

WINERIES
Graham Beck Wines
WINERY | Who needs French Champagne when you have top-class South African Méthode Cap Classique at very afforda-ble prices? Graham Beck Wines, on the road between Worcester and Robert-son, produces some very sophisticated wines. Cellarmaster Pieter Ferreira is known as Mr. Bubbles for his wonderful sparkling wines, which are so popular that the farm no longer produces any still wines. The iconic Cap Classique flagship, Cuvée Clive, is the undisputed favorite in the range. ⊠ R60, about 10 km (6 miles) northwest of Robertson, Robertson ☎ 023/626–1214 ⊕ www.grahambeck. com ≊ Tasting R75–R125.

Rooiberg Winery
WINERY | Capetonians have long consid-ered Rooiberg Winery, between Worces-ter and Robertson, one of the best value-for-the-money wineries in the area. If you don't have time to taste much, delve straight into the reds from the reserve range, which count a few award winners in their ranks. The Bodega de Vinho restaurant serves light meals and delectable pastries, making this a good place to stop for lunch. ⊠ R60, Robert-son ✛ About 10 km (6 miles) northwest of Robertson ☎ 023/626–1663 ⊕ www. rooiberg.co.za ≊ Tastings free.

Springfield Estate
WINERY | Abrie Bruwer, owner and winemaker at Springfield Estate, has a fan club, and for good reason. If the wine doesn't meet Bruwer's stringent standards, it isn't released. Although the Whole Berry Cabernet has its loyal following, this innovative estate is also known for its unusual approach to white wines, especially Chardonnay. The Méth-ode Ancienne Chardonnay is made in the original Burgundy style, a technique that uses wild yeast and no fining or filtration. It has tropical fruit flavors, layered with lime and cream. The creamy Wild Yeast Chardonnay, with its all-natural fermen-tation, is an unwooded version of the above and comes highly recommended. Another great white is the Special Cuvée. It originates from the estate's prime Sauvignon Blanc vineyard and has notes of passion fruit and nettle. Miss Lucy, an unusual white blend of Sauvignon Blanc, Semillon, and Pinot Gris, was created as an ode to the ocean. Free cellar tours are available weekdays. ⊠ R317, Robertson ☎ 023/626–3661 ⊕ www.springfield-estate.com ≊ Tastings free ☉ Closed Sun.

Van Loveren Winery
WINERY | FAMILY | This winery between Robertson and Bonnievale produces around 60 wines, as well as whisky, bran-dy, and wine coolers, so there's some-thing to suit most palates. In addition to sampling the wines, be sure to visit the unusual grounds of this family-owned farm. An established garden of native and exotic plants and trees surrounds a fountain that supplies the entire farm. Instead of visiting the usual tasting room, sit out under the trees and have the various wines brought to you. It's very relaxed and friendly, and you may feel like part of the family before you know it. The tasting room offers 10 different tastings, including pairings with cheese, chocolate, and a selection of sweets. There are even nonalcoholic tastings and a pairing for kids. ⊠ Off R317, Robertson

✣ *15 km (9 miles) southeast of Robertson* ☎ *023/615–1505* 🌐 *www.vanloveren.co.za* 🎫 *Tastings R60–R130.*

🍴 Restaurants

@ Four Cousins Restaurant

$$$ | INTERNATIONAL | FAMILY | Right at the entrance to the town, this laid-back eatery is a great lunch stop, especially if you're traveling with kids. It serves pizza, pasta, and hearty meat dishes at tables in a shady, tree-lined garden. **Known for:** family-friendly atmosphere; wide-ranging menu; hearty breakfasts. [$] *Average main: R185* ✉ *54 Voortrekker Ave., Robertson* ☎ *023/615–1505* 🌐 *www.fourcousins.co.za* 🕒 *No dinner Sun.*

Bosjes Kombuis

$$$ | SOUTH AFRICAN | FAMILY | With stunning views of the Slanghoek Mountains, Bosjes Kombuis has a seasonal menu that marries rustic ingredients with fine dining presentation, creating an experience that is unpretentious and yet very special. If you don't make it in time for lunch, there's a lovely café in the gardens that serves tea and cake. **Known for:** beautiful farm setting; minimalist dining room; family-friendly vibe. [$] *Average main: R170* ✉ *Bosjes, R43* ☎ *023/004–0496* 🌐 *bosjes.co.za* 🕒 *Closed Mon. and Tues.*

McGregor

20 km (12 miles) south of Robertson.

Saved from development by a planned mountain pass that never materialized, McGregor is the epitome of the sleepy country hollow. Tucked away between the mountains, it's one of the best-preserved examples of a 19th-century Cape village. As you approach McGregor from Robertson, farmsteads give way to small cottages with distinctive red-painted doors and window frames.

McGregor has become popular with artists who have settled here permanently and with busy executives from Cape Town intent on getting away from it all. Frankly, this is an ideal place to do absolutely nothing, but you can take a leisurely stroll through the fynbos, watch birds from one of several blinds on the Heron Walk, or follow one of the hiking or mountain-bike trails. There is a magnificent trail across the Riviersonderend Mountains to Greyton. Known as the Boesmanskloof Trail, the 14 km (8.7 mile) hike can be tackled in a day but you need to be reasonably fit.

GETTING HERE AND AROUND

McGregor is a 15-minute drive from Robertson.

👁 Sights

Eseltjiesrus Donkey Sanctuary

WILDLIFE REFUGE | FAMILY | On the road into McGregor, Eseltjiesrus Donkey Sanctuary provides a safe space for neglected and abused donkeys. Kids can meet Alice, Lulu, and the other four-footed residents while you relax at the restaurant, which serves light lunches. ✉ *Langeberg Rd., McGregor* ☎ *023/625–1593* 🌐 *www.donkeysanctuary.co.za* 🕒 *Closed Mon.–Wed.*

WINERIES

McGregor Wines

WINERY | An unpretentious destination, McGregor Wines makes good, inexpensive wines. Try the unwooded Chardonnay; previous vintages won Veritas Gold awards. Their fortified wines are perfect for sipping near a log fire in winter. The white Muscadel and the Cape Ruby Port are very different, but both are delicious. In 2019, McGregor merged with larger, Robertson-based winery Roodezandt, but it retains its own labels and identity. ✉ *Main road to McGregor, McGregor* ☎ *023/625–1741* 🌐 *www.roodezandt.co.za* 🎫 *Tastings free* 🕒 *Closed Sun.*

McGregor is one of the best-preserved examples of a 19th-century Cape village.

Hotels

Green Gables Country Inn

$$ | B&B/INN | FAMILY | In an 1860 manor house, Green Gables is decorated with antiques and feels very much like an upscale home. **Pros:** tranquil setting; you'll soon feel part of the village; friendly owners. **Cons:** limited accommodations; not the place for alone time; not many dining options in the area. [$] *Rooms from: R1500* ✉ *Smith St. at Mill St., McGregor* ☎ *023/625–1626* 🌐 *www.greengablesmcgregor.co.za* 🛏 *4 rooms* 🍴 *Free Breakfast.*

Activities

HIKING

Vrolijkheid Nature Reserve

HIKING & WALKING | The 19-km (12-mile) Rooikat Trail through the Vrolijkheid Nature Reserve takes about eight hours to complete. It's a strenuous, circular route winding up into the Elandsberg Mountains, so an early start is recommended. There are shorter hikes as well, including the 1-km Braille Trail. Five self-catering cottages accommodate a maximum of four people and are fully equipped. Day visitors need to get a permit at the entrance of the reserve. It's on the honor system, so you put your money in a box. If you don't want to hike, there are two bird blinds and a mountain-bike trail. ✉ *5 km (3 miles) outside McGregor, McGregor* ☎ *087/087–8250* 🌐 *www.capenature.co.za* 🎟 *R50.*

Montagu

29 km (18 miles) northeast of Robertson.

Montagu bills itself as "the Gateway to the Little Karoo," and its picturesque streets lined with Cape Victorian architecture lend this some credence. Montagu's main attraction is its natural hot springs, and many of the Victorian houses have been transformed into B&Bs and guesthouses. The mountains that feed the springs also provide plenty of opportunities for outdoorsy types, with superlative hiking, mountain biking, and rock climbing within easy reach of the town.

GETTING HERE AND AROUND

Montagu is a 20-minute drive from Robertson.

VISITOR INFORMATION

CONTACTS Montagu/Ashton Tourism Bureau. ✉ *27 Bath St., Montagu* ☎ *023/614–2471* 🌐 *www.montagu-ashton.info.*

Sights

Avalon Springs

HOT SPRING | FAMILY | The area's only hot springs open to day visitors, Avalon Springs is not the most stylish, and the architecture leaves a lot to be desired. But if you look beyond this and the numerous signs carrying stern warnings and instructions, you'll get some good insights into South African culture as people splash around in the various pools. If you're not staying at the resort, you can rent bikes from the village and cycle to the springs, where you can spend a few hours before heading home again. Try to visit on a weekday, as it can get unpleasantly crowded on weekends. ✉ *Uitvlucht St., Montagu* ✥ *3 km (2 miles) outside Montagu* ☎ *023/614–1150* 🌐 *www.avalonsprings.co.za* 🎫 *Weekdays R100, weekends R120.*

Langeberg Tractor Ride

SCENIC DRIVE | FAMILY | The three-hour Langeberg Tractor Ride takes you to the summit of Long Mountain and back. The tractor winds up some tortuously twisted paths, revealing magnificent views of the area's peaks and valleys. After a short stop at the summit, a similarly harrowing descent follows, but you won't be disappointed by the views or the driver's chirpy banter. If you're here in spring or summer when the flowers are in bloom, you might even get to pick some gorgeous proteas on the way down. Following your trip, you can enjoy a delicious lunch of *potjiekos* (traditional stew cooked over a fire in a cast-iron pot). Reservations are essential. ✉ *Protea Farm, R318, Montagu* ☎ *023/614–3012* 🌐 *www.proteafarm.co.za* 🎫 *R170.*

Hotels

Montagu Country Hotel

$$ | HOTEL | This delightful hotel was originally built in Victorian times but was extensively remodeled in Art Deco style after a fire in the early 1930s. **Pros:** well-trained staff; glorious deck for coffee and people-watching; wellness center with mineral baths. **Cons:** decor isn't for everyone; some rooms get chilly in winter; Sundays can be very quiet. [$] *Rooms from: R1700* ✉ *27 Bath St., Montagu* ☎ *023/614–3125, 082/899–3670* 🌐 *www.montagucountryhotel.co.za* 🛏 *32 rooms* 🍴 *Free Breakfast.*

7 Church Street

$$ | B&B/INN | In the heart of the village sits this guesthouse in a lovingly restored Victorian home; each room is individually and stylishly decorated with hand-embroidered linens. **Pros:** within walking distance of the hot springs; peaceful and secluded location; great mountain views. **Cons:** might be too quiet for some; sizable supplement for single travelers; breakfast can be a drawn-out affair. [$] *Rooms from: R1800* ✉ *7 Church St., Montagu* ☎ *023/614–1186* 🌐 *www.7churchstreet.co.za* 🛏 *5 suites* 🍴 *Free Breakfast.*

Gordon's Bay

13 km (8 miles) south of Somerset West; 30 km (19 miles) northwest of Betty's Bay.

Pretty Gordon's Bay is built on the steep slopes of the Hottentots Holland Mountains overlooking the vast expanse of False Bay. You can often see whales and their calves swim by in October and November. This is a good point to start on the fantastic coastal route known as Clarence Drive, one of the country's

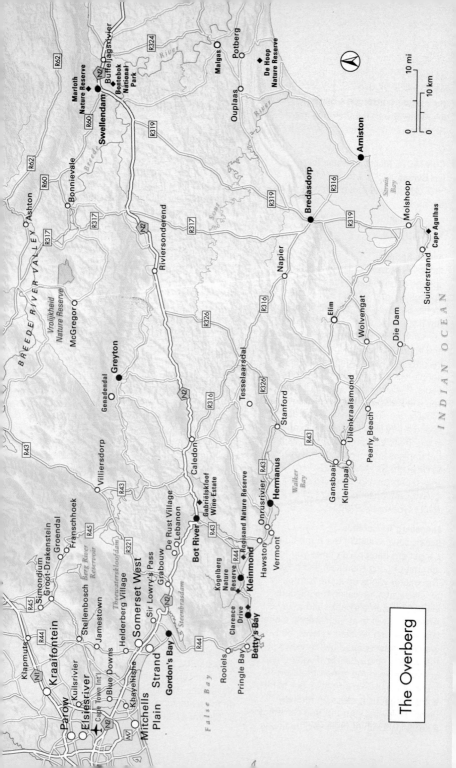

The Overberg

most scenic routes. There are numerous paths down to the seashore from the road between Gordon's Bay and Rooiels, and it's worth walking down to watch the waves pounding the rocky coast. Take care, because this section of coast is notorious for rogue waves.

GETTING HERE AND AROUND
Gordon's Bay is 55 km (34 miles) southeast of Cape Town, reachable along the N2 and R44.

Sights

★ Clarence Drive
SCENIC DRIVE | It spans less than 25 km (15½ miles), but it is without question one of the most beautiful stretches of road in South Africa. Clarence Drive—less poetically known as the R44—begins as you leave Gordon's Bay headed south. Sandwiched between ocean and mountain, the road winds around more than 70 bends on its way to the hamlet of Rooi Els. There are plenty of places to pull over though, and you'll make good use of them because Clarence Drive is a photographer's dream. On a clear day you'll see right across False Bay all the way to Cape Point. Keep an eye out for baboons when you're driving; they're usually in no great hurry when crossing the road. ✉ *Clarence Dr., Gordon's Bay, Somerset West.*

Betty's Bay

30 km (19 miles) southeast of Gordon's Bay.

Betty's Bay—or just Betty's, as the hamlet is fondly known—is worth visiting for its penguins and its botanical garden. The unfussy village is made up of weekenders wanting to escape the hustle and bustle of the city. The scenery is wild and untamed, and the weather is unpredictable, so you may have to hunker down inside when the summer wind is howling or when the winter rains set in.

If you're in the area, the colony of African penguins at Stony Point is definitely worth exploring. They are one of only two mainland colonies in southern Africa (the other is at Boulders Beach on the Cape Peninsula). The Stony Point colony lies about 600 yards from the parking area along a rocky coastal path. Along the way you pass the concrete remains of tank stands, reminders of the days when Betty's Bay was a big whaling station. It's easier to spot the birds at Boulders Beach, but Stony Point attracts far fewer visitors and you often have the penguins all to yourself. The African penguin is endangered, so the colony has been fenced off for protection, but this still doesn't stop leopards from making occasion visits.

Stony Point is on the western edge of Betty's Bay. Follow Porter Drive for 2¼ km (1¾ miles) until you reach a sign marked "mooi hawens" and a smaller sign depicting a penguin.

GETTING HERE AND AROUND
Head out of Cape Town on the N2 toward Somerset West. Once you've made your way through the town (the traffic can be torturous on a Friday afternoon), take the R44 turnoff to Gordon's Bay. From there the road hugs the coast. It takes 45 minutes from Cape Town to Gordon's Bay if there are no traffic jams and then about 30 minutes to Betty's Bay, but this will vary depending on the traffic and weather—and how often you stop to admire the view.

VISITOR INFORMATION
The Hangklip-Kleinmond Tourism Bureau has information on Betty's Bay.

CONTACTS Hangklip–Kleinmond Tourism Bureau. ✉ *Protea Centre, 29 Main Rd., Kleinmond* ☎ *028/271–8474* ⊕ *www.kleinmondtourism.co.za.*

Stretching all the way from Gordon's Bay to Rooi Els, Clarence Drive is one of South Africa's prettiest drives.

Sights

Harold Porter National Botanical Garden

GARDEN | FAMILY | This 440-acre nature reserve is in the heart of the coastal fynbos, where the Cape floral kingdom is at its richest. The profusion of plants supports 96 species of birds and a wide range of small mammals, including troops of chacma baboons. You couldn't ask for a more fantastic setting, cradled between the Atlantic and the towering peaks of the 3,000-foot Kogelberg Range. Walking trails wind through the reserve and into the mountains via Disa and Leopard's kloofs, which echo with the sound of waterfalls. Back at the main buildings, a pleasant restaurant serves light meals. Book at least two weeks in advance for a guided tour to take you around the gardens. ✉ *Clarence Dr. at Broadwith Ave., Betty's Bay* ☎ *028/272–9311* ⊕ *www.sanbi.org/gardens/harold-porter* ✉ *R35.*

Restaurants

Hook, Line and Sinker

$$ | SEAFOOD | At this seafood restaurant, expect fresher fish than you'll find just about anywhere else. It's prepared simply, usually with salsa verde or just garlic butter. **Known for:** local hang-out; warm, welcoming dining room; down-to-earth dishes. *Average main: R135* ✉ *382 Crescent Rd., Pringle Bay* ☎ *083/632–7534* ⊕ *hooklineandsinkerpringlebay.business.site* ⊘ *No dinner Sun.*

Hotels

Villa Marine

$$ | B&B/INN | Welcome to the beach house of your dreams. **Pros:** excellent breakfast; lovely infinity pool overlooking the ocean; unrivaled coastal location. **Cons:** evenings can get chilly in winter; not many restaurants nearby; it's tough to drag yourself away from the views. $ *Rooms from: R2000* ✉ *73 Marine Dr., Pringle Bay* ☎ *028/273–8081* ⊕ *www.villamarine.co.za* ⇨ *7 suites* ⊘ *Free Breakfast.*

Kleinmond

25 km (15½ miles) southeast of Gordon's Bay.

The sleepy coastal town of Kleinmond presides over a magnificent stretch of shoreline, backed by the mountains of the Palmietberg. A harbor development near the old slipway is where you'll find most of the town's restaurants and shops.

GETTING HERE AND AROUND
Kleinmond is about 15 minutes east of Betty's Bay.

VISITOR INFORMATION
CONTACTS Hangklip–Kleinmond Tourism Bureau. ⊠ *Protea Centre, 29 Main Rd., Kleinmond* ☎ *028/271–8474* ⊕ *www. kleinmondtourism.co.za.*

◉ Sights

Kogelberg Nature Reserve
NATURE PRESERVE | Midway between Betty's Bay and Kleinmond is Kogelberg Nature Reserve, a 66,000-acre area of fynbos that extends from the mountains almost to the sea and includes most of the course of the Palmiet River. Declared a UNESCO World Heritage Site in the 1990s, it has fauna and flora found nowhere else in the world. Take one of the well-marked nature walks through the reserve and you are sure to see some of the area's magnificent birds, including the Hottentot buttonquail, the orange-breasted sunbird, and the African purple swamphen. One of the reserve's best-kept secrets is its eco-friendly cabins that can sleep up to four people. ⊠ *Kleinmond* ☎ *087/288–0499* ⊕ *www. capenature.co.za* 🎫 *R60.*

Rooisand Nature Reserve
NATURE PRESERVE | FAMILY | Stroll along the boardwalk at Rooisand Nature Reserve and you might catch a glimpse of the famous Bot River horses that live in *vlei*, or wetlands along the shores of the Botrivier Lagoon. There are lots of theories about just how the horses got here. One has it that they were turned loose by soldiers during the Boer War. More likely they are descendants of the sturdy horses used to help settle the wild regions of the Overberg. This area is also a birder's paradise, and you might see white cattle egrets riding piggyback on the horses. ⊠ *Off R44, Kleinmond* ☎ *087/288–0499* ⊕ *kleinmondtourism. co.za/rooisand-nature-reserve-wild-horses* 🎫 *Free.*

🍴 Restaurants

KabelJoe's Seafood Restaurant
$$ | SEAFOOD | FAMILY | Harbour Road has a string of eateries you can choose from, but you can't go wrong at this popular place with views of the ocean. Obviously, fish and seafood are the star of the show. **Known for:** freshest seafood; laid-back atmosphere; friendly staff. 💲 *Average main: R159* ⊠ *35 Harbour Rd., Bot River* ☎ *028/271–3336* ⊕ *kabeljoesseafood. co.za.*

🛏 Hotels

★ The Arabella Hotel Golf & Spa
$$$ | HOTEL | FAMILY | The edge of the spectacular Botrivier Lagoon is where you'll find the luxurious Arabella Hotel & Spa. Your private balcony gazes down on this birder's paradise, and you just might spot rare species on the water's edge. **Pros:** world-famous golf course; plenty of activities to keep everyone entertained; perfect location near the beach and the mountains. **Cons:** part of a large chain; you'll need a car to get around; windy during summer months. 💲 *Rooms from: R2567* ⊠ *Arabella Country Estate, R44, Kleinmond* ☎ *028/284–0000* ⊕ *www. arabellacountryestate.co.za* 🛏 *145 rooms* ⫟ *Free Breakfast.*

Activities

GOLF
Arabella Golf Club

GOLF | The setting of this top-rated course is so beautiful that you'll probably forget all about golf by the 8th hole, which looks out over the lagoon, the mountains, and the sea in the distance. Flamingos are a common sight near the greens. But don't lose your head to the views—the course is fairly challenging. ⊠ *Arabella Country Estate, R44, Kleinmond* ☎ *028/284–0105* ⊕ *www.arabellacountryestate.co.za* 🖂 *R1,535* 🏌 *18 holes, 6651 yards, par 72* ☞ *Facilities: driving range, putting green, golf carts, rental clubs, restaurant, bar.*

RAFTING

You can navigate the Palmiet River all year, but whitewater rafting is most exciting in winter.

Gravity Adventures

WHITE-WATER RAFTING | The Palmiet River, which runs through the Kogelberg Nature Reserve, is perfect for whitewater rafting adventures. In winter, Gravity Adventures offers rafting trips in two- or four-seater inflatable rafts. During summer, when the currents are more gentle, they offer tubing along the same route. Whatever the season, remember to take along plenty of sun protection. ⊠ *21 Selous Rd., Claremont* ☎ *021/683–3698* ⊕ *www.gravity.co.za* 🖂 *R650.*

SA Forest Adventures

WHITE-WATER RAFTING | For adrenaline-fueled whitewater rafting adventures down the Palmiet River, turn to SA Forest Adventures in Kleinmond. If this isn't exciting enough, ask about their sand-boarding trips, where you get to ski down sand dunes that overlook Betty's Bay. ⊠ *Harbour Rd., Unit B1, Kleinmond* ☎ *021/795–0225* ⊕ *www.saforestadventures.co.za* 🖂 *R550.*

Bot River

25 km (16 miles) northwest of Kleinmond.

Set amid vast wheat fields, Bot River is a pretty little farming town on the banks of its namesake river. The community itself doesn't have a lot going on, but the surrounding region draws in day-trippers, largely for its off-the-beaten-track wineries.

GETTING HERE AND AROUND

East of Kleinmond, the R43 bends northeast to bypass the Rooisand Nature Reserve. Bot River is a 30-minute drive from there.

 Sights

WINERIES
Beaumont Family Wines

WINERY | You can't miss the old white gates of Beaumont Wines. This is a fabulous family-run winery. It's just sufficiently scruffy to create an ambience of age and country charm without actually being untidy. But, charm aside, it's the wine you come here for, and it really is worth the detour. Beaumont produces a range of dependable, notable wines, like their flagship Hope Marguerite, a wooded Chenin Blanc. ⊠ *Compagnes Drift Farm, R43* ☎ *028/284–9194* ⊕ *www.beaumont.co.za* 🖂 *Tastings R75.*

Gabriëlskloof Wine Estate

WINERY | As you're heading inland to explore the Overberg or the Garden Route, be sure to stop at the impressive Gabriëlskloof, 29 km (18 miles) northeast of Kleinmond. Try the award–winning Shiraz with notes of pepper and cherries in the garden or in front of a log fire in the tasting room. You can also sample the estate's extra-virgin olive oil, and perhaps purchase some from the deli. The Gabriëlskloof restaurant is a great place to stop for lunch. The menu changes regularly, but the food is always no-fuss house-cooked fare made with fresh local produce. ✉ *R43* ☎ *028/284–9865* 🌐 *www.gabrielskloof.co.za* 🎫 *Tastings R50* 🕒 *Closed Sun.*

🍴 Restaurants

The Restaurant at Wildekrans Wine Estate
$$$$ | ECLECTIC | A 20-minute drive from Kleinmond, The Restaurant lies on the grounds of the sprawling Wildekrans Wine Estate. The menu is small and seasonal and features dishes prepared with flair, like the honey and turmeric pork cutlet. **Known for:** stunning interior; impressive wine list; al fresco dining. [$] *Average main: R210* ✉ *Wildekrans Wine Estate, R43* ☎ *028/284–9488* 🌐 *www.wildekrans.com* 🕒 *Closed Mon. and Tues. No dinner Sat.–Thurs.*

Hermanus

34 km (21 miles) southeast of Kleinmond.

Pristine beaches extend as far as the eye can see at Hermanus, the major coastal town in the Overberg. Grotto Beach was awarded Blue Flag status (an international rating system for eco-friendly shores) decades ago, and it's still a favorite. Though the resort town has lost much of its charm—thanks to fast-food joints and other tourist-attracting amenities—it's still definitely worth a visit. If you're in Hermanus on the weekend, visit the Saturday morning organic farmers market—one of the best on the Cape.

GETTING HERE AND AROUND

Hermanus is about a 40-minute drive from Kleinmond on the R41 and the R43. In summer expect delays, as the traffic into town is often gridlocked.

VISITOR INFORMATION

CONTACTS Hermanus Tourism Bureau. ✉ *Lord Robert St. at Mitchell St., Hermanus* ☎ *028/312–2629* 🌐 *www.hermanustourism.info.*

👁 Sights

Hermanus sits atop a long line of cliffs, which makes it one of the best places in South Africa for land-based whale-watching. The town is packed during the Whale Festival in late September. The 11-km (7-mile) Cliff Walk allows watchers to follow the whales, which often come within 100 feet of the shore as they move along the coastline.

Keep an ear and an eye out for the whale crier, who makes his rounds during the season. Using a horn made from dried kelp, he belts out notes in something akin to Morse code to indicate where you can spot the whales. You first have to find him, though, since you need to read the sandwich board he wears in order to decipher the code.

Old Harbour Museum
HISTORY MUSEUM | FAMILY | Hermanus was originally a simple fishing village. Its Old Harbour, the oldest surviving example in South Africa, has been declared a national monument. The Old Harbour Museum bears testimony to the town's maritime past. A small building at the old stone fishing basin displays a couple of the horrific harpoons used to lance whales and sharks, as well as some interesting whale bones. The white building next to the parking lot on Market Square houses the Old Harbour Museum Photographic Exhibition. Here are photos of old Hermanus and of many of the town's fishermen proudly displaying their catches of fish, sharks, and dolphins. The museum's third—and most interesting—component is the Whale House, with an interactive display and entertaining movie that's great for kids. The daily crafts market held behind De Wetshuis Photo Museum is fun for browsing. ✉ *Old Harbour, Marine Dr., Hermanus* ☎ *028/312–1475* 🌐 *www.old-harbour-museum.co.za* 🎫 *R20.*

Rotary Way

SCENIC DRIVE | On the outskirts of town, a pair of white gateposts set well back from the main road signal the start of Rotary Way. This scenic drive climbs along the spine of the mountains above Hermanus, offering incredible views of Walker Bay and the Hemel-en-Aarde Valley. It's a highlight of a trip to Hermanus and shouldn't be missed. The entire mountainside is laced with wonderful walking trails, and many of the scenic lookouts have benches. The start of the drive is about 2½ km (1½ miles) west of the Old Harbour. ✉ *Off R43, Hermanus.*

WINERIES

Bouchard Finlayson

WINERY | With only 44 acres under vine, Bouchard Finlayson nevertheless thrills critics and wine lovers year after year. Winemaker Peter Finlayson makes good use of the cool sea breeze and unique terroir of the estate to create some fantastic deep-south wines. They're particularly well known for excellent Pinot Noir. You might wish to lay down a few bottles of the much-lauded Tête de Cuvée Galpin Peak Pinot Noir, a velvety and fruity wine. ✉ *Hemel-en-Aarde Valley Rd., Hermanus* ☎ *028/312–3515* 🌐 *www.bouchardfinlayson.co.za* 🎫 *Tastings from R35.*

Creation Wines

WINERY | About 17 km (11 miles) up Hemel-en-Aarde Road, Creation Wines is a little off the beaten track but well worth the drive. Like other wineries in this region, it is best known for its excellent Pinot Noir. Try the Art of Pinot Noir, with flavors of cherry and plum and a background earthiness. The estate is also known for its pairing options: you can opt for the chocolate and wine pairing or the hour-long wine and canapé pairing. Even the designated driver is catered for with a pairing experience using tea instead of wine. Open for lunch, the restaurant has an ever-changing chalkboard menu. ✉ *Hemel-en-Aarde Rd., Hermanus* ☎ *028/212–1107* 🌐 *www.creationwines.com* 🎫 *Tastings from R10.*

Hamilton Russell Vineyards

WINERY | In a thatch building overlooking a small dam, Hamilton Russell Vineyards produces only two varietals: Chardonnay and the temperamental Pinot Noir. Their wines are regarded as some of the best in the world, regularly winning all manner of accolades and awards. ✉ *Hemel-en-Aarde Valley Rd., Walker Bay* ☎ *028/312–3595* 🌐 *www.hamiltonrussellvineyards.com* 🎫 *Tastings R50.*

🍴 Restaurants

Burgundy

$$$ | **SEAFOOD** | In one of the village's original stone fishing cottages, Burgundy is one of the town's oldest and best-loved restaurants. Unsurprisingly, there's plenty of seafood on the extensive menu—try the creamy abalone with fresh sage—as well as a large choice of grilled meat dishes. **Known for:** good vegetarian selection; bustling atmopshere; al fresco dining. [$] *Average main: R175* ✉ *Marine Dr., Hermanus* ☎ *028/312–2800* 🌐 *www.burgundyrestaurant.co.za.*

★ **Ficks**

$$ | **TAPAS** | This popular restaurant and bar boasts a truly incomparable setting, right on the rocks on the edge of a natural rock pool in the Atlantic Ocean. Dine on the deck and you'll hear the crashing of the waves and maybe spot some whales swimming by. **Known for:** laid-back atmosphere; idea spot for sundowners; wonderful ocean views. [$] *Average main: R115* ✉ *8 Marine Dr., Hermanus* ☎ *028/312–4082* 🌐 *www.ficks.co.za* 🕒 *No dinner Sun.–Thurs.*

Fishermans Cottage

$$$ | **SEAFOOD** | **FAMILY** | This whitewashed stone cottage dating back to 1870 serves some of the best food in town. The menu focuses on seafood, but don't let that put you off the non-seafood options like smoked pork belly or chicken curry with freshly made roti. **Known for:** local wines; outdoor dining on picnic tables; seasonal ingredients. $ *Average main: R165* ✉ *Main St. at Harbour Rd., Hermanus* ☎ *028/312–3642* ⊕ *www.fishermanscottage.co.za* ⊗ *Closed Mon. No dinner Sun.*

★ Mogg's Country Cookhouse

$$ | **ECLECTIC** | Don't be put off by the bumpy dirt road heading up the Hemel-en-Aarde Valley—this restaurant on an orchard at the top of the valley is worth the dusty trip. The seasonal menu is scribbled on a chalkboard, with dishes like caramelized pear, Gorgonzola, avocado, and walnut salad, or smoked trout and sautéed prawns with a lime-wasabi vinaigrette. **Known for:** housemade desserts; relaxed and friendly setting; tucked-away location. $ *Average main: R150* ✉ *Nuwe Pos Farm, Hemel-en-Aarde Valley Rd., Hermanus* ☎ *076/314–0671* ⊕ *www.moggscookhouse.com* ⊗ *Closed Mon. and Tues. No dinner.*

Hotels

If you want to avoid the crowds of Hermanus, consider lodging in the nearby hamlet of Stanford.

Auberge Burgundy Guesthouse

$$ | **B&B/INN** | If you want to be in the center of the village, this stylish guesthouse puts you a stone's throw from the famous whale-watching cliffs. **Pros:** 200 feet from the sea; close to everything Hermanus has to offer; very friendly staff. **Cons:** no children under 12; some steps to climb; some suites face the street. $ *Rooms from: R1650* ✉ *16 Harbour Rd., Hermanus* ☎ *028/313–1201* ⊕ *www.auberge.co.za* ⌂ *18 rooms* ⏐○⏐ *Free Breakfast.*

★ Birkenhead House

$$$$ | **B&B/INN** | If whale-watching is on your agenda, you're unlikely you'll come across a better spot than the one of Birkenhead House. **Pros:** pretty pool; extraordinary clifftop setting; excellent service. **Cons:** far from town; not everyone wants

all-inclusive rates; opulence like this doesn't come cheap. $ *Rooms from: R8900* ✉ *11th St. at 7th Ave., Voelklip, Hermanus* ☎ *021/671–5502* ⊕ *www.theroyalportfolio.com/birkenhead-house* ⌂ *11 rooms* ⏐○⏐ *All-Inclusive.*

Blue Gum Country Estate

$$ | **B&B/INN** | **FAMILY** | On the banks of the Klein River, Blue Gum is a wonderful place to relax away from the hustle and bustle of Hermanus. **Pros:** great restaurant; perfectly peaceful surroundings; lots to keep kids occupied. **Cons:** few dining options nearby; solo travelers pay full price; off the beaten track on a gravel road. $ *Rooms from: R1800* ✉ *Off R326, Stanford* ☎ *065/626–5456* ⊕ *www.bluegum.co.za* ⌂ *7 rooms.*

★ Grootbos Private Nature Reserve

$$$$ | **RESORT** | **FAMILY** | A 30-minute drive from Hermanus, this luxury lodging sits on 2,500 acres overlooking Walker Bay. Privacy is paramount in the soothing suites, which have fireplaces, sunken bathtubs, and private sundecks opening onto mountains as far as the eye can see. **Pros:** lots of activities; a strong commitment to conserving nature; secluded natural surroundings. **Cons:** a little pricey; not much to do on rainy days; you'll need a few days to experience it all. $ *Rooms from: R19000* ✉ *R43, Gansbaai* ☎ *028/384–8053* ⊕ *www.grootbos.com* ⌂ *27 suites* ⏐○⏐ *All-Inclusive.*

★ The Marine

$$$$ | **HOTEL** | **FAMILY** | One of the Southern Hemisphere's most spectacular seaside properties, The Marine has an incomparable clifftop setting. **Pros:** old-world service and attention to detail; relaxing treatments at the full-service spa; welcoming to families with young children. **Cons:**; not as quiet as you'd think; can feel a little stuffy. $ *Rooms from: R6400* ✉ *Marine Dr., Hermanus* ☎ *021/794–5535* ⊕ *www.themarinehotel.co.za* ⌂ *40 rooms* ⏐○⏐ *Free Breakfast.*

The Vishuis

$ | B&B/INN | Walking distance to many shops and restaurants, this renovated fisherman's cottage is now a stylish urban retreat. **Pros:** beautifully decorated; convenient location; excellent value. **Cons:** rooms share a communal lounge; no on-site amenities; no views to speak of. [$] *Rooms from: R1300* ✉ *7 Hope St., Hermanus* ☎ *082/576–1355* 🌐 *www.thevishuis.co.za* 🛏 *4 rooms.*

Shopping

Wine Village

WINE/SPIRITS | This shop carries a good selection of South African wines, including wines from neighboring vineyards like Hamilton Russell and Bouchard Finlayson. ✉ *1 Hemel-en-Aarde Rd., Hermanus* ☎ *028/316–3988* 🌐 *www.winevillage.co.za.*

Activities

East of Hermanus, the R43 hugs the narrow strip between the mountains and the Klein River Lagoon. The pool is popular with water-skiers, boaters, and anglers.

KAYAKING

Walker Bay Adventures

KAYAKING | FAMILY | Enjoy some easy paddling from the Old Harbour with Walker Bay Adventures. Guides lead you through the water in safe, stable double sea kayaks. From July to December, Walker Bay is a whale sanctuary, and this is the only local company with a permit to operate excursions to see the gentle giants up close. ✉ *Old Harbour, off Marine Dr., Hermanus* ☎ *082/739–0159* 🌐 *www.walkerbayadventures.co.za* 🎫 *R450.*

WHALE-WATCHING AND SHARK DIVING

Although Hermanus is great for land-based whale-watching, you get a different perspective on a boat trip into Walker Bay. Boats leave on 2½-hour whale-watching trips from both Hermanus and Gansbaai.

Dyer Island Cruises

BOATING | FAMILY | Focused on conservation, this company is a good bet for whale-watching. You're likely to see some of the Marine Big Five—whales, dolphins, penguins, seals, and sharks—on the guided boat trip. A free visit to the African Penguin and Seabird Sanctuary is also included. Transfers to and from Cape Town can be arranged. ✉ *5 Geelbek St., Kleinmond* ☎ *082/801–8014* 🌐 *www.whalewatchsa.com* 🎫 *Expect to pay R1450 per adult.*

White Shark Diving Company

WILDLIFE-WATCHING | Shark diving is extremely popular, and Gansbaai has a number of operators working from the small harbor, including White Shark Diving Company. A 4½-hour trip includes breakfast, snacks on the boat, and a light lunch afterward. If you don't want to take the plunge—which you do in a cage—you can just watch the sharks from the boat. A volunteer program gives you the chance to contribute to great white shark research and marine conservation. ✉ *Kleinbaai Harbour, 9 Kus Dr., Gansbaai* ☎ *082/559–6858* 🌐 *www.sharkcagediving.co.za* 🎫 *R2,250.*

Bredasdorp

89 km (55 miles) east of Hermanus.

Every spring, this sleepy little town comes to life when it hosts the Foot of Africa Marathon. The race is no walk in the park. Word has it that the undulating landscape has the fittest athletes doubting their perseverance.

GETTING HERE AND AROUND

Travel time from Hermanus is around 1 hour 15 minutes and from Stanford 50 minutes. From Hermanus you travel on the R43 to Stanford; then you take the R326 and then the R316. The route is well signposted.

There are numerous day hikes that explore De Hoop Nature Reserve.

VISITOR INFORMATION

CONTACTS Cape Agulhas Tourism Bureau. ✉ *19 Long St., Bredasdorp* ☎ *028/425–5581.*

 Sights

Bredasdorp Shipwreck Museum

OTHER MUSEUM | Housed in a converted church and rectory, the Bredasdorp Shipwreck Museum has an extensive collection of objects salvaged from the hundreds of ships that have gone down in the stormy seas off the Cape. In addition to the usual cannons and figureheads, the museum displays a surprising array of household articles rescued from the sea, including entire dining-room sets, sideboards, and phonographs. Be sure to visit the buildings out back, which contain old wagons and the first fire engines used in South Africa. ✉ *6 Independent St., Bredasdorp* ☎ *028/424–1240* 🖅 *R50* ⊙ *Closed Sat. and Sun.*

Cape Agulhas

LIGHTHOUSE | From Bredasdorp, it's just 39 km (24 miles) through rolling farmland to the tip of the African continent. Although this cape is not nearly as spectacular as Cape Point, it's rather fitting for the end of a wild and wonderful continent. For R35, you can climb the Cape Agulhas lighthouse. Selfies are obligatory at a sign signifying the point where the Atlantic and Indian Oceans meet. ✉ *Lighthouse St., Cape Agulhas.*

★ De Hoop Nature Reserve

NATURE PRESERVE | Covering 88,900 acres of isolated coastal terrain as well as the undersea world below the waves, this reserve deserves its status as a UNESCO World Heritage Site. Massive sand dunes, rolling mountains, and rare lowland fynbos are home to eland, bontebok, and Cape mountain zebra, as well as more than 250 species of birds. (Keep an eye out for the blue crane, South Africa's national bird.) Though the reserve is only three hours from Cape Town, it feels a world away.

This is a fantastic place to watch whales from the shore—not quite as easy as in Hermanus, but much less crowded. You can also hike the enormously popular Whale Trail, which runs through the reserve. A shuttle service takes your bags to each new stop, so all you have to carry is a small day pack and a water bottle between overnight stops. Book up to a year in advance to enjoy the Whale Trail, or try to snag a last-minute cancellation. Self-catering cottages sleep up to four people and range from basic to fully equipped.

You can still enjoy De Hoop without doing the Whale Trail; there are delightful day hikes, beautiful and largely unpeopled beaches and excellent bird-watching, including a viewing platform where you can lie down and watch Cape vultures swooping overhead.

Access is via a dirt road between Bredasdorp and Malgas. From Bredasdorp take the R319 to Swellendam. At about 6 km (4 miles) turn right at the sign posted De Hoop/Malgas/Infanta. Follow the road for 35 km (21.2 miles) until you see the sign for the reserve ⊠ *Between Bredasdorp and Malgas, Bredasdorp* ☎ *028/542–1253* ⊕ *www.capenature.co.za* ✉ *R50.*

Elim

TOWN | Little has changed in the last 200 years in the Moravian mission village of Elim, founded in 1824. Simple white-washed cottages line the few streets. All the residents belong to the Moravian Church. You're welcome to attend services, when just about the whole town turns out in their Sunday best. Elim is the only town in the country that has a monument dedicated to the freeing of the slaves in 1838. It's also home to the country's oldest working clock and biggest wooden waterwheel. There's a tourism office near the waterwheel with a small museum detailing the history of the village. Grab a bite in the tearoom next to the waterwheel. Elim is 36 km (22 miles) west of Bredasdorp. ⊠ *Off the R319 between Cape Agulhas and Bredasdorp.*

Malgas

TOWN | On the dirt road from Bredasdorp is the small hamlet of Malgas, a major port in the 19th century before the mouth of the Breede River silted up. In addition to a tiny village, you will find the last hand-drawn car ferry in the country. It's fascinating to watch the technique, as the ferry operators "walk" the ferry across the river on a huge cable, leaning into their harnesses. ⊠ *Malgas.*

Arniston (Waenhuiskrans)

25 km (15½ miles) southeast of Bredasdorp.

Although its official name is Waenhuiskrans, and that's what you'll see on some maps, this lovely, isolated vacation village is almost always called Arniston. It's named after a British ship that was wrecked on the nearby reef in 1815. Beautiful beaches, water in Caribbean shades of blue, and mile after mile of towering white dunes attract anglers and vacationers alike.

For 200 years a community of local fisherfolk has eked out a living here, setting sail each day in small boats. Today their village, Kassiesbaai (meaning "Suitcase Bay," supposedly for all the suitcases that washed ashore after the frequent shipwrecks), is a national monument. It's fascinating to wander around the thatch cottages of this still-vibrant community.

Waenhuiskrans is Afrikaans for "wag-on-house cliff," a name derived from the vast cave 2 km (1 mile) south of town that is theoretically large enough to house several wagons and their spans of oxen. Signs point the way over the dunes to the cave, which is accessible only at low tide. You need shoes to protect your feet from the sharp rocks, and you should wear something you don't mind getting wet. It's definitely worth the trouble,

Bontebok National Park is South Africa's smallest national park.

however, to stand in the enormous cave looking out to sea.

GETTING HERE AND AROUND
It takes about 20 to 30 minutes to drive here from Bredasdorp. Don't bother with public transport. Rent a car and you'll have the freedom to explore this vast area.

 Hotels

Arniston Spa Hotel
$$ | **HOTEL** | **FAMILY** | The setting, a crescent of white dunes, has a lot to do with the Arniston Spa Hotel's appeal, so request a sea-facing room and enjoy the ever-changing colors of the horizon and the grandstand view of the whales swimming by between June and November. **Pros:** good spot for children; great views of the beach; spa treatments. **Cons:** a bit noisy during high season; very few dining options nearby; can be windy in summer. ⓢ *Rooms from: R2060* ✉ *1 Arniston Rd., Arniston* ☎ *028/445–9000* ⊕ *www. arnistonhotel.com* 🛏 *67 rooms* ⅋ *Free Breakfast.*

Swellendam

72 km (45 miles) north of Arniston (Waenhuiskrans).

Beautiful Swellendam lies in the shadow of the imposing Langeberg Range. Established in 1745, it is the third-oldest town in South Africa, and many of its historic buildings have been elegantly restored. Even on a casual drive along the main street you'll see a number of lovely Cape Dutch homes, with their traditional whitewashed walls, peaked gables, and thatch roofs.

GETTING HERE AND AROUND
Swellendam is about an hour's drive from Arniston. Long distance buses pass by fairly frequently.

 Sights

Bontebok National Park
NATIONAL PARK | **FAMILY** | Covering just 6,880 acres of coastal fynbos, Bontebok National Park the smallest of South Africa's national parks. Don't expect to

see big game here—the park contains no elephants, lions, or rhinos. What you will see are bontebok, graceful white-face antelope nearly exterminated by hunters in the early 20th century, as well as red hartebeest, Cape grysbok, steenbok, duiker, and the endangered Cape mountain zebra. There are simple accommodations in the reserve and camping facilities. For day visitors there are a number of short but beautiful walks—seeing wildlife on foot is a wonderful experience. ✉ *Off N2, Swellendam* ✣ *4 km (2½ miles) west of Swellendam, signposted from the N2* ☎ *028/514–2735* 🌐 *www.sanparks.org* 🎟 *R150.*

Drostdy Museum

HISTORY MUSEUM | The Drostdy was built in 1747 by the Dutch East India Company to serve as the residence of the *land-drost,* the magistrate who presided over the district. The building is furnished in a style that dates back to the late 1700s and early 1800s. A path leads through the Drostdy herb gardens to Mayville, an 1855 middle-class home that blends elements of Cape Dutch and Cape Georgian architecture. Across Swellengrebel Street stand the old jail and an outdoor exhibit of tools used by the town's blacksmiths, wainwrights, coopers, and tanners. ✉ *18 Swellengrebel St., Swellendam* ☎ *028/514–1138* 🌐 *www.drostdy.com* 🎟 *R30.*

Dutch Reformed Church

CHURCH | Swellendam's Dutch Reformed Church is an imposing white edifice built in 1911 in an eclectic style. The gables are baroque, the windows Gothic, and the steeple a replica of one in Belgium. Surprisingly, all the elements work together wonderfully. Inside is an interesting tiered amphitheater with banks of curving wood pews facing the pulpit and organ. ✉ *7 Voortrek St., Swellendam* ☎ *028/514–1225* 🎟 *R20; services free* 🕒 *Closed Sat.*

Marloth Nature Reserve

NATURE PRESERVE | If you need to stretch your legs, take a hike in the Marloth Nature Reserve. Four easy walks, ranging from two to six hours, explore some of the mountain gorges. An office at the entrance to the reserve has trail maps and hiking information. If you're doing a day walk, park outside the entrance boom. Although you can stay in the reserve until sunset, the gates close at the time advertised. ✉ *Off Andrew White St., Swellendam* ☎ *028/514–1410* 🌐 *www.capenature.co.za* 🎟 *R50.*

🍴 Restaurants

La Sosta

$$$$ | **ITALIAN** | A restaurant of this caliber is a real find in small-town South Africa. The husband-and-wife team of Salvatore and Nina Branda create beautifully composed dishes combining South African produce with avant-garde Italian cooking. **Known for:** family run; good local wine list; lovely garden setting. [$] *Average main: R465* ✉ *145 Voortrek St., Swellendam* ☎ *028/514–1470* 🌐 *www.lasostarestaurant.com* 🕒 *Closed Sun. and Mon.*

🛏 Hotels

Augusta de Mist

$ | **B&B/INN** | This elegant Cape Dutch homestead, established in 1802, now serves as a comfortable retreat on 3½ acres of fynbos. **Pros:** fabulous decor; quiet, peaceful setting; friendly owner knows the area. **Cons:** Wi-Fi doesn't reach to all rooms; some steps to climb; no children under 14. [$] *Rooms from: R1000* ✉ *3 Human St., Swellendam* ☎ *028/514–2425* 🌐 *www.augustademist.com* 🛏 *6 suites* 🍽 *Free Breakfast.*

De Kloof Luxury Estate

$$$ | **HOTEL** | In beautifully manicured gardens, De Kloof Luxury Estate is a chic boutique hotel that offers five-star accommodations in one of the town's oldest Cape Dutch manors. **Pros:** lovely pool area; lush and tranquil setting; breathtaking scenery. **Cons:** only a prix-fixe menu option for dinner; Egyptian geese tend to break the silence; prior approval is needed for children under 8. [$] *Rooms from: R2995* ✉ *8 Weltevrede St., Swellendam* ☎ *028/514–1303* 🌐 *www.dekloof.co.za* 🛏 *8 suites* 🍴 *Free Breakfast.*

A Hilltop Country Retreat
$ | **B&B/INN** | **FAMILY** | In the foothills of the Langeberg Mountains, A Hilltop Retreat offers spacious and luxurious self-catering accommodations. **Pros:** great value; beautiful setting in the mountains; children are welcome. **Cons:** rooms are close together; no ovens in the kitchenettes; a steep walk back from town. [$] *Rooms from: R1800* ✉ *7 Bergsig Ave., Swellendam* ☎ *028/514–2294* 🌐 *www.ahilltop.co.za* 🛏 *10 rooms* 🍴 *No Meals.*

★ **Schoone Oordt**
$$$$ | **HOTEL** | **FAMILY** | The ultimate luxury getaway, this renovated Victorian manor house—with original ceilings, wooden floors, and antique furnishings—manages to seamlessly combine five-star decadence with unpretentious family hospitality. **Pros:** tons of history; glorious gardens with a swimming pool; family-friendly atmosphere. **Cons:** you might pile on a few pounds if you stay too long; Wi-Fi can be sporadic; rooms are not in the main house. [$] *Rooms from: R3900* ✉ *1 Swellengrebel St., Swellendam* ☎ *028/514–1248* 🌐 *www.schooneoordt.co.za* 🛏 *11 rooms* 🍴 *Free Breakfast.*

Activities

HORSEBACK RIDING

Two Feathers Horse Trails
HORSEBACK RIDING | You can take a little trot or a longer excursion on horseback through the stunning Marloth Nature Reserve. Full-day rides can be arranged on request and include a picnic lunch. ✉ *5 Liechtenstein St., Swellendam* ☎ *082/494–8279* 🎫 *R650.*

Greyton

94 km (58 miles) west of Swellendam.

The charming village of Greyton, filled with thatch cottages and quiet lanes, is a popular weekend retreat for Capetonians. The village offers little in the way of traditional sights, but it's a great base for walks into the surrounding mountains. There are plenty of small B&Bs and guesthouses, but no large hotels.

GETTING HERE AND AROUND

If you're driving from Swellendam, take the N2 west. Expect the trip to take an hour to an hour and a half.

VISITOR INFORMATION

CONTACTS Greyton Tourism Bureau. ✉ *29 Main Rd., Greyton* ☎ *028/254–9564* 🌐 *www.greytontourism.com.*

Sights

Genadendal (*Valley of Grace*)
TOWN | The neighboring village to Greyton is Genadendal, a Moravian mission founded in 1737. The first school in the interior opened its doors in 1738. In 1838, the first Teachers Training College in South Africa was established. Seeing this impoverished hamlet today, it's difficult to comprehend the major role the mission played in the early history of South Africa. Some of the first written works in Afrikaans were printed here, and the Coloured community greatly influenced the development of the language as it is spoken today. None of this went down well with the white government of the time. By 1909 new legislation prohibited Coloured ownership of land, and in 1926 the Department of Public Education closed the settlement's teachers' training college, arguing that Coloured people were better employed on neighboring farms.

In 1980 all the buildings on Church Square were declared national monuments, but despite a number of community-based projects, Genadendal has

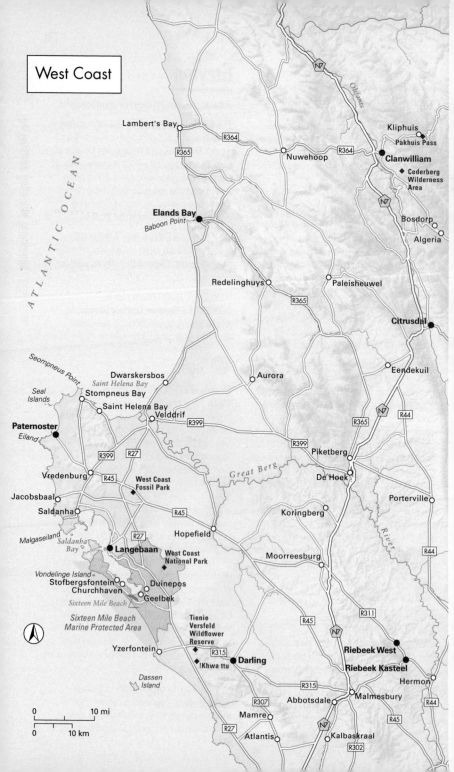

endured a long slide into obscurity. You can walk the streets and tour the historic buildings facing Church Square. Ask at the Genadendal Mission Museum for somebody to show you around. ✉ Genadendal ☎ 028/251–8582.

Genadendal Mission Museum

HISTORY MUSEUM | On the site of the original mission station, the Genadendal Mission Museum is spread through 15 rooms in three buildings. The collection includes items from early in the settlement's history, including the country's oldest pipe organ, brought in 1832. Wall displays examine mission life in the Cape in the 18th and 19th centuries, focusing on the early missionaries' work. ✉ Church Sq., Genadendal ☎ 028/251–8582 💲 R15 🕑 Closed Sun.

 Hotels

The Post House Hotel

$ | B&B/INN | In one of Greyton's oldest buildings, the Post House is now a convivial hotel with a cheery, small-town welcome. **Pros:** pretty courtyard; walking distance to numerous restaurants; meet the locals in the pub. **Cons:** Wi-Fi can be slow; pool is rather small; pub can get noisy on weekend nights. 💲 Rooms from: R1450 ✉ 22 Main Rd., Greyton ☎ 028/254–9995 ⊕ www.theposthouse.co.za 🛏 16 rooms ⦿ No Meals.

 Activities

HIKING

Boesmanskloof Trail

HIKING & WALKING | Take the 14-km (8½-mile) Boesmanskloof Trail through the Riviersonderend Mountains between the exquisite hamlets of Greyton and McGregor. It's a gorgeous hike past steep gorges, sprawling rock pools, and tumbling waterfalls. You do need a permit to do the hike; buy one from the Greyton or McGregor tourism offices. Take water and adequate protective clothing, as the weather can change quickly. 🎫 Permits R30.

Darling

82 km (51 miles) north of Cape Town.

Covered in wildflowers, Darling comes alive every year for the Wildflower and Orchid Show, held in September, and for the hugely popular music festival called Rocking the Daisies, held each October on Cloof Wine Estate.

Darling is also famous for the Voorkamerfest (or "Front Room Festival"), when different homes host a variety of performers for the weekend and you can enjoy pop-up food stalls and wine tastings.

GETTING HERE AND AROUND

Darling is an easy hour's drive from Cape Town along the N7 north and then west on the R315. Alternately, you could go north on the R27 out of town, then east on the R315.

VISITOR INFORMATION

CONTACTS Darling Tourism Bureau. ✉ Darling Museum, Pastorie St. at Hill St., Darling ☎ 022/492–3361 ⊕ www.hellodarling.org.za.

 Sights

Darling Brew

BREWERY | **FAMILY** | Launched in 2010, Darling Brew has become one of the Western Cape's most-loved craft beer brands. The beers can be found at many local restaurants and bars, but it's more fun to visit the microbrewery. You can sample craft beers in the tasting room, which also serves typically South African snacks and meals. While heavyweights have their pick of seven regular and nine specialty beers, lightweights can opt for the "beginner's beer tasting." Some of the favorites include the Slow Beer, a refreshing, golden lager, and the Bone Crusher, a Belgian witbier. ✉ 48 Caledon St., Darling ☎ 076/092–8313 ⊕ www.darlingbrew.co.za.

★ **!Khwa ttu**

HISTORY MUSEUM | If you love culture and history, you'll love !Khwa ttu, a nature reserve and education center on a former wheat farm. This is a place to learn about the San people and their history. You can do a self-guided tour, but it makes sense to pay extra and take the tour with a knowledgeable guide. A laid-back restaurant serves local food and wine, and simple accommodations are available. Visitors can take part in numerous outdoor activities, including hiking and biking. ✉ *R27, West Coast Rd, Darling* ✣ *70 km (43 miles) from Cape Town* ☎ *022/492–2998* 🌐 *www.khwattu.org* 🎟 *Self-guided tour R80.*

Tienie Versfeld Wildflower Reserve

NATURE PRESERVE | From August to early October, the wonderful Tienie Versfeld Wildflower Reserve is an unpretentious, uncommercial little gem showing off a range of South African veld plants. Look out for the geophytes—plants uniquely adapted for this type of environment—which come in a striking array of sizes and colors. ✉ *R315, Darling* ✣ *12 km (7½ miles) west of Darling* 🌐 *www.sa-venues.com/game-reserves/wc_tienie-versveld.htm* 🎟 *Free.*

WINERIES

Darling Cellars

WINERY | This large producer makes wines under a number of labels. Look out for the Premium range as well as the award-winning Darling Cellars Blanc de Blanc sparkling wine. Other suggestions include the Reserve Bush Vine Sauvignon Blanc, with notes of cut grass, passion fruit, green figs, traces of guava on the nose, and a zingy aftertaste. Don't miss out on the Sweet Darling range, a selection of white, red, and rosé wines made from local grapes. It's all good, drinkable stuff at very affordable prices. ✉ *R315, Darling* ☎ *022/492–2276* 🌐 *www.darlingcellars.co.za* 🎟 *Tastings R30.*

Groote Post Vineyard

WINERY | **FAMILY** | Former dairy farmer Peter Pentz had enough of getting up at 4 am to milk his cows, so together with his son, Nick, he turned instead to grapes at Groote Post Vineyard. The large, environmentally sensitive winery got off to a fantastic start when its maiden 1999 Sauvignon Blanc was judged one of the best in the Cape, and Groote Post has been winning awards ever since. Try the Groote Post Kapokberg Sauvignon Blanc, packed with flavors of granadilla, green fig, and green pepper. The restaurant, Hilda's Kitchen, is an excellent choice for lunch and makes scrumptious picnic baskets teeming with local cheeses and cured meats, quiches, and chocolate brownies (order these in advance). Game drives through the unique *renosterveld* ("rhino vegetation" in Afrikaans) are offered during the summer; advanced bookings are essential. ✉ *Off R307, Darling* ☎ *022/492–2825* 🌐 *www.grootepost.com* 🎟 *Tastings R30.*

🛏 Hotels

Darling Lodge

$ | **B&B/INN** | You'll soon feel at home at this pretty Victorian B&B in the heart of the village. **Pros:** only 20 minutes from the coast; centrally located in Darling; perfect accommodations for families. **Cons:** Wi-Fi can be unreliable; no air-conditioning; limited number of rooms. [$] *Rooms from: R1080* ✉ *22 Pastorie St., Darling* ☎ *022/492–3062* 🌐 *www.darlinglodge.co.za* 🔑 *6 rooms* 🍴 *Free Breakfast.*

🎟 Performing Arts

★ **Evita se Perron**

THEATER | One of Darling's main attractions is Evita se Perron, the theater started by satirist and social activist Pieter-Dirk Uys. The cabaret venue is on the platform of Darling Station (*perron* is the Afrikaans word for "railway

Pieter-Dirk Uys: Everyone's Darling

It's fitting that Pieter-Dirk Uys and his alter ego, Evita Bezuidenhout, live in a village called Darling. He's the darling of South African satire, and his speech is peppered with dramatic and warmhearted "dahlings." *Tannie* (Auntie) Evita is as much a South African icon as braais and biltong.

Evita Bezuidenhout debuted in a newspaper column written by playwright Pieter-Dirk Uys in the 1970s. He dished the dirt as though he were an insider at the National-ist Party. Evita hit the stage in the early 1980s, when apartheid was in full swing and the ruling Nationalist Party was short on humor.

Uys's first production, *Adapt or Dye*, was performed at a small venue in Johannesburg at 11 pm, a time when he hoped the censors would be in bed. The titles of his shows and some characters (all of which he plays himself) are intricately wound up with South African politics and life.

Over the years, Uys's richest material has come from the government. Most politicians have been happy to be lampooned, because laughing at themselves made them seem more human. If there's any criticism leveled at Uys, it's that he held back too much. He would argue that too many punches don't put people in seats; too many tickles can be vacuous.

Uys is not just about comedy and satire, however. He's deeply commit-ted to transforming society. He has channeled his considerable energy into tackling HIV/AIDS. At schools he demonstrates how to put a condom on a banana. This he swiftly replaces with a rubber phallus, explaining with a twinkle that "men and boys don't have bananas between their legs. A condom on a banana on the bedside table is not going to protect you!" Of course, the kids shriek with laughter. As always, humor is his weapon of mass distraction.

—Karena du Plessis

platform"). The performer has made his alter ego, Evita Bezuidenhout, a household name in South Africa. Performances—which are in equal parts poignant and hilarious—usually take place Saturday afternoon and evening and Sunday afternoon. Come early to enjoy a two- or three-course meal in the restaurant. ⊠ *Darling Station, 8 Arcadia St., Darling* ☎ *022/492–2101* ⊕ *www.evita.co.za* ✉ *R200.*

Langebaan

50 km (31 miles) northwest of Darling.

One of the most popular destinations on the coast, Langebaan is a great base from which to explore the region. The sheltered lagoon makes for fantastic water sports, especially windsurfing, kite surfing, and sea kayaking. The town has a truly laid-back, beachy feel. To quote a local: "There is nowhere in Langebaan you can't go barefoot." Lots of Capetoni-ans have weekend houses and head here on Friday afternoon with boats, bikes, and boards in tow.

The town comes alive in summer as youngsters crowd the beach and flex their muscles, during the off-season Langebaan quickly reverts to a quiet settlement where people retire to fish and mess about on boats.

GETTING HERE AND AROUND

It's about 40 minutes by car from Darling to Langebaan.

VISITOR INFORMATION

CONTACTS Langebaan Tourism Bureau. ✉ *Municipal Bldg., Bree St., Langebaan* ☎ *022/772–1515.*

Sights

West Coast Fossil Park

NATURE SIGHT | FAMILY | About 20 minutes from Langebaan, West Coast Fossil Park is one of the richest fossil sites in the world. It was discovered by chance while the area was being mined for phosphates in the 1950s. Since then, more than 200 kinds of fossilized animals have been collected, including the fearsome African bear, which used to roam this area. The park has been declared a national monument, and the curators have done much to make the park as accessible as possible. There are interactive guided tours, cycling trails through the areas, and interesting archaeological workshops for all ages. There's also a children's play park and a coffee shop where you can have a toasted sandwich. ✉ *R45, Langebaan* ☎ *022/766–1606* 🌐 *www.fossilpark.org.za* 🎟 *R50, tours R100* 🕐 *Closed Mon.*

West Coast National Park

NATIONAL PARK | FAMILY | Even if you don't stop at the West Coast National Park, consider driving along the scenic road that runs through it. The park is a fabulous mix of wetlands and coastal fynbos. On a sunny day the lagoon assumes a magical color, made all the more impressive by blinding white beaches and the sheer emptiness of the place. Birders can have a field day identifying waterbirds, including curlew and bar-tailed godwits. The little mountain at the tip of the reserve where ships would drop off their mail on their trip around the Cape, is open only in flower season, which changes from year to year but falls somewhere between August and early October.

It's easy to run out of superlatives when describing West Coast flowers, but imagine acres of land carpeted in multicolored blooms as far as the eye can see. If you're lucky, you may catch glimpses of zebra, wildebeest, or bat-eared foxes. Keep an eye out for tortoises crossing the road. There is a handful of cute cottages dotted around the park if you'd like to stay over, or for something a little more unusual, check out the houseboats permanently moored in the lagoon. Accommodations get booked up months in advance for flower season, so plan ahead. ✉ *Off the R27, Langebaan* ✣ *11 km (7 miles) north of the R315* ☎ *022/772–2144* 🌐 *www.sanparks.org* 🎟 *R220.*

Restaurants

★ Die Strandloper Seafood Restaurant

$$$$ | SEAFOOD | For a no-frills lunch on the beach, book a table at Die Strandloper. Bring your own drinks and games and expect to linger for the afternoon. **Known for:** rustic setting; bring your own libations; kid-friendly atmosphere. [$] *Average main: R350* ✉ *Off Jon Olaffson Rd., Langebaan* ✣ *2½ km (1½ miles) north of town* ☎ *022/772–2490* 🌐 *www.strandloper.com* 💳 *No credit cards* 🕐 *Closed Mon., Wed., and Thurs.*

Geelbek Restaurant

$$ | SOUTH AFRICAN | FAMILY | In an old homestead dating back to 1761, this is the spot for traditional Cape dishes like fragrant Malay chicken curry, hearty bobotie, and *denningsvleis*, a Cape Malay lamb stew flavored with tamarind.

You can climb the lighthouse at Columbine Nature Reserve for a small fee.

This is also a great place for tea. **Known for:** fish and seafood dishes; historic setting; traditional cuisine. $ *Average main: R135* ⊠ *West Coast National Park, Northern Entrance Rd., Langebaan* ☎ *084/406–7434* ⊕ *www.sanparks.org/ parks/west_coast/tourism/restaurant.php* ☾ *No dinner.*

 Hotels

The Farmhouse Hotel
$$ | HOTEL | In a farmstead originally built in the 1860s, this hotel has thick whitewashed walls, tile floors, and timber beams. **Pros:** relaxed atmosphere; great views over the lagoon; daily tea and scones. **Cons:** area can be very windy; few rooms have air-conditioning; avoid noisy rooms above the kitchen. $ *Rooms from: R1890* ⊠ *5 Egret St., Langebaan* ☎ *022/772–2062* ⊕ *www.thefarm- househotel.com* ⇥ *18 rooms* ⦿ *Free Breakfast.*

Friday Island
$ | HOTEL | FAMILY | If you can't wait to hit the water, then this guesthouse is a great choice. **Pros:** right on the beach; perfect for family vacations; very friendly service. **Cons:** sports center can get noisy; the area can get pretty windy; can draw a boisterous crowd. $ *Rooms from: R1220* ⊠ *92 Main St., Langebaan* ☎ *081/071–9701* ⊕ *www.fridayisland. co.za* ⇥ *12 rooms* ⦿ *No Meals.*

 Activities

The sheltered Langebaan Lagoon is a haven for watersports enthusiasts, but you don't have to be energetic all the time. There are expansive stretches of beach that are good for walking, sunbathing, and kite flying. Be warned, however: the water might look calm and idyllic, but it's cold, and the wind can blow unmerci- fully for days at a stretch. It's fantastic for wind- or kite surfing, but not so great if you want to spend a peaceful day under your umbrella with a book.

Cape Sports Centre

WATER SPORTS | You'll find everything you need here to kite surf, windsurf or canoe. You can rent gear or take lessons from qualified instructors. Cape Sports Centre also has a café and bar. ✉ *98 Main St., Langebaan* ☎ *022/772–1114* 🌐 *www.capesports.co.za.*

Paternoster

47 km (29 miles) northwest of Langebaan.

Paternoster is a mostly unspoiled village of whitewashed thatch cottages perched on a deserted stretch of coastline. The population here consists mainly of fisherfolk who for generations have eked out a living harvesting crayfish and other seafood, and city folk who fancy a change of pace.

GETTING HERE AND AROUND

Paternoster is about a half-hour drive from Langebaan. Take Langebaanweg out of town until you reach the junction with the R45. Turn left and head northwest toward Paternoster. At Vredenburg the road name changes to the R399.

Sights

Columbine Nature Reserve

NATURE PRESERVE | Along the coast just south of Paternoster, the 692-acre Columbine Nature Reserve is a great spot for spring wildflowers, coastal fynbos, and succulents. Cormorants and sacred ibis are common here, and the population of the endangered African black oystercatcher is growing each year. Die-hard anglers revel in the abundant fish. There is also a squat lighthouse that you can climb for a small fee. A round-trip through the reserve is 7 km (4 miles). It's very exposed, however, so don't plan to walk in the middle of the day or you'll end up with some serious sunburn. The dusty road has no name, but head south out of town and ask directions along the way. It's impossible to get lost—there aren't that many roads to choose from. ✉ *Paternoster* ✥ *8 km (5 miles) south of Paternoster* ☎ *022/752–2718* 🎫 *R29.*

Restaurants

The Noisy Oyster

$$ | **SEAFOOD** | Quirky and brightly decorated, this unpretentious gem is not to be missed. Because the freshest local ingredients are used, the menu changes frequently. **Known for:** freshly caught seafood; al fresco eating; local characters. $ *Average main: R150* ✉ *St. Augustine Rd., Paternoster* ☎ *022/752–2196* 🌐 *www.facebook.com/noisyoysterpaternoster* 🕒 *Closed Mon. and Tues. No dinner Sun.*

Oep ve Koep

$$ | **SOUTH AFRICAN** | Don't be fooled by the appearance of this tiny rustic bistro with retro garden area. The sensational and ever-changing blackboard menu is the ultimate in fresh, local fare. **Known for:** fresh fish; foraged ingredients; daily menu. $ *Average main: R150* ✉ *St. Augustine Rd., Paternoster* ☎ *072/741–3709* 🌐 *www.oepvekoep.co.za* 🕒 *No dinner.*

Voorstrandt

$$ | **SEAFOOD** | **FAMILY** | This corrugated-iron shack on the beach stood empty for years, then suddenly metamorphosed into a buzzing seafood restaurant. As well as the usual seafood and fish, you'll find fish curries, deep-fried calimari, and smoked snoek samosas on the menu. **Known for:** good children's menu; watch the whales in the bay; freshly caught seafood. $ *Average main: R135* ✉ *Strandloper St., Paternoster* ☎ *022/752–2038* 🌐 *www.voorstrandt.com.*

There are numerous trails through the twisted rock formations that make up the Cederberg mountains.

★ Wolfgat

$$$$ | SEAFOOD | The tasting menu at this award-winning restaurant from Chef Kobus van de Merwe focuses on all that is local and sustainable, including fresh seafood, seaweed, foraged plants, and pickings from the garden. The food is sublime, but very experimental, so make sure you're up for something new and inventive. **Known for:** innovative dishes; endless ocean views; hard-to-get reservations. [$] *Average main: R1050* ✉ *10 Sampson St., Paternoster* 🌐 *www.wolfgat.co.za* 🕒 *Closed Mon.–Wed. No dinner Thurs. and Sun.*

Hotels

Abalone House & Villas

$$ | HOTEL | This boutique hotel set in gorgeous gardens balances a muted color scheme and bold paintings adorning the walls. **Pros:** short walk to the beach; lovely restaurant; great value. **Cons:** service can be slow; breakfast isn't included; not all rooms have an ocean view. [$] *Rooms from: R1800* ✉ *3 Kriedoring St., Paternoster* ☎ *022/752–2044* 🌐 *www.abalonehotel.co.za* 🛏 *10 suites.*

Paternoster Lodge & Restaurant

$ | B&B/INN | This lodge makes the most of the sweeping views of the Atlantic Ocean; the rooms might be simply decorated, but who needs artwork when at every turn you catch glimpses of the azure sea? At any rate, the rooms are comfortable and—a big plus—they all open onto verandahs. **Pros:** kids under 5 stay free; easy stroll to the beach; breakfast served in your room. **Cons:** rooms are close together; no swimming pool; the wind can blow. [$] *Rooms from: R1800* ✉ *64 St. Augustine Rd., Paternoster* ☎ *083/551–7502* 🌐 *www.paternosterlodge.co.za* 🛏 *7 rooms* 🍴 *Free Breakfast.*

Elands Bay

75 km (46½ miles) north of Paternoster.

Mention eBay auctions here, and most people will stare at you blankly. But mention the E'bay left-hand break, and you'll get nods of approval and instant admission into the inner circle of experienced surfers, who make the pilgrimage to Elands Bay to experience some of the Western Cape's best surfing.

This lovely destination is at the mouth of the beautiful Verlorenvlei Lagoon. Verlorenvlei (Afrikaans for "lost wetland," a testimony to its remoteness) is a birder's delight; you're likely to see around 240 species, including white pelicans, purple gallinules, African spoonbills, African fish eagles, and purple herons. Nearby are some fantastic walks to interesting caves with well-preserved rock art that dates back to the Pleistocene era, 10,000 years ago.

GETTING HERE AND AROUND

Elands Bay is a 1½-hour drive from Paternoster. To get here, double back on the R399 to Vredenburg, then take the R399 north to Velddrif. You'll join the R27 at a junction just outside Velddrif. Follow the signs to Elands Bay through town and continue on to what looks like a secondary road. It may not seem to have a number, but it's still the R27.

 Restaurants

★ Muisbosskerm

$$$$ | SOUTH AFRICAN | For the true flavor of West Coast life, come to this open-air seafood restaurant on the beach south of Lambert's Bay. You'll watch fish cooked over blazing fires, snoek smoked in an old drum covered with burlap, and bread baked in a clay oven. **Known for:** it's all-you-can-eat; fish sizzles on grills and in giant pots; you won't find a more laid-back setting. $ *Average main: R350 ⊠ Elands Bay Rd., Elands Bay ⊕ 5 km (3 miles) south of Lambert's Bay ☎ 027/432–1017 ⊕ www.muisbosskerm. co.za.*

Clanwilliam

46 km (28½ miles) northeast of Elands Bay.

It's no surprise that half the streets are named after trees or plants. Clanwilliam is at the edge of one of the natural jewels of the Western Cape—the Cederberg Wilderness Area, which takes its name from the cedar trees that used to cover the mountains. In spring the town is inundated with flower-watchers. Clanwilliam is also the center of the rooibos-tea industry.

Clanwilliam was home to Dr. Christiaan Louis Leipoldt, poet and Renaissance man. He is buried in a lovely spot in the mountains a little way out of town; you can visit his grave, which is on the way to the Pakhuis Pass. You could also pop into the Clanwilliam Museum, which houses a room devoted to Leipoldt.

GETTING HERE AND AROUND

Driving to Clanwilliam takes close to three hours from Cape Town without stopping, but half the fun is checking out what local farm stalls have to offer and stopping to admire the scenery. In spring this trip will take much longer, as you'll likely want to stop to photograph the flowers that carpet the countryside.

VISITOR INFORMATION

CONTACTS Clanwilliam Tourism Bureau.
⊠ *34 Main Rd, Clanwilliam ☎ 027/482–2024 ⊕ www.clanwilliam.info.*

The open caves and rock formations that make up the Stadsaal Caves are particularly impressive to see at sundown.

Sights

★ Cederberg Wilderness Area

MOUNTAIN | Clanwilliam is close to the northern edge of the Cederberg, a mountain range known for its San rock paintings, its bizarre rock formations, and, once upon a time, its cedars. Most of the ancient cedars have been cut down, but a few specimens still survive in the more remote regions. The Cederberg is a hiking paradise—a wild, largely unspoiled area where you can disappear from civilization for days at a time. About 172,900 acres of this mountain range constitute what has been declared the Cederberg Wilderness Area. Try to visit in spring when the area is carpeted in orange, yellow, and white flowers. You can get hiking permits from Cape Nature or the local tourism offices in Clanwilliam or Citrusdal. Be sure to tell somebody if you are planning to hike in the area.

A scenic dirt road that heads south out of town, past the tourism bureau and museum, winds for about 30 km (18 miles) into the Cederberg to Algeria, a Cape Nature campsite with self-catering cottages and tent sites set in an idyllic valley. Algeria is the starting point for several excellent hikes into the Cederberg. The short, one-hour hike to a waterfall is great, but it's worth going into the mountains for a day or two, for which you will need to book and obtain a permit through CapeNature or from one of the local farms, many of which have simple, self-catering cottages on their land. ⊠ *Algeria Forest Station, Clanwilliam* ⊕ *www.capenature.co.za.*

Clanwilliam Museum (*Ou Tronk Museum*)
HISTORY MUSEUM | Also known as the Ou Tronk Museum, this small collection is based in the former town jail (*ou tronk* means "old jail"). The display is old-fashioned and not particularly well curated, but still gives a sense of remarkable native son Dr. Christiaan Louis Leipoldt and early settler life in the mountains. The wagons, carts, and rudimentary household equipment speak of much harder times, when pioneers headed

San Rock Art

The Cederberg has astonishing examples of San rock art, and there is a concerted effort to find ways of managing these sites. On your explorations you'll come across paintings of elephants, eland, bees, people, and otherworldly beings that seem to be half human and half beast. Some examples are in pristine condition, whereas others are battered and scarred from a time when hikers saw nothing wrong with scribbling their names across the art.

For centuries, people believed the rock art was simply a record of what happened during the daily lives of the San. But since about 1970, there has been a belief that the art is much richer and carries enormous spiritual meaning that tells us about the inner lives of the San. Drawings of an eland, for instance, are not simply depictions of animals the San have seen or hope to hunt. Rather, the eland serves as an intermediary between the physical and spiritual worlds.

The Stadsaal Caves in the Cederberg have some fine examples of San rock paintings. A slightly more accessible location is the Sevilla Rock Art Trail at the Traveller's Rest on Pakhuis Pass, where you can find nine sites along a 5-km (3-mile) hike.

into the high country wanting to farm or escape colonial control in the cities. ⊠ *Main Rd., Clanwilliam* ☎ *027/482–2024* ⊕ *clanwilliammuseum.webs.com* 🖃 *R15* ⊙ *Closed Sun.*

Pakhuis Pass

SCENIC DRIVE | East of Clanwilliam, the R364 becomes a spectacularly scenic road called Pakhuis Pass. Fantastic rock formations glow in the early morning or late afternoon. A steep, narrow road to the right leads to the mission town of Wupperthal, with its characteristic thatch houses and sleepy air. This used to be a thriving Moravian mission station, and remnants of the old industries remain. A baker still turns out soft, yeasty loaves that are snapped up as fast as they come out of the oven, and you can see shoes being made in the local shoe factory. The main industry here today though is the cultivation of rooibos tea. You can drive this road in an ordinary rental car, but be very careful in wet weather. ⊠ *Pakhuis Pass, Clanwilliam.*

Ramskop Wildflower Garden

GARDEN | At its best in August—when the Clanwilliam Flower Show takes place at the old Dutch Reformed church—the Ramskop Wildflower Garden is a wonderful opportunity to see many of the region's flowers all growing in one place. The best time to go is between 11 am and 3 pm, when the sun is at its apex and the flowers are open. You pay to enter the flower garden at the entrance of the Clanwilliam Dam, on the road out of town past the garden. They won't charge you if the weather isn't great and the flowers aren't at their best—that's small-town hospitality for you. There is a simple coffee shop in the garden. Expect opening times to vary for no particular reason. ⊠ *Ou Kaapseweg, Clanwilliam* ☎ *027/482–8012* 🖃 *R20–R30.*

Stadsaal Caves & Rock Paintings

CAVE | Located deep in the Cederberg, this complex of caves is wonderful at sunset, when the rays light up the russet landscape. It's highly likely that the San once called these caves home, and as you wander through the different

This San rock art site near the Stadsaal Cave has centuries-old paintings of elephants and people etched onto the rocks.

caverns, you could imagine it making a pretty spectacular place to live. Nearby is a San rock art site, where you'll find centuries-old paintings of elephants and people etched onto the rocks. Although it's a long and bumpy drive to get here from the N7, it's still one of the most accessible rock art sites in the Cederberg because it requires only a gentle stroll from the car park. Permits to visit the caves and rock art can be purchased at Algeria Campsite or at Sanddrif Farm, home of Cederberg Private Cellar. When you pay for your permit you'll be given the combination to a lock on the entry gate. ⊠ Clanwilliam ✛ 35 km southeast of Algeria Forest Station ☎ R50.

WINERIES

★ Cederberg Private Cellar

WINERY | The Cederberg mountain range might be the last place you'd expect to find a vineyard, but that's what makes Cederberg Private Cellar so unusual.

When old man Nieuwoudt, known to everyone as "Oom Pollie," planted the first vines in 1973, all his sheep-farming neighbors thought he had gone mad. Today, however, winemaker David Nieuwoudt and his small team are laughing all the way to the awards ceremonies. At an altitude of around 3,300 feet, this is the highest vineyard in the Western Cape, and consequently is almost completely disease-free. All the wines are excellent; in fact, you'll struggle to see the labels for all the wine accolades pasted on the bottles. The Cederberg Observatory is an open-air wonder run by passionate stargazers who help you spot faraway galaxies with their super-powerful telescopes. The little farm shop usually stocks delicious koeksisters served with strong coffee. ⊠ Dwarsrivier Farm, Algeria turnoff from the N7, Clanwilliam ☎ 027/482–2827 ⊕ www.cederbergwine. com ☎ Tastings R50 ⏱ Closed Sun.

Rooibos Tea 🍴

Chances are you will either love or hate *rooibos* (red bush) tea, which South Africans drink in vast quantities. It has an unusual, earthy taste, and is naturally sweet. People drink it hot with lemon and honey or with milk or as a refreshing iced tea with slices of lemon and a sprig of mint. It's rich in minerals like copper, iron, potassium, calcium, fluoride, zinc, manganese, and magnesium. Best of all, it has no caffeine.

Trendy chefs are incorporating it into their cooking, and you might see rooibos-infused sauces or marinades mentioned on menus. Good coffee shops also serve red cappuccinos and lattes—a delicious and healthful alternative to their coffee counterparts.

Rooibos leaves are coarser than regular tea and look like finely chopped sticks. When they're harvested, they're green; then they're chopped, bruised, and left to ferment in mounds before being spread out to dry in the baking summer sun. The fermentation process turns the leaves red—hence the name. Rooibos is endemic to the Cederberg, and Clanwilliam has latched onto this, developing the Rooibos Route (🌐 *www.rooibos-route.co.za*), a collection of local attractions where you can learn about the cultivation and processing of the tea, taste it in all its forms and even buy cosmetics that feature the plant.

🛏 Hotels

★ Bushmans Kloof Wilderness Reserve & Wellness Retreat
$$$$ | **HOTEL** | The stark beauty of the mountains, the incredible rock formations, and the tumbling waterfalls of this nature reserve were probably as attractive to the San of long ago as they are to visitors today. **Pros:** you can fly to the reserve from Cape Town; incredible rock art; wildflowers in August and September. **Cons:** you'll need pants a size bigger by the time you leave; kids only allowed at Koro Lodge; very expensive rates. [$] *Rooms from: R7860* ✉ *Off Pakhuis Pass, Clanwilliam* ☎ *087/743-2399* 🌐 *www.bushmanskloof.co.za* 🛏 *16 rooms* 🍴 *Free Breakfast.*

Traveller's Rest
$ | **RESORT** | If you're on a tight budget, this farm is the place to stay. **Pros:** nearby rock-art route; very reasonable rates; cottages are self-catering. **Cons:** amenities are very basic; Wi-Fi can be hit and miss; service at the restaurant can be slow. [$] *Rooms from: R700* ✉ *Off Pakhuis Pass, Clanwilliam* ☎ *082/554-9303* 🌐 *www.travellersrest.co.za* 🛏 *25 cottages* 🍴 *Free Breakfast.*

🛍 Shopping

Strassberger Shoe Factory
SHOES | *Veldskoen*—or *vellies*, as they're fondly known—are something of a South African institution. All you have to do is think of the singer David Kramer and his signature red shoes to understand the place they hold in most South Africans' hearts. Vellies used to be the preserve of hardy farmers, who would wear these sturdy shoes with socks and shorts in winter, and with shorts but no socks in summer. Thankfully, the styles have changed somewhat, and now you can get the softest shoes made to order from the Strassberger Shoe Factory. The shoemakers you see working here come from generations of craftspeople dating back to when the Moravian missionaries first

started shoemaking in Wupperthal. ✉ *12 Ou Kaapseweg, Clanwilliam* ☎ *027/482–1439* 🌐 *www.strassbergers.co.za.*

Citrusdal

53 km (33 miles) south of Clanwilliam.

As you might guess from the name, Citrusdal is a fruit-growing town. It sits by the Olifants River valley, surrounded by the peaks of the Cederberg, and is known as the gateway to the Cederberg. For the most part it's a sleepy farming town with not much going on, but in spring the smell of fruit blossoms as you come over the Piekenierskloof Pass is incredible.

GETTING HERE AND AROUND

It takes about 45 minutes on the N7 from Clanwilliam to Citrusdal. It's a two-hour drive from Cape Town.

VISITOR INFORMATION

CONTACTS Citrusdal Tourism Bureau. ✉ *89 Muller St., Citrusdal* ☎ *022/921–3210* 🌐 *www.citrusdal.info.*

Hotels

The Baths

$$ | **RESORT** | **FAMILY** | After a grueling hike in the Cederberg, there's no better way to relax than at the Baths, where hot mineral water gushes from a natural spring. **Pros:** great for families; beautiful setting; excellent value. **Cons:** not all rooms have air-conditioning; there aren't any shops or restaurants nearby; weekends can get very busy. [$] *Rooms from: R1500* ✉ *The Baths Rd., Citrusdal* ✣ *16 km (10 miles) outside Citrusdal; follow signs* ☎ *022/921–8026* 🌐 *www.thebaths.co.za* 🛏 *22 cottages* 🍴 *No Meals.*

Kagga Kamma Nature Reserve

$$ | **RESORT** | Located in the Swartruggens area of the Cederberg, Kagga Kamma offers well-appointed suites carved out of an unworldly red-sandstone outcrop—whoever thought sleeping in a rock cave could be luxurious? If caves aren't your thing, there are also Hut suites that are designed to resemble Khoi and San dwellings. **Pros:** onsite spa; air-conditioned rooms; tour of choice included in your stay. **Cons:** those averse to nature should think twice. [$] *Rooms from: R2670* ✉ *Kagga Kamma Nature Reserve, Citrusdal* ✣ *201 km (125 miles) southeast of Citrusdal* ☎ *023/004–0077* 🌐 *www.kaggakamma.co.za* 🛏 *15 units* 🍴 *All-Inclusive.*

Riebeek West and Riebeek Kasteel

104 km (65 miles) south of Citrusdal.

Drive over Bothman's Kloof Pass to these twin towns named after Jan van Riebeeck, the 17th-century Dutch explorer of the Cape. The towns developed only a few miles apart because of a disagreement about where to build a church. In the end, two separate places of worship were built, and two distinct towns grew up around them.

These days there is more to see and do in Riebeeck Kasteel. There are wine estates producing some great red wines and port, and the region is particularly known for its world-class olives and olive oil. The *kasteel*, or castle, in question is the Kasteelberg (Castle Mountain), which stands sentinel behind the towns.

Disenchanted city dwellers have been buying up cottages here to use as weekend getaways. It's not hard to understand why. Children play in the street and people keep sheep in their huge gardens—a far cry from Cape Town life. There are numerous restaurants, some galleries, and plenty of olive products to buy.

GETTING HERE AND AROUND

The Riebeek Valley is an hour and a half from Citrusdal via the N7 and R311 without traffic.

VISITOR INFORMATION

CONTACTS Riebeek Valley Tourism. ✉ *11 Plein St., Riebeek Kasteel* ☎ *022/001–0096* 🌐 *www.riebeekvalley.info.*

Sights

WINERIES

Allesverloren

WINERY | The red wines here are big, bold, and delicious. Packed with black-currant and tobacco flavors, and with a lingering fruitcake finish, the port (called the Allesverloren Fine Old Vintage) is an award-winner and perfect for cool winter evenings. A family-friendly restaurant and pub on the premises means you can dine in a beautiful setting. Translated from Afrikaans, Allesverloren means "all is lost." The bleak name derives from a story from the early 1700s, when the widow Cloete owned this farm. Legend has it that she left the farm for a few weeks to attend a church gathering in town, and in her absence the resentful tribespeople set her homestead alight. When she came back to a smoldering ruin, she declared, "Allesverloren," and the name stuck. These days though, there's plenty to celebrate and plenty of reasons to visit. ✉ *R311, between Riebeek Kasteel and Riebeek West* ☎ *022/461–2320* 🌐 *www.allesverloren.co.za* 🎫 *Tastings R35* 🕒 *Closed Sun.*

Kloovenburg Wine Estate

WINERY | This family-run farm has many awards under its belt and is probably best known for its excellent Shiraz, a ruby red wine with smoky flavors and a chocolate aftertaste. Also worth taking home is the Merlot, with sweet berry and oak flavors and excellent aging potential. The Eight Feet is a fun but very drinkable testimony to the generations of du Toits who have worked the land: it alludes to the eight grape-stomping feet of the owners' four sons. Don't miss out on Annalene du Toit's olive products. Kloovenburg olive oils are exceptional, and they manufacture olive oil beauty products, too. ✉ *R46* ☎ *022/448–1635* 🌐 *www.kloovenburg.com* 🎫 *Wine tastings R50, olive tastings R50.*

Restaurants

The Barn

$$ | MEDITERRANEAN | FAMILY | This friendly, long-running place on the main approach road to Riebeek Kasteel is a lovely spot to sit outside and enjoy a glass of the local wine. The menu is a meaty affair, with a range of perfectly cooked steaks and a tender, juicy ostrich fillet. **Known for:** Mediterranean flavors; outdoor tables overlooking the valley; children's play area. [$] *Average main: R150* ✉ *34 Church St, Riebeek Kasteel* ☎ *071/844–2726* 🌐 *www.thebarnriebeek.com* 🕒 *Closed Mon. No dinner Sun.*

Hotels

Riebeek Valley Country Retreat

$ | HOTEL | With a great view over vineyards and mountains, this small luxury hotel in a converted farmhouse is an oasis from the sweltering Swartland summer heat (and great as a winter getaway, as well). **Pros:** indoor heated pool; soothing spa treatments; excellent breakfast. **Cons:** no in-house dinners available; organic outdoor pool is akin to a large pond; avoid Room 8, located near the noisy kitchen. [$] *Rooms from: R1350* ✉ *4 Dennehof St., Riebeek West* ☎ *081/409–6624* 🌐 *www.riebeekvalleyhotel.co.za* 🛏 *30 rooms* 🍴 *Free Breakfast.*

Chapter 6

THE NORTHERN CAPE

Updated by
Keith Bain

⊙ Sights	🍴 Restaurants	🛏 Hotels	⊜ Shopping	☻ Nightlife
★★★★★	★★★☆☆	★★★☆☆	★☆☆☆☆	☆☆☆☆☆

WELCOME TO THE NORTHERN CAPE

TOP REASONS TO GO

★ **Getting Off the Beaten Path:** Its size and slightly mysterious character mean that this remains South Africa's least discovered province, where less is indisputably more.

★ **Scenery:** Amid mesmerizing semi-arid desolation and virtual moonscapes, there are awesome and beautiful landscapes featuring the curious communal nests built by sociable weavers, the unusual-looking quiver trees, and the incredible red sand of the Kalahari dunes.

★ **Springtime Flower Season:** The magnificent wildflowers in Namaqualand, easily reached from Cape Town, must be seen to be believed.

★ **Starry Skies:** You'll find skies rife with billions of bright-burning stars all across the province.

★ **Desert Game:** Excellent game reserves mean an experience very different from Kruger; you'll see more cheetahs and rhinos and fewer elephants.

The Northern Cape's vastness makes it a difficult place to travel, and, on a first trip, you'll probably see only a small part of it, perhaps Namaqualand in flower season, the Kalahari, or Kimberley. Namaqualand is most easily visited from Cape Town and the Western Cape, whereas Kimberley and the Kalahari are far more accessible from Johannesburg.

1 Kimberley. Known for possessing the largest manmade hole on Earth, the Northern Cape's capital harbors a lot of history, although it's an increasingly congested and crime-ridden city.

2 Upington. This large, bustling agricultural town benefits from its location on the banks of the Orange River and is a good base from which to explore the Northern Cape's lovely wineries.

3 Augrabies Falls National Park. Centered on a fiercely noisy and visually tremendous terraced waterfall, this nature preserve is a place of mesmerizing, often otherworldly beauty.

4 Kgalagadi Transfrontier Park. The planet's largest cross-border nature and wildlife preserve is possessed of a stunning, if desolate, beauty, and drives through it afford opportunities for incredible game sightings.

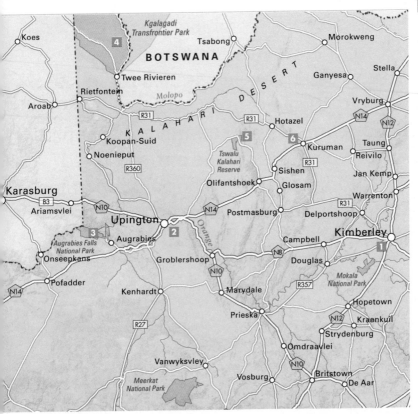

5 Tswalu Kalahari Reserve. Superlative service, accommodations, and amenities such as the country's most enchanting restaurant are matched by the extraordinary setting and wonderful game viewing.

6 Kuruman. A place to spend the night on a drive between Kimberley and Upington or the Kalahari.

7 Garies. A cute one-horse town that turns into a wonderland during the brief springtime Flower Season.

8 Kamieskroon. Another tiny town that brims with magic when the spring-time blooms appear.

9 Springbok. The biggest town in Namaqualand isn't the loveliest place, but it is an important base and gateway to the region during Flower Season.

10 Port Nolloth. A faraway town offering pretty seaside respite from the dry and sometimes dusty interior.

The Northern Cape's appeal is in its sense of isolation; its sparse but remarkable vegetation; its occasional lunar landscapes, which often elicit comparisons with America's Wild West; and its clear, star-bewitched night skies. All told, it covers an area of 372,889 square km (143,973 square miles), roughly a third bigger than the entire United Kingdom, but it has a population of just 1.3 million people, most of whom are concentrated in a handful of towns.

Many of the Northern Cape's attractions are linked to mining, which has been the province's economic backbone for more than a century. First there was the copper mania of the 1840s in Namaqualand, evidence of which is found in towns like Okiep and Nababeep. The deepest copper mines in the world are still operating here, although they are nearing the end of their productive lives. But the history of copper mining was eclipsed 30 years later by the mad scramble for diamonds in Kimberley, now the provincial capital and trading a bit on its heyday heritage.

The so-called City of Diamonds was, in the 1870s, the scene of one of the world's greatest gemstone rushes. Thousands of get-rich-quick hopefuls trekked to the hot, dusty digging fields in what is, more or less, South Africa's geographical center. In Kimberley, five diamond-bearing volcanic pipes were discovered within a few miles of one another—a phenomenon unknown anywhere else in the world. But it's the far northern town of Port Nolloth that is the real deal in terms of authentic (and colorful) diamond tales. In its Aukwatowa museum, curator and veteran navy and diamond diver George Moyses is a vibrant, unorthodox mine of information who can keep you engaged for hours. In addition to copper and diamonds, the province's geology features other gemstones as well as granite, lime, gypsum, manganese, and zinc. There are even oil and gas fields off the Namaqualand coast.

Although only a fraction of the province is regarded as arable because of low rainfall, the Orange River (known as the Gariep—or "mighty river" by the Nama) flows the breadth of the province, emptying into the Atlantic Ocean at Alexander Bay on the Namibian border. South Africa's largest and longest river supplies water to numerous irrigation schemes that sustain farming, most noticeably in the so-called Green Kalahari, a pleasant, roughly 70-km (43-mile) stretch between the hot Kalahari town of Upington and Augrabies, named for the sheer loudness of its waterfall.

The province also has the country's second-largest protected wildlife area. The Kgalagadi Transfrontier Park is Africa's first national border–straddling nature reserve, and, together with an adjoining national park in Botswana, it forms one of the world's largest conservation areas. Ecotourism also draws springtime pilgrims to see the spectacular blooms that transform Namaqualand—an area that's more accessible by road from Cape Town—into a floral wonderland.

Although it's hard to find luxurious accommodations and fine cuisine here, when you do, they will be truly noteworthy. One surprising, almost bewildering, example is the destination restaurant, Klein JAN (meaning "Little Jan"), established by South Africa's first Michelin-starred chef, Jan Hendrik van der Westhuizen, within the remote, luxurious, and private Tswalu game reserve. It is, in every respect, a dining experience unlike any other, marvelously focused on the province's surprising agricultural bounty and defiantly content to be situated—quite literally—in the middle of nowhere.

The harshly beautiful Northern Cape begs to be driven (indeed, flying is a luxury), and there's plenty to see if you're not afraid to ask questions and to go where your curiosity leads you. With a little time and patience, you'll find villages where charming locals demonstrate old-fashioned good manners, humbling hospitality, and appreciation of visitors—albeit in very broken, accented English.

Indeed, this place of infinite natural wonders is the ancestral land of descendants of the very first people, the Khoisan, some of whom still live a semi-nomadic life and commune with the spirits in dances around open fires. In 2017, the ‡Khomani Cultural Landscape was declared a UNESCO World Heritage Site, recognizing not only the cultural traditions of the Khosian, but also their singular worldview, which emphasizes sustainability and living close to the land, and their ethnobotanical knowledge. The site encompasses a vast area of the arid southern Kalahari and forms part of the Kgalagadi Transfrontier Park. One way to meet these remarkable people and see their ancient skills first hand is by staying at the community-owned !Xhaus Lodge, within the Kgalagadi Transfrontier Park, where you'll be guided by Khoisan trackers.

MAJOR REGIONS

Kimberley, the provincial capital of the Northern Cape, is known as the "City of Diamonds." It's an easy trip of about 4 to 4½ hours from Johannesburg on a good highway, but it's almost 11 hours from Cape Town. The city has acquired a rather rough edge in recent years, but its Big Hole—the largest manmade hole on Earth—continues to be a source of fascination.

Still, it is not for its cities that anyone visits the Northern Cape, but rather for the remote, often astonishingly beautiful rural landscapes where some of the finest game-viewing awaits. With Namibia to its west and Botswana to its north, **the Kalahari** is an arid area of dunelands and semi-desert terrain. With minimal rainfall, much of the region is uninhabited—by humans, that is. It is home to the oryx, springbok, and black-maned lion.

In an odd little finger of the country jutting north between Botswana in the east and Namibia in the west lies South Africa's section of the vast **Kgalagadi Transfrontier Park,** a wildlife reserve that straddles national borders. A few hours from the Kgalagadi is the privately owned, malaria-free **Tswalu Kalahari Reserve,** offering swanky digs—including Klein JAN, a restaurant you will not soon forget—and superlative game-viewing experiences.

If you have time and your own car, it's worth exploring the Kalahari's seemingly forgotten hamlets, even if only to visit a farm stall or spend the night in a quirky inn or uniquely decorated farm guesthouse. Blips on the map such as **Askham** and **Van Zylsrus** offer singular perspectives on life in a land where, amid lonely landscapes and dusty roads, the hospitality can be breathtaking.

Stretching west along the R64 from **Upington,** the gateway to the Kalahari, to **Kakamas** and beyond, the southern part of the Kalahari turns the dry-and-dusty stereotype on its head. Although Upington is known for its extreme heat (and is consequently where several European vehicle manufacturers conduct weather-and-climate tests on new car models), it is also the main town in the so-called Green Kalahari, the basin of the Orange River, South Africa's largest.

The hunter-gatherer San (Bushmen) marked the dry Kalahari as their home, but the fertile land along the Orange was occupied by the pastoral Khoi people. Here, irrigation has created a literal oasis that includes thousands of acres of vineyards and the largest date farm in the Southern Hemisphere. Particularly in the vicinity of Kakamas and Keimoes, roadside irrigation canals are punctuated by waterwheels, which elevate water so that it can be directed into the vineyards. Just north of these farming communities is **Augrabies Falls National Park**, a place of incredible rock formations and impressive scenes of water powerfully flowing through narrow gaps in the stone canyon.

Namaqualand—a huge, semi-desert region hundreds of miles north of Cape Town and west of Kimberley—is another highlight. In spring, this mostly unpopulated area with few facilities and comforts puts on what must be the greatest flower shower on Earth. Vast fields that seemed barren only a month earlier suddenly blossom with *vygies* (a type of succulent fynbos), Namaqualand daisies, and other blooms, which are, alas, again gone within two months. **Garies** and **Kamieskroon** are good bases for exploring Namaqualand, though you must book accommodations well in advance for flower season, after which many facilities close.

As in parts of the American West, distances are vast, with a harsh, hilly landscape dotted with giant boulders. Here, though, you'll find the swollen-trunked *kokerbome* (or "quiver trees," so named because Bushmen cut arrow quivers from them). If you want to see these unusual and photogenic trees, and are exploring the Northern Cape outside of flower season, visit the area in and around Augrabies.

Khoisan populations have lived in Namaqualand for thousands of years. The first Europeans were Dutch settlers from the Cape who came in search of the copper they knew existed because the Khoi had used it in trade. Though Simon van der Stel, a governor of the Cape Colony, sank test shafts in 1685 and realized there were rich quantities of copper in the hills around Okiep and Carolusberg, it wasn't until the 1840s, when the Okiep Copper Mining Company came to Namaqualand, that copper was mined on a large scale.

Today, the region's commercial activity is clustered in the *dorps* (small towns) of Okiep, Concordia, and Nababeep, as well as in the region's most prominent town, **Springbok**. The area is littered with heritage sites harking back to the early copper days, from the smokestack in Okiep to the Messelpad Pass, south of Springbok. The fishing and diamond center of **Port Nolloth** is a lovely drive from Springbok, particularly during flower time.

Planning

Getting Here and Around

AIR

The small Kimberley Airport (KIM), 12 km (7½ miles) southwest of town, is served by SA Airlink, which flies direct from Johannesburg and Cape Town. CemAir flies between Kimberley and Johannesburg. A five-minute drive from the city center, Upington International Airport (UTN) has the longest runway in the Southern Hemisphere—5 km (3 miles)—and has been the site of global land-speed records. It's connected to Cape Town and Johannesburg by very expensive flights operated by SA Airlink.

If traveling from Johannesburg to Namaqualand, you can fly to Upington and rent a car from the airport, where companies like Avis, Budget, and Europcar operate. It's a lovely four-hour drive from Upington to Springbok. More affordable, though, would be to fly to Cape Town and drive north along the Cape West Coast, perhaps spending a few night in small towns along the way.

Most people with limited time fly into the Kalahari via Upington, where many lodgings provide airport shuttle service. In addition to cars, you can also rent a 4x4 at Upington airport; quantities are limited though, so be sure to reserve well in advance. One excellent service is offered by the family-run Kgalagadi Lifestyle Lodge, which is just 5 km (3 miles) from the entrance to Kgalagadi Transfrontier Park: You can rent a 4x4 from its small Oryx 4x4 Hire dealership as part of an overnight package and have a transfer from the airport included as well, so you only have to drive the bulkier vehicle when it's needed. The lodge can also pre-book your park entry.

AIRPORT CONTACTS Kimberley Airport.
✉ Comp Patterson Rd., Diskobolos, Kimberley ☎ 053/830–7101.

BUS

For those travelers with plenty of time, Intercape Mainliner runs daily bus services between Upington and Johannesburg/Tshwane (approximately 10½ hours, R470–R955); Cape Town and Upington (about 12 hours, R590–R925); and Kimberley and Johannesburg (7 hours, R340–R855) or Cape Town (13 hours, R500–R1085). Intercape also operates daily bus services up the West Coast from Cape Town to Springbok (9 hours), stopping at various towns in the Western Cape and in Garies in the Northern Cape.

CAR

From Johannesburg, it is an easy 4½-hour drive (480 km/298 miles) to Kimberley on the N12 and N14; however, the trip from Cape Town is considerably longer, at 954 km (600 miles), and takes 10 or 11 hours. The trip from Kimberley to Upington is another 4 hours, and it's another 2½ hours from Upington to the Kgalagadi Transfrontier Park. The drive from Upington to Augrabies Falls is almost 2 hours along an excellent leg of the N14.

Namaqualand is considerably closer to Cape Town than to Johannesburg. The drive from Johannesburg to Springbok, the "capital" of Namaqualand, is 1,344 km (835 miles) and takes a little over 12 hours driving straight through with only refreshment stops; from Cape Town, it's only 7 hours driving (562 km/349 miles).

Upington and the Kalahari are usually approached from Kimberley along the scenic and winding R64, a distance of 411 km (257 miles). The N14, on the northern side of the Orange River, is a slightly longer—450 km (313 miles)—alternative, but it's straighter and faster. Upington is 375 km (233 miles) from Springbok along an excellent paved road. There are several 4x4 trails within the

Northern Cape Itineraries

3 Days: Unless you're here in the middle of summer, consider spending all three days in the Kalahari. If your budget doesn't stretch to Tswalu's admittedly extreme rates, then fly into Upington and take advantage of a direct transfer to Kgalagadi Lifestyle Lodge, where you can rent a 4x4 to explore the world's largest transfrontier reserve and also take in a few of the unique attractions scattered around this remote and arid border area. Consider spending another day (perhaps before flying out of Upington) to visit Augrabies National Park—the rock formations and sight of water gushing through the narrow canyon at Augrabies Falls is utterly sensational.

5 Days: If it's spring (August–September), it's worth splitting your time between the Kalahari and the florally phenomenal Nieuwoudtville, Springbok, or Port Nolloth where you can experience the best of Namaqualand's "Flower Season."

If you visit between October and mid-May, Port Nolloth makes an excellent entry point for the Richtersveld, South Africa's last true wilderness. The Port Nolloth region is an undiscovered country of shipwrecks, diamonds, and crayfish, and is well worth at least two nights and a day in itself. Crayfish season begins in October, so try to find a crayfish braai (barbecue) on the beach somewhere. Note, though, that there is no fresh fish in the winter months.

In summer, Upington is a good base for day trips to Pella and Klein Pella (visually arresting date-palm plantations), Witsand (wildlife and white sand dunes), a couple of wine estates along the Orange River, and Augrabies Falls, but be sure to make your visits in early morning or late afternoon, leaving time for a rest or a swim in the midday heat.

7 or More Days: If you enjoy huge, empty spaces, take a week to drive from Kimberley to Springbok, experiencing the Kalahari en route. Although there are memorable places to stop and stay along the way, this is a long and lonely trip and really should be considered only if the flowers will be in bloom when you reach Namaqualand (July–mid-October).

From Kimberley, drive toward Upington but then turn north to the vast Kgalagadi Transfrontier Park some two hours away. Upon your return, head just past Upington and toward the little farming settlement of Kanon-Eiland (literally "cannon island") on the Orange River for a memorable guesthouse experience at African Vineyard (it has a truly marvelous spa, too). You can visit award-winning brandy and wine estates for lunch, tastings, and cellar tours. Be sure to head north to visit Augrabies Falls National Park, where you can choose between a relatively classy guesthouse or a basic chalet right inside the reserve.

On Day 5, drive to Springbok, the heart of Namaqualand. Stay two nights here or in nearby Okiep while exploring the picturesque towns of Leliefontein (and the nearby Namaqua National Park) to the south and Port Nolloth to the northwest. Head south down the N7 to Cape Town, where the madding crowds will catch you by surprise after the loneliness of the beautiful Northern Cape.

Kgalagadi at Bitterpan and Gharagab, but it is not necessary to have four-wheel-drive to reach or get around the reserve.

Most towns, game parks, and even remote areas have gas, but use common sense and anticipate long distances by refueling when passing a gas station. Roadside car wrecks bear testimony to what locals say is the biggest danger on these roads: falling asleep at the wheel.

Many of the roads out of Kimberley can be almost bumper-to-bumper with extremely large trucks, most of them servicing mines in the area (especially in and around places like Kuruman); exercise caution and be vigilant when overtaking (which you will need to do often). If you are nervous about taking small cars on gravel roads, ask in advance how much of the road is dirt and also what the quality of the gravel is like. Some roads look innocent on a map but are heavily rutted and extremely dusty.

Namaqualand is more than 320 km (200 miles) north of Cape Town and 900 km (563 miles) west of Kimberley. With the great distances involved and the absence of any real public transportation, the only way to get around is by car. Roads are generally well paved, but signage to tourist attractions is not always good. From Springbok to Hondeklipbaai there is an 80-km (50-mile) stretch of sandy gravel road. Traffic to Springbok picks up on Friday and Saturday, when people from neighboring communities converge on the town.

CAR-RENTAL CONTACTS Namaqualand 4x4 Hire. ✉ *15 Jurie Kotze St., Springbok* ☎ *027/712–1905.* **Titus Car Rental.** ✉ *7 van den Heever, Springbok* ☎ *027/718–2544.*

TRAIN

Train services in South Africa have become increasingly unreliable. Some of the disruptions have been caused by the pandemic, others have been related to problems with lines, coaches, or system-ic issues, such as a major derailment in

February 2020 that halted all services for a year. Regardless, service can be dodgy, and it's best not to travel solo on any public train.

Trains between Kimberley and Johannesburg (8 hours) run intermittently, typically two or three times per week. Trains stopping in Kimberley from Cape Town are not currently operating but should ultimately return. Information on these routes can be obtained from Shosholoza Meyl (⊕ *www.shosholozameyl.co.za*).

If money is no object, consider a luxurious ride in with either The Blue Train or Rovos Rail. Both offer a "journey is the destination" experience with stops in Kimberley, specifically to check out The Big Hole. These are not, however, convenient if your goal is simply to get to the Northern Cape.

Hotels

Just about every small town has guesthouses, and the bigger centers like Kimberley and Upington are brimming with them—from basic units with cooking facilities to luxurious B&Bs. There are also comfortable farm accommodations, which can be a saving grace late at night on a long, lonely, provincial road.

In and near the parks and nature reserves, accommodations are in public rest camps, lodges, bungalows, and cottages, as well as in increasing numbers of luxury lodges. Though the price categories given for all lodgings reflect the cost for two people, many places (especially chalets in the national parks) can sleep more than two people and are, therefore, often a better value if you're traveling as a family or in a group.

Although many high-end safari lodges are all-inclusive, with all meals, alcoholic beverages, and activities (like game drives) included the rate, many places have adjusted their pricing to accommodate the increased demand among domestic travelers, which means there may be several pricing options, some all-inclusive, some not.

One of the big sadnesses of the pandemic is that smaller independent hotel operators have been forced to sell to larger chains. Be wary of groups like Country Hotels, which have swooped in and gobbled up a few old favorites in key areas—not only have the quaint touches disappeared, but the service may have gone completely down the tubes while the prices may have risen.

Hotel reviews have been shortened. For full information, visit Fodors.com.

Restaurants

The Northern Cape has never been gastronomically exciting, but some standout additions offer food as good as anything you'll find in Cape Town. Indeed, slap-bang in the middle of nowhere (Tswalu Kalahari Reserve to be precise) is one of the world's most imaginative dining experiences: Restaurant Klein JAN, which emphasizes the Northern Cape's produce and culinary traditions.

In the larger towns of Kimberley, Upington, and Springbok—where locals generally prefer red meat and regard chicken as salad—it may be hard to accommodate very specific tastes or fussy eaters. Which in no way means you will not find delicious food. Your most memorable meal might be the legendary delicacy Karoo lamb—often roasted on a braai (barbeque). It can be savored not only on the farms of the Karoo but also in restaurants in Kimberley, Upington, and the Kalahari.

Vegetarians will find their needs very difficult to meet in large towns and almost impossible to meet in small villages (if you are vegan, proceed with extra caution). However, fresh fruits, especially grapes and dates, are delicious and abundant during summer in the Orange River valley, from Upington to Kakamas. Look out for homemade preserves like peach chutney and apricot jam, too, which can often be found in the region's ubiquitous farm stalls (sometime only signposted in the Afrikaans, *padstal*).

Other than the more sophisticated hotels and such national chains as Spur (a steakhouse) and Panarottis (pizza and pasta), many restaurants are closed on Sunday evening. Unless you are a large group, reservations are not essential or even expected. Dining in the Northern Cape, even in Kimberley, is a casual affair in all but the few chic establishments.

Restaurant reviews have been shortened. For full information, visit Fodors.com.

RESTAURANT AND HOTEL PRICES
Restaurant prices are the average cost of a main course at dinner or, if dinner is not served, at lunch. Hotel prices are the lowest cost of a standard double room in high season.

What it Costs in South African rand			
$	$$	$$$	$$$$
RESTAURANTS			
under R100	R100–R150	R151–R200	over R200
HOTELS			
under R1,500	R1,500–R2,500	R2,501–R3,500	over R3,500

Tours

Aukwatowa Tours

GUIDED TOURS | The complex history of this region is one of the many reasons a good guide is imperative. Conrad Mouton is an ex-soldier–turned–tour guide who communicates his passion for the environment and the inhabitants of the far reaches of the Northern Cape, where he takes tours to South Africa's last wilderness, the Richtersveld, and within Port Nolloth. His shipwreck and crayfish (in season) tours—crayfish braais (barbecues) and excellent sunsets "guaranteed"—plus his vast knowledge of regional flora afford visitors a local introduction to this remarkable province. His tours are simply brilliant. Note that Conrad has a second tour business, Richtersveld Tours, with similar offerings. ⊠ *47 Flosse St., Port Nolloth* ☏ *083/335–1399* ⊕ *www.aukwatowa-tours.co.za, www.richtersveldtours.co.za.*

★ Cape Fox Tours & Photography

SPECIAL-INTEREST TOURS | Operating since 1998, zoologist and photographer Jaco Powell is quite simply the best at what he does in the Northern Cape: organize excursions and immersive activities—from full-blown safaris to history, cultural, or even ghost tours of Kimberley. Jaco, who co-authored the popular guidebook, *Kgalagadi Self-Drive*, specializes in photography tours across southern African, including those in both the Kgalagadi Transfrontier Park and to Augrabies Falls. But he also offers trips featuring once-in-a-lifetime experiences like taking part in a conservation exercise involving the live capture of a rhino alongside game rangers and vets. (The rhino's measurements are taken along with blood samples, and then it is microchipped for security purposes, thus contributing to the protection of the species. Each guest gets the opportunity to assist with their "own" rhino, even administering the antidote for the tranquilizer.) ⊠ *Kimberley* ☏ *082/572–0065* ⊕ *www.kalaharisafari.com.*

Kalahari Safaris

SPECIAL-INTEREST TOURS | "If the sand of the Kalahari gets in your shoes, you always come back," says Pieter Hane-kom, who was trained in bush lore by the San Bushmen and calls the Kalahari one of the last true wilderness areas on Earth. Pieter brings his experience and expertise to small groups of travelers, and his company caters to just about every budget. ⊠ *Farm Groenkuil, Upington* ☏ *082/435–0007* ⊕ *www.kalaharisafaris.co.za.*

Kalahari Tours & Travel

SPECIAL-INTEREST TOURS | Dantes Lieben-berg customizes trips to the Kgalagadi Transfrontier Park that range from two days to two weeks. Other specialties include Witsand Nature Reserve, Augra-bies Falls, the wider Kalahari region, Namaqua flower tours (in season), and farther afield to the rest of South Africa, Namibia, Zimbabwe, and Botswana. His all-inclusive, three-day, desert experience, which includes interacting with the San community, is a must. Tours range from the four-star variety to backpacker style. Plus, his company is committed to responsible tourism and supports local communities and projects whenever possible. ⊠ *22 Groen-punt Way, Upington* ☏ *054/338–0375, 082/493–5041* ⊕ *www.kalahari-tours. co.za.*

Visitor Information

Local guides and hotels are more reliable, knowledgeable, and helpful than local government tourist offices. In Kimberley, trekking to the visitor information center is far more trouble than it's worth. In Springbok, the Namakwa Tourism office is across from the Puma gas station on Voortrekker Street, but you will ultimately find more information at area lodgings.

Namakwa Tourism

⊠ *Voortrekker St., Springbok* ☏ *027/712–8035* ⊕ *www.namakwa-dm.gov.za.*

Northern Cape Tourism Authority

Don't expect to get much joy from a personal visit to this lackluster government agency; there's more information available online. ⊠ *Tourism House, 14 Villiers St., Kimberley* ☏ *053/832–2657* ⊕ *www. experiencenortherncape.com.*

When to Go

By South African standards the Northern Cape's climate is exceptionally hot in summer (late November–February), often rising to above 35°C (95°F). Although it's hot in Kimberley, it can be just about intolerable in Upington and the Kalahari. Conversely, the region can get seriously cold in winter (mid-May–early August), sometimes dropping below 0°C (32°F). In fact, the province has the dubious honor of being home to the hottest town in South Africa in summer (Upington) and one of the coldest in winter (Sutherland, in the Karoo), so come prepared to sweat or shiver (mostly at night).

The best time to see the flowers in Namaqualand is usually between the middle of August and the end of September, depending on when and how much rain has fallen. Various festivals, many of them celebrating some or other agricultural tradition, take place across the province, and sometimes in the unlikeliest of places. The region also hosts several sporting events, such as long-distance multiday trail running and mountain biking, though dates change annually.

Kimberley

480 km (298 miles) west of Johannesburg; 954 km (600 miles) northwest of Cape Town.

Kimberley was born in the dust, dreams, and disappointments of a rudimentary mining camp that eventually became, in some quarters, a city of grace and sophistication. Today, Kimberley is home to about 200,000 people who are spread out around its diamond mines—giant holes in the Earth, like inverted *koppies* (hills). The Big Hole is the main draw, though there are a host of comfortable guesthouses and a few historical attractions as well.

Kimberley's colonial beginnings date from 1869, when alluvial diamonds were found and mined on the banks of the Vaal River near Barkly West, about 30 km (19 miles) away. These were all but forgotten, though, upon the discovery of five pipes bearing the diamondiferous Kimberlite, or "blue ground," so called because of its color. In 1871, the richest pipe of all, the Kimberley Mine (now known as the Big Hole), was discovered. Diggers from around the world flocked to stake claims, and, at times there were as many as 30,000 people burrowing into the hole like a giant colony of termites. It became one of the richest diamond mines in history, producing more than 14.5 million carats before its closure in 1914.

The history of the diamond fields is dominated by eccentric and controversial personalities, like Barney Barnato, who came to South Africa with so little, he had to walk to the diamond fields, yet died a magnificently wealthy man. Then there was Cecil John Rhodes, the diamond magnate and colonizer who aspired to paint the map of Africa red for Britain and to build a railroad from Cape Town to Cairo.

Both Rhodes and Barnato were shrewd businessmen. When other miners gave up upon encountering what they thought was bedrock (but was actually unweathered, hard-blue ground fabulously rich in diamonds) these two men snapped up the claims at bargain prices, while increasing their shares in the mines. Eventually Barnato and Rhodes merged their companies into the De Beers Consolidated Mines Ltd. Today, De Beers is the world's most powerful diamond-mining company, and it owns the Big Hole tourist attraction, where you can sleep, drink, eat, shop, and even get a haircut.

Kimberley also played a part in the Anglo-Boer War (1899–1902) as evidenced by many monuments, buildings, and statues. The city's proximity to the border of the then-Boer Republic of the

Orange Free State and its renown as a diamond town occupied by prominent British citizens (including Rhodes) made it a target during the conflict. For four months in the summer of 1899, the town was under siege, its citizens enduring dwindling rations, disease, Boer shell fire, and other hardships. British efforts to relieve the beleaguered town were thwarted by the Boers at the Battle of Magersfontein. Eventually, though, a sustained cavalry charge led by Major-General John French broke through.

GETTING HERE AND AROUND

If you arrive in Kimberley by air, you'll find only two local taxi companies. Although Rikki's Taxis try to meet most flights on arrival, their presence isn't guaranteed, so it's best to reserve a taxi in advance.

If you're only staying a day or two, you don't really need a car, particularly if you hire a good guide. If you plan to explore more of the region, you'll find Avis, Budget, Europcar, Hertz and others car rental agencies at the airport. Driving in the city is difficult, though, as the streets are confusing (GPS can help) and congested, and other cars and trucks shoot out of nowhere. Also, do not park on the streets anywhere in the city center; even parking directly outside museums or hotels is an invitation for opportunistic crime. Gas stations are plentiful, and the roads out of town are very straight and generally do not have shoulders.

Kimberley was the first South African city to have tram service, and a restored 1914 tram travels from one side of the Big Hole to City Hall. The cost is R10 for the short, out-and-back ride, but there's no schedule. Trams leave from the Big Hole when at least four people are ready to go—if there is someone on duty.

AIRPORT CONTACTS Kimberley Airport.
✉ *Comp Patterson Rd., Diskobolos, Kimberley* ☎ *053/830–7101.*

AIRPORT TRANSFERS Rikki's Taxis.
✉ *Kimberley* ☎ *053/842–1764, 083/342–2533* ⊕ *www.rikkistaxis.co.za.*

TOURS

The Kimberley Ghost Route is a popular tour, starting at night with sherry inside the Honoured Dead Memorial and then proceeding to several of Kimberley's (purportedly) haunted places, such as the Kimberley Club (where one room is apparently so frightening that your guide will offer to pay you if you check in *and* manage to stay the night) and Rhodes's boardroom. The tour ends with a visit to the historic Gladstone Cemetery, where a certain Mr. Frankenstein and his wife are buried.

Prices vary according to the size of the group, which must consist of at least 10 people. Book this one at least two days in advance, and make sure you specify that you want to go inside the haunted buildings, or the tour will be disappointing. The best guides for the ghost tour can be booked through Jaco Powell, who is also your best contact for immersive history tours of the city and beyond.

Jaco Powell
GUIDED TOURS | Jaco, who will pick you up for his 10-person-minimum Kimberley Ghost Trail, also has other day tours, including culture-themed excursions that take in Galeshwa, the McGregor Museum, and the Wildebeest Kuil San petroglyph site; an Anglo-Boer War–themed tour; and a diamond-mining tour with visits to active alluvial digs and the chance to meet diggers. ✉ *Kimberley* ☎ *082/572–0065* ⊕ *www.kalaharisafari. com.*

VISITOR INFORMATION

Kimberley's Northern Cape Tourism Authority does have information on the entire province, but it's best accessed either online or in one of the brochures that it publishes. The Kimberley Visitors Information Centre has maps and brochures on the Northern Cape and the

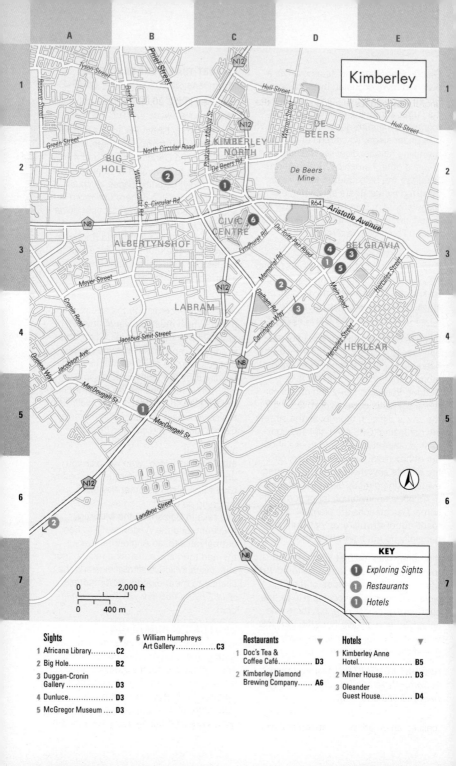

Kimberley

KEY

1 *Exploring Sights*
1 *Restaurants*
1 *Hotels*

Kimberley region, but its staff probably won't be able to assist you in any meaningful way, and it's in a dodgy part of the city where it isn't safe to park your car. Local tour guides are a better source of reliable direction that's informed by actual on-the-ground experience.

CONTACTS Kimberley Visitors Information Centre. ⊠ 121 Bultfontein Rd., Kimberley ☎ 053/830–6779 ⊕ www.kimberley.co.za.

◉ Sights

Although for most people the main reason to visit Kimberley is seeing the Big Hole, there are also several noteworthy examples of Victorian architecture, particularly in the city's first residential suburb, Belgravia, which was associated with the town's mines. De Beers, another suburb that grew up around the De Beers mine, was originally part of Johannes Nicholas De Beer's farm. (Both the Kimberley and De Beers mines are now closed, leaving three extant mines.)

Also on land originally owned by De Beers and of even greater historical interest, the residential area around the Civic Centre is similar to Cape Town's District Six in sociopolitical terms. Called Malay Camp, it was where freed Asian slaves (largely Muslim and erroneously lumped together under the name Cape Malays) settled. Given to the municipality in 1939, today it is a treed garden area stretching out from the municipal building.

In addition, one of South Africa's oldest townships, Greenpoint, is south of Kimberley, though, despite its age, no standing buildings predate the 1930s. Galeshewe is another settlement to the west of the city.

Africana Library

LIBRARY | Housed in the old Kimberley Public Library (1887) is one of the country's premier reference libraries, where books are shelved from floor to ceiling, an ornate wrought-iron staircase connects the floors, and locally published, limited-edition books are for sale. Included in the 20,000-volume collection are such rarities as the Setswana Bible, the first-ever Bible in an African language, printed by Robert Moffat in the 1850s, as well as four books dating from the 1400s. The library is said to be haunted by the ghost of Bertram Dyer, the country's first qualified librarian. After he was caught defrauding the library of money, he committed suicide. He now purportedly stacks files on the floor and rattles teacups in the kitchen. ⊠ 63–65 Du Toitspan Rd., Kimberley ☎ 053/830–6247 ⊕ www.africanalibrary.co.za ☑ Donations accepted ⊗ Closed Sat. and Sun.

★ Big Hole

HISTORIC SIGHT | FAMILY | If you do one thing in Kimberley, visit the Big Hole, which, at 2,690 feet deep, is the world's largest hand-dug hole. Although water now fills most of its depth, it's still impressive, particularly from the observation post. You also get to explore facsimile tunnels for a sense of what it might have been like for miners—there's even a simulated dynamite blast that can take you unawares. At the end of the tunnels, comprehensive museum displays document the history of both the city and the mine. Replicas of the world's most famous diamonds, including the Eureka, a 21-carat yellow diamond that was South Africa's first recorded diamond discovery in 1866, are also on view.

Touring the extensive, open-air Kimberley Mine Museum, on the lip of the mine, is like stepping back in time to wander through a mining town with a host of authentic 19th-century buildings, many of which were moved here from the city center. They include the first house erected in Kimberley (1877), which was originally brought piece by piece from Britain to the diamond fields by ship and ox wagon; Barney Barnato's boxing academy; and the very popular Occidental Bar, which serves pub-style food and is reminiscent of a Wild West saloon. There is also a hotel, The New Rush Guesthouse, whose good-value accommodations are in a variety of the museum site's old buildings and have antique furniture and slipper bathtubs that enhance the time-travel sensation. ✉ Tucker St., Kimberley ☎ 053/839–4600 ⊕ www.thebighole.co.za ☜ R130.

Duggan-Cronin Gallery

ART MUSEUM | This gallery houses early photographs of southern Africa and its inhabitants taken by A. M. Duggan Cronin, an Irishman who arrived in 1897 to work as a night watchman for De Beers. A keen photographer, he traveled widely through southern Africa, capturing his impressions—mostly of African peoples—on film. While the gallery is actually on Egerton Road, access is now via the McGregor Museum. ✉ McGregor Museum, Atlas St., Herlear, Kimberley ☎ 053/839–2700 ⊕ www.museumsnc. co.za ☜ Donations accepted ☉ Closed Sat. and Sun.

Dunluce

HISTORIC HOME | A well-known Kimberley landmark, the family home of merchant John Orr has a colonial wraparound verandah painted a distinctive green and white. Sadly, its upkeep is lacking, and you can only visit it on a tour (pre-booked through the McGregor Museum), during which you'll hear about the swimming pool (the first in Kimberley) and the red dining room, which took a shell through its ceiling during the Anglo-Boer War siege. ✉ 10 Lodge Rd., Belgravia, Kimberley ☎ 053/839–2700 ⊕ www. museumsnc.co.za ☜ R35 ⬠ Admission only by pre-arrangement.

McGregor Museum

HISTORY MUSEUM | This graceful Kimberley landmark, built at Rhodes's instigation, was first used as a sanatorium, then an upscale hotel, and later as a girls' convent school. Rhodes (now a much-maligned figure who occupies a shady realm within the South African colonial discourse) himself stayed here during the siege, and you can see rooms he once occupied.

Today the building houses a museum that focuses on Northern Cape history (prehistoric to early 20th century) within a global context. It contains quite a good display on the Anglo-Boer War and the even more impressive Hall of Ancestors—an extensive exhibition on the history of humanity that includes prehistoric human skulls dating back some 3 million years. The natural history of the area can be seen in the EnviroZone, and a chapel once stood on what is today the Hall of Religion. Note, though, that much of this museum is in need of a refresh, and some of its displays are akin to high-school projects. ✉ 7–11 Atlas St., Herlear, Kimberley ☎ 053/839–2700 ⊕ www.museumsnc. co.za ☜ R30 ☉ Closed Sun.

William Humphreys Art Gallery

ART MUSEUM | This renowned art museum in Kimberley's Civic Centre is at once sedate and lively. It's an air-conditioned haven of tranquility on a hot summer day, and its impressive collection features South African works as well as those by Dutch, Flemish, British, and French masters. One area is devoted to local work, and a very popular exhibit highlights the rock art of the Northern Cape. Free guided tours (preferably booked in advance) cater to specific interests on request. Be mindful of parking your car outside the museum; it may be worth asking someone to keep an eye on it, or catching a taxi here. ✉ Civic Centre, Cullinan Crescent, Kimberley ☎ 053/831–1724, 053/831–1725 ⊕ www.whag.co.za ☜ R5; R100 for guided tour ☉ Closed Sat. and Sun.

Did You Know?

Kimberley's Big Hole, which, at 2,690 feet deep, is the world's largest hand-dug hole.

Restaurants

Doc's Tea & Coffee Café

$ | CAFÉ | FAMILY | Cecil John Rhodes used to stop for a drink at Halfway House, halfway between the Kimberley and Bultfontein mines, and because he was short, and it was difficult for him to mount and dismount, he was served on his horse. Today, Halfway House is a lively hotel with several restaurants—the best of which is Hussar Grill, a nationwide chain that many regard as the best steakhouse in Kimberley—and this lovely, relaxing courtyard café, where you can get excellent coffee, pizzas and flatbreads, and lovely cakes. **Known for:** sparkling service; great breakfasts; milkshakes and bubble teas. $ *Average main: R75 ✉ Halfway House Hotel, 229 Du Toitspan Rd., Belgravia, Kimberley ☎ 053/831–6324 ⊕ www.halfwayhousehotel.com.*

Kimberley Diamond Brewing Company

$$ | SOUTH AFRICAN | FAMILY | After a 20-minute drive out of Kimberley, you arrive at a blip-on-the-map farm town known as Ritchie, where George van der Merwe grows pecan nuts and brews a range of beers named for key moments and figures from Kimberley's history. He also has a restaurant where you can sample some beer; join George for a brewery tour; and settle in for steaks, burgers, or pizza. **Known for:** tranquil setting; crafts beers and artisanal gins; relaxed, family-friendly atmosphere. $ *Average main: R150 ✉ 1st Ave., Ritchie, Kimberley ☎ 066/212–7090 ⊕ www.kdbc.co.za ⊘ Closed Mon. to Thurs.*

Hotels

★ Kimberley Anne Hotel

$$ | HOTEL | A small hotel with a big heart, this family-owned luxury oasis near the edge of town lives up to its single-minded ambition of providing the most professional service in Kimberley. **Pros:** classy decor that pays tribute to the Northern Cape's heritage; lots of modern conveniences and ultra-comfortable beds; excellent food in the small on-site restaurant. **Cons:** it's not walking distance to any attractions (but it is mere minutes from the airport); lacks a garden; the music in the lobby and restaurant can be lively. $ *Rooms from: R1915 ✉ 60 MacDougall St., Kimberley ☎ 053/492–0004 ⊕ www.kimberleyanne.co.za ⇨ 16 rooms ⧉ Free Breakfast.*

Milner House

$ | B&B/INN | In a tranquil part of the already sedate Belgravia neighborhood, this big, old, beautiful B&B offers all the comforts of home, with modern rooms, wooden furnishings, and a cottage feel. **Pros:** hospitable staff; lovely restaurant where good breakfasts are served; shady garden that's usually full of birds. **Cons:** there's a lack of privacy with people coming and going throughout the day; management can be disorganized; rooms have laminate floors not in keeping with the Victorian decor. $ *Rooms from: R1400 ✉ 31 Milner St., Belgravia, Kimberley ☎ 072/994–0696 ⊕ www.milnerhouse.co.za ⇨ 6 rooms ⧉ Free Breakfast.*

★ Oleander Guest House

$ | B&B/INN | Close to several attractions in the historic Belgravia suburb, Oleander is a beautifully renovated Victorian property with luxurious accommodations and an excellent restaurant that serves sophisticated food as well as burgers, pizza, and vegetarian or gluten-free dishes. **Pros:** smooth service; restaurant, Laurier Blanc, offers one of Kimberley's best dining experiences; well-appointed guest rooms and smart decor throughout. **Cons:** extensive security features can feel a bit disconcerting; French windows opening onto the pool area don't afford great privacy; some rooms are on the small side. $ *Rooms from: R1200 ✉ 28 Carrington St., Belgravia, Kimberley ☎ 053/832–7088 ⊕ www.oleander.co.za ⇨ 11 rooms ⧉ Free Breakfast.*

Upington

411 km (257 miles) northwest of Kimberley.

Home to about 84,000 residents, Upington is a thriving agricultural center on the north bank of the Orange River. In the 1870s, a Koranna (a group within the Na'ama culture) captain named Klaas Lucas invited missionary Christiaan Schröder to come to Olyvenhoudtsdrift (literally "Ford at the Olive-wood Trees"), as Upington was first known. Construction on the first mission buildings, now part of the Upington museum complex, was started in 1873.

The town was renamed after Sir Thomas Upington, a Cape attorney general who was responsible for ridding the area of its notorious bandits in the 1880s. Although convention has it that the first person to irrigate crops from the Orange was Schröder himself, more recent historical research has revealed that this honor should go to Abraham September, a freed mixed-race slave, who first led water from the Orange in about 1882.

Sights

Bezalel Estate Cellars

WINERY | Stop here if you are a fan of cognac and liqueurs or you want to sample some of the region's lesser-known wines. From his pot still, Tinus Bezuidenhout produces and sells really good brandies and high-quality liqueurs. It's a family business, so either Tinus or his son, Martiens, will likely be pouring generous tastings, something all except the designated driver will appreciate. There is also a walk-through of the distillery and maturation cellar, and a restaurant, Le Marché, serving Kalahari biltong and avocado salad, Kalahari venison pie, and beef-and-brandy burgers. It also sells a wonderful range of deli products, from Kalahari salt and barbecue sauce to wild marula jam produced on the farm. Tinus knows

everyone in the area, so think of him as a tourism resource, too. ☒ *Dyasonsklip, off the N14, Upington ✛ between Upington and Keimos* ☎ *054/491–1325* ⊕ *www. bezalel.co.za* ☒ *Free* ⊘ *Colsed Sun.* ☞ *Tastings between R30 and R120 for 1 or 2 hours.*

Camel and Rider Statue

PUBLIC ART | About 2 km (1 mile) from the Kalahari-Oranje Museum, in front of the Upington police station, this bronze monument honors the police who used camels as mounts when they patrolled the Kalahari in frontier days. If this rather lonely sight is in any way intriguing, you may want to plan a visit to the **Camel Farm** (⊕ *camelmilksouthafrica.co.za*) in a breathtakingly remote Kalahari location about 90 minutes from the Twee Rivieren entrance to the Kgalagadi Transfrontier Park. Its dairy farmer will introduce you to his gentle, free-roaming, long-eyelashed camels, and his herd is entirely descended from the first camels brought here for police and military use. ☒ *Schröder St., Upington.*

Kalahari-Oranje Museum

HISTORY MUSEUM | Conveniently adjacent the Red Ox Steakhouse, the Kalahari-Oranje Museum comprises simple whitewashed buildings that were erected by missionary Christiaan Schröder in the 1870s. It has displays on agriculture and local history and collections of minerals and artifacts used by the area's San. Just outside the complex is the Donkey Monument, a bronze sculpture by Hennie Potgieter that is a testimony to the role played by the animal in developing the Lower Orange River Valley. ☒ *4 Schröder St., Upington* ☎ *054/331–2640* ☒ *R30* ⊘ *Closed Sat. and Sun.*

Sakkie se Arkie (*Sakkie's Ark*)

TRANSPORTATION | **FAMILY** | If you're missing the sea, a sedate sunset cruise on the Orange River could be just the thing. Sakkie se Arkie (literally "Sakkie's Little Ark") is a little family operation offering a 90-minute trip on a double-decker raft

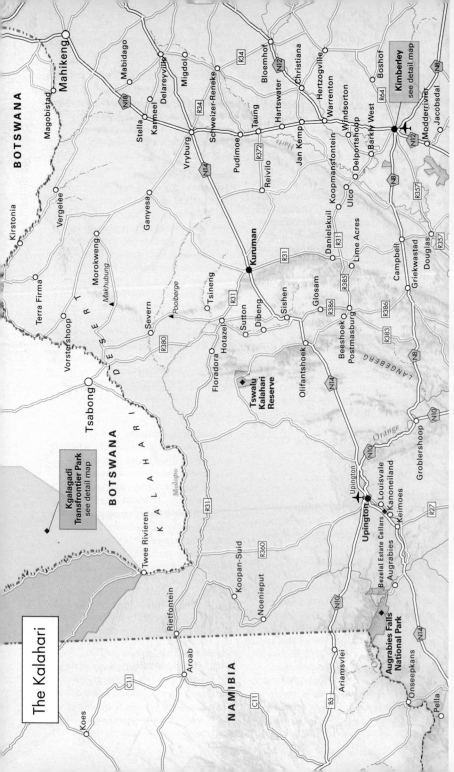

The Kalahari

complete with a cash bar. You might see catfish, monkeys, and eagles and other birds. But the main ingredients for the fun are the lively crowd, the gentle sensation of the cruise, and the wonderful cocktails made by Sakkie's wife. It generally only operates on weekends, but it might head out during the week if there are enough people interested. ✉ *Park St., Upington* ☎ *082/564–5447, 082/575–7285* 🌐 *www.arkie.co.za* 🎟 *R150 per person* 🕒 *Closed weekdays unless there's demand.*

🍴 Restaurants

Die Kerkmuis at Orange River Cellars

$$ | **SOUTH AFRICAN** | **FAMILY** | The name of this laid-back cellar/tasting room, which spills out onto an open terrace and garden where children can run around and play, means "The Church Mouse" and a nod to what is a humble venue that is always striving for greatness. Service is incredibly friendly, and the food ranges from must-try pancakes stuffed with milk tart to delectable sirloin steaks, pork ribs, or gourmet burgers (made with two types of meat). **Known for:** all-day dining with a laid-back, family-friendly atmosphere; the widest variety of menu options in town; wines made from locally sourced grapes. [$] *Average main: R120* ✉ *Orange River Cellars Wine Tasting Centre, 158 Shröder St., Middelpos, Upington* ☎ *054/495–0040, 079/594–1339* 🌐 *www.orangeriverwines.com/tasting-centre* 🕒 *Closed Sun.*

Red Ox Steakhouse

$$$$ | **STEAKHOUSE** | **FAMILY** | Burgers made with the finest ingredients, slabs of meat grilled to perfection, and absolute pride taken in making every plate a miniature masterpiece—Red Ox has high ambitions, as evidenced by both the food and the smart decor, which features lots of mirrors and a collection of paintings by the late landscape artist Walter Meyer. In addition to the menu of meat dishes (vegetarians note that, the menu states, quite explicitly, "No Meat, No Life"), there's a Sunday breakfast buffet, daily chalkboard specials, and options inspired by local tastes. **Known for:** meat and, rather exclusively, meat; steaks and burgers that are equally excellent; some local specialities. [$] *Average main: R240* ✉ *Schröder St., Upington* ☎ *060/329–3806* 🌐 *www.redoxupington.ncfamouslodges.com.*

🛏 Hotels

★ **African Vineyard**

$ | **B&B/INN** | Set in labyrinthine gardens amid expansive vineyards on Kanoneiland (Cannon Island) in the Orange River just outside Upington, this handsome guesthouse has a mix of large rooms filled with imaginative, handcrafted and/or up-cycled furniture and fittings and more modest, but equally homey, doubles. **Pros:** excellent on-site spa; truly unique setting; superb gardens where breakfasts and dinners are often served. **Cons:** it's a popular wedding and conference venue, so can be booked out; budget rooms are very compact and can lack privacy; out of the way if you're just looking for an overnight stop. [$] *Rooms from: R1368* ✉ *Plot 79, Kanoneiland, Upington* ✥ *25 km (15 miles) southwest of Upington* ☎ *060/503–8449, 079/855–7565* 🌐 *www.africanvineyard.co.za* 🛏 *14 rooms* 🍽 *Free Breakfast.*

★ **Le Must Residence**

$ | **B&B/INN** | Dark-hued, immensely stylish, and filled with vintage furniture, excellent period pieces, and immaculate antiques, this glamorous but unpretentious hotel almost feels like a museum, albeit one with comfortable rooms, including a gigantic marvel of a Presidential Suite. **Pros:** it has a lush garden and you can walk down to the river; an absolute beauty filled with individuality and charm; for lovers of vintage the thrills are endless. **Cons:** it won't suit those who prefer a standardized contemporary look; the people running the guesthouse can be a bit disorganized; standard rooms have only showers. $ *Rooms from: R1200* ✉ *14 Budler St., Upington* ☎ *082/828–1885* ⊕ *www.lemustupington.com* ⤳ *9 rooms* ❍❘ *Free Breakfast.*

River Place Manor

$ | HOTEL | FAMILY | With its back to a small vineyard and a prime location on the banks of the Orange River, this small, spic-and-span, family-owned hotel has lawns that roll right down to the water's edge. **Pros:** neat, tidy accommodations; lovely riverside location and all but two rooms face the water directly; excellent restaurant, especially if you like steak. **Cons:** no lunch, and on Sunday night, when the restaurant is closed, you may need to order takeout; beds in the standard rooms are quite small; decor is pretty standard. $ *Rooms from: R1440* ✉ *36A Steenbok Ave., Middelpos, Upington* ☎ *054/332–3102, 082/491–2338* ⊕ *www. riverplacemanor.co.za* ⤳ *17 rooms* ❍❘ *Free Breakfast.*

Witsand Kalahari Nature Reserve Lodge

$ | RESORT | FAMILY | If you can't make it to Kgalagadi, stay a few nights in a three-bedroom chalet or a simple bungalow at this beautiful lodge, owned by the provincial government and situated in the southern Kalahari within the 3,500-hectare (8,650-acre) Witsand Nature Reserve at the foot of the Langberg Mountains. **Pros:** the sounds of the desert bush lull you to sleep; well off the beaten track; good game sightings and the chance to experience Witsand's roaring sand dunes. **Cons:** adequate facilities but few creature comforts, and some rooms need TLC; no food is available (self-catering only); pink walls and pine furniture don't constitute on-trend design. $ *Rooms from: R990* ✉ *Witsand Kalahari Nature Reserve* ✛ *220 km (137 miles) east of Upington on the road to Griquatown and then another 45 km (28 miles) down a sometimes rocky road to Witsand* ☎ *083/234–7573* ⊕ *www.witsandkalahari.co.za* ⤳ *17 rooms* ❍❘ *No Meals* ☞ *Rate*

is for 2 people in a cottage; the 2-person rate for a 3-bedroom chalet is R1,490. A conservation fee of R70 per adult and R50 per child is payable.

Augrabies Falls National Park

120 km (75 miles) west of Upington; 40 km (25 miles) northwest of Kakamas.

The Khoi, pastoralists who lived in this area for thousands of years before the arrival of Europeans, called these falls Aukoerabis (Place of Great Noise), and though Augrabies is a relatively small national park (696,850 acres), its falls are truly impressive. There have been reported sightings of a river monster in the gorge, but, instead of a creature, it's probably just shoals of giant barbels, which reach about 7 feet in length.

👁 Sights

★ Augrabies Falls National Park

NATURE PRESERVE | FAMILY | South Africa's largest falls by volume of water, Augrabies plunges 653 feet over terraces and into an 18 km (11 miles) long gorge, which was carved into smooth granite over millions of years. It is strangely otherworldly, mesmerizing to behold. Legend has it that an unplumbed hole beneath the main falls is filled with diamonds washed downriver over millennia and trapped there.

You can hike in the park for an hour or several days, and you don't need a guide. Markers will direct you along routes that range from the short Dassie Nature Trail to the three-day Klipspringer Hiking Trail. You can also drive to the park's beautiful, well-appointed lookout points showcasing the gorge below the falls; scenic stops are highlighted on the maps provided with your entry permit. All are easily accessible and well marked. Unfenced

Augrabies Falls plunges 653 feet over terraces and into an 18 km (11 miles) long gorge.

Ararat provides the best views. Oranjekom, which is fenced and has a shaded hut, is particularly welcome in the blistering summer heat. The Swartrante lookout offers a view over rugged, barren areas of the park. Some areas suggest that you've arrived on another planet; others might evoke the Arizona Badlands.

If you have a 4x4, you can spend a good six hours following the 94-km (60-mile) Wilderness Road into some of the reserve's most remote parts. Midway along it is a scenic picnic spot where there are toilets and a braai (barbecue) area.

Depending on how things are with the pandemic, you might have to undergo a quick COVID-19 screening at the main gate. The visitor center, with an information office, shop, and restaurant, is a few miles down the road; this is also where you'll pay entry fees and where boardwalks to the main falls viewing areas and the SANParks rest camp are situated. ✉ *Augrabies* ☎ *054/452–9200* 🌐 *www.sanparks.org/parks/augrabies* 🎟 *R240 per person per day.*

🍴 Restaurants

Die Koker Kombuis @ Die Mas

$$ | **INTERNATIONAL** | **FAMILY** | This lovely, casual restaurant at Die Mas van Kakamas Vineyards is a good place for a long, languid, pizza-and-wine lunch or a wine, brandy, or gin tasting that you can combine with the menu's reasonably priced and lovingly prepared pasta dishes or steaks. While waiting for your order, you can sit on the terrace overlooking the vineyards, and children can take a short stroll along a wooden walkway to see farm animals and a herd of springbuck that live nearby. **Known for:** wood-oven-fired pizza; wine and spirits tastings; vineyard views. [$] *Average main: R105* ✉ *Die Mas van Kakamas Vineyards, Kakamas* ☎ *066/378–7034, 072/421–1691* 🌐 *www.diekokerkombuis.co.za* 🕒 *Closed Sun. and Mon.*

There are ostriches in the Kalahari Desert.

Hotels

Augrabies Rest Camp

$ | RESORT | FAMILY | South African National Parks (SANParks) offers clean, self-catering, brick-faced chalets that can sleep two people or a small family and are near the visitor center and the main falls viewing areas. **Pros:** you can cook for yourself, inside or outside your chalet; beautiful environment that's generally peaceful; great hikes and walks directly from your doorstep. **Cons:** chalets are an architectural eyesore and maintenance is lacking; restaurant's food is not the best and the overpriced on-site shop is poorly stocked; can get crowded (at which point the noise levels rise). $ *Rooms from: R1050 ⊠ Augrabies Falls National Park, Augrabies ☎ 012/428–9111 for reservations, 054/452–9200 ⊕ www.sanparks. org ⇨ 59 rooms ⍾ No Meals ☞ A daily conservation fee of R240 per person applies.*

Dundi Lodge

$$ | HOTEL | This small guesthouse offers big hospitality and the closest thing to cosseting luxury that you'll find in the immediate vicinity of Augrabies Falls. **Pros:** immense upstairs "executive" suite with a huge balcony and lovely view; excellent dinner menu; best-looking rooms for miles. **Cons:** downstairs rooms aren't quite as lavish or large as the one suite upstairs; after the adventure of getting here, room interiors (including laminated floors) may seem conventional; bathrooms are on the small side. $ *Rooms from: R1560 ⊠ 4 Airport Blvd., Rooipad, Augrabies ☎ 054/451–9200 ⊕ www.dundilodge.co.za ⇨ 8 rooms ⍾ Free Breakfast.*

★ Tutwa Desert Lodge

$$$$ | RESORT | FAMILY | Tutwa is far flung but far from ordinary, a slice of luxury amid both Kalahari wilderness and Orange River oasis—you can head off on a game drive and return for a paddle on the river, potentially spotting more animals from your canoe. **Pros:** lots of attention to detail in the sumptuous digs; extraordinary setting with both semi-desert and river-oasis ecosystems; sensational faraway atmosphere. **Cons:** not all rooms have great views (ask for one overlooking the watering hole); unless you charter a plane, getting here requires an hour's drive on a gravel road; family-friendly vibe won't suit those who want a romantic getaway. $ *Rooms from: R9390* ✉ *Southern Cross Game Reserve, Schuitdrift, Augrabies, Augrabies* ☎ *054/451–9200* ⊕ *www.tutwalodge.co.za* ⟿ *9 rooms* ⎜⎡⎜ *All-Inclusive* ⟿ *2-night minimum stay.*

Kgalagadi Transfrontier Park

260 km (162 miles) north of Upington on the R360.

If you're looking for truly remote wilderness with surreal landscapes, and you're not averse to foregoing luxury and getting sand in your hair, then the uniquely beautiful Kgalagadi—pronounced hala-*hardy* and meaning "place of thirst" in the San language—is for you.

In an odd little finger of the country jutting north between Botswana in the east and Namibia in the west lies South Africa's second-largest national park (after Kruger). Kgalagadi was launched in 2000, when South Africa's vast Kalahari Gemsbok National Park merged with Botswana's even larger Gemsbok National Park to create southern Africa's first transfrontier, or "peace park." It's now one of the world's largest protected wilderness areas, consisting of more than 38,000 square km (14,670 square miles), of which 9,600 square km (3,700 square miles) fall in South Africa.

Passing through the Twee Rivieren Gate, where the rest camp is to the left, you'll encounter a vast desert under enormous, usually cloudless skies and a sense of space and openness. There is no border fence, so your documents will be scrutinized upon entry, and you'll be unaware of slipping back and forth between the two countries while in the park.

The Kgalagadi Transfrontier Park is less commercialized and developed than Kruger. Its roads aren't paved, and you'll encounter far fewer people. Although there's less game than in Kruger, there's also less vegetation, so the animals are far easier to spot. The landscape of endless dunes punctuated by blond grass and the odd thorn tree is dominated by two *wadis* (dry riverbeds): the Nossob, which forms the border between South Africa and Botswana, and its tributary, the Auob. The Nossob flows only a few times a century, and the Auob flows only once every couple of decades or so.

A single road runs beside each riverbed. Along the way, wind pumps dredge up underground water into man-made reservoirs that not only help the animals to survive during periods when it's utterly dry, but also provide unsurpassed game-viewing and photography viewpoints. There are 82 such water holes, 49 of them along the tourist roads.

A third "main" road traverses the park's interior to join the other two. The scenery and vegetation on this road change dramatically from two river valleys dominated by sandy banks to a grassy escarpment. Two more dune roads and several 4x4 routes also have been developed. From Nossob camp, a road leads to Union's End, the country's northernmost tip, where South Africa, Namibia, and Botswana meet. Allow a full day for this dusty drive, which is 124 km (77 miles) one way. Note that the park infrastructure is particularly basic in Botswana, where a 4x4 is essential.

Most commonly seen animals include springbuck, sometimes in extremely large herds; oryxes (aka gemsbok), with their impressive long, straight horns;

wildebeest; ostriches; jackals; and lions, quite possibly lying right out in the open—at least when it's not roasting hot. The park also has leopards, cheetahs, eland, blue wildebeests, jackals, giraffes, meerkats, and mongooses. Rarer species include elusive aardvarks, pretty Cape foxes, and adorable bat-eared foxes. Among birders, the park is known as one of Africa's raptor meccas, filled with bateleurs, lappet-faced vultures, pygmy and red-necked falcons, and gabar goshawks.

Perhaps the key to appreciating this barren place is understanding how its creatures have adapted to their harsh surroundings. The oryx, for example, has a sophisticated cooling system allowing it to tolerate extreme changes in body temperature, and certain insects inhale only every half hour or so to preserve the moisture that breathing expends.

Note that park management struggles to maintain the water holes and the tourist roads. It is, however, a constant battle against the elements, with the elements often winning. ■TIP→ **The speed limit is never more (and sometimes considerably less) than 50 km (30 miles) per hour, and you should obey it even if others don't. Also, look out for tortoises on the roads.**

All organized game drives and walks are accompanied by SANPark rangers, who carry rifles; are subject to availability; and require reservations, which you should make when booking your accommodations. The park's legendary sunset drives—during which you might see nocturnal animals like the brown hyena or bat-eared fox by spotlight—typically depart at 5:30 in summer (earlier in winter) from Twee Rivieren Camp and Nossob. To watch the sun rise over the Kalahari and possibly encounter a lion, join one of the guided morning walks.

WHEN TO GO

The park can be super-hot in summer and freezing at night in winter (literally below zero, with frost on the ground). If, however, you don't mind dealing with the cold, the winter months of June and July can be good times for a visit. The best time, though is autumn—late February to mid-April—as it's cool after the rains, and many of the migratory birds are still around. Regardless of when you visit, make reservations far in advance, even up to 11 months out.

GETTING HERE AND AROUND

Upington International Airport is 260 km (162 miles) south of Kgalagadi Transfrontier Park. Many lodgings provide shuttle service, or you can rent a car at the airport. If you reserve a car through an agency in Upington, you can pick it up from the Twee Rivieren Camp.

If you drive from Johannesburg, you have a choice of two routes: either via Upington, along a road that is almost entirely paved, or via Kuruman, Hotazel, and Van Zylsrus, with a 150-km (93-mile), nerve-wracking, badly corrugated, gravel stretch between Van Zylsrus and Askham.

VISITOR INFORMATION

There's a daily conservation fee for all visitors, which can be paid at the Twee Rivieren reception desk. Reservations for most accommodations, bush drives, wilderness trails, and other park activities must be made through South African National Parks, and it's recommended to book all of the above well in advance.

South African National Parks

It's usually safest and quickest to book through the central booking office in Tshwane, although oftentimes when that office says "full," the camp itself has vacancies. ☎ *012/428–9111* ⊕ *www. sanparks.org.*

Sights

Kalahari Trails Meerkat Sanctuary

WILDLIFE REFUGE | FAMILY | About 30 minutes from the Twee Rivieren entry gate to Kgalagadi Transfrontier Park, this private nature reserve was established by the late zoology professor Anna Rasa who wanted to focus on the region's smaller creatures. Her son, Richard, now oversees the 9-acre property, where activities include up-close looks at meerkats being nursed back to health; walks to see animals you wouldn't necessarily spot on drives in the Transfrontier Park; sundowner and nighttime drives, where a spotlight makes it easier to see nocturnal creatures such as aardvarks; and nighttime scorpion "hunts" using flashlights to look for these arachnids, which are collected for identification and then later released (except for the few that are fed to the meerkats).

The main treat, though, is the chance to observe the resident meerkat family in its natural environment, walking with them as they move out into the landscape, foraging as they go. There are also some basic rooms (some with en-suite bathrooms) and bush-camp accommodations if you don't mind roughing it; overnight guests are able to explore the property on foot. ⊠ *R360, Bokspits, Kgalagadi Transfrontier Park* ✧ *37 km (23 miles) south of the Twee Rivieren entrance to the Kgalagadi Transfrontier Park* ☎ *063/087–7732, 073/963–8577* ⊕ *www.kalahari-trails.co.za* ✉ *Daytime dune game drive R200; nighttime game drive R250; guided walks R150; scorpion hunt R100.*

★ Kgalagadi Transfrontier Park

WILDLIFE REFUGE | Called Kalahari Gemsbok National Park when it was first incorporated in 1931, Kgalagadi was combined with Botswana's Gemsbok National Park to create this internationally protected area of nearly 9 million acres. Unlike Kruger, South Africa's other mammoth national park, this is a desert park, with sparse vegetation and sand dunes. The game seen here is mostly concentrated around two roads that follow the park's two (mostly) dry riverbeds. These are dotted with man-made watering holes.

Black-maned Kalahari lions, springbok, oryx, pygmy falcons, and martial eagles are among the star animal attractions. You will not find the broad range of large mammals that you see in Kruger, but because of the sparse vegetation and limited grazing areas, animals are more visible here. Among the noteworthy plant species are plenty of beautiful camel-thorn acacia trees; you will also spot many of the large communal nests of sociable weavers that are something of a visual signature all across the Kalahari.

The park has several lodges and rustic rest camps, and while its isolation means that it's never as crowded as Kruger, the pandemic saw a marked increase in South African visitors. According to SANParks reports, the rest and wilderness camps here are almost always full, so don't delay in making reservations. ⊠ *Twee Rivieren Rest Camp, R360, Kgalagadi Transfrontier Park* ☎ *054/561–2000* ⊕ *www.sanparks.co.za* ✉ *R416 per person per day.*

Hotels

Accommodations within the park are in three traditional rest camps and several very isolated but highly sought-after (reserve well in advance) wilderness camps that are spread around the park. The rest camps have shops selling food, curios, and some basic equipment.

The shop at Twee Rivieren has the best variety of (sometimes fresh) fruit and vegetables and essentials such as milk and meat. This camp also has a restaurant, though during the pandemic it only served takeout, and its post-COVID future seemed uncertain. Twee Rivieren is also the only camp with cell-phone

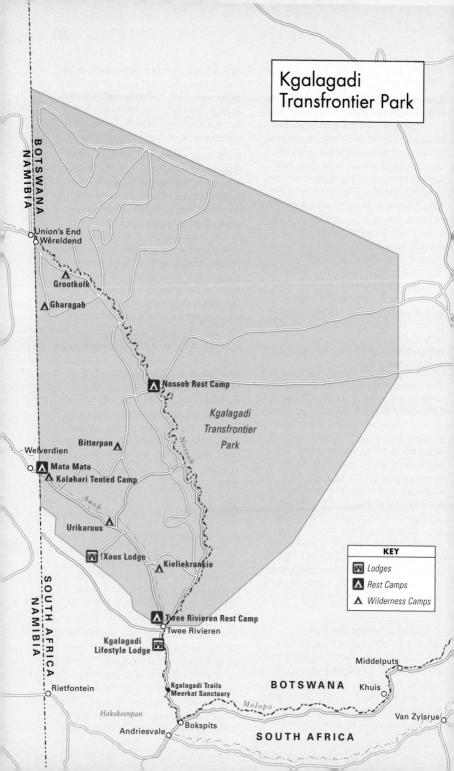

Kgalagadi Transfrontier Park

BOTSWANA
NAMIBIA

Union's End
Wêreldend

▲ Grootkolk

▲ Gharagab

◼ Nossob Rest Camp

Kgalagadi Transfrontier Park

Bitterpan ▲

Welverdien

▲ Mata Mata
▲ Kalahari Tented Camp

Anob

▲ Urikaruus

🏠 !Xaus Lodge   ▲ Kieliekrankie

SOUTH AFRICA
NAMIBIA

Nossob

◼ Twee Rivieren Rest Camp
○ Twee Rivieren

🏠 Kgalagadi Lifestyle Lodge

Rietfontein

Kgalagadi Trails
Meerkat Sanctuary

Hakskeenpan

Andriesvale   ○ Bokspits

Molopo

BOTSWANA

Middelputs

Khuis

Van Zylsrus

SOUTH AFRICA

KEY

🏠	Lodges
◼	Rest Camps
▲	Wilderness Camps

San Culture and Language

The Northern Cape has a long and rich human history. Also called the !Xam, the hunter-gatherer San (most of whom prefer to be called Bushmen, as it describes their skill) have a culture that dates back more than 20,000 years, and their genetic origins are more than 1 million years old, contemporary humans' oldest. Fast-forward a few years—about 2,000 years ago, to be inexact—when Korana or Khoi (Khoe) herders migrated south, bringing their livestock and settling along the Orange (Gariep/Garieb), Vaal, and Riet rivers. During the 18th and 19th centuries, the Griquas—thought to be part Khoi and part African and Malay slaves—moved into the Northern Cape with their cattle and sheep.

At one time 20–30 languages pertaining to various San/Bushmen clans flourished, but colonialism brought with it devastating results for most of these languages, which lost out to Tswana and Afrikaans. In the nick of time in the 1870s, British doctor Wilhelm Bleek (who spoke !Xam) and Lucy Lloyd recorded the last activities of !Xam culture and tradition. (Some of these records can be found at the McGregor Museum in Kimberley.)

Still, thousands of Northern Cape residents today acknowledge an ancestral connection to the largest San or !Xam group of the 18th and 19th centuries. The two biggest remaining groups are the !Xu and the Khwe, who live at Schmidtsdrift, 80 km (50 miles) from Kimberley. Among the best-known groups in South Africa, though, is the Khomani San, some of whom still speak the ancient Nu. For a good overview on the languages, culture, and peoples who migrated to the Northern Cape, check out the McGregor Museum.

reception and 24-hour electricity. The others use gas for hot water and refrigeration and solar power for lights; what electricity there is may run for only part of the day.

For all national park accommodations, which are almost always full, contact South African National Parks (⊕ www.sanparks.org). If you are already at the park, there's a slim chance that you can arrange an extra night's stay directly with local staff.

For a private semi-luxurious lodge, !Xaus, owned by the ‡Khomani San community, is deep in the park's western reaches. Because it's roughly 50 km (32 miles) in from the gate, guests are met by a vehicle at the Kumqwa rest area, where they park their car. From there, it is exactly 91 dunes to the lodge in a 4x4—and well worth it.

If you really want the most hassle-free park experience, and it's not too important for you to be inside the reserve itself, the Kgalagadi Lifestyle Lodge has the best facilities and very reasonable rates. Not only can you be assured of getting three far-above-average meals a day, you can also order fresh meat to cook on your own *braai* (barbecue), along with side salads or other vegetables. The lodge is just 5 km (3 miles) from the Twee Rivieren entrance, and the affable owner rents 4x4s that enhance the game-viewing experience on the reserve's gravel roads.

LODGES
★ Kgalagadi Lifestyle Lodge
$ | RESORT | FAMILY | Hotelier, chef, entrepreneur, designer, furniture-maker, and warm-hearted host, the Kalahari-born-and-raised SJ Koortzen is passionate about hospitality, and at his

"nothing's-too-much-trouble" lodge just 5 km (3 miles) from the entrance to the reserve, he does everything possible to make guests feel comfortable and welcome—based here, you will be well-fed, well-rested, and well-prepared for park adventures. **Pros:** lots of attention paid to the overall guest experience; very good value with many amenities, including an excellent restaurant; owners treat staff like family so there's a wonderful sense of community. **Cons:** some chalets are far from the restaurant, shop, and pool (the only area with Wi-Fi); you may find the accommodations a little smarter and less rustic than anticipated; you're not inside the reserve but rather 5 km (3 miles) from the gate. $ Rooms from: R1100 ⊠ R360, Kgalagadi Transfrontier Park ⌖ 5 km (3 miles) from the Twee Rivieren entrance to Kgalagadi Transfrontier Park ☎ 054/325–0935, 054/050–1320 ⊕ www.kgalagadi-lodge.co.za ⇘ 23 chalets ⧈ No Meals.

★ !Xaus Lodge

$$$$ | RESORT | To experience one of South Africa's most beautiful and isolated parks without hassle and gain insight into an ancient culture, book a stay at this comfortable and enchanting lodge, owned by the ‡Khomani San and Mier communities and located deep in the desert, 32 km (20 miles) along a track across the red dunes of the Kalahari. **Pros:** opportunities to interact with the indigenous people; a unique wilderness setting; only private lodge within the transfrontier park. **Cons:**; it will not suit you if you need lots of creature comforts; the chalets could do with some TLC. $ Rooms from: R10750 ⊠ 91st Dune, off the Auob River Road, Kgalagadi Transfrontier Park ☎ 021/701–7860 ⊕ www.xauslodge.co.za ⇘ 12 units ⧈ All-Inclusive.

REST CAMPS
Mata Mata

$ | RESORT | This camp, on the Namibian border, some 120 km (74 miles) from Twee Rivieren, has good game-viewing due to the proximity of the watering holes and is particularly well known for giraffe sightings. **Pros:** you'll appreciate the pool in summer; far smaller than Twee Rivieren and therefore sees fewer people; great watering holes where animals can be viewed, especially giraffes. **Cons:** far from the park's Twee Rivieren entrance; usually full and can feel crowded thanks to the 21 camp sites; it can be dry and dusty year-round. $ Rooms from: R1300 ⊠ Kgalagadi Transfrontier Park ☎ 012/428–9111 for reservations ⊕ www.sanparks.org ⇘ 15 units ⧈ No Meals.

Nossob Rest Camp

$ | RESORT | In a central area of the park—on the Botswana border, 166 km (103 miles) from Twee Rivieren—this camp offers basic brick chalets and family-size cottages that can sleep three to six people and have adequate bathrooms with showers (no tubs—you are in the middle of nowhere, after all). **Pros:** half the chalets have had a facelift and it's well worth asking for one of them; there's good game viewing from the camp itself; wonderful bush atmosphere with a heightened sense of remoteness. **Cons:** when camp sites fill (which is often) it can feel crowded; regular maintenance and general sprucing-up tend to get neglected; not the most attractive camp and can feel somewhat barren. $ Rooms from: R1300 ⊠ Kgalagadi Transfrontier Park ☎ 012/428–9111 for reservations ⊕ www.sanparks.org ⇘ 20 units ⧈ No Meals.

Twee Rivieren Rest Camp

$ | RESORT | FAMILY | The reserve's main southern entrance is home to park headquarters and this camp, where facilities include a pool; a restaurant; a fairly well-stocked shop; and accommodations ranging from two-bedroom, kitchen-equipped family cottages that sleep six people to bungalows with two single beds and a sleeper couch. **Pros:** access to must-do guided nature walks and morning and evening drives; fairly well-equipped chalets; gas station and a grocery store selling basics on site. **Cons:** there can be a lot of humans concentrated in this one area; not exactly built to suit the environment and is consequently a bit unattractive; biggest and noisiest camp in the park. $ *Rooms from: R1425* ⊠ *Kgalagadi Transfrontier Park* ☎ *012/428–9111 reservations* ⊕ *www. sanparks.org* ⇨ *31 units* ❤️❤️ *No Meals.*

WILDERNESS CAMPS

Kgalagadi is the first national park to provide accommodations deep in the wilderness, where several unfenced wilderness camps with their own watering holes for game-viewing put you in the heart of the Kalahari. These enchanting camps are very popular, so make your reservations well in advance—up to 11 months ahead, if possible.

Each camp is slightly different, but all are similarly priced and have the same facilities, namely, an equipped kitchen with a gas-powered refrigerator, solar-powered lights, gas for hot water, and a deck with braai facilities. You must bring your own drinking water and firewood; although there is water in the kitchenettes and bathrooms, it is far from palatable.

■ TIP→ **Under no circumstances should you bring children under 12, and never wander from your accommodations after dark. There's a very real chance of face-to-face encounters with nocturnal hunters like lions, leopards, or hyenas.**

Bitterpan

$$ | **RESORT** | This elevated camp overlooks an enormous expanse of sand and a watering hole, where you can watch game come and go from your deck or communal areas. **Pros:** only four cabins; spectacular game-viewing from

your accommodations; beautiful desert scenery. **Cons:** long drive to get here from anywhere else; extremely basic; only accessible with a 4x4. $ *Rooms from: R2125* ⊠ *Kgalagadi Transfrontier Park* ☎ *012/428–9111 for reservations* ⊕ *www. sanparks.org* ⇨ *4 units* ❤️❤️ *No Meals.*

Gharagab

$$ | **RESORT** | In the park's far northern reaches, close to the Namibian border, this camp provides stunning elevated views of Kalahari dunes and thornveld savanna, and although you need a 4x4 (with low-range capability and high clearance) to negotiate the two-track road that travels here, it's worth every dusty mile for the chance to feel like you're alone on Earth. **Pros:** with only four units you're guaranteed peace and quiet; you've probably never experienced such solitary wilderness; great views from your private deck. **Cons:** you need to enough drinking water to sustain you as none is available here; it may flay your nerves if solitude doesn't become you; accessed by serious 4x4s only (if you get stuck, there's no one to help you out). $ *Rooms from: R2125* ⊠ *Kgalagadi Transfrontier Park* ☎ *012/428–9111 for reservations* ⊕ *www. sanparks.co.za* ⇨ *4 units* ❤️❤️ *No Meals.*

Grootkolk

$$ | **RESORT** | In the far north of the South African portion of the park, surrounded by camel-thorn trees and close to the Nossob River bed, this small camp offers good game-viewing, though the heavily corrugated road that leads here and the unattractive cabins are definite tradeoffs for the chance (with patience) to see lions, cheetahs, hyenas, and antelope like oryx or springbok. **Pros:** sublime wilderness setting; watering hole that's spotlighted at night can be thrilling; for some, getting here will be part of the adventure. **Cons:** cabins aren't the prettiest; lack of amenities and remoteness means you must arrive fully equipped; it's a long drive from anywhere, and the isolation is not for the fainthearted. $ *Rooms from:*

R2125 ✉ *Kgalagadi Transfrontier Park* ☎ *012/428–9111 reservations* 🌐 *www.sanparks.org* 🛏 *4 units* 🍴 *No Meals.*

Kalahari Tent Camp

$$ | RESORT | Many regard the location of this camp, which overlooks the dry bed of the Auob River, to be one of the most beautiful in the park, so try to stay for more than one night. **Pros:** children under 12 are permitted, although you should still be extremely cautious; it's just 3 km (less than 2 miles) from Mata Mata, which has a shop and gas; relatively attractive and spacious tents. **Cons:** camp-style kitchens are not the best equipped; not as intimate as some camps and the presence of children may be disruptive; it lacks the sense of remoteness of other wilderness camps. [$] *Rooms from: R1875* ✉ *Kgalagadi Transfrontier Park* ☎ *012/428–9111 for reservations* 🌐 *www.sanparks.org* 🛏 *15 units* 🍴 *No Meals.*

Kieliekrankie

$$ | RESORT | Perched high on a big sand dune only 8 km (5 miles) from the game-rich Auob River road, this small camp overlooks seemingly infinite red Kalahari sands, creating an amazing sense of space and isolation. **Pros:** being surrounded by red Kalahari sands is unforgettable; sublime sense of solitude; not too far from Twee Rivieren but still feels remote and peaceful. **Cons:** the so-called "dune cabins" aren't the prettiest on the inside; you really need a 4x4 to get here without getting stuck; brick-built cabins don't exactly scream "wilderness." [$] *Rooms from: R2125* ✉ *Kgalagadi Transfrontier Park* ☎ *012/428–9111 reservations* 🌐 *www.sanparks.org* 🛏 *5 units* 🍴 *No Meals.*

Urikaruus

$$ | RESORT | Five cabins with basic kitchens, bedrooms, and bathrooms are set on stilts among camel-thorn trees at a site affording beautiful vistas overlooking the dry bed of the Auob River. **Pros:** the game viewing at the camp itself is excellent; of the wilderness camps, this is one you can reach with a sedan; the location is simply stunning. **Cons:** apart from the "honeymoon" cabin, all bedrooms have only single beds; as with all wilderness camps, the kitchens are pretty basic; you must be self-sufficient (e.g, bringing your own drinking water and firewood). [$] *Rooms from: R2125* ✉ *Kgalagadi Transfrontier Park* ☎ *012/428–9111 reservations* 🌐 *www.sanparks.org* 🛏 *5 units* 🍴 *No Meals.*

Tswalu Kalahari Reserve

250 km (155 miles) southeast of Kgalagadi Transfrontier Park; 262 km (163 miles) northeast of Upington; 145 km (90 miles) northwest of Kuruman.

Near the Kgalagadi Transfrontier Park is the malaria-free Tswalu Kalahari Reserve, at 1,000 square km (386 square miles) Africa's largest privately owned game reserve and the perfect place to photograph an oryx against a red dune and big blue sky. Initially founded as a conservation project by the late millionaire Stephen Boler (how he made his money is a story in itself), primarily to protect and breed the endangered desert rhino, he left it to the Oppenheimer (of De Beers diamonds fame) family in his will. Today, it spreads over endless Kalahari dunes covered with tufts of golden veld as well as much of the Northern Cape's Korannaberg mountain range.

Its initial population of 7,000 animals has grown, and it's now home to lions, cheetahs, buffalos, giraffes, and a range of antelope species—including rare roan and sable antelope, black wildebeest, and mountain zebra. Because a farm road cuts through the reserve, fences separate the reserve's two precincts, with the lion population currently only in one part. The benefit of this is that the reserve's main Tarkuni lodge is unfenced and as family-friendly as possible, and some of the antelope (notably the sable) remain off the lions' dinner menu. That said, there are plans to construct a third lodge and possibly introduce a lion pride in the currently lion-free area. Also in the pipeline is having the road delisted so that the dividing fences can be taken down. As with most conservation endeavors, Tswalu is ever-changing, so only time will tell how it will evolve.

True to the region's aridity (annual rainfall is only about 9¾ inches), the land has a lower carrying capacity than is found in areas around Kruger National Park, for example, and therefore there's less game. But the lack of vegetation makes animal sightings spectacular. You'll definitely spot meerkats, and roan and sable might stride right past your lodge.

The reserve is also home to several significant research projects, not least of which is an ongoing study of pangolins (scaly anteaters), the world's most heavily trafficked mammal, hunted as much for their scales as for their meat. Although sightings are not guaranteed, seeing one of these mysterious nocturnal creatures will be a highlight of your trip. Other after-dark creatures here include aardvark and aardwolf, and you will almost certainly spot bat-eared foxes, a real delight with their dainty faces. Regardless, Tswalu's vast, surreal landscape pure magic in and of itself.

GETTING HERE AND AROUND

Direct, scheduled, daily flights operate from Johannesburg (1 pm) and from Cape Town (7:30 am) to Tswalu, and seats on these small, private airplanes should be booked directly through the reserve. It's also easy enough to catch a commercial flight to Kimberley or Upington and be picked up from there by the lodge; private road transfers can similarly be arranged from just about anywhere.

It is also totally feasible to drive yourself to the reserve; you'll be provided very clear driving instructions that get you and your vehicle (an ordinary sedan is fine) to the gate, where you'll be met and escorted to your lodge. If you are driving yourself, consider breaking up the trip with an overnight stay en route (somewhere like Kathu, Kuruman, or even Hotazel), so that you arrive fresh and ready to absorb the reserve's majesty.

Sights

★ Tswalu Kalahari Reserve

WILDLIFE REFUGE | FAMILY | This game reserve northeast of Upington is one of the most child friendly in southern Africa, and children are not only welcomed but also well accommodated. The dedication of the rangers and attentiveness of the staff also allows for flexibility and special opportunities, from sleeping under the stars on the "Malori" open deck to enjoying an in-room Champagne breakfast in lieu of going out on a game drive. In addition, every group of guests is guaranteed its own game-viewing vehicle with a dedicated ranger and a tracker who knows the terrain and the animals intimately.

The reserve plays a very important conservation role. Backed by funds from the De Beers family, its desert black rhino population represents one-third of South Africa's remaining animals. In addition to rhino sightings, the on-foot experience with a colony of meerkats is a highlight, as are visits to 380,000-year-old rock engravings from the earliest residents of these phenomenal landscapes.

If you wish to see a pangolin, consider prearranging a visit with the reserve's specialist researcher. A few hours with Dr. Wendy Panaino will improve your odds of spotting one of these elusive, shy, adorable creatures. You can also explore parts of the reserve on horseback. Two stables welcome riders of all skill levels to participate in anything from short, gentle outings to adventurous

Although pangolin sightings are rare, it is possible in Tswalu Kalahari Reserve.

outrides that offer utterly unique views of the reserve and its wild creatures.

Your stay will include a meal at the memorable Klein JAN restaurant, a true original in the culinary universe. Other meals will also be fabulous, too, with breakfast and lunch served whenever you please and, perhaps, a surprise dinner on the dunes. ✉ *Farm Korannaberg 296, Van Zylsrus, Tswalu Kalahari Reserve* ☎ *053/781–9331 for reservations, 053/781–9211 for inquiries* 🌐 *www.tswalu.com.*

🍴 Restaurants

★ Klein JAN

$$$$ | SOUTH AFRICAN | Guests at either of Tswalu Kalahari Reserve's lodges are treated to a dinner at Klein JAN, the first restaurant in the country by Jan Hendrik van der Westhuizen (South Africa's only Michelin star–awarded chef), though others do drive (or fly) in when the eight-course lunch with wine pairings is offered. The setting is a century-old farmhouse, and meals are experiential and immersive—eye-opening introductions to the produce, culinary traditions, and flavors of the Northern Cape, with every morsel or sip seemingly designed to surprise as well as satisfy you, to fire up not only all your senses but also your imagination. **Known for:** food that truly captures the specialness of the Northern Cape and its produce; breathtaking inventiveness; setting and experience unlike anything else—anywhere. [$] *Average main: R2500* ✉ *Boscia House, Tswalu, Farm Korannaberg 296, Van Zylsrus, Tswalu Kalahari Reserve* ☎ *053/781–9441* 🌐 *www.janonline.com/restaurantkleinjan* ☞ *Prix-fixe for multiple courses, wine pairings, and other drinks; no à la carte menu.*

🛏 Hotels

★ The Motse

$$$$ | RESORT | FAMILY | Antelope often traipse by Tswalu's exquisite main lodge, where the communal area features a series of terraced indoor and outdoor lounges that spill down to a pair of pools and a floodlighted watering hole and where guest quarters consist of beautiful, freestanding, thatch-and-stone suites, known as "legae." The decor is minimalist and infinitely stylish, echoing the landscape in color and texture and incorporating local stone and wood, interesting art and artifacts, and unique light fixtures. **Pros:** special children's room and babysitting services and nannies available; you feel immersed in the surroundings from the moment you arrive; gorgeous, bespoke room decor. **Cons:** you will need to save up for a stay at this once-in-a-lifetime lodge; hard to leave your cosseting quarters for game drives (worth it, though); as it's child friendly, you might want to request a room away from the communal areas. [$] *Rooms from: R61000* ✉ *Tswalu, Farm Korannaberg 296, Van Zylsrus, Tswalu Kalahari Reserve* ☎ *053/781–9211, 053/781–9331 for reservations* 🌐 *www.tswalu.com* 🛏 *9 suites* 🍴 *All-Inclusive.*

Tswalu Tarkuni Lodge

$$$$ | **HOUSE** | **FAMILY** | In a private section of Tswalu, this exclusive, self-contained homestead—decorated similarly to the reserve's Motse lodge and offering much the same level of luxury—is perfect for families and other small groups since it sleeps up to 10 people in 5 suites and comes with its own chef, game vehicle, and tracker. **Pros:** exceptional service; ultimate exclusivity; immaculate design that echoes the landscape. **Cons:** you may miss the presence of other travelers; prohibitively expensive; unless you're used to having a staff entirely dedicated to your needs, the attention might be overwhelming. [$] *Rooms from: R124800* ✉ *Tswalu, Farm Korannaberg 296, Van Zylsrus, Tswalu Kalahari Reserve* ☎ *053/781–9317, 053/781–9331* 🌐 *www.tswalu.com* 🛏 *5 suites* 🍴 *All-Inclusive* ☞ *Rate, which is for up to 4 people, rises with each additional couple, up to R223000 if you use all 5 suites.*

Kuruman

250 km (156 miles) northeast of Upington; 236 km northwest of Kimberley.

Kuruman has long been the hub of a large dairy, cattle, and game-farming region, though, nowadays, it tends to service the growing number of area mines, which hasn't transformed the town for the better. Despite its flat, wide streets, it can feel crowded and busy, and neither cleanliness nor law and order seem high on the municipal priority list.

Still, the town is a convenient place to overnight on a drive between Kimberley and Upington or Kimberley and the Kalahari. As opportunistic crime is an issue, avoid staying at hotels in the city center, opting instead for The Hedge Guesthouse, which is in a safer, more upscale, residential neighborhood, or the Red Sands Country Lodge (also a good place to eat), about 15 km (9 miles) outside of town on the N14 towards Kathu.

Hotels

The Hedge Guesthouse

$$ | **B&B/INN** | The Hedge is an expression of passion—and a love of bright colors—on the part of its owner, Lynn-mari Olivier, a lifelong Kuruman and Kalahari resident, whose house-turned-B&B is in a residential area of Kuruman. **Pros:** comfortable rooms and a huge, lovely garden with a pool; best in-town option; decorated with love and affection. **Cons:** picks up noise from nearby roads (and the rooster next door); no access to any indoor public areas except during breakfast; some guests get rowdy on weekends. [$] *Rooms from: R1500* ✉ *36 Cowburn St., Kuruman* ☎ *076/021–3370, 053/712–0038* 🌐 *www.thehedgeguesthouse.co.za* 🛏 *10 rooms* 🍴 *Free Breakfast.*

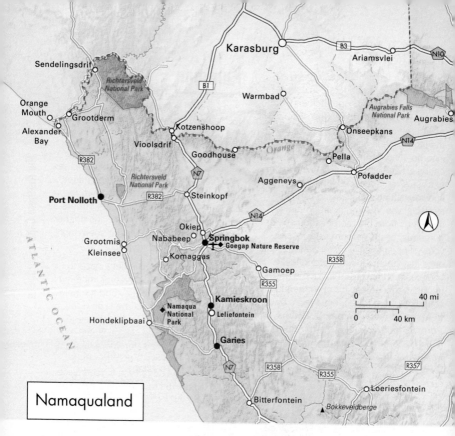

Namaqualand

Red Sands Country Lodge

$$ | **RESORT** | **FAMILY** | On a private nature reserve near the slopes of the Kuruman Hills on the outskirts of town, this casual, simple, well-kept lodge is a great place to stop for the night, with Kaufmann's Kitchen, the best restaurant for miles (complete with a bar), and clean, modern rooms in thatched rondavels or self-catering chalets. **Pros:** feels personal, and management is hands-on; you're surrounded by nature and interiors are pretty decent, with pops of citrusy colors; best food for miles. **Cons:** it's a nature reserve but you won't see huge game or predators; don't expect full-on luxury; the brick-face buildings aren't exactly the height of architectural elegance. $ Rooms from: R1600 ⊠ N14 between Kuruman and Kathu ⊹ 15 km (9 miles) west of Kuruman ☎ 053/712–0033, 082/801–4414 ⊕ www.redsands.co.za ⬅ 32 rooms ⦿ No Meals.

Garies

58 km (36 miles) northeast of Vanrhynsdorp.

Garies is a one-horse town cradled amid sunbaked, granite-dominated hills, and one of the best flower routes runs just north of it for 100 km (60 miles) to Hondeklipbaai, on the coast. The road winds through rocky hills before descending onto the flat coastal sandveld. Flowers in this region usually bloom at the end of July and early August. If you're lucky, fields along this route will be carpeted with purple vygies, but also look for Namaqualand daisies, aloes, and orchids. Quiver trees are common along this route, too.

Hotels

Agama Tented Camp

$$$ | **RESORT** | The tents at this bush camp—which is a short drive, partially along an easy dirt road, north of Garies and is open in and out of Namaqualand's world-renowned wildflower season—are on raised wooden decks and have basic bathrooms, gas heat, and spacious decks but no electricity (although you can charge phones in the dining tent). **Pros:** good meals; phenomenal scenery, especially in the (spring) flower season; very intimate experience. **Cons:** no children under 12; no cell reception (although there is Wi-Fi); isolation could be an issue for some out of flower season. [$] *Rooms from: R3500* ✣ *20 km (12 miles) north of Garies* ☎ *072/040–0614* 🌐 *www.agamacamp.co.za* 🛏 *7 tents* 🍴 *All-Inclusive.*

Namaqua Flower Beach Camp

$$$$ | **RESORT** | Operated by a glamping specialists, Chiefs Tented Camps, this upscale outdoor experience—namely, for just four weeks, Chiefs sets up 15 tents, each with an attached bathroom (hot water supplied on request), comfy beds, and good linens—puts you front and center for the riot of color when millions of tiny flowers reveal themselves briefly in spring, creating a vast natural carpet of unending patterns. **Pros:** a real chance to unplug from the grid; sublime seaside setting; intimate and magical glamping experience. **Cons:** chemical portable toilets are the only real hindrance; it can be bitterly cold in winter, especially if it rains, so come prepared; not for you if the sound of the sea is likely to keep you awake. [$] *Rooms from: R5940* ✉ *Groenriviermond* ✣ *70 km (44 miles) from Garies, on the coast* ☎ *071/260–6367, 083/652–5489* 🌐 *www.flowercamps.co.za* 🛏 *15 tents* 🍴 *All-Inclusive.*

Kamieskroon

49 km (30 miles) north of Garies; 72 km (45 miles) south of Springbok on the N7.

Another base for exploring Namaqualand in spring, Kamieskroon is the only place to stay close to Namaqua National Park—unless you're in the park itself. The Kamieskroon Hotel (which will be 100 years old in 2025), although no great shakes for accommodations, is a good source of information on wildflowers in Namaqualand. The SANParks information center at the gate to the park is also helpful.

Sights

Leliefontein

TOWN | A 29-km (18-mile) detour from Kamieskroon brings you to this old Methodist mission station at the top of the Kamiesberg, which has spectacular views across the desert to the sea. The church, a national monument, was finished in 1855, but the adjacent parsonage is much older. The wildflowers in Leliefontein bloom much later than those on the coast, often lasting as late as the end of October. Even if there are no flowers, it's a beautiful drive back down the Kamiesberg to Garies, 72 km (45 miles) away. ✉ *Leliefontein.*

Namaqua National Park

NATURE PRESERVE | During its flower season (early-August through September), Namaqua National Park can usually be counted on for superb wildflower displays, even when there are no flowers anywhere else. Covering an area of almost 200,000 acres and located 21 km (11 miles) west of Kamieskroon, the park is the world's only arid biodiversity hot spot. Look for Namaqua daisies in oranges and yellows as well as succulents, such as the many-colored vygies in hues of purple, magenta, and orange.

Park roads are good, though the nearest gas station is in Springbok, 87 km (54 miles) away. Driving from Soebatsfontein toward Springbok yields spectacular views over the coast from the top of the Wildeperdehoek Pass. Two short hiking trails take a few hours each, and you can ride bikes and make use of various picnic sites throughout the park. Recent upgrades include new routes and rest camps, and the reintroduction of game (tsessebe, oryx, springbok, and eland). There's a seasonal visitor center at the Skilpad entrance. ✉ *Skilpad Rd., Kamieskroon* ☎ *027/672–1948* 🌐 *www.sanparks.co.za* 🎟 *R100.*

Hotels

Namaqua Flower Skilpad Camp
$$$$ | **RESORT** | During flower season, this rustic-smart tented camp puts you in the middle of things—surrounded by low-lying mountains and, of course, fields of orange, yellow, and white flowers, with spectacular views all around. **Pros:** real off-the-grid experience; sublime and remote place to experience a one-of-a-kind annual phenomenon; warm, comfortable beds in cozy tents. **Cons:** nobody likes a chemical portable toilet; tents are extremely limited and can be fully booked up to a year in advance; a bit pricey for what you get. [$] *Rooms from: R5940* ✉ *Skilpad Nature Reserve, Namaqua National Park, Kamieskroon* ✣ *30 km (19 miles) from Kamieskroon* ☎ *071/260–6367, 083/652–5489* 🌐 *www.flowercamps.co.za* ⏲ *Closed Oct.–July* 🛏 *15 tents* 🍴 *All-Inclusive* ☞ *An additional fee must be paid to enter the national park.*

Springbok

117 km (73 miles) north of Kamieskroon; 375 km (233 miles) southwest of Upington.

The capital of Namaqualand is set in a bowl of rocky hills that form part of the Klipkoppe, a rocky escarpment that stretches from Steinkopf, in the north, to Bitterfontein, in the south. Quiver trees proliferate in the area, and flower season brings the town alive as the landscape becomes covered in natural carpets of multicolored blooms.

Though the town owes its existence to the discovery of copper, its architecture is mostly modern, with very few buildings dating from the 1800s. Compared with most of the *dorps* (towns) in the Northern Cape, Springbok is a buzzing little settlement, with a fair number of things to see in the area if you need to take a break from flower gazing.

Sights

Goegap Nature Reserve
NATURE PRESERVE | **FAMILY** | Each spring, this reserve transforms into a wildflower mosaic, which you can explore on either of two short—4- and 6-km (2½- and 4-mile)—walking trails; mountain biking within the reserve is also permitted. A count has recorded 581 different plant species within the reserve, and there are animals to see, too, including Hartmann's mountain zebras, oryxes, springbuck, klipspringers, duikers, and steenbuck. There are also some 94 different bird species, including ostriches, Cape eagle-owls, martial eagles, Verreaux's (or black) eagles, Ludwig's bustards, and Damara canaries.

Did You Know?

If you're looking to see amazing wildflowers, head to the Goegap Nature Reserve in the spring.

Goegap is also home to the Hester Malan Wildflower Garden, which displays an interesting collection of succulents, including the bizarre halfmen or "half person" (*Pachypodium namaquanum*), featuring a long, slender trunk topped by a passel of leaves that makes it resemble an armless person—hence the name. There are picnic sites, and, during flower season, there's a small on-site kiosk where you can get a bite to eat. Quaint, simple, gas- and solar-powered, three-bedroom chalets cost as little as R1,000 per night per couple. The nightly rate for smaller, more basic "bush huts," with no electricity and shared ablutions, is R250. ⊠ *R355, Springbok* ✚ *16 km (10 miles) southeast of town via airport road* ☎ *027/718–9906* 💲 *R30.*

Namaqualand Museum

HISTORY MUSEUM | Displays here tell the history of Namaqualand, the town of Springbok, and the people who've lived here. Items range from some 17th-century pieces to an old fridge and washing machine made of *kokerboom* (wood from the distinctive "half-man" tree). The museum is housed in an old synagogue. The earliest Jewish traders had a significant impact on the growth of business not only in the area, but in the country as a whole, and, up until the early 1970s, Springbok had a small Jewish community. ⊠ *Monument St., Springbok* ☎ *027/718–8100* 💲 *Donations accepted* ⊗ *Closed Sat. and Sun.*

🍽 Restaurants

Herb Garden Restaurant

$ | **INTERNATIONAL** | **FAMILY** | This tucked-away, family-friendly restaurant is a little gem in Springbok's otherwise limited dining scene. Emphasis is on fresh ingredients (you really do taste the difference), and there are lovely specials from time to time, including spit-roasted pig served with delicious, homemade sides. **Known for:** very welcoming service; excellent burgers, steaks, and wood-oven-fired

pizza; really good coffee. 💲 *Average main: R95* ⊠ *4 Kruis St., Springbok* ☎ *027/712–1247, 074/848–1163, 081/527–1280.*

 ## Hotels

Apollis Cottage

$ | **B&B/INN** | Remote in location, 30 minutes from Springbok, this is the real deal if you want comfort and solitude with big skies in a desertlike location. **Pros:** good value for money; remote location provides solitude (and very starry skies) in a beautiful setting; clean, comfortable accommodations. **Cons:** while the area is beautiful, the buildings are a little bland; tiled floors and modern room decor don't quite fit with the surroundings; bedroom color combinations aren't to everyone's taste. 💲 *Rooms from: R1160* ⊠ *Homeb 6, Springbok* ✚ *20 km (12 miles) off the N2* ☎ *087/233–9194, 061/296–2807 WhatsApp* ⊟ *No credit cards* 💤 *3 rooms* ⦿ *Free Breakfast.*

★ Naries Namakwa Retreat

$$$$ | **HOTEL** | This lovely retreat in the countryside west of Springbok and overlooking the Spektakelberg Mountains and has five, large, individually decorated rooms (with impressive en-suite baths) in an upscale Dutch Cape–style guesthouse; three quaint, architecturally unique Mountain Suites designed to emulate the surrounding boulders; and two self-catering cottages. **Pros:** the Mountain Suites afford a truly memorable experience; beautiful location in the mountains with wondrous views; excellent meals are available. **Cons:** don't come here if you require Wi-Fi and uninterrupted cell reception; not suitable for young children (those under 12 aren't permitted in the dining room); not for you if you're looking for a crowd. 💲 *Rooms from: R3570* ⊠ *Naries Rd., off the R355 towards Kleinzee, Springbok* ✚ *27 km (17 miles) west of Springbok, along the R355* ☎ *076/238–2934, 021/872–0398 for reservations* ⊕ *www.naries.co.za* 💤 *10 units* ⦿ *Free Breakfast.*

Okiep Country Hotel

$ | **HOTEL** | **FAMILY** | About 8 km (5 miles) from Springbok, in South Africa's oldest mining town, this hotel is one of the finest places to stay in Namaqualand, not only for the above-average accommodations and dining, but also for the friendly owner, Malcolm Mostert, who has created a homey atmosphere and who is a great source of information about what to see and do in the area. **Pros:** good value and lots of space to relax in; hands-on, longtime owner-manager who can help you learn about the region; hearty meals in the lovely restaurant. **Cons:** not the most intimate option in the area; unlike the rest of the hotel, bedrooms don't convey much sense of history; the brown-and-white contemporary styling of the rooms may not appeal to all. [$] *Rooms from: R1050* ✉ *Main St., Okiep* ☎ *027/744–1000* 🌐 *www.okiep.co.za* 🛏 *37 rooms* 🍴 *Free Breakfast.*

Springbok Inn

$$ | **HOTEL** | Just outside town, this large-for-Springbok, no-frills, cookie-cutter hotel (it's owned by the Northern Cape's Country Hotels chain) offers clean linen, decent beds, a pool, and adequate (though not thrilling) food. **Pros:** fairly neat and reasonably clean rooms; has a swimming pool and outdoor seating areas; 24-hour reception and free Wi-Fi. **Cons:** lacks personality thanks to bland and uninspiring decor; service fails to live up to expectations; overpriced for what you get. [$] *Rooms from: R2100* ✉ *Voortrekker Rd., Springbok* ☎ *027/718–1832* 🌐 *www.springbokinn.co.za* 🛏 *117 units* 🍴 *Free Breakfast.*

Springbok Lodge & Restaurant

$ | **HOTEL** | This simple, family-run lodge, (*not* to be confused with the Springbok Inn run by the Country Hotels chain) has a huge variety of rooms in different buildings and a vibe all its own—the former owner, "Oom Jopie," assembled loads of insider information as well as vast collections of minerals and old photographs that help make this old place (the main building, whose exterior is a bit of an eyesore, went up in 1929) one of those fabled roadside stops. **Pros:** loads of local information available and quite a sense of history; cheap (in every sense) and cheerful; decent food. **Cons:** small beds and cheap, basic furniture; merely functional with few amenities beyond a bar and restaurant; no discernible style. [$] *Rooms from: R875* ✉ *37 Voortrekker St., Springbok* ☎ *027/712–1321* 🌐 *springbok-lodge.business.site* 🛏 *75 rooms* 🍴 *No Meals.*

An Excellent Flower Drive

This 320-km (200-mile) rectangular route heads north on the N7 from Springbok to Steinkopf and then west on the paved R382 to Port Nolloth. From there, a dirt road leads south through the Sandveld to Grootmis, then east along the Buffels River before climbing the Spektakel Pass back to Springbok. If the rains have been good, the route offers some of the region's best flower viewing. Try to time your return to Springbok to coincide with the sunset, when the entire Spektakel Mountain glows a deep orange-red.

Port Nolloth

110 km (69 miles) northwest of Springbok.

A lovely drive from Springbok, particularly during flower time, the town started life as a copper port, but it's better known today as a fishing and diamond center. With only one (decent) road leading into it, the flat, desertlike coastal *dorp* is a ghost town at night, as the little life that exists by day dies completely after dark. If the few establishments in town are full, MacDougall Bay a mile down the coast has accommodations.

It's also the springboard to the Richtersveld, the vast region of mountains and desert to the north, which is well known for its exquisite succulents and other flora but should be visited only on an organized tour or once you have armed yourself with a considerable amount of information. It's extremely remote, and you'll definitely need a 4x4 or *bakkie* to avoid breakdowns. If you're a newbie to deserts, a guide will help you get the most out of your visit to the Richtersveld. In fact this arid country comes alive when interpreted, whether that means learning about its flowers or the Richtersveld Mountains (look out for Conrad Mouton of Aukwatowa Tours).

This bay is safe for swimming, although the water is freezing cold almost any time of the year. Head over to the harbor to check out the diamond-vacuuming boats, with their distinctive hoses trailing astern. Divers use the hoses to vacuum under boulders on the seabed in search of any diamonds that have washed into the sea from the Orange River over many millennia. It's a highly lucrative endeavor but not without its dangers; at least one diver has been sucked up the vacuum hose to his death.

Former diamond diver George Mouyses, at the rough-and-ready and totally offbeat Port Nolloth Museum, has done it all (except for the diamond-vacuum). He can keep you enthralled for hours and asks only for a small donation for his time, which may feel invaluable as you depart. The museum otherwise contains an enormous quantity of historical artifacts, from 16th-century slave bracelets from a ship that went aground to fragments of Khoi clay pots, not to mention such oddities as whale barnacles and antique matchboxes from an old Johannesburg hotel.

 Hotels

The Beach House Port Nolloth

$ | **HOUSE** | **FAMILY** | Old and new meet in these laid-back beachfront accommodations consisting of a three-bedroom house dating from the 1870s and a one-bedroom cottage—each serves as a separate self-catering vacation rental. **Pros:** lovely beachside location; very well priced; pleasing mixture of history and modern conveniences. **Cons:** it's self-catering so no meals are available; the main beach road passes directly by the house; not for you if you need slick, modern design. $ *Rooms from: R1400* ✉ *74 Beach Rd., Port Nolloth* ☎ *074/107–2422* ⊕ *www.portnollothbeachhouse. co.za* ➥ *2 units* ⭕ *No Meals* ☞ *Price is for 4 people; the house sleeps up to 8 (R1,800). The cottage is R800 per night.*

Bedrock Lodge

$ | **B&B/INN** | Comprising some of the oldest houses in town, some dating from 1855, and made up of three rooms in the main house and a handful of self-catering cottages, Bedrock is delightful, with interiors decorated with Africana and antiques that give it the atmosphere of an old-fashioned inn. **Pros:** very reasonable prices; beautiful period-piece accommodations; convenient location, with the town's museum on site. **Cons:** more nostalgia than luxury; the main road in front can get noisy; some furnishings are a little dated. $ *Rooms from: R1200* ✉ *2 Beach Rd., Port Nolloth* ☎ *027/851–8865, 083/259–8865* ⊕ *www.bedrock-lodge.co.za* ➥ *8 units* ⭕ *Free Breakfast* ☞ *Self-catering from R880 per 4-person cottage.*

Chapter 7

THE GARDEN ROUTE AND THE LITTLE KAROO

7

Updated by
Kate Turkington

 Sights
★★★★☆

 Restaurants
★★★★★

 Hotels
★★★★☆

 Shopping
★★★★★

 Nightlife
★☆☆☆☆

WELCOME TO THE GARDEN ROUTE AND THE LITTLE KAROO

TOP REASONS TO GO

★ **Whale-Watching:** Some of the best boat-based whale- and dolphin-watching in the world can be found at Plettenberg Bay on the Garden Route. You can often watch these friendly cetaceans frolicking from the shore.

★ **Animal Encounters:** The Crags area, just outside Plettenberg Bay, is the place to go if you want to spend a day with animals. Visit rescued primates, the world's largest free-flight aviary, or free-roaming big game at Sanbona Wildlife Reserve.

★ **Adventure Sports:** If you're itching for a taste of freefall, you've come to the right place. The highest commercial bungee jump in the world can be found at Bloukrans Bridge.

★ **Scenic Hiking:** Enjoy the best of nature on an escorted, guided, portered, and catered hike, locally called "slackpacking." The three coastal hikes in Plettenberg Bay's Robberg Nature Reserve are reputed to be among the most beautiful in the world.

1 Mossel Bay. Its sandy beaches, including one of the only north-facing beaches in South Africa, offer an average of over 320 days of sunshine a year. There's lots to see and do, making for a memorable visit to this friendly little town steeped in history.

2 George. About 20 minutes from the ocean, this is the Garde Route's largest town with a fascinating transport museum and an excellent public golf course.

3 Wilderness. Beaches, mountains, forests, and lagoons make this little town one of South Africa's favorite holiday destinations. It's super busy in season, but you can escape the crowds by hiking nearby trails or enjoying outdoor activities in the Wilderness section of Garden Route National Park.

4 Knysna. This popular holiday town has inviting shops, galleries, restaurants, and cafés.

5 Plettenberg Bay. Plett, as the locals call it, is a sophisticated retreat brimming with expensive vacation homes, exclusive hotels, and elegant restaurants and bars. Superb sandy beaches, gorgeous coastal hikes, and loads of water- and land-based

activities make this a must-visit destination.

6 The Crags. This forested area is known for a famous primate refuge called Monkeyland and for Birds of Eden, a stunning free-flight aviary filled with thousands of tropical and local birds.

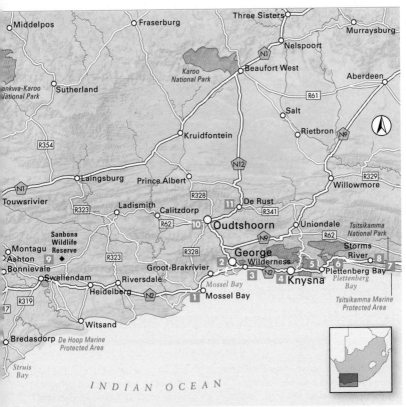

7 Tsitsikamma. Expect nature at her wildest here. Thick forests and ancient rivers roll down deep gorges to rocky shores pounded by the breakers of the Indian Ocean. Hike, boat, or bike, or just drink in the scenery.

9 Sanbona Wildlife Reserve. Arguably the Western Cape's most authentic Big Five reserve, animals like elephants, lions, and cheetahs roam free in these 135,000 acres.

8 Storms River. This tiny village is one of South Africa's top adventure and ecotourism destinations. Take a flying leap at the world's biggest bungee jump, enjoy a thrilling canopy tour, or just chill.

10 Oudtshoorn. Often described as the "Ostrich Center of the World," this dusty Victorian town was once a boomtown. Since 1870, farmers have bred ostriches for their feathers, their meat, and their hides.

11 De Rust. This quaint village is the gateway to the Klein Karoo. Stock up on olive oils or travel the spectacular Meiringspoort Pass.

The Garden Route, which generally refers to the 208-km (130-mile) stretch of coastline from Mossel Bay to Storms River, encompasses some of South Africa's most spectacular and diverse scenery, with long beaches, gentle lakes and rivers, tangled forests, impressive mountains, and steep, rugged cliffs that plunge into a wild and stormy sea. It's this mix that has earned the Garden Route its reputation for being one of the most scenic routes in South Africa. Though the ocean may not be as warm as it is in KwaZulu-Natal, the accommodations are just as superb.

The backpacking crowd loves the Garden Route for its great beaches, outdoor activities, and budget lodgings, whereas more sophisticated visitors revel in the excellent seafood, local crafts, and superior guesthouses and hotels—many with attached spas—where pampering is the name of the game. A Garden Route trip also makes a fabulous family vacation destination where little ones can frolic on a beach, visit an animal sanctuary, or go for a magical forest walk. Few would wish to pass up the opportunity to see whales and dolphins. With numerous guided, catered, and portered multiday hikes and loads of pretty day walks, the Garden Route is ideal for avid ramblers.

A trip into the Little Karoo in the interior, on the other hand, offers a glimpse of what much of South Africa's vast hinterland looks like. This narrow strip of land, wedged between the Swartberg Mountains in the north and the Outeniqua Mountains in the southeast, is a world of rock and scrub, famous for its ostrich farms and the subterranean splendors of the Cango Caves. Unlike more classic safari destinations, the Little Karoo's treasures are not handed to you on a plate. Scour the apparently dry ground to spot tiny and beautiful plants. Hike into the hills to admire the fascinating geological formations of the Cape Fold Mountains and to look for rock art.

Or simply pause and drink in the space and the silence.

MAJOR REGIONS

The best way to explore this region is by car. There are two practical routes from Cape Town to Port Elizabeth. You can follow the N2 along the Garden Route, or you can take Route 62, which goes through the Little Karoo. These two roads are separated by the Outeniqua Mountains, which are traversed by a number of scenic passes. So it is possible—even desirable, if you have the time—to hop back and forth over the mountains, alternating between the lush Garden Route and the harsher Little Karoo. The inland border of the Little Karoo is formed by the Swartberg Mountains; the Great Karoo is on the other side, beyond the mountains.

Known as the Garden Route, this beautiful 208-km (130-mile) stretch of coast takes its name from a year-round riot of vegetation. Here you'll find some of the country's most inspiring scenery: forest-cloaked mountains, rivers and streams, and golden beaches. The area draws a diverse crowd, from backpackers and adventure travelers to family vacationers and golfers. The main towns along the route are (from west to east) Mossel Bay, George, Wilderness, Knysna, Plettenberg Bay, the Crags, Tsitsikamma, and Storms River.

Presenting a striking contrast to the Garden Route is the semiarid region known as the Little Karoo (also known as the Klein Karoo). In addition to the stark beauty that comes with its deep gorges and rugged plains, the Little Karoo offers the chance to stay at the Sanbona Wildlife Reserve; visit the Cango Ostrich Farm and explore the impressive Cango Caves in **Oudtshoorn**; and relax at vineyards in **De Rust**.

Planning

Getting Here and Around

AIR

The only major airport serving the Garden Route and the Little Karoo is George Airport, 10 km (6 miles) southwest of town. George is served by Safair and Kulula airlines with daily flights from Cape Town, Durban, and Johannesburg. Flying times are 2 hours from Johannesburg, 1½ hours from Durban, and 1 hour from Cape Town.

For additional airline contact information, see Air in Travel Smart.

AIRPORT George Airport. (*GRJ*) ⊠ *George Airport, George* ☎ *044/876–9310* ⊕ *www. airports.co.za.*

BUS

Intercape Mainliner offers a regular service between Cape Town and Port Elizabeth, stopping at all major Garden Route destinations on the N2, although they often don't go into town but drop passengers off at gas stations along the highway.

CAR

Most of the towns in this chapter can be found along the N2 highway. The road is in good condition and well signposted. A cautionary note: there is a wide shoulder along most of the route, but pull onto it to let faster cars overtake you *only* when you can see a good few hundred yards ahead. Also, stick to the speed limit, as speed traps are common.

An alternative to the N2 is the less traveled—some say more interesting—inland route, dubbed Route 62, even though some of it is on the R60.

Garden Route & Little Karoo Itineraries

3 Days: Choose a home base in the Garden Route: Wilderness, Knysna, and Plettenberg Bay are all excellent options. You'll encounter wonderful crafts shops and studios in all these towns, so keep your wallet handy. On your first day, take a half-day walk through Plett's Robberg Nature Reserve, visit the Woodville Big Tree in Wilderness, or explore Knysna's Garden of Eden. Devote the afternoon to a boat or kayak trip. You may see dolphins, seals, or whales, particularly around Plett.

Dedicate the second day to whatever activity suits your fancy—lounging on the beach, paddling, horseback riding, or rappelling. If you're staying in Plett, you could drive out to Storms River on the third day to do the treetop canopy tour. If you're staying farther west, head over one of the scenic passes to Oudtshoorn, visit the Cango Caves, and take a different scenic drive back.

5 Days: Spend days four and five at the Little Karoo's Sanbona Wildlife Reserve, where you may see the Big Five and take in spectacular scenery.

Health and Safety

The whole area is malaria-free, the climate is mild, and the water is safe to drink. Avoid sunburn by wearing a hat and slathering on sunscreen, and take care when swimming, as some beaches have dangerous currents. Never feed wild animals, especially vervet monkeys, who can become a nuisance.

Most towns have late-night pharmacies, and if they don't, pharmacies usually have an emergency number on the door. Call the general-emergencies number (10111 from landline; 112 from mobile phone) for all emergencies. If you break down while driving, call your car-rental company.

Hotels

The region would not have such allure if it weren't for its exclusive seaside getaways, colonial manor houses, and rustic inland farms. Many of the better establishments are set on little islands of well-tended gardens within wild forests. Breakfast is usually included in the rates, and if your guesthouse serves dinner, eating the evening meal with other guests can be pleasant after a day of exploring. On the flip side, some cottages are self-catering (with cooking facilities), giving you the chance to pick up some local delicacies and make yourself a feast.

Note that the prices listed are for high season, generally October to April. In some cases these prices are significantly higher than during low season, and they may go up higher still for the busiest period, mid-December to mid-January. If you're traveling during South Africa's winter, be sure to inquire about seasonal specials.

Hotel reviews have been shortened. For full information, visit Fodors.com.

Restaurants

Most medium-size towns along the Garden Route offer a decent selection of restaurants, and the smaller towns of the Little Karoo usually have one or two standbys. On the Garden Route the emphasis is often on seafood in general and oysters in particular. (Knysna has an oyster festival in July.) Restaurants in the Little Karoo feature fresh ostrich meat and mutton or lamb, which is delicious accompanied by a good South African red wine. Look out for farm shops between towns. These make excellent comfort stops where you can buy traditional home-baked fare, dried fruit, and other snacks for the road.

Restaurant reviews have been short-ened. For full information, visit Fodors. com.

RESTAURANT AND HOTEL PRICES

Restaurant prices are the average cost of a main course at dinner or, if dinner is not served, at lunch. Prices are the lowest price for a standard double room in high season.

What it Costs in South African rand			
$	$$	$$$	$$$$
RESTAURANTS			
under R100	R100–R150	R151–R200	over R200
HOTELS			
under R1,500	R1,500–R2,500	R2,501–R3,500	over R3,500

Visitor Information

Most local tourism bureaus are very helpful. Typical hours are weekdays 8:30 to 5, Saturday 8 to 1. In peak season (generally October to April) you may find them open longer. In very quiet periods the staff may close up shop early.

When to Go

There's no best time to visit the Garden Route, although the water and weather are warmest November through March. The weather can be notoriously fickle, so pack accordingly.

The high season is from mid-December to mid-January, when South African schools break for the summer holidays and families flock to the coast. Between May and September, the weather cools down a bit and there's often some rain. The winter months are the low season, and some establishments choose this time of year to take a break. But even in these colder months it's rarely cold for more than two or three days at a stretch, after which you'll get a few days of glorious sunshine. Wildflowers bloom along the Garden Route from July to October, the same time as the annual Southern Right whale migration along the coast.

The Little Karoo can be scorchingly hot in summer. In winter, days are generally warm and sunny, though it can get bitterly cold at night.

Mossel Bay

384 km (238 miles) east of Cape Town.

Mossel Bay has one of the few north-facing (read: very sunny) beaches in South Africa, which means it's very popular with local families. Dolphins—sometimes hundreds at a time—pass through the bay in search of a snack, and whales swim past during their annual migration (July–October). Take a cruise out to Seal Island, home to a breeding colony of more than 2,000 Cape fur seals or, if you're feeling brave, a cage dive to view white sharks looking for a meal.

Mossel Bay has historic stone buildings (some of which are exceptionally well preserved), an excellent museum complex, and some of the best oysters along the coast.

GETTING HERE AND AROUND

At the western end of the Garden Route, Mossel Bay lies 384 km (238 miles) east of Cape Town along the N2 highway. It usually takes about four hours to drive here from Cape Town—unless you stop to take in a view or browse in a roadside produce or crafts store.

VISITOR INFORMATION

CONTACTS Mossel Bay Tourism. ✉ *Mossel Bay Tourism Office, Church St. at Market St., Mossel Bay* ☎ *044/691–2202* ⊕ *www.visitmosselbay.co.za.*

 Sights

Bartolomeu Dias Museum Complex

MUSEUM VILLAGE | Named for the 15th-century Portuguese navigator, the Bartolomeu Dias Museum Complex concentrates on the early history of Mossel Bay, when it was a regular stopover for Portuguese mariners en route to India. The most popular exhibit is the full-size replica of Dias's ship (a caravel), which was sailed from Lisbon to Mossel Bay as part of the quincentenary celebrations in 1988. When you see how small it is, you'll realize just how brave these sailors were. If you pay extra to board it, you'll find it all pretty authentic, except for the modern galley and heads. Look out for the Post Office Tree. In 1501 Pedro de Alteide left a letter here, which was picked up and delivered by another Portuguese navigator on his way to India. That's how South Africa's first post office was born. De Alteide was so grateful that he built a small chapel here, reputed to be the first place of Christian worship in South Africa. Pop a postcard into the shoe-shaped mailbox and it will arrive with a special postmark. ✉ *Church St. at Market St., Mossel Bay* ☎ *044/691–1067* ⊕ *www.diasmuseum.co.za* 🖼 *R20* ☞ *Opening and closing times vary.*

🍴 Restaurants

Café Gannet

$$$ | SEAFOOD | Mossel Bay's premium seafood house serves fresh oysters and seafood alongside inventive dishes like ostrich fillet with caramelized onions and port-soaked apricots. In summer, it's virtually mandatory to sip a cocktail on the deck of the Blue Oyster bar with its great sea view. **Known for:** black mussels; kingklip en croute; coastal oysters. 🖼 *Average main: R170* ✉ *Church St. at Market St., Mossel Bay* ☎ *044/691–1885* ⊕ *www.cafegannet.co.za.*

★ Carola Ann's

$ | EASTERN EUROPEAN | Carola Ann's is one of the town's not-to-be-missed eateries. The proprietor is passionate about food, and she brings her international experience to whipping up tasty, innovative dishes from locally sourced meat, fish, and veggies in a charming historic house close to the Dias Museum. **Known for:** baked cheesecake; superb service; Mediterranean fare. 🖼 *Average main: R90* ✉ *38 Marsh St, Mossel Bay* ☎ *064/154–6393* ⊕ *www.facebook.com/carolaannfoodforlife* ⊗ *Closed Sun.*

Delfino's

$$ | ITALIAN | With tables on the lawn right next to the beach, Delfino's has a fantastic view of the bay and the Cape St. Blaize lighthouse. It's great place to spend a sunny afternoon or lazy evening. **Known for:** lovely views; weekend breakfast buffet; lively atmosphere. 🖼 *Average main: R110* ✉ *2 Point Rd., Mossel Bay* ☎ *044/690–5247* ⊕ *www.delfinos.co.za.*

The Kingfisher Seafood Restaurant

$$ | SEAFOOD | Painted kingfisher blue, this popular seafood restaurant overlooking the beach and the St. Blaise lighthouse is where the locals hang out. Head to the deck shaded by umbrellas and enjoy some of the area's best fresh seafood. **Known for:** stunning location; seafood platter; tuna poke bowl. 🖼 *Average main: R120* ✉ *7 Point Rd., Mossel Bay* ☎ *044/690–6390* ⊕ *www.facebook.com/thekingfishermosselbay.*

 Hotels

Point Hotel

$$ | HOTEL | Situated next to the Cape St. Blaize lighthouse, the Point Hotel has great views past a huge tidal pool to the rugged coastline stretching west. **Pros:** good breakfast; stone's throw from the ocean; sea-facing balconies. **Cons:** far from town; lower floor views are obstructed by rocks; crowded in season. $ *Rooms from: R2500* ⊠ *Point Rd., Mossel Bay* ☎ *044/691–3512* ⊕ *www. pointhotel.co.za* ↪ *49 rooms* ⦿| *Free Breakfast.*

Protea Hotel Mossel Bay

$$ | **HOTEL** | Just a few steps from the Bartolomeu Dias Museum Complex, this stylish hotel is close to most of what's happening in Mossel Bay. You can take in the great views of the harbor and the beach while relaxing at the Blue Oyster Pool Lounge. **Pros:** very central location; stylish rooms; great views. **Cons:** swimming pool is on the small side; crowded in season; street-facing rooms can be noisy. $ *Rooms from: R2000* ⊠ *Church St. at Market St., Mossel Bay* ☎ *044/691–3738* ⊕ *www.proteahotels. com* ↪ *31 rooms* ⦿| *Free Breakfast.*

Santos Express Train Lodge

$ | **B&B/INN** | It might be called the Santos Express, but this train isn't departing any time soon. **Pros:** all the cabins face the sea; a 10-minute walk to town; funky, fun accommodations. **Cons:** compartments are very cramped; only suites have private bathrooms; no air-conditioning. $ *Rooms from: R350* ⊠ *Munro Rd., Santos Beach, Mossel Bay* ☎ *083/900–7797* ⊕ *www.santosexpress.co.za* ↪ *32 rooms* ⦿| *Free Breakfast.*

🏃 Activities

BOATING
Romonza Boat Trips

BOATING | **FAMILY** | For a closer look at the Cape fur seals lounging around on Seal Island, sail there on a 54-foot yacht. One-hour Seal Island trips are offered year-round and cost R200. Whale-watching trips, offered from July to October, cost R850. ⊠ *Church St., Mossel Bay* ☎ *044/690–3101* ⊕ *romonzaboattrips. co.za.*

Aloe of Albertinia

The small and rather shabby town of Albertinia, about 40 km (25 miles) west of Mossel Bay, is an interesting place to break up your journey into the Garden Route. It's the center of production for aloe ferox, which has greater therapeutic benefits than the better-known aloe vera. Two factories here sell products on-site.

HIKING
★ Oystercatcher Trail

HIKING & WALKING | Book well in advance for a guided trek along the Oystercatcher Trail. The experience lasts several days and takes you along beaches and over rocky shorelines. The trail starts in Mossel Bay near the Cape St. Blaize Lighthouse and continues to the mouth of the Gouritz River. Knowledgeable guides point out birds and plants and discuss local history and customs along the way. Nights are spent in guesthouses or thatched cottages where delicious traditional foods are prepared for you on open fires. *Difficult.* ⊠ *Bonito St., Boggomsbaai, Boggoms Bay* ☎ *0820781696* ⊕ *www.oystercatchertrail. co.za* ↪ *R7860 per person.*

George

45 km (28 miles) northeast of Mossel Bay; 50 km (31 miles) southeast of Oudtshoorn.

About 11 km (7 miles) from the sea, George is the largest town and the de facto capital of the Garden Route. Although the surrounding countryside is attractive and there is a thriving farming and crafts community on its outskirts, George itself is mostly appealing if you're a golfer or a steam train enthusiast eager to visit its excellent transportation museum.

The Outeniqua Hop route passes hops fields like this one between George and Oudtshoorn.

GETTING HERE AND AROUND

The only true airport serving the Garden Route and the Little Karoo is George Airport, 10 km (6 miles) southwest of town. Most people who fly in here rent a car to continue their journey. It takes about half an hour to get to Mossel Bay and Oudtshoorn. **■TIP→ The area between George and Wilderness is notorious for speed traps, especially in the Kaaimans River Pass, just west of Wilderness.**

TOURS

Outeniqua Hop

SCENIC DRIVE | If you're itching to explore the countryside, follow the Outeniqua Hop, a fun route past farms growing strawberries or hops (used in beer making) and numerous craft outlets. Pick up a map from George Tourism at 124 York Street. 🌐 *www.outeniqua-hop-route.co.za.*

VISITOR INFORMATION

CONTACTS George Tourism Information. ✉ *124 York St., George* ☎ *044/801–9295* 🌐 *www.georgetourism.co.za.*

👁 Sights

Outeniqua Transport Museum

TRANSPORTATION | This museum in a hangar-like building is a steam train lover's delight, with 13 beautifully restored locomotives and other examples of vintage vehicles. One of the highlights is the original " White Coach" (now a bit shabby) in which England's Princess Elizabeth and her sister Princess Margaret slept during their 1947 visit to South Africa. ✉ *2 Mission Rd., George* ☎ *044/801–8289* 🌐 *www.outeniquachootjoe.co.za* 🎫 *R20.*

🍴 Restaurants

The Deacon House

$ | **CONTEMPORARY** | A lovely colonial-style house is the setting for this charming restaurant. Eat beneath shady umbrellas in the lush gardens where inviting paths are flanked by nicely trimmed hedges and low stone walls. **Known for:** specialty coffee; Scots porridge; the Deacon Burger with ostrich, brie, and figs. [$] *Average main: R95* ✉ *2 Barrie Rd., Heatherlands,*

George ☎ 044/050–3572 🌐 deacon-house.co.za 🕓 Closed Mon. No dinner.

Meade Café

$ | CONTEMPORARY | In an 18th-century townhouse, this light and airy bistro-style restaurant has a lovely outdoor seating area. The kitchen serves breakfast and lunch favorites like eggs Benedict and fish-and-chips. **Known for:** signature quiche; buttery croissants; chicken mango curry. *[$] Average main: R95 ✉ 91 Meade St., George ☎ 044/873–6755 🌐 meadecafe.co.za 🕓 Closed Sun. No dinner.*

Hotels

Fancourt

$$$$ | RESORT | If you're one of those people who believe that humans have opposable thumbs for the sole purpose of gripping a golf club, you'll *love* Fancourt, a luxury golf resort in the shadow of the Outeniqua Mountains. **Pros:** on-site spa; three top-rated golf courses; great kids' program. **Cons:** cocooned away from real world; little nightlife in George; you might feel out of place if you don't golf. *[$] Rooms from: R5750 ✉ Montagu St., Blanco ☎ 044/804–0000 🌐 www.fancourt.com 🛏 133 rooms 🍴 Free Breakfast.*

Shopping

Outeniqua Family Market

MARKET | FAMILY | With more than 130 food and craft stalls, this family-friendly market has something for everyone. It's a great place to grab something to go for breakfast or lunch, or dine in at the covered picnic tables; there are even bathrooms. If you plan to spend the day, there's live entertainment, great craft vendors, and kids' rides, activities, and a large playground. The market is open Saturdays from 8 am until 2 pm. *✉ N2 Hwy. and Knysna Rd., George ✥ opposite the Garden Route Mall 🌐 outeniquafamilymarket.co.za 🕓 Closed Sun.–Fri.*

Country Markets

The Garden Route has some fantastic local markets where you can stock up on fresh produce and arts and crafts. With more than 130 stalls, Outeniqua Farmers' Market (*🌐 outeniquafamilymarket.co.za*) in George is held every Saturday 8 to 2. Harkerville Saturday Market (*🌐 www.harkervillemarket.co.za*) in Plettenberg Bay is the place for excellent arts and crafts, and Wild Oats Community Farmers' Market (*🌐 www.wildoatsmarket.co.za*) in Sedgefield brims with locally produced foods. Both are open on Saturday 8 to noon.

Activities

GOLF

The Links, Outeniqua, and Montagu golf courses, all at Fancourt, regularly make the list of South Africa's top 20 courses. There are some other notable courses in the area, including the public George Golf Club.

Wilderness

12 km (7 miles) southeast of George.

Wilderness is a popular vacation destination for good reason. Backed by thickly forested hills and cliffs, the tiny town presides over a magical stretch of golden sand beaches between the Kaaimans and Touw rivers. There's also a spectacular system of waterways, lakes, and lagoons strung out along the coast, separated from the sea by towering dunes. Many of the Garden Route's other attractions are within an hour or two's drive, making Wilderness a good base for exploring.

GETTING HERE AND AROUND

Many hotels offer a transfer from George Airport, but your best bet is to rent a car there and drive yourself. The roads are good and you'll be able to see a lot more of the country.

TOURS

Eden Adventures

ADVENTURE TOURS | FAMILY | Near Garden Route National Park, Eden Adventures offers canyoneering in Kaaimans Gorge, which includes a leisurely walk through the forest to the confluence of the Kaaiman and Silver rivers. You jump into deep pools and swim through canyons on your way back. Wet suits are provided. Other adventures in their bag of tricks include abseiling (also called rappelling), canoeing, and kayaking. Custom tours can also be arranged. ⊠ *Fairy Knowe Hotel, Wilderness* ☎ *044/877–0179* ⊕ *www. eden.co.za.*

VISITOR INFORMATION

CONTACTS Wilderness Tourism. ⊠ *Wilderness House, 198 George Rd., Wilderness* ☎ *044/877–0045* ⊕ *www.wilderness-info. co.za.*

Sights

Wilderness Section of the Garden Route National Park

NATURE PRESERVE | This 299,000-acre reserve stretches eastward along the coast for 31 km (19 miles). A wetlands paradise, the park's two blinds draws birders from all over the country hoping to see African fish eagles, great crested grebes, and red-knobbed coots. Several walking trails wind through the park alongside lakes, rivers, and the sea. A relatively gentle, accessible option is the 45-minute Woodville Big Tree Walk, which takes you past an 800-year-old yellowwood tree and into the indigenous forest. ⊠ *Wilderness* ☎ *044/877–0046* ⊕ *www. sanparks.org* 🎟 *R120.*

Photo Op

From George, the N2 descends steeply to the sea through a heavily forested gorge formed by the Kaaimans River. Look to your right to see a curved railway bridge spanning the river mouth. This is one of the most photographed scenes on the Garden Route. As you round the point, a breathtaking view of mile upon mile of pounding surf and white beach unfolds before you. There is an overlook from which you can often see dolphins and whales in the surf. If you look up, you may see a colorful paraglider floating overhead.

🍴 Restaurants

Pomodoro

$ | ITALIAN | FAMILY | Friendly service, great food, and good value are the highlights of this eatery serving authentic Italian food with a local flavor. Try the pizza with butternut squash, goat cheese, and chopped tomatoes or the prawns panfried with fennel, garlic, and caper butter—both local favorites. **Known for:** central location; crispy thin-crust pizza; slow-roasted lamb shank. Ⓢ *Average main: R85* ⊠ *George Rd. at Leilas La., Wilderness* ☎ *044/877– 1403* ⊕ *www.pomodoro.co.za.*

Salinas Seafood Restaurant

$$$ | CONTEMPORARY | Locals and holidaymakers love this well-established restaurant whose two spacious decks overlook the main beach, the lagoon and the distant mountains. Sip a cocktail as you enjoy a gorgeous sunset view before dining on tasty seafood, a succulent steak or the fresh fish of the day. **Known for:** grilled fresh local fish; seafood curry; beef kebabs. Ⓢ *Average main: R190* ⊠ *458 Zundorf Lane, Wilderness* ☎ *044/877–0001* ⊕ *www.salinas.co.za.*

★ Serendipity

$$$$ | **SOUTH AFRICAN** | Start your evening at this award-winning restaurant with pre-dinner drinks on the patio overlooking the river, then move inside to a candlelit table for a fabulous five-course menu that takes classic South African ingredients and gives them an original, modern twist. The menu changes frequently with acclaimed chef Lizelle Stolze combining locally sourced fresh meat, fish and vegetables that are beautifully presented and paired with husband Rudolf's selection of fine wines. **Known for:** attention to detail; some of the region's best food; excellent service. $ *Average main: R579* ✉ *Freesia Ave., Wilderness* ☎ *044/877–0433* ⊕ *www.serendipitywilderness.com* ⊘ *Closed Sun. No lunch.*

★ Zucchini

$$ | **SOUTH AFRICAN** | This popular spot is all about free-range, organic, locally sourced, and seasonal ingredients, and chances are the garnishes on your plate will have been freshly picked from the organic herb garden outside. The vegetarian-friendly menu changes regularly and features a range of dishes served either roasted or raw. **Known for:** lots of choices for vegetarians; coffee roasted on site; rustic atmosphere. $ *Average main: R140* ✉ *Timberlake Farm Stall, N2, Wilderness* ☎ *044/882–1240* ⊕ *www.zucchini.co.za.*

 ## Hotels

Ebb and Flow Restcamp, Wilderness Section of the Garden Route National Park

$ | **RESORT** | **FAMILY** | Along a lovely, meandering stretch of river, this camp is divided into northern and southern sections that include a variety of accommodations ranging from log cabins to forest huts. **Pros:** good base for exploring; plenty of outdoor activities; lovely wooded setting. **Cons:** river sometimes floods; crowded in

high season; utilitarian accommodation. $ *Rooms from: R710* ✉ *Dumbelton Rd., Wilderness* ☎ *044/877–1197* ⊕ *www.sanparks.org* ⤳ *181 rooms* ⦿ *No Meals.*

★ Views Boutique Hotel & Spa

$$$$ | **HOTEL** | This boutique hotel offers stupendous views of the seemingly endless beach from floor-to-ceiling windows and private verandahs. **Pros:** changing exhibits featuring local artists; unbeatable ocean views; an on-site deli with fresh food. **Cons:** a few miles from village center; limited on-site dining options; some less expensive rooms lack sea views. $ *Rooms from: R3560* ✉ *South St., Wilderness* ☎ *044/877–8000* ⊕ *www.viewshotel.co.za* ⤳ *27 rooms* ⦿ *Free Breakfast* ⌔ *No children under 14.*

The Wilderness Hotel

$$ | **HOTEL** | **FAMILY** | This tried-and-true hotel is just a short stroll from the golden beaches. **Pros:** favorite with families; great base for touring; lots to do on the premises. **Cons:** not all rooms have balconies; small public lounge area; very busy in high season. $ *Rooms from: R1910* ✉ *6 George Rd., Wilderness* ☎ *044/877–1110* ⊕ *thewildernesshotel.co.za* ⤳ *150 rooms* ⦿ *Free Breakfast.*

Xanadu

$$ | **B&B/INN** | Spectacular floral arrangements, deep-pile carpets, and voluminous drapes framing the sea-view windows add to the sense of opulence at this beachfront guesthouse. **Pros:** bathrooms are modern and large; a short walk to the beach; great service from hands-on owner. **Cons:** only one restaurant in area; breakfast is communal; too far to walk into town. $ *Rooms from: R2500* ✉ *Xanadu, 43 Die Duin, Wilderness* ☎ *083/357–8000* ⊕ *xanaduvilla.co.za* ⤳ *6 rooms* ⦿ *Free Breakfast.*

Shopping

Wild Oats Community Farmers Market
MARKET | Featuring locally-produced foods, this community-minded market is open Saturdays, 8 am–noon. There are take-home meals and hot breakfast items available including free-range meats, cheese, locally-sourced vegetables, and fresh baked goods. ✉ *N2 Hwy., Sedgefield, Wilderness* ✛ *Between Wilderness and Knysa* ⊕ *www.wildoatsmarket.co.za* ⊗ *Closed Sun.–Fri.*

🏃 Activities

The Wilderness section of the Garden Route National Park is great for walks, paddling, and birding.

HIKING
★ **Garden Route Trail**
HIKING & WALKING | Mark Dixon is the highly qualified nature guide behind this operation. His emphasis is on enjoying the natural environment rather than covering great distances. Excursions include day walks and multiday hikes in the forest and around the lakes and beaches of this beautiful part of the world. His signature offering is the five-day trek along the Garden Route Coastal Trail, starting at the Ebb and Flow Restcamp in Wilderness and ending at Brenton on Sea near Knysna. Another popular offering is the Moonlight Meander on the beach at full moon. ✉ *Wilderness* ☎ *044/883–1015, 082/213–5931* ⊕ *www.gardenroutetrail.co.za.*

Knysna

40 km (25 miles) east of Wilderness.

Knysna (pronounced *nize*-nuh) is one of the most popular destinations on the Garden Route. The focal point is the beautiful Knysna Lagoon, ringed by forested hills dotted with vacation homes. Several walking and mountain-bike trails wind through Knysna's forests, many offering tremendous views back over the ocean. With luck you may spot the Knysna turaco, a brilliantly plumed forest bird, or the brightly colored but even more elusive Narina trogon.

Towering buttresses of rock, known as the Heads, guard the entrance to the lagoon, funneling the ocean through a narrow channel. The sea approach is often hazardous, which is why Knysna never became a major port. Instead it developed into a popular resort town with the attendant hype, commercialism, and crowds, especially in summer. About the only aspect of the town that hasn't been modernized is the single-lane main road (the N2 goes straight through the middle of town), so traffic can be a nightmare.

Walking is the best way to get around the town center, which is filled with shops, galleries, restaurants, and coffeehouses. Knysna's main claims to fame are cultivated oysters and locally brewed Mitchell's beer, on tap at most bars and pubs.

GETTING HERE AND AROUND
The N2 highway travels straight through the center of Knysna and can get extremely busy (and noisy) in the high season.

VISITOR INFORMATION
CONTACTS Knysna Tourism. ✉ *40 Main Rd,, Rexford, Knysna* ☎ *044/382–5510* ⊕ *www.visitknysna.com.*

👁 Sights

Heads
VIEWPOINT | You can't come to Knysna without making a trip out to the Heads, at the mouth of the lagoon. The rock sentinels provide great views of both the sea and the lagoon. Only the developed, eastern side is accessible by car, via George Rex Drive off the N2. You have two options: park at the base of the Head

and follow the walking trails that snake around the rocky cliffs just feet above the crashing surf, or drive to the summit with panoramic views and easy parking. ✉ *Knysna.*

Holy Trinity Church

CHURCH | One of the most interesting buildings in the area stands across the lagoon in the exclusive community of Belvidere. The Anglican Holy Trinity Church, built in 1855 from local stone, is a lovely replica of a Norman church of the 11th century. The interior is notable for its beautiful stinkwood and yellowwood timber and stained-glass windows. ✉ *Church St., Belvidere, Knysna* ☎ *087/742–2527* 🌐 *holytrinitybelvidere.org* 🎟 *Free.*

Beaches

Although Knysna is very much a seaside destination, there are no beaches actually in the town. There are some fabulous ones nearby.

Brenton-on-Sea

BEACH | The beach at Brenton-on Sea, past Belvidere, is a long stretch of sand popular for its 6-km (4-mile) walk to neighboring Buffalo Bay. Although spectacular, this beach is not particularly good for swimming because of a strong undertow. Lifeguards are present in season, but only swim between the flags. The beach is about 12 km (7½ miles) west of Knysna. **Amenities:** food and drink; lifeguards; parking; toilets. **Best for:** sunrise; sunset; walking. ✉ *Brenton-on-Sea.*

Buffalo Bay Beach

BEACH | About 20 km (12 miles) from Knysna, Buffalo Bay is a sandy beach on a half-moon bay. Safe swimming and excellent conditions for surfing and bodyboarding make this an ideal family destination. A popular beach walk takes you toward Brenton-on-Sea. The village has been spared overdevelopment because of its proximity to the nearby Goukamma Nature Reserve. **Amenities:** food and drink; lifeguards; parking; showers; toilets; water sports. **Best for:** family, surfing; swimming; walking. ✉ *Buffalo Bay.*

Leisure Isle

ISLAND | In the middle of Knysna Lagoon, Leisure Isle has just a few tiny strands of beach. It does have great views out toward the Heads of Knysna and nature trails and wheelchair-accessible boardwalks where you can spot emerald cuckoos and black oystercatchers. Green Hole on the east shore is a public park with toilets, showers, picnic spots. The surrounding mudflats of the lagoon provide bait for the local fisherfolk. **Amenities:** parking. **Best for:** solitude; windsurfing; small nature reserve. ✉ *Knysna* 🌐 *leisureisleknysna.co.za.*

Restaurants

★ Ile de Pain

$$ | ECLECTIC | Almost every South African you meet along the Garden Route will tell you to visit Ile de Pain. Its stellar reputation is well deserved, because owners Liezie Mulder and Markus Farbinger have an uncompromising attitude toward quality that shows in their superb wood-fired breads and mouth-watering pastries. **Known for:** enthusiastic staff; folks come from far and wide for the baked goods; plenty of choices for vegetarians. [$] *Average main: R100* ✉ *8-10 The Boatshed, Thesen Island, Knysna* ☎ *044/302–5707* 🌐 *www.iledepain.co.za* 🕒 *Closed Sun. and Mon. No dinner.*

34° South

$$ | SEAFOOD | Right on the water's edge in what appears to be a former warehouse, bustling 34° South manages to combine elements of a fishmonger, a bar, a bistro, a deli, a coffee shop, and a seafood restaurant. Choose from the huge array of fresh fish (including sushi), opt for a rustic pizza, or just fill a basket with tasty breads, pickles, cheeses, meats, and other delights. **Known for:** vibey atmosphere; Knysna oysters; good wine selection. $ *Average main: R100* ⊠ *Knysna Quays* ☎ *044/382–7331* ⊕ *www.34south.biz.*

Zachary's Grill Room

$$$$ | ECLECTIC | At the Pezula Resort Hotel and Spa, Zachary's Grill Room is well worth the 10- to 15-minute drive from Knysna. Although its locally known as a gourmet destination, the restaurant's color-theme of soft brown, honey, and orange makes it comfortable and inviting. **Known for:** elegant dining; superb local steaks; vegan chickpea curry. $ *Average main: R250* ⊠ *Pezula Resort Hotel and Spa, Lagoon View Dr., Knysna* ☎ *044/302–3333.*

 ## Hotels

There are more bed-and-breakfasts than you can possibly imagine, as well as some fantastic guesthouses, hotels, and resorts, so you will not be short of choices.

Belvidere Manor

$$$ | B&B/INN | There are lovely views of the lagoon at this attractive restored 1849 Cape Georgian manor house. **Pros:** homey British-style pub; a pretty pool on the lawn; great views of the lagoon. **Cons:** no air-conditioning; in the center of a retirement village; nearby dining options are limited. $ *Rooms from: R2720* ⊠ *169 Lower Duthie Dr., Knysna, Knysna* ☎ *044/387–1055* ⊕ *www.belvidere.co.za* ⮡ *34 rooms* ❏ *Free Breakfast.*

Brenton on the Rocks

$$ | B&B/INN | FAMILY | This understated bed-and-breakfast is perched on a cliff in the quiet coastal hamlet of Brenton-on-Sea, so there are breathtaking ocean views from the suites and spacious public rooms. **Pros:** restaurant nearby; pretty heated pool on the terrace; on a gorgeous spot over the water. **Cons:** not on the main beach; very busy in season; standard doubles have limited views. $ *Rooms from: R1890* ⊠ *276 Steenbras St., Brenton-on-Sea, Brenton-on-Sea*

☎ *044/381–0489, 083/249–3644* ⊕ *brentononrocks.weebly.com* ⮡ *9 rooms* ❏ *Free Breakfast.*

The Lofts Boutique Hotel

$$ | APARTMENT | These attractive apartments right on the edge of Kynsna Lagoon are converted from an old boatshed and have retained the original timber framework. **Pros:** quirky clever design; great location on Thesen Island; perfect for couples or a small family (not toddlers). **Cons:** lots of steps; no beach; no shower in downstairs bathroom in self-catering apartment. $ *Rooms from: R2009* ⊠ *The Boatshed, Long St, Thesen Island, Knysna* ☎ *044/302–5710* ⊕ *www.the-lofts.co.za* ⮡ *18 rooms* ❏ *Free Breakfast.*

St. James of Knysna

$$ | B&B/INN | Immerse yourself in elegance at this gleaming white country house sitting right on the edge of Knysna Lagoon. **Pros:** beautiful grounds; complimentary lagoon cruise; two outdoor pools. **Cons:** a bit out of town; one pool is on the small side; must book far in advance. $ *Rooms from: R1540* ⊠ *The Point, Knysna* ☎ *044/382–6750* ⊕ *www.stjames.co.za* ⮡ *15 rooms* ❏ *Free Breakfast.*

Turbine Hotel & Spa

$$$ | HOTEL | In a former timber mill, this eco-friendly boutique hotel has incorporated some of the heavy machinery into the decor. **Pros:** shops and restaurants nearby; unique boiler-room chic; location is unbeatable. **Cons:** design is not to everyone's taste; no beaches in the vicinity; neighborhood can get crowded. $ *Rooms from: R3640* ⊠ *36 Sawtooth La., Thesen Island, Knysna* ☎ *044/302–5746* ⊕ *www.turbinehotel.co.za* ⮡ *26 rooms* ❏ *Free Breakfast.*

Knysna Houseboats

Located in the Knysna estuary, Thesen Islands is linked by a causeway and bridge to the vibey town of Knysna on the Garden Route, very popular in-season with local holidaymakers. Once the base for a timber company, the residential marina rents luxurious self-drive houseboats with a kitchen, dining table, outdoor decks, and sleeping space for four adults. Venture out into the lagoon if weather permits; if you're a bit hesitant about docking, there's someone to moor your boat for you between sunrise and sunset. Don't want to cook? Order a picnic basket, fresh Knysna oysters, a bottle of bubbly, a braai pack, or whatever you fancy from the houseboat staff, or even takeaways from the local restaurants. Fishing and swimming add to the fun.

Activities

BOATING

Springtide Charters

WILDLIFE-WATCHING | This well-regarded charter company operates a 50-foot yacht called the *Outeniqua* that takes you on scenic cruises across the lagoon and through The Heads (weather permitting). Treat yourself to the popular sunset cruise, which includes platters of fruit and cheese and a couple of glasses of bubbly. Springtide Charters also operates the *Ocean Odyssey*, Knysna's only accredited close-encounter whale-watching vessel. ⊠ *22 Long St., Knysna* ☎ *044/382–0321* ⊕ *www.springtide. co.za.*

GOLF

Pezula Championship Golf Course

GOLF | The challenging 18-hole Pezula Championship Golf Course winds its way over and among the cliff tops of Knysna's Eastern Head. One of South Africa's most scenic courses, it's a popular stop for golfers on the Garden Route. Also on-site is a comfortable clubhouse, and lessons from resident pros are available. ⊠ *Lagoonview Dr., Knysna* ☎ *044/302– 5310* ⊕ *www.pezulagolf.com* 🖭 *R765* ⅄ *18 holes, 6521 yards, par 72.*

HIKING

Diepwalle Elephant Walk

HIKING & WALKING | Head to the Diepwalle Forestry Station and follow this lovely trail deep into the ancient forest past giant yellowwoods, lush ferns, and colorful fungi. The full trail is about 20 km (12 miles) long and takes six to seven hours. For those who don't have a whole day to spare, there are three color-coded shorter routes: the easy, 9-km (5½-mile) Black Route, the moderate 8-km (5-mile) White Route, and the tough 7-km (4 1/2-mile) Red Route. These should take between two and four hours, depending on your pace. ⊠ *Diepwalle Forest Estate, Union-dale Rd., off N2, Knysna* ✛ *24 km (15 miles) east of Knysna* ☎ *044/302–5600* ⊕ *www.sanparks.org* 🖭 *R168.*

★ Garden of Eden

HIKING & WALKING | Just a short drive from Knysna, this not-to-be-missed corner of the Garden Route National Park is called the Garden of Eden. It's an easy, half-hour stroll along wheelchair-friendly boardwalks through Harkerville Forest. You're soon in a fairytale forest of ancient yellowwoods, verdant mosses, and lush ferns. You may even spot a shy duiker, an antelope that favors heavily wooded areas. There are picnic tables, too. ⊠ *Off N2, between Knysna and Plett, Knysna* ☎ *044/382–5600* ⊕ *www.sanparks.org* 🖭 *R38.*

Harkerville Trail

HIKING & WALKING | The 28-km (17-mile) Harkerville Trail passes through old-growth forests, pine plantations, and stands of fynbos (a type of evergreen native to the region). This is not a beginner's trail. It takes two days and has some fairly taxing sections along the coast. Homesick Californians can hug a familiar tree in a small stand of towering redwoods (*Sequoia sempervirens*), planted as part of a forestry experiment years ago. Overnight accommodations are in a simple hut with mattresses, water, and firewood, so you'll need to bring your own bedding and food. ✉ *Harkerville Forest Station, Off N2, Knysna ⊕ 15 km (9 miles) east of Knysna* ☎ *044/382–2095* ⊕ *www.sanparks.org* 🎫 *R390.*

Knysna Forest Tours

HIKING & WALKING | If you don't fancy heading off into the forest on your own, take a guided walk or even a trail run through the area with Knysna Forest Tours. A full-day outing, including lunch, will cost R1,010. Its parent company, Tony Cook Adventures, also offers surfing, kiteboarding, and stand-up paddleboarding. ✉ *Thesen Island, Knysna* ☎ *082/783–8392* ⊕ *www.knysnaforest-tours.co.za.*

MOUNTAIN BIKING

The Garden Route is ideal for trail riding, and Harkerville, 20 km (12 miles) east of Knysna, is where mountain bikers congregate. Here you'll find four color-coded circular trails of varying length and difficulty starting and ending at the Garden of Eden. The most challenging of these is the Red Route, which is a 22-km (13½-mile) ride through forest with some coastal scenery along the way. Green (14 km/9 miles) is moderately difficult, while Blue (11 km/7 miles) and Yellow (13 km/8 miles) are pretty easy. There's a fifth trail, 22-km (13½-mile) Petrus se Brand, that is not circular but can be ridden in either direction between Diepwalle and Garden of Eden. It's tight and twisty, and you'll

zip downhill over the springy forest floor, dodging enormous trees. ☎ *044/302–5600* ⊕ *www.sanparks.org.*

Plettenberg Bay

Surrounded by forests, lagoons, and vineyards, Plettenberg Bay is South Africa's top beach resort. Plett, as the locals call it, is one of the best places in the world to watch whales and dolphins. Boat and kayaking trips run from Central Beach. The fancy empty houses along Beachy Head Road (known as Millionaire's Mile) sit empty when it's not high season. During July and December, when school is out, inland visitors arrive en masse. You can still find yourself a stretch of lonely beach if you walk all the way to the end of Keurboomstrand or drive to Nature's Valley.

GETTING HERE AND AROUND

The airport in Plett has limited flights to and from Cape Town and Johannesburg on weekends. There's no public transportation in Plett, so your best bet is renting a car and driving yourself.

VISITOR INFORMATION

CONTACTS Plettenberg Bay Tourism Association. ✉ *Marine Dr. at Main Rd., Shop 35, Plettenberg Bay* ☎ *044/533–4065* ⊕ *www.pletttourism.co.za.*

 Sights

Robberg Nature Reserve

NATURE PRESERVE | There are three fabulous walks through Robberg Nature Reserve, all with equally spectacular scenery. Even the shortest one needs you to be steady on your legs because there are rocks to clamber up and down. The shortest takes about half an hour and offers great views of the ocean. A longer walk taking 90 minutes passes above a seal colony. Taking at least three hours (or even four or more if you have a more leisurely pace), the longest walk goes right to the end of the peninsula and often offers views of dolphins and whales offshore. It's worth taking a picnic, because you'll want to stop and admire the wildflowers along the way. A fascinating archaeological excavation at Nelson's Bay Cave has a display outlining the occupation of the cave over thousands of years. ✉ *Robberg Rd., Plettenberg Bay* ✣ *Near the airport* ☎ *044/533–2125* 🌐 *www.capenature.co.za* 🎟 *R50.*

Beaches

Plett presides over a stretch of coastline that has inspired rave reviews since the Portuguese first set eyes on it in 1497. They dubbed it *bahia formosa*, meaning "beautiful bay." Of its 11 beaches, four are Blue Flag beaches ranked among best in the world. Three rivers flow into the sea here, the most spectacular of which—the Keurbooms—forms a large lagoon. For swimming, surfing, sailing, hiking, and fishing, you can't do much better than Plett, although the water is colder than it is around Durban and in northern KwaZulu-Natal. ■ **TIP→ Keep in mind that lifeguards are usually only on duty during the summer months, from November to April.**

Central Beach

BEACH | All the dolphin-watching boats and kayaking trips leave from Central Beach. A constant stream of tenders going out to the fishing boats moored in the bay makes this area quite busy, but it's still a great spot. Just avoid the boat ramp area and swim in the southern section. **Amenities:** food and drink; lifeguards; parking; toilets. **Best for:** surfing; swimming; walking. ✉ *Plettenberg Bay.*

Keurboomstrand

BEACH | Named after the native keurboom tree, this sandy beach is about 10 km (6 miles) from Plett on the eastern edge of the bay. If you're fit you can walk all the way from here to Nature's Valley, but you need to watch the tides. Otherwise, you can stroll about a mile down the beach, relax for a while, and then walk back. **Amenities:** food and drink; lifeguards; parking; showers; toilets. **Best for:** walking. ✉ *Plettenberg Bay.*

Lookout Beach

BEACH | Always one of Plettenberg Bay's most popular beaches, Blue Flag-certified Lookout Beach is a favorite spot for swimmers and surfers. Families enjoy paddling on the lagoon side of what is essentially a large sandy spit. **Amenities:** food and drink; lifeguards (in season); parking; toilets; water sports. **Best for:** surfing; swimming; walking. ✉ *Plettenberg Bay.*

Robberg Beach

BEACH | Just past the Beacon Island Resort is Robberg Beach, a great swimming beach that continues in a graceful curve all the way to the Robberg Peninsula. You can catch a glimpse of dolphins and whales just behind the breakers. Robberg 5 Beach is popular for surfing and bodyboarding. **Amenities:** food and drink; lifeguards; parking; showers; toilets. **Best for:** swimming; sunbathing. ✉ *Beachy Head Dr., Plettenberg Bay.*

Restaurants

Enrico's Ristorante

$$$ | **ITALIAN** | The chef always makes an effort to come out of the kitchen to greet patrons at this popular Italian eatery perched above the rocks on Keurboom Beach. The atmosphere is lively and loud and there's usually a big crowd on weekends and during holidays. **Known for:** you can't beat the location; area's best Italian fare; authentic tiramisu. [$] *Average main: R175* ✉ *296 Main St., Keurboomstrand, Plettenberg Bay* ☎ *044/535–9818* 🌐 *www.enricorestaurant.co.za* 🕒 *Closed Mon.*

The Fat Fish

$$$ | **SEAFOOD** | This place is favorite with both locals and visitors, and you'll realize why the minute you tuck into some of the freshest, tastiest food in Plett. The super-friendly staff will talk you through the seafood-heavy menu, but you can't go wrong with the fish-and-chips. **Known for:** great views of the ocean; bustling location; delicious seafood. $ *Average main: R200* ✉ *Hopwood St., Plettenberg Bay* ☎ *044/533–4740* ⊕ *www.thefatfish. co.za.*

Ski Boat Club

$$ | **CAFÉ** | Fishing boat crews, ski boat skippers, and other folks who are in the know frequent this casual eatery located right on the beach. Expect a bit of a wait, but it's worth it if you're looking for a great deal. **Known for:** full English breakfast; great views of the ocean; lively atmosphere. $ *Average main: R100* ✉ *Central Beach, Plettenberg Bay* ☎ *044/533–4147* ⊕ *www.plettskiboat-club.co.za* ☾ *No dinner.*

 # Hotels

Plett has plenty of fabulous places to spend the night. Because the dining options aren't as extensive as other seaside destinations, guests often eat in their hotels.

★ Bitou River Lodge

$$$ | **B&B/INN** | About 3 km (2 miles) upstream from Keurboom Lagoon, this award-winning B&B has a tranquil location on the banks of the Bitou River. **Pros:** views from private verandahs; beautiful river runs past the property; hands-on owner cares about guests. **Cons:** doesn't serve dinner; 10-minute drive to restaurants; no air-conditioning in the rooms. $ *Rooms from: R3200* ✉ *Off the N2, Plettenberg Bay* ✛ *About 3 km (2 miles) on the R340 to Wittedrif* ☎ *044/535–9577, 082/978–6164* ⊕ *www.bitou.co.za* ☞ *5 rooms* ❘○❘ *Free Breakfast.*

The Bungalow

$$$$ | **B&B/INN** | **FAMILY** | At this pleasant lodging overlooking Plett's lovely Hobie Beach, you'll soon be dipping your toes in the Indian Ocean. **Pros:** pretty pool; on one of the best beaches; rooms big enough for families. **Cons:** beach is crowded in season; the overall area is quite small; rooms are cheek-by-jowl with each other. $ *Rooms from: R3950* ✉ *5 Meeding St., Plettenberg Bay* ☎ *044/533–1864* ⊕ *www.capesummervil-las.co.za/the-bungalow-plett* ☞ *7 rooms* ❘○❘ *Free Breakfast.*

★ Emily Moon River Lodge

$$$$ | **B&B/INN** | Only 10 minutes away from the hubbub of Plettenberg Bay, this delightfully quirky lodge on the banks of the Bitou River combines an enchanting mix of African, Asian, and Polynesian decor. **Pros:** in-room massages; stunningly original decor and design; bicycles and river canoes you can borrow. **Cons:** not all rooms have air-conditioning; some rooms have steps to climb; restaurant can get crowded on weekends. $ *Rooms from: R4200* ✉ *Rietvlei Rd., Plettenberg Bay* ☎ *044/501–2500* ⊕ *www.emilymoon. co.za* ☞ *16 rooms* ❘○❘ *Free Breakfast.*

Grand Africa Rooms & Rendezvous

$$$ | **B&B/INN** | Walking into the Grand is like entering a different world. **Pros:** central location; eclectic, stylish decor throughout; outdoor swimming pool. **Cons:** no children under 12; located on the main road; rooms can be a bit dark. $ *Rooms from: R3200* ✉ *27 Main Rd., Plettenberg Bay* ☎ *044/533–3301* ⊕ *www.grandafrica.com* ☞ *11 rooms* ❘○❘ *Free Breakfast.*

Hunter's Country House

$$$$ | **HOTEL** | **FAMILY** | Just 10 minutes from town, this tranquil property is set amid gardens that descend into a forested valley. **Pros:** service is outstanding; three excellent restaurants; breakfasts are sublime. **Cons:** limited Wi-Fi access; a 20-minute drive to most activities; accommodations are very pricey.

💲 Rooms from: R3700 ✉ off N2, Plettenberg Bay ✛ 10 km (6 miles) west of Plettenberg Bay ☎ 044/501–1111 ⊕ www.hunterhotels.com 🛏 23 suites ¶◯¶ Free Breakfast.

★ The Plettenberg

$$$$ | HOTEL | High on a rocky point in Plettenberg Bay, this luxury hotel has unbelievable views of Keurbooms Lagoon and the Tsitsikamma Mountains. **Pros:** attentive front-desk staff; the views are incredible; minutes from the beach. **Cons:** expensive rates; some rooms look out onto the car park; standard rooms are on the small side. 💲 Rooms from: R5540 ✉ Lookout Rocks, Plettenberg Bay ☎ 044/533–2030 ⊕ www.collectionmcgrath.com 🛏 37 rooms ¶◯¶ Free Breakfast.

Sky Villa Boutique Hotel

$$$$ | HOTEL | This stylish hilltop hotel has 360-degree views over the Keurbooms River, the Indian Ocean, and the Tsitsikamma and Langkloof mountains. **Pros:** excellent restaurant; the views are breathtaking; magnificent design. **Cons:** bar closes in bad weather; 15-minute drive from town; cutting edge design won't appeal to traditionalists. 💲 Rooms from: R4140 ✉ 27 Barons View Estate, Plettenberg Bay ☎ 087/550–2967, 082/767–3393 ⊕ www.capesummervillas.co.za 🛏 14 rooms ¶◯¶ Free Breakfast.

Tsala Treetop Lodge

$$$$ | HOTEL | Immerse yourself in nature at this lodge where impeccably designed chalets perched on stilts gaze out the forest canopy. **Pros:** unique treetop experience; a one-of-a-kind lodging; wake to birds singing. **Cons:** pools not heated; very pricey rates; not suitable for those with a fear of heights. 💲 Rooms from: R15055 ✉ off N2, Plettenberg Bay ✛ 10 km (6.2 miles) west of Plettenberg Bay ☎ 044/501–1111 ⊕ www.hunterhotels.com 🛏 16 rooms ¶◯¶ Free Breakfast.

🛍 Shopping

Harkerville Saturday Market

MARKET | FAMILY | This craft and farmer's market is held every Saturday, 8 am to noon. It's a great place to stop for breakfast or lunch, to go or to stay, with options ranging from coffee and pastries to dried fruit and nuts, seasonal fresh fruit and veggies, and prepared meals. The craft market has unique hand-crafted items and there's music and place for kids to play. ✉ Harkerville Saturday Market, N2 Hwy., Plettenberg Bay ✛ about 18 km Knysna, 12 km (7.5 miles) from Plettenberg Bay ⊕ www.harkervillemarket.co.za ⊘ Closed Sun.–Fri.

Old Nick Village

CRAFTS | Originally a pottery and weaving studio, Old Nick has grown to include workshops and galleries selling colorful ceramics, handwoven textiles, designer clothing, and more. There's enough that you could spend a whole day here. Nice Neighbour serves delicious food. ✉ N2, east of town, Plettenberg Bay ☎ 044/533–1395 ⊕ www.oldnickvillage.co.za.

🏃 Activities

BIKING
The Bike Shop

BIKING | Rent your bike from the friendly and knowledgeable staff at this established shop. They'll give you up-to-date advice on the best trails in the area. Not up to tackling a trail? Then choose an electric bike and putter around town. ✉ 998 Piesang Valley Rd., Plettenberg Bay ⊕ www.thebikeshop.co.za.

KAYAKING
Dolphin Adventures

KAYAKING | This operator offers regular sea kayaking trips in sleek but stable tandem kayaks throughout the year. If you're nervous about the open ocean, there are also the more placid waters of the Keurboom

Lagoon. ⊠ *Central Beach, Plettenberg Bay* ☎ *083/590–3405* ⊕ *www.dolphinadventures.co.za.*

Plettenberg Bay

KAYAKING | Kayaking on Plettenberg Bay is a great way to see the sights and possibly catch a glimpse of a whale or dolphin. Though you aren't likely to see as many creatures as the people on the big boats will, it's a far more intimate and exciting experience if you do. You can paddle past the Cape fur seal colony on Robberg. ⊠ *Plettenberg Bay, Plettenberg Bay.*

WHALE-WATCHING

Plettenberg Bay is one of the world's best locations for boat-based whale and dolphin watching. Most days, you'll spot at least two types of whales. If you're lucky, you might see six. Along the way are Cape fur seals, as well as seabirds like Cape gannets and African penguins.

Ocean Blue Adventures

BOATING | This operation offers a 1½- to 2-hour whale-watching trip that head out on a route they call the "humpback highway." Sightings are not guaranteed, but these experienced skippers know where the whales are. Along the way they take you past Robberg Peninsula, home to a colony of Cape fur seals. ⊠ *Hopwood St., Central Beach, Plettenberg Bay* ☎ *044/533–5083* ⊕ *www.oceanadventures.co.za* 🖃 *From R570.*

Ocean Safaris

WILDLIFE-WATCHING | This group runs regular whale-watching trips right from Central Beach. These last 1½ to 2 hours and let you spot much more than just whales. You're likely to see friendly dolphins, Cape seals, and sometimes even sharks. ⊠ *1 Hopwood St., Central Beach, Plettenberg Bay* ☎ *082/784–5729* ⊕ *www.oceansafaris.co.za* 🖃 *R570 to R850.*

The Crags

16 km (10 miles) northeast of Plettenberg Bay.

Although technically part of Plett, the Crags has a very different feel. It's in a forested area and is home to a primate refuge as well as a free-flight aviary. Although there's no beach, the Crags is close to the lagoon and beach at Nature's Valley. There are loads of accommodations and exciting activities, most of which are part of a marketing initiative called Cruise the Crags.

GETTING HERE AND AROUND

The Crags falls within the greater Plett area, so the same travel information applies. There's no public transportation to and around the Crags, so renting a car and driving yourself is your best option.

VISITOR INFORMATION

CONTACTS Cruise the Crags. ☎ *082/261–0542* ⊕ *www.cruisethecrags.co.za.*

Sights

Birds of Eden

WILDLIFE REFUGE | FAMILY | Built over a valley cutting through an old-growth forest, this magical sanctuary is a free-flight aviary spanning five dome-enclosed acres. More than 3,500 birds of 220 species fly, flutter, and perch here, some of which are quite tame. The main focus is African birds, and you'll see African grey parrots, Cape canaries, and greater flamingos. Take time to sit on one of the benches and listen to their calls—it's like being in the Amazon. You can grab a bite at the little restaurant overlooking the flamingo pond. Buy a memento or a gift at the well-stocked gift shop as you leave. ⊠ *Birds of Eden, N2 ✦ 16 km (10 miles) east of Plettenberg Bay* ☎ *044/534–8906* ⊕ *www.birdsofeden.co.za* 🖃 *R320.*

Detour: En Route

As you travel eastward on the N2, detour onto the R102, a far more interesting and scenic route. The road passes through farmland before dropping suddenly to sea level via the Groot River Pass. The road worms back and forth through a tunnel of impenetrable greenery pressing in on either side. At the bottom of the pass, turn right into **Nature's Valley**, where the Groot River forms a magnificent lagoon hemmed in by bush-cloaked hills. An almost fairy-tale settlement can be found here beneath a canopy of native trees. At a small restaurant-cum-shop near the beach, weary hikers give their boots a solemn resting place if they're not fit for another hike.

From Nature's Valley, the R102 climbs out of the Groot River valley and meets up again with the N2. There no choice than to return to the main road because the incredibly scenic Bloukrans Pass is closed to through traffic. Look out for the turnoff to the Tsitsikamma section of the Garden Route National Park and the wild and beautiful Storms River Mouth. The pretty and rather remote village of Storms River is another 4 km (2½ miles) farther east. Adventure lovers congregate here for the canopy tours, mountain biking, and hiking trails.

7

The Garden Route and the Little Karoo THE CRAGS

Monkeyland

WILDLIFE REFUGE | FAMILY | Don't be put off by the cutesy name. This award-winning refuge houses abused and abandoned primates, most of which were once pets or confined to zoos. They now roam in a huge enclosed area of the forest and are free to play, socialize, and do whatever it is that keeps primates happy. There are lemurs, gibbons, spider monkeys, vervet monkeys, howler monkeys, and many more. Guided walks are offered throughout the day, and the tamer residents often play with guests. Entrance to the viewing deck and restaurant is free, but you'll only get close up and personal if you take one of the guided walks. Prepare to be enchanted. ⊠ *Monkeyland, N2, 16 km (10 miles) east of Plettenberg Bay, The Crags* ☎ *044/534–8906* ⊕ *www. monkeyland.co.za* ✈ *R320.*

 Hotels

Hog Hollow Country Lodge

$$$$ | B&B/INN | On the edge of a forested gorge with the Tsitsikamma Mountains in the background, this lovely lodge puts you close to many of the Garden Route's most popular attractions. **Pros:** plenty of privacy and space; professional and friendly service; commanding forest views. **Cons:** Wi-Fi only in the main lounge area; not suitable for those with mobility issues; vervet monkeys might pester you on your verandah. ⓢ *Rooms from: R4150* ⊠ *Askop Rd., The Crags* ☎ *044/534–8879, 082/896–5975* ⊕ *www.hog-hollow.com* ➥ *19 rooms* ⓞ *Free Breakfast.*

Kurland Hotel

$$$$ | HOTEL | On the road to Tsitsikamma, this magnificent 1,500-acre estate offers spacious suites that make you feel like you're staying in your own country home. **Pros:** pony rides for the kids; it's the best place to catch a polo match; supremely comfortable accommodations. **Cons:** far from beach; no other dining options nearby; a 15-minute drive from Plettenberg Bay. ⓢ *Rooms from: R5590* ⊠ *N2, The Crags* ☎ *044/534–8082* ⊕ *www.kurland. co.za* ➥ *13 rooms* ⓞ *Free Breakfast.*

The five-day Otter Trail is so popular that it's usually booked up a year in advance.

Tsitsikamma

31 km (19 miles) east of Nature's Valley; 42 km (26 miles) east of Plettenberg Bay.

Run as its own park, the Tsitsikamma section of the Garden Route National Park is a narrow belt of coastline extending for 80 km (50 miles) from Oubosstrand to Nature's Valley. It includes some of the most spectacular coastal scenery in the country, including deep gorges, evergreen forests, tidal pools, and empty beaches.

GETTING HERE AND AROUND

Pickup can be arranged with most lodges. There's no public transportation in this area, so your best bet is renting a car and driving yourself. The roads are in good condition.

 Sights

Tsitsikamma Section of the Garden Route National Park

NATIONAL PARK | If you want to hike through some of the most fantastic scenery along the Garden Route, head to this park between Nature's Valley and Plettenberg Bay. One of the best ways to experience it is the five-day Otter Trail, one of South Africa's most popular hikes. However, it's usually booked out a year ahead. The somewhat easier Dolphin Trail is also incredibly popular.

A less strenuous option is to visit Storms River Mouth, where the river enters the sea through a narrow channel between sheer cliffs. From the Tsitsikamma Visitor Center, a trail descends through the forest and over a narrow suspension bridge strung across the water. It's a spectacular walk, a highlight of any trip to the Garden Route. On the other side of the bridge, a steep trail climbs to the top of a bluff overlooking the river and the sea. Other trails, ranging from 1 to 3 km

(½ to 2 miles), lead to a cave once inhabited by hunter-gatherers or through the coastal forest. ☎ *042/281–1607* ⊕ *www. sanparks.org* ☞ *R262*.

Hotels

Storms River Mouth Rest Camp
$$ | **RESORT** | **FAMILY** | Almost within soaking distance of the pounding surf, the setting at Storms River Mouth Rest Camp is nothing short of spectacular, making it a must-visit for international visitors. **Pros:** spectacular scenery; you couldn't get closer to the sea; on-site restaurant and shop. **Cons:** not much to do when it rains; nearby trails can be crowded; there's a daily conservation fee. **$** *Rooms from: R1815* ☒ *Storms River Mouth* ☎ *042/281–1607* ⊕ *www. sanparks.org* ☞ *243 rooms* ◎ *No Meals*.

Activities

BOATING
Spirit of Tsitsikamma
BOATING | **FAMILY** | For a close look at the Storms River Gorge—which is otherwise inaccessible—take a trip on the *Spirit of Tsitsikamma*. The boat departs every 45 minutes from the jetty below the suspension bridge. ☒ *Storms River Mouth Rest Camp* ☎ *042/281–1607* ⊕ *www. sanparks.org* ☞ *R150*.

HIKING
★ Dolphin Trail
HIKING & WALKING | Starting at Storms River Mouth, this trail through ruggedly beautiful scenery takes you east along the coast. It covers 17 km (10½ miles) over two days, though you carry only a day pack. The rest of your luggage is transported to the next spot for you. Accommodations are in comfortable cabins and lovely guesthouses with awesome views. The price includes a guide, all meals, transportation, and three nights' accommodations. ☒ *Storms River Mouth Rest Camp* ☎ *042/280–3588* ⊕ *www.dolphintrail.co.za* ☞ *R8,000*.

Otter Trail
HIKING & WALKING | One of South Africa's most popular hikes, the five-day Otter Trail runs along the coastline from the mouth of the Storms River to Nature's Valley, passing rocky cliffs, deserted beaches, rushing rivers, and towering old-growth forests. The challenging trail is 45 km (27 miles) long, and there are a lot of steep climbs along the way. Basic accommodations are in huts equipped with sleeping bunks and chemical toilets. You must carry in all food and carry out all trash. Only 12 people are allowed on the trail per day, making it vital to book at least a year in advance. Some spots could open up at the last minute, but don't count on it. ☒ *Storms River Mouth* ☎ *012/426–5111* ⊕ *www.sanparks.org* ☞ *R1,450*.

Storms River

4 km (2½ miles) east of Tsitsikamma section of the Garden Route National Park.

Although it's a small, isolated village, Storms River absolutely buzzes with activity. One hotel, a couple of guesthouses, and a few backpacker lodges all cater to both adrenaline junkies and nature lovers.

GETTING HERE AND AROUND
Storms River Mouth is 18 km (11 miles) south of the Storms River Bridge. There's no public transportation around the area, so you will need your own transport.

Restaurants

Marilyn's 60's Diner
$ | **AMERICAN** | **FAMILY** | Slick back your hair, put on your blue suede shoes, and sashay into this red-and-white checkered diner for a burger and fries or an indulgent chocolate toffee sundae. Posters of Elvis, the Beatles, and Marilyn Monroe adorn the turquoise walls while music from a jukebox plays classic tunes. **Known for:**

Within Tsitsikamma National Park, a spectacular trail descends through the forest and over a narrow suspension bridge strung across Storms River. Hiking it is a Garden Route highlight.

surprisingly good diner favorites; decor is a blast from the past; fun atmosphere. [$] *Average main: R60* ✉ *Darnell St., Koukamma, Storms River* ☎ *042/281–1711* 🌐 *www.marilyns60sdiner.co.za.*

Hotels

At the Woods Guest House
$$ | **B&B/INN** | Built with care and attention to detail, this lovely guesthouse is a winner. **Pros:** a small but pretty swimming pool; comfortable common areas; knowledgeable owner. **Cons:** some rooms don't have mountain views; no air-conditioning; limited dining options in the area. [$] *Rooms from: R2000* ✉ *Formosa St.* ☎ *082/328–2371* 🌐 *www.atthewoods.co.za* 🛏 *8 rooms* 🍴 *Free Breakfast.*

Tsitsikamma Village Inn
$$ | **HOTEL** | Built around a hunting lodging dating back to 1888, this beloved lodging has whitewashed cottages neatly arranged around a village green. **Pros:** adventure center close by; three restaurants on-site; gardens filled with flowers. **Cons:** very busy in season; on the town's main road; sometimes filled with tour groups. [$] *Rooms from: R1900* ✉ *Darnell St.* ☎ *042/281–1711* 🌐 *www.tsitsikammahotel.co.za* 🛏 *49 rooms* 🍴 *Free Breakfast.*

Activities

BUNGEE JUMPING

★ Face Adrenalin
LOCAL SPORTS | If you only try bungee jumping once in your life, do it from the Bloukrans River Bridge with Face Adrenalin. At 700 feet, it's the highest commercial bungee jump in the world. The span is the third-highest bridge in the world and the highest in the Southern Hemisphere. Pay a little extra for a video to show your friends back home. If you have no intention of flinging yourself off a bridge, opt for the walking tour. Even that's not for the faint of heart, as it is pretty high, exposed, and scary. ✉ *Off the N2* ✣ *Between Plett and Storms River* ☎ *042/281–1458* 🌐 *www.faceadrenalin.com* 🎟 *R1400.*

CANOPY AND FOREST TOUR
★ Storms River Adventures
ZIP LINING | Want a bird's-eye view of the treetops? Storms River Adventures will take you deep into the forest, outfit you with a harness, and "fly" you on long cables from platform to platform. Friendly, knowledgeable guides are with you the whole way. A video of your adventure costs a little extra. The outfitter also offers the gentler Woodcutter's Journey, an open-vehicle tour of the forest. You learn about the flora and fauna and the interesting history of the region. You end it all with lunch or tea at a beautiful picnic site next to the Storms River, a spot where wagons would stop more than a century ago. Other all-weather trips include a 2-km (1.2-mile) or 5.9-km (3.6-mile) guided forest walk. ⊠ *Main Rd., Storms River* ☎ *042/281–1836* ⊕ *www. stormsriver.com* ✒ *R695.*

MOUNTAIN BIKING
Storms River Mountain Bike Trail
BIKING | **FAMILY** | This trail, in the Plaatbos Area of Garden Route National Park, is a scenic, circular 22-km (14-mile) trail that navigates the old Storms River Pass. It's tough, so fitness is a prerequisite here. The 5-km (3-mile) descent through the forest to the bottom of the pass offers beautiful gorge views and a refreshing dip in the river. The starting point is near the police station at Storms River. Pick up a self-issue permit at the start of the trail. ⊠ *Storms River, Main Rd., Storms River* ☎ *042/281–1557* ⊕ *www.sanparks.org.*

Tsitsikamma Segway Tours
BIKING | Book a fascinating two-hour tour through the indigenous forest on a Segway, or rent a mountain bike to travel the same route. ⊠ *54 Formosa St., Storms River Village* ☎ *081/320–3977* ⊕ *www. segwayfun.co.za* ✒ *R750.*

Sanbona Wildlife Reserve

270 km (168 miles) east of Cape Town.

On Route 62—the world's longest wine route—Sanbona Wildlife Reserve is a scenic three-hour drive from Cape Town or three-and-a half hours from George. Run by a non-profit organization dedicated to conservation, Sanbona Wildlife Reserve in the heart of the Klein Karoo is arguably the Cape's most authentic wildlife reserve. Remote, tranquil, and beautiful, Sanbona also offers luxurious accommodations.

GETTING HERE AND AROUND
There's no public transportation in the area, so you will need a car to get around. The drive from Cape Town is about three hours along the N1, the R60, and the R62.

Sights

★ Sanbona Wildlife Reserve
WILDLIFE REFUGE | Sanbona Game Reserve couldn't be more different than Kruger National Park and the Lowveld. The gorges and ridges of the towering Cape Fold mountains, the semi-arid terrain of the Karoo plains, and unique vegetation of the fynbos (scrubland) make this a must for visitors to the Cape. Expect to feel dwarfed by the vast landscape. Even elephants look tiny compared to their majestic surroundings. The roads are rough and the distances long, but the overall experience is breathtaking.

Roughly the size of Singapore, this enormous area supports a free-roaming population of animals that were indigenous to the Western Cape before European settlers arrived. Here you'll find the Big Five (lion, rhino, elephant, buffalo, and leopard), although the area is so vast and desolate that you're certainly not guaranteed to spot them all. Guides make use of tracking devices to locate them. A unique experience is to spend time on foot with wild cheetahs that have grown accustomed to being approached by rangers.

Wildlife isn't all you'll find here. Be sure to climb up to some rare examples of San rock art, some reputed to be over 3,500 years old. Crystal-clear night skies deliver exceptional stargazing.

Conservation is the primary concern of the non-profit Caleo Foundation, and it shows in every detail from the building materials to the hand-carved furniture to your personal water bottle. Three luxury lodges cater to all types of guests. Historic Tilney Manor has an old-world feel, Gondwana Lodge is geared toward families, and the strikingly beautiful Dwyka Tented Camp is styled as a bush safari camp and is perfect for couples. If you want to get even more immersed in the wilderness, choose a two-day hike from Explorer Camp where you sleep in tents and dine under the stars around a crackling fire. ✉ *Off R62, Montagu* ✥ *43 km (27 miles) from Montagu* ☎ *021/010–0028* 🌐 *www.sanbona.com.*

Hotels

★ Dwyka Tented Camp
$$$$ | ALL-INCLUSIVE | One of the most scenic in South Africa, this luxury tented camp sits on a horseshoe bend of a dry riverbed at the foot of soaring cliffs. **Pros:** soothing spa treatments; a more spectacular setting would be hard to find; outstanding accommodations. **Cons:** unsuitable for mobility-impaired guests; wildlife is not as abundant as in other areas of the park; unpaved paths to tents are a bit rough and not well lit. [$] *Rooms from: R16500* ✉ *Sanbona Wildlife Reserve, Montagu* ☎ *021/010–0028* 🌐 *www.sanbona.com* 🛏 *9 rooms* 🍴 *All-Inclusive.*

Gondwana Lodge
$$$$ | HOTEL | FAMILY | Within easy striking distance of the best game-viewing areas, this lodge overlooking the Bellair Dam is unashamedly family-friendly. **Pros:** on-site spa; staff is attentive and accommodating; lots of options for families. **Cons:** not ideal for a secluded stay; not ideal for couples; steep stairs to the upper level. [$] *Rooms from: R15616* ✉ *Sanbona Wildlife Reserve, Montagu* ☎ *021/010–0028* 🌐 *www.sanbona.com* 🛏 *12 rooms* 🍴 *All-Inclusive.*

Tilney Manor
$$$$ | ALL-INCLUSIVE | At historic Tilney Lodge, the staff waits outside to greet new arrivals with hot face towels to freshen up after the hour-long drive from the reserve entrance. **Pros:** indoor and outdoor dining; hands-on staff will attend to your every need; on-site spa. **Cons:** formal atmosphere in lodge; communal dinner tables; Wi-Fi does not reach all rooms. [$] *Rooms from: R15616* ✉ *Sanbona Wildlife Reserve, Montagu* ☎ *021/010–0028* 🌐 *www.sanbona.com* 🛏 *6 rooms* 🍴 *All-Inclusive.*

Oudtshoorn

85 km (53 miles) north of Mossel Bay.

Oudtshoorn has been famous for its ostriches since around 1870, when farmers began raising them to satisfy the European demand for feathers to adorn women's hats. In the years leading up to World War I, ostrich feathers were almost worth their weight in gold thanks to the continuing demands of fashion, and Oudtshoorn experienced an incredible boom. Many of the beautiful sandstone buildings in town date from that period, as do the "feather palaces," huge homes built by prosperous feather merchants. Although feathers are no longer on trend, these huge birds are now bred for their tough and distinctive leather and almost completely fat- and cholesterol-free meat.

Almost as much of a moneymaker, though, is the tourist potential of these weird and wonderful birds. In addition to visiting an ostrich farm, you can buy

The 20-million-year-old Cango Caves are filled with amazing stalactite and stalagmite formations.

ostrich products ranging from the sublime (feather boas) to the ridiculous (taxi-dermied baby ostriches emerging from cracked eggs). Several farms compete for the tourist buck, offering almost identical tours and a chance to eat an ostrich-based meal. Be warned—these can be real tourist traps: glitzy, superficial, and crowded.

Most of the restaurants, guesthouses, and attractions listed here are on Baron van Reede Street. This street becomes the R328, which heads north from Oudtshoorn to the Cango Caves, the Swartberg Pass, and Prince Albert.

GETTING HERE AND AROUND
The most convenient and efficient way of getting around is driving yourself. The roads are good, and parts are very scenic. Intercape buses now travel to Oudtshoorn.

VISITOR INFORMATION
CONTACTS Oudtshoorn Tourism Bureau.
⊠ *12 Baron van Reede St., Oudtshoorn*
☎ *044/279–2532* ⊕ *www.oudtshoorn.com.*

 Sights

★ Cango Caves
CAVE | Between Oudtshoorn and Prince Albert, the huge and stunningly beautiful 20-million-year-old Cango Caves, filled with weird and wonderful stalactite and stalagmite formations, are deservedly one of the most popular attractions in the area. Only a small fraction of the caves, which extend for several miles through the mountains, is open. There's some damage from vandals, especially to the first chamber, but things get more magnificent the more the tour progresses. One of the highlights is Cleopatra's Needle, which stands 29 feet high and is at least 150,000 years old. You can choose between two tours: the hour-long standard tour and the aptly named adventure tour, which lasts 1½ hours. The latter is exhilarating, but the temperatures and humidity are high, there's not much oxygen, and you'll be shimmying up narrow chimneys on your belly, wriggling your way through tiny tunnels, and sliding on your bottom. Wear old clothes and shoes

Scenic Garden Route Drives

Part of the beauty of the Garden Route and Little Karoo is the spectacular passes that connect the two, as well as those between the Little and Great Karoo. Be sure to drive at least one during your visit.

Between Oudtshoorn and George you'll encounter the Outeniqua Pass (via the N12) or the more historic Montagu Pass (off the N9 after it diverges from the N12). The latter is on a narrow gravel road that's a great example of Victorian road-building techniques. There's arched bridge, a railway viaduct, and expertly laid dry-stone embankments. An old tollhouse still sits at the bottom of the pass.

The Robertson Pass, between Oudtshoorn and Mossel Bay, is on a paved road and has some fabulous views. One of the most interesting things about this route (especially if you're traveling from Mossel Bay) is that you can see the abrupt change of vegetation as you crest the ridge.

For a great loop between the Great and Little Karoo, drive counterclockwise from Oudtshoorn through De Rust and the spectacularly scenic Meiringspoort. This road runs along the bottom of a deep gorge, crossing the pretty Meirings River 25 times in the process. Halfway through the pass is a rest area where a path leads to a 200-foot waterfall. Local legend has it that a mermaid lives in the pool at the base.

Head west on the R407 to the pretty Karoo town of Prince Albert, then south over the Swartberg Pass on the R328 back to Oudtshoorn. (The views are more dramatic from this direction.) This pass, built between 1881 and 1886, is regarded as the legendary road engineer Sir Thomas Bain's masterpiece. At times the road barely clings to the mountainside, held only by Bain's stone retaining walls. From the top, at 5,230 feet, you can look out toward the hot plains of the Great Karoo and the distant mountains of the Nuweveldberg.

with a good tread. ✉ *Off R328, Oudtshoorn* ✥ *29 km (18 miles) north of Oudtshoorn* ☎ *044/272–7410, 082/303–0029* 🌐 *www.cango-caves.co.za* 🎟 *R150.*

Cango Ostrich Farm

FARM/RANCH | **FAMILY** | One of the least commercialized ostrich farms, Cango has guides that explain the bird's extraordinary social and physical characteristics. There are lots of interactive opportunities, including feeding and petting the ostriches and posing with one for a photo. From September to February, you may see babies hatching. The farm is conveniently located en route to the Cango Caves. ✉ *R328, Oudtshoorn* ✥ *14 km (9 miles) north of Oudtshoorn* ☎ *044/272–4623* 🌐 *www.cangoostrich.co.za* 🎟 *R120.*

🍴 Restaurants

Jemima's Restaurant

$$$$ | **SOUTH AFRICAN** | Named after the mythical guardian angel of love, good taste, and good cooking, this restaurant would not disappoint its muse. All the ingredients are sourced locally from farmers in the district, and the menu focuses on such local delicacies as olives, mutton, and, of course, ostrich. **Known for:** tasty deserts; a meat-lover's paradise; extensive list of local wines. [$] *Average main: R260* ✉ *94 Baron van Reede St., Oudtshoorn* ☎ *044/272–0808* 🌐 *www.jemimas.com.*

Coffee and Quick Bites

Wilgewandel

$$ | **SOUTH AFRICAN** | **FAMILY** | At the turnoff to the Cango Caves, Wilgewandel serves well-cooked simple fare like hamburgers, sandwiches, and ostrich steaks. Shady outdoor tables overlook a big lawn and duck-filled pond. **Known for:** traditional South African cuisine; gourmet milkshakes; sweet treats. [$] *Average main: R100* ✉ *R328, Oudtshoorn* ✣ *2 km (1 mile) from the Cango Caves* ☎ *044/272–0878* 🌐 *www.wilgewandel.co.za.*

Hotels

★ **De Zeekoe Guest Farm**

$$ | **B&B/INN** | **FAMILY** | The warmest of welcomes awaits you at this homey guest farm surrounded by the Swartberg and Outeniqua mountains. **Pros:** unpretentious and authentic farm atmosphere; exceptionally friendly staff; simple on-site spa. **Cons:** very hot in summer, very cold in winter; often busy with tour groups; no canoeing or other water sports during droughts. [$] *Rooms from: RR2080* ✉ *Off the R328, Oudtshoorn* ✣ *7 km (4.3 miles) from Oudtshoorn* ☎ *082/531–3019* 🌐 *www.dezeekoe.co.za* 🛏 *21 rooms* 🍴 *Free Breakfast.*

Hlangana Lodge

$$ | **B&B/INN** | Conveniently situated on road out to the Cango Caves, this warm and friendly lodge has bright, airy rooms with modern furnishings. **Pros:** laid-back atmosphere; staff is super friendly and helpful; near good restaurants. **Cons:** doesn't serve dinner; lodge is on the main road; rooms not very private. [$] *Rooms from: R1600* ✉ *Baron van Reede St., at North St., Oudtshoorn* ☎ *044/272–2299* 🌐 *www.hlangana.co.za* 🛏 *27 rooms* 🍴 *Free Breakfast.*

Kleinplaas

$ | **RESORT** | **FAMILY** | Although Kleinplaas means "small farm," this lodging isn't really a farm despite the ostriches and ducks on the premises. **Pros:** good for kids; conveniently located at edge of town; friendly clientele. **Cons:** not particularly scenic; not much privacy; not all chalets have air-conditioning. [$] *Rooms from: R1250* ✉ *171 Baron van Reede St., Oudtshoorn* ☎ *044/272–5811* 🌐 *www.kleinplaas.co.za* 🛏 *54 rooms* 🍴 *Free Breakfast.*

★ **La Plume Guest House**

$$ | **B&B/INN** | On a working ostrich farm, this stylish guesthouse has rooms that are individually decorated with beautiful antiques; all of the bathrooms have elegant clawfoot tubs. **Pros:** terrific attention to detail; beautiful views of the valley; picnic lunches on request. **Cons:** not for trendy types; no room phones; a 10-minute drive from town. [$] *Rooms from: R2040* ✉ *Volmoed, Oudtshoorn* ✣ *14 km (9 miles) west of Oudtshoorn* ☎ *044/272–7516, 082/820–4373* 🌐 *www.laplume.co.za* 🛏 *19 rooms* 🍴 *Free Breakfast.*

Le Petit Karoo

$$ | **B&B/INN** | Perched high on a hill, this trio of bush tents with fabulous mountain views feels like your own little private paradise. **Pros:** charming owners; breakfasts are delicious; tents have their own hot tubs. **Cons:** dinner requires reservations; tents can get hot in summer; it's a little too rustic for some. [$] *Rooms from: RR2080* ✉ *Off R328, Oudtshoorn* ✣ *14 km (9 miles) north of Oudtshoorn* ☎ *073/834–0666* 🌐 *www.lepetitkaroo.com* 🛏 *8 rooms* 🍴 *No Meals.*

★ **Rietfontein Ostrich Palace**

$$ | **B&B/INN** | The world's oldest working ostrich farm is still owned and managed by descendants of the original Potgieter family. **Pros:** authentic and historic vibe; swimming pool with panoramic views; child-friendly accommodations. **Cons:** not all rooms have bathtubs; no single rooms available; very hot in summer, very cold in winter. [$] *Rooms from: R2000* ✉ *R62, Oudtshoorn* ✣ *18 km (11 miles) from Calitzdorp* ☎ *044/050–1109* 🌐 *www.rop.co.za* 🛏 *7 rooms* 🍴 *Free Breakfast.*

Rosenhof Country House

$$$$ | B&B/INN | For luxury and indulgence in the heart of Oudtshoorn, look no further. **Pros:** on-site spa and gym; breakfast served in the garden gazebo; lovely gardens full of flowers. **Cons:** close to main road; small pool area; patios aren't very private. $ *Rooms from: R5200* ✉ *264 Baron van Reede St., Oudtshoorn* ☎ *044/272–2232* ⊕ *www.rosenhof.co.za* ⤳ *12 rooms* ⟊ *Free Breakfast.*

Shopping

Oudtshoorn has loads of stores selling ostrich products, but it pays to shop around because prices vary significantly. The shops along Baron van Reede Street have a great variety but are a tad pricey.

Cape Karoo Ostrich Emporium

OTHER SPECIALTY STORE | This company provides more than 65% of ostrich leather products sold around the world. If you're looking for a pair of fancy boots, dress shoes, or a purse, this is the place. Check out the little Karoo angels with ostrich feather wings. ✉ *15 Rademeyer St, Oudtshoorn* ☎ *044/279–2127* ⊕ *www.capekarooshop.com* ⊗ *Closed Sun.*

Lugro Ostrich

OTHER SPECIALTY STORE | This small workshop manufactures ostrich handbags, wallets, and belts in a plethora of gorgeous colors, as well as smaller items such as key rings. These can be bought in the shop on the premises. ✉ *133 Langenhoven Rd., Oudtshoorn* ☎ *082/788–7916* ⊕ *www.lugro-ostrich.co.za* ⊗ *Closed Sun.*

De Rust

40 km (25 miles) northeast of Oudtshoorn.

De Rust is a sleepy little Victorian Karoo village. The main road is lined with crafts stores, coffee shops, restaurants, and wineshops.

GETTING HERE AND AROUND

There's no public transportation here. You will need your own vehicle to travel around, but the roads are good and the scenery is very beautiful.

VISITOR INFORMATION

CONTACTS De Rust Tourism Bureau. ✉ *11 Schoeman St., De Rust* ☎ *044/279–2532* ⊕ *www.oudtshoorn.com.*

Sights

Domein Doornkraal

WINERY | On a real working farm, this shop sells wines from 25 cellars and has an excellent selection of pot-still brandies, dessert wines, and dry wines. They also make their own superb range of fortified wines and an inexpensive blend of white wines like Chenin Blanc, Sauvignon Blanc, and Colombard. The shop also stocks local olive oils from 10 local suppliers, fruit preserves, honey, and cookies, all sourced from local farmers and bakers. In season, they operate a small outdoor restaurant focusing on old-fashioned home cooking. ✉ *R62, 10 km (6 miles) southwest of De Rust, De Rust* ☎ *082/763–5296* ⊕ *www.doornkraal.co.za.*

Mons Ruber Estate

WINERY | This estate is named after the red hills that dominate the landscape and whose soil creates the perfect environment for growing grapes with a high sugar content. So it's not surprising that this winery specializes in dessert wines and makes a fine brandy. There is a lovely restored 19th-century kitchen and an easy hiking trail that stretches into the hills. ✉ *N12, 15 km (9 miles) southwest of De Rust, De Rust* ☎ *044/251–6550* ▣ *Free.*

Chapter 8

THE EASTERN CAPE

8

Updated by
Keith Bain

 Sights
★★★★★

 Restaurants
★★★★☆

 Hotels
★★★★☆

 Shopping
★★☆☆☆

 Nightlife
★☆☆☆☆

WELCOME TO THE EASTERN CAPE

TOP REASONS TO GO

★ **Look at the Wildlife:** With its rich and varied topography and fauna, the Eastern Cape supports a wide range of game, but best of all—it's malaria-free.

★ **Take a Dive on the Wild Side:** Diving with a "baitball"—fish tightly swimming together—off the Wild Coast is the ultimate adrenaline dive. Sharks, Cape gannets, Bryde's whales, and even humpbacks have been known to join the feast.

★ **Culture and History:** From rustic Xhosa villages to colonial mansions, the range and depth of the Eastern Cape's cultural heritage is amazing.

★ **See the Other Side:** Traversing the spectacular Wild Coast on foot, horse, bicycle, or ATV allows you to interact with locals. If you're more interested in culture, a visit to Bulungula will let you meet locals and generally interact on a far more personal level.

★ **Step Back in Time:** The dusty streets of Nieu Bethesda have no lights— and that's half the charm. The tiny, remote, mountain-enfolded village is lined with historic houses.

1 Gqeberha. Formerly Port Elizabeth (and still signposted as such), this port city is the Eastern Cape's largest metro with significant history, beautiful beaches, and relatively quick access to Big Five wildlife reserves.

2 Cape St Francis. A popular seaside resort with a permanent holiday atmosphere.

3 Addo Elephant National Park. A short drive inland from Gqeberha, it's one place where huge elephant herd sightings are guaranteed.

4 Shamwari Game Reserve. Established to restore agricultural land to its natural state, it's now stocked with game and a variety of upmarket lodges.

5 Kwandwe Private Game Reserve. A remote wilderness dotted with a handful of very pleasant lodges and private-use villas, its terrain is magnificent and its game drives are hugely productive with varied animal sightings.

6 Graaff-Reinet. Horseshoed by mountains in a scenic part of the Karoo, South Africa's fourth-oldest town offers history and gorgeous scenery.

7 Nieu Bethesda. A scenic drive north of Graaff-Reinet, this pretty hamlet is surrounded by mountains and feels like a trip back in time.

8 Samara Private Game Reserve. Near Graaff-Reinet, this is a visually magnificent—and vast— refuge for wildlife that had become locally extinct

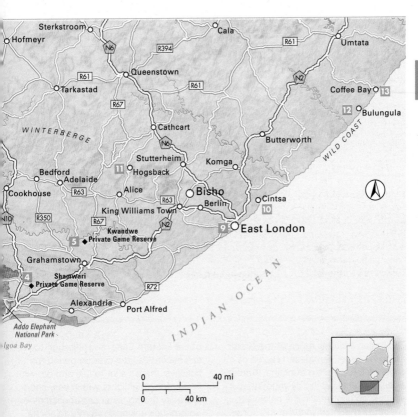

until this former farmland was returned to its original state and animals, many of them rescued, brought in.

9 East London. South Africa's only river port is the gateway city for trips along the Wild Coast, albeit not necessarily a city in which you'll want to linger.

10 Cintsa. A laid-back, bohemian coastal village at the southern end of the Wild Coast.

11 Hogsback. Fresh air, magnificent gardens, and an artistic-bohemian population define this dreamy mountain village.

12 Bulungula. A remote, rural community on the Wild Coast.

13 Coffee Bay. A laid-back hideaway for surfers, hippies, beachcombers, and anyone wanting to engage with a bit of local rural life.

South Africa's most diverse province, the Eastern Cape includes some of the country's best vacation destinations including the country's finest and least crowded beaches; Afro-montane forests (one of South Africa's eco-regions) and heathlands; a number of fantastic malaria-free game reserves; and some of the country's most interesting cultural attractions. But the region's main attraction is its coastline, still largely undeveloped and running for some 640 km (400 miles) from temperate to subtropical waters.

The region includes much of the Great Karoo—a large, semidesert region of ocher plains, purple mountains, dramatic skies, and unusual, hardy vegetation; it abuts KwaZulu-Natal in the northeast, Lesotho's mountain lands in the north, and the Garden Route to the southwest.

Frontier Country and the Sunshine Coast offer the perfect mix of well-maintained sunny coastal towns, beaches and resorts, historic and cultural sites, and a plethora of great game reserves all within a relatively concentrated (and malaria-free) area. Combined with good roads and infrastructure and a fine climate almost throughout, it's not hard to see why this part of the Eastern Cape is a particularly popular playground for South African tourists. It's richer and more developed here than in many other parts

of the Eastern Cape, and although towns can become a little overrun during the holidays, there's a lot to see and do, with most of the highlights within very short and easy driving distances of each other. Sometimes unkindly referred to as the Detroit of South Africa, Gqeberha is the Sunshine Coast's (as well as the whole of the Eastern Cape's) main urban hub and has great transport links to and from the rest of the region and beyond. Both the city and the surrounding region also boast many of the province's best accommodations options and restaurants.

For a generous taste of the Great Karoo, head inland and spend a few days in Graaff-Reinet, a well-preserved town packed with heritage architecture, surrounded by mountains and enfolded by the incredibly scenic Camdeboo National

Park. There are private game reserves in the vicinity, too, and 50 km (31 miles) away is one of the prettiest hamlets in the country, Nieu Bethesda, where time stands still.

Another noteworthy region on the Eastern Cape is the Wild Coast. Unfortunately, the area lost a lot of its allure during the political uncertainty of the 1980s—more because of the perceived threat of violence than anything else. Hotels went out of business, the overnight huts on the fantastic Wild Coast Hiking Trail fell into disrepair, and the Transkei—the name given to this previously designated Xhosa "homeland" by the former apartheid government—sank further into economic depression. For many years it was only die-hard locals with strong emotional ties and small groups of backpackers who frequented these still-lovely and little-known places. Happily, the area has gone through a significant revival in recent years. Coastal hotels have been renovated one by one, and community projects are continually being put in place to ensure that the tourist dollar goes where it should. In addition to long, lovely beaches, the Wild Coast has crystal clear turquoise lagoons, some of which can be paddled for miles. The area's still largely unspoiled, and the people who live here are mostly subsistence farmers and fisherfolk. It's not uncommon for a family who can't afford a loaf of bread to dine (reluctantly) on oysters and lobster.

Then there's the Amatole region that comprises the casual coastal hub of East London as well as the idyllic, secluded bay at Cintsa just a little farther along the coast. Head inland for an hour or so and you'll find yourself in the foothills of the dramatic mountain range that gives this area its name. The forests, waterfalls, peaks, and rock formations of Amatole are an outdoor enthusiast's dream, and some of the picturesque towns and villages in the valleys below are strangely reminiscent of rural England; this area was said to be the inspiration behind J.R.R. Tolkien's Middle Earth and the living trees in *The Lord of the Rings*. It's also an important region in South Africa's history of struggle—Nelson Mandela, among others, attended university here, and Black Consciousness leader Steve Biko was born here. Though a popular region with a handful of South Africans in the know, Amatole isn't on many international tourists' maps yet. That's slowly beginning to change, but for now it's another large part of Amatole's appeal.

MAJOR REGIONS

The Eastern Cape is a huge province with considerable variety and many tiny gems. The towns, and even the cities, of the province are relatively small and often quaint, and the distances between them are often fairly large. Since the only airports are in Gqeberha, East London, and Mthatha (which you are strongly urged to avoid), the best way to experience the region is on a self-driving tour, leaving yourself plenty of time to explore (but be prepared for some poorly maintained roads across most of the easternmost region that many still refer to as the "Transkei").

Formerly known as Settler Country, the Eastern Cape's **Frontier Country** stretches from the outskirts of **Gqeberha** (the province's main city, until recently known as Port Elizabeth–or simply PE–and still signposted and referred to as such) to Port Alfred in the east, Makhanda (formerly known as Grahamstown, and still signposted as such) in the northeast, and the Zuurberg Mountains in the north. The area also encompasses the pretty beach town of **Cape St Francis,** and **Addo Elephant National Park** and such private game reserves as **Shamwari** and **Kwandwe**. The **Sunshine Coast** overlaps part of this area, running roughly from Cape St Francis for 500 km (310 miles) as far as East London via Gqeberha.

The semi-arid Karoo is a vast region covering much of central South Africa, and straddling the adjacent Western Cape and Northern Cape provinces. In the Eastern Cape, one of the country's most historically important towns— **Graaff-Reinet**—enjoys one of the Karoo's most stunning settings, within a horseshoe of mountains, right next to Camdeboo National Park and the geologically astonishing Valley of Desolation. Nearby are several private game reserves, including **Samara**, known for reintroducing cheetah to the area, and—to the north— **Nieu Bethesda**, a pretty hamlet in a breathtaking valley where you will meet a variety of modern-era pioneers, people who've left their cities and towns in search of a more authentic way of life. The village, which has dirt roads, no street lights, and plenty of characterful historic houses, is home to the locally-famous Owl House, established by the outsider artist Helen Martins.

The **Amatole** region takes its name from the spectacular Amatola mountain range, which is home to a number of ancient indigenous forests, waterfalls, and rare flora and fauna, all presided over by impressive peaks that reach up to 5,905 feet above sea level. This undulating region stretches along the coast from just beyond Port Alfred almost as far as Port St. Johns, overlapping with the Wild Coast from East London onward. The largest city in the region, **East London** has excellent transport links with the rest of the country and is a good starting point for heading into the hinterland with the picturesque mountain village of **Hogsback** found more or less at its heart. All of this sets the backdrop for the six-day Amatola Trail, considered one of the country's toughest multi-day hikes, and definitely one of the finest. There are also game parks, beautiful beaches, and a number of cultural pursuits to discover in Amatole, in addition to a rich history. Aside from the region's important role in South Africa's anti-apartheid struggle, towns like Cathcart and Adelaide began their life as 19th-century British military outposts

intended to defend the border of the Cape Colony and the white farmers in the area from the Xhosa nation to the east. One of the frequent border wars between these two sides was dubbed the Amatola War. There's still something distinctly reminiscent of rural England about parts of the region, albeit with a distinctly African twist, and farming remains a central facet of life.

As the name suggests, the **Wild Coast** is a haven of unspoiled wilderness, although a recent decision to allow Shell to conduct tests off the coastline have raised major environmental and ecological concerns. Strictly speaking, it originally reached from the Kei River mouth to Port Edward (which were the borders of the once nominally independent Transkei), but today it has spread almost to the outskirts of East London. Whereas other areas of the country have become tourist playgrounds, the coast's lack of infrastructure has resulted in the large and mostly undeveloped swath of country east of **Cintsa**, which might be considered the Wild Coast's westernmost village. From here, the coastline consists of more than 280 km (174 miles) of desolate white-sand beaches, ragged cliffs, and secluded bays. Inland it's green and forested, with abundant birdlife. The mostly Xhosa population farm the land communally, domestic animals roam free, and traditional thatched *rondavel* huts dot the landscape. With mild year-round weather, this is a great destination for the adventure-seeker, heaven for hikers, and an excellent place to discover authentic Xhosa culture while dipping into the more bohemian, laid-back way of life the region's tiny villages offer. If you're looking for tranquility, epic beaches and relaxation, the tiny hamlets of **Bulungula** and **Coffee Bay** are ideal places to discover the spirit of the Wild Coast. Also dotted along the coast are slightly larger resort villages, some with long-established family hotels, pretty campsites, and backpacker resorts—these can be quite busy during South Africa's summer holiday (December/January).

For many, this section of the Eastern Cape is also a glimpse of a very different South Africa; among one of the country's poorest regions, here more than most places it's worth seeking out travel operators and accommodation providers that endeavor to practice responsible tourism—a number of low-key lodges (such as Bulungula) have been established in partnership with local communities in order to help to raise employment levels while simultaneously giving visitors unique insights into the traditional Xhosa culture. Seek them out, especially if you're open to traveling more slowly.

Finally, it's worth pointing out that **Mthatha**, home to the Nelson Mandela Museum, might be a place you pass through as it has no noteworthy places to stay or eat; the city—a major economic hub for a vast, primarily rural region—experiences high incidences of theft, can feel congested, and offers little that's likely to feel like you're on holiday.

Planning

When to Go

The region's climate is mild throughout the year, with temperatures at the coast ranging between winter lows of 5°C (41°F) and summer highs of 32°C (90°F). Summer—November to April—is the most popular time to visit, especially for sun worshippers. (The beaches are best avoided at Christmas and New Year's when they become severely overcrowded with reveling locals.) But even winter (June to early September) has its attractions like the sardine run in June or early July (see "The Food Chain Up Close" box, later in this chapter), is a significant draw, and both Gqeberha and East London host a number of sporting festivals, notably Iron Man triathlons, especially in summer.

Getting Here and Around

AIR

Small and easy to navigate, Chief Dawid Stuurman International Airport (PLZ) in Gqeberha is the primary air entry point for the Eastern Cape and has a number of daily services from Johannesburg (1½ hours) and Cape Town (1 hour) with SA Airlink, as well as British Airways (operated by Comair), and low-cost FlySafair. You can also fly here direct from Durban. Despite the airport's new name, there are currently no direct international flights.

Tiny King Phalo Airport (ELS) in East London is the best point of entry for the Amatole region and the Wild Coast and is served daily by SA Airlink, British Airways (operated by Comair), and FlySafair.

For information on airlines, see Air in Travel Smart.

CONTACTS Chief Dawid Stuurman International Airport (Gqeberha). ✉ *Allister Miller Dr., Gqeberha* ⊕ *www.airports.co.za/airports/Chief-Dawid-Stuurman-international-al-airport.* **King Phalo Airport (East London).** *(ELS)* ✉ *66 Settlers Way, East London* ☎ *043/706–0306* ⊕ *www.acsa.co.za.*

BUS

Intercape has pretty reliable and reasonably priced bus services, divided between their Mainliner and Sleepliner buses; the latter is their more premium service. In Gqeberha, buses depart and arrive from their depot in Perridgevale (corner of Nile and Storey roads). Be sure to arrange to be picked up in advance, or hail an Uber.

For information on buses, see Bus in Travel Smart.

CAR

Traveling by car is the easiest and best way to tour the Eastern Cape. The major rental agencies have offices at the various airports in the region and in downtown Gqeberha. One-way rentals are available. Most roads are in fairly

Eastern Cape Itineraries

3 Days: Fly into Gqeberha in the morning. Do a historical tour in the afternoon followed by dinner at your guesthouse or one of the restaurants in town. The next morning, drive out to Shamwari, Kwandwe, or Addo; plan to spend two days in one of these reserves (staying at one of the private luxury lodges or, at Addo, at an inexpensive SANParks camp) and then drive back to Gqeberha to fly out. Or if you choose to visit Kwandwe, you can cut the game-viewing down to one day, keep heading north from Makhanda (formerly known as Grahamstown, just don't plan to stay there), and spend the third day exploring the pretty village of Hogsback and taking a brisk hike into the Amatola Mountains. Alternatively, you could spend two days in Gqeberha or its beautiful coastal environs—soaking up the sun, playing a round of golf, taking a cultural tour, and just relaxing—and the third day on a day trip to Addo for an animal fix.

5 Days: With five days you could fly in and out of East London to join the Wild Coast Meander tour with Wild Coast Holiday Reservations —your days filled with walking this wonderful coastline, and each night spent at a different beach hotel. Or head from East London to Bulungula and spend two days and three nights immersing yourself in the local culture; then drive to Addo, Shamwari, or Kwandwe for a good game fix. If you spend these last couple of nights at one of the private lodges, you can revel in the indulgence of absolute luxury after a few days of roughing it. Or if game parks aren't your thing, head to Hogsback and hike through the mountains and forests for a day or two before returning to East London (or Gqeberha) to fly out. Or, spend one more day on the Sunshine Coast soaking up some culture, lounging on the beach, or playing golf.

7 Days: Start off as you would for the three-day itinerary but spend two days in Gqeberha and three days at your game destination. Then opt for some beach time on the Sunshine Coast, at Coffee Bay, or Cintsa. Alternatively, fly into East London to join the Wild Coast Meander or head inland toward the Amatola mountain range, with a few cultural stop-offs along the way; then spend two days at Addo, Shamwari, or Kwandwe. Head to Gqeberha or its environs and try to work in time to relax on the beach, play golf, or join a tour before flying out.

good shape, although you do need to keep an eye out for potholes, especially (but not exclusively) in rural areas and all across the Wild Coast. East London's roads are noticeably riddled with holes, and in many parts of the province you will be driving on gravel or dirt roads; these are generally accessible by normal sedan, although you might feel more comfortable traveling to lodges and anywhere on the Wild Coast with a high-clearance vehicle.

For information on car-rental agencies, see Car in Travel Smart.

Safety and Precautions

One thing to keep in mind is that although most of the suburban areas of Gqeberha are safe, a few parts of Central can be dicey. The lower section along Govan Mbeki is lively and vibrant, and the upper section is quiet and peaceful, but the parts in between have been seeing increasing incidents of crime. It's still best to get advice from your hotel or the tourism office before wandering around. The same goes for East London where you are best off sticking to less crowded neighborhoods such as Nahoon and Gonubie; smaller towns and villages tend to be less affected by crime, but are by no means free of petty theft, including incidental break-ins at guesthouses and lodges.

Though the area surrounding Makhanda> (formerly Grahamstown) is extraordinarily beautiful (if sadly litter-strewn in some rural quarters), the town itself has become a little rough around the edges, slightly disheveled, potholed, and forlorn in recent years. While there remain a few comfortable and charming guesthouses should you need to overnight, it's best treated as a pass-through town only; there are several fuel stations to pick from.

Mthatha is a major crime hub and it is reported that you could witness car parts being stolen off trucks waiting at red traffic lights—in broad daylight. It's best avoided entirely.

The Eastern Cape is malaria-free, and the climate is generally good. Water services have been highly unpredictable in many towns and cities and you are advised to follow advice on whether or not you can drink tap water—many places now provide filtered rain or borehole water to drink. Some places, such as Nieu Bethesda, have excellent spring water on tap. Avoid driving in rural areas at night: the roads are unfenced and animals wander onto—or even sleep on—the warm tarmac, which is a serious hazard. In many places, particularly the Wild Coast, cows are regularly found on roads and even highways. Be sure to bring protection against sunburn, and be careful swimming in the sea—the Wild Coast beaches don't have lifeguards.

In case of an emergency, call the general emergencies number (☏ *10111*). For vehicle breakdown, call your car-rental company.

Hotels

Most hotels along the coast get booked up over summer vacation (December and January), and the Wild Coast hotels are even busy over the winter school vacation, usually around June. Most establishments run winter specials, but there are exceptions. Hotels on the Wild Coast often offer packages for the sardine run, usually in June or early July, but it's always a bit of a gamble, as the sardines aren't always reliable.

Reservations can be secured via the lodging's website, or by phone. Another thing to keep in mind is that some of the more remote or rural lodgings in the Eastern Cape (particularly on the Wild Coast) still have limited or unreliable Wi-Fi provided for guest use, though all lodgings in urban areas and in the game reserves have good, fast connections these days. Be warned that South Africa's ongoing electricity disruptions as a result of planned load shedding by the national energy supplier can interrupt power and Wi-Fi in some hotels, guesthouses and lodges, although many are able to switch to generators or use stored-up solar energy. ■ TIP→ **If the ability to connect to the Web is important to you, it's always worth clarifying the type of service available when you make your reservation.**

Hotel reviews have been shortened. For full information, visit Fodors.com.

Restaurants

Generally speaking, the restaurants of the Eastern Cape are good and you will come across an increasing number of adventurous chefs and food experimenters doing very special things in the kitchen. Food at upmarket safari lodges tends to be exceptional, and there are concerted efforts to introduce local dishes to their guests. Not surprisingly, most restaurants are reasonably casual, and there are none where men would be expected to wear a dinner jacket or a tie; while some safari lodge guests like to dress up a bit before dinner, it's perfectly acceptable to eat in whatever you wore on a late-afternoon game drive (though you'll probably want to shower and change).

Restaurant reviews have been shortened. For full information, visit Fodors.com.

RESTAURANT AND HOTEL PRICES

Restaurant prices are the average cost of a main course at dinner or, if dinner is not served, at lunch. Hotel prices are the lowest cost of a standard double room in high season.

What it Costs In South African rand			
$	$$	$$$	$$$$
RESTAURANTS			
under R100	R100–R150	R151–R200	over R200
HOTELS			
under R1,500	R1,500–R2,500	R2,501–R3,500	over R3,500

Tours

African Dive Adventures

ADVENTURE TOURS | Although based in KwaZulu-Natal, this long-standing tour company offers Sardine Run Packages along the Wild Coast from a seasonal satellite base at the Ocean View Hotel in tranquil Coffee Bay. The best time to see this remarkable natural phenomenon, which draws an array of shark species as well as pods of dolphins, whales, and even gannets plunging into the sea from the skies above, is usually between late June and late July. You'll often be joined by co-owner Roland, who can spin a good yarn or two from his many thousands of dives in this area, as can the company's highly experienced dive

masters and instructors, who'll make you feel right at home both in and out of the water. Note that the sardine run is not guaranteed and the natural phenomenon has occasionally failed to materialize, presumably due to over-fishing, but possibly because of disruptions in the ocean caused by climate change. ⊠ *Ocean View Hotel, Coffee Bay* ☎ *082/456-7885 mobile* ⊕ *www.afridive.com* ⌨ *€ 2,100, 5 nights and 4 days of diving, with accommodation and food included.*

Mosaic Tourism

GUIDED TOURS | From a short and informative city or township tour with knowledgeable local guides to an all-day game-viewing excursion, the award-winning Mosaic offers a variety of immersing tailor-made tours in and around Gqeberha and right across the Eastern Cape. ⊠ *Garden Court Kings Beach, La Roche Drive, Humewood* ☎ *071/771-4418 mobile* ⊕ *www.mosaictourism.co.za.*

★ Wild Coast Holiday Reservations

WALKING TOURS | The Wild Coast has been a favorite hiking destination for years, and it was this women-owned, East London–based enterprise that pioneered organised walks along this stretch of coastline. The Wild Coast Meander and the Wild Coast Amble are five- or six-day guided hikes during which you walk between hotels and/or resorts on the southern section of the coast; the Meander includes one tough day covering 21 km (13 miles), so it's not to be taken lightly. A popular option is the Wild Coast Combo Trail (56 km [35 miles]), which includes luggage transfers and covers distances that are more or less the same each day; it starts at Wavecrest, includes a stay at Haga Haga, and ends at Crawfords Beach Lodge in Cintsa. Farther north, the Wild Coast Pondo Trail (69 km [43 miles] in and around Mbotyi) traverses more remote and less densely populated terrain; it's a series of treks to and from a comfortable base camp over far more spectacular, but also much steeper, tougher terrain than what you'll find on the other hikes. The trips are all fully catered, and you can arrange to have your luggage driven or portered. Shorter walks can be organized by request. This really is the best of both worlds. You walk on deserted beaches during the day and stay in comfy hotels with all the modern conveniences at night, and there are opportunities to add extra nights along the way if you prefer a more languid pace. ✉ *2 Muirfield Rd., Bunkers Hill, East London* ☎ *043/735–2976* ⊕ *www.wildcoastholidays.co.za.*

Visitor Information

CONTACTS Nelson Mandela Bay Tourism. ✉ *Donkin Reserve, Belmont Terrace, Central* ☎ *041/585–8884 Donkin, 041/583–2030 Boardwalk* ⊕ *www.nmbt.co.za.*

Gqeberha

770 km (477 miles) east of Cape Town.

Gqeberha (the new official name of Port Elizabeth [a.k.a. PE] occurred in 2020 as part of ongoing attempts to reconcile the country's colonial past—signposts have not changed yet, though, and most people still call it PE) may not have the range of attractions found in Cape Town or on the Garden Route, but it's a pleasant town that's worthy of a couple of days' exploration.

A large part of the town's charm lies in its small size and laid-back environment, but Gqeberha is not a total sleepy hollow. If you feel the need for a bit of nightlife, head to the Summerstrand's Boardwalk complex near the beach for its restaurants, cafés, theater, and casino; the beachfront here also has a few lively spots and is almost always bustling with joggers, strollers, surfers, and beachcombers. There are some beautiful beaches (although you'll need to visit them early in the day in summer, as the wind tends to pick up by midday)

and some historic buildings in the older part of the city, called Central, where you need to be on your toes and avoid walking around at night.

GETTING HERE AND AROUND
Gqeberha is a good base for exploring some other fantastic destinations, both wild and cultural, including Addo Elephant National Park. If you're traveling to any of the game reserves east of the city (such as Shamwari or Kwandwe), it may be a good idea to spend the night in Gqeberha, as many places advise you to check-in before lunch and it could be a scramble to get there if you're driving or flying in that morning.

Gqeberha's suburbs can be a little confusing. Humewood and Summerstrand are its two main coastal suburbs, with Humewood closer to the city center. The Humewood Golf Course, one of South Africa's best, is in Summerstrand, not Humewood, however (just to keep you on your toes). That said, it's a small city that also feels small and is, with a GPS, relatively easy to get around.

There's a minibus shuttle at Gqeberha's Chief Dawid Stuurman International Airport that will drop you off at your hotel (about R110 one way, much less than a metered taxi), but you'll need to book in advance. Airport Cabs (⊕ *airport-cabs. co.za*) will take you from the airport to anywhere you need to go, including distant pockets of the Eastern Cape, with set rates for each destination; their 24-hour number can also be reached using WhatsApp (☎ *081/ 707–5199*).

CONTACTS Blunden Coach Tours. ✉ *Gqeberha* ☎ *041/451–4803* ⊕ *www.blunden. co.za.*

TOURS
★ **Alan Tours**
GUIDED TOURS | In the business for years, Alan Fogarty's tours of Gqeberha, Addo, and more distant corners of the Eastern Cape come with heaps of valuable insight—plus a genuine passion for the

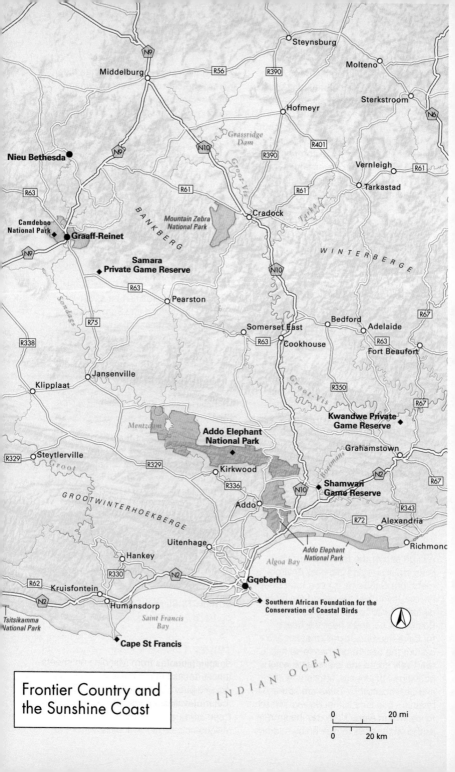

Frontier Country and
the Sunshine Coast

region's history, culture, and natural treasures. Safari-focused tours to Addo are on offer, but a real thrill for anyone wanting to take home unique memories is his "Big Seven" itinerary, rated one of the best tours in the country. "It's a wildlife experience that will knock your socks off," Alan says of the land-and-sea safari package that couples a morning spent in Algoa Bay searching for whales, dolphins (there are around 22,000 in the sheltered bay), and other ocean-going creatures; and it truly is a mindblowing marine excursion, during which you'll also see fur seals and circumnavigate St. Croix Island with its large African penguin breeding colony, and get to see a 220,000-strong gannet colony, the largest gannetry in the world. After the boat safari, the tour heads to Addo Elephant National Park for a more traditional game drive, albeit heightened by the presence of a better-than-most guide. Other tours include an excursion to Cape Recife, and Alan's "Western Country Road" tour which takes in one end of the marvelous Baviaanskloof, the surfing town of Jeffreys Bay, and a couple of flower reserves (with lunch at Van Staden's Wildflower Reserve). While touring, you also learn about pre-colonial history and discover fascinating details about the Khoi Khoi, the region's earliest human residents. You can also sign up for shark cage diving which includes a boat safari to wild-and-wonderful Bird Island, and St. Croix, too. ⊠ *Gqeberha* ☎ *072/358–4634* ⊕ *www.alantours.co.za* ✉ *Tours from R1,450 per person; "Original Big 7 Safari" from R3,850 per person.*

Raggy Charters

BOAT TOURS | **FAMILY** | For a conservation-minded sea-going adventure, set off with this boating outfit to explore St. Croix Island marine reserve where a large colony of endangered African penguins breed. Between June and early January, humpback whales—which mate and calve in Algoa Bay—can be spotted, and the boat trips will likely include sightings of all sorts of sea creatures, from dolphins to Cape gannets, terns, albatrosses, shearwaters, and skuas. They also offer shark cage diving and deep-sea fishing excursions. ⊠ *Dom Pedro Jetty, Nelson Mandela Bay Yacht Club* ✚ *Harbour entrance is at 16 Lower Valley Rd.* ☎ *073/152–2277* ⊕ *www. raggycharters.co.za.*

VISITOR INFORMATION
Gqeberha's Nelson Mandela Bay Tourism is open weekdays 8–4:30.

◉ Sights

Route 67

PUBLIC ART | Consisting of 67 public artworks by the Eastern Cape's local artists, the route symbolizes the 67 years that the late Nelson Mandela dedicated to the South African fight for freedom. The route runs from the city center to Donkin Reserve and the old lighthouse above that overlook the harbor and the ocean beyond. Here there's a large pyramid built by the city's former governor Rufane Shaw Donkin in honor of his deceased wife, Elizabeth, for whom the city—originally called Port Elizabeth—was named. Stretching from the pyramid toward a towering South African flag is a long and colorful mosaic that references various important aspects of the historic and cultural legacy of the city and the Eastern Cape. Beneath the huge flag is a life-size metal cutout of Mandela (he was taller than you might think) with his fist raised in triumph, and snaking down the steps behind him is a line of South Africans (also life-size) of all ages, colors, and creeds lining up to vote in the 1994 elections. Sixty-seven colored steps lead from this point back to the city below, and along the way you'll find a number of inspiring quotes from Mandela on sheets of metal made to look like pages ripped from a book. Combined with all the other colorful wall paintings, sculptures, and texts, the route has both revitalized and contextualized some of the previously

more run-down areas of central Gqeberha, and tells important stories about
where South Africa came from and
where it is headed. ⊠ *Donkin Reserve,
Central.*

**Southern African Foundation for the Conser-
vation of Coastal Birds** (*SANCCOB*)
WILDLIFE REFUGE | If you'd like to glimpse
penguins up close, this dedicated seabird
rehab facility at the Cape Recife Nature
Reserve offers informative small-group
tours, on the hour, from 9 am until 2 pm.
Guests learn about the habits and behav-
iors of African penguins, and watch them
waddle, hear them squawk, and—during
certain hours—see them being fed. The
tour also offers insight into the many
threats facing these endangered birds.
Be sure to schedule time to explore the
nature reserve, a coastal conservancy
with excellent bird-watching, and a
lighthouse built in 1849. ⊠ *Cape Recife
Nature Reserve, Marine Dr.* ☎ *41/583–
1830* ⊕ *www.sanccob.co.za* 🎫 *R45.*

Beaches

The beaches listed here are lined with
restaurants, shops, and coffee bars, and
there are flea markets on weekends.
Beyond Hobie Beach the seafront is still
built up with houses and apartments, but
the frenetic commercialism is missing.

Hobie Beach
BEACH | The 137-meter (450-feet) long
Shark Rock Pier is a Gqeberha landmark
and definitely worth traversing for the
view back towards Summerstrand it
affords. It also marks one end of Hobie
Beach, where sailing catamarans and jet
skis launch, and where some of the city's
best-loved annual sporting events and
festivals are held. The section of beach
nearest the pier is great for swimming
and sunbathing, and there are also rock
pools to explore; it can get very busy on
a hot summer's day. With a view of the
pier, Blue Waters Café serves very good
food and is a great spot at sunset; you

will doubtless also witness countless
joggers making use of the long promenade strip that stretch along the seafront.
There are plenty of restaurants along the
other side of the promenade, including
Ginger (offering what's considered the
city's most upmarket dining) at the Beach
Hotel; next door, the Boardwalk Casino
and Entertainment World is a major draw
for families, with places to eat, drink,
shop, play, and even spend the night.
Amenities: food and drink; lifeguards;
parking; showers; toilets. **Best for:**
swimming; sunbathing; walking. ⊠ *Hobie
Beach, Marine Dr., Summerstrand.*

Humewood Beach
BEACH | FAMILY | Humewood Beach runs
from King's Beach to Shark Rock Pier.
This beach has fine white sand and is a
great place for families, with shaded areas supplied by an overhead promenade.
A convenient parking lot is behind the
beach, and there are excellent facilities,
including picnic tables, plus lifeguards
on duty during peak times. Some grassy
areas lead into Happy Valley, but it's not
recommended that you walk into the
valley, as it's often completely deserted and you may be in danger of being
mugged. The beach slipway has a little
reef, and the water beside it is great for
snorkeling. Humewood Beach is close to
the bustling Boardwalk Hotel and all its
facilities (including a casino and mall) and
the Beach Hotel, where Ginger Restaurant is located. **Amenities:** lifeguards;
parking (free); showers; toilets. **Best for:**
snorkeling; swimming. ⊠ *Marine Dr.*

King's Beach
BEACH | FAMILY | Within the bay and
starting closest to the city center and
harbor (which is best avoided), the first
beach you come to is King's Beach, so
named because King George VI slept in
the Royal Train here during a visit to the
city before World War II. You may want
to avoid the far end of King's Beach, as
it can get pretty crowded. The beach
is one of three Blue Flag beaches in

Gqeberha (along with Hobie Beach and Humewood Beach), meaning that it has met international standards of cleanliness, safety, and facilities. It's another very family-friendly beach, too. The Macarthurs Baths pool complex is along the promenade. The Garden Court King's Beach Hotel offers rooms with views across King's Beach. **Amenities:** lifeguard; parking (free); showers; toilets. **Best for:** swimming; walking. ✉ *Kings Rd.*

McArthur Baths

BEACH | FAMILY | The section of beach near McArthur Baths is great for swimming and very popular. If you'd rather swim in flat water, head for the bath complex. Open from September through April, for a small fee you can use a range of pools, two of which are heated to a few degrees above sea temperature. There's no natural grass here, however, so you will need to rent a lounge chair to be comfortable. **Amenities:** lifeguard; showers; toilets. **Best for:** swimming. ✉ *Beach Rd.*

Pollock Beach

BEACH | FAMILY | Adjacent to the suburb of Summerstrand, Pollock Beach is one of the better swimming beaches, with a lovely small natural tidal pool. It also offers great surfing. (Generally the surfing in Gqeberha isn't too challenging, unlike at Jeffreys Bay, just over an hour's drive to the west, which has some pretty exciting waves.) The far end of Pollock Beach is best avoided, as it can get crowded with somewhat boisterous, picnicking, partying crowds. **Amenities:** food and drink; lifeguard; parking (free); toilets. **Best for:** partiers; surfing. ✉ *10th Ave., off Marine Dr.*

Sardinia Bay

BEACH | FAMILY | For a truly fantastic Gqeberha beach experience, very little can beat Sardinia Bay Beach, outside the bay and about a 20-minute drive from the main beaches. Here, miles and miles of deserted, snow-white sand are great for long walks. It's best to come on weekends, however, as during the week it can be isolated and there have been a few incidents of muggings. On weekends there are plenty of people, and you will be perfectly safe. It's also a popular beach for scuba-diving and this part of the coast has been declared a marine reserve, so no fishing is allowed. There are also fire pits so come prepared for a braai. **Amenities:** food and drink; lifeguard; parking (free); toilets. **Best for:** snorkeling; swimming; walking. ✉ *Sardinia Bay Dr.*

🍴 Restaurants

The beachfront is lined with reasonably priced hotels and restaurants, as well as a few higher-quality ones. Richmond Hill is the area to go to if you want to be able to pick from dozens of venues, many of them side-by-side, each proffering unique cuisines and varied menus.

Ginger

$$$$ | SOUTH AFRICAN | This is Gqeberha's most well-established fine-dining option, a stylish stalwart along the bustling beachfront, located in the Beach Hotel opposite Shark Rock Pier and boasting sea views. Glass doors open onto a sunny terrace, or you can sit inside at tables placed around the bar to enjoy an expansive array of contemporary dishes with local flair. **Known for:** upmarket prices; sumptuous seafood; lovely beach-facing location. [$] *Average main: R240* ✉ *The Beach Hotel, Marine Dr., Summerstrand* ☎ *041/583–1229* 🌐 *www.ginger-restaurant.co.za* 🕒 *No dinner Sun.*

★ **Muse**

$$ | CONTEMPORARY | Former hotel chefs, Allan and Simone Bezuidenhout have brought a touch of true class to Gqeberha's traditionally mediocre dining scene with this intimate, handsome, dark-hued restaurant adorned with leather seats and Allan's own artwork. The menu focuses on imaginative versions of classic dishes like a traditional lamb rump with dry ice infused with fynbos to bring the scent of the Karoo (where the lamb comes from) onto the plate, as well as beautiful pizzas, aromatic curries, light meals, and pastas. **Known for:** the caramel dessert with ganache and popcorn is a crowd-pleaser; uses only the freshest fish, and only if it's sustainable; classic dishes with an unexpected twist inspired by local ingredients. $ *Average main: R145* ⊠ *1b Stanley St., Richmond Hill, Central* ☎ *041/582–1937, 073/991–5011* ⊕ *www.muserestaurant.co.za* ⊗ *Closed Mon. and Sun.*

Hotels

★ Forest Hall Guesthouse

$ | **B&B/INN** | **FAMILY** | Located in the leafy and affluent suburb of Walmer, just a 5- to 10-minute drive from the airport, this friendly family-owned guesthouse is a charming place to pause and recuperate for a night or two before traveling on from Gqeberha. **Pros:** there's a sense of history about the place; owners are approachable and helpful; prices are very reasonable. **Cons:** aside from breakfast meals are by special request only; you might regret being this far from the beach (although it's not such a long drive); when it gets full it can be noisy and the breakfast room can feel crowded. $ *Rooms from: R1100* ⊠ *84 River Rd., Walmer* ☎ *041/581–3356* ⊕ *www. foresthall.co.za* ⇨ *17 rooms* ⊙ *Free Breakfast.*

★ Hacklewood Hill Country House

$$$$ | **B&B/INN** | For supreme comfort in a gracious setting with great historical ambience, try this inn set in English-style gardens in the leafy suburb of Walmer. **Pros:** very reasonably priced considering the museum-grade furnishings and décor; among the most beautiful guestrooms you'll ever set eyes on; excellent dining experience (with wines to match). **Cons:** staff have regrettably taken on a degree of stiff formality; you might regret not being able to walk to the beachfront; not for you if you prefer a contemporary

aesthetic. $ *Rooms from: R3560* ⊠ *152 Prospect Rd., Walmer* ☎ *041/581–1300* ⊕ *www.hacklewood.co.za* ⇨ *8 rooms* ⊙ *Free Breakfast.*

Island Vibe Harbour Masters House

$ | **HOTEL** | On a hill adjacent Fort Frederick, this historic building overlooks the harbor and adds a bit of heritage flavor to what are essentially laidback backpacker digs albeit with a twist. **Pros:** lovely views, especially from the upstairs balcony; it has a more grown-up feel than most backpackers; the heritage architecture is a bonus. **Cons:** this part of the city is not as safe as it once was, so walking around at night is a very bad idea; no meals are provided; the shared bathrooms are in a modern facility on the ground floor. $ *Rooms from: R700* ⊠ *2 Fort St., Central* ☎ *041/582–3443* ⊕ *www.islandvibe.co.za* ⇨ *8 rooms, 3 dorms* ⊙ *No Meals.*

★ Mantis No5 Boutique Art Hotel

$$$ | **HOTEL** | Established and owned by Adrian Gardiner, the founder of Shamwari Private Game Reserve, this is the most refined hotel in Gqeberha and an utterly original variation on the colonial theme offered by Hacklewood and Forest Hall, for example. **Pros:** much more affordable than hotels of this ilk would be in most other cities; perfect location if you want to stroll to the beach; elegant, onsite restaurant. **Cons:** you may find the museum-level layout a bit stiff and restricting; lacks views; some staff come off as a tad snooty. $ *Rooms from: R2540* ⊠ *5 Brighton Dr., Summerstrand* ☎ *041/502– 6000* ⊕ *www.mantiscollection.com/ hotel/mantis-no-5-boutique-art-hotel* ⇨ *7 suites* ⊙ *Free Breakfast.*

Singa Lodge

$ | **HOTEL** | Intimate, welcoming, and designed to feel like a home-away-from-home in residential Summerstrand, this is a popular pre- or post-safari stop, especially for visitors who have booked their Eastern Cape game-viewing experience at Pumba Private Game Reserve, which shares owners with Singa. **Pros:** aesthetically interesting interiors; obliging staff; homey environment. **Cons:** some might not appreciate the idiosyncratic styling; it's down-to-earth rather than slick; not for you if you prefer an anonymous hotel. [$] *Rooms from: R1450* ✉ *15 Scarborough St., Summerstrand* ☎ *041/503–8500* 🌐 *www.singalodge.com* 🛏 *12 suites* 🍴 *Free Breakfast.*

Activities

Humewood Golf Course

GOLF | Consistently ranked among the country's top courses, the challenging championship Humewood Golf Course is set in undulating dunes on the edge of Algoa Bay, making it one of South Africa's few natural links courses. The late South African golfer Bobby Locke considered it the finest course in the country and compared it favorably to the best of British links courses. At 7,030 yards and exposed to stiff sea breezes, it's not for the fainthearted. ✉ *Marine Dr., Summerstrand* ☎ *041/583–3011* 🌐 *www.humewoodgolf.co.za* 🎫 *R490 for 18 holes* ⛳ *18 holes, 7,030 yards, par 72.*

Cape St Francis

111 km (69 miles) southwest of Gqeberha (Port Elizabeth); 693 km (430 miles) east of Cape Town.

Weaving its way between beautiful nature reserves, indigenous fynbos, wetlands, plush marinas, and rolling sand dunes, Cape St Francis is a pretty beachfront eco-village at the heart of the St Francis Peninsula, which extends to the equally pristine St Francis Bay and the even more remote Oyster Bay. Hugely popular with South African tourists during the summer holiday season, it retains an air of calm and tranquility throughout the year, and there's plenty of sunshine even in the depths of winter, when the area's mostly empty. There's a historic lighthouse (the highest masonry building in southern Africa), a challenging links golf course, a handful of good restaurants and watering holes, and any number of fine accommodations options among the pretty whitewashed, thatch-roofed Cape Dutch–style beach cottages and villas that dominate the area's architecture. It's also a great destination for surfers and water-sports enthusiasts.

GETTING HERE AND AROUND

The best way to get here is to rent a car in Gqeberha and drive yourself; it's an easy and pleasant 1½-hour drive on the N2 and then the R330, and the roads are decent. There's no direct public transport between Cape St Francis and Gqeberha. There are local minibus taxis around, but they run fairly infrequently, as evinced by the many hitchhikers you'll see on the side of the road. You can also book a private shuttle from Gqeberha's airport with J-Bay Cabs. St Francis Bay is roughly 10 km (6 miles) north of Cape St Francis, and Oyster Bay is 14 km (9 miles) west of St Francis Bay on a dirt road.

For information on car rentals, see Car in Travel Smart.

Restaurants

Nevermind

$$$ | **SOUTH AFRICAN** | **FAMILY** | Next to the Seal Point Lighthouse, this restaurant, bakery, and deli has brought a sophisticated touch to the laidback holiday resort of Cape St Francis. At the helm is Wesley Randles, a celebrated Cape Town chef who moved to the Eastern Cape with his family, which has allowed him to be more adventurous with fresh seafood ingredients, bake decadent treats (like chocolate-filled doughnuts), and integrate a profound knowledge of sensual flavors with a knack for creative plating. **Known for:** crispy chokka (the local name for squid) and other seafood; beautiful baked treats; one-of-a-kind location. [$] *Average main: R200* ✉ *Seal Point Lighthouse,*

Cape St Francis ☎ 066/421–1532 🌐 sealpointlighthouse.com/restaurant/.

Hotels

Cape St Francis Resort

$$ | RESORT | FAMILY | This big, bright beachfront resort offers a wide range of accommodations, from luxury self-catering villas with direct beach access over the dunes to spic 'n' span private backpacker rooms with shared bathrooms. **Pros:** very family-friendly; great location; a wide range of activities can be organized at reception. **Cons:** it's not the quietest place with so many children about; because of the size, it can feel a little impersonal; it can get overcrowded during holidays. [$] *Rooms from: R2008* ✉ *Da Gama Way, Cape St Francis* ☎ *042/298–0054* 🌐 *www.capestfrancis.co.za* 🛏 *83 rooms, 6 villas* 🍴 *Free Breakfast.*

★ **Oyster Bay Lodge**

$$$ | B&B/INN | Set on a secluded coastal reserve that incorporates magnificent dunes, woods, river deltas, lagoons, a 3½-km (2-mile) expanse of beach, free-roaming horses, and a plethora of birdlife, Oyster Bay Lodge truly is a hidden gem that, once reached, feels like you've arrived at the ends of the earth. **Pros:** room rates are very reasonable; location, activities and food are superb; service is smooth. **Cons:** some of the standard rooms don't get a lot of daylight; it's a long drive if you want to visit Cape St Francis; not the easiest place to get to (from St Francis Bay it's gravel all the way). [$] *Rooms from: R3014* ✉ *Humansdorp* ✥ *2 km (1¼ miles) west of Oyster Bay village; take the 632 Palmietvlei exit off the N2 hwy. and follow signs to Oyster Bay Lodge for 24 km (15 miles)* ☎ *042/297–0150* 🌐 *www.oysterbaylodge.com* 🛏 *14 rooms* 🍴 *Free Breakfast.*

Addo Elephant National Park

72 km (45 miles) north of Gqeberha.

At just under 445,000 acres, Addo Elephant National Park is home to elephants, buffalo, black rhino, leopards, spotted hyena, hundreds of kudu and other antelopes, and lions.

GETTING HERE AND AROUND

The closest airport to Addo Elephant Park is Chief Dawid Stuurman International Airport (PLZ) in Gqeberha. Flights arrive daily from all of South Africa's main cities via British Airways, SA Airlink, and the budget airline FlySafair. Flights from Cape Town take roughly 1 hour and from Johannesburg 1½ hours.

Traveling by car is the easiest and best way to tour this area, as public transport is limited and unreliable. Some roads are unpaved and their conditions are highly variable. Most lodges will organize airport transfers for their guests.

For information on airlines, see Air in Travel Smart.

TOURS

Schotia Safaris

SPECIAL-INTEREST TOURS | If you're short on time or budget, Schotia offers a good value, family-run, no-frills safari experience taking place in a privately owned wildlife reserve bordering the eastern side of Addo; situated just 45 minutes from Gqeberha, it's incredibly convenient. It's also something of a sure thing: Due to its small size (4,200 acres) and the fact that it's very densely stocked (more than 2,000 animals and 40 species) you're almost guaranteed to see a wide variety of wildlife—lion, giraffes, hippos, white rhinos, crocodiles, zebras, elephants, and all kinds of buck. The popular six-hour Tooth and Claw safari starts at 2:30 pm

Addo Elephant National Park has more than 600 elephants.

and includes a game drive and a tasty, generous buffet dinner served in an attractive open-air area with roaring fires. After dinner you're taken on a short night drive back to the reception area—keep your eyes peeled for rarely-spotted nocturnal animals. Other options are to combine an Addo game drive, with lunch, and the Tooth and Claw safari, or a very long (and thrilling) day out that includes a boat safari to see Algoa Bay's marine wildlife. A half-day Sea Safari is also possible, commencing from Gqeberha's harbour. Basic accommodation is also available on the reserve. Transfers from your Gqeberha or Addo accommodation are included in all tours, apart from the half-day Sea Safari which commences from the harbor in Gqeberha. ✉ *Orlando Farm, Paterson, Addo Elephant National Park* ☎ *042/235–1436, 083/654–8511* ⊕ *www.schotiasafaris.com* ✉ *From R133.*

Sights

Addo Elephant National Park

WILDLIFE REFUGE | **FAMILY** | Smack in the middle of a citrus-growing and horse-breeding area, Addo Elephant National Park is home to more than 600 elephants not to mention plenty of buffalo (around 400 of them), black rhino, leopards, spotted hyena, hundreds of kudu and other antelopes, and lions. At present the park has just under 445,000 acres, including two islands, St Croix and Bird, which can be visited as part of tours out of Gqeberha. The most accessible parts of the park are the original, main section and the Colchester, Kabouga, Woody Cape, and Zuurberg sections.

The original section of Addo still holds most of the game and is served by Addo Main Camp. The Colchester section, in the south, which has one SANParks camp, is contiguous with the main area. The scenic Nyathi section is separated from the main section by a road and railway line. Just north of Nyathi is the mountainous Zuurberg section, which doesn't have a large variety of game but is particularly scenic, with fabulous hiking trails and horse trails, and it's where you might glimpse Cape mountain zebra, mountain reedbuck, blue duiker, red rock rabbits, and—if you are extremely fortunate—aardwolf. There are also hippos in the Sundays River, at the base of the Zuurberg range.

You can explore the park in your own vehicle, in which case you need to heed the road signs that claim "dung beetles have right of way." Addo is home to the almost-endemic and extremely rare flightless dung beetle, which can often be seen rolling its unusual incubator across the roads. Watch out for them (they're only about 2 inches long), and watch them: they're fascinating. Instead of driving you could take a night or day game drive with a park ranger in an open vehicle from the main camp. A more adventurous option is to ride a horse among the elephants. Warning: no citrus fruit may be brought into the park, as elephants find it irresistible and can smell it for miles. ⊠ *Addo Elephant National Park* ☎ *042/233–8600* ⊕ *www.addoelephant-park.com* 🎟 *R360.*

Hotels

Addo Elephant National Park Main Camp
$ | **RESORT** | **FAMILY** | One of the best SANParks rest camps, this location has a range of self-catering accommodations, such as safari tents, forest cabins, rondavels, cottages, and chalets, all of which are serviced daily. **Pros:** you can see elephants without even leaving the camp; great value; you get to enter the game area before the main gates open and go on night drives. **Cons:** can feel crowded; the restaurant's food is average at best; only basic supplies are available from the shop. $ *Rooms from: R1070* ⊠ *Addo Elephant National Park* ☎ *042/233–8600, 012/428–9111 for*

reservations, *042/233–8674 for restaurant* ⊕ *www.sanparks.org* 🎟 *60 rooms* ⎮○⎮ *No Meals.*

Camp Figtree Mountain Safari Lodge
$$$$ | **B&B/INN** | It's not within Addo Elephant National Park, but this lodge's perch on the top of a high ridge in the Zuurberg mountain range—the altitude, coupled with the vastness of the views that drop away in front of you—adds something sensational to your stay. **Pros:** wonderful meals prepared by an imaginative chef; unpretentious, warm hospitality; gorgeous drop-away mountain views from an incredible high-up location. **Cons:** younger children are not allowed to stay in the luxury tents; not for you if suffer from any height-related phobias; it's a bit of a drive to reach Addo (but worth it). $ *Rooms from: R4490* ⊠ *Addo Elephant National Park* ☎ *042/007–0239, 082/611–3603* ⊕ *www.campfigtree.com* 🎟 *13 rooms* ⎮○⎮ *Free Breakfast.*

★ Elephant House
$$$ | **B&B/INN** | It's hard to believe that what looks and feels like a 150-year-old farmstead was, in fact, purpose-built from scratch in 1998—its deep verandahs, roughly whitewashed walls, thatched roofs and a mixture of heirlooms and old prints and sepia photographs, Persian rugs, and deep, cushy sofas, all carefully assembled to make it feel like it's a generations-old family home surrounded by a magnificent jungle-garden. **Pros:** excellent proximity to the national park; intimate and homely environment with hosts who treat you like guests in their own home—staying here it feels more like an experience than simply a standardized, functional hotel stay; the owners are genuinely involved in community uplift and care about their environmental impact. **Cons:** while you're near the reserve, you're not inside it so still need to drive to see animals; also not for you if you need everything spic 'n' span and the gardens manicured; if you prefer the anonymity of a hotel, this may

not be your cup of tea. [$] *Rooms from: R2860* ✉ *Just off the R335, near Addo village, Addo Elephant National Park* ✣ *8 km (5 miles) from Addo's main entrance* ☎ *042/233–2462* 🌐 *elephanthouse.co.za* 🛏 *8 rooms, 6 cottages* 🍴 *Free Breakfast.*

★ **Gorah Elephant Camp**
$$$$ | RESORT | On a private concession within the main section of Addo, this picturesque colonial-themed camp has accommodations in spacious, luxurious safari tents with thick thatch canopies and interiors furnished in fine antiques from the colonial era. **Pros:** you get to watch animals going about their business directly from your private deck and from the main lodge; the food and service are top-notch; tents are oriented to maximize privacy. **Cons:** some might find the colonial-era throwback atmosphere a bit inappropriate; the tents can get very cold at night in winter; the tents don't have bathtubs. [$] *Rooms from: R17,290* ✉ *Addo Elephant National Park* ☎ *044/501–1111* 🌐 *gorah.hunterhotels.com* 🛏 *11 rooms* 🍴 *All-Inclusive.*

RiverBend Collection
$$$$ | ALL-INCLUSIVE | FAMILY | Situated on a 34,594-acre private concession within the Nyathi section of Addo Elephant National Park, River Bend consists of two exclusive-use houses—Peppergrove House and Long Hope Villa—and RiverBend Lodge, which has eight superb villas. **Pros:** you can see animals without even going on game drive; children are welcome, and are never put on the same safari vehicle as other guests; the food is excellent, and there's a great little spa. **Cons:** you're never quite rid of the sight of vehicles on roads in the distance; if you want a private plunge pool, you'll need to reserve the honeymoon suite; the English country decor in the public areas may not be your cup of tea. [$] *Rooms from: R21480* ✉ *Addo Elephant National Park, Addo Elephant National Park* ☎ *042/233–8000* 🌐 *www.riverbendcollection.co.za* 🛏 *8 rooms, 2 houses* 🍴 *All-Inclusive.*

Shamwari Game Reserve

72 km (45 miles) from Gqeberha.

Once barren farmland, the 62,000 acre Shamwari Private Game Reserve is a conservation triumph, home to an abundant wildlife population as well as indigenous plants.

GETTING HERE AND AROUND

The closest airport to Shamwari Game Reserve is Chief Dawid Stuurman International Airport (PLZ) in Gqeberha, about 72 km (45 miles) away.

For information on airlines, see Air in Travel Smart. For information on car rentals, see Car in Travel Smart.

Sights

Born Free Shamwari Big Cat Sanctuary
WILDLIFE REFUGE | Within Shamwari are two Born Free big cat sanctuaries, which guests have the option of visiting, usually as part of one of their games drives. Here African leopards and lions rescued from zoos, circuses, and even nightclubs around the world are allowed to roam in large enclosures for the rest of their lives, as they cannot safely be returned to the wild. Although these are interesting tourist attractions, the main purpose is educational, and about 500 local schoolchildren tour the centers every month. Their other purpose is to incentivize visitors to contribute financially; seeing the animals cut off from the wilderness they're meant to live in is quite depressing, and if you're sensitive to the plight of animals abused by humans, you might want to give the sanctuaries a skip. ✉ *Shamwari Game Reserve* 🌐 *www.bornfree.org.uk.*

★ **Shamwari Private Game Reserve**
WILDLIFE REFUGE | An easy 1½-hour drive from Gqeberha, Shamwari is, in every sense of the word, a conservation triumph. Unprofitable farmland has been turned into a successful tourist destination, wild animals have been

Once barren farmland, the 62,000-acre Shamwari Game Reserve is working to restore the property to its natural state complete with flora and fauna.

reintroduced, and alien vegetation has been eradicated. The reserve, which officially opened in 1992, is constantly being expanded and now stands at about 62,000 acres. Its mandate is to conserve not only the big impressive animals (which are abundant), but everything else: indiginous plants, buildings, history, and the culture of the area. The reserve's seven lodges are all top notch, each with a unique flavor. During the summer months (October to April), you can also enjoy a unique walking safari experience at Shamwari's Explorer Camp. ✉ *Shamwari Game Reserve* ☎ *042/203–1111* ⊕ *www.shamwari.com.*

Shamwari Wildlife Rehabilitation Centre

WILDLIFE REFUGE | Unlike the Born Free sanctuaries at Shamwari where the big cats you see are destined never to return to the wild, the animals being nurtured back to health at this center that opened at the end of 2019 will have a brighter future. Animals found in the large enclosures here have been injured or orphaned and are being prepared for a return to

the wild. Some, like meerkats, might have been born in captivity and yet will ultimately be able to fend for themselves and find a home on the reserve. The center's reception room features incredibly detailed information panels about a variety of ongoing conservation struggles and there are plenty of reminders of the epidemic of species extinction that is a direct result of human activity. As with visits to the Born Free centers, you can ask to tour the rehab center during one of your game drives. ✉ *Shamwari Game Reserve* ⊕ *www.shamwari.com.*

 Hotels

Bayethe Tented Lodge

$$$$ | RESORT | If you're yearning for the atmosphere afforded by canvas in the bush but still prefer unbridled luxury, then these air-conditioned safari "blended canvas" suites under thatch roofs are ideal. **Pros:** the king-size beds have comfortable 400-thread-count sheets; each tent has an amazing outside shower and deck; tents have fabulous bathrooms. **Cons:**

children under 12 aren't permitted; if you don't like showering outside, you'll need to specifically request one of three tents that have an indoor shower; it's slightly more rustic than the other Shamwari lodges. $ *Rooms from: R17670* ✉ *Shamwari Game Reserve* ☎ *042/203–1111* ⊕ *www.shamwari.com* 🛏 *12 rooms* ❍ *All-Inclusive.*

⭐ Eagles Crag

$$$$ | RESORT | Magnificently refurbished in 2018, this gorgeous lodge, designed to take full advantage of its lofty views, has a charming contemporary sleekness that's very different from the other Shamwari properties. **Pros:** a carefully selected choice of top local wines and spirits is included; the rooms are enormous; the food and service are excellent. **Cons:** there's always a chance that the impressive design will steal your attention from the surrounds. $ *Rooms from: R21500* ✉ *Shamwari Private Game Reserve, Shamwari Game Reserve* ☎ *042/203–1111* ⊕ *www.shamwari.com* 🛏 *9 rooms* ❍ *All-Inclusive.*

⭐ Long Lee Manor

$$$$ | RESORT | Originally built in 1910 as the manor house of one of the private farms that would later be incorporated into Shamwari, this studiously designed and richly furnished Edwardian property continues to evoke the colonial era and all the opulence that went with it, albeit now with a more contemporary twist. **Pros:** the whole place exudes considerable elegance; slick service from beginning to end; has an innovative boma and the food is exceptional. **Cons:** it's quite hotel-like, so may not be for you if you want something that feels more like a lodge or safari camp; noise from adjacent rooms can sometimes be overheard; it's one of the bigger lodges at Shamwari, so not the most intimate. $ *Rooms from: R17850* ✉ *Shamwari Game Reserve* ☎ *042/203–1111* ⊕ *www.shamwari.com* 🛏 *18 rooms* ❍ *All-Inclusive.*

Riverdene Family Lodge

$$$$ | ALL-INCLUSIVE | FAMILY | Riverdene combines the great food and service of Shamwari's other lodges with a much more child-friendly atmosphere and a rather unprecedented number of facilities designed to keep youngsters engaged and entertained, making it the ultimate safari lodgings for younger families. **Pros:** extremely friendly atmosphere; children will remember this safari for years to come; rooms even have microwaves so you can warm baby's meals and milk. **Cons:** some may not appreciate the more contemporary aesthetic; not the place for privacy or romance; all those children means it can get noisy. $ *Rooms from: R17010* ✉ *Shamwari Game Reserve* ☎ *042/203–1111* ⊕ *www.shamwari.com* 🛏 *9 rooms* ❍ *All-Inclusive.*

Sarili

$$$$ | ALL-INCLUSIVE | FAMILY | Named for a Xhosa chief and in fact pronounced *sag-ee-leh*, this five-bedroom private villa puts guests in the heart of a marvelous wilderness area where you have the run of magnificent grounds with exquisite views onto a thrilling—and vast—landscape populated by animals that regularly make an appearance. **Pros:** exquisite views; suitable for the entire family (it's also entirely fenced, so safe for children); impeccably stylish. **Cons:** no chance for interaction with other travelers; not for you if having a private staff feels intrusive; if you're traveling with friends, there may be some "debate" over who gets the best rooms. $ *Rooms from: R96000* ✉ *Shamwari Game Reserve* ☎ *042/203–1111* ⊕ *www.shamwari.com* 🛏 *5 rooms* ❍ *All-Inclusive.*

⭐ Sindile

$$$$ | ALL-INCLUSIVE | The view from Shamwari's new flagship lodge will take your breath away: Built in a more contemporary style than the older Shamwari lodges, and situated in what might just be the reserve's most perfect-for-a-lodge location, the eye is constantly drawn across the ravine, over the rolling plains, to a water hole where animals gather, and on towards distant hills marching across the horizon. **Pros:** being fenced, you can walk to your room unescorted at night; it's a smaller and more intimate lodge with an emphasis on privacy; the views are exquisite. **Cons:** for some, being fenced might be a drawback; some might find the pathways to the rooms tricky; for parents the drawback is that children under 16 aren't permitted. $ *Rooms from: R23650* ✉ *Shamwari Game Reserve* ☎ *042/203–1111* ⊕ *www.shamwari.com* 🛏 *9 rooms* 🍴 *All-Inclusive.*

Kwandwe Private Game Reserve

157 km (97 miles) northeast of Gqeberha; 38 km (24 miles) northeast of Makhanda (previously known as Grahamstown as still signposted as such).

The more than 55,000-acre Kwandwe Private Game Reserve is a conservation triumph as it's reintroduced native vegetation (eradicating alien plants) and is now home to more than 7,000 mammals, including the Big Five.

GETTING HERE AND AROUND
Kwandwe is a 30-minute drive from Makhanda, and air and road shuttles are available from Gqeberha, which is a 2-hour drive.

 Sights

★ Kwandwe Private Game Reserve
WILDLIFE REFUGE | Tucked away in the Eastern Cape, near the historic university "city" of Makhanda (formerly known as Grahamstown, and now increasingly run down), Kwandwe is a conservation triumph as more than 55,000 acres of various vegetation types and scenic diversity, including rocky outcrops, great

plains, thorn thickets, forests, desert scrub, and the Great Fish River were just ravaged farmland and goat-ridden semidesert two decades ago. Today it's home to more than 7,000 mammals, including the Big Five and the elusive black rhino, and it's likely you'll see fauna you don't always see elsewhere, such as black wildebeest, bat-eared foxes, and the endangered blue crane (*Kwandwe* means "place of the blue crane" in isiXhosa). If you spend more than a couple of nights here, you'll likely see a huge and impressive array of animals, including leopards, lions, and herds of elephants marching across the terrain. If you come in winter, you'll see one of nature's finest floral displays, when thousands of scarlet, orange, and fiery-red aloes are in bloom, attended by colorful sunbirds. The reserve also has a strong focus on community development, as evinced by the Community Centre and village within the reserve, both of which are worth a visit. ✉ *Kwandwe Private Game Reserve, Grahamstown* ☎ *046/603–3400* ⊕ *www.kwandwe.com.*

 Hotels

Aside from the four exclusive-use villas within the reserve, visitors can choose between two lodges—the classic colonial-with-an-African-twist Great Fish River Lodge or the modern-chic Ecca Lodge. Both are gorgeous, but offer very different experience thanks to their unique locations. No matter where you stay, you'll be cosseted, pampered, well fed, and taken on hugely memorable wildlife adventures. All the lodges listed here have cable TV in a communal area and massages available upon request. The child-friendly lodges have movies and games.

Ecca Lodge
$$$$ | **RESORT** | **FAMILY** | Velvet cushions and rugs that echo the African sky at dawn, rough-hewn rock walls that recall the hills that dot the reserve, and decor

that includes handwoven baskets, animal hides, and neutral shades offset by pale greens and blues, create the fresh, contemporary aesthetic of this intimate, classy lodge that caters to families with young children. **Pros:** magnificent showers, outside and indoors; superb food and an extensive self-service bar; fresh room design, with colorful, cheerful accents under a white ceiling. **Cons:** because it's family-friendly, the sounds of children may freak you out; service can be up and down; the modern design may have you longing for a more traditional aesthetic. [$] *Rooms from: R20740* ✉ *Kwandwe Private Game Reserve* ☎ *046/603–3400* 🌐 *www.kwandwe.com* 🛏 *6 suites* 🍴 *Free Breakfast* ☞ *A R400 conservation fee per person per night also applies.*

Fort House

$$$$ | HOUSE | FAMILY | Previously used exclusively by Kwandwe's owners, this well-stocked and handsomely decorated 4-bedroom house is available to rent for exclusive use by a family or group. **Pros:** you can create your own schedule; exclusive use of the 4-bedroom mansion; good chance of spotting animals from the deck, garden, or pool. **Cons:** the house lacks elevation; the study's collection of wall-mounted hunting rifles might be a turn-off for some; you might feel a bit isolated. [$] *Rooms from: R70,800* ✉ *Heatherton Towers, Fort Brown District, Kwandwe Private Game Reserve* ☎ *046/603–3400* 🌐 *www.kwandwe.com* 🛏 *4 rooms* 🍴 *All-Inclusive* ☞ *A R400 conservation fee per person per night also applies.*

★ **Great Fish River Lodge**

$$$$ | RESORT | Public areas—dining room, cozy lounges, library, and a long terrace—sprawl along one bank of the Great Fish River (one of the few rivers in the region flowing continuously, despite a prolonged drought) with floor-to-ceiling windows that bathe the interior stone walls, Persian rugs, fireplaces, deep armchairs, bookcases, and collection of old prints and photographs in clear light. **Pros:** ultrafriendly staffers go out of their way to satisfy your personal needs; spectacular river and cliff views from every room; there's an effort to serve interesting food at every meal. **Cons:** does not accommodate children under 12; avoid if an unfenced camp makes you nervous; some rooms are a distance from the main lodge (request a nearby room if need be). [$] *Rooms from: R20740* ✉ *Heatherton Towers, Fort Brown District, Kwandwe Private Game Reserve* ☎ *046/603–3400* 🌐 *www.kwandwe.com* 🛏 *9 rooms* 🍴 *All-Inclusive* ☞ *A R400 per person per night conservation fee also applies.*

Melton Manor

$$$$ | RESORT | FAMILY | Slightly bigger than Uplands Homestead, the Manor accommodates up to eight guests and offers the same superb service and exclusivity. **Pros:** creative food; you feel surrounded by wilderness; lovely service. **Cons:** as you're in your own group you miss out on the opportunity to meet other travelers; it's not quite as opulent as Fort House. [$] *Rooms from: R54180* ✉ *Heatherton Towers, Fort Brown District, Kwandwe Private Game Reserve* ☎ *046/603–3400* 🌐 *www.kwandwe.com* 🛏 *4 rooms* 🍴 *Free Breakfast* ☞ *A conservation fee of R400 per person per night also applies.*

Uplands Homestead

$$$$ | RESORT | FAMILY | If you're a small family or a bunch of friends and want to have a genuine, very exclusive, out-of-Africa experience, then stay at this restored 1905 colonial farmhouse. **Pros:** steeped in history; perfect for that special family occasion or friends' reunion; great food and service. **Cons:** not a good option if you want to meet other guests; the colonial nostalgia might be a little overwhelming for some; can only be booked for families or parties of up to six. [$] *Rooms from: R44,330* ✉ *Heatherton Towers, Fort Brown District, Kwandwe*

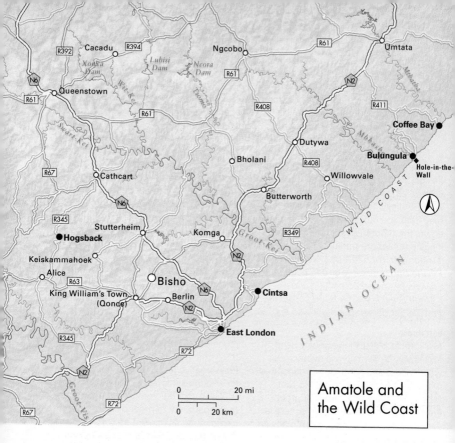

Amatole and the Wild Coast

Private Game Reserve ☎ *046/603–3400*
⊕ *www.kwandwe.com* ☾ *Closed June*
⇥ *3 rooms* ⏧ *Free Breakfast* ⌨ *A R400*
conservation fee per person per night
also applies.

Graaff-Reinet

*263 km (163 miles) northwest of
Gqeberha.*

In the Great Karoo, amid vast stretches
of semi-arid nothingness, sheep and
game ranches interrupted by monumen-
tal rock formations, sheer cliffs, and crag-
gy gorges, Graaff-Reinet is South Africa's
fourth-oldest town, enveloped by the
gorgeousness of the Camdeboo plains.
Occupying a horseshoe-shaped bend in
the Sunday's River, the town is virtually
surrounded by the Camdeboo National

Park, with the Valley of Desolation—a
geological marvel of weathered rust- and
coral-coloured dolerite pillars—one of the
highlights.

Established in 1786 and known for its
well-preserved Cape Dutch, Victorian,
and Karoo architecture, the town has
retained something of a vintage aesthetic, with wide streets and some 220
historic monuments, many restored and
serving a second life as guesthouses,
hotels, and museums. The immediacy of
the surrounding mountains and envelop-
ing Camdeboo plains adds something of
a mystical quality to the town, and there
are roads calling for exploration in almost
every direction.

Apart from an intriguing colonial history—
it was at one stage its own republic, after
declaring independence from the Cape—
the town also produced such notable

anti-apartheid heroes as Robert Sobukwe, a teacher who founded the Pan Africanist Congress; his home became a museum in 2022.

The town has in recent years also upped its game in terms of dining options, shops, and tours that take in curious attractions. Local guides can show you a host of wonders—trips to a nearby tequila farm, tastings of a local rum, and visits with local artisans and crafters. You could easily spend two or three days here before your safari at one of the nearby private game reserves (such as Samara). Another delightful outing is the 45-minute drive to the pretty Karoo hamlet of Nieu Bethesda , which generates a special kind of enchantment in a breathtakingly beautiful valley.

GETTING HERE AND AROUND

Graaff-Reinet is best reached by car; it's a 3-hour drive from Gqeberha on the R75. Having your own vehicle will enable you to explore the town (which is quite spread out) and the surrounding area including Camdeboo National Park.

That said, hotels or local tour companies such as Toerboer or Karoo Connections can arrange transfers from Gqeberha or Addo. These tour companies can also put together a tailored program of sightseeing with knowledgeable guides.

Intercape has a bus service linking Graaff-Reinet with Gqeberha, the Garden Route, and various other towns across the Eastern Cape and elsewhere. The town also has an airstrip, so you can also fly in—as some people do from Plettenberg Bay.

TOURS

Karoo Connections

PRIVATE GUIDES | With more national monuments than any other South African town, Graaff-Reinet's streets are packed with curiosities. The Graaff-Reinet Museum is a collection of four significant monuments, of which one is stately Reinet House, a Cape Dutch parsonage built in

1812. Other buildings worth noting are the Victorian pseudo-gothic style Dutch Reformed Church which resembles England's Salisbury Cathedral. To bring these and other architectural marvels to life, David McNaughton and his team from Karoo Connections serve up impressive historical tours, packed with well-researched information and a studious love of the places they take you to. They'll talk you through the museum displays and explain how and why Graaff-Reinet briefly became an independent colony. They also do tours of uMasizakhe township, where you can visit Robert Sobukwe's birthplace, experience Xhosa hospitality, and perhaps attend a gospel church service or have a beer in a shebeen-style tavern. They do transfers from Gqeberha and can show you around the Great Karoo, taking in places like Nieu Bethesda and other historic towns in the region; they have tours that include the Valley of Desolation. ⊠ *7 Church St.* ☎ *049/892–3978* ⊕ *www.facebook.com/karootours.*

★ Toerboer

SPECIAL-INTEREST TOURS | Big-bearded Dawid de Wet is full of lovely ideas—and he knows how to show visitors to Graaff-Reinet a good time. He's also passionate about the outdoors and sharing the visual splendor of the Great Karoo with his guests. His tour company, Toerboer (which literally means "Touring Farmer"), has an excellent 3-day "Craft Reinet" tour (it can be personalized to fit your time restraints) that introduces guests to a variety of artists and crafters, as well as wine and artisanal liquor (there's a tasting of Dawid's own Afrikanis rum) tastings, and a visit to a farm where agave is grown for a local tequila. The tour also goes to Nieu Bethesda where, among other places, you'll visit Two Goats, a craft brewery and coffee roastery where you can tuck into a cheese platter. On the tour, you also meet a leather maker and meet a group of women who create items by upcycling plastics. Dawid also puts together guided hikes and mountain-biking expeditions, as well as day tours of Graaff-Reinet and Nieu Bethesda. Some packages include overnight stays in one of his handsomely restored cottages, while others—mostly day hikes or cycling tours—involve staying in mobile camps where you sleep on mattresses on stretchers with bush showers and porta-potties. His "Three Peaks Challenge" is a hike that takes in three distinct Karoo peaks—Toorberg, Nardousberg, and the challenging Kompasberg. ✉ *Our Yard, 38 Noord St.* ☎ *083/538–2865* ⊕ *www.toerboer.co.za.*

Sights

Camdeboo National Park
NATIONAL PARK | Home to the Valley of Desolation, and some 43 different mammal species, this game-viewing area covers 19,000 hectares (46,950 acres). You may see the endangered Cape mountain zebra, or catch a glimpse quizzical bat-eared foxes, see klipspringers bounding over rocks, and can spend time in the Kwelimanzi hide if you're especially interested in birds. There are a few picnic areas in the park as well as some hiking trails that vary in length and difficulty.

The entire protected area can be explored by car, on foot (the Crag Lizard walking trail is just under a mile and starts at the Valley of Desolation parking lot), or even by mountain bike (cyclists from Graaff-Reinet can be seen puffing up the reserve's inclines most mornings). Summers are very hot (plan your visit in the early morning or late afternoon) and winters can be very cold. ✉ *Graaff-Reinet* ⊕ *www.sanparks.org/ parks/camdeboo/* ✉ *R150.*

Obesa Nursery
GARDEN | This astonishing cactus and succulent specialty nursery is worth getting lost in for a while, as its expansive garden wends and winds like a fantastical maze among thousands upon thousands of spiky plants and quirky sculptures and animal skulls. Johan Bouwer, a retired lawyer with eccentric tendencies and very strong, colorful opinions on just about everything (including American politics—you've been warned), started his cactus collection in about 1960. The garden, which is believed to house over 2 million plants and around 5,500 different species (some of them extremely rare) is the result of a relentless obsession and unfettered passion. ✉ *49 Murray St.* ☎ *079/496–8067* ⊕ *www.obesanursery. com* ✉ *R30* ⊘ *Closed Sat.–Sun.*

Valley of Desolation
NATURE SIGHT | Within Camdeboo National Park, these tall, slender dolerite towers stand some 150 meters (492 feet) tall, rising from the valley floor like russet-colored sentinels at attention, as they have for around 200 million years; in the background, the Sneeuberg mountain range is simply sublime. The scene is extraordinary, and it's no less mystifying any time of day, but try to time your visit for sunset as the rock towers glow crimson in the softening pink light of the Camdeboo dusk. There are a few picnic areas. ✉ *Camdeboo National Park, Off the R63 to Murraysburg* ⊹ *14 km (8.7 miles) from Graaff-Reinet; the entrance gate for the park is 5 km (3 miles) out of town* ☎ *049/892–3453* ⊕ *www.sanparks. org* ✉ *R150.*

Restaurants

De Camdeboo Restaurant
$$ | SOUTH AFRICAN | Apart from the fabulous breakfast spread that's laid out for guests staying at The Drostdy, the hotel's restaurant is also the best lunch and dinner venue in town, catering to a range of tastes and dietary preferences, not to mention offering cool dishes (like gazpacho) when it's hot under the Karoo sun, and offer lots of nourishment and warming comfort food when winter bares its teeth. From pizzas and burgers made with ground venison, to Karoo lamb curry and tasty venison loin, you

The sentinel-like rock formations in Camdeboo National Park's Valley of Desolation have been around for 200 million years.

can expect plenty of rewarding flavors. **Known for:** abundant use of local produce as well as venison and lamb; wonderful pizzas and burgers; beautiful breakfasts. [$] *Average main: R145* ✉ *Drostdy Hotel, 30 Church St.* ☎ *049/892–2161* 🌐 *www.newmarkhotels.com.*

Hello You

$$$ | **SOUTH AFRICAN** | While locals love to stop in for coffee, breakfast, and brunch, this house-converted-into-a-restaurant is also an excellent place to tuck into a selection of popular South African dishes such as *slaphakskeentjies* (boiled onions served in an egg sauce) or *mosbolletjies* (a kind of sweet dessert bread). There's also pizza, burgers, and BBQ chicken on the menu, but look out for anything featuring Karoo lamb. **Known for:** cocktails made with local rum; delicious coffee; great place to try authentic South African dishes. [$] *Average main: R185* ✉ *52 Somerset St.* 🌐 *www.facebook.com/helloyougrt* 🕒 *Closed Sun.*

🛏 Hotels

De Kothuize

$ | **HOUSE** | **FAMILY** | Most of these self-catering cottages are located on Parsonage Street, which is something of a historic hub for Graaff-Reinet and architecturally one of its best-preserved streets. **Pros:** excellent value; you're in the heart of the town's best heritage street; the cottages have been impressively restored and furnished. **Cons:** the booking office can be a bit disorganized; there is no concierge to help you navigate the town's attractions. [$] *Rooms from: R800* ✉ *4 Parsonage St.* ☎ *049/892–3469* 🌐 *www.dekothuize.co.za* 🔑 *2 rooms, 7 cottages* 🍴 *No Meals.*

★ **The Drostdy**

$$$ | **HOTEL** | While the cobblestone lanes and authentic architecture make it feel like you're in a bygone era, the Drostdy Hotel is very much a luxurious boutique property, albeit rich with history. **Pros:** unexpectedly affordable given the quality; wonderful, almost village-like

atmosphere, with lots of open-air areas; lots of diverse spaces to explore. **Cons:** you may not like the many hunting trophies in some public areas; so-called Bachelor's rooms are quite small; service, which is very friendly, can be a bit hit and miss (but you should suck it up as many staffers are students). $ *Rooms from: R2520* ✉ *30 Church St.* ⛪ *Entrance on Parliament St.* ☎ *049/892–2161, 021/427–5900 for reservations* ⊕ *www. newmarkhotels.com* ⇥ *48 rooms* ⦿ *Free Breakfast.*

Nieu Bethesda

About a 40-minute drive north of Graaff-Reinet, Nieu Bethesda is among the country's prettiest settlements, largely unspoiled and (mercifully) still bereft of tarmac, street lights, and anything vaguely resembling congestion. Home to the Owl House, where outsider artist Helen Martins created a fantastical sculpture garden, this time-warp hamlet is a quintessential Karoo *dorp* (town) where life continues much as it did many moons ago. It's still a place of slow walks, donkey cart rides, and passing time on the verandah, watching the world go by.

Set within a fertile valley enfolded by the Sneeuberg range, the town only emerged from a period of prolonged isolation a couple of decades ago—the resulting lack of development between the 1940s and 1980s has had the ironic impact of giving the town a wonderful "lost in time" atmosphere. While the holidays are busy, the remainder of the year is tranquil and almost therapeutic; people here adhere to a kind of authentic, unfettered way of life that's genuinely touched by the Karoo's special magic, or as one resident explained it, "You fall under Nieu Bethesda's spell." If you're walking about, take note of the "leiwater" furrows alongside the streets; it's a way of dispensing water from the surrounding mountains to people's gardens, which

explains why just about every garden is lush and beautiful.

For a tiny hamlet surrounded by mountains, the village has a surprising number of artists and galleries including the Owl House. There's also a brewery and coffee roasters (Two Goats), the Kitching Fossil Museum where guides will take you out into the veld to look at rocks and fossils, one of the country's best second-hand bookstores, a lovely farm stall (Tot Hier Toe Padstal), a number of really great restaurants, and even an "honesty shop" where you simply leave your cash for whatever vintage or antique item you choose. There's even a labyrinth in the garden of the Gregg Price Gallery, and a couple of old water towers have been transformed into budget accommodations. There's a tremendous sense of community and cooperation in the town, evidenced by the friendliness of the residents. Don't be surprised if you're invited to join a local event.

It's worth asking for directions to "Marette's bench," an elevated viewpoint just beyond the town's rural outskirts where you'll get a marvelous view back across the valley. Do set aside an hour or two to visit the "Stone Folk," a series of rock and wire sculptures of human figures positioned in a gorgeous rocky landscape a few kilometers outside town— it's marked on the side of the road where you just open the gate and explore. And, at some point in the evening, survey the sky. The lack of light pollution means that, if there are no clouds, the heavens will be glistening with stars.

GETTING HERE AND AROUND

If you're self-driving, there are two roads from the N9 leading to Nieu Bethesda, but only one is paved (most of the way); the signposted turn-off onto the paved road to the town is 27 km (17 miles) north of Graaff-Reinet. You'll drive on the paved road for 20 km (12 miles), and then, after a hairpin bend, follow a gravel road for 4 km (2.5 miles), keep right

The entrance to the Owl House is just as unique as the museum and its former owner, artist Helen Martins.

when the road forks and soon find yourself on Martin Street, the "main road."

Fill up with fuel before leaving Graaff-Reinet as there's no gas station in Nieu Bethesda. There aren't any ATMs or banks; a few places only accept cash. There is only one shop (Die Winkel, which literally means "The Shop") selling groceries and provisions, but you won't find luxuries such as wine on its shelves. Most residents do a weekly or monthly shop in Graaff-Reinet, grow their own, or trade among themselves.

 Sights

★ The Owl House

ART MUSEUM | This is what Nieu Bethesda is best known for, and why tourists began traveling to this small, once-forgotten hamlet in the first place. Its creator, Helen Martins, was the subject of the Athol Fugard play, *The Road to Mecca*, which was made into a film starring Kathy Bates. The story of Helen Martins, who was born in 1897 and died

in 1976, has been extensively elaborated upon, and the truth may never be known. Whether she was mad with grief, a visionary, or a mystic genius, the reclusive Martins externalized her loneliness by spending the last 30 years of her life (she eventually committed suicide) transforming her home into a jewel-box with bits of mirror and colorful crushed glass all designed to beautifully reflect the candlelight. Her wondrous vision then spread into her backyard, where she and her assistant Koos Malgas spent over a decade creating the country's most famous sculpture garden, a mystical world cluttered with concrete sirens (which everyone mistakenly calls mermaids), sphinxes, serpents, glittering peacocks, camels, owls, and wise men. The figures and scenes find their inspiration in the Bible, in William Blake, in the poetry of Omar Khayyam, and also in the visions and personal obsessions of Martins herself. Her house and yard are now a gallery and museum at the heart of the village and worthy of an hour or two of your time. ⊠ *The Owl House, Martin St.*

☎ *049/841–1733* 🌐 *www.theowlhouse.co.za* 🎟 *R60; R90 combo ticket includes the Kitching Fossil Centre.*

🍴 Restaurants

★ Stirlings at the Ibis

$ | SOUTH AFRICAN | Roasted wild garlic ice cream pretty much sums up the experimental nature of the entirely new cuisine that is evolving at this low-key gourmet-with-a-difference restaurant attached to The Ibis guesthouse. Barbara Weitz has been inspired by the abundance of little-known and underhyped medicinal plants that grow wild in the Karoo, and while she makes all kinds of teas with some of what she forages in the veld and grows in her garden, she has been inspired to go one step further and create never-tried-before dishes using ingredients you will never have come across anywhere and will probably never taste again. **Known for:** unusual flavors, including many that tend towards bitter; one-of-a-kind dishes made from Karoo ingredients; the passion and creativity of the chef. [$] *Average main: R100* ✉ *The Ibis, Martin St.* ☎ *072/110–6254* 🌐 *www.theibislounge.co.za* ☞ *The tasting menu is R225 per person.*

🛏 Hotels

★ The Bethesda

$ | B&B/INN | In a small town filled with beautiful houses, this is one of the best B&Bs, each room a stunning example of Karoo-chic stylishness. **Pros:** town highlights are all within walking distance; every space is handsomely decorated and well thought out; unpretentious, despite being masterfully put together. **Cons:** you may have to put up with occasional sound of merriment from the restaurant; with only 5 rooms, it's usually full; you may find yourself unwilling to leave the premises. [$] *Rooms from: R1010* ✉ *317 Martin St., Nieu Bethesda* ☎ *082/877–8053, 082/805–2693* 🌐 *www.thebethesda.co.za* 🛏 *5 rooms* 🍽 *Free Breakfast.*

Ganora Guestfarm

$ | B&B/INN | FAMILY | Steeped in an oh-my-gosh landscape, this historic farm affords guests the opportunity to spend time really getting to know the Karoo while staying in a white-washed farm cottage or a renovated old sheep *kraal.* Spend your free time looking for Bushman rock art, swimming in crystal-clear rock pools, hiking, climbing mountains, riding mountain bikes, watching birds, and even seeing sheep being sheared. **Pros:** your host's knowledge of fossils is incredible; a chance to stay on an authentic working farm; children (and grown-ups) love getting close to the lambs. **Cons:** lunch and dinner must be booked in advance; you'll need more than a day or two to experience everything; it's not within walking distance to town. [$] *Rooms from: R1180* ✉ *Ganora Farm* ✥ *7 km (4 miles) from Nieu Bethesda* ☎ *049/841–1302* 🌐 *www.ganora.co.za* 🛏 *13 rooms* 🍽 *Free Breakfast.*

The Ibis

$ | B&B/INN | On the town's main road within walking distance to everything, The Ibis offers heartfelt hospitality in a very personal environment—plus the immediacy of the on-site restaurant, Stirlings, where one-of-a-kind dinners are served. **Pros:** heartfelt hospitality that makes you feel right at home; an authentic Nieu Bethesda home; home to one of the best dining experiences in the province. **Cons:** not for you if you prefer the spic 'n' span hotel treatment; you won't find anonymity if that's what you prefer. [$] *Rooms from: R1000* ✉ *Martin St.* ☎ *072/110–6254* 🌐 *www.theibislounge.co.za* 🛏 *3 rooms* 🍽 *Free Breakfast.*

Samara Private Game Reserve

55 km (34 miles) southeast of Graaff-Reinet; 258 km (160 miles) northeast of Gqeberha.

The 67,000-acre, malaria-free Samara Private Game Reserve encompasses 11 former farms and is home to a variety of reintroduced species, including cheetah, lion, Cape mountain zebra, white rhino, and giraffe.

GETTING HERE AND AROUND

If you're driving directly from Gqeberha to the reserve, travel towards Graaff-Reinet for 258 km (160 miles), and then turn right onto the R63 toward Pearston/Somerset East for 7 km (4 miles). Turn left onto the Petersburg gravel road and drive 23 km (14 miles) to reach Karoo Lodge.

Air charters to Samara (gravel airstrip) can be arranged on request; the lodge will also arrange transfer from Gqeberha's airport, or from Addo lodges.

Sights

Samara Private Game Reserve

WILDLIFE REFUGE | Surrounded by the melancholic beauty of the Great Karoo with its scattered *koppies* and ridges of flat-topped mountains, Samara is a 67,000-acre private game reserve tucked beneath the Sneeuberg mountain range in the fabled plains of Camdeboo National Park some 45 minutes from the historic town of Graaff-Reinet. Owners Sarah and Mark Tompkins opened the reserve in 2005 with a promise to return former farmland to its natural state—the malaria-free reserve encompasses 11 former farms and is home to a variety of reintroduced species, including cheetah, lion, Cape mountain zebra, white rhino and desert-adapted black rhino, giraffe, black wildebeest, and a variety of antelope; there are also meerkats and aardvarks. By day, it's a build-your-own-adventure of game drives, picnics atop the lofty heights of Mount Kondoa, and exploring the reserve's topographical diversity at a civilized pace. Due to the lower density of predators and the sparseness of vegetation, rangers stop the game-viewers often so that guests can experience some of their safari on foot. One of its signature experiences is the opportunity to track a telemetry-collared rehabilitated cheetah, and then get within whispering distance of her. The relatively low density of dangerous game also means this reserve is well-suited to families with children. ✉ *Petersburg Rd., off the R63 to Pearston, Graaff-Reinet* ☎ *049/940–0059, 031/262–0324* 🌐 *www.samara.co.za.*

Hotels

★ **Karoo Lodge**

$$$$ | **ALL-INCLUSIVE** | **FAMILY** | From the moment you reach this lovingly restored, 19th-century, green-roofed farmhouse set among purple mountains, 800-year-old trees, and rolling plains where cheetahs, rhinos, and giraffes roam, you'll forget another more stressful world even existed. **Pros:** great for families; the setting possesses a mesmerizing beauty; wonderfully exclusive and yet full of personality. **Cons:** the colonial decadence might not suit everyone; farmstead rooms don't provide quite such a magical experience as the free-standing cottages; not for you if you're fearful of being surrounded by vast empty space. [$] *Rooms from: R13,650* ✉ *Samara Private Game Reserve, Petersburg Rd., off the R63 to Pearston, Graaff-Reinet* ☎ *049/940–0059, 031/262–0324 for reservationa* 🌐 *www.samara.co.za* 🛏 *9 rooms* 🍴 *All-Inclusive* ☞ *R315 conservation fee per person per night is additional.*

The Manor

$$$$ | **ALL-INCLUSIVE** | If you're looking for
the perfect place to share a safari with
a group of people, this is a fabulous
option—although suites can also be
rented individually. **Pros:** exquisite meals,
served either in the villa, or occasionally
out in the bush; brings a contemporary,
Afro-chic design twist to the safari lodge
design game; staff are extremely attentive. **Cons:** the contemporary decor touches may not be to your taste; although
more exclusive, there's less chance to
hear the game-viewing experiences of
others guests.; you miss out on the more
sociable atmosphere of Karoo Lodge.
$ *Rooms from: R16,800* ⊠ *Samara
Private Game Reserve, Petersburg Rd.,
off the R63 to Pearston, Graaff-Reinet*
☎ *049/940–0059, 031/262–0324 for
reservations* ⊕ *www.samara.co.za* 🛏 *4
rooms* ◎ *All-Inclusive* ☞ *R315 conservation fee per person per night additional
cost.*

East London

*285 km (177 miles) east of Gqeberha;
150 km (93 miles) east of Makhanda
(Grahamstown).*

The gateway to both the Wild Coast and
the Amatole region, East London was
built around the mouth of the Buffalo
River, which forms South Africa's only
river port. Although fairly urban, East
London is still close to the rural heart-
land, so it retains a pleasantly small-town
air. There's a great museum here, and you
can take a half-day city tour, an escorted
visit to a local township, or a full-day tour
of a rural village. Note that, although the
beaches on the outskirts of the city are
wonderful, those close to the central
business district are crowded and not
very pleasant.

GETTING HERE AND AROUND
East London's King Phalo Airport has
all the expected facilities. For a transfer
to your hotel or further afield, contact
super-reliable Velile Ndlumbini of Imonti
Tours.

Intercape has pretty reliable and reasonably priced bus services from the country's major cities, including Johannesburg
and Cape Town, but the distances are
long and the buses not especially comfortable. All the buses stop and depart
from the coach terminal in town.

*For information on buses, see Bus in
Travel Smart.*

It's easiest and best to tour this region
by car. The major rental agencies have
offices at East London's airport and in
the city's downtown. One-way rentals
are available. Roads are wide, often dual
lane, and well maintained. Northeast of
East London there are long sections of
road that are relatively broad and well
maintained, but they are all unfenced—
meaning livestock can wander onto the
road—and most stretches have potholes.

*For information on car rentals, see Car in
Travel Smart.*

TOURS
Imonti Tours

GUIDED TOURS | Based in East London,
Imonti Tours runs a wide variety of
immersive and inventive tours that range
from three- to four-hour experiences in
a local township to multi-day cultural
trips that take in a variety of historical-
ly-significant destinations that you might
have otherwise missed. On a township
tour, you will visit a *sangoma* (traditional healer) and a local shebeen where
you can enjoy a *braai* (barbecue) lunch,
have drinks with residents and listen to
live jazz. On Sundays, the tour includes
a church visit. A tour of a rural Xhosa
village takes the whole day. Imonti's
full-day Nelson Mandela Early Childhood
Tour takes in Mandela's childhood home
in Qunu (which is also where he lived

his final years), as well as Mvezo and Mqhekezweni, both significant places from his youth, and also takes you to the Nelson Mandela Museum near Mthatha, all the while taking in some beautiful Transkei scenery. It's a full 10-hour tour that includes lunch. There are tours that show you around East London, and one that curates a number of sites related to iconic figures from the anti-apartheid "struggle," and there's a fantastic 6-day tour of the Wild Coast during which you'll learn heaps about traditional Xhosa culture. ⊠ *9 Chamberlain Rd., Office 34D Tecoma Arcade, East London* ☎ *083/487–8975, 043/721–2082* ⊕ *www.imontitours. co.za.*

VISITOR INFORMATION
Tourism Buffalo City, in East London, is open weekdays 8–4:30.

CONTACTS Buffalo City Tourism. ⊠ *Orient Beach Pools Complex, Lower Esplanade St., East London* ☎ *043/705–3556, 043/721–1007, 043/642–1215* ⊕ *www. buffalocitytourism.co.za.*

 Sights

East London Museum
SCIENCE MUSEUM | FAMILY | There's definitely something fishy going on at the East London Museum. In addition to a whole section on the discovery of the coelacanth, the museum has a large display of preserved fish, including an enormous manta ray. For a different kind of fishy, check out what is claimed to be the world's only surviving dodo egg. Probably the most worthwhile exhibit, though, is the extensive beadwork collection; it's culturally interesting and just plain beautiful. ⊠ *319 Oxford St., Southernwood, East London* ☎ *043/743–0686* ⊕ *www.elmuseum.za.org* 🎫 *R25 adults, R15 children* 🕒 *Closed weekends* ☞ *Also open on 1st and 3rd Sat. of each month, until 1pm.*

Steve Biko Centre
HISTORY MUSEUM | The state-of-the-art heritage center, which opened in 2012, is in Ginsberg township in King William's Town (now officially known as Qonce), where Steve Biko grew up. It's actually about a 40-minute drive out of East London, but it's well worth a visit for anyone interested in South Africa's "struggle" history, as well as the development of its young democracy. There's a museum, an archive, a library resource center, a commemorative garden honoring human rights activists, performance and production spaces, training rooms, and a community media center. The center is also the focal point for a heritage trail that consists of various sites that pay tribute to Steve Biko, the South African activist and leading Black Consciousness Movement proponent who died in police custody in 1977 at the age of 31. Biko has often been held up as one of the greatest martyrs of the anti-apartheid movement. Imonti Tours offers a Buffalo City Heritage Tour which includes stops at the center, as well as historic sites in East London, Mdantsane, and Bisho. ⊠ *1 Zotshie St., Ginsberg, Qonce, King William's Town* ☎ *043/605–6700* ⊕ *www. sbf.org.za* 🎫 *Free* 🕒 *Closed Sun.*

 Beaches

Gonubie Beach
BEACH | FAMILY | Gonubie Beach is at the mouth of the Gonubie River, about half an hour northeast of the city. The riverbank is covered in dense forest, with giant *strelitzias* (wild banana trees) growing right to the water's edge. A lovely white sandy beach, tidal pools, and a 500-yard-long wooden walkway make this a fantastically user-friendly beach. It's also a good place to watch whales and dolphins, and compared to some of the more central beaches it's pretty quiet. There are picnic tables, fire pits, and a playground. Gonubie is ultimately not just a beach destination, but quite likely the

closest to downtown East London you should consider staying. **Amenities:** food and drink; lifeguard; parking (free); showers; toilets. **Best for:** sunset; swimming; walking. ⊠ *Riverside Rd., Gonubie.*

Nahoon Beach

BEACH | FAMILY | Nahoon Beach, at the mouth of the Nahoon River, is about a 10-minute drive from the city. There's some fantastic surf—but only for people who know what they're doing. It's also just a beautiful beach for sunbathing, watching surfers, and evening walks, and the lagoon is good for swimming and snorkeling. The walk from the parking lot to the beach takes you through a beautiful forest, which helps make the beach feel secluded despite its proximity to the city. There are picnic tables, fire pits, and a playground, making a perfect spot for a braai. Nearby, The Beach Break cafe sells wonderful coffee and breakfasts and all kinds of scrumptious wraps, burgers, toasted sandwiches (or sarnies, as they call them here), and excellent cakes. It's a very pleasant spot pre- or post-beach. **Amenities:** food and drink; lifeguards; parking (free); toilets. **Best for:** sunsets; surfing; walking. ⊠ *Beach Rd., Nahoon.*

🍽 Restaurants

Sanook Cafe

$$ | INTERNATIONAL | Constantly busy and bustling thanks to its simple formula of good, well-presented gourmet burgers and thin-crust pizzas topped with only the freshest ingredients, combined with sharp but always friendly service. The decor and layout of the place are equally simple and effective, with heavy wooden tables and exposed brick walls and pillars, and lots of air and light, despite the tightness of the space. **Known for:** central location; excellent burgers; lively atmosphere. $ *Average main: R125* ⊠ *11 Chamberlain Rd., Berea, East London* ☎ *043/721–3215* ⊕ *www.sanook.co.za* ☻ *Closed Sun.*

Sanook Eatery

$$ | INTERNATIONAL | The creators of what was East London's first discernibly "trendy" eating spot (Sanook Cafe), have added a few new venues to their small empire including Sanook Eatery. Situated a way out of the maelstrom of the city, you can breathe a bit easier while you tuck into the usual selection of excellent pizzas, gourmet burgers, and Buddha bowls, or summon something more sophisticated such as dukkah-crusted fillet, a stack of ostrich, or a marvelous sirloin steak rubbed with traditional biltong spice. **Known for:** delicious breakfasts; next-level burgers and pizzas; marvelous sirloin steak. $ *Average main: R120* ⊠ *13A Beacon Bay Crossing, Bonza Bay Rd., Beacon Bay, East London* ☎ *043/748–2494* ⊕ *www.sanook.co.za* ☻ *Closed Sun.*

🛏 Hotels

Driftwood Studios

$ | HOUSE | Established as an extension of a private home and set up as an artists retreat, this small family-run spot has three overnight options—a bedroom in the main house under the kitchen; a beautiful self-catering treehouse in the forest; or a two-bedroom cottage with its own kitchen. **Pros:** beautiful and artfully created rooms, surrounded by nature; remote and far from the bustle of any urban activity; easy access to the beach. **Cons:** not like a traditional hotel, if that's what you prefer; it's far from the city (if that's what you crave); there are free-roaming chickens on the property. $ *Rooms from: R960* ⊠ *26 Rainbow Valley Complex, Kwelera, East London* ☎ *043/737–4431, 083/479–2750* ⊕ *www.driftwoodstudios.co.za* 🛏 *3 rooms* � *No Meals.*

The Edge Boutique Bed & Breakfast

$$ | B&B/INN | East London's most sophisticated guesthouse benefits tremendously from its location—not only is it in the best suburb, far from the hectic buzz of

the city but it occupies a beautiful position with a high vantage over the lovely Gonubie River. **Pros:** one of the rooms has the biggest bathroom you'll ever lay eyes on; the best rooms are huge and come with lovely river views; there's a gorgeous wine cellar in the basement. **Cons:** not all rooms have river views; only breakfast is served; avoid rooms 1 and 2 which look onto the neighbours who can be noisy. $ *Rooms from: R1500* ✉ *1 Smith St., Gonubie* ☎ *043/740–3515, 076/300–3434* ⊕ *www.edgebb.co.za* ↻ *7 rooms* ⦿ *Free Breakfast.*

Mpongo River Lodge
$$ | **B&B/INN** | **FAMILY** | It might not technically be *in*East London, but this old-fashioned lodge in the heart of a small game reserve beyond the outskirts of one of the city's rural suburbs benefits from being far from the maelstrom and surrounded by nature. **Pros:** friendly staffers and laidback atmosphere; lush setting, with (harmless) animals that wander into the buildings; far from the crowds. **Cons:** a bit of a drive out of town, and the last bit of (dirt) road is badly potholed; food's okay but not marvelous; some may find the old-school safari lodge décor a bit dated. $ *Rooms from: R1560* ✉ *Premier Resort Mpongo Private Game Reserve, N6 National Road, Macleantown District, East London* ⊕ *35 km (22 miles) from East London* ☎ *043/742–9000* ⊕ *www. premierhotels.co.za/hotels/eastern-cape/ east-london/mpongo-private-game-reserve/mpongo-river-lodge/* ↻ *11 rooms, 3 chalets* ⦿ *Free Breakfast.*

Cintsa

40 km (25 miles) northeast of East London.

This lovely, quiet little seaside town a half-hour drive from East London is a winner. A nice long beach, pretty rock pools, and a beautiful lagoon on which to paddle make it a coastal paradise. Not

much happens here, which is its main attraction. The town—if it can be called a town—is divided by the river mouth into an eastern and a western side. It's a drive of about 10 km (6 miles) between them, although you can walk across the river at low tide (most of the time). The town has a couple of restaurants and small shops, plus a variety of accommodations to suit most tastes.

GETTING HERE AND AROUND
It's best to tour this area by car, and the road from East London to Cintsa is paved and in decent condition. Intercape buses go as far as East London on the coast but don't continue via Cintsa.

Hotels

Buccaneers Lodge and Backpackers
$ | **RESORT** | Half hostel, half B&B, this very casual establishment is a shirts-and-shoes-optional sort of place, and can get quite lively. **Pros:** you can mix restaurant meals with self-catering; has an airport shuttle; sociable environment. **Cons:** it can be noisy; cheaper accommodations are a little basic; it can feel cut off from Cintsa's village hub. $ *Rooms from: R550* ✉ *Cintsa West, Cintsa* ⊕ *From the N2 toward Durban, follow signs for Wild Coast and Jikileza, take the Cintsa West turnoff and follow signs for the lodge on the left* ☎ *043/734–3012* ⊕ *www.cintsa. com* ↻ *26 rooms* ⦿ *No Meals.*

★ Prana Lodge
$$$$ | **RESORT** | With seven luxury suites tucked away inside a thick, lush indigenous dune forest (plus one on a dune with magnificent views), this exclusive hideaway was Cintsa's first and best luxury offering—you'll find few better spots in which to unwind anywhere on the Wild Coast. **Pros:** the lodge is a romantic retreat; fantastic relaxation and wellness location; the setting will restore and energize you. **Cons:** can feel a bit cut off from Cintsa's village and from the beach, too; only one of the suites have sea

views; there's a bit of a walk between suites and public areas. $ *Rooms from: R6600* ✉ *Chintsa Dr., Chintsa East* ☎ *043/704–5100* 🌐 *www.pranalodge.co.za* *8 suites* 🍽 *Free Breakfast.*

Hogsback

139 km (87 miles) northwest of East London; 170 km (105 miles) northwest of Cintsa.

This peaceful and picturesque village is the perfect place from which to embark on some of South Africa's best hiking trails and experience a number of its finest waterfalls and oldest Afro-montane forests. Hogsback allegedly takes its name from the shape of the three striking peaks that overlook the village, referred to as the Three Hogs. One of the village's earliest inhabitants was a gardener from Oxford by the name of Thomas Summerton, who set about trying to re-create the English countryside in his new homeland; he's responsible for many of the pretty gardens, apple orchards, and tree-lined avenues that give the village its distinctly rural English feel. Today, Hogsback has become a mecca for artists and artisans, as well as a few other endangered species. The village has long been associated with J. R. R. Tolkien's *Lord of the Rings,* though there is nothing to actually prove this connection. But spend some time in this magical place and it's not hard to see why the rumors might have gained so much credence.

GETTING HERE AND AROUND

As is the case throughout most of Amatole, it's best to tour this area by car, and the roads to and from East London (2 hours) and Cintsa (2½ hours) are pretty good for the most part, aside from the occasional pothole. Once you're in the village itself, most of the points of interest are within walking distance of the accommodations.

Restaurants

Happy Hogs
$ | **INTERNATIONAL** | With huge portions of delicious food made with extra-large servings of love, Hogsback's old faithful is located in heart of the town's main drag. The restaurant got a new injection of energy in 2021, and locals and visitors continue to come for the great-value menu which features something to satisfy every possible taste, especially the popular Sunday lunchtime roasts. **Known for:** excellent value and large portions; Sunday roasts; varied selection for all tastes. $ *Average main: R100* ✉ *Main Rd., Hogsback* ☎ *083/275–0030* ⊙ *Closed Tues.*

★ **The Touraco Table**
$$ | **INTERNATIONAL** | Laurent Chauvet and his partner Angus Park created one of the village's finest eateries (It's BYOB) as an extension of their home. Always authentic and always executed with great care, Laurent's impeccable cooking features the best possible ingredients to create an amazing internationally-inspired meal from the delicious soup course right through to the homemade ice creams and slightly legendary baked Alaska. **Known for:** a constantly changing menu; authentic world cuisine; charming, art-filled dining room. $ *Average main: R150* ✉ *Touraco, 15 Summerton Dr., Hogsback* ☎ *083/568–8271 Laurent, 082/923–6053 Angus* 🌐 *www.touraco-hogsback.co.za* ⊙ *Closed Mon.–Thurs. No lunch.*

Hotels

★ **The Edge Mountain Retreat**
$ | **B&B/INN** | **FAMILY** | This property boasts some of the best views in Hogsback, as well as 15 acres of handsome gardens (in which there's also one of South Africa's best labyrinths), a range of self-catering cottages that are perfect for families or groups—some are perched right on the cliff's edge and perfect for romance-seeking couples—and 10

The Food Chain Up Close 🍴

Hailed by locals as "the greatest shoal on Earth," the sardine run is, in terms of biomass, the world's largest animal migration. Cold water traveling up the coast moves closer to shore and brings with it untold millions of sardines (actually pilchards). These tiny fish are, of course, highly edible, so they have quite a following. Cape gannets, Cape fur seals, common and bottlenose dolphins, sharks, and Bryde's whales all follow this movable feast. The run coincides with the northern migration of the humpback whales, so the sea is teeming with life. Local fishing folk revel in the huge catches to be had simply by wading into the shallows with makeshift nets, and sightseers can watch for the bubbling water and attendant cloud of seabirds that signal shoals moving past.

There are boat trips aplenty to take you out for a closer look, but the real thrill is in diving the run. It's awesome just being amid all those fish, but you often are also among a thousand common dolphins. What everyone is really hoping for is a "baitball"—when dolphins herd a big school of sardines into a circle, keep them there by swimming around them, and pick them off at will. Sharks almost always join in, and an acrobatic seal or two might take advantage of the free lunch. Bryde's and even humpback whales have been known to take a (rather large) passing bite out of the ball, and the sight of Cape gannets from underwater as they dive-bomb the fish is memorable. African Dive Adventures (🌐 *www.afridive.com*) offers Sardine Run Packages along the Wild Coast from a seasonal base at Coffee Bay. The best time to see the run is usually between late June and late July, although there is always a small chance the entire affair will fail to materialize at all.

simple but comfortable en-suite rooms with whitewashed walls. **Pros:** lovely for families; breathtaking views; loads of space. **Cons:** don't expect snappy service as it can be a bit laid-back; it's farther than most lodgings from the village center (although this might be precisely its allure); food standards in the restaurant have declined. [$] *Rooms from: R750* ✉ *Bluff End, Hogsback* ☎ *82/603–5246* 🌐 *www.theedge-hogsback.co.za* 🛏 *26 units* 🍴 *Free Breakfast.*

Laragh-on-Hogsback

$ | HOUSE | FAMILY | Within their sprawling, handsome, tree-filled garden, not-quite-retirees Norman and Jenny Newman have created three adjoining self-catering cottages with cozy interiors. **Pros:** fabulous garden setting; lovely location in what is essentially Hogsback's "countryside"; spic 'n' span and everything's in good nick. **Cons:** there's a very slight chance you'll get lost among the trees; the upstairs loft room isn't very private; meals aren't typically part of the deal. [$] *Rooms from: R1,050* ✉ *1 Orchard La., Hogsback* ☎ *045/962–1187* 🌐 *www.laragh-on-hogsback.co.za* 🛏 *3 suites* 🍴 *No Meals.*

Bulungula

295 km (183 miles) northeast of East London.

Bulungula is a tiny community near the mouth of the Bulungula River, about a 25-km (16-mile) walk from Coffee Bay's Hole-in-the-Wall. There are no shops, no banks, and no post office. There isn't even a decent road. The one lodge is run in partnership with the local community, making it a completely different destination for adventure travelers. Bulungula is a great place to just chill out on the beach, but there are also loads of great activities—all owned and run by members of the community in conjunction with the lodge. You can choose from a horseback ride, a canoe or fishing trip, an educational walk through the bush with an herbalist, a visit to a local restaurant, or a day spent with the women of the village, learning how they live. You might learn to carry water and firewood on your head, harvest wild foods and cook them for your lunch, make mud bricks, work in the fields, or weave baskets.

This is a really worthwhile destination, although it's not for everyone. But because Bulungula is such a small, isolated community, crime is practically nonexistent and it is very safe.

GETTING HERE AND AROUND

You'll need to travel on unpaved roads to get to Bulungula. The driving time from East London is 4½ hours. The lodge will provide you with a detailed map if you're driving yourself. Your best bet is to leave your car in the secure parking provided by the lodge at a small grocery store about 1½ km (1 mile) away, from which you can walk to the lodge (downhill for 45 minutes) or be picked up. If you arrive after 5 pm, leave your vehicle at the larger grocery store 15 km (9 miles) away and arrange for a pickup, as it's not advisable to drive the dirt road in the dark. In both instances, the owners of the stores will look after your vehicles for R15 per night. The lodge also runs a shuttle service to and from the bus stop at Mthatha.

Hotels

★ Bulungula Lodge

$ | B&B/INN | This Fair Trade lodging (Bulungula's only lodge) is owned by the local community, which is not an uncommon thing on the Wild Coast, but what makes it different is that the local people are fully integrated in the running of the lodge. **Pros:** warm and friendly staff; interaction with local Xhosa people means you learn a lot about their culture; eco-friendly credentials and Fair Trade Tourism accredited. **Cons:** tricky to get to; not much privacy or solitude; accommodations are simple and low on creature comforts. [$] *Rooms from: R540* ✉ *Bulungula River Mouth, Nqileni Village, Mthatha* ☎ *047/577–8900, 083/391–5525* 🌐 *www.bulungula.com* 🛏 *10 rooms* 🍴 *No Meals.*

Coffee Bay

295 km (183 miles) northeast of East London.

The village of Coffee Bay is a bit run-down, but the beaches and the scenery are great. The surf is superb, but don't head out alone if you don't know what you're doing.

You can do a fabulous 37-km (23-mile) hike from Coffee Bay to Bulungula (or vice versa) via Hole-in-the-Wall, across the cliff tops, and along the beach. It's best to take a guide, who can cut about two or three hours from the journey by taking a shortcut through rolling hills dotted with thatched huts. Arrange a guide through Bulungula Lodge, where you should plan to overnight at the end of your hike; the lodge can transport your luggage while you walk.

Nelson Mandela Museum

The Nelson Mandela Museum (⊕ www.nelsonmandelamuseum.org.za) was built in honor of the great freedom fighter and statesman who called parts of the Eastern Cape home for much of his life. The museum comprises three sections: the Bhunga Building in Mthatha; the Nelson Mandela Youth and Heritage Centre in Qunu where he spent his childhood and later life; and an open-air museum at Mvezo, where he was born.

The museum in Mthatha has exhibits that trace the political and personal journey of this beloved politician, some of which is told in his own words from his biography *A Long Walk to Freedom*.

The center in Qunu, the area where Mandela spent part of his childhood and the years prior to his death, is a beautifully designed building that combines natural stone and unfinished wattle branches to create an interesting pattern of light and shade that complements the black-and-white photographs documenting Mandela's early life and his period of activism and incarceration. There's also a reconstruction of his prison cell on Robben Island, and you can take a short walk to a smooth rock face that Mandela and his young friends used to use as a slide, and maybe even have a go at it yourself.

Mvezo was the birthplace of Mandela. Although the foundations of the house in which Mandela was born are visible and there is a small open-air museum, Mvezo is more a place of pilgrimage than a museum (since there isn't very much to see here). It's best to visit Mvezo as part of a tour—both because it's hard to find and because you'll get much more out of it with a knowledgeable guide—which you can arrange through the museum, or with Imonti Tours.

8

The Eastern Cape COFFEE BAY

GETTING HERE AND AROUND

Coffee Bay is about 4 hours from East London. The Coffee Shack will pick guests up from the Shell Ultra City just outside the crime-infested city of Mthatha. Avoid any temptation to travel via Mthatha.

If you are driving, take the N2 to Viedgesville (about 20 km [12 miles] south of Mthatha) and then follow signs for Coffee Bay road. The coastal road is paved, but there are lots of potholes, and you're advised to travel only during daylight.

Coffee Bay itself is small, so you can walk to most places or take local minibus taxis to get around.

Sights

Hole-in-the-Wall

NATURE SIGHT | What makes Coffee Bay stand out from all the other lovely destinations is its proximity—only 9 km (5½ miles)—to the spectacular Hole-in-the-Wall, a natural sea arch through a solid rock island. You can go here on a rather adventurous road from Coffee Bay, and it's included on almost any tour of the Wild Coast. The Xhosa name, Esikaleni, means "place of the water people," and it is believed to be a gateway to the world of the ancestors. If you try swimming through it in rough seas, it certainly will be, but some intrepid souls have made it on calm (very calm) days. ⊠ *Coffee Bay* ✛ *About 9 km (5½ miles) south of Coffee Bay along a coastal path.*

Hotels

Coffee Shack

$ | **B&B/INN** | The main (but certainly not the only) attraction of this vibey beach-side backpackers' lodge are the surfing lessons; book pretty far ahead to secure rooms with private bathrooms, although the shared facilities are pretty decent, with quaint, artistic touches. **Pros:** dinner is free on Sunday night, and there's a free supply of oysters and mussels if the ocean allows; private rooms are situated on the quieter part of the lodge, designated "Beach Side"; stay for four nights and get the fifth free. **Cons:** meals are not included in the rate; you need to book far in advance; the party atmosphere can get wild and noisy. [$] *Rooms from: R480* ✉ *Coffee Bay, Mqanduli, Coffee Bay* ☎ *047/575–2048* 🌐 *www.coffeeshack.co.za* 🛏 *9 rooms* 🍴 *No Meals.*

Ocean View Hotel

$$ | **HOTEL** | **FAMILY** | This old Wild Coast hotel is light and bright, with white walls and blue fabrics with marine motifs. **Pros:** it's close to the beach and it's child-friendly; the best rooms have sea views and have been spruced up; there are plenty of adventure activities to participate in. **Cons:** service isn't always the friendliest; it's a family resort, and children are often left to their own devices; rooms are a bit basic, and the cheapest rooms have no view. [$] *Rooms from: R2100* ✉ *Main Rd, Coffee Bay* ☎ *047/575–2005, 047/575–2006* 🌐 *www.oceanview.co.za* 🛏 *30 rooms* 🍴 *Free Breakfast* ☞ *Rate includes dinner.*

Swell Eco Lodge

$ | **MOTEL** | About an hour north of Coffee Bay, thatched-roofed, eco-friendly huts designed after Xhosa rondavels hug the Wild Coast. **Pros:** a place to unplug and unwind; whale spotting from your window; pickup and drop off transfers available. **Cons:** no meals provided; peace and tranquility might not be for everyone; getting to the lodge is difficult via a gravel road. [$] *Rooms from: R1000* ✉ *Mdumbi, Coffee Bay* ✣ *an hour north of Coffee Bay via* 🌐 *www.swellecolodge.com/* 🛏 *9 huts* 🍴 *No Meals.*

Chapter 9

DURBAN AND KWAZULU-NATAL

Updated by
Melanie van Zyl

 Sights
★★★★★

 Restaurants
★★★★★

 Hotels
★★★★☆

 Shopping
★★★★☆

 Nightlife
★★★☆☆

WELCOME TO DURBAN AND KWAZULU-NATAL

TOP REASONS TO GO

★ **Beautiful Beaches:** Durban has some of the world's safest and most beautiful beaches, which extend all the way up the Dolphin (north) Coast, as well as south down the Sapphire Coast, the Hibiscus Coast, and into the Eastern Cape.

★ **Reliving History:** Explore the city's museums or go farther afield to the battlefields of the Anglo-Zulu and Anglo-Boer wars, making sure you visit the legendary sites of Isandlwana, Rorke's Drift, and Blood River.

★ **Game-Viewing:** Although smaller than Kruger, the easily accessible Hluhluwe-iMfolozi Park, Mkuze, Phinda, and Pongola game reserves have the Big Five, and more.

★ **Amazing Natural Wonders:** KZN has two World Heritage Sites—the uKhahlamba-Drakensberg and iSimangaliso Wetland Park—as well as numerous game reserves.

★ **A Vibrant City:** Durban, Africa's busiest port, has a distinct feel, flavored by its diverse populations.

Hugging the country's east coast, Durban's amount of sunshine has earned the city the nickname "South Africa's playground." Head inland to the KwaZulu-Natal Midlands and the dramatic Drakensberg Mountains; farther north you'll find the Big Five roaming in various game reserves.

1 **Durban.**

2 **Umhlanga.**

3 **Valley of a Thousand Hills.**

4 **Dolphin Coast.**

5 **South Coast.**

6 **KwaZulu-Natal Midlands.**

7 **The Drakenberg.**

8 **Ladysmith.**

9 **Spioenkop.**

10 **Dundee.**

11 **Rorke's Drift.**

12 **Hluhluwe-iMfolozi Park.**

13 **iSimangaliso Wetland Park.**

14 **Phinda Private Game Reserve.**

15 **Thanda Private Game Reserve.**

16 **Manyoni Game Reserve.**

17 **Zimanga Private Game Reserve.**

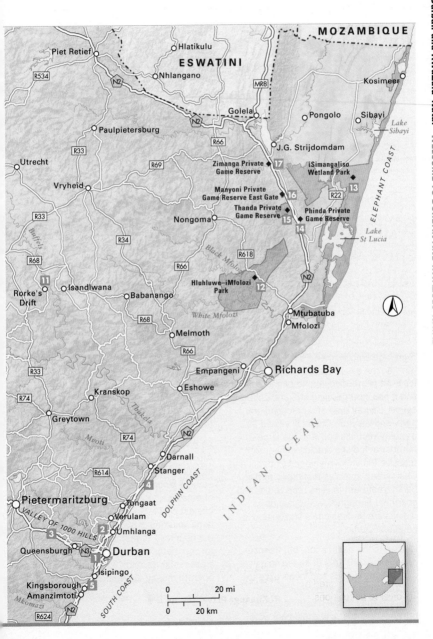

Durban has the pulse, the look, and the complex face of Africa. Then there's the summer heat, a clinging sauna that soaks you with sweat in minutes. If you wander into the Indian Quarter or drive through the Warwick Triangle—an area away from the sea around Julius Nyerere (Warwick) Avenue—the pulsating city rises up to meet you. Traditional healers closely guard animal organs for *muti* or medicine, vegetable and spice vendors crowd the sidewalks, and minibus taxis hoot incessantly as they trawl for business. It's by turns colorful, stimulating, and hypnotic.

It's a place steeped in history and culture and it has a burgeoning arts and culture scene. Gandhi lived and practiced law here, and Winston Churchill visited as a young man. It's home to the largest number of Indians outside India; the massive Indian townships of Phoenix and Chatsworth stand as testimony to the harsh treatment Indians received during apartheid, though now thousands of Indians are professionals and business-people in Durban.

Durban is the destination, but its main draw is the 320 days of sunshine a year that entices visitors and locals alike to the vast stretches of beautiful beach. The proximity to the beach has given the province's largest city a laid-back vibe that makes it a perfect vacation destination and the ideal springboard from which to visit the diverse beauty of the rest of the province of KwaZulu-Natal.

As one of the few natural harbors on Africa's east coast, Durban developed as a port city after the first European settlers landed in 1824 with the intention of establishing a trading post. It's the busiest port in South Africa, as it exports large volumes of sugar and is home to the country's largest import/export facility for the motor industry. The port also has a passenger terminal for cruise liners that operate mostly between November and May.

The city's Esplanade, known as the Golden Mile (an area much larger than the name implies as it now stretches all the way to the harbor) consists of high-rise hotels flanked by a popular promenade and beaches, with the Moses Mabhida Stadium in the background. The colonial-inspired suburbs of Berea and Morningside overlook the city and offer boutique hotels and packed restaurants.

Residential and upscale commercial development has seen coastal spots like Umhlanga to the north earn cult status with tourists, and collections of small villages along both the north and south coasts have access to pristine beaches. Add to the mix two World Heritage Sites (uKhahlamba-Drakensberg Park and iSimangaliso Wetland Park), and KwaZulu-Natal itself embodies South Africa's mantra: the world in one country. More importantly, it's truly representative of the country's diversity.

Durban's booming lifestyle scene can be enjoyed the moment you step onto the ocean-flanked Golden Mile, filled with cyclists (you can even rent a tandem bicycle), skateboarders, runners, and coffee aficionados enjoying the broad boardwalk. On weekends, locals and visitors head to the markets around the Moses Mabhida Stadium and the trendy boutiques near Station Drive Precinct.

KwaZulu-Natal—commonly referred to as KZN—is a premier vacation area for South Africans, and, despite being a comparatively small province, has the country's second-largest province population, at more than 10 million people. It's all but impossible to resist the subtropical climate and the warm waters of the Indian Ocean. In fact, the entire 480-km (300-mile) coastline, from the Wild Coast in the south to the Mozambique border in the north, is essentially one long beach, attracting hordes of swimmers, surfers, and anglers.

KwaZulu-Natal's two-part moniker is just one of the many changes introduced since the 1994 democratic elections. Previously the province was known simply as Natal (Portuguese for "Christmas"), a name bestowed by explorer Vasco da Gama, who sighted the coastline on Christmas Day in 1497. KwaZulu, "the place of the Zulu," was one of the nominally independent homelands created by the Nationalist government (1948–94), but with the arrival of democratic South Africa the two were merged to form KwaZulu-Natal. The province is now defined as the Kingdom of the Zulu, and the local Zulu population (about 2.2 million) is characterized by warm hospitality and a connection to the land of their ancestors. The Indian population—originally brought here by the British in the late 1860s as indentured laborers, working in grim conditions on the sugarcane plantations—has also made an indelible mark and now represents about 1 million of Durban's total population of 3.5 million.

MAJOR REGIONS

South Africa's third-largest city, **Durban** is southern Africa's busiest port (chiefly cargo). The city's chief appeal to tourists is its long strip of high-rise hotels and its popular promenade—known as the Esplanade or Golden Mile (though it's actually several miles long)—fronting its beaches. **Umhlanga**, to the north of Durban, is a coastal destination with access to pristine beaches.

To find beaches unmarred by commercial development, you need to travel north to the **Dolphin Coast** or south to the aptly named **South Coast**. Moving inland takes you to the **KwaZulu-Natal Midlands**, just off the N3 between Durban and Johannesburg. Here racehorse and dairy farms stud rolling green hills and lush pastures that are reminiscent of England. The Midlands Meander (an ever-growing series of routes set up by the local tourism board) is a great way to experience the area's farms, food, and crafts shops.

Zululand stretches north from the Tugela River all the way to the border of Mozambique. Prominent towns (though these are all relatively small) in this region are the industrial towns of Empangeni and Richards Bay, Eshowe, Pongola, and Ulundi. It's also a region of rolling grasslands, gorgeous beaches, and classic African bush, and it's the place Boers battled Zulus, Zulus battled Britons, and Britons battled Boers. Some of the most interesting historic sites, however, involve the battles against the Zulus. Names like **Isandlwana, Rorke's Drift,** and **Blood River** have taken their place in the roll of legendary military encounters. Other towns to explore include **Ladysmith, Spioenkop, and Dundee.**

The Battlefields (Anglo-Zulu and Anglo-Boer) are inland, to the north of the Midlands and northeast of the **Drakensberg**. The towns dotted among the Zululand battlefields tend to be a little dusty and forlorn during the dry winter months, but this is an area to visit more for its history than its scenic value.

The Elephant Coast is also referred to as Maputaland and extends from the iMfolozi River all the way north to Kosi Bay. Flanked by coastal forests, teeming with tuskers, turtles, and drenched in tradition, it's renowned for its biodiversity and natural wonders. Over the years, several rewilding projects have resulted in a glut of game reserve options that cater to Big Five seekers, avid birders, and ocean-lovers alike. This region includes the **iSimangaliso Wetland Park** (home to pristine dive sites of **Sodwana Bay, St Lucia Lake, and Mkhuze Game Reserve**), Hluhluwe-iMfolozi Game Reserve, and **Phinda, Thanda, Manyoni, and Zimanga Private Game Reserves.**

Planning

When to Go

The height of summer (December and January) brings heat, humidity, higher prices, and crowds, who pour into "Durbs," as it's fondly known, by the millions. Locals know never to brave the beach on holidays or over the Christmas season except for an hour or two from 6 am—one of the nicest times there. June and July are Durban's driest months, and although you can never predict the weather, expect warm, dry days and cool nights.

The best time to tour KwaZulu-Natal is early autumn through winter and into spring (April to October), with the coast particularly pleasant in winter—you'll see people swimming. April is a lovely time to visit the city (avoid Easter weekend if you can), with warm air and sea temperatures.

Some facilities in the Zululand game reserves close in summer because of the extreme and unpleasantly high temperatures.

FESTIVALS AND EVENTS

Ballito PRO. Around the end of June and the beginning of July, top surfers and surfing fans head to Ballito for one of the longest-running professional surfing events in the world, established in 1969. Summer editions now run too during the festive December season. ⊕ *www. theballitopro.com.*

Comrades Marathon. This is the world's oldest and largest ultra-marathon—approximately 90 km (56 miles) between Pietermaritzburg and Durban, the race route changes annually but typically takes place during winter. It's a South African institution, creating an unparalleled camaraderie between runners and streetside cheerleaders. Many runners have earned their "life" permanent race number after competing in the grueling marathon 10 times. ⊕ *www.comrades.com.*

Durban International Film Festival. Running for almost four decades, DIFF is a highlight on the KwaZulu-Natal and South African arts calendars. The largest film festival in southern Africa, it's a celebration of local, African, and international film, offering paid and free screenings plus virtual access. Many filmmakers and actors have cut their teeth here and gone on to international acclaim. ⊕ *www. durbanfilmfest.com.*

FNB Dusi Canoe Marathon. Paddlers compete in this 120-km (76-mile) kayak race between Pietermaritzburg and Durban along the Msindusi (Dusi) River. It's regarded as one of the toughest canoe events in the world and takes place over three days. The race is run by Natal Canoe Club. ⊕ *www.dusi.co.za.*

Sardine Run. Dubbed "The Greatest Shoal on Earth," the Sardine Run is regarded as one of nature's most amazing migrations. Starting along the South Coast and moving up to Durban, sardine shoals of 20–30 km (12–18 miles) are followed by some 23,000 dolphins, 500 whales, 1,000 sharks, and countless birds. The spectacle can be viewed from the beach or below the water at various dive spots. You can even grab a bucket and catch your own dinner. Ancillary events take place on land. ⊕ *www.tourismsouth-coast.co.za.*

Splashy Fen. South Africa's longest-running and most renowned annual music festival showcases the country's top bands, famous performers, and up-and-coming musicians. The outdoor event takes place every Easter long weekend on a Midlands farm in the Underberg. It's great fun and has an eclectic selection of the best local bands and a great Woodstock-esque vibe. ⊕ *www.splashyfen.co.za.*

Vodacom Durban July. South Africa's most prestigious horse race sees tens of thousands of spectators descend on Greyville Racecourse to partake in one of the year's biggest social events and to watch the ponies run. Fashionistas have a day in the sun, often in over-the-top designs as they compete for "best-dressed" prizes. ⊕ *www.vodacomdur-banjuly.co.za.*

Getting Here and Around

■ TIP→ **Street names have all been updated, but the old ones remain in brackets, as some maps and locals still refer to streets by the old names.**

AIR

Durban's King Shaka International Airport, at La Mercy on the north coast, sits about 17 km (11 miles) from Umhlanga and about 32 km (20 miles) north of Durban; it operates under the management of the Airports Company South Africa.

South African Airways (SAA) flies to Durban via Johannesburg. Domestic airlines serving Durban are SAA, BA/Comair, Kulula, Airlink, FlySafair, and Lift. The easiest way to book a ticket to or from Durban is online. Kulula and FlySafair are budget-priced airlines, so expect to buy your own snacks and drinks on board. SAA is usually the more expensive option, unless you're looking for a ticket at short notice (next day or two), when it may turn out to offer the lowest price.

The most inexpensive ground transfer into Durban and back is the Airport Shuttle Service, which costs R100 and departs every 30 to 45 minutes after incoming flights arrive and leave the city center every hour. Its drop-off points are flexible within the city and include all hotels on the North Beach and South Beach, the Central Business District, the International Convention Centre, and the Moses Mabhida Stadium. On request, the driver is likely to drop you anywhere en route. Call ahead and the bus will pick you up at any hotel in the city; there's no need to reserve for the trip into Durban. A taxi ride into Durban will cost around R320. If you plan to go farther afield, call Magic Transfers or catch a cab or an Uber that will conveniently pick you up from a demarcated area just outside the terminal building.

For airline contact information see Air in Travel Smart South Africa.

AIRPORTS Airports Company South Africa. ✉ *Durban* ☎ *032/436–6000* ⊕ *www. airports.co.za.* **King Shaka International Airport.** ✉ *King Shaka Dr., La Mercy* ☎ *032/436–6758* ⊕ *kingshakainternational.co.za.*

BUS

Translux Transfers offer long-distance bus service to cities all over South Africa from Durban. All intercity buses leave from the Durban Station on Masabalala Yengwa Avenue (N.M.R. Avenue), between Archie Gumede Road (Old Fort Road) and Sandile Thusi Road (Argyle Road). Bear in mind that you can often fly for much the same prices as traveling by bus, especially if you book well in advance or find a discount.

eThekwini Transport Authority operates three primary bus services in and around the city: Durban Transport, Mynah, and People Mover buses. All of the fleet's buses are air-conditioned and equipped with electronic ramps for wheelchair access and strollers. All bus stops are staffed by security people. Small Mynah buses are ideal for short trips within the inner city, costing a couple of rand per ride; you pay as you board and exact change isn't required. Larger, more comfortable People Mover buses make longer city trips, including to the Golden Mile, the Central Business District (aka CBD), and out to the beachfront and back; fares are roughly R6 per ride or R55 for 10 rides, and buses arrive every 15 minutes between 6:30 am and 10 pm. Durban Transport services city-to-suburb routes. If you plan to make frequent

use of public transportation, it would be worth investing in a Muvo Card. This is a single secure smartcard that can be used interchangeably across the three bus lines.

The main bus depot is on Monty Naicker Road (Pine Street) between Samora Machel (Aliwal) and Dorothy Nyembe (Gardiner) streets. Route information is also available at an information office at the corner of Samora Machel Street and Monty Naicker Road.

CONTACTS eThekwini Transport Authority. (*Durban City Transport*) ✉ *Durban* ☎ *031/311–1111* ⊕ *www.durban.gov.za.* **Muvo Card.** ✉ *Durban* ☎ *080/000–6886* ⊕ *www.muvo.co.za.*

CAR

Durban is relatively easy to navigate because the sea is a constant reference point. Downtown Durban is dominated by two parallel one-way streets, Dr. Pixley kaSeme Street (West Street) going toward the sea and Anton Lembede Street (Smith Street) going away from the sea, toward Berea and Pietermaritzburg; together they get you in and out of the city center easily. Parking downtown is a nightmare; head for an underground garage whenever you can. As with the rest of South Africa, wherever you go, self-appointed car guards will ask if they can watch your car. The going rate for a tip—if you want to give one—is R10, depending on how long you're away. The guards between North and South beaches are said to be very trustworthy. ∎TIP→ **Don't leave any belongings visible in the car or your keys with anyone.**

The M4 (Ruth First Highway), which stretches north up to the Dolphin Coast—from Umhlanga to Ballito, about 40 km (25 miles) and beyond—is a particularly pretty coastal road, offering many views of the sea through lush natural vegetation and sugarcane fields. It's much nicer than the sterile N2 highway,

Durban & KwaZulu-Natal Itineraries

2 Days: If you have just two days, spend them in Durban. Start with an early morning walk or cycle along the Golden Mile to watch the surfers before grabbing brunch at Surf Riders Cafe, popular with locals. ■TIP→ **Leave large jewelry and valuables in your hotel safe. Safety has improved dramatically but exercise caution as the sun sets—don't walk alone on poorly lit sections of the promenade.`**

Spend three or four hours on a guided walking tour of the Indian District or downtown Durban. Tours (reservations are a must—you can call to book) leave from Durban Tourism Office at the bottom of Florida Road, or book something more unusual with Durban Walking Tours. Wilson's Wharf, which overlooks the Durban harbor, and Morningside's trendy Florida Road offer great options for lunch or dinner. You can also spend the afternoon strolling around Mitchell Park, which is known for its colorful flower beds at the top of Florida Road (also be sure to visit the small zoo here). On your second day, visit the aquarium at uShaka Marine World, one of the largest and best in the world, perhaps lunching on seafood at Cargo Hold, adjacent to the shark tank or find something fancy at 9th Avenue Waterside. In the afternoon, visit the Natal Sharks Board for a show and fascinating shark dissection—yes, they actually do a dissection (Tuesday through Thursday only). You could also visit the Umgeni River Bird Park, whose live bird shows are a must-see (11 and 2 daily, except Monday).

5 Days: Spend at least one day in Durban before or after you explore KwaZulu-Natal following the Zululand and the more northern section option, which takes in the coastal strip and some of the northern game parks and private lodges. Start out with a tour of the battlefield sites of Isandlwana, Rorke's Drift, and the Talana Museum at Dundee. Afterward, travel north and take the R103 to pick up the Midlands Meander, which stretches north all the way to Mooi River, through the tranquil KZN Midlands.

If you decide to head up the north coast, spend a night at Shakaland or Rhino Ridge for their authentic overnight homestay to get the total Zulu cultural experience. Then schedule at least two days in Hluhluwe-iMfolozi Park or Phinda Private Game Reserve to see the wildlife for which these reserves are known. A trip to iSimangaliso Wetland Park to see hippos and crocodiles in the wild at St Lucia lake is another great experience.

7–10 Days: Spend a day or two exploring Durban and Umhlanga and then head up to Zululand to start your grand loop. Visit iSimangaliso Wetland Park on your way to the incredible wildlife of Hluhluwe-iMfolozi Park or Phinda Private Game Reserve. A three-day trek in the wilderness of iMfolozi could be the high point of your trip. For something more sedate, spend three days at Thonga Beach Lodge in the Maputaland Coastal Reserve, close to the Mozambique border; it's especially interesting during turtle-breeding season, November through early March. On the way back to Durban, drive through the battlefields.

which takes a parallel path slightly inland and offers no views.

Avis, Budget, Europcar, and Tempest have rental offices at the airport. Rates start at around R500 per day, including insurance and 200 km (125 miles), plus R2.10 per additional kilometer (½mile), or about R600 for the weekend. Avis offers unlimited mileage to international visitors, as long as you can produce your return ticket, international driver's license, and passport as proof.

Unless you're on a tour, it's almost impossible to see Zululand and the Battlefields without your own car. Your best bet is to rent a car in Durban and perhaps combine a trip to the battlefields with a self-driving tour of KwaZulu-Natal's game reserves. Roads are in good condition, although some of the access roads to the battlefields require more careful and slower driving, as dirt roads can be bumpy and muddy when wet.

RICKSHAW

Colorfully decorated rickshaws are unique to Durban—you won't find them in any other South African city. Though their origins lie in India, these two-seat carriages with large wheels are pulled exclusively by Zulu men dressed in feathered headgear and traditional garb. Limited to the beachfront, the rickshaw runners ply their trade all day, every day, mostly along the Golden Mile section. The going rate is about R100 per person for about 15 minutes, and R20 for a photo (don't assume you can take a picture without paying for the privilege). With numerous other modes of transport for hire here, like bicycles and go-karts, the rickshaws are at the end of their life cycle, since many consider the practice cruel.

TAXI

Taxis are metered and start at R10, with an additional R12 per kilometer (half mile); after-hours and time-based charges apply. Fares are calculated per vehicle for up to four passengers. Expect to pay about R60 from City Hall to North Beach and R400 to Durban International Airport. The most convenient taxi stands are around City Hall, in front of the beach hotels, and outside Spiga d'Oro on Florida Road in Morningside. Some taxis display a "for-hire" light, whereas others you simply hail when you can see they're empty. Major taxi companies include Eagle Taxi and U Cabs (previously Umhlanga Cabs).

There's no need to contact a taxi yourself. They will either be easy to find or your hotel or restaurant can call one for you. Otherwise, Uber and app-based taxi services have made hailing one from anywhere in the city a breeze.

CONTACTS **Eagle Taxi Cabs.** ✉ *Durban* ☎ *080/033–033, 031/337–8333* ⊕ *www. eagletaxicabs.co.za.* **U Cabs.** ✉ *Durban* ☎ *082/454–1577* ⊕ *www.ucabs.co.za.*

Beaches

The sea near Durban, unlike that around the Cape, is comfortably warm year-round: in summer the water temperature can top 27°C (80°F), whereas in winter 19°C (65°F) is considered cold. The beaches are safe, the sand is a beautiful golden color, and you'll see people swimming year-round. KwaZulu-Natal's main beaches are protected by shark nets and staffed by lifeguards, and there are usually signs giving the wind direction, water temperature, and warnings about any dangerous swimming conditions. Directly in front of uShaka Marine World, **uShaka Beach** is an attractive public beach. The **Golden Mile,** stretching from South Beach all the way to Snake Park Beach, is packed with people who enjoy the waterslides, singles' bars, and fast-food joints. A little farther north are the **Umhlanga beaches,** and on the opposite side of the bay are the less commercialized but also less accessible and safe beaches on **Durban's Bluff.**

Another pretty beach and coastal walk, just north of the **Umhlanga Lagoon,** leads to miles of near-empty beaches backed by virgin bush. You should not walk alone on deserted beaches or carry jewelry, phones, or cameras, and never walk the beaches at night. ■TIP➔ **A great way to see Durban's beaches is by bicycle.**

Hotels

Many of Durban's main hotels lie along the Golden Mile, but there are some wonderful boutique hotels and bed-and-breakfasts (especially in Berea, Morningside, and Umhlanga) that offer a more personalized experience. ■TIP➔ **Prices, especially along the coast, tend to rise with the summer heat.**

Hotel reviews have been shortened. For full information, visit Fodors.com.

Restaurants

The dining scene in Durban is small but on par with global trends, so expect to find a little of everything at a very good price. Durban offers some superb dining options, provided you eat to its strengths. Thanks to a huge Indian population, it has some of the best curry restaurants in the country, and the Italian food options are numerous at various price points.

Durbanites eat lunch and dinner relatively early because they're early risers, particularly in summer, when it's light soon after 4. They're also generally casual dressers—you'll rarely need a jacket and tie, and jeans and tanks are de rigueur. ■TIP➔ **Durban North's Mackeurtan Avenue has transformed into a restaurant strip that gives the famed Florida Road a run for its money.**

For more information on South African food, see the What to Eat and Drink feature in the Experience chapter. Restaurant reviews have been shortened. For full information, visit Fodors.com.

RESTAURANT AND HOTEL PRICES

Restaurant prices are the average cost of a main course at dinner or, if dinner is not served, at lunch. Hotel prices are the lowest cost of a standard double room in high season.

What it Costs In South African rand			
$	$$	$$$	$$$$
RESTAURANTS			
under R100	R100–R150	R151–R200	over R200
HOTELS			
under R1,500	R1,500–R2,500	R2,501–R3,500	over R3,500

Safety and Precautions

Durban has not escaped the crime evident in every South African city. Though far less prevalent nowadays, in the city center but also elsewhere, smash-and-grab thieves occasionally roam the streets, looking for bags or valuables in your car, even while you're driving, so lock any valuables in the trunk and keep your car doors locked and windows up at all times. Although there's no need to be fearful, be observant wherever you go. Hire a guide to take you around Durban, don't wander around the city center aimlessly or linger outside your hotel alone at night, and keep expensive cameras and other possessions concealed. The Durban Beachfront (with recently upgraded security features), Umhlanga, and the outlying areas are safe to explore on your own, though you'll need a taxi or car to get between them. If you plan to take a dip while you're at the beach, ask a neighboring beachgoer or lifeguard to keep an eye on your belongings, or put them in a locker—available in the vicinity of North and South beaches and on Umhlanga Main Beach.

It is essential that visitors to the northern parts of the province, including Zululand, take antimalarial drugs, particularly during the wet summer months.

Shopping

Durban offers a great array of shopping experiences, from the Beachfront, where you can buy cheap beadwork and baskets, to enormous shopping malls such as Gateway in Umhlanga. In general, bargaining is not expected, though you might try it at the Beachfront or with hawkers anywhere. Look out for goods indigenous to the province: colorful Zulu beadwork and tightly handwoven baskets.

Tours

DURBAN TOURS

★ Durban Green Corridor

ECOTOURISM | This non-profit organization offers responsible eco-tours led by passionate youngsters. Daily shuttles are great value outings to visit Durban's hidden gems and are more nature-based—think canoeing, caves, hikes, picnics, and river swims. These trips depart on specific days from the GreenHub and include transport, all entry fees, activities, and excellent local guides. ⊠ *Green Hub, Durban* ☎ *013/322–6026* ⊕ *www.durban-greencorridor.co.za/shuttlebus* 🖅 *R400* ☞ *Minimum four people.*

Durban Tourism

WALKING TOURS | Three-hour walking tours depart from the KwaMuhle Museum when booked. The Oriental Walkabout explores the Indian District, including Victoria Market and several mosques, and the Historical Walkabout covers major monuments and museums. Reservations are essential; a two-person minimum applies. Durban Tourism can also provide details of various guided township tours by local tour operators such as SBRM Tours, Jikeleza Tours & Travel, and Kude Travel & Tours, which offer an insight into the social history and modern-day

challenges of the townships. ☎ *031/322–4164, 073/549–1111 to book directly with guide* ⊕ *www.visitdurban.travel* 🖅 *R100.*

★ Durban Walking Tours

WALKING TOURS | Take in the historical sights of Durban with two energetic local ladies. A shared love of reading, research, and passion for naval history and art-deco architecture has granted them an eye for uncovering the extraordinary. Their great network of characters will unlock secrets of the city and each tour examines an area, suburb, or theme often glossed over by other operators. Walks will grant you an inside glimpse at the forgotten glamor of Morningside's mansions, see you strutting old elephant highways, or entering a secret underground tunnel at the harbor. ⊠ *City Centre* ☎ *082/777–7073* ⊕ *www.durbanwalkingtours.co.za* 🖅 *R250* ☞ *6–10 people; no children under 10.*

Isle of Capri

BOAT TOURS | This company offers sightseeing cruises around Durban Bay or out to sea, plus whale- and dolphin-watching tours and party cruises for the young at heart. Boats depart from Wilson's Wharf on Margaret Mncadi Avenue. ⊠ *14–18 Boatman's Rd., Canal Rd., Victoria Embankment* ☎ *031/305–3099, 082/851–4787* ⊕ *www.isleofcapri.co.za* 🖅 *R100.*

Ricksha Bus Tours

BUS TOURS | An inexpensive way to see the main attractions Durban has to offer is to join one of the bus tours, operated by Durban Tourism. They depart daily at 9 am and 1 pm from the North Beach Tourism Office and take 2½ to 3 hours to complete the circuit. The route includes the Beachfront, uShaka Marine World, Emmanuel Cathedral, Victoria Market, Florida Road, City Hall, KwaMuhle Museum, Mitchell Park, Moses Mabhida Stadium, Suncoast Casino, and more, and a tour guide provides commentary en route. ⊠ *Durban* ☎ *031/322–4209*

⊕ www.visitdurban.travel/destination/ricksha-bus-city-tour/ ✉ R100.

Sarie Marais Pleasure Cruises

BOAT TOURS | Trips around the bay or out to sea are offered by this company, one of the oldest in Durban. Half-hour harbor cruises run on the hour 9–4 and hour-long sea cruises run noon–3 daily. Deep-sea fishing and educational excursions are possible, or hire a boat and captain your own harbor cruise. Charters for up to 57 people are also available. ☒ Wilson's Wharf, 14–18 Boatman's Rd., Victoria Embankment ☎ 031/305–2844 ⊕ www.sariemaraiscruises.co.za ✉ Harbor cruise R80; sea cruise R130.

ZULULAND AND THE BATTLEFIELDS TOURS

The visitor information offices at Dundee's Talana Museum and in Ladysmith have lists of registered battlefield guides. Information about battlefield guides and guides specializing in authentic Zulu culture can be obtained at any information center or tourism office.

★ Battlefields Route

SELF-GUIDED TOURS | This route, with its 82 battlefields, several museums, old fortifications, and places of remembrance, has the largest concentration of important battles and war-related sites in South Africa. It's best to choose your particular area of interest and then to decide in advance the sites you would like to visit. ■ TIP→ Hire a local guide to really get the best out of your stay. Read up about the battles and sites before your trip, and keep a good road map in your vehicle. ☒ The Battlefields, Rorke's Drift ☎ 082/801–0551 ⊕ www.battlefieldsroute.co.za.

Pat Rundgren

GUIDED TOURS | An official registered guide, Pat Rundgren offers 68 battlefield tours dealing with the Anglo-Zulu and Anglo-Boer wars. He will tailor tours to your requirements, but his most popular day tour is Isandlwana and Rorke's Drift for the Zulu War, or Spioenkop/Ladysmith

for the Boer War. He has also introduced a three-day tour which includes a visit to Nambiti, a Big Five game reserve. Prices range according to length of trip and type of accommodations. Pat also offers "novelty" tours to coincide with annual reenactments of battles at Isandlwana in January and Talana in October. For those wanting to get a more active tour, there is the option to explore on a mountain bike. He operates via the Talana Museum in Dundee. ☒ Isandlwana ☎ 034/212–4560, 072/803-2885 ✉ From R1,500 for day trip (not including site entrance fee and lunch).

Visitor Information

Durban Tourism sits at the bottom of the bustling Florida Road and is the easiest, safest visitor hub for inquiries. You can find information about almost everything that's happening in the province of KwaZulu-Natal. It's open weekdays 8–4:30. There's also a satellite office, conveniently located along the Golden Mile, one of the city's premier destinations. Umhlanga Rocks Tourism is open weekdays 8:30–4:45 and Saturday 9–1, and Sapphire Coast Tourism (covering Amanzimtoti to Umkomaas) is open weekdays 8–4 and Saturday 9–2.

Battlefields Route is a good source for information on The Battlefields. For a good overview covering this area, go to Tourism KwaZulu-Natal's website.

CONTACTS Durban Tourism Beach Office. ☒ 2 K.E. Masinga Rd., Beachfront ☎ 031/322–4172 ⊕ www.visitdurban.travel. **Durban Tourism Office.** ☒ 90 Florida Rd., Durban ☎ 031/322–4164 ⊕ www.visitdurban.travel. **Sapphire Coast Tourism.** ☒ 95 Beach Rd., Amanzimtoti ☎ 031/322–2852 ⊕ www.sapphirecoasttourism.co.za. **Tourism KwaZulu-Natal.** ☒ Durban ☎ 031/366–7500 ⊕ www.zulu.org.za. **Umhlanga Tourism Info Center.** ☒ 15 Chartwell Dr., Shop 1A, Chartwell Centre, Umhlanga ☎ 031/561–4257 ⊕ www.umhlangarockstourism.co.za.

Durban

A vibrant, bustling city, it's well worth spending a day or two in Durban to get to grips with its colorful history, eye-catching heritage, and flavorful cuisines before catching some sun or a surf at the cosmopolitan beachfront. To get the most from your visit, explore the Central Business District (CBD), which includes the City Center; the Indian Quarter; the Beachfront; and Berea and Morningside. The city center is best visited on a guided walking tour to achieve full exposure to authentic town life; tours can be booked through Durban Walking Tours or Durban Tourism.

City Center

The center of the city is indicative of South Africa's developing world status and first-world leanings. Large office buildings dominate streets filled with crowded taxis and buses, but every so often you'll stumble across a building that speaks of an imperial past. It can get horribly humid from December through February, so if you visit then, avoid walking too much during the midday heat. Browse the air-conditioned museums when it's hot, and save walking outside for later in the afternoon, making sure you get to the museums and galleries before they close, around 4:30.

Sights

Durban Art Gallery
ART GALLERY | A vibrant, contemporary mix of local, southern African, and international work is presented here, though the main focus is on work from KwaZulu-Natal. Exhibits have included the cultural diversity of art and craft from KwaZulu-Natal and the rest of South Africa. Look out, too, for the traditional, patterned *hlabisa* baskets, regularly displayed at the gallery. Exhibits change every few months. ⌧ *City Hall, Anton Lembede [Smith] St. entrance, 2nd fl., City Centre* ☎ *031/311–2264* ⊕ *www. durban.gov.za/City_Services/ParksRecreation/musuems/dag/Pages/default.aspx* ⌧ *Free.*

Durban Natural Science Museum
SCIENCE MUSEUM | FAMILY | Despite its small size, this museum provides an excellent introduction to Africa's numerous wild mammals (the displays include a stuffed elephant and leopard, as well as smaller mammals like wild dogs and vervet monkeys), plants, birds, reptiles, and insects. It's a great place to bring the kids or to familiarize yourself with the local wildlife before heading up to the game parks in northern KwaZulu-Natal. At one popular gallery, the KwaNunu Insect Arcade, giant insect replicas adorn the wall; another, the bird gallery, showcases a variety of stuffed birds, including flamingos, ostriches, eagles, and penguins. Then there's the enormous Tyrannosaurus dinosaur dominating the exhibition. There are exciting, temporary art exhibitions next door. ⌧ *City Hall, 234 Anton Lembede [Smith] St., 1st fl., City Centre* ☎ *031/311–2256* ⌧ *Free* ⊘ *Closed Good Friday and Christmas Day.*

Farewell Square
PLAZA/SQUARE | In the heart of Durban, the square (also known as Luthuli Square) is a lovely shady plaza bordered by some of the city's most historic buildings, including City Hall, the Central Post Office, and the Royal Hotel. Walkways lined with stately palms and flower beds crisscross the square and lead to monuments honoring some of Natal's important historic figures. The square stands on the site of the first European encampment in Natal, established by Francis Farewell and Henry Fynn in 1824 as a trading station to purchase ivory from the Zulus. A statue representing Peace honors the Durban volunteers who died during the Second South African War (1899–1902), also known as the Boer

War or Anglo-Boer War. The Cenotaph, a large stone obelisk, commemorates the South African dead from the two world wars. In the same block is the Old Court House Museum, one of the city's oldest buildings. Apart from the historic attractions, it's an energetic, bustling part of the city center, with street stands selling inexpensive flowers, clothes, and food for the locals. You'll really feel the vibe of the city here. ⚠ **Pay attention to your valuables while walking in the square.** ✉ *Bounded by Anton Lembede [Smith], Dr. Pixley Kaseme [West], and Dorothy Nyembe [Gardiner] Sts. and the Church St. pedestrian mall, City Centre* ⊕ *www. heritagekzn.co.za.*

Florida Road
STREET | Florida Road leads a double life. By day, shoppers and tourists stroll up and down the tree-lined avenue, browsing art galleries and boutiques and indulging in lazy lunches; by night it transforms into a neon-lighted nightclub, where hordes of young and not-so-young revelers overflow from restaurants, lounges, and bars.

The thing that sets Florida Road apart is its historic character, with fine Edwardian architecture, well-preserved historic buildings, and half a dozen churches creating a timeless atmosphere that attracts the city's trendy set to meet and eat. Don't miss the hundreds of locks that adorn the fence at Mandela Legacy Park.

Since the strip is only about 0.8 km (less than ½ mile) long, you can enjoy it on foot in fine weather, but Mynah buses pass regularly, so there's transportation if you need it, and taxis are another option. The city has erected detailed and well-marked boards for walkers to navigate the city's most popular areas, including Florida Road and surrounds. ✉ *Florida Rd., City Centre.*

KwaMuhle Museum
HISTORY MUSEUM | Pronounced kwa-*moosh*-le (with a light *e*, as in *hen*), this small museum, housed in what used to be the notorious Department of Native Affairs, tells of Durban's apartheid history. During apartheid the department was responsible for administering the movement of Black people in and out of the city, dealing with the dreaded passes that Blacks had to carry at all times, and generally overseeing the oppressive laws that plagued the Black population. Ironically, the name means "place of the good one," Kwa meaning "place of" and "Muhle" meaning "good one" (after J. S. Marwick, the benevolent manager of the municipal native affairs department from 1916 to 1920). Exhibits provide the often heartbreaking background on this period through old photographs and documents, replicas of passbooks, and lifelike models of people involved in the pass system, including *shebeen* (informal bar) queens, who had to apply for permits to sell alcohol at a time of prohibition. ✉ *130 Bram Fischer [Ordnance] Rd., City Centre* ☎ *031/311–2237* ✆ *Free* ⊘ *Closed Good Friday and Christmas Day.*

Moses Mabhida Stadium
NOTABLE BUILDING | FAMILY | This handsome structure, an architectural jewel in Durban's skyline, was built for the 2010 World Cup soccer tournament and seats just under 63,000. Named after General Moses Mabhida, the secretary general of the South African Communist party, it's a busy, multiuse stadium that is busy year-round with activities for tourists. You can take a guided tour of the stadium (R60 for adults) or glide around on a Segway (R285). The People's Park is free and open to the public with rolling green lawns, a café with free Wi-Fi, and plenty of parking. Then there's also the interesting museum which traces the life of the stadium's namesake. ■ **TIP→ The vibrant I Heart Market is held here on the first Saturday of the month, a premier food and lifestyle market loved by local families and visitors.** ✉ *44 Isaiah Ntshangase Rd. [Walter Gilbert]* ☎ *031/322–9936* ⊕ *www. mmstadium.com* ✆ *Free.*

🍴 Restaurants

Big Easy Wine bar + Grill Durban by Ernie Els

$$$ | AFRICAN | Inside the dramatically revamped Hilton Hotel in Durban's CBD, this wine bar and grill is frequented by suited business folk and vacationers who choose to stay centrally. A distinctly South African menu—think smoked *snoek* (a local barracuda) and corn cakes, oxtail marrow fritters, duck curry, and a *braai* (barbecue) sharing platter—and a masterful wine list, including Ernie Els's signature wines, round the offering. **Known for:** comprehensive wine list; business traveler vibe; elegant setting. $ *Average main: R200* ✉ *12–14 Walnut Rd.* ☎ *031/336–8166* ⊕ *www.bigeasydurban.co.za.*

Roma Revolving

$$$ | ITALIAN | In business since 1973, this slowly revolving restaurant, which takes about an hour to do one full rotation, offers what has to be the most spectacular views of the city, especially the harbor. It's run by the original Italian owners, and the extensive menu runs the gamut from pasta to seafood. **Known for:** special-occasion dinners; kitschy setting; old-school vibe. $ *Average main: R190* ✉ *John Ross House, Margaret Mncadi Ave., 32nd fl., City Centre* ☎ *031/337–6707* ⊕ *www. roma.co.za* ⊘ *Closed Mon. and Tues. No lunch Mon.–Thurs. No dinner Sun.*

☕ Coffee and Quick Bites

Royal Coffee Shoppe

$ | CAFÉ | This is a popular, if old-school meeting place for daytime breaks and for pre- and post-theater crowds. Crystal chandeliers, etched glass, formally dressed staff, and live piano music in the nearby lounge at lunchtime create a rich atmosphere of old-time colonial Durban. **Known for:** tea and scones; affordable toasted sandwiches; iced coffee. $ *Average main: R80* ✉ *Royal Hotel, 267 Anton Lembede [Smith] St., City Centre* ☎ *031/333–6000* ⊕ *www.coastlands.co.za/hotels/the-royal.*

Beachfront

Of any place in Durban, the Beachfront most defines the city. Either you'll hate it for its commercial glitz, or love it for its endless activity. It extends for about 8 km (5 miles) from Durban Point, past uShaka Marine World all the way past North Beach and the Suncoast Casino to Blue Lagoon, on the southern bank of the Umgeni River. The area received a R500-million upgrade that included creating a 65-foot-wide uninterrupted promenade and an additional pedestrian walkway linking the Beachfront to the Kings Park Sports Precinct and the Moses Mabhida Stadium. There are refreshment stands and places to relax every 980 feet. The section of Beachfront between South Beach and the Suncoast Casino is particularly safe, as police patrol often. It's lovely to take a stroll along here early or late in the day when it's less busy. Walk out onto one of the many piers and watch surfers tackling Durban's famous waves.

Depending on the weather, parts of the Beachfront can be quite busy, especially on weekends. There's always something to see, even in the early mornings, when people come to surf or jog before going to work. ⚠ **Pay attention to your valuables during busy public holidays.**

👁 Sights

Suncoast Casino & Entertainment World

CASINO | Part of the rejuvenation of Durban's Golden Mile, this casino is done in the art-deco style for which Durban is famous. Colorful lights make it a nighttime landmark, but it's established itself as a daytime hot spot as well. There are deck chairs beneath umbrellas on a grassy sundeck and a pretty beach. A paved walkway dotted with benches is a pleasant place to sit and watch cyclists, inline skaters, and joggers. Fairly regularly there's a band playing directly in

Exploring the Florida Road Strip

To get the most of your visit, start in the morning at the top of the road where it meets Innes, opposite Mitchell Park, and work your way downhill. Along the way, a bevy of coffee shops beckon for a light bite and good coffee (if you need a little pick-me-up), and clothing boutique Gorgeous adds a bit of glamour.

Chic home design outlet Ceclie & Boyd's showcases opulent style in a repurposed original home, while the Elizabeth Gordon Gallery features established South African artists in mixed media *(see the Shopping section of Morningside)*. Botica's leather bags and shoes woo passersby and Smokers will want to seek out the road's high-quality tobacconists selling imported cigars and cigarettes, of which Mojo Cairo Tobacconist, a coffee and cigar lounge, is the best.

Most of the numerous restaurants remain open all day, so there's no shortage of lunch or dinner venues. As the sun goes down and Florida Road puts on its party face, restaurants begin filling up, and pubs and lounges—Dropkick Murphy's, Sinderella, and Keys on Florida—do a brisk trade. Find Italian fare at Mama Lucianna's, Spiga d'Oro, and Lupa Osteria; Afro-Portuguese at 258 Mozambique; hot and spicy food at House of Curries; proudly local fried chicken at Afro's Chicken Shop; and succulent steaks at Butcher Boys Grill.

Should you choose to stay overnight on Florida Road, Quarters on Florida or the Benjamin *(see the Hotels section of Morningside)* are two classy boutique hotels at the lower end of the road, offering some respite from the hustle and bustle.

front of the complex on weekends, with amphitheater-like stairs where you can sit and enjoy the show. ⊠ *20 Suncoast Blvd., Beachfront* ☎ *031/328–3000* ⊕ *www.suncoastcasino.co.za* ⊠ *Free.*

★ **uShaka Marine World**
AQUARIUM | FAMILY | This aquatic complex combines the uShaka Sea World aquarium and the uShaka Wet 'n Wild water park. The largest aquarium in the Southern Hemisphere, it has a capacity of nearly 6 million gallons of water, more than four times the size of Cape Town's aquarium. Enter through the side of a giant ship and walk down several stories to enter a "labyrinth of shipwrecks"—a jumble of five different fake but highly realistic wrecks, from an early-20th-century passenger cruiser to a steamship. Within this labyrinth are massive tanks, housing more than 350 species of fish and other sea life and the biggest variety of sharks

in the world, including ragged-tooth and Zambezi (bull sharks). Try to catch the divers hand-feeding fish and rays in the morning. The complex includes dolphin, penguin, and seal shows, and a variety of reptiles and amphibians populate the Dangerous Creatures exhibit.

The extensive water park comprises slides, pools, and about 10 different water rides. The intensity ranges from toddler-friendly to adrenaline junkie. Durban's moderate winter temperatures make it an attraction pretty much year-round, though it's especially popular in summer. Right out front, the uShaka beach is also one of the best in the city with lifeguards on duty. ■ TIP→ **Avoid on public holidays, and call ahead during winter when hours may change.** ⊠ *1 King Shaka Ave., Beachfront* ☎ *031/328–8000* ⊕ *www.ushakamarine.com* ⊠ *Sea World R157; Wet 'n Wild R157. Dangerous*

Located at the southern end of the Golden Mile, just past uShaka Beach, Vetch's Pier (a.k.a. Vetchie's) has been in existence since the 19th century.

Creatures Exhibit R62 ☞ Children under 3 get in for free.

 Beaches

Golden Mile

BEACH | From Vetch's Pier in the south to Suncoast in the north, the Golden Mile is a series of golden, sandy beaches divided by piers. Beaches are cleaned regularly, and each has a beach report board warning of bluebottles, jellyfish, strong currents, or dangerous conditions. Bodyboarders favor North Beach, and New Pier and Bay are preferred surfing spots. Swimmers should remain between the flags or beacons and away from the sides of piers, where strong currents wash straight out to sea. Chairs and umbrellas can be rented. Just off the sand, popular beachfront hotels like the Edward, Blue Waters, Elangeni, Belaire, Tropicana, and Garden Court jostle for visitors' favor. Rent a bicycle, Segway, or go-kart from a few points along the beachfront and fully enjoy the promenade when you tire of sunbathing. **Amenities:** food and drink; lifeguards; parking; showers; toilets. **Best for:** surfing; swimming. ⊠ *O. R. Tambo Parade, Beachfront.*

★ uShaka Beach

BEACH | In front of uShaka Marine World aquarium and water theme park this beach has small waves and calm conditions, making it great for families. Sand sculptors are often here, too, creating intricate artwork. Grassy banks offer an alternative to the sand (which isn't always as clean as the more central beaches), and the local surf school is busy all year round. A block inland, in the rejuvenated Point area, is the trendy Docklands hotel. **Amenities:** parking. **Best for:** swimming; walking. ⊠ *Escombe Terr., Beachfront.*

Restaurants

Cargo Hold

$$$ | SEAFOOD | You might need to book several weeks in advance to secure a table next to the shark tank here, but if you do it'll be one of your most

memorable dining experiences. Enjoy a carpaccio of smoked ostrich or tomato veloute—while massive ragged-tooth sharks drift right by your table and sand sharks stir up the sandy bottom. **Known for:** tourists; unique setting; shipwreck decor. $ *Average main: R175 ✉ uShaka Marine World, 1 Bell St., Beachfront ☎ 031/328–8065 ⊕ www.ushakamarine. com/cargohold/.*

Havana Grill
$$$ | SOUTH AFRICAN | Attention to detail and freshly prepared, quality food combine to make this one of Durban's finest restaurants serving steak—prepared and aged in the in-house butchery—and seafood. It offers spectacular sea vistas (ask for a table with a view when making your reservation) and a chic interior, with white leather-upholstered chairs, wall-length couches, and antelope horns on the walls. **Known for:** local wine list; fresh seafood. $ *Average main: R190 ✉ Suncoast Casino & Entertainment World, Shop 42, 20 Suncoast Blvd., Beachfront ☎ 064/757–1141 ⊕ www.havanagrill. co.za ☞ Parents with young children are requested to make sure little ones are on their best behavior.*

★ Surf Riders Cafe
$ | BURGER | FAMILY | This beachfront spot serves a solid menu of all-day breakfasts (they close around 5 pm), burgers, and freshly pressed juices. Try the sunrise smoothie with orange juice, mint, plain yogurt, and honey and one of several eggs Benedict combos—portions are small, made with high-quality ingredients, and hit the spot. **Known for:** long lines on weekends; soft-serve ice cream perfect for a beach stroll; laid-back vibe. $ *Average main: R100 ✉ South Beach, 17 Erskine Terr. ☎ 062/747–7037.*

Coffee and Quick Bites

★ Mahā Café
$ | EUROPEAN | This casual cafe restaurant in the reinvigorated Point Waterfront district is great for coffee (especially if you're averse to the crowds of uShaka Marine World) and a fancy breakfast that won't break the bank. **Known for:** within easy reach of the promenade; fresh all-day dishes; great coffee. $ *Average main: R80 ✉ 5 Mahatma Gandhi Rd., Beachfront ☎ 082/817–2957 ⊕ www. thepointwaterfront.co.za/maha-cafe/.*

Milky Lane
$ | CAFÉ | Take respite from the summer sun and enjoy a cool treat at this ice-cream parlor, one of 20 or so restaurants, fast-food outlets, and coffee shops in the Suncoast Casino complex. Even in winter, the creamy ice-cream waffles and creative shakes are a welcome indulgence. **Known for:** decadent waffles; classic soft serve; milk shakes of every flavor. $ *Average main: R40 ✉ Sun Coast Mall, Marine Parade, Shop L11 ☎ 031/332–1849 ⊕ www.milkylane.co.za.*

🛏 Hotels

Blue Waters Hotel
$ | HOTEL | Ideally located on North Beach, 250 meters from the Suncoast Entertainment Complex, the Blue Waters Hotel is an excellent value, and always busy with both vacationers and locals attending conferences and weddings. **Pros:** parking available (but not for big SUVs); enviable location; front-facing rooms have balconies and sea views. **Cons:** children can be noisy; elevators are slow and always full. $ *Rooms from: R1100 ✉ 175 Tambo [Snell] Parade, Beachfront ☎ 031/327–7000 ⊕ www.bluewatershotel.co.za ⇨ 92 rooms ❍ Free Breakfast.*

Garden Court Marine Parade

$ | **HOTEL** | You can't beat the location of this pleasant hotel midway between South and North beaches and only a five-minute drive from the city center. **Pros:** friendly staff; central location on Golden Mile; sea views. **Cons:** inadvisable to walk in area after dark; recommended restaurants a taxi ride away; very corporate feel to the hotel. [$] *Rooms from: R1500* ✉ *167 Tambo (Marine) Parade, Beachfront* ☎ *031/337–3341, 011/461–9744 for reservations only* 🌐 *www.tsogosun.com/garden-court-marine-parade* 🛏 *352 rooms* 🍴 *Free Breakfast.*

Southern Sun Elangeni & Maharani

$$ | **HOTEL** | Overlooking North Beach along the Golden Mile, this combination of two adjacent high-rise hotels is a two-minute drive from the city center and attracts a mix of business, conference, and leisure travelers. **Pros:** helpful tour and travel desk; sea views; discounted rates on weekends. **Cons:** lacks some character; not for those who prefer an intimate hotel experience. [$] *Rooms from: R1795* ✉ *63 Tambo [Snell] Parade, Beachfront* ☎ *031/362–1300* 🌐 *www.tsogosun.com/southern-sun-elangeni-maharani* 🛏 *753 suites* 🍴 *Free Breakfast.*

Suncoast Hotel and Towers

$$ | **HOTEL** | This hotel mostly attracts businesspeople and gamblers, but it's a stone's throw from the beach and has some great sea views. **Pros:** access to beach; closest hotel to Moses Mabhida Stadium; has a good spa. **Cons:** open-plan bathrooms aren't for everyone; like with all Golden Mile hotels, it gets filled with participants during major sporting events; smallish rooms. [$] *Rooms from: R1945* ✉ *20 Battery Beach Rd., Beachfront* ☎ *031/314–7878* 🌐 *www.tsogosun.com/suncoast-towers* 🛏 *201 rooms* 🍴 *Free Breakfast.*

Morningside

Dating back to Durban's colonial past, Morningside is an upscale suburb featuring prestigious residential properties such as the Dr. John L. Dube House, where the state president resides when in Durban. Below Jameson Park and Mitchell Park a slew of fashionable restaurants, boutique hotels, pubs, and clubs welcome patrons to trendy Florida Road.

Sights

Mitchell Park

CITY PARK | **FAMILY** | The magnificent rose garden, colorful floral displays, and leafy lawns here are a real treat on a hot summer day. Attached to the park is a small zoo, named after Sir Charles Mitchell, an early governor of Natal. It was opened at the turn of the 19th century, and the Aldabra tortoises that were donated to the park in the early 1900s—now massive—are still in residence. There are also small mammals, reptiles, tropical fish, and birds in large aviaries. The park has a popular playground. ✉ *Bordered by Innes, Nimmo, and Ferndale Rds., and Havelock Crescent, Morningside* ☎ *031/303–2275* 🎫 *Gardens free; zoo R13 adults, R11 children.*

Restaurants

★ **Mali's Indian Restaurant**

$$ | **SOUTH INDIAN** | An unexpected find within a residential section of the Morningside neighborhood, Mali's is loved by chefs and locals for its broad Indian menu serving specialities from the North and South, like steamed idli with sambar, masala dosai, and vadai—dishes you'll be hard-pressed to find in many Indian eateries. While the biryanis and tandoori dishes are very good in this homey restaurant with its cozy dining room, the Chinese-influenced offerings like the deep-fried mushroom Manchurian and Szechuan

chicken noodles have a loyal follow-ing. **Known for:** mango lassi; Chettinad chicken; unique Indian flavors. $ *Average main: R110* ⊠ *77 Smiso Nkwanyana Rd.* ☎ *031/312–8535* ⊕ *www.malis.co.za.*

★ Spiga d'Oro

$ | ITALIAN | Perched at the top of the ever-popular Florida Road, Spiga is something of a Durban institution, and it certainly represents the attitude and overall feeling of Durban—unpreten-tious with an animated atmosphere that makes diners feel part of the crowd. The Italian menu is not always classical in its interpretation, but you can count on it being delicious and a good value (pasta dishes come in medium or large portions). **Known for:** seafood pasta; buzzy atmosphere; bruschetta di pomodoro. $ *Average main: R100* ⊠ *465 Innes Rd., Morningside* ☎ *031/303–9511* ⊕ *www. spiga.co.za.*

☕ Coffee and Quick Bites

Love Coffee

$ | CAFÉ | On Lilian Ngoyi Road in Win-dermere, which some say is the "new" Florida Road, Love Coffee is your best bet for noncommercial, top-notch coffee in a veritable hole-in-the-wall, of the con-temporary, well-designed kind. The bran muffins, rooibos cappuccino, fresh juice, packed salads, toasted sandwiches and brief breakfast menu are highly recom-mended. **Known for:** great coffee; afforda-ble sandwiches; up-and-coming location. $ *Average main: R65* ⊠ *484 Lilian Ngoyi Rd., Morningside* ☎ *084/493–2802* ⊕ *www.lovecoffee.durban.*

🛏 Hotels

The Benjamin

$$ | HOTEL | In one of Durban's trans-formed historic buildings, this small hotel offers excellent value, and its location on trendy Florida Road is ideal for restau-rants and nightlife and only a short dis-tance from the city center and beaches.

Pros: approximately five minutes from beaches and city center; within walk-ing distance to restaurants; covered swimming pool. **Cons:** no elevator; no on-site restaurant for lunch or dinner; limited secure parking. $ *Rooms from: R1900* ⊠ *141 Florida Rd., Morningside* ☎ *031/303–4233* ⊕ *www.benjamin.co.za* ⇥ *41 rooms* ❑ *Free Breakfast.*

Quarters on Florida

$$ | HOTEL | Four converted Victorian homes comprise the city's most intimate boutique hotel, a contemporary Europe-an-style property that's been reinvented with a colonial African makeover. **Pros:** close to restaurants and nightlife of Flor-ida Road; tasteful rooms; on-site restau-rants. **Cons:** limited off-street parking; no pool; despite efforts, street-facing rooms are noisy. $ *Rooms from: R1900* ⊠ *101 Florida Rd., Morningside* ☎ *031/303–5246* ⊕ *www.quarters.co.za* ⇥ *24 rooms* ❑ *Free Breakfast.*

🍸 Nightlife

Drop Kick Murphy's

PUBS | A modern take on an Irish pub, this bar, right in the heart of Florida Road's lively center, offers a range of craft beers, signature cocktails, and comfort food like the local classic chicken livers panfried in peri-peri (hot sauce made from bird's eye chili), Philly Chili Steaks, deep-fried chick-en wings, and a salad with homemade fish cakes. Happy Hour from 5 to 6 each day offers half-price on drinks and cock-tails and 25% off burgers, craft beers, and draughts. A late-night (9:30–mid-night) food menu keeps the hungry fed, and friends gather here to watch rugby matches and contribute to the festive atmosphere. Expect loud Irish singing at times. ⊠ *219 Florida Rd., Windermere* ☎ *031/303-2980.*

TO
UMHLANGA

Durban

KEY

1 Exploring Sights

1 Restaurants

1 Quick Bites

1 Hotels

INDIAN

OCEAN

Golden Mile Beach

BEACH
FRONT

uShaka Beach

POINT

ISLANDVIEW

Bluff Beaches

Parade

Mahatma Gandhi Rd.

side Rd.

| 0 | | 1/2 mi |
| 0 | | 1/2 km |

Sights ▼

1 BAT Centre **F7**
2 Campbell Collections... **D4**
3 Durban Art Gallery....... **F6**
4 Durban Botanic Gardens.................. **D5**
5 Durban Natural Science Museum **F6**
6 Farewell Square **E6**
7 Florida Road............. **E4**
8 Hare Krishna Temple of Understanding **A7**
9 Herb Market............. **D6**
10 Jumah Mosque **E6**
11 Kendra Hall and Ekta Mandir **D5**
12 KwaMuhle Museum..... **E6**
13 Kwazulu-Natal Society of Arts Gallery............... **C6**
14 Madressa Arcade **E6**
15 Mitchell Park........... **D3**
16 Moses Mabhida Stadium **F3**
17 Suncoast Casino & Entertainment World **F4**
18 Umbilo Shree Ambalavaanar Alayam Temple **A7**
19 Umgeni River Bird Park.................. **E1**
20 uShaka Marine World **G7**
21 Victoria Street Market **E6**
22 Wilson's Wharf........... **E7**

Restaurants ▼

1 Big Easy Wine bar + Grill Durban by Ernie Els...... **F6**
2 Cargo Hold............... **G7**
3 Havana Grill **F4**
4 Jack Salmon Fish House................ **G1**
5 Mali's Indian Restaurant................ **E2**
6 9th Avenue Waterside **E7**
7 Roma Revolving........... **F6**
8 Spiga d'Oro.............. **D3**
9 Surf Riders Cafe **G7**

Quick Bites ▼

1 Capsicum at Britannia Hotel.......................**C2**
2 Govinda's Pure Vegetarian Restaurant............... **A7**
3 Hollywood Bunny Bar **B1**
4 John Dory's............... **E7**
5 Love Coffee **E3**
6 Mahā Café............... **H7**
7 Milky Lane............... **G5**
8 Patel's Vegetarian Refreshment Room...... **E6**
9 Royal Coffee Shoppe.... **F6**

Hotels ▼

1 The Benjamin **E4**
2 Blue Waters Hotel **F4**
3 Garden Court Marine Parade.......... **G6**
4 Quarters on Florida **E4**
5 Southern Sun Elangeni & Maharani.... **F5**
6 Suncoast Hotel and Towers **F4**

The Tollgate Bridge near Berea is one Durban's iconic landmarks.

Shopping

★ Cécile & Boyd

OTHER SPECIALTY STORE | Super-stylish interiors here cleverly combine the best of African and colonial design in a contemporary space. ✉ *253 Florida Rd., Morningside* ☏ *031/303–1005* ⊕ *www. cecileandboyds.com.*

Elizabeth Gordon Gallery

ART GALLERIES | This small gallery in a cozy Edwardian house carries a wide selection of work—including prints—by local and international artists and photographers. ✉ *120 Florida Rd., Morningside* ☏ *031/303–8133* ⊕ *www.elizabethgordon.co.za* ⊘ *Closed Sun.*

Berea

Durban's colonial past is very much evident in this suburb overlooking the city. Built on a ridge above the sea, it's characterized by old homes with wraparound balconies, boutique hotels, and strips of fashionable restaurants. Durban formed the coastal hub of the British Colony of Natal, declared in 1843 after the annexation of the former Boer Republic of Natalia. In 1910 Natal combined with three other colonies to form the Union of South Africa. One of the most sought-after addresses in the upscale Berea suburb is Musgrave Road. Tree-lined avenues feature luxury homes and apartment blocks interspersed with parks, schools, and sports clubs. The Musgrave Centre shopping hub is a major drawing card.

Sights

Campbell Collections

HISTORY MUSEUM | Amid bustling, suburban Berea, Muckleneuk is a tranquil Cape Dutch home in a leafy garden. It was built in 1914 upon the retirement of Sir Marshall Campbell, a wealthy sugar baron and philanthropist who lived here with his wife, Ellen, and daughter, Killie. Today it is administered as a museum by the University of KwaZulu-Natal, and is furnished in similar style to when the Campbells lived here, with some excellent pieces of the family's Cape Dutch furniture. In addition to the William Campbell Furniture Museum (William was the son of Sir Marshall) there is an extensive collection of works by early European traveler artists, such as Angas, and paintings by prominent 20th-century Black South African artists, including Gerard Bhengu, Daniel Rakgoathe, and Trevor Makhoba. The Mashu Museum of Ethnology displays the best collection of traditional Zulu glass beadwork in the country, plus African utensils, like tightly woven wicker beer pots, carvings, masks, pottery, and musical instruments. There are also weapons dating from the Bambatha Uprising of 1906, during which Blacks in Natal rebelled against a poll tax and were brutally put down. Paintings of African tribespeople in traditional dress by artist Barbara Tyrrell, who traveled around South Africa from the 1940s to 1960s gathering valuable anthropological data, add vitality to the collection. The Killie Campbell Africana Library, open to the public, is a treasure trove of historical information on KwaZulu-Natal. It includes the papers of James Stuart, a magistrate and explorer during the early 20th century; the recorded oral tradition of hundreds of Zulus; a collection of pamphlets produced by the Colenso family in their struggle for the recognition of the rights of the Zulu people; and a good collection of 19th-century works relating to game hunting. ⊠ *220 Gladys Mazibuko [Marriott] Rd., at Stephen Dlamini [Essenwood] Rd., Berea* ☎ *031/207–3432, 031/260–1710* ⊕ *campbell.ukzn.ac.za* 🖅 *Muckleneuk daily tours R20 (reservations essential); library free* ☞ *Bring exact cash.*

Durban Botanic Gardens
GARDEN | FAMILY | Opposite the Greyville Racecourse, Africa's oldest surviving botanical garden is a delightful 150-year-old oasis of greenery interlaced with walking paths, fountains, and ponds. The gardens' orchid house and collection of rare cycads are renowned. The Garden

of the Senses caters to the blind, and there's a lovely tea garden where you can take a load off your feet and settle back with a cup of hot tea and cakes—crumpets with "the works" are the best in town. On weekends it's a popular place for wedding photographs. During the Music at the Lake events, which happen on some Sundays, various musical acts perform in the gardens (additional fee) and people take along picnics. ⊠ *70 St. Thomas Rd., Berea* ☎ *069/598-1396* ⊕ *www.durbanbotanicgardens.org.za* 🖅 *Free.*

Beaches

Bluff Beaches
BEACH | South of Durban's harbor, these beaches offer a less crowded alternative to the more central city beaches, although it can get rough at times, with big waves. Brighton Beach and Anstey's Beach are popular surf spots, with southerly surf swells breaking on the rocky reef below. Cave Rock at low tide is a paradise for anyone who enjoys exploring rock pools; at high tide it's a wave ride for the fearless. **Amenities:** lifeguards. **Best for:** surfing; swimming. ⊠ *Marine Dr., Berea.*

Shopping

★ African Art Centre
ART GALLERIES | An outstanding collection of art and crafts from local artisans is on offer at this nonprofit center dedicated to promoting their work. Purchases can be shipped overseas. ⊠ *500 Esther Roberts Rd., Morningside* ☎ *031/312–3804* ⊕ *www.afri-art.co.za.*

★ The Morning Trade Market
MARKET | FAMILY | Founded by Anna Savage, who established the popular I Heart Market at the Moses Mabhida Stadium, this market is a showcase of organic and wholesome food and local produce at The Alliance Cafe. It's a great way to gather with the locals and pick up

excellent bread, cheese, yogurt, freshly squeezed juices, and farm-fresh veggies while sipping on a great coffee and settling in for languid brunch. Open Sundays from 9 to midday. ⊠ *22 Sutton Crescent* ☎ *064/809-2066* ⊕ *www.themorningtrade.co.za* ⊘ *Closed Mon.–Sat.*

Indian Quarter

It's said that the largest Indian population outside of India resides in Durban, and the influence on the city is much in evidence, from the architecture to the cuisine. Under apartheid's Group Areas Act that designated where various race groups could live and own businesses, Indian traders set up shop on Dr. Yusuf Dadoo Street (Grey Street). Here, at the Indian Quarter known in recent times as the Grey Street Casbah you can eat vegetarian curry, bargain for goods, buy fabrics, or just browse shops whose ownership spans generations, and soak up the Eastern vibe. ■TIP→ **You can find inexpensive freshly baked goods at street corners made by local bakers. Look out for filled doughnuts, queen cakes, and Madeira slices.** In addition, this part of town can be quite grubby, and in the midday summer heat it can get unpleasantly humid.

◉ Sights

★ Herb Market
MARKET | Southern Africa's largest and most extensive traditional medicine market, known locally as the *Muti* (traditional medicine, pronounced moo-tee) Market, has tables and tables filled with bunches of fresh and dried herbs, plant matter, and (controversially) animal bones, skin, and other parts, possibly including endangered species. The market also serves as a distinctive traditional-medicine facility, where *sangomas* (traditional healers) offer consultations to locals in a bustling, urban atmosphere. If you're feeling bold, you might wish to consult a sangoma on matters of health, wealth, or personal

problems. Remember to always respect the traders and do not take photographs of people or the goods for sale, particularly any animal matter. If you are with a guide, ask them to negotiate picture-taking on your behalf, if you must—there's no guarantee though. Speaking of guides, you can hire one through Durban Tourism or book a comprehensive tour through Markets of Warwick that includes all the neighborhood's markets. ⊠ *Warwick Junction, Julius Nyerere Ave.* ☎ *031/309–3880* ⊕ *www.marketsofwarwick.co.za.*

Jumah Mosque
RELIGIOUS BUILDING | Built in 1927 in a style that combines Islamic and colonial features, this is the second-largest mosque in the Southern Hemisphere (the biggest sits in Johannesburg). Its colonnaded verandahs, gold-domed minaret, and turrets give the surrounding (not-so-gleaming) streets much of their character. Tours (the only way to visit) are free and can be arranged through the Islamic Propagation Center, in a room at the entrance of the mosque, or through the Durban Tourism offices.

■TIP→ **If you plan to go inside, dress modestly: women should bring scarves to cover their heads and shoulders and skirts should extend to the ankles; men should not wear shorts.** It's a good idea to keep a *kikoi* (a lightweight African sarong readily available in local markets) in your bag to use as a skirt or scarf. Men can use them, too, to cover bare legs. You'll have to take off your shoes as you enter, so wear socks if you don't want to go barefoot. No tours are offered during Islamic holidays, including Ramadan, which varies but lasts a whole month in the latter part of the year. ⊠ *Dr Yusaf Dadoo [Grey] St. at Denis Hurley [Queen] St., Indian District* ☎ *031/304–1518* ⊠ *Free.*

Madressa Arcade
MARKET | There's a Kiplingesque quality to this thoroughfare, recalling the bazaars of the East. Built in 1927, it's little more

Bunny Chow

Contrary to what you may think, bunny chow is not about lettuce and carrots. This Durban specialty, prevalent in the Indian Quarter and around town, is a hollowed-out loaf of bread traditionally filled with bean, vegetable, chicken, or mutton curry. Though historical sources can't confirm it, the dish is said to have been popularized in the late 1930s and 1940s during apartheid, when Blacks were prohibited from entering a restaurant or lingering at the tables. Many credit Kapitan's Restaurant, in the city center, as the first to sell a bunny chow, though Patel's Vegetarian Refreshment Room may contest that. Another theory supports the story that bunny chow is derived from the term "Bania" or "Baniya," used to describe the Gujarati merchants who ran the Indian shops like Kapitans

and Patels. Others postulate that the bunny chow was a convenience meal already developed by home cooks, and made popular by the traders who sold it cheaply. Whatever the true history, the bunny chow has found a permanent and loving home in Durban.

Good bunnies can be found at several eateries across the city. Try **Hollywood Bets at Springfield Park** for outstanding broad beans and mutton curry bunnies. Ignore the betting environment—there's an air-conditioned interior, covered deck, and Bunny Bar for takeaways. **Patel Vegetarian Refreshment Room**, which has been satisfying customers since 1912; and **Capsicum at Britannia Hotel**, an incredibly busy restaurant and take-away business supported by locals.

than a narrow, winding alley perfumed by spices and thronged with traders plying a mishmash of drab goods. You can buy everything from cheap plastic trinkets to household utensils and recordings of Indian music. Bursts of color—from bright yellow fabric to dark red spices—create a refreshing and photogenic sight. You can buy striking costume jewelry that would cost three times as much at major shopping centers. Leave large bags and valuables at your hotel to browse unencumbered. ⊠ *Entrances on Denis Hurley [Queen] and Cathedral Sts., Indian District.*

Victoria Street Market

MARKET | Masses of enormous fish and prawns lie tightly packed on beds of ice while vendors competing for your attention shout their respective prices. In the meat section, goat and sheep heads are stacked into neat piles (a spectacle for those with iron stomachs), and

butchers slice and dice every cut of meat imaginable. The noise is deafening. In an adjacent building—where all the tour buses pull up—you'll discover a number of curio shops whose proprietors are willing to bargain over wood and stone carvings, beadwork, and basketry. You'll also find shops selling spices with creative names like Mother-in-Law's Revenge and Exterminator, recordings of African music, and Indian fabrics. The current structures stand on the site of an original, much-loved market, a ramshackle collection of wooden shacks that burned down during the years of Nationalist rule. ■TIP→ Go with a guide and make a visit to Joe's Corner shop or to the Thirupathi Spices Shop where Sanusha Moodliar, the shop's charismatic heir, will prepare you the freshest spice packs to take home (as she did for Gordon Ramsay). It's not cheap, but it's worth it. ⊠ *Denis Hurley [Queen] St. at Jospeh Nduli [Russell] St., Indian*

District ☎ *031/306–4021, 031/309-
3880 Markets of Warwick guided tours*
⊕ *www.marketsofwarwick.co.za* ✉ *R100
per person for a guided tour* ☞ *Minimum
three people.*

☕ Coffee and Quick Bites

Capsicum at Britannia Hotel

$ | INDIAN | FAMILY | The tables are
somewhat grimy and the red interior
is unattractive, yet the clientele here
remains loyal. You can get a wide range
of curries and "exotic" bunnies, with
curry fillings like tripe, trotters, and the
more regular sugar beans, mutton, and
chicken curries. **Known for:** mango lassi;
soji (Semolina served with cream and
almonds); "exotic" bunny chows. $ *Average main: R45* ✉ *Britannia Hotel, 1299
Umgeni Rd.* ☎ *031/303–2266* ⊕ *www.
hotelbrits.co.za.*

★ Hollywood Bunny Bar

$ | INDIAN | FAMILY | Though you'll be sur-
rounded by the big screens of Hollywood
Bets broadcasting live horse races and
games, don't be put off. The air-conditioned restaurant, with a large covered
deck and dedicated Bunny Bar for takeout, serves up some of the best bunny
chow in Durban. **Known for:** lunchtime
specials; affordable quarter bean bunny
chow; lamb curry. $ *Average main: R65*
✉ *Springfield Park, 126 Intersite Ave.*
☎ *031/263–2073* ⊕ *www.hollywoodbets.
net.*

Patel's Vegetarian Refreshment Room

$ | INDIAN | Founded in 1912, this place
has built a family legacy of good traditional Indian food. Serving only vegetarian
dishes in the form of curries, the restaurant is run by Mr Manilal Patel, now in
his late 70s, who lives in the apartment
above the shop, and gets up around 2 am
each day to start the day's prep. **Known
for:** difficult parking; variety of vegetarian
options; affordable, good curry. $ *Average main: R25* ✉ *202 Dr Yusuf Dadoo St.*
☎ *031/306–1774.*

🛍 Shopping

Victoria Street Market (*Indian Market*)
MARKET | FAMILY | The most vibrant
cross-cultural market in the city is a
century-old trading area where more
than 150 vendors sell everything from
recordings of African music to rolls of
fabric, curios, brass ornaments, Chinese
goods, incense, and curry spices. Bargaining is expected here, much as it is in
India, though not for spices. Also known
among locals as the Indian market, it's
worth booking a tour of this and the
adjacent markets with Markets of Warwick (R100 per person, minimum three).
✉ *Denis Hurley [Queen] St. at Bertha
Mkhize St., Indian District* ☎ *031/309–
3880* ⊕ *www.marketsofwarwick.co.za.*

Victoria Embankment

Margaret Mncadi Avenue (formerly
Victoria Embankment or the Esplanade)
skirts Durban harbor from Maydon Wharf
with its sugar terminal in the west, past
Wilson's Wharf and the yacht mall to the
docksides in the east.

👁 Sights

BAT Centre

ARTS CENTER | This vibrant center (buoyed
by a current contemporary revival) is
abuzz with artists and musicians. Most
days—and some nights—you can watch
sculptors and painters at work, hear
poetry readings, and see Africology
(African teachings and traditions) dancers
and musicians. The center is home to
several small galleries that showcase the
work of local artists. The center contains
a coffee bar overlooking the bay and
shops that sell an excellent selection of
high-quality African crafts, including fabrics and ceramics. ✉ *Small Craft Harbour,
45 Maritime Pl., Victoria Embankment*
☎ *031/332–0451* ⊕ *www.batcentre.co.za.*
✉ *Free.*

Restaurants

★ 9th Avenue Waterside

$$$$ | EUROPEAN | Durban desperately needed a first-rate seafood offering and this upmarket restaurant perched at the scenic harbor delivers. Think crispy fried calamari with black garlic aioli and pickled cauliflower, grilled baby crayfish with passion fruit and lemon verbena coconut broth, and magnificent seafood pasta. **Known for:** seasonal cuisine; harbor views; fine dining. Ⓢ *Average main: R300* ✉ *9th Avenue Waterside, 2 Maritime Pl, Harbour, Victoria Embankment* ☎ *031/940-4628* ⊕ *www.9thavewaterside.co.za* ✆ *Closed Mon.* ☞ *No kids under 12 years old during dinner service.*

Greyville

Between the foot of the Berea ridge and the beachfront, this suburb of older homes and apartment blocks is dominated by the legendary Greyville Racecourse, where Durban's social highlight, the Durban July horse race, takes place. Greyville is bounded in the south by the Botanical Gardens and in the north by Morningside.

⊙ Sights

Kendra Hall and Ekta Mandir

RELIGIOUS BUILDING | One of the most easily accessible and opulent temples in the city, the Kendra, next to the Durban Botanic Gardens, opened in 2001 after two years of intricate work by sculptors in India. The structure is unmistakably Eastern, with golden domes that tower above a palm tree supported by ornately decorated columns and arches that give the temple an East-meets-West look. Inside are two halls: a small one on the ground level and a larger one upstairs, which is a popular venue for weddings and leads to the temple. Huge statues of Hindu gods, notably Ganesha, Krishna,

Need a Break?

Head over to Wilson's Wharf in the Maydon Wharf neighborhood, where you can have a cool cocktail or a meal on a deck overlooking the harbor at one of several restaurants ranging from an oyster bar to fast-food outlets like the affordable John Dory's.

If you're in the Victoria Embankment neighborhood, check out 9th Avenue Waterside restaurant. It gets booked up in advance, but the upstairs cocktail bar is often open for walk-ins to enjoy a sunset and sundowner from 4 to 9 pm from R155 per person.

and Rama, are garlanded and clothed in exquisite Indian fabric. You can join an early morning or evening prayer daily at 6:30 am and 6:30 pm. ✉ *5 John Zikhali [Sydenham] Rd., Greyville* ☎ *031/309–1824* ⊕ *www.kendra.org.za* ✑ *Free.*

Maydon Wharf

Maydon Wharf is an extensive cargo handling section of Durban's harbor, sandwiched between the suburb of Congella and the ocean. Its northern section features the Wilson's Wharf entertainment node, with a number of restaurants and the Catalina Theatre.

⊙ Sights

Wilson's Wharf

PEDESTRIAN MALL | On the edge of the harbor, this pleasant, privately developed section of waterfront is a lovely place to while away a few hours, soaking up the atmosphere, admiring the harbor view, and maybe having a meal or drink at one of the open-air restaurants on the expansive wooden deck. In addition to restaurants and fast-food outlets, there are boat rentals, sightseeing cruises (try Sarie Marais Pleasure Cruises or Isle of Capri), and a small market with stands selling local crafts or cheaper trinkets from India and China. ✉ *Boatman's Rd., Maydon Wharf* ☎ *031/907–8968, 031/305–2844 Sarie Marais Pleasure Cruises* 🌐 *www.wilsonswharfonline.co.za.*

Coffee and Quick Bites

John Dory's

$ | **SEAFOOD** | You won't find the most exceptional seafood here, but the views, affordable price range, and menu variety more than make up for it. Order a gourmet milkshake and watch all the yachts and boats bobbing about in the Durban harbor. **Known for:** upper deck views; half-price sushi specials; decadent milkshakes. [$] *Average main: R100* ✉ *Wilson's Wharf, Boatmans Rd., Maydon Wharf* ☎ *031/304–7669* 🌐 *www.johndorys.com.*

Chatsworth

The predominantly Indian inner-city suburb of Chatsworth is a vibrant, cosmopolitan mix of old and new architecture complemented by myriad home-based businesses and a couple of large shopping malls. It comprises seven residential wards along the Higginson Highway, bounded to the north by the Umhlatuzana River and to the south by the Umlaas River. It's home to one of South Africa's most spectacular Hare Krishna temples.

Sights

Hare Krishna Temple of Understanding

RELIGIOUS BUILDING | This magnificent lotus-shaped temple, opened in 1985, is at the heart of activities run by the city's International Society for Krishna Consciousness. Gold-tinted windows add a glow to the interior, floored with imported Italian marble and intricate artwork. Colorful laser drawings depicting the life of the Hindu god Krishna cover the ceiling, and statues of Krishna and his consort Radha are elaborately dressed in traditional Indian attire. Love fests and traditional singing and dancing take place on Sunday (1:30–5) and all are welcome. You need to remove your shoes when entering the temple. ✉ *50 Bhaktivedanta Swami Circle, Unit 5, Chatsworth* ☎ *031/403–3328, 062/526–3606 WhatsApp Hotline* 🌐 *www.iskcondurban.net* 🎟 *Free.*

Coffee and Quick Bites

★ **Govinda's Pure Vegetarian Restaurant**

$ | **VEGETARIAN** | This is an inexpensive yet excellent vegetarian restaurant catering to Hare Krishna devotees, who do not use onions, garlic, or mushrooms in their food. The traditional Indian rice dish biryani (breyani as it's known locally) is a favorite. **Known for:** egg-less cakes and desserts; takeaways; paneer butter masala. [$] *Average main: R60* ✉ *Hare Krishna Temple of Understanding, 50 Bhaktivedanta Swami Circle, Unit 5, Chatsworth* ☎ *078/849–4291* 🌐 *www.iskcondurban.net* 🕒 *Closed Wed.*

Durban North and Glenashley

Along the eastern coastline north of the Umgeni River, you'll find the well-established middle- to upper-income suburb of Durban North, the highlight of which is the superb Umgeni River Bird Park. One of the city's older suburbs, Glenashley sits between Durban North and La Lucia. Palatial properties line its beachfront, whereas more modest yet upscale homes fill the inland area. The Ruth First Highway (M4) connects these suburbs southward to the city and northward to the more upscale Umhlanga Rocks region.

Sights

Umgeni River Bird Park

NATURE SIGHT | FAMILY | Ranked among the world's best, this bird park shelters beneath high cliffs next to the Umgeni River and has various walk-through aviaries containing more than 800 birds. The variety of birds, both exotic and indigenous, is astonishing. You'll be able to take close-up photographs of macaws, giant Asian hornbills, toucans, pheasants, flamingos, and three crane species, including the blue crane, South Africa's national bird. Try to time your visit to take in the free-flight bird show, which is a delight for both children and adults. Drinks and light lunches are available at the park's kiosk. ✉ *490 Riverside Rd., off the M4, Durban North* ☎ *031/322–5750* ⊕ *www.umgeniriverbirdpark.co.za* 🎫 *R67; free bird show Tues.–Sun. at 11 am and 2 pm.*

 Restaurants

⭐ Jack Salmon Fish House

$$ | SEAFOOD | A short drive north of the city, the small suburb of Glenashley has an elevated position that offers diners a pleasant sea view, but this restaurant's fresh seafood, prepared in unique and traditional ways, is the drawing card, with excellent service keeping the place busy during lunch and dinner. For starters, opt for the sushi or the Falkland Island calamari tubes stuffed with prawns and peri-peri dressing and then char-grilled. **Known for:** panna cotta; fresh seafood; excellent view. 💲 *Average main: R140* ✉ *Glenore Centre, Shop 15, 1 Aubrey Dr., Glenashley* ☎ *031/572–3664* ⊕ *www.jacksalmon.co.za.*

Glenwood

Dotted with parks, schools, churches, and sports clubs, Glenwood is a quiet family suburb. Helen Joseph Road is the social hub, where restaurants, bistros, pubs, and clubs attract hordes of partygoers on weekends.

◉ Sights

⭐ KwaZulu-Natal Society of Arts Gallery

PUBLIC ART | This arts complex, known as KZNSA, houses four exhibition areas, in addition to a crafts shop, the Durban Center for Photography, and a classy open-air cafe. The center does not have a particular focus but is committed to promoting emerging talent in the province. Exhibition media ranges from photos and paintings to video installations. The center's clean architectural lines and leafy setting, with ever-changing colorful murals on the exterior, make this a popular venue with Durban's trendy set, and it's a lovely place to cool off after a hot morning touring the town. The gallery and crafts shop support and promote local art, so it's worth seeking out for tasteful souvenirs. Local musicians are often given a platform on Friday nights. ■**TIP**→ **The daytime-only restaurant is a wonderful child-friendly pit stop with affordable lunches such as prosciutto and mozzarella toasted sandwiches or no-frills beef burgers for under R65.** ✉ *166 Bulwer Rd., Glenwood* ☎ *031/277–1705* ⊕ *www.kznsagallery.co.za* 🎫 *Free* 🕙 *Closed Mon.*

Cato Manor

This neighborhood came about when Black South Africans settled in the area during the 1920s, renting land from Indian landlords. The area saw race riots in the 1950s and 1960s when squatters and police clashed, but since the 1980s new infrastructure and urban development has created a more formal, working-class suburb with schools, a market, and a community center.

 Sights

Umbilo Shree Ambalavaanar Alayam Temple

RELIGIOUS BUILDING | One of Durban's most spectacular Hindu shrines is in Cato Manor. The temple's facade is adorned with brightly painted representations of the Hindu gods, notably Ganesha, Shiva, and Vishnu. The magnificent doors leading to the cellar were salvaged from a temple built in 1875 on the banks of the Umbilo River and subsequently destroyed by floods. The culmination of a long fast results in the carrying of "kavadi," a sacrifice in honor of Lord Murugan, held annually in March, where unshod fire walkers cross beds of burning, glowing coals. There are no set visiting hours. The kavadi-carrying devotees, often adorned in pins and needles walking in a deeply meditative state known as "trance," draw huge crowds of spectators and well-wishers. If the temple is open you'll be welcome to go inside; if not, the exterior of the building is still worth seeing. ⊠ *890 Bellair Rd., Cato Manor* ✢ *Take the M13 (from Leopold St.) out of the city; at the major fork in road after Westridge Park and the high school, veer left onto Bellair Rd.* ☎ *031/261–6509* ⊕ *www.usaat.co.za* ⊠ *Free.*

Activities

BOATING

It's easy to charter all manner of boats, from a paddleboat (a flat fiberglass board that you paddle) for a few rand to a deep-sea fishing vessel for a few thousand. Inexpensive harbor tours lasting a half hour, booze cruises, and dinner cruises can all be booked from the quayside at Wilson's Wharf. Shop around to find something that suits your budget, taste, and time frame.

FISHING

Deep-sea fishing is a popular activity, as there's almost always something biting. Summer (November–May) brings game fish like barracuda, marlin, sailfish, and dorado, whereas winter is better for the bottom fishes, like mussel crackers, salmon, and rock cod.

★ Aqua Nautical Adventures

FISHING | With daily departures at 6 am, this company deploys luxury 30- and 48-foot catamarans and a 30-foot Lee Cat, equipped with electric flush loos, a covered cabin for respite from the sun, and a even a bed if you're worn out from fighting a mahimahi (dorado). They provide all equipment and professional staff will barbecue lunch on board for a nominal fee, or you could bring your own meat and braai (barbecue) it yourself in South African fashion. Half-day and full-day tours for game fish deep-sea and harbor fishing, with stunning views of Durban city, start at R6500 for a maximum of eight or ten depending on the vessel. The company operates on a strict catch-and-release policy for all billfish (such as marlin) with a limited number of catch allowed per customer for other fish. ⊠ *Wilson's Wharf, 18 Boatmans Rd.* ☎ *073/500–4704* ⊕ *www.aquanautical. co.za.*

Casea Charters

FISHING | Trips on a ski boat depart from Granny's Pool, in front of Umhlanga's Cabana Beach. Various trips are available, ranging from one to six hours. The popular three- and four-hour trips are priced per person at R950 and R1100 respectively; otherwise you need to get a group together and hire the whole boat (R2750–R7200 depending on the length of time you want). Fish for dorado, yellowfin tuna, king and queen mackerel, garrick, rock cod, salmon, and other species. Bait and equipment are supplied, but bring your own food and drinks. You can keep the fish you catch. Booking is essential, and you need to obtain a fishing license (from any post office) in advance of the trip. ✉ *1 Lighthouse Rd.* ☎ *071/611–8276, 083/690–2511* ⊕ *www. caseacharters.co.za.*

Lynski Charters

FISHING | Deep-sea fishing trips for barracuda, sailfish, marlin, shark, and reef fish head out from Durban's harbor at 5 am in a 30-foot game-fish boat, returning at 2 pm. They charge a set fee for up to 6 people fishing for a day trip, although the boat can take 12 people. The price includes equipment, tackle, and bait. Bring your own refreshments. ✉ *Durban Harbor, Off Maritime Pl.* ☎ *064/501–3846* ⊕ *www.lynski.co.za* ✉ *R950 per person for 5-hours or from R6,000 for five hour private charter.*

GOLF

Durban is a great destination for golfers, with a number of internationally acclaimed courses in subtropical settings. Lush, forest-fringed fairways make for a scenic and challenging golfing experience, and thanks to Durban's sunshine and perennially warm climate, golf can be enjoyed throughout the year.

Beachwood Country Club

GOLF | The layout is challenging to the links-course golfer, with most fairways running parallel in a N-NE/S-SW direction. The 6th and 9th fairways feature doglegs, and 74 bunkers lure wayward shots. Four holes have water features and tree-lined fairways. Set high in the dunes, the par-4 6th is a hugely demanding hole at 448 yards from the back tee. The hole doglegs left, with a stream, bush, and water hazard to be negotiated before reaching the green. ✉ *Beachwood Pl., off Fairway* ☎ *031/035–1530* ⊕ *www. beachwood-countryclub.com* ✉ *R170 Mon., R260 Tues., R290 Wed.–Fri., R360 weekends. R290 for golf cart hire.* ⛳ *18 holes, 6016 yards, par 71.*

★ Durban Country Club

GOLF | Durban Country Club was the first public course on the African continent to be rated in the Top 100 Golf Courses of the World by *Golf Magazine USA*. Lush subtropical vegetation, sand dunes, and elevated views of the Indian Ocean and the striking Moses Mabhida Stadium lend this course its unique and challenging appeal. Classic features include large undulating fairways on the 5th, 8th, and 17th, and massive sand dunes that form part of the design. The 1535-foot par-5 3rd hole—high tee-off to a narrow fairway with dense vegetation and a left-hand fairway bunker—is rated among the world's best. ✉ *Walter Gilbert Rd.* ☎ *031/313–1777* ⊕ *www.durbancountry-club.co.za* ✉ *R700 day rate* ⛳ *18 holes, 6683 yards, par 72.*

Mount Edgecombe Country Club

GOLF | This two-course championship estate—Mount Edgecombe One and Mount Edgecombe Two—is set in rolling hills inland from Umhlanga. Designed by Sid Brews in 1936, Course One was upgraded in 1992 and modernized by Hugh Baiocchi to meet USGA specifications. Both feature indigenous vegetation that attracts a variety of birdlife. Course One's water features and multi-tiered greens demand accurate play, whereas Course Two has more undulating terrain that tests the serious golfer and hones the amateur's skill. Signature holes are the 13th to 16th, referred to by locals as "Amen corner." ✉ *Golf Course Dr., Gate 2, Mount Edgecombe* ☎ *031/502–1010* ⊕ *www.mountedgecombe.com* ✉ *weekdays R495, weekends R630 and golf cart hire R400* ⛳ *18 holes, 6302 yards, par 71.*

Royal Durban Golf Club

GOLF | Tucked in the center of the Greyville Racecourse, the Royal Durban Golf Club course, built in 1898, appears deceptively easy. However there's no wind protection, so hitting narrow fairways is difficult, and subtle green breaks are challenging. On the plus side, it's centrally located, surroundings are attractive, the course is flat, and trees are minimal. The par-4 7th is the most difficult with palm trees punishing a sliced or blocked tee shot. First tee-off is at 6:30 am. ⊠ *16 Mitchell Crescent, Gate 15, Greyville* ☎ *031/309–1373* ⊕ *www. royaldurban.co.za* ✉ *Day rate: R450 all wk* 🏌 *18 holes, 6444 yards, par 73.*

Umhlali Country Club

GOLF | This Peter Matkovich–designed golf course is a premier golf destination on the North Coast. It features sweeping greens, exotic palms, and manicured fairways that offer an easy walk for golfers of all abilities. Strategically positioned tee boxes and seven water holes test the mettle of competitive golfers, and longer handicappers can take advantage of front markers. The 4th and 8th present more of a challenge, with greens surrounded by water. ⊠ *Compensation Rd., Ballito* ☎ *032/947–1181* ⊕ *www.umhlaliclub. co.za/sports/golf* ✉ *R420 weekdays, R525 weekends* 🏌 *18 holes, 6228 yards, par 72.*

HELICOPTER TOURS

JNC Helicopters

LOCAL SPORTS | Flips (a short flight on a helicopter) are undertaken with up to three people leaving from Virgina Airport. Take a scenic trip to Umhlanga (10 minutes), Umdloti (14 minutes), Durban harbor (14 minutes), or to Ballito (25 minutes). Seeing the coast from the air is quite breathtaking. ⊠ *Virgina Airport, Hangar 1, 220 Fairway, Umhlanga* ☎ *031/563–9513* ⊕ *www.jncheli.co.za* ✉ *12 mins, Durban harbor R2,600 for 3 people; 20 mins, harbor plus Umhlanga R3,400 for 3 people; 30 mins, Ballito R4,500 for 3 people.*

SURFING

Surfing has a fanatical following in Durban, and several local and international tournaments are staged on the city's beaches, at nearby Umhlanga, Ballito,

or on the Bluff. Crowds of more than 10,000 are not unusual for night surfing competitions or the annual Ballito Pro championship (formerly the Gunston 500), a top World Qualifying Series event on the world surfing circuit. When the conditions are right, New Pier is one of the best beach breaks in the world.

Just on the other side of Durban's protected bay, Cave Rock, on the Bluff, offers a seething right-hander that can handle big swell. It can be a tough paddle and is not for amateurs. Farther down the South Coast, surfers head for Scottburgh, Green Point, Park Rynie, or Southbroom. North of Durban, popular spots include Umhlanga, Ballito, Richard's Bay, and Sodwana Bay.

The more popular spots can get crowded, and locals are known to be territorial about certain sections. Be sure to obey the laws of surfing etiquette. Usually the best waves are found at dawn and dusk. If the southwester blows, the Durban beaches are your best bet. In the winter months look out for an early-morning land breeze to set up good waves along the whole coastline.

Surfing lessons are offered at uShaka Beach, where experienced coaches supply boards and advice. Surf shops along the beachfront will put you in touch with surf coaches, including professional surfers and bodyboarders who offer one-on-one coaching and group lessons. You can also rent surfing equipment from the surf shops, by the hour or by the day, at nominal rates during peak vacation season.

Learn2Surf

SURFING | Run by a surfer-lifeguard, this surf school just north of uShaka Beach at Addington Beach caters to beginners and improvers, for individuals or groups—and can even organize surf parties. Equipment is supplied. Prices depend on your individual requirements. ⊠ *Erskine Terr., Beachfront* ☎ *083/414–0567 SMS hotline*

⊕ www.southafrica.learn2surf.net/
🖃 R300 per lesson, per person; various
rates apply.

Ocean Ventures

SURFING | Based on the beachfront at
uShaka Marine World, this company
offers surf instruction suitable for begin-
ners for R250 per hour as well as ocean
kayaking. You can rent surfboards and
bodyboards here, too. ✉ uShaka Marine
World, 1 Bell St., South Beach, Beachfront ☎ 031/332–9949, 073/687–3326
⊕ www.oceanventures.co.za 🖃 R250 per
hr, per person for private surf lesson.

PADDLING
★ The Green Hub

CANOEING & ROWING | Durban Green
Corridors is a non-profit organization
that offers responsible eco-tours from
passionate youngsters. For something
different in the city, canoe around the
Umgeni River lagoon on a guided trip
upriver to Connaught Bridge and back
towards the mouth. You can also walk
through the nearby mangroves on a
guided tour. Based at Blue Lagoon at the
start of the promenade, there's also very
affordable bicycle rental. ✉ Green Hub
⊕ www.durbangreencorridor.co.za/green-
hub-umngeni-adventures 🖃 R175 guided
or R85 rental.

★ Xpression On The Beach

STAND UP PADDLEBOARDING | Learn how
to Stand Up Paddle on the glassy ocean
waters or cruise one of the city's hidden
canals. Based on the beachfront, this
surf store provides rentals for everything
you need on the promenade—bicycles,
go-karts, skateboards, surf and stand-
up paddleboards. This is also the only
"Surfing South Africa Accredited Surf
School" in Durban. Book a private lesson
or mingle with locals at the one-hour
Saturday SUP club for less. ✉ Xpression
☎ 031/001–1052 ⊕ www.xpressiononthe-
beach.com/durban/ 🖃 R250.

Umhlanga

17½ km (11 miles) north of Durban via M4

Umhlanga's sophisticated charm and
lovely beaches have entrenched it as one
of the most sought-after vacation destinations for locals and foreigners, and it
has many of Durban's top hotels. Also
known as Umhlanga Rocks (meaning
"Place of the Reeds"), this area used to
be a small vacation village, but Durban's
northward sprawl has incorporated it into
a popular and upscale residential and
business suburb, much like Sandton is to
downtown Johannesburg. To the north
are the nicest sea views; to the south is
Umhlanga's lighthouse.

Sights

Gateway Theatre of Shopping

STORE/MALL | **FAMILY** | The largest mall
in the Southern Hemisphere, Gateway
has been designed to let in natural light
and is surprisingly easy to navigate.
Shopping ranges from surfing parapher-
nalia and imported and local fashions to
electronics, Indian spices, and designer
wedding frocks. Gateway also has a large
variety of entertainment options including
an IMAX theater, indoor trampoline
park, funfair, karting track, and sports
arena. ✉ New Town Centre, 1 Palm Bd.
☎ 031/514–0500 ⊕ www.gatewayworld.
co.za.

Hawaan Forest

FOREST | This 114-acre coastal forest
grows on a dune that dates back 18,000
years and has 175 species of indigenous
trees, fungi (during wet months), and
various species of birds. Guided walks
take two to three hours and are conduct-
ed on the first Saturday of every month
(except in January or February), but if you
call ahead you may be accommodated
at another time. ∎**TIP**→ **Be sure to wear
closed-toe shoes.** ✉ Portland Dr. at Herald
Dr. ☎ 031/561–2271 ⊕ www.breakersre-
sort.co.za 🖃 R30.

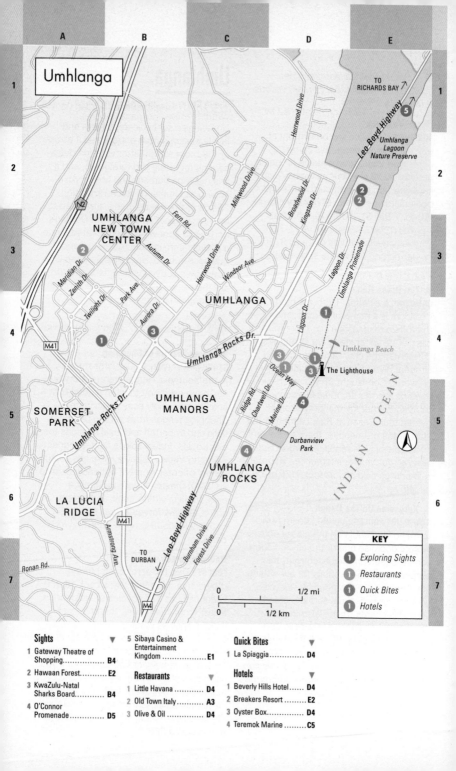

Umhlanga

A B C D E

1

TO RICHARDS BAY

Leo Boyd Highway

Umhlanga Lagoon Nature Preserve

Herrwood Drive

Millwood Drive

Broadwold Dr.

Kingston Dr.

2

2

UMHLANGA NEW TOWN CENTER

N2

Fern Rd.

Meridian Dr.

Zenith Dr.

Autumn Dr.

Herrwood Drive

Windsor Ave.

Lagoon Dr.

Umhlanga Promenade

3

Twilight Dr.

Park Ave.

Aurora Dr.

UMHLANGA

M41

Umhlanga Rocks Dr.

Lagoon Dr.

Umhlanga Beach

4

SOMERSET PARK

Umhlanga Rocks Dr.

UMHLANGA MANORS

Ocean Way

The Lighthouse

Ridge Rd.

Chartwell Dr.

Marine Dr.

Durbanview Park

INDIAN OCEAN

5

LA LUCIA RIDGE

M41

Armstrong Ave.

TO DURBAN

Leo Boyd Highway

UMHLANGA ROCKS

Burnham Drive

Forest Drive

6

Ronan Rd.

M4

0   1/2 mi

0   1/2 km

KEY

1 Exploring Sights
1 Restaurants
1 Quick Bites
1 Hotels

7

Sights ▼

1 Gateway Theatre of Shopping................ **B4**

2 Hawaan Forest.......... **E2**

3 KwaZulu-Natal Sharks Board............ **B4**

4 O'Connor Promenade **D5**

5 Sibaya Casino & Entertainment Kingdom **E1**

Restaurants ▼

1 Little Havana **D4**

2 Old Town Italy **A3**

3 Olive & Oil **D4**

Quick Bites ▼

1 La Spiaggia **D4**

Hotels ▼

1 Beverly Hills Hotel **D4**

2 Breakers Resort **E2**

3 Oyster Box................ **D4**

4 Teremok Marine **C5**

★ **KwaZulu-Natal Sharks Board**

COLLEGE | FAMILY | Most of the popular bathing beaches in KwaZulu-Natal are protected by shark nets maintained by this shark-research institute, the world's foremost. Each day, weather permitting, crews in ski boats check the nets, releasing healthy sharks back into the ocean and bringing dead ones back to the institute, where they are dissected and studied. One-hour tours are offered, including a shark dissection (sharks' stomachs have included such surprising objects as a boot, a tin can, and a car license plate!) and an enjoyable and fascinating audiovisual presentation on sharks and shark nets. An exhibit area and good curio shop are also here. You can also join the early morning trip from Durban harbor to watch the staff service the shark nets off Durban's Golden Mile. Depending on the season, you will more than likely see dolphins and whales close at hand, but the real kicker are the sunrise views across the city. Booking is essential for trips to the shark nets, and a minimum of six people is required; no one under age six is allowed.

■TIP→ **Book well in advance for this—it may turn out to be a highlight of your trip.** ⊠ *1a Herrwood Dr.* ☎ *031/566–0400, 082/403–9206 for boat tour reservations* ⊕ *www.shark.co.za* ⊠ *Presentation R50, boat trips R350* ⊘ *Dissection show days Tues.–Thurs. only* ☞ *Boat tour fee includes complementary ticket to shark dissection show.*

O'Connor Promenade

PROMENADE | FAMILY | Join tourists and locals for a gentle stroll or vigorous run along the 3-km (2-mile) paved stretch that reaches from Durban View Park in the south to Umhlanga Lagoon Nature Reserve in the north. This is a great way to check out the local coastline and bathing areas, and you'll pass Umhlanga's landmark lighthouse (closed to the public) and the pier, with steel arches designed to look like a whale's skeleton.

It's also known as the Umhlanga Rocks Promenade. ⊠ *Umhlanga Beach* ⊠ *Free.*

Sibaya Casino & Entertainment Kingdom

CASINO | Sibaya is expansive—in size, appearance, and number of activities—but is worth seeing for its grandiose, Zulu-themed design. The buildings themselves, for example, echo a giant and opulent Zulu *kraal* (compound/dwelling). Huge bronze statues of Zulu warriors and buffaloes at the entrance provide a truly African welcome. Wherever you are at Sibaya—all 48 hectares (119 acres) of it—a breathtaking view of the ocean is only a window or a balcony away. As you might expect, there are plenty of dining options, and there's a 36-room, five-star hotel as well as a lodge with 118 rooms. It's quite a way out of town, north of Umhlanga and about halfway between the city center and Ballito. If you have only a few days, you won't want to spent them at a casino. ⊠ *1 Sibaya Dr.* ☎ *031/580–5000* ⊕ *www.suninternational.com/sibaya* ⊠ *Free.*

⦿ Beaches

★ **Umhlanga Beaches**

BEACH | Some of the country's finest beaches are on this stretch of the coast, and they can be less crowded than those in central Durban. Safe and clean—Umhlanga Rocks beach has a Blue Flag award—the beaches are easily accessed via pathways from parking lots down to a promenade skirting the busy beachfront. Vacation apartments and premier hotels like the Oyster Box, Cabanas, and Beverly Hills line this paved walkway southward to Umhlanga's famous lighthouse. If you're driving here, arrive early at peak times so you'll have a better chance of finding a parking spot. **Amenities:** food and drink; parking. **Best for:** jogging; sunrise; surfing; swimming; walking. ⊠ *Lighthouse Rd. or Marine Dr.* ⊠ *Free.*

Part of the O'Connor Promenade, the Whalebone Pier is a great place to stroll and catch the sunset.

🍴 Restaurants

Little Havana

$$$ | **STEAKHOUSE** | This award-winning steak house has a modern dining room—expect well-dressed diners on romantic dates or small business teams strategizing over lunch. The steaks are unmissable (try the chimichurri sirloin), though the line fish with coconut and lime and the caponata gnocchi will satisfy those without carnivorous tastes. **Known for:** excellent steaks; local wine list; Cuban vibe. [$] *Average main: R180* ✉ *Granada Sq., 16 Chartwell Dr.* ☎ *031/561–7589, 081/393–8205* 🌐 *www.littlehavana.co.za.*

Old Town Italy

$$ | **ITALIAN** | This chic outpost of Old Town Italy is a cleaned-up, thoroughly modern version of an old-fashioned Italian delicatessen, with a restaurant serving simple, wholesome fare, that seats patrons indoors and outside on the pavement—a favorite in warm weather. Order a platter of the finest Italian salumi or cheeses; heartier appetites may look to the lemon caper chicken or steak Florentine. **Known for:** inviting decor; Italian wines. [$] *Average main: R150* ✉ *Meridian Park, 39 Meridian Dr.* ☎ *031/566–5008* 🌐 *www.oldtown.co.za.*

Olive & Oil

$$ | **MEDITERRANEAN** | You can't go wrong with the fantastic and well-priced Mediterranean-inspired fare here. The best way to start your meal is with a meze platter to share before moving on to main courses like calamari, steaks, pastas with Sicilian and Moroccan flavors, and the easy-on-the-budget pizzas. **Known for:** excellent value; outdoor seating; family-friendly setting. [$] *Average main: R150* ✉ *Chartwell Centre, Shop 19, 15 Chartwell Dr.* ☎ *031/561–2618* 🌐 *oliveandoil.co.za/branches/umhlanga.*

☕ Coffee and Quick Bites

La Spiaggia

$ | **AFRICAN** | **FAMILY** | As close to the Indian Ocean as you can get, this restaurant overlooking the main bathing beach has outside tables that are always packed with families sipping milk shakes or friends sharing a bottle of wine and having a bite to eat off a menu with broad appeal. Not the best food on offer in the area, but an unbeatable location. **Known for:** Kahlúa coffee milkshake; sea views; pizza. [$] *Average main: R100* ✉ *O'Connor Promenade* ☎ *031/561–4388.*

Hotels

Beverly Hills Hotel

$$$$ | HOTEL | In a high-rise building right on the beach, this upscale hotel is popular with both vacationers and businesspeople and has a long-standing reputation for gracious hospitality. **Pros:** hotel has its own demarcated piece of beach with lounge chairs; unbeatable sea views. **Cons:** some rooms and many of the bathrooms are smaller than you might expect; prices increase in-season; a dedicated local crowd may give this hotel a cliquey feel. [$] *Rooms from: R4580* ✉ *2 Lighthouse Rd.* ☎ *031/561–2211* 🌐 *www.tsogosun.com/beverly-hills* 🛏 *89 rooms* 🍴 *Free Breakfast.*

Breakers Resort

$$ | RESORT | FAMILY | This property enjoys an enviable position at the northern tip of Umhlanga, surrounded by the wilds of the Hawaan Forest and overlooking the unspoiled wetlands of Umhlanga Lagoon. **Pros:** family-friendly; sprawling gardens; great pool. **Cons:** furniture is basic; overrun with families in-season; taxi is required to get to local restaurants, especially at night. [$] *Rooms from: R1800* ✉ *88 Lagoon Dr.* ☎ *031/561–2271* 🌐 *www.breakersresort.co.za* 🛏 *80 rooms* 🍴 *No Meals.*

★ **Oyster Box**

$$$$ | HOTEL | This iconic multi-award-winning hotel has achieved a perfect marriage between old colonial and African contemporary style in its luxurious accommodations and offers an eye-popping range of services and complimentary extras. **Pros:** free shuttle to Gateway Shopping Centre; fabulous food (vegan options too) and service; award-winning spa. **Cons:** colonial uniforms are dated; public areas fill up with nonresidents attending various events in the hotel; the resident vervet monkeys can make a nuisance of themselves—lock your room doors. [$] *Rooms from: R8850* ✉ *2 Lighthouse Rd.* ☎ *031/514–5000* 🌐 *www.oysterboxhotel.com* 🛏 *86 rooms* 🍴 *Free Breakfast.*

★ **Teremok Marine**

$$$$ | HOTEL | Translated from Russian as "little hideaway," this delightful boutique lodge has eight huge, individually styled rooms, each offering a different sensory experience—its own specific body-product fragrance and mood CD—and the three rooms at the top have beautiful ocean views. **Pros:** free transfers to village; close to Umhlanga village and one block from the sea; personalized service and concierge recommendations. **Cons:** no minibars in the room; open-plan bathrooms in all but one room; 1 km (½ mile) from nearest restaurants. [$] *Rooms from: R4890* ✉ *49 Marine Dr.* ☎ *031/561–5848* 🌐 *www.teremok.co.za* 🛏 *8 rooms* 🍴 *Free Breakfast.*

Valley of a 1000 Hills

45 km (27 miles) northwest of Durban.

In the early part of the 19th century, before cars were introduced, wagons traveled from the port of Durban up along the ridge of this region of plunging gorges, hills, and valleys into the hinterland, where the mining industry was burgeoning. Today the Old Main Road (M103) still runs between Durban and Pietermaritzburg, winding through a number of villages and offering stunning views of hills and valleys dotted with traditional Zulu homesteads. It is along this route that the Comrades Marathon—South Africa's most famous road race—is run.

For purposes of exploring, the area has been organized into routes by the local tourism office. A favorite with Durbanites, the routes wind through villages and past coffee shops, art galleries, restaurants, quaint pubs, small inns, farms, and nature reserves. There are a number of excellent B&Bs, small inns, and lodges in the area, often with fantastic views of the gorges.

GETTING HERE AND AROUND

The main route—the T1, or Comrades Route—follows the M13 out of Durban, up Field's Hill, through the village of Kloof, and past Everton, Gillits, and Winston Park; it then joins the Old Main Road (M103) at Hillcrest. A number of small shopping centers along the M103 sell a variety of goods, from crafts to old furniture, and there are some excellent coffee shops, restaurants, and small hotels as well as cultural attractions. At the end of the M103 is the small town of Monteseel, known for its climbing routes. Drive along the dirt roads to the signposted overlook for one of the best uninterrupted views of the Thousand Hills. Other well-marked routes in the area are the T2 Kranzkloof Route, T3 Assagay Alverstone Route, T4 Isithumba Route, and T5 and T6 Shongweni Shuffle, all of which make for scenic drives.

VISITOR INFORMATION

CONTACTS 1000 Hills Tourism Association. ✉ *47 Old Main Rd.* ☎ *031/322–2855* 🌐 *www.1000hillstourism.co.za.*

Sights

PheZulu Safari Park

MUSEUM VILLAGE | FAMILY | Popular with big tour buses, PheZulu is the equivalent of fast-food tourism, good for people who want a quick-fix African experience. A tour of the cultural village, in collaboration with the Gasa clan, with its traditional beehive huts gives some insight into African traditions, and there are performances of traditional Zulu dancing, but the operation is not as vibrant or professional as the cultural villages up north in Zululand. An old-fashioned crocodile farm and snake park is fairly interesting, if a little tacky. The curio shop is enormous; you can probably get just about any type of African memento or booklet imaginable. Impala and zebra are frequently spotted on the hour-long game drive (additional fee). Accommodations are available on the property and can be booked online. ✉ *Old Main Rd., Drummond* ☎ *031/777–1205* 🌐 *www.phezulusafaripark.co.za* 🎟 *Village tour and Zulu dancing R100, game drive R220, reptile park tour R60* 🕒 *Closed Mon.*

Restaurants

★ The LivingRoom @ Summerhill Estate Culinary Retreat

$$$$ | SOUTH AFRICAN | Don't let the relaxed homey feel fool you; this is the most exciting meal you can have in the Durban area right now. Each course of the sustainable nose-to-tail menu is bold, flavorful, and carries a Kwa-Zulu Natal story, told by the head chef, German-born, Durban-raised Johannes Richter, who incorporates the property's fresh produce with handcrafted items like fish sauce made by fermented specimens caught on the annual sardine run and homemade sourdough served with lashings of spiced masala butter, as well as local ingredients such as maas (traditional milk) and amaranth (a protein-packed grain). **Known for:** a great spot for date night; exciting fine dining; creative vegetarian options. [$] *Average main: R1255* ✉ *Summerhill Estate, 9 Belvedale Rd., Durban* ✥ *a 15-minute drive from Durban's City Centre in the suburb of Westville* ☎ *063/529–1966* 🌐 *www.summerhillkzn.com* ☞ *7 courses R730 / including wine pairing R1,255.*

Treat Cafe

$ | CAFÉ | FAMILY | Tucked away from the road, this café with its fresh palette and friendly service welcomes guests with farm-style food, hearty breakfasts, and healthy lunches; opt for outdoor seating overlooking the Alverstone Valley. The café is a great spot for a cup of coffee and a slice of their famous lemon meringue pie. **Known for:** on-site spa; good coffee and light meals in a relaxing setting; beautiful local gifts. $ *Average main: R100* ⊠ *61 Old Main Rd.* ☎ *031/777–1586* ⊕ *www.talloula.co.za/ treat-cafe/* ⊗ *Closed Tues.*

🛍 Shopping

The Puzzle Place
TOYS | FAMILY | With quirky wooden puzzles for the young and young-at-heart, this small shop provides a selection of locally themed puzzles, including brainteasers and 3-D puzzles. Consider the various well-crafted Africa and Big Five-shaped puzzles as unusual curios to take back home. ⊠ *1000 Hills Village, 138 Old Main Rd.* ☎ *072/986–1168* ⊕ *www. puzzleplace.co.za.*

Dolphin Coast

48 km (30 miles) northwest of Durban.

About an hour north of Durban, the Dolphin Coast (North Coast) lies along the warm waters of the Indian Ocean, with lifeguards and shark-netted beaches making it a popular vacation choice. Bordered by the Tugela River in the north and Zimbali in the south, it includes Ballito, Chaka's Rock, Salt Rock, Sheffield Beach, Blythedale, and Zinkwazi. Four excellent golf courses, a crocodile farm, cultural villages, and historical Indian, British, and Zulu sites are easily accessible at KwaDukuza, Shakaskraal, and Sheffield.

Large shopping malls straddle the entry into Ballito, and the Gateway Theatre of Shopping and La Lucia malls are just a 15-minute drive away. All types of accommodations are covered, from hotels to camping, and a host of restaurants are available.

Culture and history form an integral part of life on the Dolphin Coast. Indian, Zulu, and colonial cultures can all be explored on one estate at The Kingdom in Sheffield. You can visit the King Shaka Memorial in KwaDukuza/Stanger, the Dukuza Museum, or the grave and home of Nobel Peace Prize winner Chief Albert Luthuli in Groutville. There are also many temples and mosques in the Shakaskraal and KwaDukuza/Stanger area.

GETTING HERE AND AROUND
A rental vehicle will afford you the flexibility needed to visit select destinations. You can take the N2, but the M4 north is a more scenic option. King Shaka International Airport lies 22 km (14 miles) north.

VISITOR INFORMATION
CONTACTS North Coast Tourism. ⊠ *Ithala Trade Center, 29 Canal Quay Rd.* ☎ *031/366–7500* ⊕ *www.zulu.org.za/ travel/regions/north-coast/.*

🍴 Restaurants

Mozambik
$$$ | AFRICAN | FAMILY | Sample the authentic tastes of Mozambique without ever crossing the border at this funky, vibrant restaurant. The eatery's rustic charm extends from the interior design to the service to the food, which has Portuguese, Arab, Indian, and Goan influences. **Known for:** lively atmosphere; specialty seafood dishes; kids' area. $ *Average main: R165* ⊠ *Belvista Centre, 12 Library Lane, Ballito* ☎ *066/242–2973* ⊕ *www. mozambik.co.za.*

★ Two Shrimps
$$$ | ECLECTIC | Smack-dab against the ocean with the sound of waves tumbling just outside, Two Shrimps at The Canelands Beach Club & Spa, a converted former luxury beach house, offers incredible views and contemporary classics. This is the place for seafood, so splurge on the seafood platter for two, the peri-peri prawns, or the saffron-infused poached crayfish. **Known for:** proximity to

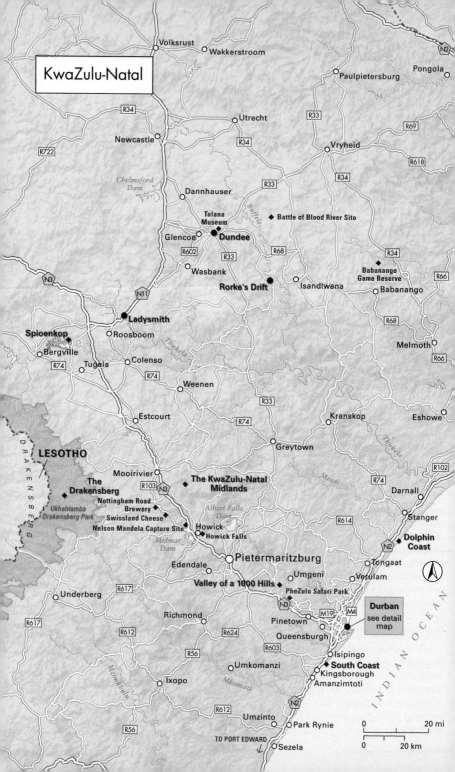

KwaZulu-Natal

LESOTHO

Volksrust
Wakkerstroom
Paulpietersburg
Pongola
R34
Utrecht
R33
R69
Newcastle
R34
Vryheid
R618
R722
R34
N3
Chelmsford Dam
Dannhauser
R33
Talana Museum
Battle of Blood River Site
Glencoe · Dundee
R602
R33
R68
Babanango Game Reserve
R34
Wasbank
R66
Rorke's Drift
Isandlwana
Babanango
N11
R68
Ladysmith
Roosboom
Melmoth
Spioenkop
Bergville
R66
R74
Tugela
Colenso
R74
Weenen
Estcourt
R74
R33
Kranskop
Eshowe
Greytown
DRAKENSBERG
R102
Mooirivier
The KwaZulu-Natal Midlands
R74
Darnall
The Drakensberg
R103
N3
Albert Falls Dam
R614
Stanger
Nottingham Road Brewery
Ukhahlamba Drakensberg Park
Swissland Cheese
N2
Dolphin Coast
Nelson Mandela Capture Site
Howick
Howick Falls
Midmar Dam
Tongaat
Pietermaritzburg
Verulam
Edendale
Umgeni
Underberg
Valley of a 1000 Hills
PheZulu Safari Park
Durban see detail map
R617
N3
M19
M4
Richmond
Pinetown
R612
Queensburgh
R603
Isipingo
R56
Umkomanzi
South Coast
Ixopo
Kingsborough
Amanzimtoti
R617
INDIAN OCEAN
R612
Umzinto
Park Rynie
TO PORT EDWARD
Sezela

0   20 mi

0   20 km

the ocean; seafood; views. $ *Average main: R200* ⊠ *2 Shrimp La., Salt Rock* ☎ *032/525–2300* ⊕ *www.thecanelands. co.za/dining.*

South Coast

60 km (37 miles) southwest of Durban.

Vacation towns like Scottburgh, Margate, Ramsgate, Trafalgar, and Palm Beach dot KwaZulu-Natal's southern coast, which stretches for more than 200 km (125 miles) from Durban in the north to Port Edward in the south. The area has some of the country's best beaches, set against a tropical background of natural coastal jungle and palm trees. In fact, Blue Flag status has been conferred on Alkantstrand, Lucien, Marina (San Lameer), Ramsgate, Southport, Trafalgar, and Umzumbe beaches.

The South Coast is also famous for the annual sardine run, dubbed the Greatest Shoal on Earth, which usually occurs in June or July. Colder currents in Antarctica at this time bring millions of sardines to local waters, and they often wash right up on the beach. Dolphins, seabirds, sharks, and whales follow in a feeding frenzy. Paddle into the sea and collect your own lunch in a bucket.

GETTING HERE AND AROUND
The best and really only way to explore this area is with your own transportation. Main roads (the N2 and R61) are easy to navigate, and following the coastal road (turn off the R61 toward the coast) is picturesque.

If you're looking to explore the South Coast, Sapphire Coast Tourism and Tourism South Coast can provide relevant information.

VISITOR INFORMATION
CONTACTS Sapphire Coast Tourism. ⊠ *95 Beach Rd., Amanzimtoti* ☎ *031/322–2852* ⊕ *www.sapphirecoasttourism.co.za.* **Tourism South Coast.** ⊠ *16 Bisset St., Port*

Shepstone ☎ *039/682–7944* ⊕ *www. visitknsouthcoast.co.za.*

 Sights

★ Beaver Creek Coffee
FARM/RANCH | **FAMILY** | Coffee grown in the seaside town of Port Edward? You best believe it! At Beaver Creek, four coffee trees have grown since 1984 to more than 60,000 today. Family-run (three generations have worked here), this coffee plantation and roastery is open to the public for daily hour-long tours of the estate called Crop to Cup (R75 per person) to better understand the process, outlining the flavors you can expect from the different coffee regions and what goes into creating a meticulous hand-harvested cup of coffee. The Estate Café (8 am–4 pm) brews freshly roasted coffee and serves light meals. Buy bags of beans or ground coffee as a unique souvenir from this region. You can also book a two-hour barista course to learn to make a great cup at home using various brewing methods—by appointment only (R500). ⊠ *Izingolweni Rd., Port Edward* ☎ *039/311–2347* ⊕ *www. beavercreek.co.za.*

 Hotels

San Lameer Villas
$$ | **APARTMENT** | **FAMILY** | The vacation rental properties in this exclusive resort between Ramsgate and Palm Beach offer a great getaway for a group of friends or a family, and golfers are drawn by the on-site championship course. **Pros:** lively atmosphere; on a Blue Flag beach; championship golf course on-site. **Cons:** busy in-season; it's a car ride away from off-site restaurants; estate is very large. $ *Rooms from: R2000* ⊠ *Lower South Coast Main Rd., San Lameer* ☎ *039/313–0450* ⊕ *www.sanlameer.co.za* ↬ *62 rooms* ⍾ *No Meals* ⌀ *Minimum two-night stay required.*

Umzumbe Surf House

$ | **HOUSE** | As one of the first cottages built in the area over 100 years ago, this laidback and airy white-washed beach house enjoys a prime position on the quiet coastline, and it's one of the few spots where you can walk straight from your bed onto the sandy shores in under a minute. **Pros:** easy to access with regular airport shuttle schedule; beachfront location and on-site surf school; chilled atmosphere. **Cons:** not advisable to use the beach at night; nearest restaurant requires driving. $ *Rooms from: R1000* ✉ *11 Green Lane Rd., (2 Track Extension)* ☎ *073/536–8728* ⊕ *www.umzumbesurf-camp.com* 🛏 *8 rooms* ⦿*No Meals.*

The KwaZulu-Natal Midlands

104 km (65 miles) northwest of Durban.

Set amid the rolling green foothills of the Drakensberg, the Midlands encompass waterfalls, lakes, reservoirs, forests, fields, Zulu villages, game reserves, and battle sites. The climate is pleasant most of the year, though summers tend to be hot, with a brief afternoon thunderstorms. Nights in the mountains can get bitterly cold, even in summer. The area has long been an enclave for craftspeople—weavers, potters, woodcrafters, metalworkers, cheese makers, and beer brewers—who escaped the cities.

As a way to draw customers to the area, the crafters created a growing number of routes, called the Midlands Meander, in 1985, which include more than 160 shops, galleries, cultural activities, restaurants, and accommodations. Running through the towns of Curry's Post and Howick in the northeast and the little village of Nottingham Road, Mooi River, Balgowan, the Dargyle District, Lion's River, and Midmar in the southwest, the routes provide a great opportunity to shop for authentic, high-quality South African arts and crafts while enjoying the tranquility and beauty of the countryside. The area is filled with top accommodations and dining options.

The most popular time to do the Meander is in the autumn (March to May), when it's not too hot or too cold. Many South Africans love the winters here; it often snows, particularly on the higher ground, and many establishments burn fires. Don't be surprised to experience four seasons in one day! No matter what time of year you visit, though, there's always something to see and do, most of which involves shopping for local crafts or indulging in artisanal produce.

GETTING HERE AND AROUND

The only way to explore this area is in your own transportation. Roads are easy to navigate, and all establishments are well marked. The N3 is the quickest route between places, but the R103 is a scenic route that passes through all areas.

VISITOR INFORMATION

If you plan to explore the area, contact the Midlands Meander Association for its magazine that includes maps of the routes and details of the various establishments. Members of the association also stock the magazine for sale or for free if you are a paying guest at one of the accommodation establishments.

■ TIP→ **More-remote artisans may follow their own schedules**

CONTACT Midlands Meander Association. ☎ *033/330–8195* ⊕ *www.midlandsmeander.co.za.*

Sights

Howick Falls

VIEWPOINT | Although this area in the heart of the KwaZulu-Natal Midlands is mainly about dining, shopping, and the arts, this lovely waterfall is definitely worth a stop. In the town of Howick, the Umgeni River plunges an impressive 300

This dramatic steel sculpture, known as the Nelson Mandela Capture Site, marks the spot where Mandela was finally captured on August 5, 1962 after 17 months on the run.

feet into a deep pool in the gorge. Local people and sangomas (traditional Zulu healers) believe the waterfall is inhabited by ancestral spirits and has mystical powers. Take photographs from the viewing platform, or if you have more time, there are numerous hikes of varying difficulty that provide different vantages of the falls. Contact or visit the Howick Tourism Office, which is just a few hundred yards from the falls, for information. ⊠ *Falls Dr., Howick.*

★ Nelson Mandela Capture Site

VISITOR CENTER | FAMILY | In 2012, on the 50th anniversary of Nelson's Mandela's capture, this breathtakingly dramatic steel sculpture was unveiled and the visitor center opened. You will never have seen anything quite like this—don't miss it. The magnitude of what happened here is remarkable: on August 5, 1962, after 17 months on the run, Nelson Mandela, disguised as a chauffeur, was arrested at this very spot on his way from Durban to Johannesburg. He was convicted of incitement and illegally leaving the

country and was sentenced to 5 years in jail before being prosecuted in the Rivonia Trials that led to his 27-year incarceration, most of it served on Robben Island. The new immersive exhibition is a marvel with a 360-surround film screened onto the towering walls accompanied by copious clippings and artifacts that'll keep you engrossed for ages. Plan at least two hours for your visit; the last admission is at 4 pm. The cafe is open on weekends from 10 to 4 for light lunches and coffee. ⊠ *R103, Howick* ⊹ *From the N3 take the Tweedie Interchange and get onto the R103; the monument is just outside Howick* ☎ *072/351–0967* ⊕ *www.the-capturesite.co.za* ⊠ *R100* ⊗ *Cafe closed Mon.–Fri.*

Nottingham Road Brewery

BREWERY | On the same premises as Rawdon's Hotel, this rustic microbrewery has developed a cult following. With names like Pickled Pig Porter, Whistling Weasel Pale Ale, Pye-Eyed Possum Pilsner, and Wobbling Wombat Summer Ale, you may have a tough time choosing which brew to taste first, so order a tasting paddle to sample them all. Call ahead if you would like to do a tour of the small brewery; otherwise just pop into the shop to stock up on beer, accessories, and clever merchandising. Guaranteed you'll head home with a "pickled as a pig" or "I'm as possed as a pye-eyed pissum" T-shirt. ⊠ *Rawdons Estate, Nottingham Rd., Nottingham Road* ☎ *033/266–6728* ⊕ *www.nottsbrewery. co.za/.*

Swissland Cheese

FARM/RANCH | **FAMILY** | Expect to be greeted by white free-roaming Saanen goats grazing happily in luscious green pastures when you visit this family-owned-and-run cheesery. In the Swiss-chalet-style tasting room, you can sample a range of goat cheeses including *chevin*—similar to a cream cheese but a little crumblier—and a mild blue cheese, and learn about the cheese-making practices that Fran Isaac and her family have been following here for more than two decades. Relax on the lawn with a picnic hamper you can choose at the deli or at the restaurant next door. If you're here between August and May, you can watch the daily goat-milking between 3 and 4:30 pm. ⊠ *R103 Old Main Rd., Balgowan* ☎ *082/418–3440* ⊕ *www. swisslandcheese.net* ⊙ *Closed Tues.– Thurs., Christmas, and New Year's Day* ☞ *High-clearance vehicles are advised.*

🍴 Restaurants

Blue Cow Deli at Gourmet Greek

$ | **GREEK FUSION** | **FAMILY** | The producer of arguably the best small-batch double-cream yogurt in the country, Blue Cow Deli at Gourmet Greek, situated on a small estate in the heart of the Meander, offers a café-style menu of Greek-inspired items and you can take tubs of yogurt and wedges of cow's milk cheese home. You won't find these products outside the province, so indulge while you can. **Known for:** dairy tours; yogurt and

cheese; area's best breakfast. **$** *Average main: R60* ⊠ *No. 10 D369, Lions River* ☎ *033/234–4338* ⊕ *www.thegourmet-greek.com* ⊙ *Closed Mon. and Tues.*

 Hotels

Brahman Hills Hotel & Spa

$$ | **HOTEL** | **FAMILY** | Brahman Hills is a contemporary slick country hotel with serviced self-catering cottages ideal for couples or families. **Pros:** good food and coffee at the main building; self-catering cottages offer solitude and hot tubs; set on a nature reserve with zebra and buck roaming. **Cons:** lacks the typical Midlands intimacy; focused on weddings and functions; hotel rooms are small and close to each other. **$** *Rooms from: R1745* ⊠ *Old Curry's Post Rd., Mount West* ☎ *033/266–6965* ⊕ *www.brahmanhills. co.za* ⟿ *48 rooms* ⦿ *No Meals.*

★ Fordoun Hotel and Spa

$$$ | **HOTEL** | In the heart of a lush dairy farm that dates back to the 1800s, original stone buildings have been converted into a five-star luxury hotel and spa. **Pros:** complimentary sauna, steam room, and gym; tranquil country setting; wholesome country fare at the restaurant and contemporary wine list. **Cons:** not all suites face mountains or dam; can get cold at night in rooms, though fireplaces and electric blankets are provided. **$** *Rooms from: R2700* ⊠ *R103, Nottingham Road* ✛ *3 km (2 miles) off N3* ☎ *033/266–6217* ⊕ *www.fordoun.com* ⟿ *31 suites* ⦿ *Free Breakfast.*

Granny Mouse Country House

$$ | **B&B/INN** | One of the best-loved and oldest hotels on the Meander, Granny Mouse has cozy thatch rooms, all slightly different, with a bush view, fireplace, and homey, though upmarket, atmosphere. **Pros:** lovely setting in rolling green countryside; highly regarded restaurant; on-site spa. **Cons:** popular wedding venue so can be noisy; country feel isn't for everyone; slightly dated interiors. [$] *Rooms from: R2290* ✉ *R103, Balgowan* ✣ *25 km (15½ miles) south of Nottingham Rd. exit off N3* ☎ *033/234–4071* 🌐 *www.grannymouse.co.za* 🛏 *32 rooms* 🍴 *Free Breakfast.*

Hartford House
$$$ | **B&B/INN** | Deliciously luxurious, if rather formal, this 1875 inn, high up on the Meander in the foothills of the Drakensberg, is steeped in history and misty beauty. **Pros:** all suites are thoughtfully appointed; gourmet getaway; beautiful English-styled garden. **Cons:** service exceedingly polite; can feel a little formal; food is excellent, but a little traditional. [$] *Rooms from: R2680* ✉ *Hlatikulu Rd., off road to Giant's Castle, Mooi River* ☎ *033/263–1081* 🌐 *www.hartford.co.za* 🛏 *17 rooms* 🍴 *Free Breakfast.*

Rawdons Country Hotel
$$ | **RESORT** | In the heart of the lush KwaZulu Natal Midlands, this lake-side English cottage-style hotel offers lawn tennis, walking trails, a distillery, and a brewery, with beers best enjoyed at the Boars Head Pub. **Pros:** recently updated rooms; good base for exploring the Midlands; Nottingham Road Brewery onsite. **Cons:** popular wedding destination; peace and tranquility might not be for everyone; older properties can be noisy. [$] *Rooms from: R1530* ✉ *Nottingham Rd., Nottingham Road* ☎ *033/266–6044* 🌐 *www.rawdons.co.za* 🛏 *20 rooms* 🍴 *Free Breakfast.*

Shopping

Though on the whole the route is known for its quality, you can also find some establishments that are not quite up to the standards of others. If you've only a limited time, head for the concentration of crafts shops on the R103 between Nottingham Road and Lion's River. Or visit the one-stop Piggly Wiggly Country Village, which showcases the work of many of the Meander members. If you have a couple of days, base yourself at one of the hotels and explore the Meander using the large-format, free guide available at most Meander stops. Many of the better establishments offer shipping services for those unusual items large and small.

ART AND CRAFTS

★ **Ardmore Ceramic Art**
CERAMICS | Ardmore Ceramics, known for its exquisite and elaborate pieces, was established on the Ardmore farm in 1985 by ceramic artist Fée Halsted who was soon joined by the now late Bonnie Ntshalintshali, 18 years old at the time. The on-site museum dedicated to Bonnie is testament to her role in making Ardmore the brand it is today, with exhibitions in top galleries and private homes around the world, including a collaboration with Hermès and auctions by Christie's of London. There are glorious luxury fabrics, table decor, and more featuring the iconic Ardmore prints for sale, too. None of the ceramics are below R1,000 and some go up to an eye-watering R500,000. They offer tours of the site with artists busy at work, too—call in advance to arrange. ✉ *Caversham Rd., Lidgetton* ☎ *033/940–0034* 🌐 *www.ardmore-design.com/.*

Culamoya Chimes
OTHER SPECIALTY STORE | **FAMILY** | As you enter the gardens of Culamoya Chimes, in the Dargle District, your ears will be gently assailed with harmonious chimes of every description. There's a 13-foot chime in the garden as well as other chimes inside the shop that mimic the sounds of Big Ben and St. Paul's Cathedral down to gentle tinkles of fairy magic. The chimes are handmade and can be shipped to your home. ✉ *3 km (2 miles) off R103, Lidgetton* ☎ *082/565–5503* 🌐 *www.culamoyachimes.co.za* 🕒 *Closed Mon.*

Piggly Wiggly Country Village
MARKET | **FAMILY** | If you're short on time, but still want to experience some of the best of the Midland Meander's arts and

crafts, drop in at the one-stop Piggly Wiggly, where a wide range of shops—all representing Meander destinations and selling their products—are clustered around a central green with a Piggly putt-putt course and train ride for kids. There are fast-food outlets serving pizza and hamburgers, but be sure to sample the award-winning cappuccino and a slice of freshly baked cheesecake at Piggly Wiggly's famous coffee shop. On weekends, the reptile show and petting zoo at the Dingo Farm and Reptile Park is sure to keep little ones entertained (R60) while you peruse the antique book shop or lick a nougat ice cream. ⊠ 1 Dargle Rd., Lions River ☎ 060/344–9359 ⊕ www.pigglywiggly.co.za ☞ Piggly Wiggly Coffee Shop does not take reservations.

CLOTHING
Spiral Blue
JEWELRY & WATCHES | FAMILY | Here you'll find a veritable Aladdin's cave of colorful cotton, silk, and tie-dye garments and scarves, leather slippers, silver jewelry with precious and semiprecious stones, homewares, and esoteric gifts. Candles, incense, curtains, chimes, unusual door knobs, and even hammocks will keep you amused and browsing this fun space. Few things say "Midlands arts and crafts" like this iconic store. There's a garden outdoors if the kids get restless. ⊠ Lions River, R103, Shop No. 407, Lions River ☎ 033/234–4799 ⊕ www.spiralblue.co.za.

FOOD AND CANDY
Peel's Honey Merrivale Farmstore
FOOD | FAMILY | Established in 1924, Peel's Honey is the oldest honey label in the country. Snack on peanut honey brittle, or other tasty treats, or take a jar of creamed honey with you for padkos (the popular South African word for "road food," to munch as you drive). The new store sits inside a refashioned shipping container and also stocks other regional goods such as Terbodore Coffee. It's just off the N3 below the Midmar Dam. ⊠ 1 Boston Rd., Merrivale ☎ 033/330–3762 ⊕ www.peelshoney.co.za.

SHOES, LUGGAGE, AND LEATHER GOODS
Tsonga
SHOES | Makers of gorgeous handcrafted handbags and leather shoes for men, women, and children, Tsonga has its roots and inspiration in Lidgetton, where the iconic hand-stitching detail, a skill of the local women, originates. Inspired by the people he grew up around, founder Peter Maree created an African-influenced collection that provided valuable skills to this impoverished community. The Thread of Hope farm has become a training center where the motto is a hand up, not a hand out. Tsonga's shoes are based on a wide, ultra-cushioned sole and are supremely comfortable. With stores in South Africa, Australia, and France, you'd do well to visit the original outpost. Note, this isn't a factory store selling bargains, though you can occasionally find items on sale. ⊠ R103, Lidgetton, Lions River ☎ 087/379-6904 ⊕ www.tsonga.com.

Activities

ZIPLINES
Karkloof Canopy Tours
ZIP LINING | FAMILY | Zip along steel cables through the treetops of the Karkloof Forest, the second-largest indigenous forest in South Africa. The 1,800-foot-long foefie (zip) course is divided into 10 slides—the longest an exhilarating 656 feet long—that are interspersed with wooden platforms. Designed by a civil engineer, safety is paramount, and two trained guides (well versed in the forest and ecology) accompany each group; group size ranges from one to eight people. Tours (R595) take two hours and leave every hour in most weather conditions; call ahead to reserve your spot. Anyone from the ages of 7 to 70 can participate, but there's a weight limit of 130 kg (286 pounds). Light refreshments, lunch, and

a 4x4 trip up the mountain are included. ✉ *Karkloof Rd., Howick* ✛ *From Howick, take Karkloof Rd. for 19 km (12 miles) and follow signs to Canopy Tours for another 2 km (1¼ miles)* ☎ *076/241–2888* ⊕ *www.canopytour.co.za/locations/karkloof/* ✄ *R695.*

The Drakensberg

240 km (150 miles) northwest of Durban.

Afrikaners call them the Drakensberg: the Dragon Mountains. To Zulus they are uKhahlamba (pronounced Ooka-hlamba)—"Barrier of Spears." Both are apt descriptions for this wall of rock that rises from the Natal grasslands, forming a natural fortress protecting the mountain kingdom of Lesotho. Although you don't come here for big game, or much game at all, it's well worth visiting this World Heritage Site, the first in South Africa to be recognized for both its natural and cultural attractions, with some of the finest rock art in the world.

If possible plan your visit to the Berg during the spring (September and October) or late autumn (late April through June), because although summer sees the Berg at its greenest, it's also the hottest and wettest time of the year. Vicious afternoon thunderstorms and hailstorms are an almost-daily occurrence. In winter the mountains lose their lush overcoat and turn brown and sere. Winter days in the valleys, sites of most resorts, are usually sunny and pleasant, although there can be cold snaps, sometimes accompanied by overcast, windy conditions. Nights are chilly, however, and you should pack plenty of warm clothing if you plan to hike high up into the mountains or camp overnight. Snow is common at higher elevations.

GETTING HERE AND AROUND
The main resort area of the Drakensberg is almost a direct shot along the N3 from Durban. A car is not strictly necessary for

a trip to the Berg, although it is certainly a convenience, and though a 4x4 would be an advantage, it, too, is not a necessity. Gas stations can be found in Bergville, Winterton, and at the foot of Champagne Castle. Driving in this area is time consuming. Trucks often slow up traffic, and you should watch for animals on and attempting to cross the road.

VISITOR INFORMATION
CONTACTS Drakensberg Experience Tourism Association. ✉ *The Drakensberg* ⊕ *www.drakensbergexperience.com.* **Ezemvelo KZN Wildlife.** ☎ *033/845–1999* ⊕ *www.kznwildlife.com.*

 Sights

The Natal Drakensberg is not conducive to traditional touring because of the nature of the attractions and the limited road system. It's best to check into a hotel or resort for two or three days and use it as a base for hiking and exploring the immediate area. If you decide to stay at one of the self-catering camps, do your shopping in one of the bigger towns, such as Winterton or Harrismith for Tendele, and Bergville or Estcourt for Giant's Castle, Kamberg, and Injasuti. For more information on touring the area, visit the Drakensberg Experience Tourism Association website).

The Drakensberg
MOUNTAIN | The Drakensberg is the highest range in southern Africa and has some of the most spectacular scenery in the country. The blue-tinted mountains seem to infuse the landscape, cooling the "champagne air," as the locals refer to the heady, sparkling breezes that blow around the precipices and pinnacles. It's a hiker's dream, and you could easily spend several days here on the gentle and challenging slopes, just soaking up the awesome views.

The Drakensberg is not a typical mountain range—it's actually an escarpment separating a high interior plateau from

San Paintings

Besides the hiking opportunities and the sheer beauty of the mountains, the other great attraction of the Berg is the San (Bushman) paintings. The San are a hunter-gatherer people who once roamed the entire country from 8,000 years ago to the 1800s. With the arrival of the Nguni peoples from the north and white settlers from the southwest in the 18th century, the San were driven out of their traditional hunting lands and retreated into the remote fastnesses of the Drakensberg and the Kalahari Desert. San cattle raiding in Natal in the late 19th century occasioned harsh punitive expeditions by white settlers and local Bantu tribes, and by 1880 the last San had disappeared from the Berg. Today only a few clans remain in the very heart of the Kalahari Desert. More than 40,000 of their paintings enliven scores of caves and rock overhangs throughout the Berg in more than 550 known San rock-art sites—one of the finest collection of rock paintings not only in the country, but also in the world. They tell the stories of bygone hunts, dances, and ceremonies as well as relating and representing spiritual beliefs and practices. Images of spiritual leaders in a trance state, their visions, and their transformation of themselves into animals have now been studied and written about, although some of the meanings are still not fully understood. ■TIP→ **Be sure to bring binoculars and a cotton shirt and hat to cover up from the sun.**

the coastal lowlands of Natal. It's a continuation of the same escarpment that divides the Transvaal Highveld from the hot malarial zones of the lowveld in Mpumalanga. However, the Natal Drakensberg, or Berg, as it is commonly known, is far wilder and more spectacular than its Transvaal counterpart. Many of the peaks—some of which top 10,000 feet—are the source of crystalline streams and mighty rivers that have carved out myriad valleys and dramatic gorges. The Berg is a natural watershed, with two of South Africa's major rivers, the Tugela and the Orange, rising from these mountains. In this untamed wilderness you can hike for days and not meet a soul, and the mountains retain a wild majesty missing in the commercially forested peaks of Mpumalanga. 🌐 *www.drakensbergexperience.com.*

Hotels

Cathedral Peak Hotel
$$$ | **HOTEL** | **FAMILY** | You'll get breathtaking views from almost every spot in this friendly, delightful hotel nestled among the mountains, 43 km (18 miles) from Winterton. **Pros:** well-organized activities make it ideal for families; good horse trails around; central location near activities and shopping. **Cons:** crowded in season; can get loud with bands of children running about; decor and rooms a little tired. [$] *Rooms from: R2990* ✉ *Cathedral Peak Rd., Winterton* ☎ *036/488–1888* 🌐 *www.cathedralpeak.co.za* 🛏 *105 rooms* 🍴 *Free Breakfast.*

★ **Cleopatra Mountain Farmhouse**
$$$ | **B&B/INN** | This truly enchanting hideaway tucked away at the foot of the Drakensberg Range near Rosetta overlooks a trout-filled lake encircled by mountains and old trees. **Pros:** excellent service; exclusive yet modish accommodations;

gourmet breakfasts and dinners—come hungry. **Cons:** there's a formula—guests gather for a drink and dine at one set time, so you can't come and go as you please; if you're a fan of minimalistic decor, you'll have a hard time here; stay away if you're on a diet. [$] *Rooms from: R3200* ✉ *Highmoor Rd., off Kamberg Rd., Kamberg* ☎ *033/267–7243, 071/687–7266* 🌐 *www.cleopatramountain.com* 🛏 *11 rooms* 🍴 *Free Breakfast.*

Thendele Camp

$ | **RESORT** | **FAMILY** | Smack in the middle of Royal Natal National Park west of Bergville, amid some of the most spectacular mountain scenery in the Drakensberg, this very affordable popular camp makes a great base for hikes into the mountains. **Pros:** family-friendly; great views from every room; superb launch pad for hiking. **Cons:** supplies are limited; no luxury amenities nearby; not for urban party animals. [$] *Rooms from: R1400* ✉ *Royal Natal National Park* ☎ *036/438–6411* 🌐 *www.kznwildlife.com/Tendele.html* 🛏 *29 rooms* 🍴 *No Meals.*

Activities

HIKING

Stretching for almost 1000 km (621 miles), the Drakensberg Mountains offer some of the best hiking opportunities in South Africa, but the options can be overwhelming. The region's trails have few facilities and the routes traverse remote wilderness without passing through any towns, so hikers must be totally self-sufficient, which means carrying all food and camping supplies in a backpack for the duration of the multi-day hike. Some hikes have water points, but qualified mountain guides are best equipped to advise on such details due to seasonality. Commit to a hiking base depending on your needs. Want a luxurious location to return to after a day wandering the mountains? Then the Champagne Valley, with its golf course, spas, bakeries, and a brewery provides plenty of side attractions after tackling one of the gorgeous day hikes at Monk's Cowl. For remote wilderness that requires you to carry a tent, the Mnweni Pass provides a challenge for fit hikers. If you have just one night, then an adventure to the top of the Amphitheatre is your best bet. For total immersion, the rustic hutted five-day Giant's Cup trail is renowned for its straightforward trails and accessibility.

Hikes must be booked through the government-run KZN Wildlife (🌐 *www.kznwildlife.com*), and permits to enter the wilderness area typically cost between R85 and R100 per night. Reservations with a private guide cost roughly R400 a day.

Amphitheatre Overnight Hike

HIKING & WALKING | The 5-km (3-mile) long, 1200-meter (394-foot) high cliff face of the Amphitheatre looks impenetrable, but the iconic landmark is conquerable for fit hikers with a head for heights. The trailhead is at the Sentinel car park, in the Maloti Drakensberg Transfrontier Conservation Area, 7 km (4.3 miles) on a poor road from Witsieshoek Mountain Lodge, which also offers guides to escort you up. Tackle the chain ladders and marvel at the Tugela Falls—one of the world's tallest—from above. ✉ *Witsieshoek Mountain Lodge* ☎ *058/713–6361* 🌐 *www.witsieshoek.co.za* 🎟 *R1345 per guide.*

Giant's Cup Trail

HIKING & WALKING | Traversing the foothills of the uKhahlamba-Drakensberg Park World Heritage Site for nearly 60 km (37 miles), this is the most accessible multi-day trail in the range. Over five days, you'll be hiking with panoramic views, crossing crystal rivers, swimming in rock pools, and sleeping in the comfort of rustic huts (a rarity in the Berg) from Sani Pass to Bushman's Nek. This trail is accessed from the southern section of the mountain range, in the picturesque Underberg area. ✉ *Bushmans Nek* ☎ *033/845–1000 reservations* 🌐 *www.kznwildlife.com* 🎟 *R600.*

Mnweni Circuit

HIKING & WALKING | Mnweni means "the place of fingers" in isiZulu and refers to the pointed rock spires that fire high into the mountain heavens. Usually done as a two-day hike, this tough trail climbs several high, seriously steep passes, leading to the top of Lesotho, and through a rugged, remote, showstopping area of the Drakensberg that is far less frequented. The trails are unmarked and it's best to hire a guide. Hikes start from the Mnweni Cultural Centre (270 km [168 miles] from Durban), which is best accessed from Bergville. If you need to rent gear, Scuttle (⊕ www.scuttle.co.za) offers an affordable range of equipment, but book it in advance so they can deliver. ■TIP→ **Support the Mnweni Cultural and Hiking Centre by hiring a local guide. All are trained, familiar with the area, and hold first aid qualifications. Guide hire costs R1000 per day per group, and an overnight permit costs R60 per hiker. Don't forget to sign the rescue register.** ✉ *Mnweni Cultural Center, Bergville* ☎ *079/615–5941* 🎫 *R60.*

Monk's Cowl Day Hikes

HIKING & WALKING | Monks Cowl is the gateway to some of the most magnificent mountain trails in the central Champagne Valley. Day hikes range from one to six hours and are graded from easy to difficult. Park your car at the Monk's Cowl campsite and ask for a route map from the office. Explore the foothills and river valleys to visit the pretty, forested Sterkspruit Falls, the Gorge, iNandi Falls, or venture up the Sphinx onto the little 'berg. The trails are well-marked and you should be fine without a guide, but never underestimate the weather. Take snacks, water, a hat, and a rain jacket for every possibility. ✉ *Monks Cowl Camp* ☎ *036/468–1103* ⊕ *www.kznwildlife.com* 🎫 *R70.*

Ladysmith

160 km (99 miles) northwest of Pietermaritzburg.

Ladysmith, dating back to the middle of the 19th century, became famous around the world during the South African War, when it outlasted a Boer siege for 118 days. Nearly 20,000 people were caught in the town when the Boers attacked on November 2, 1899. Much of the early part of the war revolved around British attempts to end the siege. The incompetence of British general Sir Redvers Buller became apparent during repeated attempts to smash the Boer lines, resulting in heavy British losses at Spioenkop, Vaalkrans, and Colenso. Finally, the sheer weight of numbers made possible the British defeat of the Boers in the epic 10-day Battle of Tugela Heights and ended the siege of Ladysmith on February 28, 1900.

Today Ladysmith is a small provincial town with a haphazard mix of old colonial and newer buildings and the same inhospitable climate (scorchingly hot in summer, freezing in winter). Seek out the elegant, historic Town Hall built in 1893 and visit the gleaming white Soofie Mosque on the banks of the Klip River—this national monument is regarded as one of the most beautiful mosques in the Southern Hemisphere. On Murchison Street (the main street) is Surat House, a shop built in the 1890s, where Gandhi used to shop on his way through Ladysmith. On the same street is the Siege Museum, and in its courtyard stands a replica of a Long Tom, the 6-inch Creusot gun used by the Boers during the siege to terrify the inhabitants of Ladysmith. In front of the town hall are two howitzers used by the British and christened Castor and Pollux.

GETTING HERE AND AROUND
There are only two ways to get around the battlefields: with your own rental car or with an organized tour.

Boers, Brits, and Battlefields

The Second Anglo-Boer War (1899–1902), now referred to as the South African War, was the longest, bloodiest, and costliest war fought by Britain for nearly 100 years. The Brits and the Boers, Afrikaner descendants of 17th-century Dutch settlers fighting for independence from Britain, engaged in numerous battles in which the little guys (the Boers) often made mincemeat of the great British colonial army sent out to defeat them. Britain marched into South Africa in the spring of 1899, confident that it would all be over by Christmas. However, the comparatively small bands of volunteers from the republics of the Transvaal and the Orange Free State were to give Queen Victoria's proud British army, as Kipling wrote, "no end of a lesson." Today history has also revealed the part played by hundreds of thousands of Black South Africans in the war as messengers, scouts, interpreters, and laborers—hence the renaming of the war.

The most famous—or infamous—battle was fought on top of Spioenkop, in KwaZulu-Natal, where the mass grave of hundreds of British soldiers stretches from one side of the hill to the other. Of interest is that three men who were to change the course of world history were there on that fateful day: war correspondent Winston Churchill (who wrote "The shallow trenches were choked with dead and wounded"), Mahatma Gandhi (who was a stretcher bearer), and Louis Botha, the first prime minister of the Union of South Africa.

VISITOR INFORMATION

CONTACTS Emnambithi/Ladysmith Information Bureau. ✉ *Siege Museum, Town Hall, 151 Murchison St., Ladysmith* ☎ *036/637–2992, 082/575–0898* 🌐 *www.ladysmithtourism.co.za.*

Sights

Ladysmith Siege Museum

HISTORY MUSEUM | Formerly an 1884 market house, this is regarded as the best South African (Anglo-Boer) War Museum in South Africa. Step back into history and into the siege itself with electronic mapping, old uniforms, memorabilia, artifacts from the period, and black-and-white photos. The museum can arrange guided tours, but it also sells two pamphlets that outline self-guided tours: the Siege Town Walkabout and the Siege Town Drive-About. ✉ *151 Murchison St., Ladysmith* ☎ *036/637–2992* 🌐 *www.battlefieldsroute.co.za/place/ladysmith-siege-museum* 🎟 *R12* 🕓 *Closed Sun.*

Hotels

Royal Hotel

$$ | **HOTEL** | This historic South African country hotel shares much of Ladysmith's tumultuous past—it was built in 1880, just 19 years before the town was attacked by the Boers during the South Africa (Anglo-Boer) War. Expect small rooms, although TVs and air-conditioning are standard features. **Pros:** steeped in South African (Anglo-Boer) War history; convenient, central location; great 1800s facade and front door. **Cons:** kitschy bed linens; roadside rooms are noisy; dated rooms. [$] *Rooms from: R1655* ✉ *140 Murchison St., Ladysmith* ☎ *036/637–2176* 🌐 *www.royalhotel.co.za* 🛏 *71 rooms* 🍴 *Free Breakfast.*

Spioenkop

38 km (24 miles) southwest of Ladysmith.

The Second Anglo-Boer War (1899–1902), now called South African War, was the biggest, the longest, the costliest, the bloodiest, and the most humiliating war that Great Britain had ever fought. The **Battle of Spioenkop** near Ladysmith was a focal point, where the Boers trounced the British, who suffered 243 fatalities during the battle; many were buried in the trenches where they fell.

Hotels

Spionkop Lodge
$$$ | **RESORT** | This lovely secluded lodge, with the spectacular Drakensberg Mountains as a backdrop, lies in a 700-hectare (1,730-acre) nature reserve and is a perfect base for touring the battlefields, discovering the mountains and rock art, birding, or looking for big game. **Pros:** warm hospitality; superb location; knowledgeable and friendly hosts. **Cons:** interior of rooms slightly old-fashioned; pricey for what you get; often busy with group bookings. [$] *Rooms from: R2700* ✉ *On R600 between Ladysmith and Winterton, Ladysmith* ☎ *036/488–1404* 🌐 *www.spionkop.co.za* 🛏 *11 rooms* 🍴 *Free Breakfast.*

★ **Three Tree Hill Lodge**
$$$$ | **RESORT** | **FAMILY** | This quaint little Victorian lodge is run by a safari- and mountain-guide couple who follow Fair Trade, sustainability, and social ethics, and also offer guided walks and activities. **Pros:** excellent food and gorgeous location; superb hosts; fabulous tours, including game walks and rhino tracking. **Cons:** drinks not included in price; pricey, as with all properties in the area; bleak in winter. [$] *Rooms from: R8320* ✉ *D564, Ladysmith* ✣ *25 km (16 miles) northeast of Bergville* ☎ *036/448–1171, 087/059–9016* 🌐 *www.threetreehill.co.za* 🛏 *9 rooms* 🍴 *All-Inclusive.*

Dundee

74 km (46 miles) northeast of Ladysmith.

Once a busy coal-mining town, Dundee still has straight roads wide enough for the ox wagons of pioneer days to turn in, but today it's just a small commercial center in an area of subdued farming activity.

GETTING HERE AND AROUND

To get to Dundee from Ladysmith, take the N11 north and then the R68 east. For a more scenic route, take the R602 toward Elandslaagte from the N11 and then go east on the R68.

VISITOR INFORMATION

TOURIST OFFICES Dundee Tourism. ✉ *Civic Gardens, Victoria St., Dundee* ☎ *034/218–2837* 🌐 *www.tourdundee.co.za.*

Sights

Babanango Game Reserve
NATURE PRESERVE | About three hours from Durban, and 50 km (31 miles) from Vryheid, this new reserve pairs Zulu cultural lessons with wonderful wildlife encounters. Once indentured farmland, this protected 22,000-hectare (54,363 acre) Zululand reserve underwent biodiversity rehabilitation and now encompasses mist belt grasslands, thornveld, and river frontage, and is home to animals of all sizes, from the sweet little steenbok to the surlier lion. The acacia-flecked plains and meandering valleys are home to three beautifully refurbished lodges—historically-inclined Babanango Valley Lodge, Zulu Rock Lodge in the north, and the highly anticipated riverside Travellers Camp—all managed and staffed in partnership with local communities. Nearby sites include the Isandlwana battlefield, Rorke's Drift, Devil's Pass, the grave of Piet Retief, and the location of the

Battle of Blood River. ✉ *Babanango Game Reserve, Babanango* ☎ *031/100–0362* 🌐 *www.babanango.co.za.*

Battle of Blood River Site

MILITARY SIGHT | One of the most influential events in the history of South Africa with long-reaching tragic consequences for the original inhabitants of the land, this battle, fought between the Boers and the Zulus in 1838, predates the Anglo-Zulu War by more than 40 years. After the murder of Piet Retief and his men at Mgungundlovu in February 1838, Dingane dispatched Zulu impis to kill all the white settlers in Natal. But by November Andries Pretorius's new group of 464 men and 64 wagons moved to challenge the Zulus and took a vow that should God grant them victory, they would forever remember that day as a holy day. On December 16 an enormous Zulu force armed only with spears attacked the armed Boers. At the end of the battle 3,000 Zulus lay dead, but it's said not a single Boer had fallen. The long-term effects of the battle were dramatic. The intensely religious Voortrekkers saw their great victory as a confirmation of their role as God's chosen people which led to the apartheid system that surfaced more than a century later. Two powerful monuments—one to the Boers, the other to the Zulus—today commemorate the battle. ✉ *Dundee* ✥ *Approach site via a gravel road, off R33 between Vryheid and Dundee* ☎ *034/632–1695, 087/985–1885* 🌐 *www.bloedrivier.org.za* 🎫 *R45.*

Talana Museum

MUSEUM VILLAGE | **FAMILY** | The first-rate Talana Museum, set in an 8-hectare (20-acre) heritage park, on the outskirts of Dundee, is well worth a visit. Fascinating exhibits, spread over 17 buildings, trace the history of the area, from the early San hunter-gatherers to the rise of the Zulu nation, the extermination of the cannibal tribes of the Biggarsberg, and, finally, the vicious battles of the South African (Anglo-Boer) War. The museum stands on the site of the Battle of Talana (October 20, 1899), the opening skirmish in the war, and two of the museum buildings were used by the British as medical stations during the battle. The military museum here is an excellent starting point for the Battlefields Route, where Zulus, Brits, and Boers battled it out for territory and glory. Reenactments, living history, and special events are regular features. ✉ *R33, Dundee* ✥ *2 km (1 mile) east of Dundee* ☎ *034/212–2654* 🌐 *www.talana.co.za* 🎫 *R40 (cash only).*

Coffee and Quick Bites

Miners' Rest Tea Shop

$$ | **CAFÉ** | In a delightfully restored pre-1913 miner's cottage at the Talana Museum, the tea shop serves light refreshments as well as more substantial home-cooked meals. The food is excellent and the atmosphere most welcoming. **Known for:** friendly service; Sunday buffet; quality meals. [$] *Average main: R150* ✉ *Talana Museum, Dundee* ☎ *034/212–1704, 083/985–2220* 🌐 *www.talana.co.za.*

Rorke's Drift

35 km (22 miles) southwest of Dundee.

From the British perspective the Battle of Rorke's Drift was the most glorious battle of the Anglo-Zulu War, all the more so because it took place just hours after the British humiliation at Isandlwana on January 22, 1879. For 12 hours, a British force numbering just 140 men, many of them wounded in the previous battle, fought off and ultimately repelled more than 3,000 Zulu warriors. The 1964 movie *Zulu* brought the story to the masses.

GETTING HERE AND AROUND

Rorke's Drift is southwest of Dundee on the R68.

Sights

Fugitives' Drift

HISTORIC SIGHT | This drift (ford) was where, on 22 January 1879, the British survivors of the Battle of Isandlwana crossed the Buffalo River, and it was here that Lieutenants Melvill and Coghill were killed as they tried to save the Queen's Colour. They are buried on the hillside above the drift, which is now on the grounds of what is now the Fugitives' Drift Lodge, part of a nature reserve. The Queen's Colour was later recovered and, now restored, hangs in Brecon Cathedral in Wales. **■ TIP→ There's no information on-site, so read up about it before your visit, or hire an accredited battlefields guide.** ✉ *Rorke's Drift Rd., Rorke's Drift* ☎ *034/271–8051, 034/271–8053* 🌐 *www.fugitivesdrift.com.*

Shiyane/Rorke's Drift

MILITARY SIGHT | This is by far the best of the Zulu War battlefields to see without a guide. A small museum and orientation center retells the story of the battle from the British perspective, with electronic diagrams, battle sounds, and dioramas. The British force at Rorke's Drift consisted of just 140 men, of whom 35 were ailing or wounded. They occupied a Swedish mission church and house, which had been converted into a storehouse and hospital. The Zulu forces numbered some 3,000–4,000 men, composed of the reserve regiments from the earlier battle of Isandlwana. When a survivor from Isandlwana sounded the warning at 3:15 pm, the tiny British force hastily erected a stockade of flour bags and biscuit boxes around the mission. The Zulus attacked 75 minutes later, and the fighting raged for 12 hours before the Zulus faltered and retreated. A record number of 11 Victoria Crosses (Britain's highest military honor) were awarded at Rorke's Drift. ✉ *Rorke's Drift Rd., off R68, Rorke's Drift* ☎ *034/642–1687* 🎟 *R35.*

Hotels

Fugitives' Drift Lodge

$$$$ | **RESORT** | Set in a 5,000-acre natural heritage site, this attractive lodge lies just a couple of miles from the famous battle site of Rorke's Drift and overlooks the drift where survivors of the British defeat at Isandlwana fled across the Buffalo River. **Pros:** knowledgeable hosts; lovely garden settings; you'll be contributing to the local communities through the David Rattray Foundation. **Cons:** harks back to a colonial era; can be full of groups of old military gentlemen; pricey and excludes drinks. [$] *Rooms from: R7780* ✉ *Rorke's Drift Rd., Dundee* ☎ *034/271–8051, 087/059–9012 for reservations* 🌐 *www.fugitivesdrift.com* 🛏 *9 rooms* 🍴 *All-Inclusive* ☞ *Pricing excludes battlefield tour.*

Shopping

Rorke's Drift ELC Art and Craft Centre

CRAFTS | Rorke's Drift is still a mission station, run by the Evangelical Lutheran Church, and this center at the mission sells handmade bags, handwoven rugs, curios, and beadwork, all created by local artists. It's a good one to support. ✉ *Rorke's Drift Rd., off R68, Dundee* ☎ *034/642–1627* 🌐 *www.rorkesdriftart.com.*

Hluhluwe-iMfolozi Park

264 km (165 miles) northeast of Durban.

Renowned for its conservation successes—most notably with white rhinos—this reserve is a wonderful place to view the Big Five and many other species. Until 1989 it consisted of two separate parks, Hluhluwe in the north and iMfolozi in the south, separated by a fenced corridor. Although a road (R618) still runs through this corridor, the fences have been removed, and the parks now operate as a single entity. Hluhluwe and the corridor are the most scenic areas of the park, notable for their bush-covered hills

Hluhluwe-iMfolozi Park has the Big Five including black and white rhinos.

and knockout views, whereas iMfolozi is better known for its broad plains.

👁 Sights

Hluhluwe-iMfolozi Park

WILDLIFE REFUGE | FAMILY | Reputedly King Shaka's favorite hunting ground, Zululand's Hluhluwe-iMfolozi (pronounced shloo- *shloo*-ee im-fuh- *low-*zee) incorporates two of Africa's oldest reserves: Hluhluwe and iMfolozi, both founded in 1895. These days the reserves are abbreviated as HIP. In an area of just 906 square km (350 square miles), Hluhluwe-iMfolozi delivers the Big Five plus all the plains game and species like nyala and red duiker that are rare in other parts of the country. Equally important, it encompasses one of the most biologically diverse habitats on the planet, with a unique mix of forest, woodland, savanna, and grassland. You'll find about 1,250 species of plants and trees here—more than in some entire countries.

The park is administered by Ezemvelo KZN Wildlife, the province's official conservation organization, which looks after all the large game reserves and parks as well as many nature reserves. Thanks to its conservation efforts and those of its predecessor, the highly regarded Natal Parks Board, the park can take credit for saving the white rhino from extinction. So successful was the park at increasing white rhino numbers that in 1960 it established its now famous Rhino Capture Unit to relocate rhinos to other reserves in Africa. The park is currently trying to do for the black rhino what it did for its white cousins. Poaching in the past nearly decimated Africa's black rhino population, but as a result of the park's remarkable conservation program, Africa's black rhinos safely roam this reserve—and you won't get a better chance of seeing them in the wild than here. ✉ *Hluhluwe iMfolozi* ☎ *035/562–0848* ⊕ *www.kznwildlife.com* 💳 *R260 international guests, R125 South Africans.*

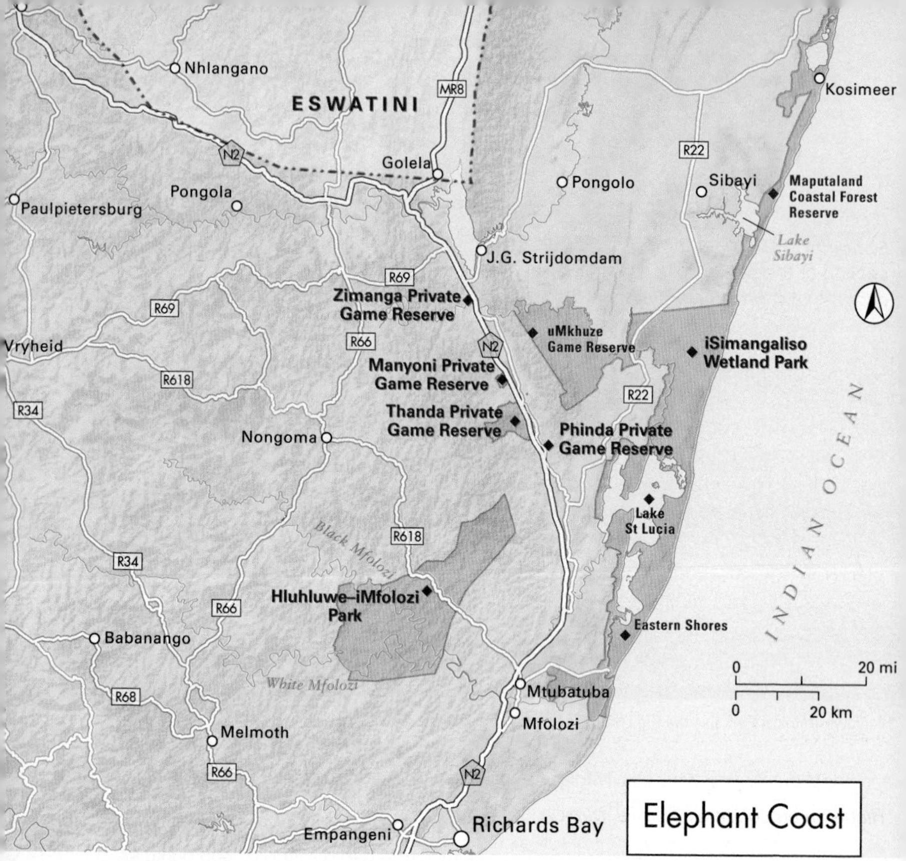

Hotels

Hluhluwe-iMfolozi offers a range of accommodations in government-run rest camps, with an emphasis on self-catering (only Hilltop has a restaurant). The park also has secluded bush lodges and camps, but most foreign visitors can't avail themselves of these lodgings, as each must be reserved in a block, and the smallest accommodates at least eight people. Conservation levies are R260 per person.

Hilltop Camp

$$ | **RESORT** | **FAMILY** | Located in the Hluhluwe half of the park, the camp's self-contained chalets have high thatch ceilings, rattan furniture, and small verandahs. **Pros:** incredible views; floodlit water hole; warm, friendly staff. **Cons:** bathrooms can smell a little moldy; outdoor grill area not covered and is dimly lit at night; watch out for marauding monkeys. [$] *Rooms from: R1850* ✉ *Hluhluwe* ☎ *035/562–0848 Hilltop Camp, 033/845–1000 reservations* 🌐 *www.kznwildlife.com/Hilltop.html* 🛏 *70 rooms* 🍴 *Free Breakfast.*

Hluhluwe River Lodge

$$$ | **HOTEL** | **FAMILY** | Overlooking False Bay lake and the Hluhluwe River floodplain—follow signs from Hluhluwe village—this fantastic-value, family-owned lodge is the ideal base for visiting the game reserves and the iSimangaliso Wetland Park. **Pros:** excellent food; only 25 minutes from Hluhluwe-iMfolozi; great for families. **Cons:** four-wheel drive recommended; 35-minute drive to the park; lots of kids in holiday times and activities cost extra. [$] *Rooms from: R3500* ✉ *Hluhluwe*

☎ *035/562–0246* 🌐 *www.hluhluwe.co.za* 🛏 *13 rooms* 🍴 *All-Inclusive.*

Mpila Camp
$ | RESORT | FAMILY | In the central iMfolozi section of the park, Mpila is reminiscent of some of Kruger's older camps. **Pros:** good value for money compared to other parks up north; free-roaming game; lovely location. **Cons:** little privacy; watch out for hyenas stealing your braai meat; needs a refurb. [$] *Rooms from: R1150* ✉ *Hluhluwe iMfolozi* ☎ *033/845–1000 reservations* 🌐 *www.kznwildlife.com/Mpila.html* 🛏 *40 rooms* 🍴 *No Meals.*

★ **Rhino Ridge Safari Lodge**
$$$$ | ALL-INCLUSIVE | Perched upon a hillside, the park's only 4-star private lodge commands breathtaking views across the park. **Pros:** shared community ownership of the lodge; legendary walking safaris; authentic Zulu homestay activity available. **Cons:** can get noisy with family groups; rates exclude bush walks. [$] *Rooms from: R8120* ✉ *Rhino Ridge Safari Lodge, Hluhluwe iMfolozi* ☎ *035/474–1473* 🌐 *www.rhinoridge.co.za* 🛏 *18 suites* 🍴 *All-Inclusive.*

Activities

BUSH WALKS
Armed rangers lead groups of eight on two- to three-hour bush walks departing from Hilltop or Mpila Camp. You may not spot much game on these walks, but you do see plenty of birds, and you learn a great deal about the area's ecology and tips on how to recognize the signs of the bush, including animal spoor (tracks). Walks depart daily at 5:30 am and 3:30 pm (6 and 3 in winter) and cost R315. Reserve a few days in advance at **Hilltop Camp reception** (☎ *035/562–0848*).

GAME DRIVES
A great way to see the park is on game drives led by rangers. These drives (R385 per person for minimum two) hold several advantages over driving through the park yourself: you sit high up in an open-air vehicle with a good view and the wind in your face, a ranger explains the finer points of animal behavior and ecology, and your guide has a good idea where to find animals like leopards, cheetahs, and lions. Your guide will also take you to a picnic spot or for lunch if you're on a longer drive. Game drives leave daily at 5:30 am in summer, 6:30 am in winter. The park also offers three-hour night drives, during which you search with powerful spotlights for nocturnal animals. These depart at 7, and you should make advance reservations at **Hilltop Camp reception** (☎ *035/562–0848*).

WILDERNESS TRAILS
The park's **Wilderness Trails** are every bit as popular as Kruger's, but they tend to be tougher and more rustic. You should be fit enough to walk up to 16 km (10 miles) a day for a period of three days and four nights. An armed ranger leads the hikes, and all equipment, food, and baggage are carried by donkeys. While in the bush, hikers bathe in the iMfolozi River or have a hot bucket shower; toilet facilities consist of a spade and toilet-paper roll. Trails, open March–October, are limited to eight people and should be reserved a year in advance.

Fully catered two- or three-night **Short Wilderness Trails** (R2920 per person) involve stays at a satellite camp in the wilderness area. You'll sleep in a dome tent, and although there's hot water from a bucket shower, your toilet is a spade.

If that sounds too easy, you can always opt for the four-night **Primitive Trail.** On this trek hikers carry their own packs and sleep out under the stars, although there are lightweight tents for inclement weather. A campfire burns all night to scare off animals, and each participant is expected to sit a 90-minute watch. A ranger acts as guide. The cost is R3465 per person.

A less rugged wilderness experience can be had on the **Base Camp Trail,** based out of the tented Mndindini camp, where you're guaranteed a bed and some creature comforts. The idea behind these trails is to instill in the participants an appreciation for the beauty of the untamed bush. You can also join the Mpila night drive if you wish. Participation is limited to eight people and costs about R4800 per person.

The **Explorer Trail**, three nights and two days, combines the most comfortable Base Camp trail with the Primitive Trail. On this trail you sleep out under the stars at a different spot each night. The cost is R3750 per person.

iSimangaliso Wetland Park

245 km (152 miles) north of Durban via the N2 and R618

iSimangaliso (formerly the Greater St Lucia Wetlands Park) is the largest protected wetland in South Africa stretching 220 km (137 miles) along the northern coast of KwaZulu-Natal from St Lucia to Kosi Bay.

Imagine a place where you can find hippos and humans living side by side, Humpback whales breach just beyond the breakers in the Indian Ocean, and the endangered black rhinoceros finds safe harbor on land. The name "iSimangaliso" means miracle and wonder, and it's found in spades when exploring this underestimated park. Declared a UNESCO World Heritage Site (South Africa's first) in 1999, the iSimangaliso Wetland encompasses a number of disparate natural African environments including the uMkhuze Game Reserve and the Maputaland Marine Reserve, an important nesting site for endangered loggerhead and leatherback turtles. The park protects the myriad river and coastal environments, including the lake and estuary of the St. Lucia River, coral reefs, sandy beaches and coastal dunes of Sodwana Bay, inland and tidal lakes, swamps, mangrove forests, papyrus wetlands, and the enchanting indigenous woodlands of the Maputaland Coastal Forest Reserve.

The park and World Heritage Site are most easily accessed from the tropical village of St Lucia, but not many know that it is divided into two sections: the Western and Eastern Shores. The simplest and most rewarding way to experience these precious wetlands is by going straight to the heart of the park—Lake St Lucia.

GETTING HERE AND AROUND

Don't expect to see the whole park in one day because it's broken up into sections. The Park's gates are accessible from two major tarred roads–the N2 and the R22–but there are multiple entry points.

The heart of the park sits in the town of St. Lucia which is 245 km (152 miles) north of Durban and is accessible via the N2 and R618. To get to Sodwana Bay, Lake Sibaya, the Coastal Forest sections and Kosi Bay, take N2 north from Durban for 267 km (166 miles) towards Hluhluwe and then use the R22. The southernmost Park entrance is Maphelane, accessible from the Kwambonambi junction off the N2.

If you're heading to a lodge in the northern Maputaland Coastal Reserve, it's best to fly into Richards Bay from Johannesburg and be picked up by your lodge—they will make all the flight and pickup arrangements. If you prefer to travel by road, that can be arranged to and from Johannesburg.

The nearest international airport is King Shaka International Airport (Durban) and the closest regional airport is at Richards Bay.

AIRPORT CONTACTS Richards Bay Airport. ⊠ *30 Fish Eagle Flight, Birdswood, Richards Bay* ☎ *035/789–9630* ⊕ *www. richardsbayairport.co.za.*

VISITOR INFORMATION

CONTACTS iSimangaliso Wetland Park.
☎ *035/590–1633* ⊕ *www.isimangaliso.com.*

WHEN TO GO

The loggerhead and leatherback turtle egg-laying season in Maputaland Coastal Forest Reserve goes from November through early March. During these months rangers lead after-dinner drives and walks down the beach to look for turtles, and you can expect to cover as much as 16 km (10 miles) in a night. From a weather standpoint, the best times to visit the lodge are probably spring (September–October) and autumn (March–May). In summer the temperature regularly soars past 38°C (100°F), but this is when the turtles come ashore to dig their nests and lay their eggs—an awesome spectacle. Swimming during winter is a brisk proposition, and August is the windiest month.

◉ Sights

★ Eastern Shores

NATURE SIGHT | An ideal beach and safari destination, the Eastern Shores (which lies on the eastern section of Lake St Lucia) features a number of straightforward, paved game-viewing roads that offer comprehensive access to the lucky packet of charming habitats at a fraction of the cost at other Big Five destinations. Take a day trip to scour the grassland, lakes, pans, and coastal dune forest for animals and birds via the lookout points (if there's time for just one, then make it Kwashaleni Tower which was designed for whale watching). Pack a bathing suit and snorkel mask too and break your day in the car with a picnic on the beach at popular Cape Vidal. ⊠ *Cape Vidal* ⊕ *www.isimangaliso.com* 🖃 *R61 per vehicle plus R56 per person.*

Lake St Lucia

BODY OF WATER | **FAMILY** | The most carefree way to enjoy the reserve is on a boat trip from St Lucia, where you'll be able to get close to hippos and immense Nile crocodiles and try to spot some of the more than 500 species of birds that call the park home. Two-hour guided trips are run by various operators and leave daily. Our tip? Skip the booze-cruise crowds and enjoy the tranquility of the dawn chorus on a morning outing. ■TIP→ **There's a nondescript arts and crafts center on the main road in St. Lucia town, filled with authentic Zulu woven baskets, storage vessels, placemats, and beaded and wooden crafts made by local women. Prices vary according to the artist and are extremely good value for excellent quality. Shop away after your boat cruise.** ⊠ *Lake St Lucia* ✛ *Access via the town of St Lucia* ☎ *035/590–1162, 035/590–1071* ⊕ *www.shakabarker.co.za* 🖃 *R350.*

Maputaland Coastal Forest Reserve

NATIONAL PARK | Expect great swaths of pale, creamy sand stretching to far-off rocky headlands, a shimmering, undulating horizon where whales blow. Watch out for pods of dolphins leaping and dancing in the morning sun. If you're here in season (November to early March), one of nature's greatest and most spiritually uplifting experiences is waiting for you—turtle tracking. Nothing—not photographs, not wildlife documentaries—prepares you for the size of these creatures. On any given night, you might see a huge, humbling leatherback, 6 feet long and weighing up to 500 kg (1,100 pounds), drag her great body up through the surf to the high-water mark at the back of the beach. There she will dig a deep hole and lay up to 120 gleaming white eggs, bigger than a golf ball but smaller than a tennis ball. It will have taken her many, many years to achieve this moment of fruition, a voyage through time and across the great oceans of the world—a long, solitary journey in the cold black depths of the sea, meeting and mating only once every seven years, and always coming back to within about 300 feet of the spot on the beach where she herself had been born. And if your luck holds, you might even observe the miracle of the hatchlings, when perfect bonsai leatherback turtles dig themselves out of their deep, sandy nest and rush pell-mell toward the sea under a star-studded sky. ✉ *Off Hwy. 2, south of Mtunzini* ✥ *300 km (186 miles) from Richards Bay* ☎ 🌐 *www.isimangaliso.com.*

uMkhuze Game Reserve

NATIONAL PARK | Wildlife—and amazing birdlife—abounds in this 400-square-km (154-square-mile) reserve in the shadow of the Ubombo Mountains. Lying between the uMkhuze and Msunduzi rivers, it makes up the northwestern spur of the iSimangaliso Wetland Park, a World Heritage Site. It has been a protected area since 1912.

If you're a birder, then you'll find yourself in seventh heaven: more than 420 bird species have been spotted here, including myriad waterfowl drawn to the park's shallow pans in summer. Several blinds, particularly those overlooking Nsumo Pan, offer superb views. Don't miss out on the amazing 3-km (2-mile) walk through a spectacular rare forest of towering, ancient fig trees. This is a good place to spot rhinos and elephants, although lions, cheetah, and leopards are much harder to find. However, there's is plenty of other game, including hippos, zebras, giraffes, kudus, and nyalas. **■ TIP→ There are variant spellings of Mkuze in the area; you may also see Mkhuze, Mkuzi or Mkhuzi.** ✉ *Off N2, Mkuze* ✥ *48 km (30 miles) northeast of Hluhluwe-iMfolozi.* ☎ *035/573–9004* 🌐 *www.isimangaliso.com* 🎫 *R61 per vehicle plus R56 per person.*

Hotels

★ Ghost Mountain Inn

$$ | **B&B/INN** | Swaths of scarlet bougainvillea run riot in the lush gardens of this family-owned country inn with tastefully furnished rooms that each have a small verandah (the newest Mountain Rooms have the best interiors). **Pros:** spa on-site; good value for money and generous buffet; strategic location for bush excursions. **Cons:** can get noisy in peak season; tour buses overnight here; hotel-like atmosphere. [$] *Rooms from: R2120* ✉ *Fish Eagle Rd., uMkhuze* ☎ *035/573–1025* 🌐 *www.ghostmountaininn.co.za* 🛏 *74 rooms* 🍴 *Free Breakfast.*

★ Makakatana Bay Lodge

$$$$ | **ALL-INCLUSIVE** | Connected via a series of wooden boardwalks (all the better to keep you out of the hippo highways) Makakatana Bay Lodge comprises elegant zen forest cottages and access to the western shores of Lake St Lucia. **Pros:** bushveld setting with easy beach access; owner-managed game lodge within the iSimangaliso Wetland Park; middle-of-nowhere seclusion. **Cons:** the beach requires a full day; droughts have dried out access to the lake before—check activity availability before booking. [$] *Rooms from: R13600* ✉ *Makakatana Bay lodge* ☎ *087/059–9015 reservations, 035/550–4189 lodge* 🌐 *www.makakatana.com* 🛏 *9 rooms* 🍴 *All-Inclusive.*

Mseni Beach Lodge

$$$ | **RESORT** | **FAMILY** | Log cabins simply decorated in ocean tones of white and blue lie on a dune ridge ensconced by coastal forest regularly visited by little duiker antelope and Trumpeter hornbills. **Pros:** close to a quiet beach; sublime cocktail deck with ocean views; air-conditioned cottages. **Cons:** steep staircase to get to the beach; restaurant gets very busy during holiday season. [$] *Rooms from: R2800* ✉ *Mseni Lodge* ☎ *072/061–9672 resort, 033/345–6531 reservations* 🌐 *www.mseni.co.za* 🛏 *16 cottages* 🍴 *Free Breakfast* ☞ *Minimum of 3 nights in high season.*

★ Thonga Beach Lodge

$$$$ | **RESORT** | Dramatically sited, this lovely beach lodge a stone's throw from the sea has air-conditioned, thatch suites decorated in chic Robinson Crusoe style with wooden floors, reed interior walls, cane and wooden furniture, gorgeous

Park of the iSimangaliso Wetland Park, Sodwana Bay is the best place to dive in South Africa.

bathrooms with sea views, and personal decks looking out over rolling coastal dunes and the blue Indian Ocean. **Pros:** Robinson Crusoe deluxe; turtle tracking straight from the lodge; spa treatments. **Cons:** booked up frequently; difficult to get to. $ *Rooms from: R9780* ✉ *Maputaland Coastal Forest Reserve* ☎ *035/474–1490, 035/474–1473 reservations* ⊕ *www.thongabeachlodge.co.za* ⇥ *24 rooms* ⚍ *All-Inclusive.*

 Activities

DIVING

Home to 1200 species of fish (compared to 1800 on the Great Barrier Reef, that's pretty impressive!) as well as other incredible invertebrates, turtles, rays, and sharks, the diving at Sodwana Bay is revered. If you want to dive in South Africa, this is the best, most beautiful base. Sodwana Bay falls under the iSimangaliso Wetland Park and is a Marine Protected Area (MPA). It is currently South Africa's only UNESCO marine World Heritage Site and shares an MPA with Mozambique

too, making it Africa's largest transfrontier MPA. This section of iSimangaliso is beloved by locals. Avoid during the holiday season when queues build at the gate and lots of dive boats make swimming difficult in the bay.

Dive conditions range from challenging to aquarium simplicity depending on currents, swell, and wind. Dive sites also vary in depth. For example, the shallowest sighting of the coelacanth fossil fish during a dive was just over 100 meters. What makes Sodwana such a pleasure for ocean submersion is the easy proximity of the reef to the shore. You can reach Two Mile Reef and its abundance of colorful creatures and coral on a short five-minute boat trip.

Amoray

SCUBA DIVING | There are lots of dive operators in Sodwana Bay, but ones situated inside the gates to the beach make for a simpler excursion without the fuss of daily gate fees and queues. Amoray is a quieter, more attentive center with mature, experienced dive masters (as opposed to gap year enthusiasts) and is a good bet for discerning scuba divers. ⊠ *Mseni Lodge* ☎ *083/928–5892* ⊕ *www.amoraydiving.com* 🖾 *R490 per dive, R330 for full gear rental per day.*

Coral Divers

SCUBA DIVING | Coral (as it's affectionately nicknamed) is a professional diving operation set within the borders of the iSimangaliso Wetland Park that attracts both young and old. The established center ranks as a PADI five-star Instructor Development Centre and Gold Palm resort offering everything from five-day PADI Open Water qualification to daily dives to Two Mile Reef to entry-level bubble-making adventures for teens. There's equipment rentals, a restaurant, self-catering accommodations, plus a free shuttle available on the hour to take you (and your very wet wetsuit) to the beach and back for dives. ⊠ *Coral Divers* ☎ *035/571–0290 resort, 033/345–6531 reservations* ⊕ *www.coraldivers.co.za* 🖾 *R380 per dive, R310 for full gear rental per day and from R5,080 for a five-day PADI Open Water Course with tented accommodation.*

TURTLE TRACKING

South Africa has the oldest turtle monitoring program in the world, clocking in at just over 50 years. South African loggerheads and leatherbacks nest on the sandy beaches of KwaZulu-Natal and monitoring is in place in the area of highest density—between the Kosi Bay/Mozambique border and south towards Mabibi and Sodwana Bay. Travelers can track turtles too with registered guides and learn more about this curious marine reptile. It's a timeless wonder to see this creature drag her load up a steep beach at midnight to lay eggs, or if you're lucky, find the hatchlings returning to sea.

★ Ufudu Turtle Tours

ECOTOURISM | This tour company operates from Sodwana Bay during the nesting season in an open 4x4 safari-style vehicle. Pete Jacobs will collect you after dinner and drive along the beach in the dark looking for signs of any emerging animals. Of the seven species of sea turtle found worldwide, five of them (leatherback, loggerhead, green, hawksbill, and olive Ridley) are found in the sea off iSimangaliso. Only two, however—the leatherback and the loggerhead—come ashore to lay. If you come across any turtles during the drive, Pete uses a red flashlight to sensitively share the egg-laying process without disturbing the female. The best time of year to see the turtles is in summer, between October and March, and hatchlings emerge between January and April. ⊠ *Sodwana Bay* ☎ *082/391–1503* ⊕ *www.ufuduturtletours.co.za* 🖾 *R950.*

Phinda Private Game Reserve

134 km (83 miles) from Richards Bay; 300 km (186 miles) from Durban.

Where Phinda excels is in the superb quality of its rangers, who can provide fascinating commentary on everything from local birds to frogs. It's amazing just how enthralling the love life of a dung beetle can be! There are also Phinda adventures (optional extras) down the Mzinene River for a close-up look at crocodiles, hippos, and birds; big-game fishing or scuba diving off the deserted, wildly beautiful Maputaland coast; and sightseeing flights over Phinda and the highest vegetated dunes in the world.

GETTING HERE AND AROUND

Phinda is 300 km (186 miles) from Durban by road, with a journey time of just over four hours. Before you decide to drive, bear in mind that you won't use your vehicle after you arrive at Phinda—all transportation is provided by open game-viewing vehicles. There are scheduled flights daily from Johannesburg to King Shaka International Airport and to Richards Bay Airport as well as regular direct flights to Phinda's own airstrip (check with the lodge for latest schedules). Phinda will also arrange road transfers from the airports.

Sights

★ Phinda Private Game Reserve
NATURE PRESERVE | FAMILY | This eco-award-winning flagship &Beyond reserve, established in 1991, is a heartening example of tourism serving the environment with panache. *Phinda* (*pin*-da) is Zulu for "return," referring to the restoration of 220 square km (85 square miles) of overgrazed ranchland in northern Zululand to bushveld. It's a triumph. Today Phinda has a stunning variety of seven healthy ecosystems including the rare sand forest (which grows on the fossil dunes of an earlier coastline), savanna, bushveld, open woodland, mountain bush, and verdant wetlands. The Big Five are all here, plus cheetahs, spotted hyenas, hippos, giraffes, impalas, and the rare, elusive, tiny Suni antelope. Birdlife is prolific and extraordinary, with some special Zululand finds: the pink-throated twin spot, the crested guinea fowl, the African broadbill, and the crowned eagle. The reserve is a little more than two hours drive from Richards Bay or four hours by road from Durban. ✉ *Phinda Game Reserve* ☎ *011/809–4300 central reservations* 🌐 *www.andbeyond.com.*

Hotels

★ Forest Lodge
$$$$ | RESORT | Hidden in a rare sand forest, this fabulous lodge overlooks a small water hole where nyalas, warthogs, and baboons frequently come to drink. **Pros:** lovely views from the pool; magical feeling of oneness with Africa's last remaining dry sand forest; modern conveniences. **Cons:** rooms are set apart, but when guests gather its not the most intimate stay; Zulu-zen might not be for traditional tastes; due for refurbishment. [$] *Rooms from: R20700* ✉ *Phinda Game Reserve* ☎ *011/809–4300 reservations* 🌐 *www.andbeyond.com* 🛏 *16 rooms* 🍴 *All-Inclusive.*

Mountain Lodge
$$$$ | RESORT | FAMILY | This attractive thatch lodge (the first built at Phinda) sits on a rocky hill overlooking miles of bushveld plains and the Ubombo Mountains. **Pros:** outstanding menu variety and exceptional dining; superior mountain views; very family-friendly. **Cons:** not the best choice for couples seeking solitude; pricey if you take the kids (pricey even if you don't take the kids); a bigger, less discreet lodge. [$] *Rooms from: R19000* ✉ *Phinda Game Reserve, off R22, Hluhluwe* ☎ *011/809–4300 reservations* 🌐 *www.andbeyond.com* 🛏 *25 rooms* 🍴 *All-Inclusive.*

Phinda Homestead
$$$$ | ALL-INCLUSIVE | FAMILY | Complete with a dedicated butler, chef, ranger and tracker, this property is the only sole-use safari villa on the reserve–and the most contemporary designer-chic of all the stays. **Pros:** state-of-the-art gym; flexibility; outdoor boma overlooks the busy water hole. **Cons:** must rent the whole villa; eclectic design not for everyone. [$] *Rooms from: R120750* ✉ *Phinda Game Reserve* ☎ *011/809–4300* 🌐 *www.andbeyond.com* 🛏 *4 suites.*

Rock Lodge
$$$$ | RESORT | Ideal for honeymooners or romantic solitude, this turreted lodge feels like it's dropped from a Moroccan movie set. **Pros:** luxurious sitting rooms; personal plunge pools and tranquility; amazing views. **Cons:** not the place for a lively atmosphere; not suitable for families (also, no kids under 12 allowed); stay away if you suffer from vertigo. [$] *Rooms from: R25800* ✉ *Phinda Game Reserve* ☎ *011/809–4300 reservations* 🌐 *www.andbeyond.com* 🛏 *6 rooms* 🍴 *All-Inclusive.*

★ Vlei Lodge

$$$$ | **RESORT** | Made of thatch, teak, and glass, with a distinctly Asian feel, your suite, which overlooks a marshland on the edge of an inviting woodland, at this comfortable lodge, tucked into the shade of a sand forest, is so private it's hard to believe there are other guests. **Pros:** superb views over the floodplains; intimate; Wi-Fi en suite. **Cons:** lots of mosquitoes and other flying insects; no children under 12. $ *Rooms from: R25800* ⊠ *Phinda Game Reserve* ☎ *011/809–4300* ⊕ *www.andbeyond.com* 🔁 *6 rooms* ❄❄ *All-Inclusive.*

Zuka Lodge

$$$$ | **RESORT** | **FAMILY** | Designed as an exclusive, single-use lodge for a family or small group of friends, Zuka (*zuka* means "sixpence" in Zulu) is a couple of miles from the bigger lodges and can now be booked per room. **Pros:** exclusivity (that's more affordable than bigger lodges); it's like having your own private holiday retreat; gives you the feeling of immediate celebrity status. **Cons:** entire property is best rented as a whole. $ *Rooms from: R19700* ⊠ *Phinda Game Reserve* ☎ *011/809–4300 reservations* ⊕ *www.andbeyond.com* 🔁 *4 rooms* ❄❄ *All-Inclusive.*

Thanda Private Game Reserve

23 km (14 miles) northeast of Hluhluwe; 400 km (248 miles) north of Durban.

One of KwaZulu-Natal's newer game reserves, Thanda offers a more intimate nature experience than some. Game may sometimes be elusive, but the highly experienced and enthusiastic rangers work hard to find the Big Five and other wildlife. Enjoyable cultural interactions with local people are a highlight of any visit.

GETTING HERE AND AROUND

Road transfers from Richards Bay and Durban airports can be arranged with the reserve.

Sights

Thanda Private Game Reserve

NATURE PRESERVE | In wild, beautiful northern Zululand, the multi-award-winning 150-square-km (60-square-mile) Thanda reserve, continues to restore former farmlands and hunting grounds to their previous pristine state, thanks to a joint venture with local communities and the king of the Zulus, Goodwill Zweletini, who donated some of his royal hunting grounds to the project. Game that used to roam this wilderness centuries ago has been reestablished, including the Big Five. *Thanda* (*tan*-da) is Zulu for "love," and its philosophy echoes just that: "for the love of nature, wildlife, and dear ones." There's a main lodge, a private villa, and a small tented camp and opportunities to interact with the local people. ⊠ *D242, off N2, Hluhluwe* ☎ *032/586–0149 reservations* ⊕ *www.thandasafari.co.za.*

Hotels

Thanda Safari Lodge

$$$$ | **RESORT** | **FAMILY** | This exquisite lodge blends elements of royal Zulu with an eclectic pan-African feel evident in the thatched, turreted dwellings perched on the side of rolling hills that overlook mountains and bushveld. **Pros:** loads of space; luxurious with a generous mini bar included; private plunge pool and boma area. **Cons:** children three and up permitted and can disrupt romantic atmosphere; spa treatments excluded; some might say it's Hollywood in the bush. $ *Rooms from: R17330* ⊠ *Off N2 and D242, Hluhluwe* ☎ *032/586–0149 reservations* ⊕ *www.thanda.com* 🔁 *9 rooms* ❄❄ *All-Inclusive.*

Thanda Tented Camp

$$$$ | RESORT | FAMILY | Perfect for a family or friends' reunion (although it's great for individual travelers, too), this intimate and luxurious eco-forward camp deep in the bush brings you into close contact with your surroundings. **Pros:** five-star luxury; eco-friendly. **Cons:** no air-conditioning; no children under eight; not for the nervous type. $ *Rooms from: R4990* ⊠ *Off N2 and D242, Hluhluwe* ☎ *032/586–0149 reservations* ⊕ *www.thanda.co.za* ⤳ *15 rooms* ⫶◯⫶ *All-Inclusive.*

Manyoni Private Game Reserve

50 km (31 miles) northeast of Hluhluwe; 300 km (186 miles) north of Durban.

One of KwaZulu-Natal's newest game reserves, Manyoni Game Reserve mirrors the story of nearby Phinda and also boasts incredible game viewing. There may be more lodges spread across this reserve, but a deeply-caring conservation team and some innovative activities plus affordable stays make this a wildly underrated Big Five destination.

GETTING HERE AND AROUND

Manyoni Private Game Reserve is 300 km (186 miles) from Durban by road, with a journey time of 3½ hours. Take the N2 north from Durban past the Hluhluwe turn off and take a left onto the D646 dirt road. From here, the Manyoni Private Game Reserve is plainly signposted. There are scheduled flights daily from Johannesburg to King Shaka International Airport and to Richards Bay Airport. Most lodges will also arrange road transfers from the airports.

 Sights

Manyoni Private Game Reserve

NATURE PRESERVE | In 2004, 17 private properties in the northern Zululand area dropped their fences to create the Manyoni Private Game Reserve. Formerly known as the Zululand Rhino Reserve, the marriage and restoration of these properties (a mishmash of old tomato farms, cotton fields, and seasonal cattle grazing) has created a 23,000-hectare game-rich private reserve. The terrain varies from bushveld to riverine woodland and open savanna thornveld that animals, such as wildebeest, zebra, and cheetah love. The reserve has over 70 mammal species and an exceptional diversity of birdlife including sought-out endemics such as the Pink-throated twinspot and elusive African broadbill. Apt then, that the name means the "place of birds" in isiZulu. However, this sanctuary is all the more special because it's been chosen as a safe space to rehabilitate rescued pangolins. This species is particularly susceptible to illness and takes ages to recover from the hardships of trafficking (they often suffer dehydration and malnutrition). If there is a pangolin in residence, you can join the conservation team on the ground as they walk with them to ensure they are eating, picking up weight, and getting strong enough to roam freely again. There's no touching or petting. ⊠ *Manyoni Game Reserve* ✛ *50 km (31 miles) northeast of Hluhluwe* ⊕ *www.manyoni.co.za.*

 Hotels

★ Rhino Sands Safari Camp

$$$$ | ALL-INCLUSIVE | This intimate and traditional safari camp enjoys a sublime forested setting aflutter with birdsong inside the southern stretch of the Manyoni Game Reserve. **Pros:** small and deeply personal; hands-on team; exceptional food and menu variety. **Cons:** no air-conditioning; other tents lie within earshot if you have noisy neighbors. $ *Rooms from: R15000* ⊠ *Rhino Sands Safari Camp* ✛ *Access via East Gate and D464 dirt road* ☎ *087/004–4027 Reservations, 082/655–0927 Safari Camp* ⊕ *www.rhinosands.com* ⤳ *4 suites* ⫶◯⫶ *All-Inclusive.*

Zimanga Private Game Reserve

8 km (5 miles) north of Mkhuze; 315 km (196 miles) north of Durban.

Every element of the Zimanga Private Game Reserve safari experience is designed for photographers. Like many reserves in the area, old farmlands have been rewilded into a seriously scenic Big Five sanctuary but here you'll see everything close up at eye level thanks to the state-of-the-art photographic hides.

GETTING HERE AND AROUND

The Zimanga Private Game Reserve Main Entrance lies 315 km (196 miles) north of Durban on the N2, roughly 8 km (5 miles) north of Mkuze town with a travel time of 3 hrs.

Charter flights are available from Virginia Airport (Durban North) or King Shaka International Airport. Charter to Zimanga is between 50 and 70 minutes depending on whether you choose a direct flight or a slightly longer scenic route over the ocean.

Sights

Zimanga Private Game Reserve

NATURE PRESERVE | South Africa's only dedicated private photographic game reserve will make anyone feel like a professional wildlife photographer. Spread over nearly 70 square km (27 square miles) of immaculate Zululand bushveld, encompassing rolling hills, reed-lined dams, and fever tree forests, Zimanga is a residence for a colorful array of birds and endangered animals. In addition to game drives, guides drop guests off for a morning or afternoon session at one of nine carefully crafted hides strategically spread across the reserve. Each hide serves a certain spectacle: some elevated, some to attract water birds or wily crocodiles, some underground, two accommodate overnight stays for four while others offer brilliant mirror reflections of elephants, rhino, and lions lapping up the water. Thanks to exhaustive testing (each hide required months to perfect positioning, lighting, focal lengths, and backgrounds without altering animal behavior) the wild subjects have no idea you're there. Pack your camera, settle into the bunker, and wait to see who arrives. The ultimate experience for diehard camera heads has to be the opportunity to sleep in one of these hides, which is equipped with Wi-Fi, a toilet and a small communal area. Bunk beds are simple and a little cramped, but when that motion sensor goes off with a creature passing by, any discomfort dissipates as you snap the night away. ✉ *Zimanga Private Game Reserve* ✥ *8 km (5 miles) north of Mkuze on the N2* 🌐 *www.zimanga.com.*

Hotels

★ **Zimanga Main Lodge**

$$$$ | **ALL-INCLUSIVE** | Just as thoughtfully constructed as the high-tech photographic hides, Zimanga Main Lodge is unobtrusive and comfortable with minimal (if a touch masculine) zen decor and low electric fencing that doesn't obscure the view of the Lebombo Mountains from your private deck. **Pros:** excellent food; state of the art photographic hides; single suites designed for solo travelers (and no single supplement fees). **Cons:** minimum 2-night package required; not suited for first safari experience. [$] *Rooms from: R21864* ✉ *Zimanga Private Reserve* ✥ *8 km (5 miles) north of Mkuze on the N2* 🌐 *www.zimanga.com* 🛏 *10 suites* 🍴 *All-Inclusive.*

JOHANNESBURG

Updated by
Iga Motylska

⊙ **Sights** ★★★★★   🍴 **Restaurants** ★★★★★   🛏 **Hotels** ★★★★★   🛍 **Shopping** ★★★★★   📺 **Nightlife** ★★★★★

WELCOME TO JOHANNESBURG

TOP REASONS TO GO

★ **History in Your Lifetime:** Constitution Hill, which houses the Constitution Court, was built on the site of a prison whose inmates included Mahatma Gandhi and Albert Luthuli.

★ **Iconic Soweto:** The site of dramatic anti-apartheid struggles, including the Hector Pieterson Museum, and the former home of Nobel Peace Prize laureate Nelson Mandela, found on the same street (Vilakazi) as Archbishop Desmond Tutu's family home.

★ **44 Stanley:** This leafy retail complex in a refurbished 1930s industrial block houses bespoke stores, galleries, cafés, restaurants, and an independent cinema.

★ **Parkhurst:** Great selection of restaurants, cafés, bars, and street-facing stores.

★ **Cradle of Humankind:** This World Heritage Site presents evolution, fossils, and paleontology in a kid-friendly manner. Sterkfontein Caves and Maropeng Visitor Centre are also nearby.

South Africa's biggest city is in the middle of Gauteng, South Africa's smallest but wealthiest province. The greater metropolitan area is a massive 1,645 square km (635 square miles), most of which is made up of suburban sprawl. The M1, a major highway, runs centrally through the city and its suburbs. Two adjoining highways circle the city: the N3 to the east and the N1 to the west; the M1 bisects this circle.

1 **City Center.** Parts of the city center—Maboneng, Braamfontein, and Victoria Yards—have been experiencing a rebirth, with trendy restaurants, boutiques, and hotels. There are also a number of important attractions including Constitution Hill.

2 **Soweto and the South.** About 20 km (12 miles) south of downtown Johannesburg, this vast township is where the 1976 anti-apartheid student uprisings began. Here you'll find the Hector Pieterson Memorial and Museum and the former home of Nelson Mandela.

3 **Rosebank and Houghton.** A chic commercial center art galleries, boutiques, restaurants, and hotels.

4 **Melrose and Illovo.** Neighborhoods bordering Rosebank.

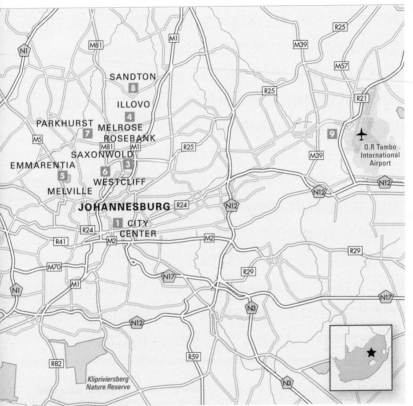

5 Melville and Emmarentia. Melville's "high street" is lined with restaurants, bars, antique stores, and thrift shops. In Emmarentia, the Johannesburg Botanical Gardens and Emmarentia Dam offer the perfect retreat in an urban park.

6 Parktown, Parkview, Saxonwold, and Westcliff. The man-made Sachsenwald Forest makes Saxonwold and its surrounds one of Johannesburg's greenest parts.

7 Parkhurst and Parktown North. Some of Jo'burg's best restaurants and bars are found in Parkhurst, where an eclectic mix of international cuisines mingle with boutiques and stores selling decor, design, and homeware by local artists.

8 Sandton. South Africa's new financial center is famed for the continent's tallest building, The Leonardo, as well as swanky hotels, trendy eateries, and the Johannesburg Stock Exchange.

9 Near OR Tambo International Airport. While there's not much to explore here, it's a convenient place to sleep before catching a red-eye flight.

Johannesburg, Jo'burg, Egoli ("City of Gold"), or Jozi, as it is affectionately known by locals, is the commercial heart of South Africa and the primary gateway for international visitors. Historically, it is where money is made and fortunes are found. The city has an unfair reputation for being an ugly, dangerous place you ought to avoid on any trip to South Africa. On the contrary, much of Johannesburg is quite pretty, largely because of the millions of trees that cover it (it has, purportedly, one of the largest human-planted forests in the world), and statistically speaking it is less dangerous than the Western Cape.

The city also epitomizes South Africa's paradoxical makeup—it's rich, poor, innovative, and historic all rolled into one. And it seems, at times, as though no one actually comes *from* Johannesburg. The city is full of immigrants: Italians, Portuguese, Poles, Chinese, Hindus, Swazis, English, Zimbabweans, Nigerians. The streets are full of merchants. Traders hawk *skop* (boiled sheep's head, split open and eaten off newspaper) in front of polished glass buildings as taxis jockey for position in rush hour. *Sangomas* (traditional healers) lay out herbs and roots next to roadside barbers' tents, and you never seem to be far from women selling *vetkoek* (dollops of deep-fried dough) beneath billboards advertising investment banks or cell phones.

Johannesburg is well worth a stopover of at least two or three days en route to other parts of the country. There's plenty to see here, including Constitution Hill in the city, not to mention the nearby city of Soweto, and the Cradle of Humankind World Heritage Site about 90 minutes away. Areas like Sandton, Rosebank, Greenside, and Parkhurst—as well as the day trips—are perfectly safe to visit on your own, though we recommend a tour guide to explore Soweto and the inner city.

Ask a *jol* (lively party) of Jo'burgers what they love about their hometown, and they may point to its high-paced energy that's laced with opportunity and a can-do attitude; summer afternoon thunderstorms; the Pirates versus Chiefs derby (the Orlando Pirates and Kaizer Chiefs are South Africa's most loved—and hated—soccer teams); spectacular sunsets; jacaranda blooms carpeting the city in purple in October and November; a great climate; the dog walks around Emmarentia Dam; the down-to-earth nature of its people; and the city's rich history.

Johannesburg's origins lie in the discovery of gold. The city sits at the center of a vast urban industrial complex that covers most of the province of Gauteng (the *g* is pronounced like the *ch* in Chanukah); colloquially most people refer to this as "place of gold." Indeed, it is home to the world's deepest gold mines (more than 3.9 km [2.4 miles] deep). More than 135 years ago it was just a rocky piece of unwanted highveld land. But in 1886 an Australian, George Harrison, discovered gold, catapulting Johannesburg into a modern metropolis that still helps to power the country's economy (though gold mining has been winding down in recent years).

With a population between 8 and 10.5 million—if you include the surrounding cities like Soweto, the East Rand, and the West Rand—greater Jo'burg is a fairly populous city by world standards (bigger than Paris but smaller than Tokyo) and is by far the country's largest city. Despite its industrial past, Jozi remains a green city, with more than 10 million trees and many beautiful parks and nature reserves, which is all the more exceptional considering it is the largest city in the world not built on a river or near a significant water source.

In the late 1980s, many of central Johannesburg's big businesses fled north from urban decay to the suburbs of Sandton and Rosebank. The former is now an upmarket commercial hub in its own right, but lately, local government and businesses have been reinvesting in the inner city, and parts are being revived. The Maboneng precinct in the city center, for instance, is a hub of trendy restaurants, novelty stores, and pop-up arts and culture events.

In addition, an extensive public transportation system serves the local working population and tourists alike. This includes the Gautrain rapid rail system that connects Sandton, Rosebank, and Pretoria with OR Tambo International Airport, moving Jo'burg steadily toward its goal of being—as the city's government is eager to brand it—"a world-class African city."

The Greater Johannesburg metropolitan area is massive—more than 1,600 square km (618 square miles)—incorporating the large municipalities of Randburg and Sandton to the north. Most of the sights are just north of the city center, which degenerated badly in the 1990s but is now being revamped.

To the south, in Ormonde, is Gold Reef City, while the sprawling township of Soweto is just a little farther to the southwest. Johannesburg's northern suburbs are its most affluent. On the way to the shopping meccas of Rosebank and Sandton, you can find the Zoo Lake and the South African Museum of Military History, in the leafy suburb of Saxonwold.

Planning

When to Go

Jo'burgers boast that they enjoy the best climate in the world: not too hot in spring and summer (mid-September–mid-April), not too cold in autumn and winter (mid-April–mid-September), and not prone to sudden temperature changes. Summer (especially between October and January) may have the edge, though: it's when the gardens and open spaces are at their most beautiful. October and November are possibly the best time of year to visit as the jacaranda trees are in full bloom.

Getting Here and Around

It's difficult but not impossible to see the Johannesburg area without a car. However, your best bet is to rent a car and a GPS navigator (or use Google Maps or the Waze app on your mobile phone). If you're reluctant to drive yourself, book a couple of full-day or half-day tours that will pick you up from your hotel or a central landmark. The City Sightseeing bus can give you an excellent overview of the city along its two routes, and it allows you to hop on and off at most of Johannesburg's attractions. Spend at least a full day doing this, and pair it with their two-hour guided tour of Soweto, if you want to go farther afield.

AIR

OR Tambo International Airport is about 19 km (12 miles) from the Johannesburg city center and is linked to the city by a fast highway, which is always busy but especially before 9 am and between 4 and 7 pm.

The most affordable, fastest, and safest way to travel to and from the airport is via the Gautrain, a high-speed train that connects Sandton, Rosebank, Midrand, downtown Johannesburg, and Pretoria directly with OR Tambo. It takes about 14 minutes to travel from the airport to Sandton and costs R181 one way, plus the cost of a Gautrain card (R19). The train runs from between 5 or 5:30 am and 9 or 9:30 pm every day, depending on the station. Gautrain also runs an extensive bus service that stops at various stations. Use the Gautrain website or app to plan your route, as well as departure and arrival times.

If your hotel or guesthouse does not have a shuttle, ask a staff member to arrange transportation for you with a reliable taxi or transfer company. Most lodgings have a regular service they use, so you should have no problem arranging this in advance.

Prices vary, depending on where you are staying, but plan on R400–R500 for a ride from your hotel or guesthouse in Sandton, Rosebank, or the city center to the airport. Some companies charge per head, whereas others charge per trip, so be sure to check that in advance. Most guesthouses or hotels will be able to drop you at the closest Gautrain station or Gautrain bus stop.

Alternatively, Magic Bus offers private transfers to all major Sandton hotels (R675 per vehicle for one or two people, R740 for three people, R780 for four to seven people). The journey takes 30 minutes to an hour.

Airport Link will ferry you anywhere in the central Johannesburg area for R580 for one person, plus R55 per additional person up to seven people (R635 for two people, R690 for three people).

In addition, scores of licensed taxis line up outside the airport terminal. By law, they must have a working meter. Expect to pay about R500 for a trip to Sandton. If, for whatever reason, the meter is not working, be sure to negotiate a price before you get into the taxi, and write the amount down on a piece of paper as confirmation.

Lines at the airport can be long: plan to arrive three hours before an international departure and at least an hour and a half before domestic departures. While the airport has its own police station, luggage theft has been a problem in recent years. Keep your belongings close to you at all times.

For airline contact information, see Air Travel in Travel Smart.

AIRPORT CONTACTS OR Tambo International Airport. ⊠ *Johannesburg* ☎ *086/727–7888, 011/921–6262 information desk* ⊕ *www.acsa.co.za.*

AIRPORT TRANSFERS Airport Link. ☎ *011/794–8300, 083/625–5090* ⊕ *www.airportlink.co.za.* **Gautrain.** ⊠ *Johannesburg* ☎ *0800/428–87246* ⊕ *www.gautrain.co.za.* **Magic Transfers.** ⊠ *Johannesburg* ☎ *011/548–0800* ⊕ *www.magictransfers.co.za/us.*

BUS

Intercity buses depart from Park station in Braamfontein in the Johannesburg city center. TransLux and Intercape Mainliner operate extensive routes around the country; you can buy tickets through ⊕ *tickets.computicket.com.*

CAR

Traveling by car is the easiest way to get around Johannesburg, as the city's public transportation is not that reliable or extensive, though this is changing (the Gautrain, for example, is incredibly reliable). The general speed limit for city streets is 60 kph (37 mph); for rural streets, it's 80 km (50 mph); and for highways, it's 100–120 kph (62 mph). Be warned that Johannesburg drivers are known as the most aggressive in the country, and minibus taxis are infamous for ignoring the rules of the road, often stopping for passengers in undesignated areas with little or no warning. Most city roads and main countryside roads are in good condition, with plenty of signage. City street names are sometimes visible only on the curb, however. Avoid driving in rush hours, 7 to 9 am and 4 to 6:30 pm, as the main roads become terribly congested.

Gas stations are plentiful in most areas. (Don't pump your own gas, though; stations employ operators to do that for you and it's seen as a courtesy to tip them anything from R2.) And remember, South Africans drive on the left side of the road, so you will need an International Driving Permit. Almost everywhere there are security guards who look after parked cars. It's customary to give these guards a small tip (R2 or R5) when you return to your car. Most big shopping centers have parking garages (starting at R8–R10).

If you plan to drive yourself around, rent a GPS (available at the airport and all reputable car-rental agencies), use Google Maps or the Waze mobile phone app. MapStudio also prints excellent complete street guides, available at bookstores and many gas stations and convenience stores. Be aware that smash and grabs are common, particularly at traffic lights and stop streets—keep your doors and windows closed, and place all valuables in the car trunk, even whilst driving.

Major car rental agencies have offices in the northern suburbs of the city and at the airport.

(For information, see Car in Travel Smart.)

TAXI

Minibus taxis form the backbone of Jo'burg's transportation for ordinary commuters, but you should avoid using them since they're often not roadworthy, drivers can be irresponsible, and it's difficult to know where they're going without consulting a local. Car taxis, though more expensive, are easier to use. They have stands at the airport and the train stations, but otherwise you must phone for one (be sure to ask how long it will take the taxi to get to you). Taxis should be licensed and have a working meter. Meters usually start at R50 (includes first 3 km [2 miles]) and are about R13 per kilometer (½ mile) thereafter. Expect to pay about R500 to the airport from town or Sandton and about R300 to the city center from Sandton.

Uber is the most entrenched e-hailing service in South Africa, with DiDi being the most recent entrant into the on-demand ride market as of mid-2021. There have been some instances of crime, particularly directed towards women, as well as driver fraud on the Bolt ride-hailing app, despite the fact that there is a 'women only' feature, which often struggles to meet demand. It's recommended to wait inside your hotel or restaurant until your vehicle arrives, as there have been cases of snatch and grabs of mobile phones.

CONTACTS DiDi. ⊠ *Johannesburg* ⊕ *za. didiglobal.com.* **Rose Taxis.** ⊠ *Johannesburg* ☎ *083/255–0933, 011/403–0000* ⊕ *www.rosetaxis.com.* **Uber.** ⊠ *Johannesburg* ☎ ⊕ *www.uber.com/cities/ johannesburg.*

TRAIN

Johannesburg's train station, Park station, is in Braamfontein, at Leyds and Loveday streets. The luxurious Blue Train, which makes regular runs to Cape Town, departs from here, as do Shosholoza Meyl trains to cities around the country, including the Trans-Karoo to Cape Town, the Komati to Nelspruit in Mpumalanga, and the Trans-Natal to Durban. Many of these trains have overnight service. They vary a lot in terms of service, comfort levels and price, and the more expensive ones such as the Blue Train and the Rovos Rail (which departs from Capital Park in Pretoria) are often booked up far in advance, though it's always worth a try if you want to make a reservation on short notice.

Locally, you can catch the Gautrain from OR Tambo, Pretoria, Sandton, or Rosebank to Park station *(see Airport Transfers in Air, above).*

Hotels

You can find just about every type of lodging in Johannesburg, from staying in Nelson Mandela's former home at Sanctuary Mandela to the colorful and vibey Radisson RED with its rooftop terrace, or the owner-run The Peech Boutique Hotel, which is set in a luscious garden. Although these varied options are all worthy places to lay your head, the truth is that most travelers stop here only to overnight or to spend a day or two in the city before they head out to their safari destination. With that in mind, we have compiled a list of places that are easy to get to from the airport and are in well-secured areas so that you will feel safe and comfortable.

Most of the good hotels are in the northern suburbs, though some are found elsewhere, including the revitalized inner city. Many are linked to nearby malls and are well policed. Boutique hotels have sprung up everywhere, as have bed-and-breakfasts and AirBnbs from Melville to Soweto. Hotels are quieter in December and January, when many local business travelers take their annual vacations. Be aware that if there's a major conference, some of the smaller hotels can be booked months in advance.

The prices of most chain hotels are calculated on a pro-rata basis and fluctuate, so it's always best to contact them directly to confirm prices during your stay.

All the hotels we list offer no-smoking rooms, and many have no-smoking floors.

Hotel reviews have been shortened. For full information, visit Fodors.com.

Nightlife

Johannesburg remains abuzz with electric energy well after dark on most days. Whether you're a punk rocker, culturati, or a suave business executive, there's always something interesting to do, even on a weeknight. Rosebank, Rivonia, and the business district of Sandton have become trendy spots for young, hip professionals and their style-conscious friends, while the main streets in the neighborhoods of Parkhurst, Melville, and Linden are lined with lively little bars and restaurants where you may catch a weekly quiz night or a round of snooker and darts. The suburb of Norwood also has a central street (Grant Avenue) with a diverse selection of mostly family-owned restaurants, while the mixed-used 44 Stanley development is ideal for a bite to eat and a spot of retail shopping. To dine, drink and dance in one go, you should venture to Sir James van der Merwe venue in Kramerville on a Wednesday from sundowners until late. Alternatively, you can also visit one of the casino complexes, such as the popular Montecasino in Fourways or Emperor's Palace next to OR Tambo International Airport.

Restaurants

Jo'burgers love eating out, and there are hundreds of restaurants throughout the city to satisfy them. Some notable destinations for food include 4th Avenue and 6th Street in Parkhurst; 7th Street and 4th Avenue in Melville; 44 Stanley, as well as Melrose Arch, Sandton, and Rosebank. Smart-casual dress is a good bet. Many establishments are closed on Sunday night and Monday.

There's no way to do justice to the sheer scope and variety of Johannesburg's restaurants in a few examples. What follows is a (necessarily subjective) list of some of the best. Try asking locals what they recommend; eating out is the most popular form of entertainment in Johannesburg, and everyone has a list of favorite spots, which changes often.

For more information on South Africa food, see What to Eat and Drink in South Africa, in the Experience chapter. Restaurant reviews have been shortened. For full information, visit Fodors.com.

RESTAURANT AND HOTEL PRICES
Restaurant prices are the average cost of a main course at dinner or, if dinner is not served, at lunch. Hotel prices are the lowest price for a standard double room in high season.

What it Costs in South African rand

	$	$$	$$$	$$$$
RESTAURANTS				
	under R100	R100–R150	R151–R200	over R200
HOTELS				
	under R1,500	R1,500–R2,500	R2,501–R3,500	over R3,500

Shopping

Whether you're after local or international designer clothes, the latest books or DVDs, high-quality African art, crafts, and curios, or glamorous gifts and souvenirs, Johannesburg offers outstanding shopping opportunities. In fact, many people, particularly from other African countries, come here with the express aim of shopping. Dozens of malls, galleries, and curio shops are scattered throughout the city, often selling the same goods at widely different prices. It's best to shop around.

Tours

Township tours (to Soweto in particular) are offered by a number of local operators. One of the best options, if your time is limited, is to take the add-on tour with the City Sightseeing bus, where resident Soweto guides give tours. JMT Tours and Safaris, and Springbok Atlas Tours & Safaris offer half-day and full-day tours of Johannesburg and Soweto. For more recommendations of reputable tour operators, inquire at Johannesburg Tourism.

Africa Explore
SPECIAL-INTEREST TOURS | Africa Explore offers half-day, full-day, and overnight tours of sights in and around Johannesburg (and throughout South Africa), including Pretoria, The Cradle of Humankind, and Pilanesberg National Park. ✉ Johannesburg ☎ 083/718–6065, 072/242–2281 ⊕ www.africa-explore.com ✈ From R990/per person sharing.

City Sightseeing Bus

BUS TOURS | FAMILY | The red, double-decker City Sightseeing bus is a hop-on, hop-off bus operator that offers a very safe and affordable way to see the city and its key attractions, particularly if you don't have a car rental. There are two routes to choose from: Johannesburg city center (Red Route) and the suburbs (Green Route). The bus departs from 12 locations every 30 minutes from 9 to 5 every day, but the best places to catch it are either at The Zone @ Rosebank (stop 1) or Gold Reef City (stop 13). Adults and kids alike will love the experience; there's a special children's soundtrack, and the adult commentary is available in 15 languages. The Red Route takes about 1½ hours if you don't get off—though you should consider at least getting off at Constitution Hill. This is also where you can jump onto the Green Route for a further hour-long drive across Jo'burg's luscious suburbs and a lookout point—you'll want to sit on the open-top level for that. There is also an option to pair either tour with a 2½-hour guided Soweto tour in a City Sightseeing shuttle bus, also highly recommended. Buy your tickets at The Zone @ Rosebank (stop 1) or on any City Sightseeing bus, but there's a discount when purchasing them online, where you can also choose from combo deals and a one- or two-day pass. ⊠ *The Zone @ Rosebank, Oxford Road, Rosebank* ☎ *0861/733–287* ⊕ *www.citysightseeing. co.za* ✉ *From R245.*

JMT Tours and Safaris

SPECIAL-INTEREST TOURS | JMT Tours and Safaris can arrange tailor-made trips for small groups to a number of destinations. Prices will vary according to where you want to go and how many people are in your group. JMT Tours and Safaris specializes in tours of Soweto but also does the Cradle of Humankind and can take you farther afield. ☎ *027/233–0073* ⊕ *jmttours.com* ✉ *From R690.*

Johannesburg Heritage Foundation

SPECIAL-INTEREST TOURS | Interested in checking out hundreds of heritage buildings and sites? Most are closed to the public, but the Johannesburg Heritage Foundation organizes walking tours of the houses and gardens, which will give you a glimpse of turn-of-the-20th-century grandeur. Prearranged tours looking at different aspects of Johannesburg's history are arranged for most weekends and take about two to three hours. It's also possible to arrange a private tour during the week, if you can do it far enough in advance, or join one of their virtual tours. ■TIP➔ **Departure points vary by the tour.** ⊠ *Johannesburg* ☎ *060/813–3377* ⊕ *www.joburgheritage.org.za* ✉ *From R100 (virtual); from R200 (walking tours).*

★ Past Experiences

SPECIAL-INTEREST TOURS | Specialist guide and owner of Past Experiences, Jo Buitendach has a passion for the inner city and the heritage value of graffiti and street art. Her walking tours weave through the inner city, where she greets the locals by name. Tours can be tailored based on your interests from shopping tours where you can buy Shweshwe fabric to following in the footsteps of Joburg's mining history, and eating Beef tibs at the Ethiopian Quarter downtown. ⊠ *Johannesburg* ☎ *083/701–3046* ⊕ *www.pastexperiences.co.za* ✉ *From R2150 for a private tour.*

Springbok Atlas Tours & Safaris

GUIDED TOURS | Springbok Atlas Tours & Safaris offers a selection of half-day and full-day tours of Johannesburg, including the city center (Maboneng) and Soweto, as well as Pretoria. Other tours explore Sun City, and the famous Pilanesberg Game Reserve. Their "Road to Democracy" tour is a highlight for anyone on a quick visit to the City of Gold. ⊠ *Johannesburg* ☎ *021/460–4700* ⊕ *www.springbokatlas.com* ✉ *From R985.*

Johannesburg Itineraries

1 or 2 Days: If you have only one day in Jo'burg, take a guided tour of Soweto and visit Constitution Hill, alternatively do a half- or full-day walking tour of downtown Jo'burg and watch sunset from the top of Africa's tallest building at Alto234 (booking essential). Spend the evening having dinner at Nelson Mandela's former home at Sanctuary Mandela, where his personal chef of almost 20 years will cook some of his much-loved dishes for you.

If you have a second day, focus on what interests you most: perhaps a trip to the Cradle of Humankind, where you can explore the sites of some of the world's most significant paleontological discoveries; a trip to Cullinan, where you can visit a working diamond mine; or a fun day or two at Sun City resort, and/or the Pilanesberg Game Reserve for a Big Five safari, just 2½ hours west of Johannesburg.

3 to 5 Days: Spend your first day touring Soweto and Constitution Hill and the inner city, followed by a dinner with African flair at Sanctuary Mandela, where you can also spend the night. The next day, leave early and do Sterkfontein Caves and Maropeng in the Cradle of Humankind, then overnight at one of the establishments in the Magaliesberg, perhaps at the luxurious Maropeng Hotel, which offers beautiful views of the Magaliesberg; the De Hoek Country Hotel; or African Pride Mount Grace Country House & Spa. Get an early start at the Pilanesberg Game Reserve, set in the hills of an ancient volcano, where you're likely to see rhinos and elephants on a game drive. Stay a night or two in one of the reserve's luxurious lodges, and treat yourself to an early-morning hot air balloon ride over the reserve followed by sparkling wine and an African sunrise.

Safety

Johannesburg is notorious for being a dangerous city—it's common to hear about serious crimes such as armed robbery and murder. That said, it's safe for visitors who avoid dangerous areas and take reasonable precautions. Do not leave bags or valuables visible in a car (put them into the car trunk), and keep the doors locked and windows up, even while driving (to minimize the risk of smash-and-grab robberies or carjackings, which mostly happen at traffic lights, intersections or stop streets); don't wear flashy jewelry or carry large wads of cash or expensive equipment. It's also advisable to keep your valuables and handbags on your person when eating at restaurants, as there have been cases of snatch and grabs at restaurants with street-side seating. ■ TIP→ **Don't visit a township or informal settlement on your own. Explore the inner city (Maboneng Precinct) with a guide.**

Unemployment is rife, and foreigners are easy pickings. If you wish to see a township or explore the inner city, check with reputable companies, which run excellent guided tours and know which areas to avoid. Constitution Hill within the city, Victoria Yards, and the various day-trip destinations—such as The Cradle of Humankind, Magaliesburg, and Pilanesberg—are perfectly safe to visit on your own. ■ TIP→ **If you drive yourself around the city, it's safest to keep your doors locked and windows up, and to not leave valuables such as bags, cameras, or phones on the seat or visible.**

That said, it is safe to drive yourself around Johannesburg. If you prefer, though, you could order a car service or transportation from your hotel for trips in and around the city.

Visitor Information

The helpful Gauteng Tourism Authority has information on the whole province, but more detailed information is often available from local tourism associations. Joburg Tourism has a good website, with information about Johannesburg and up-to-date listings of events happening around the city, as does the Johannesburg In Your Pocket website.

CONTACTS City of Johannesburg. ⊕ *www. joburg.org.za.* **Gauteng Tourism Authority.** ☎ *011/085–2500* ⊕ *gauteng.net/.* **JHBLive.** ✉ *Johannesburg* ⊕ *www.jhblive.com.* **Joburg Tourism.** ☎ *011/883–3525* ⊕ *www. joburgtourism.com.* **Johannesburg In Your Pocket.** ✉ *Johannesburg* ⊕ *www. inyourpocket.com/johannesburg.* **Soweto. co.za.** ☎ *083/535–4553, 071/204–5594* ⊕ *www.soweto.co.za.* **What's on in Joburg.** ✉ *Johannesburg* ⊕ *www.iol.co.za/ entertainment/whats-on/joburg.*

City Center

Although the city center experienced somewhat of a revival in recent years, it's not a place everyone will choose to visit—particularly alone. You'll find plenty to do downtown though, including a visit to the Maboneng Precinct, and Victoria Yards (an up-and-coming urban renewal project) on the border of the inner city. Diagonal Street runs—you guessed it— diagonally through the city center. The Hillbrow Tower (now known as Telkom Tower) is 886 feet, the tallest structure in Jo'burg, and is used for telecommunications, as is the 767-foot Brixton Tower (also called Sentech Tower) in Auckland Park. The tall, round Ponte City apartment block near Hillbrow is another focal point that can be seen from almost all parts of the city and is the starting point for Dlala Nje's immersive walking tours.

Located in the western section of the city, Newtown, which is connected to Braamfontein via the Nelson Mandela Bridge, was once one of the city's most run-down neighborhoods. Today it is one of the city's cultural precincts and has been reimagined with the launch of The Playground in early 2022, which attracts urban-hipsters over the weekends with its amazing array of specialty and artisanal foods, vintage clothing, arts and crafts, jewelry, pop-up artists stores, as well as live music and performances.

Braamfontein is where you'll find Constitution Hill and the University of the Witwatersrand, one of South Africa's oldest and most respected universities, which is also the location of the Origins Centre and the planetarium.

 Sights

★ **Constitution Hill**
HISTORIC SIGHT | Overlooking Jo'burg's inner city, Constitution Hill houses the Constitutional Court, which sits on the most important human rights cases, much like the United State's Supreme Court. The slanting columns represent the trees under which African villagers met to discuss important matters and each of the 11 chairs of the justices are covered in Nguni cowhide, representing their individuality. If not in session, you can view it and its artworks.

This is also where you will find the austere Old Fort Prison Complex (also called Number Four), where thousands of political prisoners were incarcerated, including Nobel Peace Prize laureates Albert Luthuli and Nelson Mandela, and iconic Indian leader Mahatma Gandhi. There is no fee to explore the prison ramparts (built in the 1890s) but there is an hour-long highlights tour (R100) of

Once avoided, the Maboneng Precinct is filled with art galleries, indie boutiques, coffee shops, restaurants, and rooftop bars.

the Old Fort Prison Complex every hour on the hour from 9 am to 4 pm, while the two-hour full site tour (R150) takes place at 10 am and 1 pm. Both tours visit the Women's Jail. Food I Love You, in the refurbished prison kitchen, serves breakfast, lunch, and grab-and-go bites with local flavor, while Motherland Coffee has a coffee truck on site. ⊠ *11 Kotze St., entrance on Joubert St., Braamfontein* ☎ *011/381–3100* ⊕ *www.constitutionhill. org.za* ✉ *Court free; Constitution Hill tours from R100 (tickets can only be bought via Webtickets; link found on website).*

Diagonal Street
STREET | On this street in the city center, among stores selling traditional African fabrics and household appliances, you'll find African herbalists' shops purveying a mind-boggling array of homeopathic and traditional cures for whatever ails you. If you're lucky, a *sangoma* (traditional healer) might throw the bones and tell you what the future holds. This is also the site of the old Johannesburg Stock Exchange building (the modern version is in Sandton) and the so-called Diamond Building, resembling a multifaceted diamond. ■**TIP**→ **You'll get the most out of visiting Diagonal Street on a guided walking tour—go with Past Experiences where owner and guide Jo Buitendach will introduce you to the locals and shop owners.** ⊠ *Diagonal St., City Center.*

Maboneng Precinct
NEIGHBORHOOD | If you need proof that Jo'burg is revitalizing, Maboneng Precinct (along Main street) is one example. Once a place to avoid, this neighborhood is buzzing with art galleries, indie boutiques, coffee shops, restaurants, rooftop bars, and apartments. Vendors display their wares (paintings, batik tablecloths, beadwork, and souvenirs) along the main stretch of the street. It can be a little overwhelming driving there alone, especially with so many one-way streets, and the outlying area can be a bit frenzied, so you may want to visit on a guided tour. ⊠ *Maboneng Precinct, City Center.*

Sights ▼

1 Constitution Hill **D8**
2 Diagonal Street **C9**
3 Ditsong National Museum of Military History....... **D6**
4 Johannesburg Botanical Garden and Emmarentia Dam **A6**
5 Maboneng Precinct..... **E9**
6 Melville Koppies Nature Reserve **A6**
7 Nelson Mandela Bridge..................... **C8**
8 Origins Centre............ **C8**
9 The Playground **C8**
10 Ponte City................. **E8**
11 Satyagraha House....... **F6**
12 Victoria Yards **E8**
13 Wits Planetarium **C8**

Restaurants ▼

1 Basalt **E4**
2 Bellinis **D4**
3 Bertrand Café **E9**
4 The Butcher Shop and Grill **E3**
5 Embarc................... **B5**
6 Ethos **D5**
7 Flames **C7**
8 Hell's Kitchen............ **B7**
9 Little Addis Cafe......... **B8**
10 Marble **C5**
11 Modena Italian Eatery **B5**
12 Parea Taverna **D4**
13 Saint....................... **E2**
14 Trabella Pizzeria **D4**

Quick Bites ▼

1 Bespokery **C6**
2 Glenda's................... **C4**
3 Gourmet Grocer.......... **E5**
4 JFF Rooftop Farm **C8**
5 Jo'Anna Melt Bar....... **B7**
6 Nice on 4th **B5**
7 Truffles on the Park...... **E2**

Hotels ▼

1 City Lodge Hotel at OR Tambo International Airport..................... **I7**
2 Fairlawns Boutique Hotel & Spa............... **F1**
3 54 on Bath **D5**
4 Four Seasons The Westcliff............. **C7**
5 The Houghton Hotel **F6**
6 InterContinental Johannesburg OR Tambo Airport........ **I7**
7 The Leonardo **E2**
8 The Maslow **E2**
9 The Peech Boutique Hotel **E4**
10 Radisson Blu Gautrain Hotel............ **E3**
11 Radisson RED **D5**
12 Reef Hotel **D9**
13 Sanctuary Mandela **E6**
14 Sandton Sun............. **D3**
15 The Saxon Hotel, Villas & Spa **C3**
16 Ten Bompas **C4**
17 The Troyeville Hotel **E8**

KEY

- 1 *Exploring Sights*
- 1 *Restaurants*
- 1 *Quick Bites*
- 1 *Hotels*

Nelson Mandela Bridge

BRIDGE | A symbol of the renewal process going on in the city, this modern, 931-foot-long bridge with sprawling cables spans the Braamfontein railway yard, connecting Braamfontein and the revamped Newtown Cultural Precinct to The Market Theater and Maboneng Precinct. The bridge is especially beautiful at night when it is colorfully illuminated (though walking across without a guide, even during the day, is not advised). ⊠ *Bertha St., Braamfontein, City Center* ✛ *Take Queen Elizabeth St. from Braamfontein, or follow signs from central Newtown or from M1 south.*

Origins Centre

OTHER MUSEUM | **FAMILY** | A giant world map that is handmade of aluminum wire depicts the migration of hominins at the entrance of Origins Centre. This modern museum (situated at the University of the Witwatersrand) explores the development and culture of modern humans over the past 100,000 years, and in particular rock art and stone tools—of which southern Africa has the oldest in the world. Origins is spacious and elegantly designed across three stories that house permanent and temporary exhibitions, which cater to school kids and visiting professors alike. It was renovated in 2021 and boasts interactive multimedia displays and photographs that are enhanced by a free Augmented Reality app (OriginsCentreAR), which can be used with the museum's free Wi-Fi. The museum's gift shop sells high-quality crafts made by the Khomani San in the Northern Cape as well as hard-to-source books on rock art in southern Africa. The center's coffee shop, Food Art @ Origins, serves tasty, light meals. If you don't make it to the museum, you can experience most of its exhibitions via its websites, thanks to Google Arts & Culture. ⊠ *University of the Witwatersrand, Yale Rd., Braamfontein, City Center* ☎ *011/717–4700* ⊕ *www.wits.ac.za/origins* 🎟 *R81* ⊗ *Closed Sun.*

The Playground

MARKET | Braamfontein's Juta Street Precinct has been reignited with the establishment of The Playground (at the site of what was Neighborhoods Market pre-pandemic). Housed in an underground parking lot with a rooftop and wraparound wooden deck accented by a living green wall, the venue hosts an artisan market on weekends (9 am–6 pm). It's characterized by good food, with a selection of gourmet stalls and street food vendors, coupled with cocktails and a showcase of local artists' design, art, and fashion wares. Live music and DJ sets emanate from this performance venue on Sundays.

The Playground looks out onto a towering mural of Nelson Mandela by graffiti artist Shepard Fairey titled *The purple shall govern*. It references an anti-apartheid march on September 2, 1989, during which police sprayed protestors with water cannons containing purple dye to distinguish them easily. And while you're here, just across the street, beneath the mural, is an intimate rooftop bar called The Beach where you can dig your feet into beach sand while reclining on a lounger in the shade of an umbrella. ⊠ *73 Juta St., Newtown, City Center* ☎ *060/793–6107* ⊕ *www.playbraamfontein.co.za* 🎟 *R20 (after 11 am on Sat.)* ⊗ *Closed Mon.–Fri.* ☞ *Cashless environment, credit cards accepted.*

★ Ponte City

NOTABLE BUILDING | If there's a symbol of Johannesburg, it's Ponte City, a massive, hollow 54-story cylinder of apartments that you might recall from watching *District 9*. Built in 1975, and standing at a height of 568 feet with a flashing advertisement at the top, it was, until recently, the tallest residential building in Africa. Once the apex of grand living, it became a slum in the 1990s as the middle class fled to the suburbs. It has since been revitalized, with young professionals, students, and immigrants moving in.

The Dlala Nje Foundation, on the ground floor of the building, is a safe space and community center for the neighborhood's youth. It is funded by the four fascinating tours offered by the Dlala Nje Experiences Business, which takes visitors on walking tours of the inner city's misunderstood suburbs. Leave all your prejudices behind as you explore Hillbrow, Yeoville, and Berea on a culinary, shopping, or queer tour, where you can interact with locals, many of whom are small business owners, to gain a refreshed perspective on this vastly diverse city. ⊠ *Ponte city apartments (Dlala Nje: Shop 1), 1 Lily Ave., Hillbrow* ☎ *067/082–8168* ⊕ *www.dlalanje.org* ⌧ *Depending on tour.*

★ Victoria Yards

MARKET | FAMILY | Victoria Yards is an urban renewal project on the fringe of the inner city that has reimagined abandoned warehouses into a mixed-use lifestyle complex. It supports the surrounding community through its three on-site non-profits and urban farming project, while locals and tourists explore the 50-odd artists' workshops, decor showrooms, galleries, and fashion outlets housed in its brick face buildings. The driving force behind Victoria Yards is sustainability with tenants making designer bags from vibrant *shweshwe* fabric (a printed cotton fabric) and plastic waste, homeware made from recycled industrial parts, upcycled pre-loved clothing, and a sorbet stand that buys overripe, unsold fruit from community street-side sellers to make frozen desserts.

If your appetite gets the better of you on a visit, there's an old-school "tuck shop," coffee roastery, and bakery that stands shoulder-to-shoulder to a small-batch gin distillery, as well as a bar, and a traditional walk-in fish and chip shop with wooden benches arranged in the courtyard. While it's open 7 days a week, the First Sunday Market (first Sunday of the month, 10 am–4 pm) hosts a

Did You Know?

South Africa can proudly claim four Nobel Peace Prize winners. The first was African National Congress (ANC) founder Albert Luthuli, in 1960. Anglican Archbishop Desmond Tutu won his in 1984, and Nelson Rolihlahla Mandela and ex-president F. W. de Klerk won theirs in 1993.

collection of additional vendors who sell everything from collectibles, antiques, and handmade African curios to food and drink. There is free, undercover parking available, as well as overflow on-street parking with parking guards, making it safe to visit on your own. ⊠ *16 Viljoen St., Lorentzville, City Center* ☎ *072/520–7432 mobile, 010/594–5210 landline* ⊕ *www. victoriayards.co.za* ☉ *No First Sunday Market in Jan.*

Wits Planetarium

OBSERVATORY | FAMILY | This planetarium, dating from 1960, has entertaining and informative programs on the African skies and presentations that range from space travel to the planets. Have a look at the website to find out what's on and to book tickets. ⊠ *University of the Witwatersrand, Yale Rd., Braamfontein, City Center* ☎ *011/717–1390* ⊕ *www. planetarium.co.za* ⌧ *Varies by event, average R55.*

🍴 Restaurants

Bertrand Café

$$$ | FRENCH FUSION | One of the coolest places to be seen in Maboneng, Bertrand Café exudes a shabby chic style with its mirror and portrait walls, chandelier, mix-match pops of color, and bookshelves lined with bric-a-brac. The food is a fusion of French and African flavors thanks to inspiration from the Congolese co-owner Bertrand Mampouya. **Known for:** an

Famous Residents

What other place on Earth can boast of having had two Nobel Peace Prize laureates living within a block of each other? For most of his adult life Anglican Archbishop Desmond Tutu lived on Vilakazi Street, in Soweto's Orlando West neighborhood. His neighbor would have been an attorney named Nelson Mandela, had Mandela not spent most of *his* adult life incarcerated on Robben Island (*see Cape Town*). The archbishop's family home is a gray, two-story building that holds heritage status but is not open to the public. You can, however, visit the nearby Mandela house, which became a museum in 1997 and was revamped in 2009.

ideal spot for remote working; people watching from the outside seating; good Wi-Fi. $ *Average main: R180* ⊠ *296 Fox St., City Center* ☎ *011/614–0261* ⊕ *bertrand-cafe.business.site.*

☕ Coffee and Quick Bites

JFF Rooftop Farm

$ | CAFÉ | Surely one of the most picturesque coffee shops in town, this is a fusion between a tea garden and an open-air, urban farm that sells indigenous plants, flowers, and herbs. Bask in the sunshine at this matchbox-sized, inner-city establishment as co-owner Ashleigh "Ash" Machete gives you tips on how to best look after your plants while you sip on your coffee. **Known for:** a popular stop on inner city tours; elephant graffiti by artist Falko One; only being accessible by a short but steep ladder. $ *Average main: R40* ⊠ *70 Juta St., City Center* ✛ *Behind the Kalashnikovv Gallery* ☎ *081/768–4827* ⊕ *www.jffrooftopfarm.co.za.*

Hotels

Reef Hotel

$ | HOTEL | Occupying a former office building, this chic-industrial style hotel commemorates Jo'burg's early beginnings as a gold-mining town with touches like a big black-and-white photo of a gold mine over the headboard in each well-appointed room. **Pros:** open-air rooftop bar on 16th floor open Thursday through Sunday; the restaurant was refurbished in mid-2021; great breakfast buffet. **Cons:** noise from downtown; doorless, walk-in bathrooms; very slow response on email, better to call. $ *Rooms from: R1050* ⊠ *56 Anderson Rd., Marshalltown* ☎ *011/689–1000* ⊕ *www.reefhotel.co.za* ⇄ *120 rooms* ⦿| *Free Breakfast.*

The Troyeville Hotel

$ | HOTEL | Even though it was established in 1939 to house gold prospectors coming to the city in search of their fortunes, The Troyeville Hotel is still going strong receiving a significant facelift in 2021. **Pros:** restaurant serves authentic Portuguese fare and imported drinks; walk-in coffee shop serves on-the-go eats and homemade pastéis de nata; a favorite among local patrons. **Cons:** overflow streetside parking, but with hotel security guards who will walk you to your car; breakfast not included, but can be ordered at restaurant; restaurant gets very busy when it broadcasts live sports on its big screen. $ *Rooms from: R650* ⊠ *1403 Albertina Sisulu Road, Troyeville, City Center* ☎ *079/612–0125* ⊕ *www.thetroyeville.co.za* ⇄ *5* ⦿| *No Meals.*

The Apartheid Museum takes visitors on a journey through South African apartheid history.

Soweto and the South

An acronym for *South Western Townships*, Soweto dates back to 1904, when city councilors used an outbreak of bubonic plague as an excuse to move Black people outside the town. Today the suburb, which is 20 km (12 miles) south of the city, is home to nearly 2 million residents. What it lacks in infrastructure (though it's been vastly upgraded since the first democratic elections in 1994) it more than makes up for in soul, energy, and history. The largely working-class population knows how to live for today, and Soweto pulsates with people and music.

Some areas of Soweto that are worth touring include old-town neighborhood of Diepkloof, just beyond Orlando West, and its neighbor, the new Diepkloof Extension, which dates from the mid-1970s, when bank loans first became available to Black property owners. The difference between the two is startling:

the dreary, prefabricated matchbox houses of Diepkloof next to what looks like a middle-class suburb anywhere. In nearby Dube, many of the evicted residents of Sophiatown—a freehold township (where Blacks were allowed to own property) west of the city and a melting pot of music, bohemianism, crime, and multiracialism that insulted Afrikaner nationalism—were resettled in 1959, bringing an exciting vibe to the dreary, homogenous dormitory town. The area remains a vibrant suburb, with an exciting mix of people and a festive atmosphere.

Between downtown Johannesburg and Soweto lie several suburbs less affluent than their northern counterparts, including Ormonde, where Gold Reef City and the Apartheid Museum are located.

GETTING HERE AND AROUND
If you want a whistle-stop tour of Soweto, City Sightseeing offers a 2 ½-hour add-on tour which can be combined with both or either of their other two

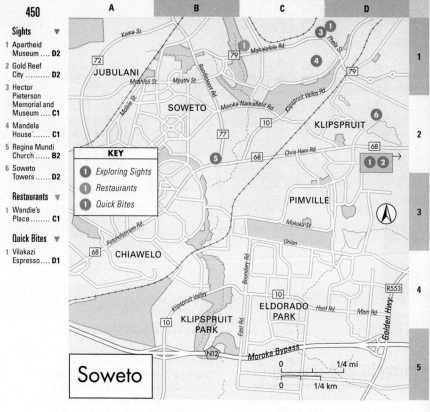

KEY

1 Exploring Sights

1 Restaurants

1 Quick Bites

Soweto

sightseeing routes. It is guided by a local who lives in and knows the township.

Otherwise, if you'd like to spend more time on the ground getting a deeper understanding of Soweto's history and its nuances—a half-day or a full-day tour will suffice—we suggest hiring a private guide. You can also choose between a number of special-interest tours, which center on art, traditional medicine, restaurants, nightlife, or memorials. Most tours start in Jo'burg, and you can arrange to be collected from your hotel. ■TIP➜ **We strongly suggest that you take a guided tour if you decide to visit Soweto. It is a chaotic, virtually indistinguishable sprawl. Even if you found your way in, you'd struggle to find your way out—let alone around.**

◉ Sights

★ Apartheid Museum

OTHER MUSEUM | The Apartheid Museum, in Ormonde, takes you on a journey through South African apartheid history—from the entrance, where you pass through a turnstile according to your assigned skin color (black or white), to the myriad historical, brutally honest, and sometimes shocking photographs, video displays, films, documents, and other exhibits. It's an emotional, multilayered journey. As you walk chronologically through the apartheid years and eventually reach the country's first steps to freedom, with democratic elections in 1994, you experience a taste of the pain and suffering with which so many South Africans had to live. A room with 121 ropes with hangman's knots hanging from the ceiling—one rope for each

Hector Pieterson & the Soweto Uprising

On June 16, 1976, hundreds of schoolchildren in Soweto marched to protest the use of Afrikaans as the primary language of education in the overcrowded, much neglected Bantu schools in the townships. This was a highly charged political issue. Not only was Dutch-based Afrikaans considered the language of the oppressor by Blacks, but it also made it more difficult for students to learn, as most spoke an African language and, as a second language, English.

The march quickly turned nasty. The police started firing into the youthful crowd. One of the first people of 200 to 500 to die in what was the beginning of a long and protracted struggle was 12-year-old Hector Pieterson. A picture taken by photographer Sam Nzima of the dying Pieterson in the arms of a crying friend, with Pieterson's sister running alongside them, put a face on apartheid that went around the globe.

Pieterson was just a schoolboy trying to ensure a better life for himself and his friends, family, and community. He and the many students who joined the liberation movement strengthened the fight against apartheid. Eventually Afrikaans was dropped as a language of instruction, and more schools and a teaching college were built in Soweto. Today, Hector Pieterson's name graces a simple memorial and museum about the conflict, and June 16 is Youth Day, a public holiday.

political prisoner executed in the apartheid era—is especially chilling. ⊠ Northern Pkwy. at Gold Reef Rd., Ormonde ☎ 011/309–4700 ⊕ www.apartheidmuseum.org ✉ R85.

Gold Reef City
AMUSEMENT PARK/CARNIVAL | FAMILY | This theme park lets you step back in time to 1880s Johannesburg to see why it became known as the City of Gold. One of the city's most popular attractions, especially for families, it has good rides that kids will enjoy and is based on the history of Jo'burg. In addition to riding the Anaconda, a scary roller coaster on which you hang under the track, feet in the air, you can (for an additional fee) descend into an old gold mine and see molten gold being poured. The reconstructed streets of the bygone era are lined with operating Victorian-style shops and restaurants. And for those with money to burn, the large, glitzy Gold Reef Village Casino beckons across the road. ⊠ Northern Pkwy. at Data Crescent,

Shaft 14, Ormonde ✛ 6 km (4 miles) south of city center ☎ 011/248–6800 ⊕ www.goldreefcity.co.za ✉ R200 general admission; additional R120 for underground mine tour or additional R190 for full heritage tour.

Hector Pieterson Memorial and Museum
MUSEUM VILLAGE | FAMILY | Opposite Holy Cross Church, a stone's throw from the former homes of Nelson Mandela and Archbishop Desmond Tutu on Vilakazi Street, the Hector Pieterson Memorial and Museum is a crucial landmark. Pieterson, a 12-year-old student, was one of the first victims of police fire on June 16, 1976, when schoolchildren rose up to protest their second-rate Bantu (Black) education system. The memorial is a paved area with benches for reflection beneath trees that have been planted by visiting dignitaries, an inscribed stone, and water feature. Inside the museum, which was updated in 2021, multimedia displays of grainy photographs and archival footage bring that fateful day

The brightly painted Soweto Towers are a well-known Johannesburg landmark.

to life and put it into the context of the broader apartheid struggle. The museum courtyard has 562 small granite blocks as a tribute to the children who died in the Soweto uprisings. Suggested visiting time is at least 30 minutes. You can also hire an on-site tour guide to take you around (recommended donation is R100). ✉ Khumalo St. at Phela St., Orlando West ☎ 011/536–0611 ⊕ www.joburg.org.za 🖃 R52 ⊘ Closed Mon.

Mandela House

HISTORY MUSEUM | FAMILY | The anti-apartheid activist and former president lived in this small house for 15 years until his arrest in 1961 (and for 11 days after his release), with his first wife, Evelyn Ntoko Mase, and then second wife, Winnie Madikizela-Mandela. The redbrick house, which was burnt to the ground in 1988 and was rebuilt with the help of the community, holds heritage status today and has been converted into a museum that contains Mandela's memorabilia and weaves a story that helps visitors better understand his daily struggles as

a life-long freedom fighter. The museum was renovated in 2008 to mark his 90th birthday. If you're unable to visit the museum, you can do a free virtual tour via the website, which includes a number of informative videos. ✉ 8115 Vilakazi St., Orlando West ☎ 011/936–7754 ⊕ www. mandelahouse.com 🖃 R120.

Regina Mundi Church

CHURCH | Central to the liberation struggle, this Catholic church was a refuge of peace, sanity, and steadfast moral focus for the people of Soweto through the harshest years of repression. Archbishop Desmond Tutu often delivered sermons in this massive church during the apartheid years. And it wasn't always so peaceful—you still can see bullet holes where police opened fire on students and residents seeking refuge. It has a Black Madonna and Child painting and beautiful stained-glass windows, including one depicting the Annunciation. ✉ 1149 Khumalo St., Rockville 🖃 R60.

Soweto Towers

VIEWPOINT | Originally a coal-fired power station, the brightly painted cooling towers are now a well-known Johannesburg landmark that's been transformed into an adrenaline junkie's paradise, where you can do bungee jumping and a scad free-fall from the top of the 33-story structure, as well as rock climbing and paintballing. The viewing deck offers 360-degree views of Soweto below. Afterward, you can relax at Chaf-Pozi, the popular restaurant located on the premises which serves authentic South African cuisine. ✉ *corner of Sheffield Rd. and Chris Hani Rd., Orlando* ☎ *071/674–4343* 🌐 *sowetotowers.co.za* 🎟 *R630 (bungee jumping)* ⏲ *Closed Mon.–Wed.*

🍴 Restaurants

★ **Wandie's Place**

$$ | AFRICAN | Smartly dressed waiters in ties serve truly African food—meat stews, sweet potatoes, beans, a stiff corn porridge, traditionally cooked pumpkin, chicken, and tripe laid out in a buffet of pots and containers—to a steady stream of hungry patrons. The food is hot, the drinks are cold, and the conversation flows, especially if you happen to meet Wandie, who frequently still runs operations. **Known for:** tour groups; eclectic decor; best-known township restaurant in Soweto. [$] *Average main: R150* ✉ *618 Makhalamele St., Dube* ☎ *081/420–6051.*

☕ Coffee and Quick Bites

Vilakazi Espresso

$ | SANDWICHES | Across the street from the Hector Pieterson Memorial and Museum, Vilakazi Espresso is recognizable for its geometric Ndebele-inspired mural and colorful graffiti artwork. It serves deep-fried and filled South African *vetkoek* (dough bread) and sandwiches, along with its wide coffee selection and smoothies. **Known for:** sit down or takeaway options; central location; quick service. [$] *Average main: R55* ✉ *7346 Vilakazi St., Soweto* ☎ *081/206–0369* 🌐 *www.vilakaziespresso.co.za.*

Johannesburg's Northern Suburbs 👁

Johannesburg has dozens of northern suburbs, ranging in size from the huge and diverse Sandton, which includes the entire township of Alexandra, among other suburbs, to the smaller, leafy Saxonwold. The northern suburbs highlighted here are by no means the only ones—they simply have the most attractions and are where most tourists stay.

Rosebank and Houghton

Rosebank is home to upmarket shopping malls, restaurants and cafes, hotels, and art galleries that are frequented by well-to-do locals and tourists. At Rosebank Mall you'll find all the international designer brands, along with the best in uniquely South African brands, boutiques, and outlets, particularly at the Soko District inside, while Exclusive Books has an excellent range of coffee-table and reference books on Africa. The Rosebank Art and Craft Market, open daily, is adjacent to the mall and is popular for its curios, and African art—it's acceptable to shop around and bargain.

Keyes Art Mile, a few roads down, is a pedestrian art precinct that stretches between the Everard Read and Circa galleries, and is dotted with public artworks by African artists. Here you'll also find the elegant Marble restaurant, alongside a string of casual eateries and home decor stores.

🍴 Restaurants

★ Ethos

$$$$ | **MEDITERRANEAN** | The relaxed fine-dining, Mediterranean-inspired fare at Ethos has as much appeal as its decor and design, which is characterized by beige hues, Doric columns, brass accents, and flowing ceiling baffles. Dishes are carefully curated to highlight how the natural flavors of various foods also complement each other in terms of texture, color, and thoughtful presentation. **Known for:** sophisticated tapas and elegant main meals; stylish eatery with comfortable ambiance; prix-fixe menus also available. [$] *Average main: R300* ✉ *Oxford Parks, Corner Eastwood and Parks blvds., Rosebank* ☎ *010/446–9906* 🌐 *www.ethosrestaurant.co.za.*

Marble

$$$$ | **SOUTH AFRICAN** | Famed for award-winning chef and co-owner David Higgs (whose cookbook, *Mile 8*, can be purchased on-site), Marble plates epicurean meals that can be expertly paired with wine. The open-plan kitchen is the restaurant's focal point, where the chef's table presents an intimate look into how Higgs and his team of 37 prepare food over a live wood fire in a quintessentially South African manner. **Known for:** multiple awards since it opened; interior design shaped by four local artists and artisans; premium flame-grilled meat. [$] *Average main: R350* ✉ *Trumpet on Keyes, Corner Keyes and Jellicoe Aves., Rosebank* ☎ *010/594–5550 Landline, 064/439–2030 WhatsApp* 🌐 *www.marble.restaurant.*

☕ Coffee and Quick Bites

Glenda's

$$ | **EUROPEAN** | This cozy, atmospheric restaurant is always busy because of the quality of its food and the gorgeous bucolic murals on its walls that complement the retro design elements, making it oh-so Instagram-worthy. The all-day menu serves breakfast, light lunches, high tea coupled with its in-house baked goods and treats, and dinner. **Known for:** being an any-time-of-day kind of place; takeaway patisserie counter; trendy cocktails, craft brews and local wines. [$] *Average main: R120* ✉ *Hyde Square, Corner Jan Smuts Ave. and North Rd., Rosebank* ☎ *011/268–6369* 🌐 *www.glendas.co.*

🛏 Hotels

54 on Bath

$$$ | **HOTEL** | Most of the visitors to 54 on Bath are international business travelers and foreign tourists drawn to the modern yet intimate elegance behind the towering brick facade and Doric columns, though the Champagne bar is popular with locals. **Pros:** friendly staff; high-speed Wi-Fi for guests throughout the hotel; direct access to malls via sky bridge. **Cons:** the hotel is looking a little dated; not on airport shuttle route, although the hotel will arrange transport for a fee; construction in the area can be noisy. [$] *Rooms from: R2590* ✉ *54 Bath Ave., Rosebank* ☎ *011/344–8500* 🌐 *www.tsogosun.com/54-on-bath* 🛏 *75 rooms* 🍴 *Free Breakfast.*

The Houghton Hotel

$$ | **RESORT** | **FAMILY** | If resort life is what you're after then look no further than the contemporary Houghton Hotel—kitted out with five swimming pools (including a ying-yang-shaped one with a tumbling water feature), award-winning spa, 24-hour gym with daily classes, adjoining 18-hole golf course, and acclaimed restaurants. **Pros:** business lounge facilities; a destination hotel; commendable service. **Cons:** many rooms look out onto the rest of the hotel; the main hotel area can feel quite built up; the size may be overwhelming for some. [$] *Rooms from: R2500* ✉ *Lloys Ellis Ave., Rosebank* ☎ *011/032–5500* 🌐 *www.thehoughtonhotel.com* 🛏 *67 rooms* 🍴 *Free Breakfast.*

Radisson RED

$$ | HOTEL | The newly-built Radisson RED wows guests with its rotating collection of African prints, as well as its contemporary decor and design elements that make its open spaces and rooms pop with color. **Pros:** grab 'n go food station in the lobby; fee shuttle to Gautrain station (650 feet away); walking distance to The Zone @ Rosebank Mall and Keyes Art Mile. **Cons:** alongside a busy road (rooms are soundproof); the rooftop bar and terrace can get quite lively on weekends; the decor and atmosphere will appeal more to younger travelers. [$] *Rooms from: R1800* ✉ *4 Parks Blvd., Oxford Parks, Rosebank* ☎ *010/023–3580* 🌐 *www.radissonhotels.com* 🛏 *222 rooms* 🍴 *Free Breakfast.*

★ **Sanctuary Mandela**

$$$$ | HOTEL | Get an insider's insight into Nelson Mandela with a stay at Sanctuary Mandela, which has converted his former Houghton home and heritage site into a boutique hotel that pays homage to the human rights activist with specially commissioned art pieces that document his lifetime. **Pros:** medium-sized swimming pool with loungers; Mandela's master bedroom has been converted into the presidential suite; Mandela's personal items, mementoes, and photographs are throughout the hotel. **Cons:** open-plan bathrooms; the space can feel a little formal; no garden, though vegetation lines the property's borders. [$] *Rooms from: R4350* ✉ *4 13th Ave., Houghton, Rosebank* ☎ *010/035–0368* 🌐 *www.sanctuarymandela.com* 🛏 *9 rooms* 🍴 *Free Breakfast.*

Shopping

AFRICAN ARTS AND CRAFTS

Everard Read Johannesburg

ART GALLERIES | Established in 1913, the gallery is one of the oldest commercial art galleries in South Africa. The privately-owned gallery acts as an agent for several important South African and African artists and sculptors, and it specializes in modern and contemporary artworks, particularly wildlife paintings and sculpture. ✉ *2 and 6 Jellicoe Ave., Rosebank* ☎ *011/788–4805* 🌐 *www.everard-read.co.za* 🕒 *Closed Sun.*

MARKETS

Bargaining can get you a great price at the city's several markets. At the Rosebank Art and Craft Market, in particular, bargain hard by offering half the asking price, and then work your way up to about two-thirds of the price, if you're interested in the item. Take your time before you buy anything, as you will see similar crafts at different stalls, and the prices may vary considerably.

Rosebank Art and Craft Market

CRAFTS | The Rosebank Art and Craft Market, between the Rosebank Mall and The Zone, has a huge variety of African crafts from Cape to Cairo, all displayed to the background beat of traditional African music. Drive a hard bargain here—the vendors expect you to! If you want to save your shopping until the end of your trip, then this should be your destination. It's the best place in Jo'burg to buy African crafts, and it's an entertaining place to visit as well. ✉ *Mall of Rosebank, Cradock Ave., Rosebank* ✣ *Next to Europa* ☎ *011/568–0850* 🌐 *www.rosebankartandcraftmarket.co.za.*

Rosebank Sunday Market

MARKET | FAMILY | The Rosebank Sunday Market, in the parking lot on the rooftop of Rosebank Mall, has become a Sunday tradition in the city. Some 600 stalls sell African and Western crafts by local artisans, antiques, art, handmade clothing, trinkets, bric-a-brac and more. It's also a great place to fill your picnic basket, with tempting specialties from Greek wraps to Thai spring rolls, and gourmet cupcakes. African musicians, dancers, and other entertainers delight the crowds between the alleyways. ✉ *The Mall of Rosebank, Level 4, Bath St. at Baker St., Rosebank* ☎ *064/735–4224* 🌐 *www.rosebanksundaymarket.co.za* 🕒 *Closed Mon.–Sat.*

Melrose and Illovo

Illovo and Melrose are two small suburbs wedged between Rosebank and Sandton. Illovo is home to several shopping centers with family-owned businesses, office parks, small restaurants and cafes. Melrose Arch, located in Melrose, is an upscale shopping, dining, residential, and business district that features a selection of noteworthy restaurants, bakeries, shops and boutiques. This European-style lifestyle center has closed off pedestrian walkways and offers pleasant accommodations in a relaxed and safe setting. Both are popular with locals and very safe to visit alone.

🍴 Restaurants

★ Basalt

$$$$ | **CONTEMPORARY** | This is fine dining at its finest, according to the 2021 Luxe Restaurant Awards which conferred the title of Fine Dining Restaurant of the Year on Basalt. This intimate, dinner-only establishment prides itself on attention to detail with immaculate plating that plays on a fusion of color, texture, and storytelling. **Known for:** regularly changing menu in line with seasons and fresh produce; a romantic night out where the prix-fixe menu is served at a leisurely pace; quality service and attention to detail. [$] *Average main: R875* ✉ *The Peech Hotel, 61 North St., Melrose Arch* ☎ *011/537–9797* 🌐 *www.basalt.restaurant* 🕓 *Closed Mon. and Tues. No lunch* ☞ *Children aged 16 or over are welcome.*

Bellinis

$$ | **SOUTH AFRICAN** | This small, casual restaurant offers memorable food and quick, professional service, whether you choose to sit down or grab a quick bite. The atmosphere can be quite noisy and energy-packed, as friends catch up over lunch and businesspeople chat animatedly about work over a plate of legendary potato rostis: try one with smoked salmon or a pepper fillet. **Known for:** bellinis; good selection of South African wines; house-baked cakes, particularly the carrot cake. [$] *Average main: R150* ✉ *18 Chaplin Rd., Illovo* ☎ *011/880–9168* 🌐 *www.bellinis.co.za* 🕓 *Closed Sun.*

Parea Taverna

$$ | **GREEK** | At this Greek taverna, music floats above the buzz of conversation, a souvlaki spit turns slowly near the door, and a refrigerated case displays an array of *meze* (small appetizers)—which you can also select as a takeaway, if you're on the go. Start with a meze platter of souvlaki, feta, olives imported from Greece, tzatziki, and dolmades, followed by the line fish, grilled on an open flame with olive oil and lemon, or *kleftiko* (lamb slow-cooked in a clay oven) and a carafe of wine. **Known for:** Chef Jabu, who has been there since it opened in 1993; produce sourced from Greece; unbeatable selection at meze cafe. [$] *Average main: R150* ✉ *3D Corlett Dr., at Oxford Rd., Illovo* ☎ *011/788–8777* 🌐 *www.parea.co.za.*

Trabella Pizzeria

$$ | **ITALIAN** | Trabella's strength is its pizza, whether it's with the Brie and cranberry topping; or smoked salmon, sour cream, and caviar, sprinkled with spring onion. If you can't decide which one to choose go with Tracy's Special, which includes every topping, with a vegetarian or meat-lovers option; the pasta and gnocchi are also good choices. **Known for:** fresh porcini mushrooms; wheat-free and gluten-free pizza bases (at additional charge); peanut butter chocolate cheesecake. [$] *Average main: R137* ✉ *Illovo Junction, Oxford Rd. 3, at Corlett Dr., Illovo* ☎ *011/442–0413* 🌐 *www.trabellapizzeria.co.za* 🕓 *Closed Mon. No lunch Sun.*

☕ Coffee and Quick Bites

Gourmet Grocer

$ | **CAFÉ** | Stop by for an on-the-go breakfast or picnic take-away, or a sit-down

Posing on a Gold Mine

In 1952, Dolly Rathebe, a young Black woman who was to become a jazz-singing legend, and a white German photographer, Jürgen Schadeberg, scrambled to the top of a gold-mine dump for a *Drum* magazine photo shoot. The photograph looks like it was taken on some strange beach: Rathebe smiles, posing in a bikini. They were spotted by the police and arrested under the Immorality Act, which forbade intercourse between blacks and whites. This dump was at Crown Mines, and is now the site of the Crown Mines Golf Club. Today there's a street in Newtown named after Rathebe, who died in 2004 at the age of 76, while the so-called "Father of South African Photography," who played an active role in the struggle against apartheid, passed in 2020 in Spain.

You still can see gold-mine dumps along the edge of town marching east and west along the seam of gold. Some are close to 300 feet high. Many people are fond of them—they are one of the city's defining characteristics—but those who live nearby are blinded by the dust, and little vegetation grows on the dumps. Officials are also concerned they contain radioactive uranium, which occurs naturally in reefs containing gold. Rich in minerals, they're slowly being chipped away and remined, and in years to come, they will probably be completely gone.

coffee and brunch at the old-style Gourmet Grocer. This is a specialist grocer, deli, bakery, coffee shop, and restaurant, all rolled into one, so you're sure to find what you're looking for, whether it's a scrumptious bagel, toasted *sarmie*, healthy snack, or decadent treat from their niche, family-run suppliers. **Known for:** continuously supporting community causes and charities; extensive selection of goods that cater to any taste and dietary preference; friendly, family-run establishment. [$] *Average main: R100* ✉ *St. Andrew St. and Wrenrose Ave., Melrose Arch* ☎ *011/442–6965* 🌐 *www.facebook.com/thegourmetgrocersa.*

Hotels

★ The Peech Boutique Hotel

$$$$ | **HOTEL** | The luscious garden with its two adjoining swimming pools is the central feature of this award-winning, owner-run boutique hotel that is equidistant from Melrose Arch, Rosebank, and Sandton. **Pros:** within safe walking distance of a park and delicatessen; fair trade certified since 2010; spectacular service and personalised attention. **Cons:** grounds can feel a little cramped; R150 fee to use the gym next door; some rooms overlook the swimming pools. [$] *Rooms from: R4300* ✉ *61 North St., Rosebank* ☎ *011/537–9797* 🌐 *www.thepeech.co.za* 🛏 *32 rooms* 🍴 *Free Breakfast.*

Melville and Emmarentia

You certainly won't be at a loss for choice when it comes to restaurants, shops, and bars that line Melville's 7th Street and 4th Avenue. The perpendicular strip in this residential neighborhood is known for its night-time vibe and for drawing a younger crowd, even on weekdays, thanks to its location near the city's two main universities: the University of the Witwatersrand (affectionately known as Wits) and The University of Johannesburg (often shortened to UJ). From tattoo

Jacaranda trees bloom from early October to early November throughout Johannesburg's streets.

parlors and second-hand book stores to thrift shops and family-owned convenience stores, you're likely to find just what you're looking for in this arty part of town.

If you do the guided hike at Melville Koppies Nature Reserve, which showcases a gorgeous silhouette of the city, Melville is the perfect place to stop for a cup of coffee or a bite to eat. Or, if you're looking for a night out, numerous restaurants and bars regularly host karaoke nights, pub quizzes, and dance parties. ■TIP→ **There are independent car guards, but it's recommended to park in the paid underground parking at 27 Boxes (4th Avenue) or as close to the main drag as possible, especially after dark.**

Close to Rosebank and Parkhurst, the suburb of **Emmarentia** is best known for the Johannesburg Botanical Gardens with its heritage rose gardens. It is a popular dog-walking and picnic spot that also hosts pop concerts in the warmer months, while Emmarentia Dam sees rowers, canoeists, and sailors gliding across its waters.

 ## Sights

Johannesburg Botanical Garden and Emmarentia Dam

DAM | FAMILY | Overlooking Emmarentia Dam, the large and beautiful botanical gardens are five minutes from Parkhurst. This gigantic parkland, dotted with trees, fountains, and ponds, is a wonderful haven. You can relax on benches beneath weeping willows surrounding the lake, where canoeists and windsurfers brave the water, or wander across to the 24-acre rose and herb gardens. The gardens' flora includes an alpine collection and a cycad collection. On weekends bridal parties use the gardens as a backdrop for photographs. ⊠ *Olifants Rd., Roosevelt Park* ☎ *011/375–5555, 011/712–6600* ⊕ *www.jhbcityparksand-zoo.com* ⊠ *Free.*

Melville Koppies Nature Reserve

RUINS | A 50-hectare (123-acres) nature reserve and heritage site on the southern side of the Johannesburg Botanical Garden, Melville Koppies preserves lands as they were before the 1886 gold discovery. The central section of the reserve is opened on Sunday mornings from 8 until 11:30 am, with safe parking at the adjacent Marks Park Sports Club and security guards stationed at various points. Visitors can undertake the 5 km (3 mile) hiking trail or the 3 km (1.8 mile) heritage trail that includes information stops that examine the archaeology, history, geology, fauna, and biodiverse highveld flora of the area. The site includes a 500-year-old Iron Age furnace. ⚠ **Don't visit the east and west sections of Melville Koppies Nature Reserve alone, as it isn't safe.** ✉ *Judith Rd., Emmarentia* ☎ *079/532–0083* 🌐 *www.mk.org.za* 🎟 *R80; special group tours during the week by prior arrangement (R1000).*

🍴 Restaurants

Hell's Kitchen

$$ | MODERN AMERICAN | The neon "Be naked when I get home" sign draws lots of attention, but so do the antlers on the wall, black subway tile bar, and the checked floor of this 1920s New York-esque speakeasy. Try their signature Hellfire, a cinnamon-infused whiskey, to go along with your *braai* (barbecue) meat, pizza, or burger. **Known for:** live music on weekend afternoons; always being busy; great bar vibe. [$] *Average main: R110* ✉ *4 7th St.* ☎ *079/980–9591* 🌐 *www.hellskitchen.co.za.*

★ Little Addis Cafe

$ | ETHIOPIAN | Kassa and his friendly staff serve up affordable and delectable Ethiopian cuisine at this small restaurant at 44 Stanley—there's a selection of options for meat lovers and vegans (as Ethiopians regularly fast by not eating animal products). While the decor may be simple, comprising of a few photos and paintings of Ethiopia, the food steals the show like Beyaynetu, a vegan combo dish where lentil stew, pumpkin, chickpea gravy, sautéed spinach, curried potatoes, pickled beetroot, and tomato salsa is laid out on injera (a sourdough flat bread). **Known for:** friendly and polite service; as authentic as it gets; best value for money by far. [$] *Average main: R75* ✉ *44 Stanely, 44 Stanley Ave.* ☎ *082/683–8675* 🌐 *little-addis-cafe.business.site* 🕒 *Closed Mon.*

☕ Coffee and Quick Bites

Jo'Anna Melt Bar

$ | SANDWICHES | Known for its hearty toasted sandwiches like the *Popeye* with a beef patty, bacon, caramelized onions, tomatoes, gherkins, cheddar, and a squirt of mustard and ketchup, Jo'Anna Melt Bar's name speaks for itself. Wash it down with the Give Me Hope Jo'anna—a mixture of locally-made Klipdrift brandy, passion fruit, and pineapple syrup shaken with a shot of red wine and a dash of bitters—at the seemingly oversized bar, which is the central feature of this small establishment. **Known for:** seating around the bar; you can also order from Dukes Burgers next door; half-price toasties on Tuesdays. [$] *Average main: R60* ✉ *7 7th St.* ☎ *072/733–5966.*

🛍 Shopping

44 Stanley

SHOPPING CENTER | The dappled sunshine courtyards of this 1930s industrial block are lined with ateliers, galleries, family-owned cafés and restaurants, as well as one-of-a-kind stores. On the border of Melville, 44 Stanley is the kind of place where you can easily spend half the day—getting a custom T-shirt printed or a dress tailored, flipping through vinyls, picking out a limited edition print, choosing a holiday memento, or simply window shopping. It's also the newfound home of a few businesses that have relocated from Maboneng, such as the independent Bioscope cinema that screens independent documentaries and film festivals, and hosts live music performances as well as stand-up comedy. While there are many options to choose from for a bite to eat at 44 Stanley, the much-loved Little Addis Café is a must if you want to give authentic Ethiopian cuisine a try. There is free street-side parking with car guards directly outside this leafy lifestyle complex, an off-street parking lot (R10) in Owl Street, or in the underground parking lot at Stanley Studios vis-a-vis. ☒ *44 Stanley Ave., Emmarentia* ⊕ *www.44stanley.co.za.*

27 Boxes

SHOPPING CENTER | FAMILY | Faan Smit Park on 4th Avenue has been converted into a landscaped urban space with 27 Boxes as its central feature. Stacked shipping containers (19ft x 6ft in size) make up this retail center, which contains 50-odd stores and eateries. From art, design, and décor to fashion and specialty gifts, you can find it all here—there's even a craft gin distillery. Be sure to check out Krag Drag clothing for a retro South African souvenir that is hard to find elsewhere like T-shirts emblazoned with emblematic South African brand logos like Chappies bubblegum or clothes and accessories made from vibrant *shweshwe* fabric. Have a look at the website for details about their pop-up weekend markets and events, which regularly include a green market and a vegan market. ☒ *76a 4th Ave., Melville, Emmarentia* ☏ *011/712–0000 landline, 067/016–2237 mobile* ⊕ *www.27boxes.co.za.*

Parktown, Parkview, Saxonwold, and Westcliff

Perched on Braamfontein Ridge, Parktown was once the address *du jour* for the city's early mining magnates. Most of the magnificent houses have since met their demise, but those that are left are worth a look, and they are all lovely areas in which to stay or to take a walk. The small but picturesque suburbs of Westcliff, Parkview, and Saxonwold are nearby.

Sights

Ditsong National Museum of Military History

MILITARY SIGHT | Located in a park along the City Sightseeing hop-on, hop-off green bus route, this museum has three exhibition halls and a rambling outdoor display focusing on South Africa's role in the major wars of the 20th century, with an emphasis on World War II. On display are original Spitfire and Messerschmidt fighters (including what is claimed to be the only remaining ME110 jet night fighter), various tanks of English and American manufacture, and a wide array of artillery. Among the most interesting objects are the modern armaments South Africa used in its war against the Cuban-backed Angolan army during the 1980s, including French-built Mirage fighters and Russian tanks stolen by the South Africans from a ship en route to Angola. More recent exhibits include the national military art collection, memorabilia from the Anti-Conscription Campaign of apartheid days, and an exhibit on the history of *Umkhonto we Sizwe* (Spear of the Nation, or MK, the African National Congress's military arm). The tall, freestanding South African (Anglo-Boer) War Memorial, which looks like a statue-adorned mini Arc de Triomphe, is the most striking landmark of the northern suburbs. ✉ *20 Erlswold Way, Saxonwold* ☎ *011/646–5513* 🌐 *www.ditsong.org.za/museum-of-military-history* 🎟 *R70.*

Restaurants

★ Flames

$$$$ | **EUROPEAN** | A golf cart whisks you up the hill followed by a glass elevator ride to this chic establishment with an infinity fountain that appears to overflow into Zoo Lake and faces the direction of Sandton and Rosebank. It's a popular sundowner spot as it beautifully displays Jo'burg's urban man-made forest and the menu showcases seasonal, regional cuisine with vegan and gluten-free options, but has a particular flair for South African meats, such as lamb chops, oxtail, pork belly, and a selection of locally-bred Wagyu prime cuts. **Known for:** Wagyu prime cuts; sundowners; high-end dining at the Four Seasons Hotel. [$] *Average main: R350* ✉ *Four Seasons Hotel The Westcliff, 67 Jan Smuts Ave., Saxonwold* ☎ *011/481–6190* 🌐 *www.flamesrestaurant.co.za* ☞ *Cashless restaurant.*

Coffee and Quick Bites

Bespokery

$$$$ | **MEDITERRANEAN** | This intimate, modern eatery specializes in small plates that cater to conscious foodies and those with restrictive diets—vegan, keto-friendly, or gluten-free or lactose-free options available. The minimalist decor draws focus to the flavors and colors of the food, which is meant for sharing so as to avoid order envy—three plates per person should do the trick. **Known for:** weekend brunches (closed for brunch during the week); quality ingredients that keep sustainability in mind; unsigned Nelson Makamo mural on the wall. [$] *Average main: R300* ✉ *66 Tyrone Ave., Parkview* ☎ *072/752–4184* 🌐 *www.bespokery.co.za* 🕒 *Closed Mon. and Tues. and mid-Dec.–mid-Jan.*

Hotels

★ Four Seasons The Westcliff

$$$$ | **HOTEL** | The iconic Four Seasons The Westcliff is the paragon of a luxurious urban resort. **Pros:** impeccable service; highly-rated spa facilities with an infinity pool and rooftop deck; spectacular views over the city's greenbelts. **Cons:** rooms spread out along a steep hill, though a golf cart drop off is always on standby; somewhat formal atmosphere, which may not be to everyone's liking; all this luxury and service comes at a high cost. [$] *Rooms from: R3600* ✉ *67 Jan Smuts Ave., Westcliff* ☎ *011/481–6000* 🌐 *www.fourseasons.com/johannesburg* 🛏 *153 rooms* 🍴 *Free Breakfast.*

Shopping

AFRICAN ARTS AND CRAFTS

Art Africa

ART GALLERIES | Art Africa brings together a dazzling selection of ethnic arts, crafts, and artifacts from across the continent and also sells funky items, such as tin lizards made from soda cans, wood-carved animals, and beaded keychains, that are produced in community empowerment projects, which uplift and benefit the craftsmen and their communities. ✉ *62 Tyrone Ave., Parkview* ☎ *011/486–3193 landline, 082/783–7730 Whatsapp.*

Goodman Gallery

ART GALLERIES | The highly successful, five-plus-decade-old Goodman Gallery presents exciting monthly exhibitions by the stars of contemporary African and African diaspora art, including William Kentridge, David Goldblatt, Kudzanai Chiurai, and Sue Williamson. Its website also hosts online viewing rooms. ✉ *163 Jan Smuts Ave., Parkwood* ☎ *011/788–1113* 🌐 *www.goodman-gallery.com* 🕒 *Closed Sun. and Mon.*

Parkhurst and Parktown North

With its pastel-colored cafés, coffee shops, and awning-fringed ice-cream parlors, the lively neighborhood of Parkhurst is somewhat reminiscent of Europe. It also has award-winning restaurants, boutiques, and specialty stores that face 4th Avenue, a bustling, tree-lined strip that's the perfect place for people watching. This upper-middle-class residential area also offers an extensive collection of quality restaurants from authentic Lebanese and fine-dining sharing plates to a modern take on Greek cuisine, contemporary Italian, tapas bars, and burger joints. Independent artists and peddlers walk along the "high street" selling their artwork, handmade crafts and curios, second-hand books, and pot plants. Be sure to book ahead, as even during the week tables fill up fast as this is the place to be seen on a relaxed, yet sophisticated, night out on the town.

The neighboring suburb of Parktown North is more low-key when it comes to the restaurants found along 7th Avenue. Here you'll find breweries and bars alongside franchise restaurants and high-end dining experiences.

Note: Do not confuse Melville's 7th Street and 4th Avenue with Parkhurst's 4th Avenue and Parktown North's 7th Avenue.

🍴 Restaurants

★ Embarc
$$$$ | MEDITERRANEAN | While Parkhurst is known for the countless restaurants that line 4th Avenue, the refined space at Embarc is in a league of its own making fine dining accessible to all through its relaxed environment. Fusing high-quality local produce and artisanal products with international flavors, coupled with a thoughtful combination of contrasting flavors and hues to create delectable dishes that can be eaten as starters or shared as mains. **Known for:** displaying and selling local artworks that enhance the ambience of the space; co-owner is a sommelier who compiled an extensive collection of local and international wines; supporting small artisans and sustainable suppliers. [$] *Average main: R500* ✉ *Corner 13th St. and 4th Ave., Parkhurst* ☎ *081/848–6480* 🌐 *www.embarcrestaurantza.com* 🕒 *Closed Mon. and Tues.*

Modena Italian Eatery
$$$ | ITALIAN | It's hard to find a table inside without a dinner booking (even during the week) at this father-and-son-owned restaurant simply because the food always delivers on taste, portion size, and how it's plated. The jovial ambience and pastel colors reminiscent of a Modena sunset add to the flavor of their modern Italian fare. **Known for:** being busy, which talks to the quality of the food; relaxed and unpretentious atmosphere; handmade and imported Italian products. [$] *Average main: R180* ✉ *Shop 10, Cobbles Shopping Centre, 4th Ave., Parkhurst* ☎ *010/900–0912* 🌐 *www.eatmodena.co.za.*

☕ Coffee and Quick Bites

Nice on 4th
$ | CAFÉ | This easygoing, unpretentious café serves only breakfast, brunch, and lunch, but is always busy, mostly because the food is so fresh and good. Breakfast is a specialty—do try one of their six wholesome breakfast egg baskets—but you could also pop by for high tea and a taste of their homemade cakes. **Known for:** busy atmosphere; fresh ingredients; healthy breakfasts. [$] *Average main: R120* ✉ *Corner of 4th Ave. and 14th St., Parkhurst* ☎ *011/788–6286* 🌐 *www.niceon4th.co.za* 🕒 *Closed Mon. No dinner.*

Sandton

Originally a residential area, Sandton is now home to the Johannesburg Stock Exchange as well as numerous hotels, restaurants, and bars, and the 234-meter (767-feet) high Leonardo—Africa's tallest building.

Sandton City Shopping Centre, which is located in the heart of the country's 'Richest Square Mile', and the adjacent open-air Nelson Mandela Square (also known as Sandton Square), is where you'll find trendy restaurants selling good but pricey food and flagship fashion outlets. There's also the small Theatre on the Square, which favors short, lightweight productions such as stand-up comedy. The enormous Sandton Convention Centre, next to Sandton Square, hosts large conferences and concerts.

But Sandton is not all glitz and glamour—a few miles from Sandton City Shopping Centre and part of the large suburb is the township of Alexandra, home to an estimated 700,000 people, mostly living in overcrowded, squalid conditions in shacks and rented rundown houses.

👁 Sights

Satyagraha House

HOTEL | A young Mahatma Gandhi spent 10 years in Jo'burg, including one year at this house in the residential neighborhood of Orchards. Today, it's been transformed into a small museum with exhibits dedicated to the freedom fighter as well as a tranquil guesthouse with seven rooms (R2320, including breakfast), both infused with his peaceful spirit. You can stop by to see exhibits even if you're not a guest (call ahead to book a guided tour), or indulge in a night of mindfulness. Vegetarian meals are served, sourced from the garden. ✉ *15 Pine Rd., Johannesburg* ☎ *011/485–5928* 🌐 *www.satyagrahahouse.com* 🎟 *R70 for a guided 30 minute tour.*

🍴 Restaurants

The Butcher Shop and Grill

$$$$ | **STEAKHOUSE** | This is a good place for hungry meat lovers, specializing in prime South African meat (as well as Wagyu and Argentinian beef) that have been aged to perfection by Alan Pick, the butcher-owner. Kudu, springbok, ostrich, and other game are staples on the menu, and only the most tender cuts are served, but there's also chicken or line fish options. **Known for:** excellent South African wine cellar; interactive butchery for in-house and take-home orders; prime location at Nelson Mandela Square. [$] *Average main: R250* ✉ *Nelson Mandela Sq., Shop 30, Sandton* ☎ *011/784–8676* 🌐 *www.thebutchershop.co.za.*

Saint

$$$$ | **ITALIAN** | Thanks to the Bermar preserving system, you can sip on bubbles by the glass at this high-end establishment while you feast on Neapolitan-style pizza prepared in an imported pizza oven, topped with handmade local Buffalo Mozzarella and served on terracotta pizza plates. But don't assume this is just an Italian restaurant or a fancy pizzeria, as renowned chef and business partner David Higgs (the very same of Marble Restaurant) adds signature dishes like wood-fired pawns, smokey Bistecca alla Fiorentina, and frutti di mare onto the ever-changing menu, to be degusted with the restaurant's extensive wine collection. **Known for:** design is prioritized, like the giant cupped hands in the bathrooms by Damien Grivas; serves limited edition and rare vintage Champagne and Méthode Cap Classique (South Africa's alternative); the bar, separated by the front of house, is a lively nightlife venue. [$] *Average main: R300* ✉ *The MARC (Shop UR 18), corner Maude St. and Rivonia Rd., Sandton* ☎ *010/594–5888* 🌐 *www.saint.restaurant.*

Coffee and Quick Bites

Truffles on the Park

$$$ | BISTRO | For a time out from Sandton's skyscrapers, head to this bistro-style eatery with floor-to-ceiling windows and a living plant wall and planters that give it an urban jungle feel; there's even access to walking paths and a children's play area. The menu features small plates, hot and cold salads, and a wide selection of main meals (try the Truffles Risotto Fillet) and vegan options. **Known for:** lovely, relaxed setting in an urban oasis with outdoor seating; extensive gin cocktail selection; large menu caters to all palates. $ *Average main: R200* ⊠ *Mushroom Park, 125 Daisy St., Sandown, Sandton* ☎ *010/025–0436* ⊕ *www.trufflesbistro.co.za* ☉ *Closed Mon.*

Hotels

Fairlawns Boutique Hotel & Spa

$$$$ | HOTEL | Located in a residential area, this gracious boutique hotel was once a private home owned by the Oppenheimer family. **Pros:** a 3-piece jazz bands plays on Sundays from 12:30–4 pm; working fireplaces add to the romance; centrally located in a peaceful suburb. **Cons:** shuttle service to Sandton City Mall at an additional cost; not great for families; service can be slow. $ *Rooms from: R7700* ⊠ *Morningside Manor, 1 Alma Rd., Sandton* ☎ *011/804–2540* ⊕ *www.fairlawns.co.za* ☛ *40 rooms* ⌾ *Free Breakfast.*

The Leonardo

$$$$ | HOTEL | Africa's tallest building, at 55-stories and 234 meters (767 feet), this hybrid skyscraper stands at the foot of Sandton with panoramic views that stretch beyond Johannesburg's borders and includes a refined retail space, a contemporary hotel with all the bells and whistles, and residential apartments and luxury penthouses. **Pros:** unbeatable views from the rooftop bar; in central Sandton; within walking distance of the Gautrain station, Sandton City and The

MARC. **Cons:** not for those who prefer smaller, boutique hotels; rather expensive; can seem exuberant and haughty. $ *Rooms from: R5000* ⊠ *75 Maude St., Sandton* ☎ *087/536–0000* ⊕ *www.theleonardo.co.za* ☛ *113 suites* ⌾ *Free Breakfast.*

The Maslow

$$ | HOTEL | Conveniently situated in the heart of bustling Sandton, the Maslow is a case study in modern, seamless sophistication and, if only for a few moments, you'll forget you're anywhere near a city. **Pros:** a very strong focus on sustainability and environmentally-friendly initiatives; one of the best business-orientated hotels in the province; is aligning itself more with the leisure traveler through its offerings. **Cons:** can feel crowded due to its popularity; many rooms overlook the roof which obscures the garden; the restaurant occasionally lets down the high standard of the hotel. $ *Rooms from: R1975* ⊠ *146 Rivonia Rd., Sandton* ☎ *010/226–4600, 011/780–7855* ⊕ *www.suninternational.com/maslow* ☛ *281 rooms* ⌾ *Free Breakfast.*

Radisson Blu Gautrain Hotel

$$ | HOTEL | Located just 55 steps from the Sandton Gautrain station, this is a popular destination for international tourists and local business travelers with well-appointed rooms, an outdoor splash pool, and a deck that overlooks Sandton's high-rise buildings. **Pros:** panoramic views of surrounding Sandton cityscape; great value for money; 24-hour gym. **Cons:** not for a romantic getaway; not child-friendly; no free parking. $ *Rooms from: R1950* ⊠ *Rivonia Rd. at West St., Sandton* ☎ *011/286–1000* ⊕ *www.radissonblu.com/hotelsandton-johannesburg* ☛ *220 rooms* ⌾ *Free Breakfast.*

Sandton Sun

$$$ | HOTEL | One of the first luxury hotels to open in Sandton, the Sun has a very upmarket designer African feel. **Pros:** linked to Sandton City, Johannesburg's premier mall, by a first-floor sky bridge;

business suites have home-automation technology and video conferencing; excellent restaurants are within easy walking distance. **Cons:** pricey; if conspicuous consumption bothers you, stay elsewhere; shopping's the name of the game here. [$] *Rooms from: R3300* ✉ *Sandton City, 5th St. at Alice La., Sandton* ☎ *011/780–5000* 🌐 *www.tsogosun.com/sandton-sun-hotel* 🛏 *334 rooms* 🍴 *Free Breakfast.*

The Saxon Hotel, Villas & Spa
$$$$ | HOTEL | In the exclusive suburb of Sandhurst, this luxurious and impeccably designed Saxon Hotel, Villas & Spa has repeatedly received awards for its excellence. **Pros:** good for business travelers or high-profile folk; refurbished in late 2020; exceptional spa on-site. **Cons:** pricey; no longer has its fine-dining option; the atmosphere can be quite snooty. [$] *Rooms from: R10250* ✉ *36 Saxon Rd., Sandhurst* ☎ *011/292–6000* 🌐 *www.saxon.co.za* 🛏 *53 rooms* 🍴 *Free Breakfast.*

Ten Bompas
$$$ | HOTEL | This 10-room hotel is decorated in a minimalist style with each suite decorated by a different interior designer. **Pros:** same-day laundry service; restocked wine cellar in 2021 with 4,000-odd bottles across 200 varietals; a breeding pair of barn owls lives on the property. **Cons:** bugs from the garden might find their way into the ground-floor rooms; slightly-outdated decor, which doesn't detract from the level of comfort; a taxi ride away from shopping or sightseeing. [$] *Rooms from: R3150* ✉ *10 Bompas Rd., Dunkeld West* ☎ *011/325–2442* 🌐 *www.tenbompas.com* 🛏 *10 suites* 🍴 *Free Breakfast.*

Performing Arts

Theatre on the Square
THEATER | Located on Nelson Mandela Square in Sandton, this intimate, 200-seater theater has hosted thousands of shows since it opened in 1997. Its extensive repertoire includes comedy shows, cultural celebrations, author interviews, jazz concerts, plays, and music recitals. Friday lunchtime concerts are a boon to Sandton-based workers. ✉ *Nelson Mandela Sq., Sandton* ✥ *Nelson Mandela Square adjoins Sandton City, with entrances and parking garage in West Street and 5th Street, Sandown.* ☎ *011/883–8606* 🌐 *www.theatreonthesquare.co.za.*

Shopping

Krugerrands, which carry images of former President Paul Kruger and a springbok on either side, are among the most famous gold coins minted today. They lost some of their luster during the apartheid years, when they were banned internationally. Krugerrands are sold individually or in sets containing coins of 1 ounce, ½ ounce, ¼ ounce, and 1/10 ounce of pure gold. You can buy Krugerrands through most city banks, and at reputable coin shops such as the Scoin chain of shops, which you'll find in upmarket malls. The most convenient branches are in the Sandton City Mall and Rosebank Mall.

South Africa is also diamond country. The world's biggest diamond, the 3,106-carat Cullinan, was found in the town of the same name (near present-day Tshwane) in 1905 and is now among the British crown jewels.

JEWELRY

Charles Greig
JEWELRY & WATCHES | Charles Greig is a reputable jeweler with a long-standing record, and a reputation for excellence, making this shop a good choice if you wish to buy a special South African piece, such as a ring or necklace containing diamonds. ✉ *Hyde Park Corner, Jan Smuts Ave., Hyde Park* ☎ *011/325–4477* 🌐 *www.charlesgreig.co.za.*

Kwaito

Kwaito is a uniquely South African music genre, rooted in house, raga (a subgenre of reggae), hip-hop, and local rhythms. It emerged from the country's townships after apartheid and gets its name, some say, from township slang for "cool talk." Its hard-pumping bass beats, lightly slowed down from a house rhythm, are topped with rambled-off lyrics in a style reminiscent of American rap. It's as much a lifestyle as it is a music genre, with its own ways of dancing and dressing.

The best-selling kwaito musicians (and kwaito DJs) have superstar status in South Africa, but they have a less unsavory reputation than their American hip-hop equivalents. Though some kwaito acts stand accused of sexism and vulgar lyrics, the kwaito attitude is generally quite respectable. Lyrics are often about banning guns or respecting women, or they comment on murder, rape, AIDS, and unemployment. One kwaito star, Zola—named after an impoverished Soweto community—enjoyed a long-running TV series, in which he worked to improve people's lives. His music is featured in the 2006 Academy Award–winning movie Tsotsi. Other chart-topping kwaito stars include the late Mandoza, whose catchy, powerful songs earned him several awards and crossover appeal; the pop sensational duo, Mafikizolo; Mdu Masilela; the Brothers of Peace; and Mzekezeke, an enigmatic masked singer.

—Riaan Wolmarans

Near OR Tambo International Airport

While you're not going to stay in this area if you have a full visit to Johannesburg planned, the fact is that if you have a layover in the city before you head out to your safari destination, or have an early flight home, you may want to stay close to the airport.

 Hotels

City Lodge Hotel at OR Tambo International Airport

$$ | HOTEL | This affordable, three-star property has a passageway that's connected to the airport building, which makes it the ideal overnight stay if you have a red-eye flight to catch. **Pros:** same-day laundry and dry-cleaning service at an additional cost; convenient location at an affordable price; hotel is soundproof. **Cons:** no business lounge; full English and Continental breakfast at an additional cost; no spa facilities. $ Rooms from: R1980 ⊠ OR Tambo Airport Rd., Kempton Park ☎ 011/552–7600 ⊕ www.clhg.com ⇥ 365 rooms ⦿ No Meals.

InterContinental Johannesburg OR Tambo Airport

$$$$ | HOTEL | A few paces from international arrivals and adjacent to the car-rental companies and bus terminal, this is a good choice for those who have a one-night layover. **Pros:** free meet-and-greet service with escort to the hotel; ideal for those who don't need to go into Johannesburg or who have a layover before a connecting flight; free Wi-Fi. **Cons:** you won't see much of Johannesburg without leaving the hotel; large and impersonal. $ Rooms from: R3850 ⊠ OR Tambo International Airport, Kempton Park ☎ 011/961–5400, 877/859–5095 ⊕ www.ihg.com ⇥ 140 rooms ⦿ Free Breakfast.

Side Trips from Johannesburg

About an hour north of Johannesburg (depending on the traffic—on a bad day it can take more than two hours), Pretoria, the country's capital, is within the larger metropolitan area of Tshwane (pronounced *chwa*-ah-neh). About an hour and a half from Johannesburg is the Cradle of Humankind, declared a World Heritage Site for its rich fossil record reflecting the history of humanity over the past 3.5 million years or so. To the north of Johannesburg, not far from the Cradle of Humankind, lies the Magaliesberg (pronounced muh- *xuh*-lees-berg, where the first *g* is pronounced like the *ch* in *Chanukah*), a gentle, ancient mountain range and leisure area, where you can get a restful break amid lovely mountain scenery, farmlands, and quiet country roads. Sun City, a multifaceted entertainment and casino complex comprising hotels, championship golf courses, and a water park, and the adjacent Pilanesberg Game Reserve are about a three-hour drive from Johannesburg—well worth a visit if you have the time.

Pretoria

48 km (30 miles) north of Johannesburg.

The city of Pretoria lies within the greater Tshwane metropolitan area, which was formed in 2000 when Pretoria and its surrounding areas—Centurion, the townships of Atteridgeville, Mamelodi, and Shoshanguve, and neighboring areas—merged under a single municipal authority. The country's administrative capital and home to many senior politicians and diplomats, Pretoria is a pleasant city, with historic buildings and the largest concentration of jacaranda trees in the country, giving it the moniker Jacaranda City.

Founded in 1855, the city was named after Afrikaner leader Andries Pretorius, one of the Voortrekkers (pronounced *fooer*-trekka) who moved from the Cape to escape British rule. In 1860 it became the capital of the independent Transvaal Voortrekker Republic. After the South African War of 1899–1902 (the Second Anglo-Boer War), the city became the capital of the then British colony, and in 1910 it was named the administrative capital of the Union of South Africa. In 1948, when the National Party came to power, Pretoria became the seat of the apartheid government. In 1964 the Rivonia Treason Trial (named for the Johannesburg suburb where 19 ANC leaders were arrested in 1963) was held here, and Nelson Mandela and seven of his colleagues were sentenced to life in prison.

GETTING HERE AND AROUND

There are a few options for getting to Pretoria. The Gautrain offers a safe, convenient, and high-speed connection between OR Tambo International Airport, Sandton, Rosebank, and Pretoria. Alternatively, a rental car gives you the flexibility to explore the city at your leisure, and private transfers are offered by all of OR Tambo's airport transfer companies *(see Air Travel, in Planning, at the beginning of the chapter).*

It takes at least an hour to travel from Johannesburg to Pretoria on the N1 (two hours if the traffic is bad, which happens quite regularly, especially between about 7 and 9 am and 4 and 7 pm).

TIMING AND PRECAUTIONS

If you want to see everything, schedule an entire day or even a couple of days here. The best time of year to visit is in the springtime (particularly September–November when the jacarandas are in full bloom). A side trip to the Cullinan Diamond Mine will take at least half a day. Pretoria is not as notorious as Johannesburg for crime, but drive with your car doors locked, and don't have bags or

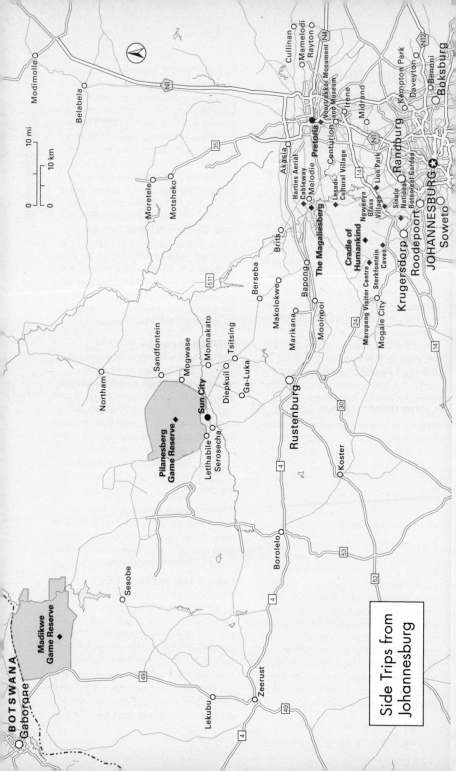

Side Trips from Johannesburg

valuables visible or you could become a target of a "hit-and-grab."

VISITOR INFORMATION

Covering Pretoria, Centurion, Atteridgeville, Mamelodi, and the surrounding areas, these public and private sector tourism websites are good resources for planning a visit to the capital city and the greater Tshwane municipality.

CONTACTS Discover Tshwane. ⊠ *Pretoria* ☎ *012/841–4212* ⊕ *www.discovertshwane.com.* **Tshwane Tourism Association.** ⊠ *CSIR International Convention Centre (Building 39), Meiring Naude Rd., Brummeria, Pretoria* ☎ *084/521–5852* ⊕ *www.visittshwane.co.za.*

 Sights

Cullinan Diamond Mine

MINE | Anyone can go to a jewelry store and bring home South African diamonds, but how many people can say they got their sparkler from an actual mine? At Cullinan Diamond Mine, you can not only buy diamonds, but get custom-made pieces from the resident jeweler, though don't expect your piece to include the world's largest diamond—the 3,106-carat Cullinan Diamond unearthed here in 1905 is now in the crown jewels in London. Two-hour surface tours of the mine take place daily at 10:30 am and 2 pm (with the second tour commencing at 12:15 pm on weekends and public holidays). The four-hour underground tours, which demand that you be quite physically fit, takes place on Tuesdays, Thursdays, and Saturdays from 8:30 am. You must reserve all tours in advance and wear comfortable closed shoes; children under 10 are not permitted on either tour. Cullinan has a series of delightful tea gardens to choose from. For pleasant outdoor dining, the Whispering Oaks Garden Cafe (closed Tuesdays) serves breakfasts and lunches. ⊠ *99 Oak Ave., Cullinan* ☎ *012/734–0081* ⊕ *www.*

diamondtourscullinan.co.za ⊠ *Surface tours R150, underground tours R600.*

Freedom Park

HISTORY MUSEUM | FAMILY | Opened in 2013, the 129-acre Freedom Park is a cultural heritage site dedicated to the struggle for freedom and human rights, while chronicling Africa's 3.6-billion-year-old history, from the dawn of humanity to South Africa's post-apartheid present. At Salvokop, a prominent hill that welcomes you to Pretoria on the highway from Johannesburg, and within view of the Voortrekker Monument, the site comprises a memorial, interactive museum containing national archives, and a garden of remembrance. The park was launched in 2002 by then President Thabo Mbeki, who said, "We dedicate this day to all the heroes and heroines in this country and the rest of the world who sacrificed in many ways and surrendered their lives so that we could be free." It is also a spiritual resting place that honors those who fought for and shaped the country's liberation struggle. If you have limited time, do the 360-degree virtual tour via the website. ⊠ *Koch Ave. at 7th Ave., Salvokop, Pretoria* ☎ *012/336–4020* ⊕ *www.freedompark.co.za* ⊠ *R150.*

Melrose House

HISTORIC HOME | Built in 1886, this opulent structure is one of South Africa's most beautiful and best-preserved Victorian homes, furnished in period style. It has marble columns, mosaic floors, lovely stained-glass windows, ornate ceilings, porcelain ornaments, and richly colored carpets. On May 31, 1902, the Treaty of Vereeniging was signed in the dining room, ending the South African War. You can view a permanent exhibit on the war or arrange for a guided tour. ⊠ *275 Jeff Masemola St., Pretoria* ☎ *012/358–0882* ⊕ *www.tshwane.gov.za* ⊠ *R25, entrance is R2 on every Wednesday (except public holidays)* ⊗ *Closed Mon.*

Union Buildings

GARDEN | Built in 1901, this impressive cream-sandstone complex—home to the administrative branch of government and now a national heritage site—was designed by Sir Herbert Baker, one of South Africa's most revered architects. This is where Nelson Mandela was inaugurated as the country's first democratically elected president in 1994. The complex incorporates a hodgepodge of styles—an Italian tile roof, wooden shutters inspired by Cape Dutch architecture, and Renaissance columns—that somehow works beautifully. Expansive formal gardens step down the hillside in terraces, which are dotted with war memorials and statues of former prime ministers. What is most striking is the nine-meter-tall bronze statue of Mandela with outstretched arms by South African sculptors André Prinsloo and Ruhan Janse van Vuuren. While there's no public access to the building, the gardens are perfect for a picnic lunch. ⊠ *Near Church Sq., Government Ave., Pretoria.*

Voortrekker Monument and Museum

HISTORY MUSEUM | This famous national heritage site is regarded as a symbol of Afrikaner nationalism and independence. Completed in 1949, the monument honors the Voortrekkers, who rejected colonial rule and trekked into the hinterland to found their own nation. The Hall of Heroes traces in its marble frieze their momentous Great Trek, culminating in the Battle of Blood River (December 16, 1838), when a small force of Boers defeated a large Zulu army without losing a single life. The Voortrekkers considered this victory a covenant with God. An adjoining museum displays scenes and artifacts of daily Voortrekker life, as well as the Voortrekker Tapestries, 15 pictorial weavings that trace the historical high points of the Great Trek. The monument is in a nature reserve, which has a picnic area. You can dine in the restaurant and tea garden if you don't like to rough it. At an additional cost, Adventure Zone offers hiking trails

(3km, 5.6km and 8km), as well as other activities such as: quad biking, drumming, fire-making and archery. Also on-site is **Fort Schanskop,** the best preserved of four area forts commissioned by President Paul Kruger in about 1897. The fort houses a South African (Anglo-Boer) War museum and gift shop. ⊠ *Eeufees Rd., Pretoria* ☎ *012/326–6770 Voortrekker Monument, 012/734–0507 Adventure Zone (Voortrekker Monument)* ⊕ *www.vtm.org.za* ⊠ *R162 per person; additional charges for Adventure Zone activities.*

🍴 Coffee and Quick Bites

Old East Precinct

$$ | CONTEMPORARY | The Old East Precinct is a suburban development in Hazelwood with a village feel to it, as a wide selection of coffee shops, restaurants, bars and bespoke stores line the leafy streets of Hazelwood Road and 16th Street. If you're hungry, you'll have plenty to choose from here, from Lexi's Healthy Eatery (our number one choice which serves a selection of vegan, but not only, dishes) to Alfie's Pizzeria and Deli, and you can never go wrong with Cowfish, which as the name suggests serves a combination of fish, seafood and meat-lovers dishes, alongside cocktails. **Known for:** being the trendiest place to eat in Pretoria; lively atmosphere with plenty of options to choose from; establishments spill out onto the sidewalk creating an open-air dining experience. Ⓢ *Average main: R120* ⊠ *Old East Precinct, Hazelwood Rd. and 16th St., Pretoria* ⊕ *www.thevillageoldeast.co.za* ⊘ *Closed Mon.*

Whispering Oaks Garden Cafe

$ | CAFÉ | Cullinan has a series of delightful tea gardens to choose from, but for pleasant outdoor dining, this cafe is the spot serving breakfast and lunch. **Known for:** homemade sweets; sweet and savory pancakes; seafood. Ⓢ *Average main: R120* ⊠ *94 Oak Ave., Cullinan, Pretoria* ☎ *073/230–4500* ⊘ *Closed Tues.*

Cradle of Humankind

72 km (45 miles) northwest of Johannesburg.

This World Heritage Site stretches over an area of about 470 square km (181 square miles), with about 300 caves. Inside these caves, paleoanthropologists have discovered thousands of fossils of hominids and other animals, dating back some 3.5 million years. The most famous of these fossils are Mrs. Ples, a skull more than 2 million years old, and Little Foot, a skeleton more than 3 million years old. Although the Cradle does not have the world's oldest hominid fossils, it has the most complete fossil record of human evolution of anywhere on Earth, has produced more hominid fossils than anywhere else.

Archaeological finds at the Cradle of Humankind include 1.7-million-year-old stone tools, the oldest recorded in southern Africa. At Swartkrans, near Sterkfontein, a collection of burned bones tells us that our ancestors could manage fire more than a million years ago.

Not all the fossil sites in the Cradle are open to the public, but a tour of the Sterkfontein Caves and the visitor center provides an excellent overview of the paleontological work in progress, and a trip to Maropeng, a much larger visitor center 10 km (6 miles) from the Sterkfontein Caves, provides even more background.

GETTING HERE AND AROUND

Public transportation to the Cradle of Humankind area is limited, so using a rental car or taking an organized tour is best. Some hotels in the area will arrange transportation on request. The Cradle of Humankind is about a 90-minute drive from Johannesburg or Pretoria, but isn't well signposted, so use a GPS or download instructions on how to get there from the Maropeng website if you don't visit on a guided tour.

VISITOR INFORMATION

The Maropeng Visitor Centre provides information about the various sites in the Cradle of Humankind, and you can pick up many different promotional pamphlets here about things to do and see in the area. *(See Sights.)*

Sights

★ Maropeng Visitor Centre
MUSEUM VILLAGE | FAMILY | Maropeng is the official visitor center of the Cradle of Humankind World Heritage Site and offers much more than information about the region: it's a modern, interactive museum dedicated to the history of humanity that kids will love. It provides information about the various fossil sites in the area. About a 90-minute drive from either Johannesburg or Pretoria, it's one of the area's top attractions. It's best visited in parallel with the nearby fossil site of Sterkfontein Caves, but to visit both you'll need to set aside at least half a day. ⊠ *Off R563 (Hekpoort Rd.), Sterkfontein* ☎ *014/577–9000* ⊕ *www.maropeng.co.za* ✉ *R100.*

Ngwenya Glass Village
ART GALLERY | FAMILY | You can watch the intricate art of glass blowing at Ngwenya Glass Village and pick out a handmade souvenir whether it's one of the Big Five, a glass-crowned cork stopper, napkin rings, paperweights, or a bespoke wine cooler. This retail village also includes a number of other stalls, in little huts arranged in a semi-circle, that sell one-of-a-kind items and food. Gilroy's Brewery is where you can stop for lunch and a pint of small-batch ales and lagers, after you've done the beer tasting experience (Saturdays, 11 am, R145). ⊠ *Shady Lane, Diepsloot, Magaliesberg* ☎ *011/796–3006* ⊕ *www.shadesofngwenya.co.za.*

★ Sterkfontein Caves
CAVE | FAMILY | It was in the Sterkfontein Caves, in 1947, that Dr. Robert Broom discovered the now famous Mrs. Ples,

The now-famous Mrs. Ples, a more than 2 million-year-old skull was found in SterkfonteinCaves in 1947.

as she is popularly known—a skull of an adult *Australopithecus africanus* that is more than 2 million years old. The find reinforced the discovery of a skull of an *Australopithecus* child, the Taung Skull, by Professor Raymond Dart in 1924, which was the first hominid ever found. At the time, Dart was ostracized for claiming the skull belonged to an early human ancestor. Scientists in Europe and the United States simply didn't believe that humanity could have originated in Africa. Today, few disagree with this theory. Another important find was the discovery in the 1990s of Little Foot, a near-complete skeleton of an *Australopithecus*, embedded in rock deep inside the caves. And even more recently, the 2013 discovery of hundreds of *Homo Naledi* fossils (dating from around 300,000 years ago) in the Cradle of Humankind area. These fossil specimens remain one of the largest hominin finds in Africa. Guided tours of the excavations and caves last an hour and are not advisable if you are claustrophobic. Wear comfortable shoes. Start with the excellent

museum, which has exhibits depicting the origins of the Earth, life, and humanity. A small on-site restaurant that serves light meals is open daily. ⊠ *Sterkfontein Caves Rd., off R563, Sterkfontein* ☎ *014/577–9000* ⊕ *www.maropeng.co.za* 🖾 *R100.*

Walter Sisulu National Botanical Garden

GARDEN | More than 240 bird species and a variety of small mammals add to a biodiverse garden named in honor of late ANC stalwart Walter Sisulu. The Witpoortjie Falls dominate the garden, providing a backdrop to a succulent rockery, cycads, an arboretum, bird and butterfly garden, wildflowers, a children's section, and bird hides. The garden is famous for a pair of Verreaux eagles that breed in early spring (August/September). There are four self-guided walking trails, the most popular of which is a brisk trail to the top of the waterfall where you can get a closer look. Eagle's Fare Restaurant serves breakfast, light meals and hearty dishes throughout the day beneath the shade of the trees or on the sunny deck. Most of the garden is accessible by wheelchair. Guided tours are offered (R170). ■ TIP→ **Email is the best way to contact the Gardens with any questions.** ✉ *End of Malcolm Rd., Poortview, Roodepoort* ☎ ⊕ *www.sanbi.org/gardens/walter-sisulu* 💲 *R65* ☞ *tickets can be purchased with a credit card at the entrance or on www.webtickets.co.za.*

Restaurants

The Carnivore
$$$$ | **AFRICAN** | Don't come expecting a quiet romantic lunch or dinner, as the huge space lends itself to a loud and sometimes frenetic scene. Game meat such as warthog, impala, and crocodile vies with tamer fare such as pork and mutton for space around an enormous open fire in the center of the restaurant. **Known for:** vegetarian and pescatarian options; churrascaria-style service; Sunday eat-as-much-as-you-can lunch. 💲 *Average main: R295* ✉ *Misty Hills Country Hotel, 69 Drift Blvd., Muldersdrift* ☎ *011/950–6000* ⊕ *www.carnivore.co.za* 🕐 *Closed Mon.*

🛏 Hotels

Forum Homini
$$$$ | **HOTEL** | This boutique hotel in a game estate within the Cradle of Humankind aptly alludes to the mysterious and fascinating story of the development of humanity in every bit of its decor and can be a good option if you want to spend some time outside but near Johannesburg. **Pros:** unique art and decor that blends into natural surroundings; luxury accommodations; wildlife can be spotted around the game estate. **Cons:** because there's no spa, treatments are done in your room; not suitable for children; hotel can be overwhelmed with wedding parties on weekends. 💲 *Rooms from: R4000* ✉ *Letamo Game Estate, R540 (off N14), Kromdraai, Mogale City* ☎ *011/668–7000* ⊕ *www.forumhomini.*

com 🕐 *Closed Mon.–Tues. and Dec. 20–Jan. 4* 🛏 *14 rooms* 🍴 *All-Inclusive.*

Maropeng Boutique Hotel
$$ | **HOTEL** | The Maropeng Boutique Hotel offers peace and tranquility with magnificent views of the Magaliesberg and Witwatersberg mountain ranges just 90 minutes from Johannesburg. **Pros:** Fair Trade certified; free shuttle between Maropeng and Sterkfontein Caves for guests; easy access to the Maropeng Visitor Centre and Cradle of Humankind. **Cons:** rooms near swimming pool can be noisy; difficult to access without a car, shuttle from airport at added cost; rooms on the small side with classic decor. 💲 *Rooms from: R1800* ✉ *R400, off the R563 Hekpoort Rd., Kromdraai* ☎ *014/577–9100* ⊕ *www.maropeng.co.za* 🕐 *No dinner service on a Sun., unless booked for a 3-night weekend stay* 🛏 *24 rooms* 🍴 *Free Breakfast.*

Toadbury Hall
$ | **HOTEL** | This quaint, thatched country hotel is well located for trips into the Cradle of Humankind World Heritage Site. **Pros:** romantic, countryside setting; attention to detail; fresh, tasty cuisine at the two in-house restaurants. **Cons:** not a family destination; no spa facilities; difficult to reach without a car. 💲 *Rooms from: R1500* ✉ *Beyers Naude Dr. Extension, Plot 64, Elandsdrift* ☎ *010/593–7523* ⊕ *www.toadburyhall.co.za* 🛏 *10 rooms* 🍴 *Free Breakfast.*

The Magaliesberg

The Magaliesberg are about 100 km (62 miles) northwest of Johannesburg and well worth a day trip or a short visit, especially if you are going onwards to Pilanesberg National Park or Sun City.

The Magaliesberg Mountains (actually rolling hills) stretch 120 km (74 miles) between Pretoria and the town of Rustenburg. The South African War once raged here, and the remains of British blockhouses can still be seen. The region is most remarkable, however, for its natural beauty—grassy slopes, streams running through the ferns, waterfalls plunging into pools, and dramatic rock formations. It's an outdoor lover's paradise: go hiking, mountain biking, ziplining, or horseback riding; swim in crystal streams; picnic in one of the natural hideaways; or take a balloon flight at dawn followed by a Champagne breakfast. It's also home to the large Hartbeespoort Dam, a water-sports hot spot. You can get a great view of the Magaliesberg from atop them by riding up in the Harties Aerial Cableway, a highly recommended attraction. ■TIP→ **There's an important distinction to make Magaliesberg (with an 'e') is the name of the mountain range, while Magaliesburg (with a 'u') is the name of the region where they are found.**

GETTING HERE AND AROUND

About a 90-minute drive northwest of Johannesburg, the region is fairly isolated, requiring a rental car or private transfer. Some of the hotels and lodges in the area can arrange transfers on request.

TIMING AND PRECAUTIONS

The main areas and attractions become crowded on weekends. On Friday evenings and Sunday afternoons there's always a wait—sometimes half an hour or more—to cross the one-way bridge over the Hartbeespoort Dam, as you head towards Pilanesberg National Park or Sun City. This has given creative roadside hawkers the opportunity to sell their handmade wares, curios and fruit to the string of waiting cars. The area is relatively small, and two to three days is more than enough time to spend exploring.

 Sights

★ Harties Aerial Cableway

VIEWPOINT | FAMILY | It will take you six minutes to get to the top of the longest mono-cableway in Africa to savor panoramic views of the Magaliesberg Mountains and Hartbeespoort Dam from an altitude of 1985 meters (6512 feet), and 345 meters (1132 feet) above the base station. At the top, a short circular pathway (less than a mile in length) takes in indigenous flora, while signposts point out geological features of interest. There's a restaurant at the bottom station, as well as three restaurants at the top which sell pizzas, pastas, sandwiches, and burgers. Treat yourself to a late afternoon cocktail on the wooden deck at the mountaintop bar, while keeping an eye out for the resident Black Cape Vultures. After buying mementoes and branded items at the curio shop, you can also paraglide from the top with a qualified tandem flight instructor. ✉ *Melodie Agricultural Holdings, Plot 3, Hartbeespoort* ☎ *012/253–9910* ⊕ *www. hartiescableway.co.za* ✒ *R250; this is a cashless facility, tickets should be bought online or using a credit card at the base station* ⊘ *Closed Mon.–Tues.*

Lesedi Cultural Village

MUSEUM VILLAGE | FAMILY | This cultural museum village is not just a place to stay and eat; it's a place to learn about the cultures and history of South Africa's Basotho, Ndebele, Pedi, Xhosa, and Zulu nations. Daily shows of singing, dancing, and tours of traditional homesteads take place from 11 am–1 pm and 4–6 pm, alongside the crafts market. The large Nyama Choma restaurant serves a buffet (costing R220) with food from all over the continent, so you can taste North African fare, East African cuisine, or opt for a South African barbecue (called a *braai*). Dishes include roast meats, a stiff corn porridge, and vegetables, often cooked over the fire in traditional African three-legged iron pots called *potjie* pots. Packages can include accommodation in a 3-star hut—you have a choice of one of five traditional homesteads—breakfast, dinner, and a tour (R980/per person sharing), but most people just come for a day visit and a meal. ✉ *Kalkheuwel, R512 (Pelindaba Rd.), Broederstroom* ☎ *071/507–1447* general info 🌐 *aha.co.za/lesedi* 🎫 *R610 with lunch, R395 without lunch.*

🍴 Restaurants

★ Black Horse Restaurant

$$ | **BISTRO** | **FAMILY** | Set in manicured, terraced gardens that stretch out onto paddocks where grazing Friesian horses idle away afternoons, the family-owned Black Horse Estate Restaurant predominantly serves bistro staples like burgers and wood-fired pizzas, though Stables Café, open during the week, can easily accommodate walk-ins. While you're here, you can also do a tasting and tour of the craft brewery, run by one of the country's youngest female brewers, and gin distillery (1 hour, R287.50 for both). **Known for:** quaint and affordable accommodation options; gorgeous outdoor setting surrounded by nature; brewery and distillery tours, tasters and gift shop. [$] *Average main: R120* ✉ *32 Zeekoeihoek Rd., Magaliesberg* ☎ *082/453–5295* 🌐 *www.blackhorse.co.za.*

🛏 Hotels

Although it's an hour drive from the city center, Hartbeespoort is these days almost a suburb of Johannesburg. You might choose to stay here for the night if you're en route from OR Tambo International Airport (or the even-closer domestic airport of Lanseria) to a game reserve like the Pilanesberg or Madikwe, rather than staying in Johannesburg itself. It's on the way, after all, and has a pleasant, relaxed atmosphere, and you could more easily squeeze in a trip up the cableway, which is well worth doing. There are loads of bed-and-breakfasts and guesthouses to choose from.

African Pride Mount Grace Country House & Spa

$$ | **HOTEL** | One of South Africa's largest hotel spas is located at this peaceful retreat near Magaliesburg. **Pros:** activity club for kids and two swimming pools; lovely location, out of the city; top-rated spa facilities. **Cons:** Remote location means it's somewhat of a drive to nearby attractions; pricey; some guests say the decor is a little tired. [$] *Rooms from: R2300* ✉ *Old Rustenburg Rd.* ✣ *Take the R24 to Hekpoort, near Magaliesburg* ☎ *014/577–5600* 🌐 *www.tsogosun.com/mount-grace-hotel-and-spa* 🛏 *121 rooms* 🍴 *Free Breakfast.*

Budmarsh Country Lodge

$$ | **HOTEL** | Surrounded by a lush garden in the heart of the Magaliesberg, this lodge has rooms with beautiful antique furniture and is a good place to base yourself if you just want to get into the country for a river ramble or a mountain hike–even the drive is scenic. **Pros:** rooms have jet baths and outdoor showers; relaxing rustic setting; peaceful library. **Cons:** odors from the neighboring cows sometimes drift through the hotel—a reality for any country-based hotel; inaccessible without a car; can be busy on weekends. [$] *Rooms from: R2500* ✉ *T1, Magalies Meander Rd., R96* ✣ *Magaliesburg* ☎ *011/728–1800* 🌐 *www.budmarsh.co.za* 🛏 *18 rooms* 🍴 *Free Breakfast.*

★ De Hoek Country Hotel

$$$$ | **HOTEL** | In France this exclusive establishment would be called an *auberge*—a five-star destination hotel with a superb restaurant suitable for an overnight or weekend jaunt—and the two-story, sandstone building along the river would not be out of place in Provence. **Pros:** statues and artworks dot its bucolic setting; magnificent spa facilities overlooking a swimming pool; friendly and attentive service. **Cons:** pricey, but a value-for-money getaway; sometimes host small private conferences; difficult to access without a car. [$] *Rooms from: R4990* ✣ *Off R24, north of Magaliesberg, adjacent to Bekker School* ☎ *014/577–9600* 🌐 *www.dehoek.com* 🛏 *35 suites* 🍴 *Free Breakfast.*

Mountain Sanctuary Park

$ | RESORT | FAMILY | This wilderness retreat offers campsites, rustic huts, and comfortable self-catering cabins and chalets with electricity, hot water, and cooking facilities. **Pros:** unspoiled nature reserve; inexpensive; peaceful, rural setting. **Cons:** some trails not well marked, so it's easy to get lost; it's a self-catering experience, so not good if you don't like to do it yourself; rustic accommodations. [$] *Rooms from: R874* ✉ *Magaliesberg* ✥ *40 km (25 miles) from Magaliesburg on dirt road, 15 km (9 miles) south of N4* ☎ *014/534–0114, 082/707–5538* 🌐 *www.mountain-sanctuary.co.za* 🛏 *23 rooms* 🍴 *No Meals* ☞ *Bedding and towels not included with huts.*

Valley Lodge & Spa

$$$ | HOTEL | While it's too big to be called a hideaway, this four-star lodge is located on a 250-acre nature reserve with a stream running through it and a bird sanctuary. **Pros:** spacious accommodations; excellent food and good wine list; peaceful surroundings. **Cons:** anyone expecting country charm will be disappointed by the urban corporate decor; pricey; can get busy with conference groups. [$] *Rooms from: R3380* ✉ *13 Jennings St.* ☎ *014/577–1301, 014/577–1305* 🌐 *www.valleylodge.co.za* 🛏 *76 rooms* 🍴 *Free Breakfast.*

Shopping

Welwitschia Country Market

CRAFTS | FAMILY | The Welwitschia Country Market sells handmade arts and crafts, which make for great souvenirs, among other gifts and trinkets at around 40 shops and stalls in the shade of giant trees. There are three restaurants and a beer garden with live music on Wednesday, Friday, Saturday, and Sunday. It's especially bustling on weekends, as there is a children's playground area. There is ample free parking and you can find detailed directions on the website. ✉ *Rustenburg Rd., Damdoryn, Hartbeespoort* ✥ *R104, 2 km (1 mile) from Hartbeespoort Dam, at Damdoryn 4-way stop* ☎ *083/302–8085* 🌐 *www.country-market.co.za* ⏲ *Closed Mon.*

Activities

★ **Bill Harrop's "Original" Balloon Safaris**

BALLOONING | A fun and fascinating way to start the day is with an early-morning balloon ride. Bill Harrop's "Original" Balloon Safaris flies daily at sunrise, weather permitting, over beautiful valleys, mountains, and glassy lakes, with views taking in the Cradle of Humankind, the sparkling Hartbeespoort waterways, as well as the Johannesburg skyline. You may even spot some wildlife below as you float over the Magalies River Valley. A one-hour flight costs from R2,595 per person, including tea and coffee pre-flight, followed by a hot breakfast and sparkling wine on landing. Private exclusive packages can also be organized for special occasions. Transfers from various Johannesburg hotels may be arranged at an additional price. ✉ *R560, near Skeerpoort Rd.* ☎ *083/457–3402, 083/443–2661* 🌐 *www.balloon.co.za.*

Magaliesberg Canopy Tour

ZIP LINING | FAMILY | If you're looking for an unusual way to explore one of the world's oldest mountain ranges—the Magaliesberg, which is dated at around 2,500 million years and partially lies within the Magaliesberg Biosphere Reserve—what better way to do it than soaring through the sky between interlocking spurs. The 2½-hour guided Magaliesberg Canopy Tour comprises of 10 zipline slides and 11 platforms that are safely secured onto the sides of these ancient cliffs. From here you may see *dassies* (rock hyraxes) sunning themselves in the sunshine, klipspringers leaping from rock to rock, and Black Eagles circling overhead in

Hot air ballooning over Pilanesberg Game Reserve is a bucket-list experience.

search of prey. As you become more confident, each of the ziplines get progressively longer (from 20 meters to 140 meters) and faster in speed (up to 40 km per hour). The last five ziplines are a little more technical, though the guides will teach you how to break yourself and follow their hand signals.

For those who are a little nervous, rest assured that the company has numerous zipline tours around the country and an excellent safety record. The tour follows a thorough safety briefing, includes safety gear, and participants are always attached via four devices across two lines (one of which is a back-up line). ⊠ *Rosewood Functions, Rietfontein, Rustenburg, Magaliesberg* ☎ *079/492–0467 mobile, 014/535–0150 landline* ⊕ *www.canopytour.co.za* ✉ *R695* ☞ *Weight limit (150kg/330lbs).*

Sun City

177 km (110 miles) northwest of Johannesburg.

A huge entertainment-and-resort complex in the middle of dry bushveld in the North West Province, Sun City is popular with golfers and families—and with South Africans and foreign tourists alike. Sun City's appeal is vastly enhanced by the Pilanesberg Game Reserve, which is only a few miles from the resort.

Developed by the same company that built the elaborate Atlantis resorts in the Bahamas and Dubai, this is a real destination resort. It was named Africa's Leading Family Resort at the 2021 World Travel Awards.

Sun City was built in 1979, in the rocky wilds of Pilanesberg Mountain, the remains of an ancient volcano. The area was in the then Bantustan of Bophuthatswana—one of several semi-self-governed areas during apartheid set aside for Black ethnic groups. As such, it was exempt from South Africa's then strict anti-gambling laws.

Today Sun City comprises four luxurious hotels; one casino with slot machines, card tables, and roulette wheels; major amphitheaters that host international stars; and an array of outdoor attractions. The complex consists of two parts: Sun City, where the focus is on sport, entertainment and gambling; and the Lost City, anchored by the magnificent The Palace of the Lost City Hotel, which offers guests an opportunity to enjoy outdoor adventure at the Valley of the Waves—a large man-made beach and swimming area with artificial waves, as well as numerous water slides like the four-story-high Temple of Courage.

For golfers, there are the 72-par, 18-hole championship Gary Player Golf Course and the Lost City Golf Course, famous for the Nile crocodiles on its 13th hole. Sun City also stages rock concerts, major boxing bouts, the annual Nedbank Golf Challenge, and many major conferences.

At the Lost City, painted wild animals march across the ceilings, imitation star-spangled skies glitter even by day, lush jungles decorate the halls, and stone lions and elephants keep watch over it all.

The Lost City has hosted a long list of celebrities, including Michael Jackson, Frank Sinatra, and Oprah, and it's where *Blended,* the 2014 movie starring Drew Barrymore and Adam Sandler was filmed.

GETTING HERE AND AROUND

Ingelosi, the official Sun City shuttle, travels between Johannesburg (pickups are in various locations, including OR Tambo) and Sun City twice daily, and once a day from Pretoria. The tickets cost R1,250 one-way for one or two people, though the per-person price drops quickly with a larger group. Otherwise, to get to the area you'll need to arrange a private transfer or a rental car.

Within the Sun City complex are free shuttle buses that ferry visitors around between the attractions and hotels.

TIMING AND PRECAUTIONS

There is plenty to keep you entertained not only in the resort but also in the area, so a few days are needed to do justice to the resort and adjacent Pilanesberg Game Reserve.

VISITOR INFORMATION

Covering the entire North West Province (including Hartbeespoort Dam, Sun City, and the Pilanesberg Game Reserve), the North West Tourism Information website offers plenty of useful information on what to do and where to stay in the province. The Sun International website also offers useful information on Sun City.

CONTACTS North West Province Tourism Information. ☎ *018/381–7341* 🌐 *www.tourismnorthwest.co.za.* **Sun International.** ✉ *Sun City Resort, R556, Sun City* ☎ *014/557–1000* 🌐 *www.suninternational.com.*

🛏 Hotels

There's a wide variety of dining options inside Sun City, from upmarket and glitzy to poolside cafés selling light meals like toasted sandwiches. There are also several affordable family-friendly chain restaurants offering casual dining for all ages, from burgers at Spur to seafood at Ocean Basket.

The Cabanas

$$ | RESORT | FAMILY | Paths thread through pleasant gardens to rooms in these small apartment blocks overlooking a man-made lake. **Pros:** includes complimentary access to The Valley of Waves; great for kids; more affordable than other Sun City accommodations. **Cons:** need to hop a shuttle for dining options; smallish rooms; not a particularly tranquil setting. [$] *Rooms from: R2040* ✉ *Sun City Resort, Sun City* ☎ *011/780–7800 reservations* 🌐 *www.suninternational.com/sun-city/cabanas* 🛏 *380 rooms* 🍴 *Free Breakfast.*

★ The Palace of the Lost City

$$$$ | **HOTEL** | You might think a hotel based on the concept of a lost African palace would suffer from theme-park syndrome, but happily, that's not the case here as sculpted cranes and leaping kudu appear to take flight from the hotel towers, elephants guard stairways and bridges, and graceful reminders of ersatz Africa strike you at every turn. **Pros:** great activities; luxury accommodations; impeccable service. **Cons:** requires a minimum booking of two nights; some would find it unbearably ostentatious and a little kitsch; pricey. $ *Rooms from: R6067* ✉ *Sun City Resort, Sun City* ☎ *011/780–7800 reservations* ⊕ *www. sun-city-south-africa.com/palace.asp* ⤴ *338 rooms* ❖ *Free Breakfast*.

Soho Hotel

$$$ | **HOTEL** | This is the original Sun City hotel, housing spacious and comfortable rooms in the complex that houses the resort's gaming casino, banks of slot machines, and other gaming activities. **Pros:** top-notch restaurants; classic turndown and chocolate-on-the-pillow service; easy access to all the entertainment facilities. **Cons:** expensive food and drink; crowded during high season; casino can be noisy. $ *Rooms from: R3081* ✉ *Sun City Resort, Sun City* ☎ *011/780–7800 reservations* ⊕ *www.sun-city-south-afri-ca.com/suncity.asp* ⤴ *340 rooms* ❖ *Free Breakfast*.

Pilanesberg Game Reserve

200 km (124 miles) northwest of Johannesburg.

Often called the Pilanesberg National Park, this 150,000-acre game reserve is centered on the caldera of an extinct volcano dating back 1.3 billion years that may well have once been Africa's highest peak. Open grassland, rocky crags, and densely forested gorges provide ideal habitats for a wide range of plains and woodland game, including rare brown hyenas, cheetahs, wildebeests, and zebras. Since the introduction of lions in 1993, Pilanesberg (pronounced pee-*luns*-berg) can boast the Big Five. One of the best places in the country to see rhinos, it's also a birdwatcher's paradise, with a vast range of grassland species, waterbirds, and birds of prey. It's also malaria-free and an excellent choice for game-viewing if you're short on time and can't make it all the way to Kruger National Park, for instance. You can drive around the park in your own vehicle or join a guided safari. The entertainment and resort complex of Sun City is nearby.

GETTING HERE AND AROUND

To get to the Pilanesberg from Johannesburg, get on the N4 highway to Krugersdorp and take the R556 off-ramp and follow the signs. The drive is about 2½ to 3 hours. There is a shuttle from Johannesburg to Sun City, just outside the park, otherwise you'll need to rent a car, hire a transfer company or take a guided tour from Johannesburg.

TOURS

Several major tour operators in Johannesburg offer trips to Pilanesberg, including Springbok Atlas Tours & Safaris and JMT Tours and Safaris *(see Tours in Planning)*. Booking these tours ahead of time is essential.

 Sights

Pilanesberg Game Reserve

NATURE PRESERVE | The 150,000-acre Pilanesberg Game Reserve is centered on the caldera of an extinct volcano. Concentric rings of mountains surround a lake filled with crocodiles and hippos. Open grassland, rocky crags, and forested gorges provide ideal habitats for a wide range of plains and woodland game, especially wildebeests and zebras, which are plentiful here. The Pilanesberg (pronounced pee- *luns*-berg) can boast the Big Five (you have a great chance of seeing elephants and rhinos here on almost any single drive) and is malaria-free. It's a bird-watcher's paradise, with a vast range of grassland species, waterbirds, and birds of prey. The entertainment and resort complex of Sun City is nearby. ✉ *Pilanesberg Game Reserve, Sun City* ☎ *014/555–1600, 018/397–1500 North West Parks Board* 🌐 *www.pilanesbergnationalpark.org* 🎫 *R40 per vehicle, R80 per person.*

Hotels

Bakubung Bush Lodge
$$$$ | **HOTEL** | Abutting Pilanesberg, this lodge sits at the head of a long valley with terrific views of a hippo pool that forms the lodge's central attraction—it's not unusual to have hippos grazing 100 feet from the terrace restaurant. **Pros:** cheerful atmosphere; malaria-free; ask for a refurbished room. **Cons:** feels vaguely institutional; always crowded; close to a main gate. [$] *Rooms from: R5360* ✉ *Bakubung, Pilanesberg Game Reserve* ☎ *014/552 6314* 🌐 *www.legacyhotels.co.za* 🛏 *100 rooms* 🍴 *Free Breakfast.*

Kwa Maritane Bush Lodge
$$$$ | **HOTEL** | **FAMILY** | The greatest asset of this hotel, primarily a time-share resort, is its location: in a bowl of rocky hills on the edge of the game reserve. **Pros:** lovely swimming pools; malaria-free; you've got the best of both worlds—bushveld on your doorstep and Sun City 20 minutes away by shuttle at an additional cost. **Cons:** it gets noisy around reception, pool, and dining areas; busy during school holidays; you can't get away from the hotel feel. [$] *Rooms from: R5360* ✉ *Kwa Maritane, Pilanesberg Game Reserve* ☎ *014/552-5300* 🌐 *www.legacyhotels.co.za* 🛏 *90 rooms* 🍴 *Free Breakfast.*

Manyane
$$ | **RESORT** | In a thinly wooded savanna east of Pilanesberg's volcanic ridges, this resort offers affordable accommodations in the Sun City area for those travelers who want to experience the region but can't pay five-star prices. **Pros:** lovely pool, which is a delight on a hot day; accommodations are very basic but a good value; there is a good restaurant if you want a break from self-catering. **Cons:** there's a lot of dust; can be full of noisy campers and late-night revelers; more down-market than other options in the area. [$] *Rooms from: R2355* ✉ *Manyane, Pilanesberg Game Reserve* ☎ *014/555–1000 reception* 🌐 *www.goldenleopardresorts.co.za/manyane.php* 🛏 *24 rooms* 🍴 *No Meals.*

Tshukudu Bush Lodge
$$$$ | **HOTEL** | The five-star Tshukudu Bush Lodge offers a fully-inclusive experience that includes brunch, high tea, a 5-course dinner, local beverages, as well as two daily game drives. **Pros:** high on a hill with panoramic views; malaria-free; luxurious and secluded accommodations. **Cons:** no children under 12 permitted; game good, but not as abundant as Kruger; it's a 132-step climb to the main lodge from the parking area, so not suitable for guests with disabilities or who get winded easily. [$] *Rooms from: R13120* ✉ *Tshukudu, Pilanesberg Game Reserve* ☎ *014/552–6255* 🌐 *www.legacyhotels.co.za* 🛏 *10 rooms* 🍴 *All-Inclusive.*

Madikwe Game Reserve

300 km (186 miles) northwest of Johannesburg (or farther, depending on which gate you enter).

Just as leopards and Sabi Sand Game Reserve are synonymous, think of Madikwe Game Reserve and wild dogs in the same way. This is probably your best chance in South Africa to have an almost guaranteed sighting of the "painted wolves."

In 1991, the 765-square-km (475-square-mile) area bordering Botswana was a wasteland of over-grazed cattle farms, overgrown bush, and rusting fences. A brilliant and unique collaboration between the North West Parks Board, private enterprise, and local communities changed all that when Operation Phoenix—one of the most ambitious game relocation programs in the world—relocated more than 8,000 animals of 27 different species to Madikwe. Soon after, it became one of the fastest-growing safari destinations in South Africa.

Madikwe today is teeming with game. Spot the Big Five, plus resident breeding packs of the endangered painted wolves—the wild dogs of Africa, and another endangered predator, cheetah. On your morning or evening game drive, you also might spot lions, elephants, and buffalo, but you'll certainly see zebras, wildebeests, and several kinds of antelope (South Africans refer to all antelope generically as "buck," whether they're male or female). Birders can look out for more than 350 bird species that occur here. Be dazzled by the crimson-breasted shrike, the lilac-breasted roller, yellow-billed and red-billed hornbills, blue waxbills, and many more.

Madikwe can't claim the great rivers, giant riverine trees, and range of habitats of Kruger or the Sabi Sands, but it has a diverse landscape including wide plains, thick bushveld, an area steeped in history, and a background of low, purple mountains. The reserve also has a host of advantages over many of the others: it's only 3½ hours from Johannesburg on good roads, it's malaria-free, it doesn't allow day visitors or self-drives making sightings more controlled and intimate, and most of its lodges are 5-star, meaning pretty much anywhere you choose to stay is likely to be of a high standard. Choose among over 20 top-class commercial lodges, get your binoculars ready, and off you go.

GETTING HERE AND AROUND

Madikwe is an easy drive on good roads from Johannesburg. Go to Sun City via Hartbeespoort Dam and follow the signs to Madikwe, which is about an hour's drive from Sun City (though your trip could be an hour longer if your lodge is in the north of the park). Ask at your lodge for detailed instructions. You'll be driven around in an open game vehicle by a staff member of your lodge; guided bush walks are also available. No day visitors are allowed.

⊙ Sights

Madikwe Game Reserve

NATURE PRESERVE | This 187,500-acre game reserve in the North West Province (about 3½ hours from Johannesburg and Pretoria) close to the Botswana border is open only to overnight visitors, who can choose from over 20 luxury lodges to stay. The reserve is famous for its wild dog population, but is also known for cheetah, the Big Five, and its general game, such as zebra, wildebeest, giraffe, and impala. It was established in 1991 and is fast becoming one of the most popular private reserves in the country, because of its size, abundance of game, proximity to Johannesburg, and the fact that it is malaria-free (so is very safe for children). ⊠ *Madikwe Game Reserve* ⊕ *www.madikwegamereserve.co.za* ⊡ *R180 gate fee.*

🛏 Hotels

Choose between the ultra-luxurious Jamala Madikwe Lodge with its fine dining and lavish décor or quite the opposite, the Mosethla Bush Camp and Eco-Lodge, with its simple pine cabins and old-fashioned donkey boiler to make hot water. Other options include either of Jaci's Lodges, which is particularly child-friendly, and Rhulani, located in the hills in the west of the reserve, and which has an air of relaxed luxury.

Always check for special offers at any of the Madikwe lodges. You can often get very affordable rates, especially off-season or if you can leave your booking to the last minute (phone any of the lodges and ask them for their last-minute rates).

Jaci's Lodges (Jaci's Safari Lodge and Jaci's Tree Lodge)

$$$$ | **ALL-INCLUSIVE** | **FAMILY** | The two lodges that make up Jaci's Lodges are family owned and have a longstanding reputation for friendliness, superb game drives, and comfortable accommodations. **Pros:** friendly, welcoming atmosphere; children welcome; great game-viewing. **Cons:** food tasty, but not in the league of Rhulani or Jamala Madikwe; pricey; if children aren't your thing, stay away from Jaci's Safari Lodge. [$] *Rooms from: R22800* ✉ *Accessed through Molatedi Gate, Madikwe Game Reserve* ☎ *083/700–2071 reservations, 083/303–0885 Jaci's Safari Lodge manager, 083/276–2387 Jaci's Tree Lodge manager* 🌐 *www.jacislodges.co.za* 🛏 *18 suites* 🍴 *All-Inclusive.*

Jamala Madikwe

$$$$ | **HOTEL** | This intimate lodge, with only five suites, is the ultimate in luxury, with its marble floors, elaborate chandeliers and plush furnishings. **Pros:** memorable food; superb accommodations; excellent game-viewing. **Cons:** more formal than some of the other lodges; some rooms have better views than others; pricey. [$] *Rooms from: R26310* ✉ *Accessed via Molatedi Gate, Madikwe Game Reserve, Madikwe Game Reserve* ☎ *082/929 3190, 082/927 3129* 🌐 *www.jamalamadikwe.com* 🛏 *5 suites* 🍴 *All-Inclusive.*

★ Mosethla Bush Camp

$$$$ | **RESORT** | If you're genuinely eco-conscious and seeking an authentic wilderness experience, then choose this unique bush camp set plumb in the middle of Madikwe's best game-viewing areas. **Pros:** most competitive prices in Madikwe; genuine commitment to the local communities and to conservation; superb local guides. **Cons:** low lighting at night; no pool; basic, rustic accommodation. [$] *Rooms from: R7590* ✉ *Madikwe Game Reserve* ✥ *Accessed through Molatedi Gate* ☎ *011/444–9345 reservations, 083/305–7809 emergencies* 🌐 *www.thebushcamp.com* 🛏 *10 rooms* 🍴 *All-Inclusive* ☞ *Rate includes accommodations, 3 meals daily, 2 game drives daily, tea/coffee.*

Rhulani Safari Lodge

$$$$ | **ALL-INCLUSIVE** | **FAMILY** | Located in the west of Madikwe, Rhulani is a multi-award-winning lodge with nine private rooms, located around an attractive communal lounge and pool area, and overlooking a waterhole frequented by elephants and other animals. **Pros:** privacy; excellent, friendly service; waterhole and hide at the lodge. **Cons:** can be cold in winter; Wi-Fi intermittent; Rhulani's position makes it slightly less accessible than some of the lodges in the center and north of Madikwe (about 30- 45 minutes longer to drive from Johannesburg). [$] *Rooms from: R17200* ✉ *Accessed through Wonderboom Gate, Madikwe Game Reserve* ☎ *014/553–3981 inquiries and reservations, 082/907–9628 inquiries and reservations* 🌐 *www.rhulani.com* 🛏 *9 suites* 🍴 *All-Inclusive* ☞ *well-stocked mini-bar in room, all meals and drinks except premium brands included.*

Chapter 11

MPUMALANGA AND KRUGER NATIONAL PARK

Updated by
Melanie van Zyl

 Sights
★★★★★

 Restaurants
★★★☆☆

 Hotels
★★★★★

 Shopping
★★★☆☆

 Nightlife
★☆☆☆☆

WELCOME TO MPUMALANGA AND KRUGER NATIONAL PARK

TOP REASONS TO GO

★ **Blyde River Canyon:** The gigantic rocks, deep gorges, and high mountains of the Three Rondawels create one of South Africa's great scenic highlights.

★ **Classic Africa:** Kruger National Park is legendary Africa, where countless wild animals, birds, insects, and reptiles freely roam the plains, rivers, and forests.

★ **Discovery Channel Comes Alive:** From grasses and flowers to trees and shrubs, from dainty bushbuck to giant giraffes, from leaping bush babies to languorous lions, you'll marvel at it all.

★ **A Total Escape:** When you're steeped in the bush, you'll forget all the pressures of today's living. This is digital detox at its best.

★ **Safari Opulence:** You're guaranteed luxury accommodations, impeccable service, and (probably) Big Five sightings at one of Sabi Sand's private game reserves. Kids are usually welcome, but check before you book.

1 Sabie. This mountain-top forestry town is surrounded by waterfalls that run off the escarpment. It's a tranquil stop between the Panorama Route and safari that awaits at the Kruger National Park.

2 Pilgrim's Rest. One of just two dedicated museum towns in South Africa, the village was declared a National Monument in 1986; its streets are lined with historic buildings filled with compelling collections.

3 Graskop. This small town may not be the prettiest, but its location on the brim of the Blyde River plateau is unbeatable for exploring the Panorama Route. A handful of the best natural sites (and Pilgrim's Rest) lie within 20 minutes drive.

4 Blyde River Canyon Nature Reserve. One of the world's biggest canyons, the Drakensberg Mountains surround this valley, which is home to attractions such as Bourke's Luck Potholes, the Three Rondavels, and God's Window.

5 Hazyview. The Kruger National Park gateway has a lush subtropical feel that's ideal for growing macadamias, bananas, mangos, and avocados.

Lodgings are typically tucked into these attractive plantations.

6 White River. Wedged between encroaching Mbombela and a network of roads that wind towards Kruger or the Panorama Route, this budding town is home to farmers, artists, and artisans.

7 Mbombela. Formerly Nelspruit, the capital of Mpumalanga is usually a pitstop for business travelers only, but if you need to stock up on supplies or overnight before a flight, this is your spot.

8 Kruger National Park. The park's diverse terrain ranges from rivers filled with crocodiles and hippos to rocky outcrops where leopards lurk and thick thorn scrub shelters lions and buffalo.

9 Sabi Sands. Adjacent to Kruger's western boundary at its southern end (no fences separate the two), South Africa's oldest private reserve is famous for its abundant game (especially leopards) and world-famous luxury lodges.

10 West of Kruger. This is where Manyeleti and Timbavati Private Game Reserves are as well as Thornybush Nature Reserve.

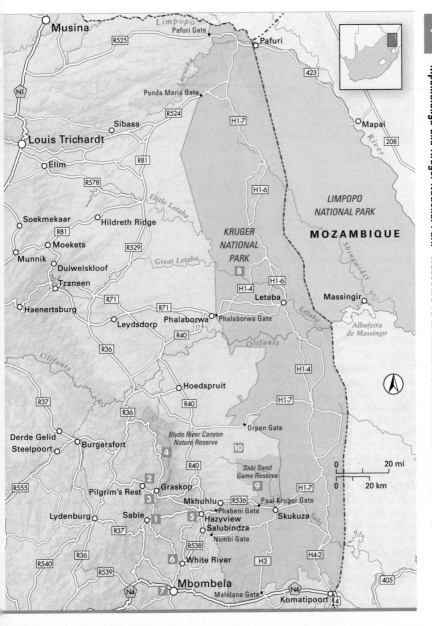

In many ways, Mpumalanga ("where the sun rises") is South Africa's wildest and most exciting province. Its local history is action-packed: local wars, international battles, and a gold rush every bit as raucous and wild as those in California and the Klondike. Nowhere else in the country can you spend one day seeing spectacular wildlife, the next climbing or gazing over the escarpment, and the third poking around some of the country's most historic towns—all within proximity of each other.

The local history is fascinating. In the late 1800s, skirmishes and pitched battles pitted the local Pedi against the Boers (the original Dutch farmers who moved here from the Cape to escape British oppression), as well as the Brits against the Boers (in the First South African War). At the turn of the 20th century, the Brits and Boers fought again (the Second South African War) when England's Queen Victoria brought some of her finest troops from all corners of the British Empire to South Africa, hoping for a final victory over the Boers. Gold and diamonds had been discovered in South Africa, and there was more at stake than political games. The Pilgrim's Rest gold strike of 1873 was minor compared with those in and around Johannesburg, but it nevertheless provided an inducement for gold-hungry settlers.

These early gold-mining days have been immortalized by Sir Percy Fitzpatrick in *Jock of the Bushveld,* a classic of South African literature. Jock was a Staffordshire terrier whose master, Percy (he was later knighted by the British crown), worked as a transport rider during the gold rush. Sir Percy entertained his children with tales of his and Jock's adventures braving leopards, savage baboons, and all manner of dangers. Rudyard Kipling, who wandered this wilderness as a reporter covering the First South African War in the early 1880s, encouraged Fitzpatrick to write down the stories. Jock is still a household name in South Africa today. You'll see lots of Jock of the Bushveld signs all over Mpumalanga, seemingly wherever he cocked a leg.

If you look at a map of South Africa, Mpumalanga is in the top right just below Limpopo. It spreads east from Gauteng to the border of Mozambique. The 1,125-km (700-mile) Drakensberg, part of the Great Escarpment, separates the high, interior plateau from a low-lying subtropical belt that stretches to Mozambique and the Indian Ocean. These lowlands, called the Lowveld, are classic Africa, with as much heat, dust, untamed bush, and big game as you can take in. This is where you find Kruger National Park, covering a 320-km (200-mile) swath of wilderness and undoubtedly one of the world's finest game parks. Apart from its ease of access (there are nine entry gates along its western border), there are plenty of excellent accommodations ranging from bushveld and tented camps to luxury lodges. Mbombela (Nelspruit), south of Kruger, is the nearest big town.

The Drakensberg area rises to the west of Kruger and provides a marked contrast to the Lowveld; it's a mountainous area of trout streams and waterfalls, endless views, and giant plantations of pine and eucalyptus. The escarpment region has some of South Africa's most spectacular scenery, including the Blyde River (Motlatse) canyon—one of the world's largest canyons and one of its greenest because of its luxuriant subtropical foliage—waterfalls, amazing vistas, great hiking, and river rafting. People come to the escarpment to unwind, soak up its beauty, and get away from the summer heat of the Lowveld. Touring the area by car is easy and rewarding—the 156-km (97-mile) Panorama Route winds along the lip of the escarpment—and you can reach many of the best lookouts without stepping far from your car. You'd miss fabulous sightseeing opportunities if you failed to stop on the way to or from Kruger to take in some of Mpumalanga's fantastic sightseeing opportunities.

MAJOR REGIONS

If you look at a map of South Africa, Mpumalanga is in the top right just below Limpopo. This is where you'll find **Kruger National Park**, one of the world's finest

game parks. **Mbombela** (Nelspruit), south of Kruger, is the nearest big town. Other towns include **Sabie, Pilgrim's Rest, Graskop, Hazyview,** and **White River.** It's also where you'll find the **Blyde River Canyon Nature Reserve.**

Bordering Kruger's eastern border, the Sabi Sand Game Reserve, more commonly referred to as the **Sabi Sands,** is a grouping of private game reserves. This is where you'll find the world-famous **MalaMala** and **Londolozi,** as well as **Djuma, Leopard Hills, Lion Sands, Sabi Sabi, Singita,** and **Dulini Private Game Reserves.**

West of Kruger, and north of Sabi Sand Game Reserve, are the less well-known, but more affordable game reserves of **Manyeleti, Timbavati, Thornybush,** and **Kapama**.

Planning

Where you stay on the escarpment may well dictate the kind of weather you get. High up, around Pilgrim's Rest and Sabie, the weather can be chilly, even in summer. Pack a sweater whatever the season. At these elevations fog and mist can be a hazard, especially while driving. On the other hand, the lowveld, especially in summer, is downright sultry.

When to Go

Kruger National Park can be hellishly hot in midsummer (November to March), with afternoon rain a good possibility, though mostly in the form of heavy short showers that don't interfere with game-viewing for long. If you plan your drives in the early morning (when the gates first open) or in the late afternoon, you will manage even if you are extremely heat sensitive. ■TIP→ **Don't drive with the windows up and the air conditioner on—you'll cocoon yourself from the reason you're there.**

11

Mpumalanga and Kruger National Park PLANNING

In summer the bush is green, the animals are sleek and glossy, and the birdlife is prolific, but high grasses and dense foliage make spotting animals more difficult. Also, because there's plenty of surface water about, animals don't need to drink at water holes and rivers, where it's easy to see them. There are also more mosquitoes around then, but you'll need to take malaria prophylactics whatever time of year you visit.

In winter (May through September), the bush is at its dullest, driest, and most colorless, but the game is much easier to spot, as many trees are bare, grasses are low, and animals congregate around the few available permanent water sources. Besides, watching a lion or leopard pad across an arid but starkly beautiful landscape could be the highlight of your trip. It gets very cold in winter (temperatures can drop to almost freezing at night and in the very early morning), so wear layers of warm clothes you can shed as the day gets hotter. Lodges often drop their rates during winter (except July), because many foreign tourists prefer to visit in the South African summer months, which coincide with the Northern Hemisphere winter.

Spring (September and October) and autumn (March to early May) are a happy compromise. The weather is very pleasant—warm and sunny but not too hot—and there are fewer people around. In October migratory birds will have arrived, and in November many animals give birth. In April some migrating birds are still around, and the annual rutting season will have begun, when males compete for females and are often more visible and active.

Getting Here and Around

AIR

Airlink best connects Johannesburg to KMIA (Kruger Mpumalanga International Airport), at Mbombela (Nelspruit), which is equipped to handle the largest and most modern aircraft. KMIA has a restaurant, curio shops, banking facilities, car-rental agencies, VIP lounges, information desks, and shaded parking. Mbombela (Nelspruit) is good for accessing southern Kruger, but if you need to reach other areas, Federal Air also flies directly to most airstrips that serve the Sabi Sand lodges; Hoedspruit Airport, close to Kruger's Orpen Gate and serving Timbavati Game Reserve, and Skukuza Airport, in the middle of Kruger.

For information on airlines, see Air in Travel Smart.

Charter flights between parks and lodges are usually booked by tour operators as part of the tour package.

CONTACTS Hoedspruit Airport. (*HDS*) ✉ *Eastgate Airport, Hoedspruit* ☎ *015/793–3681* ⊕ *www.eastgateairport. co.za.* **Kruger Mpumalanga International Airport (KMIA).** ☎ *013/753–7500* ⊕ *www. kmiairport.co.za.* **Skukuza Airport.** (*SZK*) ✉ *Skukuza* ☎ *013/735–5074* ⊕ *www. skukuzaairport.com.*

BUS

Translux runs regularly between Johannesburg and Mbombela (Nelspruit). The direct trip takes five to six hours, but there are also buses that stop along the way. A one-way ticket starts at R300. Mbombela (Nelspruit) is 50 km (31 miles) from Kruger's Numbi Gate and 64 km (40 miles) from Kruger's Malelane Gate.

Smaller and more comfortable, Citybug is another great shuttle service with daily departures between O.R Tambo airport in Johannesburg and Mbombela, but it is pricier at R490. They also have a daily route to Durban in KwaZulu-Natal for R710.

Public bus service is limited or nonexistent within Mpumalanga. If you don't have your own car, you're dependent on one of the tour companies to get around the escarpment and into the game reserves.

Mpumalanga & Kruger Itineraries

If you have more than a handful of days in the area, split them between the mountain scenery of the escarpment and wildlife-viewing in the Lowveld. You could complete a tour of the Drakensberg Escarpment area in two days, but you're better off budgeting three or more if you plan to linger anywhere. To take in parts of Kruger National Park or one of the private game lodges, which are simply a must, add another three days or more.

3 Days: One of the prime reasons for visiting Mpumalanga is for big game, so fly into the airport nearest your destination and either rent a vehicle and take off into Kruger or get picked up by the private game lodge of your choice. Driving anywhere else in such a short time is not really an option.

5 Days: Your biggest decision will be how much time to spend wildlife-watching and how much to spend exploring the escarpment and its historic towns. A good suggestion is two days for the mountains and

three in Kruger. Driving from Johannesburg, plan an overnight in Sabie after driving the awesome Long Tom Pass. The next day, head to the former mining town of Pilgrim's Rest and soak up some of the colorful local history. Spend the night there or at one of the friendly and superb value-for-the-money bed-and-breakfasts in the area, and start out early the next morning for Blyde River (Motlatse) canyon, with its hiking trails and magnificent escarpment scenery. Then it's off to Kruger, Sabi Sand, Manyeleti, Timbavati, Thornybush, or any of the other game reserves adjacent to Kruger, but make sure you get to Kruger or your private lodge in time for the afternoon game drive.

7 to 10 Days: Spend four or more days in the bush—half at Kruger and half at a private lodge, perhaps. A minimum of two nights at either one is non-negotiable. Then split the rest of your time between the escarpment and the Lowveld outside Kruger, as in the previous itinerary.

Many of these companies also operate shuttle services that transfer guests between the various lodges and to the airport. It's usually possible to hire these chauffeured minibuses at an hourly or daily rate.

Only tour-company buses actually go through Kruger, but they're not recommended. Being in a big tour bus in the park is like being in an air-conditioned bubble, totally divorced from the bush. Also, the big tour buses aren't allowed on many of Kruger's dirt roads and have to stick to the main paved roads.

For information on buses, see Bus in Travel Smart.

BUS CityBug. ☎ *087/537–1444* ⊕ *citybug. co.za.*

CAR

The road system in Mpumalanga is excellent, making it a great place to travel by car. Three principal routes—the N4, N11, and R40—link every destination in the province. From Johannesburg drive north on the N1, and then head east on the N4 to Mbombela (Nelspruit), which is close to many of Kruger's well-marked gates. It's best to arm yourself in advance with up-to-date maps, available at most large gas stations or bookstores, and plan your route accordingly.

The N4 is a toll road (approximately R165 for the one-way trip between Johannesburg and Kruger). International credit cards are not accepted at the toll booths; if you don't have a South African credit card, you will have to pay cash. Though it's a very good, well-maintained road, always look out for the ubiquitous, often reckless taxi drivers in their overcrowded *combis* (vans). Traffic jams are common on weekends and at the beginning and end of school vacations. Secondary roads are also well maintained, but watch out for goats and donkeys that stray from the villages.

The best places to pick up rental cars are at the KMIA, Hoedspruit, and Phalaborwa airports. Avis, Budget, and Europcar all have desks at KMIA and Phalaborwa, whereas Hoedspruit offers Avis and Budget. Rental cars are also available at Skukuza.

For information on car-rental agencies, see Car in Travel Smart.

Maps of Kruger are available at all the park gates and in the camp stores, and gas stations are available at the park gates and at the major camps. Once in the park, observe the speed-limit signs carefully (there are speed traps): 50 kph (31 mph) on paved roads, 40 kph (25 mph) on dirt roads. Leave your vehicle only at designated picnic and view sites, and if you do find animals on the road, allow them to pass before moving on. Sometimes you have to be very patient, especially if a breeding herd of elephants is blocking your way. ■TIP→ **Animals always have the right of way.**

Always be cautious. Kruger is not a zoo; you are entering the territory of wild animals, even though many may be habituated to the sights and sounds of vehicles.

If you are planning to go into Kruger, it's worth renting an eight-seater combi (van) or SUV. Though more expensive than a car, they provide more legroom and you'll probably spot more game and see it better from your lofty perch. It's best to reserve well in advance, particularly if you want a bigger vehicle. Opt for the "super-cover" insurance; it's not that much more expensive, but if you do get bumped by an elephant, you'll be covered.

TRAIN

Sadly, the Shosholoza Meyl/Spoornet's *Komati* train that traveled between Johannesburg and Mbombela (Nelspruit) via Tshwane (Pretoria) is no longer running. The only train service into Kruger is a rather sumptuous ride upon the Blue Train or Rovos Rail. Blue Train's two-night return trip goes from Pretoria to Numbi Train Station on set departure dates and includes a stay at Nkambeni Safari Camp (R42245 per person). Rovos Rail does a longer "African Collage" journey between Pretoria and Cape Town that stops at Kruger (R90000 per person).

For information on trains, see Train in Travel Smart.

Hotels

You may be in wildest Africa, but you'll be amazed by the very high standards you'll encounter for both service and accommodations. The private camps and lodges in the private reserves bordering the national park are renowned for offering the ultimate in luxury. With glossy-magazine decor, spa treatments, private plunge pools, and five-course meals served beneath the stars, you may forget you're in the bush until an elephant strolls past.

For the more budget-minded, the park offers self-catering huts and more pricey (but worth it) self-catering cottages in the more remote and exclusive bushveld (*bushveld* is the generic term for the wild indigenous vegetation of the Lowveld) camps. There are also private concessions that step up the pampering. Visit the South African National Parks website

(⊕ *www.sanparks.org*) to get information and book accommodations. It's essential to note that there are no elevators in any lodging facility in Mpumalanga or in Kruger. ■TIP→ **Make sure you book well in advance and, if possible, avoid July, August, and December, which are South African school vacations.**

That said, there are plenty of hotels, B&Bs, self-catering cottages, and other lodgings available just outside the park, in and around, for example, the towns of Hazyview and White River. Remember, you can still go on a game drive even if you're staying in a chain hotel, and you'll pay much, much less (you'll need to book the game drives separately through an outfitter).

If you're here to experience Mpumalanga beyond Kruger, including the Drakensberg, there are plenty of historic towns with charming inns and chain hotels, including Sabie and Pilgrim's Rest. If you stay in Hazyview or White River, you could feasibly experience both Kruger and the Drakensberg.

Hotel reviews have been shortened. For full information, visit Fodors.com.

Restaurants

Because Mpumalanga is a sought-after tourist destination, its culinary scene keeps getting better and better, both in *larney* (South African slang for "posh") restaurants and attractive cafés. Cuisines range from Mediterranean to pan-African, and many places serve local delicacies such as fresh trout, venison, Cape Malay favorites such as *bobotie* (a spicy meat-and-egg dish), and curries.

Food is cheap and cheerful in Kruger's cafeterias and restaurants, and usually excellent with fine dining and tasteful wine pairings in the private game lodges. Dinner is eaten 7:30-ish, and it's unlikely you'll get a meal in a restaurant after 9. The more expensive the restaurant,

the more formal the dress, with "smart casual" the norm. In Kruger, you might put on clean clothes for an evening meal in a restaurant, but that's how formal it gets. After an exciting night game drive in a private reserve, you'll want to change or at least freshen up, but keep the clothes very casual. Wear long sleeves and long pants because of mosquitoes. Many higher-end restaurants close on Monday, and it's always advisable to make reservations at these in advance.

Restaurant reviews have been shortened. For full information, visit Fodors. com.

RESTAURANT AND HOTEL PRICES

Restaurant prices are the average cost of a main course at dinner or, if dinner is not served, at lunch. Hotel prices are the lowest cost of a standard double room in high season.

What it Costs in South African rand			
$	$$	$$$	$$$$
RESTAURANTS			
under R100	R100–R150	R151–R200	over R200
HOTELS			
under R1,500	R1,500–R2,500	R2,501–R3,500	over R3,500

Safety

The Lowveld area, which stretches from Malelane (east of Mbombela/Nelspruit) to Komatipoort, on the Mozambique border, and up throughout Kruger National Park, is a malarial zone, and you should take antimalarial drugs. Note: malaria prophylactics may be unsuitable for children under six. Consult your doctor about the best options when planning your trip. ■TIP→ **Prevention is the best medicine: at dawn and dusk, smother yourself with insect repellent, and wear long sleeves, long pants, socks, and covered shoes. The private camps all have mosquito (mozzie)** nets, but not Kruger, so spray yourself again before you go to sleep.

If self-driving, be cautious of speed limits. Local police have been known to pull over naive tourists and ask for bribes. Take down the badge number and ask for a receipt if you are guilty of speeding.

Tours

The easiest way to visit this region is to sign up with an outfitter to organize your stay. They will take care of your accommodations and game-viewing trips into Kruger National Park and the private reserves, as well as add on a visit to the Panorama Route; they will also shuttle you from one point to another, so you don't need to hire a car. Springbok Atlas, Trips SA, Welcome Tours, and Shinzelle Safaris are just some of the many operators that lead trips in the area.

African Welcome Safaris
GUIDED TOURS | The highly respected African Welcome Safaris has more than 30 years' service under its belt and offers a wide range of trips and tours ranging from self-drive to fully escorted tours throughout Mpumalanga along the Panorama Route, to Kruger National Park, the private game reserves, and beyond. They will tailor a personal itinerary or you can choose from scheduled day or weekly trips. ✉ Norwich Pl. W, 2 Norwich Close, 4th fl., Sandton ☎ 021/797–4905 ⊕ www.africanwelcomesafaris.com.

Shinzelle Safaris
GUIDED TOURS | Full-day and overnight safari experiences in Kruger National Park, as well as day trips along the Panorama Route, are offered by this small but impressive award-winning company that offers a personal touch. It's run by a husband-and-wife team—he's the guide, she's the amazing chef. You're in good hands, guaranteed. ✉ White River ☎ 064/002–5543 ⊕ www.shinzellesafaris.co.za.

Springbok Atlas Tours and Safaris
GUIDED TOURS | An assortment of tours and excursions that cover game-viewing trips into Kruger National Park and the private reserves, as well as the Panorama Route, which links the major escarpment sights, is offered through Springbok Atlas. ✉ Head Office, 17 Chiappini St., Woodstock ☎ 021/460–4700 head office ⊕ www.springbokatlas.com.

Trips SA
GUIDED TOURS | As with most of the tour companies in the area, Trips SA offers an excellent variety of trips and tours that cover the game-viewing trips into Kruger National Park and the private game reserves, as well as the spectacularly scenic Panorama Route, which links the major escarpment sights. ✉ 90 Main St., Sabie ☎ 013/764–1177 ⊕ www.sabie.co.za.

Visitor Information

The Mpumalanga Tourism and Parks Authority has a host of information. There are also tourist information offices for Hoedspruit, Mbombela (Nelspruit), and White River. The towns of Sabie and Hazyview have websites for additional information.

In Kruger there are information centers at the Letaba, Skukuza, and Berg-en-Dal rest camps.

CONTACTS Hazyview Tourist Information. ✉ Hazyview ☎ 013/764–3399 ⊕ www.hazyviewinfo.co.za. Hoedspruit Tourist Information. ✉ Hoedspruit ⊕ www.hoedspruit.co.za. Kruger Lowveld Tourism. ✉ Kruger National Park ☎ 013/755–1988 ⊕ www.krugerlowveld.com. Mpumalanga Tourism Authority. ✉ Hall's Gateway, N4 National Hwy., Mbombela (Nelspruit) ☎ 013/759–5300, 013/755–3928 ⊕ www.mpumalanga.com. Nelspruit (Mbombela) Tourist Information. ✉ Mbombela (Nelspruit) ☎ 013/759–5300, 044/873–4595 ⊕ www.nelspruit-info.co.za. Sabie Tourist

Information. ✉ *Sabie* ☎ *013/764–1177, 013/767–1886* ⊕ *www.sabie.co.za.* **White River Tourist Information.** ✉ *White River* ☎ *013/759–5300* ⊕ *www.white-river-info. co.za.*

Sabie

355 km (220 miles) east of Johannesburg on the N12.

As you descend Long Tom Pass, the town of Sabie (sah-bee) comes into view far below, in a bowl formed by the surrounding mountains. It's by far the pleasantest and most enjoyable town in the region, with restaurants, shops, and bars. The name Sabie is derived from the Shangaan word *uluSaba,* which described the "fearful river," home to many crocodiles. Today it makes a great base for exploring.

In the 1900s gold provided the community's livelihood, but today it's been replaced by timber, and Sabie sits in the heart of one of the world's largest human-made forests—more than a million acres of exotic pine and eucalyptus. The first forests were planted in 1876 to provide the area's mines with posts and supports. Today you'll find both pine and eucalyptus forests (neither of which is indigenous to the region), with the timber being used for pulp and cardboard, mining timber, and telephone poles, as well as veneer and furniture.

Sabie itself is a busy little town with a farming feel. It boasts some of the biggest traffic humps in South Africa, ensuring that farmers' and visitors' tractors and cars drive slowly through the broad, shady, tree-lined streets. It's easy to walk from one end of the central part of town to the other, taking in sights like **Market Square,** the commercial hub of Sabie in its early days. Here St. Peter's Anglican Church, designed by the famous architect Sir Herbert Baker and built by Italians in 1913, stands in its own pleasant gardens. Also in the square is a Jock of

the Bushveld sign, said to commemorate Jock and Percy's arrival in 1885.

GETTING HERE AND AROUND

Travel 355 km (220 miles) east of Johannesburg on the N12. You'll drive on good roads through lovely scenery. Plan to explore the tiny town on foot after parking your vehicle near the main square.

TOURS
Kestell Adventures
ADVENTURE TOURS | Located just 45 minutes away from Kruger National Park and the Blyde River Canyon, this company offers numerous adventure-based activities including white-water rafting, canyoning, abseiling, caving, and forest cruises. ✉ *Sabie* ⊕ *kestelladventures. com.*

Sights

Lone Creek Falls
CITY PARK | This is the prettiest, most peaceful, and last of three local waterfalls on a dead-end road (the others are Bridal Veil Falls and Horseshoe Falls). An easy paved walkway leads to the falls, which plunge 225 feet from the center of a high, broad rock face framed by vines and creepers. The path crosses the Sabie River on a wooden bridge and loops through the forest back to the parking lot. If you're feeling energetic, follow the steep steps leading up to the top of the falls. Lone Creek is accessible to the elderly and those with disabilities because of its easy approach. ✉ *Old Lydenburg Rd., Sabie* ✛ *6½ km (4 miles) down Old Lydenburg Rd., off Main Rd.* ☎ *013/764–2580 Sabie tourism* ⊕ *www. safcol.co.za* 🎟 *R30.*

Mac Mac Falls
WATERFALL | Set in an amphitheater of towering cliffs, the Mac Mac Falls—a national treasure—is arguably the most famous waterfall in Mpumalanga. The water plunges 215 feet into the gorge as rainbows dance in the billowing spray. A small entry fee gets you through the gate

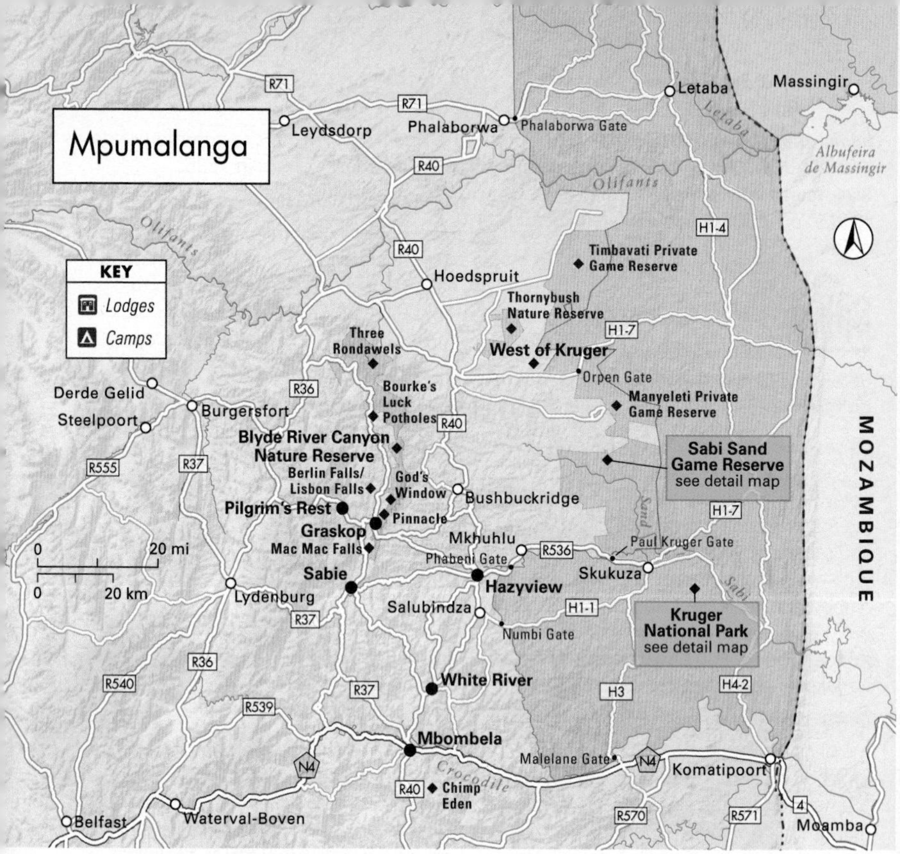

for a closer look. At the gate a number of peddlers sell very well-priced curios. In 1873, President Thomas Burger named the falls after the area's Scottish miners who panned for gold. You can't swim at the falls themselves, but you can at the Mac Mac Pools, about 2 km (1 mile) before you reach the falls. It's worth the small fee to use the picnic and braai facilities there or swim on a hot day. ✉ *R532, 15 km (9 miles) northeast of Sabie, Sabie* ☎ *013/764–1058 Sabie tourism* 🌐 *www.safcol.co.za* 🎟 *R15 for the falls; R30 for pools.*

🍴 Restaurants

Sabie Brewing Company

$ | SOUTH AFRICAN | Perch on the porch along the main drag in Sabie and sip your way through the history of this area while sampling a *chakalaka vetkoek*. The Sabie Brewing Company is home to pet chickens, affordable eats, and home-made hops. Each beer is named after a character from local folklore, such as the Shangaan Stout, which shares the tale of how the Sabie River got its name. **Known for:** wood-fired pizza; craft beer on tap; cosy fireplace. $ *Average main: R50* ✉ *45 Main Rd., Sabie* ☎ *013/764–1005* 🌐 *www.sabiebrewery.com.*

Wild Fig Tree Restaurant

$$ | ECLECTIC | This excellent, casual eatery, in the shade of a wild fig tree, is open daily for breakfast, light lunches, and dinner. Although the emphasis is on local specialties ranging from biltong pâté to impala kebabs and springbok carpaccio, try the local trout dishes or a house-made burger. **Known for:** lovely patio; local meats; cozy bar. $ *Average main: R150* ✉ *Main St. at Louis Trichardt St., Sabie*

☎ *013/764–2239* 🌐 *www.facebook.com/WildFigTreeSabie* ⏲ *Closed Sun.*

Hotels

Sabie Town House
$ | **B&B/INN** | **FAMILY** | Built of local Sabie stone, this charming bed-and-breakfast is the perfect base for exploring Mpumalanga's scenic attractions. **Pros:** excellent value for money; near Panorama Route; friendly. **Cons:** the road leading to the hotel is not in good condition; bar can get noisy at weekends. [$] *Rooms from: R1480* ✉ *25 Malieveld St., Sabie* ☎ *013/764–2292 office, 082/556–7895 cell* 🌐 *www.sabietownhouse.co.za* 🛏 *17 rooms* 🍴 *Free Breakfast.*

Pilgrim's Rest

16 km (10 miles) north of Sabie on R533.

The charming (although very touristy) village of Pilgrim's Rest—also a national monument—dates back to the 1870s gold-rush days when it was the first proper gold-mining town in South Africa. Alec "Wheelbarrow" Patterson abandoned the overcrowded Mac Mac diggings and, carting all his belongings in a wheelbarrow, left to search elsewhere for gold. He found it in Pilgrim's Creek, setting off a new gold rush in 1873. Rumors about the richness of the strike spread quickly around the world, bringing miners from California, Australia, and Europe. Within a year 1,500 diggers, living in tents and huts, had moved to the area. Most of the alluvial gold was found by individuals who recovered more than R2 million worth of gold dust and nuggets using pans, sluice boxes, and cradles. It wasn't until about 1876 that most of the tents were replaced by buildings. Most of the beautifully restored houses seen in the village today are from the more staid and elegant period of the early 1900s. It's worth walking up to the cemetery, as the old graves provide an instant history of the village.

Mpumalanga Gold Rush

On November 6, 1872, a prospector located gold in a creek on the Hendriksdal farm, now a small hamlet about 16 km (10 miles) from Sabie. Sabie itself owes its origins to an altogether luckier strike. In 1895 Henry Glynn, a local farmer, hosted a picnic at the Klein Sabie Falls. After a few drinks, his guests started taking potshots at empty bottles on a rock ledge. The flying bullets chipped off shards of rock, revealing traces of gold. Fifty-five years later, more than 1 million ounces of gold had been taken from the Klein Sabie Falls.

GETTING HERE AND AROUND

Pilgrim's Rest is on the R533, 15 km (9 miles) northwest of Graskop. You'll need a vehicle to tour the area, but plan to explore the village on foot, as most of the attractions are on Main Street. There's a great five-hour walking tour through the village with the Friends of Pilgrim's Rest, but this should be booked in advance.

TOURS

★ **Brummer Tours**
GUIDED TOURS | Tours of Pilgrims Rest and Panorama route are available including gold panning experiences, ghost tours, and guided hikes in the rain forests and mountains surrounding Pilgrims Rest areas. ✉ *Pilgrim's Rest* ☎ *082/522–1958.*

VISITOR INFORMATION

Your first stop should be the Pilgrim's Rest Information Centre, in the middle of town, opposite the Victorian-era Royal Hotel, which is the town's focal point and well worth a visit for its history. The friendly staff at the center will advise you on what to do and what tours to take, such as panning for gold and the

Established in 1873, the Royal Hotel dates from the very beginning of the gold rush in Pilgrim's Rest.

Prospector's Hiking Trail, as well as provide maps and tickets for all the museums in the village.

CONTACTS Pilgrim's Rest Information Centre. ✉ *Main St., Pilgrim's Rest* ☎ *013/768–1060 reception* ⊕ *www.pilgrims-rest. co.za.*

 Sights

★ Alanglade

HISTORY MUSEUM | Guided tours are offered at Alanglade, the former beautiful home of the Transvaal Gold Mining Estates' mine manager, set in a forested grove 2 km (1 mile) north of town. The huge house was built in 1916 for Richard Barry and his family, and it is furnished with pieces dating from 1900 to 1930. Look carefully at the largest pieces—you will see that they are segmented, so they could be taken apart and carried on ox wagons. Tour tickets are available at the information center and should be reserved in advance to ensure a guide. ✉ *Main St., Pilgrim's Rest*

☎ *013/768–1060 Pilgrim's Rest Information Centre, 082/522–1958 Brummer Tours* ⊕ *www.pilgrims-rest.co.za/sight-see/#alanglade* 🎟 *Tours R30.*

The Diggings

MUSEUM VILLAGE | To see how the whole valley looked during gold-rush days, visit the Diggings just outside the village. In the creek where the gold was originally panned, you'll find authentic displays of a water-driven stamp battery, the Gold Commissioner's hut, a transport wagon, a waterwheel, a steam engine, a sluice box, a prison tent, and wattle-and-daub huts typical of the early gold-rush years. The tour lasts about an hour, and you'll watch a gold-panning demonstration (you can even try your own hand at gold-panning). The retired prospector who conducts the tours adds to the atmosphere with yarns about the old days. Tickets are available at the information center. ✉ *R533, Pilgrim's Rest* ✛ *3 km (2 miles) south of Pilgrim's Rest* ☎ *013/768–1060 Pilgrim's Rest Information Centre,*

082/522–1958 Brummer Tours ⊕ *www.
pilgrims-rest.co.za* ✉ *R30.*

Dredzen Shop and House Museum
MUSEUM VILLAGE | Experience life after
the heady gold-rush days, and relive
the '30s and '40s, when 16 general
stores lined the streets of Pilgrim's Rest.
By 1950 mine production had taken a
nosedive, and most of the businesses
had shut down. The Dredzen Shop and
House Museum re-creates the look of
a general store during those lean years,
with shelves displaying authentic items
that would have been on sale, from jams
and preserves to candles and matches.
The attached house belonged to the
shopkeeper and re-creates the life of a
middle-class family of the period. ✉ *Main
St., Uptown* ✚ *After you come down the
hill from the cemetery, turn left on Main
St.* ☎ *013/768–1060 Pilgrim's Rest Information Centre, 082/522–1958 Brummer
Tours* ⊕ *www.pilgrims-rest.co.za* ✉ *R30.*

House Museum
MUSEUM VILLAGE | Originally a doctor's
house, the House Museum, across
and up the street from the Royal Hotel,
re-creates the way of life of a middle-class family in the early part of the
20th century. The house was built in
1913 of corrugated iron and wood and is
typical of buildings erected at the time.
Check out the late Victorian furnishings,
kitchen utensils, and the very grand
carved wooden commode (precurser to
the toilet). Purchase tour tickets at the
information center. ✉ *Main St., Uptown*
☎ *013/764–1177 Pilgrim's Rest Information Centre, 082/522–1958 Brummer
Tours* ⊕ *www.pilgrims-rest.co.za* ✉ *R30.*

Pilgrim's and Sabie News Printing Museum
OTHER MUSEUM | The tiny Pilgrim's and
Sabie News Printing Museum is full of
displays of antique printing presses and
old photos. The building, constructed in
the late 19th century as a residence, later
served as the offices of the weekly *Pilgrim's and Sabie News.* The first newspaper in Pilgrim's Rest was the *Gold News,*

published in 1874 and notable for its
libelous gossip. The editor, an Irishman
by the name of Phelan, felt obliged to
keep a pair of loaded pistols on his desk.
Purchase tour tickets at the information
center. ✉ *Main St., Uptown* ☎ *013/768–
1060 Pilgrim's Rest Information Centre,
082/522–1958 Brummer Tours* ⊕ *www.
pilgrims-rest.co.za* ✉ *R30.*

Pilgrim's Rest Cemetery
CEMETERY | The Pilgrim's Rest Cemetery
sits high on the hill above Main Street.
The fascinating tombstone inscriptions
evoke the dangers and hardship of life
in Mpumalanga a century ago. Tellingly,
most of the dead were young people
from Wales, Scotland, and England. The
cemetery owes its improbable setting to
the Robber's Grave, the only grave that
lies in a north–south direction. It contains
the body of a thief banished from Pilgrim's Rest for stealing gold from a tent,
after which he was tarred and feathered
and chased out of town; he later foolishly
returned and was shot dead. Buried
where he fell, the area around his grave
became the town's unofficial cemetery.
✉ *Pilgrim's Rest* ✚ *Follow the steep path
that starts next to the picnic area, near
the post office* ☎ *013/768–1060 Pilgrim's
Rest Information Centre, 082/522–1958
Brummers Tours* ⊕ *www.pilgrims-rest.
co.za* ✉ *Free.*

🍴 Restaurants

Vine Restaurant and Pub
$ | **SOUTH AFRICAN** | In a former trading
store dating from 1910, the Vine uses
antique sideboards, sepia photos,
and country-style wooden furniture to
recapture that heady 1800s gold rush–
era feeling. The food is straightforward
and hearty, like traditional South African
bobotie (curried ground beef topped with
egg), *potjiekos* (lamb stew), digger's
stew (beef and veggies) served in a digger's gold-prospecting pan, or *samp* (corn
porridge). **Known for:** South African pub
fare; all-day breakfast; people-watching.

$ *Average main: R80 ⊠ Main St., Downtown ☎ 013/768–1080 ⊕ www.theviner-est.co.za.*

Hotels

Royal Hotel
$$ | HOTEL | Established in 1873, this hotel dates from the very beginning of the gold rush in Pilgrim's Rest—you'll see its corrugated-iron facade in sepia photos all over town. **Pros:** good value; step-back-in-time ambience; friendly staff. **Cons:** rooms can be cold; popular with bus tours, so can be overcrowded with tourists; restaurant food unimaginative. $ *Rooms from: R1680 ⊠ Main St., Uptown ☎ 013/768–1100, 013/768–1043 ⊕ www.royalhotelpilgrims.co.za ⇌ 50 rooms* ❍❘ *Free Breakfast.*

Activities

HIKING
Golden Trail
HIKING & WALKING | This newly opened day trail winds around some of the town's best sites, starting with the story-filled cemetery. Ask the town information center for the starting point and follow the markers on this well-signposted hike. ⊠ *Pilgrim's Rest ⊕ Start at the information center ☎ 013/768–1060 Pilgrim's Rest Information Centre ⊕ www.pilgrims-rest.co.za ▨ Free.*

Graskop

25 km (16 miles) northeast of Sabie; 15 km (9 miles) southeast of Pilgrim's Rest.

Graskop (translation: "grass head") was so named because of the abundance of grassveld and few trees. Like so many of the little towns in this area, it started as a gold-mining camp in the 1880s, on a farm called Graskop that was owned by Abel Erasmus, who later became the local magistrate. After the gold mines closed down, the town served as a

major rail link for the timber industry. Today the main features of this rather featureless little town are its curio shops and eateries. Perched on the edge of the Drakensberg/Mpumalanga Escarpment, Graskop considers itself the window on the Lowveld, and several nearby lookouts do have stunning views over the edge of the escarpment. It's an ideal base for visiting scenic hot spots, including Mac Mac Falls and the beauties in and around the Blyde River (Motlatse) Canyon Nature Reserve.

Traveling east toward Hazyview, you enter the lovely Koewyns Pass, named for a local Pedi chief. Unfortunately, there are few scenic overlooks, but you'll still get sweeping views of the Graskop gorge. Look for the turnoff to Graskopkloof on your left as you leave town, and stop to get a closer view into this deep, surprisingly spectacular gorge, where in the rainy season two waterfalls plunge to the river below.

GETTING HERE AND AROUND
It's best to approach Graskop from Mbombela (Nelspruit), the biggest town in the area. It's a pleasant drive (a vehicle is essential) via White River and Hazyview. But don't hold your breath: the town is hardly memorable. Still, it's a good base for exploring the region.

◉ Sights

★ Graskop Gorge Lift
NATURE SIGHT | The same Otis elevator brand that sails down Sandton's tallest towers in Johannesburg can be found on the edge of a cliff in Mpumalanga. The Graskop Gorge Lift drops 51 meters into a magical world of indigenous forest where guests wander the brilliantly signposted boardwalks (wooden walkways and scenic suspension bridges make up a 600-meter [1,969-feet] long trail) to learn about local flora and enjoy views across the Motitsi Falls. After your walk, there are refreshments with upper-level

The Graskop Gorge Lift brings visitors down into the Graskop Gorge.

views down the gorge at The Lift Cafe and craft shopping from local vendors in the market outside. Fourteen veteran traders that previously sold from make-shift plastic and wood structures around town now operate from this sheltered, upmarket trading area. The lift is wheel-chair-friendly. ⊠ *Graskop* ✛ *Situated just outside of Graskop on the R533 towards Hazyview (on the opposite side of the gorge to the Big Swing).* ☎ *013/767–1144, 066/305–1572* ⊕ *www.graskopgorgelift-company.co.za* 🎟 *R225; R50 to visit the cafe, craft market, and viewpoint.*

🍴 Restaurants

★ Harrie's Pancakes

$ | DINER | An institution on the Panorama Route, Harrie's Pancakes has included all manner of fillings in their trademark thick, fluffy pancake rolls since 1986. There's classic lemon and cinnamon or far more decadent sweet stuffings such as the iconic South African peppermint crisp crumble with caramel sauce and milk tart custard. **Known for:** locally-grown coffee; pancakes with a South African twist; fast service. 💲 *Average main: R90* ⊠ *Corner Louis Trichardt Ave. and Kerk St., Graskop* ☎ *013/767–1273* ⊕ *www.harriespan-cakes.co.za/graskop.*

🛏 Hotels

★ Graskop Hotel

$$ | HOTEL | Tagged as "the art gallery you can sleep in" this quirky old town hotel has been lovingly restored into its current boutique offering and boasts a total of 37 en-suite rooms. **Pros:** off-street parking; quirky and fun; central base within walking distance of restaurants. **Cons:** no mini-bar fridge; rooms on the small side; can get busy with group bookings. 💲 *Rooms from: R1930* ⊠ *Cnr Main and Louis Trichardt Sts., Graskop* ☎ *013/767–1244* ⊕ *www.graskophotel.co.za* 🛏 *37 rooms* 🍽 *Free Breakfast.*

The breathtakingly beautiful Blyde River Canyon Nature Reserve encompasses 71,660 acres.

West Lodge Bed & Breakfast

$$ | **B&B/INN** | This attractive Victorian-style B&B is set in a delightful garden bursting with roses. **Pros:** great breakfast; a wide choice of eateries and the town center are only minutes away; friendly. **Cons:** some say the dinners are merely average; a tad pricey for the area. $ *Rooms from: R2020* ⊠ *12 Hugenote St., Graskop* ☎ *060/878–2107* ⊕ *www.westlodge. co.za* ⇱ *6 rooms* ⦿| *Free Breakfast.*

Blyde River Canyon Nature Reserve

15 km (9 miles) northeast of Graskop.

Also known as the Motlatse Canyon Nature Reserve, this breathtakingly beautiful 71,660 acres of red sandstone mountains, gorges, and grassland stretches 60 km (37 miles) north of Graskop, to the Abel Erasmus Pass. Its spectacular main feature is the canyon itself. Carved out of almost 2½ km (1½ miles) of red sandstone, Blyde River Canyon is the world's third biggest—and is often described as the world's greenest, on account of its lush evergreen vegetation. But there are other stunning natural spectacles to see as well, including Bourke's Luck Potholes, God's Window, Three Rondawels, and several waterfalls. All are connected by the Panorama Route north of Graskop (the R532).

GETTING HERE AND AROUND

Situated on the scenic Panorama Route, the Blyde River (Motlatse) Canyon Nature Reserve is easily accessible from Mbombela (Nelspruit), Sabie, and Graskop, and from the west of Kruger. A vehicle is essential, but if you're keen on hiking, it's hiking heaven.

 ## Sights

Abel Erasmus Pass

SCENIC DRIVE | The descent out of the nature reserve, down the escarpment, and through Abel Erasmus Pass is breathtaking. (From the Three

Rondawels, take the R532 to a T, and turn right onto the R36.) Be careful as you drive this pass. Locals graze their cattle and goats on the verges, and you may be surprised by animals on the tarmac as you round a bend. The J. G. Strijdom Tunnel serves as the gateway to the Lowveld. At the mouth of the tunnel are stands where you can buy clay pots, African masks, wooden giraffes, curios of many kinds and subtropical fruit. As you emerge from the dark mouth of the tunnel, the Lowveld spreads out below, and the views of both it and the mountains are stunning. On the left, the Olifants River snakes through the bushveld, lined to some extent by African subsistence farms. ⊠ *Graskop* ☎ *013/759–5300 Mpumalanga Tourism Authority, 015/293–3600 Limpopo Tourism Authority* ⊕ *www.mpumalanga.com.*

Berlin Falls

VIEWPOINT | A small stream, Waterfall Spruit, runs through a broad expanse of grassland to Berlin Falls. A short walk takes you to a platform overlooking the cascade, shaped like a candle. It starts off as a thin stream that drops through a narrow sluice (this looks like the candlewick), and then widens out to fall 150 feet into a deep-green pool surrounded by tall pines. If the weather's good, plan to swim and picnic here. Why the not-very-local name? The German miners who came here during the gold rush named it nostalgically after their home country. ⊠ *Off R532, Graskop* ⊹ *10 km (6 miles) north of Graskop* ☎ *013/759–5300 Mpumalanga Tourism and Parks Agency* ⊕ *www.mpumalanga.com, www.graskop.co.za* ⊠ *R15.*

Blyde River Canyon

CANYON | Starting just below the point where the Blyde (joy) River and Treur (sorrow) River converge, the world's third-largest canyon is also South Africa's second-most-visited natural attraction (after Table Mountain). Discover the spectacular scenery of red cliffs jutting up from the canyon base, quirky geological formations, indigenous rare Afromontane forest, cascading waterfalls, and an abundance of birds, small animals, and biodiversity. You can also try your hand at all sorts of adventure activities, from white-water rafting and abseiling to mountain biking and hiking. ⊠ *Along R532, Bourke's Luck* ☎ *013/767–1886 Graskop Tourism* ⊕ *www.mpumalanga.com, www.graskop.co.za* ⊠ *Individual fees at different access points.*

Bourke's Luck Potholes

VIEWPOINT | The amazing Bourke's Luck Potholes are 27 km (17 miles) north of Berlin Falls. Named after a gold prospector, the cylindrical and rather alien-looking deep potholes filled with green water are carved into the rock by whirlpools where the Treur (sorrow) and Blyde (joy) rivers converge—and where the canyon begins. Several long canyon hiking trails start from here, as do shorter walks and trails (pack a hat and sunscreen, there's very little shade). A three-hour walk, for example, could take you down into the bottom of the canyon, where you follow a trail marked by rocks painted with animal or bird symbols as the gorge towers above you. Be sure to stop by the Blyde River Canyon Nature Reserve visitor center at the entrance to the site, where interesting exhibits describe the canyon's flora, fauna, and geology. ⊠ *Graskop* ⊹ *27 km (17 miles) north of Berlin Falls on R532* ☎ *013/755–3928 Mpumalanga Tourism and Parks Agency* ⊕ *www.mtpa.co.za, www.graskop.co.za* ⊠ *R130.*

God's Window

VIEWPOINT | God's Window is the most famous of the Lowveld lookouts along the Panorama Route. It got its name because of the rock "window" that looks out at the sublime view below. Gaze out into seeming infinity from the edge of the escarpment (which drops away almost vertically). Geared to tourists, it has toilet facilities, paved parking areas, curio vendors, and paved, marked

Lisbon Falls is a good kick-off point for exploring the Panorama Route.

walking trails leading to various lookouts. The God's Window lookout has a view back along the escarpment framed between towering cliffs. For a broader panorama, make a 10-minute climb along the paved track through the rain forest to a small area with sweeping views of the entire Lowveld. The altitude here is 5,700 feet, just a little lower than Johannesburg. ✉ *Off R534, Graskop* ☎ *013/759–5300 Mpumalanga Tourism and Parks Agency* ⊕ *www.graskop.co.za, www.mpumalanga.com* ✎ *R40 per person.*

★ Lisbon Falls

WATERFALL | You'll find more gorgeous waterfalls clustered on the Panorama Route than anywhere else in southern Africa. Just north of Graskop, the dramatic falls are set in a bowl between hills just outside the Blyde (Motlatse) Canyon Nature Reserve, sending cascades 120 feet onto rocks below, throwing up spray over a deep pool. Named nostalgically by European miners who came here looking for gold in the late 1800s, this is a good kick-off point for the whole Panorama Route. Hike down (roughly 40-minutes) to the pool on a path from the parking area, and enjoy a picnic below Mpumalanga's highest waterfall. ✉ *Off R532, Graskop* ✚ *A few km north of Graskop; watch for signs* ☎ *013/759–5300 Mpumalanga Tourism and Parks Agency* ⊕ *www.safcol.co.za* ✎ *R30.*

Pinnacle

VIEWPOINT | Pinnacle is a 100-foot-high quartzite "needle" that rises dramatically out of the surrounding fern-clad ravine, as it has for countless millennia. Way down below, beneath and to the right of the viewing platform, you can see the plateau beneath the escarpment. The watercourse drops down some 1,475 feet in a series of alternating falls and cascades. Stay away from the edge if you suffer from vertigo. ✉ *Graskop* ✚ *6 km (3.7 miles) north of Graskop off R532, on R534* ☎ *013/759–5300 Mpumalanga Tourism and Parks Agency* ⊕ *www.mpumalanga.com, www.graskop.co.za* ✎ *R40 per person.*

★ Three Rondawels

VIEWPOINT | This is one of the most spectacular vistas in South Africa—you'll find it in almost every travel brochure. Here the Blyde River, hemmed in by towering buttresses of red rock, snakes through the bottom of the Blyde River canyon. The Three Rondawels are rock formations that bear a vague similarity to the round, thatch African dwellings of the same name. Before Europeans moved into the area, the indigenous local people named the formations the Chief and His Three Wives. The flat-top peak to the right is Mapjaneng (the Chief), named in honor of a Mapulana chief, Maripe Mashile, who routed invading Swazi at the battle of Moholoholo ("the very great one"). The three "wives," in descending order from right to left, are Maseroto, Mogoladikwe, and Magabolle. ✉ *R536, Graskop* ☎ *013/759–5300 Mpumalanga Tourism and Parks Agency* 🌐 *www.mpumalanga.com, www.graskop.co.za* 🎟 *R70 per person.*

Hotels

Blyde Canyon, a Forever Resort

$ | **RESORT** | **FAMILY** | If you want to make the most of the viewpoints along the Panorama Route (and get the best photographs), this old-school holiday resort with campsites, self-catering chalets, and a restaurant, is your best bet. **Pros:** family-friendly; accessibility to Bourke's Luck Potholes and Three Rondavels; great hiking base and spectacular views. **Cons:** dated lodgings; quite conference-y. [$] *Rooms from: R1450* ✉ *R532, Ohrigstad, Graskop* ☎ *086/122–6966* 🌐 *www.foreverblydecanyon.co.za* 🛏 *100 rooms* 🍴 *No Meals.*

Activities

HIKING

For the safest hiking trails, enter the Blyde River Canyon from the Forever Resort. There is a well-maintained network of paths with impressive canyon views all starting in the cliffside, taking you through fairytale indigenous forest. Trails range in length from 2 km (1.2 miles) to 5 km (3 miles) but can be combined into a longer walk of roughly 13 km (8 miles). One particular spot is called World's End, which you'll want to visit at sunrise or sunset to experience a true spectacle. It's important to note that the provincial park viewpoints close early, but if you spend the night at the Forever Resort, you'll be able to photograph well into the golden hour from within the resort grounds.

Hazyview

45 km (28 miles) east of Sabie.

Named for the heat haze that drifts up from the fruit plantations and bush in the surrounding area, Hazyview is a bustling little town. Situated in the center of the prime tourist attractions, it's also another gateway to Kruger through the nearby Phabeni, Numbi, and Kruger gates. There are plenty of good places to stay and eat, and Hazyview is also the adventure mecca of the region. Here you can try your hand at horseback riding, helicopter trips, river rafting, ballooning, quad biking, golf, and game-viewing safaris.

GETTING HERE AND AROUND

Hazyview is easily accessible from Mbombela (Nelspruit) on good, well-signposted roads. From here, it's a comfortable drive to the major attractions of the Panorama Route, including God's Window, Bourke's Luck Potholes, and the spectacular Blyde River (Motlatse) canyon.

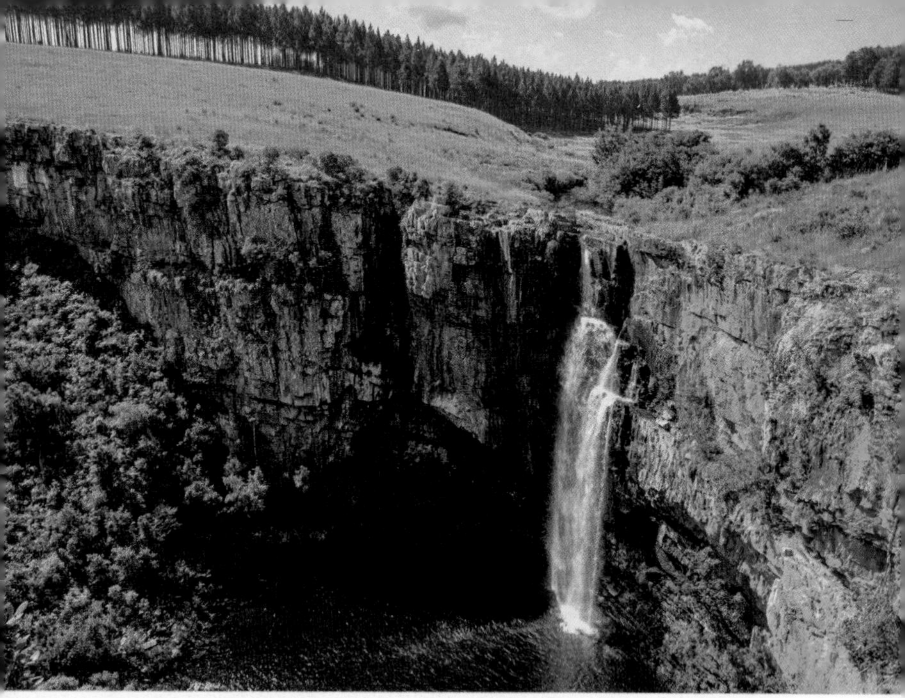

The German miners named the Berlin Falls after their home country.

VISITOR INFORMATION

CONTACTS Hazyview Tourist Information. ✉ *Hazyview* ☎ *013/764–3399* 🌐 *www.hazyviewinfo.co.za.*

Hotels

Böhm's Zeederberg Country House

$$ | **B&B/INN** | Expect a warm, sincere welcome at this owner-run guesthouse situated on spacious grounds with verdant lawns shaded by indigenous trees. **Pros:** concierge service for activity reservations; lovely terrace views; shaded swimming pool. **Cons:** pricey for the area; no TV or Wi-Fi in the rooms. [$] *Rooms from: R2500* ✉ *R536, Hazyview* ✣ *18 km (11 miles) west of Hazyview* ☎ *013/737–8101* 🌐 *www.bohms.co.za* 🛏 *10 chalets* 🍴 *Free Breakfast.*

★ **Rissington Inn**

$$ | **B&B/INN** | This lovely, reasonably priced lodge offers fine food, superb hospitality, and all the facilities you'd expect at a top lodge. **Pros:** great base for Kruger; superb value for money; fine food. **Cons:** as beautiful as it is, not for anyone looking for the luxurious perks of a five-star (i.e., no bathrobes or slippers); book well in advance; often busy. [$] *Rooms from: R2100* ✉ *Off R40, Hazyview* ✣ *1 km (¾ mile) from Hazyview and down a dirt road* ☎ *013/737–7700* 🌐 *www.rissington.co.za* 🛏 *16 rooms* 🍴 *Free Breakfast.*

White River

35 km (22 miles) southeast of Sabie.

This pleasant little town is set amid nut and tropical-fruit plantations and is one of the gateways to the escarpment's major sights, as well as to Kruger National Park. Settled by retired British army officers in the early 20th century, it still retains some of its colonial feel, but it's now much more representative of the "new" South Africa, crowded with people of all backgrounds. There's something for everyone from shopping to holistic healing.

Rock Art

An important key to understanding humankind's past, rock art is a fascinating aspect of the South African and world's heritage. Engravings (made by scratching into the rock surface), paintings, and finger paintings proliferate throughout the province and carry an air of mystery, since relatively little is known about them. Although some archaeologists have attributed the origins of rock art to ancient Egyptians, Phoenicians, and even extraterrestrial races, the rock art found here was created by ancestors of the San. Materials came from the immediate environment. Ocher (red iron-oxide clay) was used to obtain red, charcoal for black, and white clay for white. Blood, egg, and plant juices were used for binding, creating a paint with obvious staying power.

Most rock art illustrates the activities and experiences of the African medicine people, or shamans. Religious rituals, such as those for making rain and healing the sick, involved trances and inspired visions, from which rock-art images were created. The images included large animals, such as the highly regarded eland and rhino, which were believed to possess supernatural power. Half-animal, half-human representations and geometric patterns and grids are also featured. The shamans believed that when an image was drawn, power was transferred to the people and the land.

GETTING HERE AND AROUND

White River is very conveniently situated on good, well-signposted roads between Mbombela (Nelspruit) and Kruger National Park. You'll need wheels to tour the area, and be sure to shop for fresh fruit and produce at the numerous roadside stalls.

 Sights

★ Sabie Valley Coffee

OTHER ATTRACTION | From the moment you enter Sabie Valley Coffee the delicious smell of freshly roasted beans lures you in. A fascinating coffee tour, led by owner Tim Buckland, takes you through the whole coffee-making process—from orchards to roasting to packaging. Find out about a coffee grower's life, and the different kinds of beans that produce different tastes, which is why there are so many (often bewildering) coffees available today. Challenge your taste buds with a tasting of homegrown, 100% pure Arabica specialty coffees, before sampling some of the coffee-related goodies for sale: coffee liqueur, cake, and candies. Reservations are best. ⊠ Casterbridge LIfestyle Centre, R40, corner of Hazyview and Numbi Rds., White River ☎ 013/737–8169, 082/751–3400 reservations ⊕ www.sabievalleycoffee. com ⛟ Tours with tastings R140 includes coffee and cake.

White River History & Motor Museum

OTHER MUSEUM | If you're into automobiles and their history, travel to the Casterbridge Lifestyle Centre for the White River History & Motor Museum. It has an impressive collection of more than 60 vehicles, dating from as early as 1911, including a 1936 Jaguar SS100, one of only 314 ever built. ⊠ Casterbridge Lifestyle Centre, R40 at Numbi Rd., White River ☎ 013/751–1540, 082/578–3552 ⊕ www.casterbridge.co.za ⛟ Free.

Hotels

Casterbridge Hollow Boutique Hotel
$$ | **HOTEL** | Mpumalanga's first green hotel has contemporary and stylish rooms with balconies and verandahs overlooking the pool and flourishing gardens. **Pros:** classy base for day trips into the Kruger via Phabeni Gate; friendly service; spacious rooms. **Cons:** popular with weddings on weekends so could be crowded; some rooms can be noisy. [$] *Rooms from: R1500* ✉ *Casterbridge Lifestyle Centre, R40, White River* ☎ *013/751–3088* 🌐 *www.casterbridgehollow.co.za* 🛏 *30 rooms* 🍴 *Free Breakfast.*

Oliver's Restaurant and Lodge
$$$ | **B&B/INN** | This large, white-walled, red-roofed country house situated among pine trees and lush forest overlooks lovely gardens and the 1st hole of the White River Golf Course. **Pros:** excellent and friendly service; on-site spa; great food. **Cons:** about an hour from Kruger for those entering at Phabeni; pricey rates; quite formal. [$] *Rooms from: R3800* ✉ *R40, between Hazyview and White River, White River* ☎ *013/750–0479* 🌐 *www.olivers.co.za* 🛏 *14 rooms* 🍴 *Free Breakfast.*

Shopping

★ **Casterbridge Lifestyle Centre**
SHOPPING CENTER | If you need some classy retail therapy, stop off at this upmarket lifestyle center. Once a rambling mango estate, it's now home to art galleries, pottery and sculpture studios, and quirky boutiques selling designer clothes, jewelry, and much more, all set in lovely manicured gardens. The White River Art Gallery always has interesting local and national exhibitions, and when you've shopped till you dropped, tuck into a good meal at one of the eateries that serve everything from tasty pub fare and fine dining to wood-oven pizza. If wheels are your thing, pop into the vintage White River History & Motor Museum and feast your eyes on immaculately restored past motoring beauties. You'll even find Mpumalanga's first green hotel here, the Cambridge Hollow Boutique Hotel. ✉ *R40 at Numbi Rd., White River* ☎ *013/751–1540 information* 🌐 *www.casterbridge.co.za.*

Mbombela (Nelspruit)

19 km (12 miles) southwest of White River on the R40.

Mbombela (formerly Nelspruit), the capital of Mpumalanga and home of the provincial government, is a modern, vibrant subtropical city of some 56,000 people. Known as the gateway to Kruger and the Lowveld, it's also a notable stop on the main route between Gauteng and Maputo, Mozambique. The compact town sits in the middle of a prosperous agricultural community, which farms citrus (a third of South Africa's citrus exports come from here), subtropical fruit, tobacco, and vegetables. It has an international airport, excellent hospitals, great restaurants, superb botanical gardens, and the Riverside Mall, Mpumalanga's biggest shopping center. Nearby is the Jane Goodall Institute's Chimpanzee Eden.

GETTING HERE AND AROUND

Approximately a five-hour drive from Johannesburg, Mbombela (Nelspruit) is easily accessible by road. The Kruger Mpumalanga International Airport (KMIA) is 22 km (13 miles) northeast of the town.

Sights

Chimp Eden
OTHER ATTRACTION | **FAMILY** | Jane Goodall Institute's Chimp Eden provides sanctuary to chimpanzees that have been uprooted from their homes. Established in 2006, it's located on 1,000 hectares (2,500 acres) of wild lands just outside Mbombela. Visitors can observe the

chimps from several viewpoints overlooking the forest. You can also take a one-hour tour where you'll learn all about the chimps and the sanctuary, and a small restaurant provides refreshments. Tours run three times daily—10 am, noon, and 2 pm—and must be pre-booked via email or phone. ⊠ *R40 (Baberton Rd.), Mbombela (Nelspruit)* ✛ *Off N4, about 12 km (7½ miles) from Mbombela* ☎ *079/777–1514 tours* ✍ *info@jane-goodall.co.za or tours@chimpeden.com* ⊕ *www.chimpeden.com* ⊠ *R225 for chimp tour.*

Lowveld National Botanical Gardens
GARDEN | FAMILY | The gorgeous Lowveld National Botanical Gardens, just outside Mbombela, is the only one in the province. It's a must-see if you are at all interested in plant life. Apart from its collection of more than 2,000 species of plants, it has the largest collection of cycads in Africa. Take great photos from the wooden suspension bridge over a tumbling waterfall where the Crocodile and Nel rivers (which flow through the gardens) join together. In spring and summer, when many of the indigenous plants are flowering, you'll see lots of iridescent sunbirds feasting on the blossoms. But at any time of year, don't miss the lush man-made African rain forest that gives the gardens its "evergreen" moniker. The gardens are wheelchair-friendly. ⊠ *White River Rd., Mbombela (Nelspruit)* ✛ *3 km (2 miles) outside Mbombela* ☎ *013/752–8880* ⊕ *www.sanbi.org/gardens/lowveld* ⊠ *R40* ☞ *Book guided tours 2 wks in advance.*

 Hotels

⭐ **Torburnlea**
$$ | B&B/INN | Nestled into a fertile and scenic hillside on the outskirts of Mbombela, fourth-generation heirs, Andrew and Kim Hall, have lovingly restored this grand old farmhouse to a stately stay. **Pros:** wrap-around verandah for languid afternoons; owner-run with knowledgable, invested, story-telling hosts; gorgeous, spacious rooms. **Cons:** set in a residential estate, so not a "farm" setting any longer. $ *Rooms from: R2720* ⊠ *Mbombela (Nelspruit)* ☎ *072/884–8872, 013/007–0241* ⊕ *www.torburnlea.co.za* ⊠ *6 rooms* ⦿ *Free Breakfast.*

Kruger National Park

Kruger National Park is undoubtedly one of the world's best game parks, where teeming game roams freely over an area the size of Wales or Israel. Visiting Kruger is likely to be one of the greatest experiences of your life, truly providing ultimate "Wow!" moments. You'll be amazed at the diversity of life forms—the tallest (the giraffe), the biggest (the elephant), the funkiest (the dung beetle), the toothiest (the crocodile), and the glitziest (the lilac-breasted roller).

But it's not all game and safari. If you're into ancient human history, there are also major archaeological sites and fascinating San (Bushman) rock paintings. (There is ample evidence that prehistoric humans—*Homo erectus*—roamed the area between 500,000 and 100,000 years ago.) Founded in 1898 by Paul Kruger, president of what was then the Transvaal Republic, the park is a place to safari at your own pace, whether with a guide in a safari jeep or driving your own car.

Kruger lies in the hot Lowveld, a subtropical section of Mpumalanga and Limpopo provinces that abuts Mozambique. The park cuts a swath 80 km (50 miles) wide and 320 km (200 miles) long from Zimbabwe and the Limpopo River in the north to the Crocodile River in the south. It is divided into 16 macro eco-zones, each supporting a great variety of plants, birds, and animals, including 150 mammal species and more than 500 species of birds, some of which are not found elsewhere in South Africa. In 2002 a treaty was signed between South Africa, Zimbabwe, and Mozambique to form a giant conservation area, the Great Limpopo Transfrontier Park. It's a complex ongoing process, but once all the fences between Kruger, the Gonarezhou National Park in Mozambique, and the Limpopo National Park in Zimbabwe are finally removed, the Peace Park will be the largest conservation area in the world.

GETTING HERE AND AROUND

You can fly to Kruger Mpumalanga International Airport (KMIA), at Mbombela (Nelspruit); Skukuza Airport inside Kruger itself; Hoedspruit Airport, close to Kruger's Orpen Gate; or Phalaborwa Airport (if you're going to the north of Kruger) from either Johannesburg or Cape Town. *(See Air in Travel Smart.)*

Self-drive tours of Kruger are available, and you can drive to Kruger from Johannesburg in about six hours. But, self-drive tours are not recommended for first-time safari goers. Wherever you go, **don't get out of your vehicle** except at certain well-marked picnic sites or view sites, unless you want to make an international headline.

HOTELS

You have your choice of rest camps, bushveld camps, and private game lodges within the confines of Kruger National Park. And within those options, your choices include cottages, safari tents, campsites, and guest lodges that are ideal for families. It's impossible to recommend just one place to stay. One person might prefer the intimacy of Kruger's oldest rest camp, Punda Maria, with its whitewashed thatch cottages; another might favor big, bustling Skukuza. The bushveld camps are more expensive than the regular camps, but offer much more privacy and exclusivity—but no shops, restaurants, or pools. If you seek the ultimate in luxury, stay at one of the private luxury lodges in the private concession areas, some of which also have walking trails. A great way to experience the park

is to stay in as many of the camps as possible. The SANParks website has a comprehensive overview of the different camps. The private game lodges include safaris and meals in the price, whereas the rest camps and bushveld camps are self-catering, and you'll need to book your drives and walks.

Reservations for park-operated accommodations should be made through **South African National Parks.** *(For SANParks contact information, see Visitor Information in Travel Smart.)*

If air-conditioning is a must for you, be sure to check the website to confirm its availability in the accommodation of your choice.

■TIP→ **Book your guided game drives and walks when you check-in. Opt for the sunset drive. You'll get to see the animals coming to drink plus a thrilling night drive.**

Another option is to stay in one of the luxury camps located within one of the private reserves bordering Kruger, with Sabi Sand Private Game Reserve being the most renowned and most exclusive; dozens of private lodges here will take care of all your safari and dining and relaxing needs.

Or you can opt for a hotel or self-catering lodging in one of the communities just outside the park, such as Hazyview or White River, and either self-drive through the park, join a "Park & Drive" game drive at one of the gates, or make arrangements with one of the region's many outfitters. Elephant Herd Tours & Safaris (⊕ *elephantherd.co.za*) and Shinzelle Safaris (⊕ *shinzellesafaris.co.za*) are recommended. Safaribookings.com is one of the many online marketplaces that compares tour operators and safari tours.

BUSHVELD CAMPS

Smaller, more intimate, more luxurious, and consequently more expensive than regular rest camps, Kruger's bushveld camps are in remote wilderness areas of the park that are often off-limits to regular visitors. Access is limited to guests only. As a result, you get far more bush and fewer fellow travelers. Night drives and day excursions are available in most of the camps. There are no restaurants, gas pumps, or grocery stores, so bring your provisions with you (though you can buy wood for your barbecue). All accommodations have fully equipped kitchens, bathrooms, ceiling fans, and large verandahs, most with air-conditioning. Cottages have tile floors, cheerful furnishings, and cane patio furniture and are sited in stands of trees or clumps of indigenous bush for maximum privacy. Many face directly onto a river or water hole. There's only a handful of one-bedroom cottages (at Biyamiti, Shimuwini, Sirheni, and Talamati), but it's worth booking a four-bed cottage and paying the extra, even for only two people. If you have a large group or are planning a special celebration, you might consider reserving one of the two bush lodges, which must be booked as a whole: Roodewal Bush Lodge sleeps 18, and Boulders Bush Lodge sleeps 12. Reservations should be made with South African National Parks.

For SANParks contact information, see Visitor Information in Travel Smart.

PRIVATE GAME LODGES

Kruger boasts a number of private concessions that are exclusive, uncrowded, and unfenced in prime Big Five territory (meaning animals can roam freely to and fro; each concession contains two or three luxury lodges at most, ranging in style from traditional colonial to ultramodern. They're the perfect choice for visitors not interested in roughing it—though you'll pay for that luxury. You'll enjoy good food and wine, relaxation, and plenty of game-viewing throughout the day. Singita Lebombo Lodge is the crème-de-la-crème with its super-chic lodging, wooden decks overlooking a water hole, spa treatments, and fine dining. ReturnAfrica in the remote north honors the underappreciated cultural aspects of the park.

REST CAMPS

Kruger operates rest camps all over the park. These government-run rest camps offer a variety of accommodations, including campsites, safari tents, bungalows, cottages, and guesthouses, and provide electricity, shop, braai, communal kitchen facilities, laundry facilities, restaurant and/or self-service cafeteria, and petrol station. Oftentimes the rest camps offer seasonal programming and evening films showcasing Kruger's wildlife. See the complete listing on the SANParks website.

For SANParks contact information, see Visitor Information in Travel Smart.

MONEY MATTERS

Kruger accepts credit cards, which are also useful for big purchases, but you should always have some small change for staff tips (tip your cleaning person R20 per hut per day) and for drinks and snacks at the camp shops, although camp shops also accept credit cards. Some camps, including Skukuza and Letaba, have cash machines.

TIMING

How and where you tackle Kruger will depend on your time frame. If you can spend a week here, start in the north at the very top of the park at the Punda Maria Camp or in Pafuri with RETURNAfrica, where there are always fewer people. Then make your way leisurely south to the very bottom at Crocodile Bridge Gate or Malelane Gate. With only three days or fewer, stick to the south or central sections of the park and just plan to explore those areas where the game sightings are richer. No matter where you go in Kruger, be sure to plan your route and accommodations in advance (advance booking is essential) and consider the sedate speed limit of 50km/h (31 mph). And be sure to take at least one guided sunset drive; you won't likely forget the thrill of catching a nocturnal animal in the spotlight.

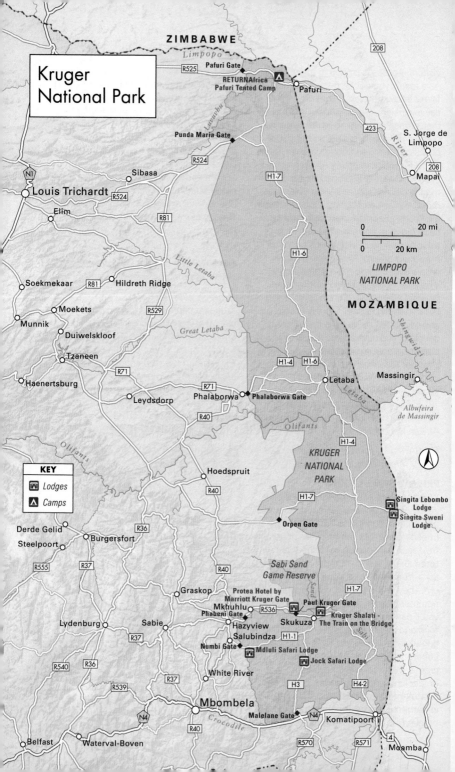

Kruger National Park

ZIMBABWE

Limpopo

R525 — Pafuri Gate
RETURNAfrica
Pafuri Tented Camp — Pafuri

208

423 — S. Jorge de Limpopo

Luvuvhu

Punda Maria Gate

208 — Mapai

N1
Louis Trichardt
Sibasa
R524
Elim
R81
H1-7

R524

Little Letaba

0   20 mi
0   20 km

LIMPOPO NATIONAL PARK

Soekmekaar
R81 — Hildreth Ridge
Moekets
R529
Munnik
Duiwelskloof
Great Letaba
H1-6

MOZAMBIQUE

Tzaneen
Haenertsburg
R71
Leydsdorp
R71 — Phalaborwa
Phalaborwa Gate
R40

H1-4   H1-6
Letaba
Massingir
Shingwidzi
Letaba
Albufeira de Massingir

Olifants

Hoedspruit
R40

KRUGER NATIONAL PARK

H1-4

H1-7

KEY
🏠 *Lodges*
⛺ *Camps*

Derde Gelid
Steelpoort
Burgersfort
R36
R555
R37

Singita Lebombo Lodge
Singita Sweni Lodge

Orpen Gate

Graskop
Lydenburg
R37
Sabie
R40

Sabi Sand Game Reserve

Sand

H1-7

Protea Hotel by Marriott Kruger Gate
Mkhuhlu
Phabeni Gate
Hazyview
Salubindza
Numbi Gate
R536
Paul Kruger Gate
Skukuza
Kruger Shalati – The Train on the Bridge
H1-1

R540
R36
R539
White River
R37

Mdluli Safari Lodge
Jock Safari Lodge

Sabie

Mbombela
N4
Belfast
Waterval-Boven
R40

Crocodile
Malelane Gate
N4 — Komatipoort
H3
H4-2
R570
R571
4
Moamba

◉ Sights

The main reason you come to Kruger, of course, is to see the amazing wildlife. Game-spotting isn't an exact science: you might see all the Big Five plus hundreds of other animals, but you could see much less. Old Africa hands claim that the very early morning, when the camp gates open, is the best time for game-viewing, but it's all quite random—you could see a leopard drinking at noon, a breeding herd of elephants mid-morning, or a lion pride dozing under a tree in the middle of the afternoon. You could also head out at dawn and find very little wildlife.

The southern and central sections of the park are the best for sightings because riverine forests, thorny thickets, and large, grassy plains studded with knob-thorn and marula trees, typical vegetation of this region, make ideal habitats for a variety of animals, including black and white rhinos, leopards, giraffes, hyenas, numerous kinds of antelope, lions, and the rare "painted wolf"—a wild dog.

As you head north to Olifants, Letaba, and Shingwedzi, you enter major elephant country, although you're likely to spot lots of other game, too, including lions and cheetahs. North of Letaba, however, the landscape becomes a monotonous blur of mopane trees, the result of nutrient-poor land that supports smaller numbers of animals, although the lugubrious-looking *tsessebe* (sess-a-bee) antelope and the magnificent and uncommon roan antelope, with its twisty horns, thrive here. Elephants love mopane, and you'll certainly see plenty of them. The Shingwedzi River Drive towards the Kanniedood Dam is one of the park's most rewarding drives, with elephants, leopards, giraffes, and other game. Park your vehicle underneath the lovely hide on this drive, then sit upstairs and take in life on the river, including waterbirds, hippos, and basking crocs.

To experience the full richness of the northern Kruger, visit the Pafuri Picnic Site (hot water and braais available), where ancient massive leadwood and jackalberry trees lean over the often dry Luvuvhu River, the haunt of the scarlet-and-green Narina trogon (a bird) and the much-sought-after Pel's fishing owl. But don't leave your picnic unattended while you look for more special birds, such as the wattle-eyed flycatcher, because the vervet monkeys will have it in a flash.

★ Kruger National Park

NATIONAL PARK | There are nine entrance gates to Kruger, namely (counterclock-wise from the north) Pafuri, Punda Maria, Phalaborwa, Orpen, Paul Kruger, Phabeni, Numbi, Malelane, and Crocodile Bridge. National access roads to all the entrance gates are paved. If you're staying at one of the park's lodges or camps, you can arrange for a late-entry escort until 9 pm for the following gates (and their nearby camps): Paul Kruger (Skukuza), Numba (Pretoriuskop), Malelane (Berg-en-Dal and Malelane), Crocodile Bridge (Crocodile Bridge), Punda Maria (Punda Maria), and Orpen (Orpen).

With excellent roads and accommoda-tions, Kruger is a great place to drive around yourself, though first-timers may want to think again about getting behind the wheel, since not everyone knows what to do when an enormous elephant with wavering ears is standing in front of your vehicle, blocking the road. Travel times in the park are tough to estimate, in addition, and a hefty fine is levied if you don't make it out of the gates on time.

An affordable solution is to join a game drive with a park ranger, who will drive you around in an open-sided four-wheel-drive. All the major rest camps offer ranger-led bush drives in open-air vehicles (minimum of two people), and, if you're not staying in the park itself, you can still join a tour led by ranger; your option for this are the Park & Ride tours, which leave from the park's entrance gates. There are also plenty of outfitters who will arrange a safari for you (as well as accommodations). Most drives depart in the early morning for either a half day or full day.

There are also bush walks on offer, something else you can't do on your own.

Whatever you do, don't miss out on a ranger-led sunset drive, when the park is closed to regular visitors. You'll sit in a large open-air vehicle, scanning the bush as dusk settles over the landscape with the ranger, who uses a powerful spotlight to pick out animals, including nocturnal creatures that you would never see otherwise. You might see bush babies (enchanting furry, big-eared, big-eyed little primates that leap from bush to bush), servals (mini-leopard-looking felines), civets (black-and-white possum look-alikes), genets (spotted catlike creatures with bushy tails), or an aardvark ambling along in the moonlight. Scrutinize branches of big trees for the giant eagle owl, with its pink eyelids, or a leopard chewing on its kill. Night is also the time when hyenas and lions hunt. These opportunities alone make a night drive an unforgettable experience. The three- to four-hour trip leaves the rest camps roughly half an hour before the gates close. ■ **TIP→ Book drives at least two weeks in advance or when you make your park reservations, and don't forget your binoculars, a snack or drink, and a warm jacket whatever the season.** ✉ *Kruger National Park* ☎ *012/428–9111 reservations* 🌐 *www.sanparks.org* 🎟 *Game drives start at R285 per adult; daily conservation fees are R440 per adult per day; Wild Cards (available at the gates or online) are more economical for stays of more than a few days.*

Hotels

HOTELS

★ Kruger Shalati: Train on a Bridge
$$$$ | ALL-INCLUSIVE | If you're looking for safari lodging that's the opposite of typical khaki trappings, the swanky suites at the Kruger Shalati sit aboard an ingeniously upcycled (and stationary) train that's been converted from 1950s coaches painstakingly collected from scrapyards across South Africa and suspended 15 meters (49 feet) above the sightings-rich Sabie River. **Pros:** excellent food options; breathtaking views; design-savvy interiors highlight South African talent. **Cons:** the train doesn't move; not for those with vertigo. [$] *Rooms from: R15900* ✉ *Skukuza, Skukuza* ☎ *013/591–6000* 🌐 *www.krugershalati.com* 🛏 *24 suites* 🍴 *All-Inclusive.*

★ Mdluli Safari Lodge
$$$ | HOTEL | Set in the fertile south of the Kruger National Park (near the Numbi Gate), this deluxe tented camp—think enormous infinity pool overlooking a water hole—has partnered with the local Mdluli Community (some 45,000 people that live adjacent to the Park) to help them earn back 2,100 acres of land inside the borders of the iconic Kruger that was seized by the government in 1967. **Pros:** underpriced relative to other exclusive lodges; community-empowerment and lovely lodge-style ambience; family-friendly resort and safe to walk the grounds. **Cons:** some tents are close together; it's big and can sleep 100 guests. [$] *Rooms from: R9720* ✉ *Mdluli Safari Lodge, Kruger National Park* ☎ *078/687–2546 reception, 087/980–0431 lodge* 🌐 *www.mdlulisafarilodge.co.za* 🛏 *50 suites* 🍴 *All-Inclusive.*

Protea Hotel by Marriott Kruger Gate
$$$ | HOTEL | FAMILY | Overlooking the Sabie River with quick access to the Kruger National Park, this sprawling hotel is large and somewhat impersonal but offers good-value accommodation in a

prime location when checking into the right room. **Pros:** air-conditioning, Wi-Fi, room service and other hotel creature comforts; easy and affordable proximity to Kruger; on-site spa that's easy on the pocket. **Cons:** game drives can be generic and not catered to individual interests; not all rooms renovated. *[$] Rooms from: R5900 ✉ Protea Hotel Kruger Gate, Skukuza ☎ 013/735–5671 lodge, 086/111–9000 central reservations 🌐 www.marriott.com/hotels/travel/mqp-kg-protea-hotel-kruger-gate 🛏 145 rooms 🍴 Free Breakfast ☞ includes buffet dinner, but game drives cost extra.*

PRIVATE GAME LODGES

★ Jock Safari Lodge

$$$$ | **RESORT** | This lodge, one of South Africa's loveliest, is set among 14,826 acres of private concession in southwest Kruger—the park's first with game-rich traversing rights as a result—with twelve comfortable, spacious suites, each with a plunge pool and stunning views over the Biyamiti River. **Pros:** riverfront location with private viewing deck; authentic safari experience. **Cons:** no tracker to assist the field guide (as is the case at other private lodges outside Kruger); busy in season. *[$] Rooms from: R20930 ✉ Jock Safari Lodge, Kruger National Park ☎ 041/509–3000 reservations, 041/509–3001 reservations 🌐 www.jocksafarilodge.com 🛏 12 rooms 🍴 All-Inclusive.*

★ RETURN Africa Pafuri Tented Camp

$$$ | **ALL-INCLUSIVE** | While the southern section of Kruger is prone to overtourism, this luxurious tented camp lies in the underrated and remote northern realm of the Kruger National Park and stretches for more than a kilometer along the banks of the winding Luvuvhu River. **Pros:** terrific biodiversity; community-empowerment initiatives; culturally-rich safari activities. **Cons:** accessible by road, but it's a long drive to get there; quite a big camp (can sleep 100 people when full). *[$] Rooms from: R14500 ✉ Kruger National Park ☎ 011/646–1391 🌐 www.returnafrica.com/escapes/pafuri-tented-camp/ 🛏 20 tents 🍴 All-Inclusive.*

Singita Lebombo Lodge

$$$$ | **RESORT** | Named for the nearby Lebombo mountain range, the breathtakingly beautiful Singita Lebombo—winner of numerous international accolades and eco-driven in concept—hangs on the edge of a cliff (inspired by eagle nests) with wooden walkways that connect the aptly named "lofts" (suites) seamlessly fusing the outdoor and indoor areas. **Pros:** brilliant bar with expert mixologists; on-site cooking school with cookings classes; great curio shop and spa; stunning avant-garde architecture and youthful feel. **Cons:** avoid if you prefer a traditional safari lodge; very pricey (rate excludes tourism and carbon offset levy). *[$] Rooms from: R69120 ✉ Kruger National Park ☎ 021/683–3424 reservations 🌐 www.singita.co.za 🛏 15 rooms 🍴 All-Inclusive.*

Singita Sweni Lodge

$$$$ | **RESORT** | More intimate than its sister camp, Lebombo, Sweni is built on wooden stilts with six huge river-facing suites glassed on three sides, wooden on the other. **Pros:** outdoor day beds transform to stargazing loungers; tiny and intimate; great location. **Cons:** all of Singita's properties are situated in malaria-risk areas; dim lighting. *[$] Rooms from: R69120 ✉ Kruger National Park ☎ 021/683–3424 reservations 🌐 www.singita.co.za 🛏 7 rooms 🍴 All-Inclusive.*

Activities

HIKING

You can take a morning or afternoon bushwalk from most of the Kruger rest camps to understand the smaller ecosystems at work, but for those with the time (and courage), Kruger's ten walking trails also offer the chance to experience a three-day, two-night hike. Led by an armed ranger and local tracker, you walk in the mornings and evenings, with an

Spotting Kruger's Big Game

Watching game in the bush is very different from watching it on the Discovery Channel with its nonstop action. The former demands energy, concentration, patience, and luck, and with these you'll probably see wonderful game at Kruger, including the Big Five. The easy (and most expensive) option is to stay at an all-inclusive lodge in a private game reserve, where knowledgeable rangers take you out in open vehicles or on foot and find game for you. If you're staying in self-catering accommodations inside the park or on its outskirts, you can sign up with an outfitter that specializes in game drives and likewise will find game for you (make sure they're SATSA bonded). Or, rent a vehicle and strike out on your own into Kruger's unknown territory. There's nothing quite like the thrill of finding your "own" elephant or identifying that psychedelic turquoise-and-lilac bird for yourself. Bring a couple of good field guides and a pair of binoculars, available at bookstores and Kruger camp shops.

Drive slowly, stop at water holes, and keep your eyes and ears open. Talk to other visitors, and read the "game sightings" notice board and visitor's book at each camp. If other vehicles are stopped on the road, be courteous. Don't drive in front or beside them and block their view, but edge along and find out what's being looked at. Don't forget to absorb the total bush experience—big and little creatures, trees, plants, sounds, colors, shapes, and smells. Look for the Little Five: the elephant shrew, lion ant, leopard tortoise, buffalo weaverbird, and rhinoceros beetle. You'll sometimes find these in camp along with hundreds of birds that are habituated to visitors, good for up-close pictures. Note that it's not advisable to self-drive through the park if you're a first-timer; not everyone knows what to do when a herd of elephants crosses the road in front of you.

■TIP→ **If you're a birder, it's a good idea to spend a morning or afternoon in camp when most visitors are out on a drive. You'll get great sightings.**

afternoon siesta, approximately 19 km (12 miles) a day.

There are two types to choose from. The Wilderness Trail is more slackpacking in design and departs each day from a fenced-in base camp. The Backpack Trail requires you to bring a tent and backpack to carry everything you need for three days of walking and wild camping from point A to point B.

Both trails encourage a sense of companionship among the group, which decides together on speed and length of walks, but this isn't about pushing endurance records. Many hikers can recount face-to-face encounters with everything from rhinos to lions. No one under 12 is allowed; those over 60 must have a doctor's certificate.

WILDERNESS TRAILS

Hikers sleep in rustic two-bed huts and share a bathroom (flush toilets, bucket showers). Meals are simple (stews and barbecues); you bring your own drinks. Summer is uncomfortably hot (and trails are cheaper), but nights can be freezing in winter—bring warm clothes and an extra blanket. Reservations must be made 13 months ahead; the cost is about R5600 per person per trail.

Bushmans Trail. In the southwestern corner of the park, this trail takes its name

How to Self-Drive Kruger National Park

Feeling overwhelmed? You're not to blame. The rambling Kruger National Park is like a country—smaller than Belgium and about the same area size as Israel or Slovenia.

You can absolutely drive yourself through Kruger, but if it's your first safari, there will be struggles. It's always best to get your bush bearings first at a lodge with experienced guides that know how to read animal behavior before striking out alone.

While it's not for the faint of heart, or a person who doesn't like to camp, there are several advantages to driving yourself through this iconic landscape. Experience the thrill of finding creatures with your own senses, unbounded freedom, and flexibility to take your time at sightings. Children can also make as much noise as they want (or grumpy teens can plunge into a device if they *have* to), and you'll still end the day absorbing quintessential African ambiance from your own campfire. It's also much kinder to the budget.

Step 1: Rent a vehicle. Most of the main roads are tarred, and driving is straightforward. You certainly don't need a 4WD vehicle, but high clearance is a helpful advantage to gain elevation over tall grass (especially after the rains in summer) to better spot all those animals. When choosing a rental, consider whether you want to camp or overnight in self-catering bungalows in the park. You can rent a fully equipped camper vehicle with all the boxes, bells, tents, and whistles for an unrestricted adventure. With two decades of safari expertise, the Johannesburg-based Bushtrackers 4x4 Rental can cater to every camping need with itinerary advice and booking, plus equipment rentals.

Step 2: Where to stay. Park your vehicle at a level site along Kruger's fence (Berg-en-Dal and Satara enjoy excellent outlooks) with direct views into the bush. Big mammals, such as elephants, rhinos, and even hyenas, are commonly seen through the wires. There is always a simple ablution block (bathrooms), washing up facilities, and access to camp luxuries, such as the pool or restaurants for a night off from cooking alfresco. The only downside? Having to pack up the house every time you want to go on a drive. ■TIP→ **Pack enough binoculars for everyone to enjoy that faraway sighting of a leopard in the distance. Remember, you cannot go off-road or leave your vehicle inside the park.**

Step 3: Plan your route. You cannot get from Berg-en-Dal to Satara in a day. Map the ideal Kruger circuit (give yourself at least three days) and bear in mind the 50 kmh (31 mph) speed limit. Always be generous with time allotments and allow for stops at picnic sites, unusual sightings, and bathroom breaks.

Step 4: Wake up early. The park gates open at dawn for a good reason. This is when those big toothy creatures are at their most active.

Bushtrackers 4x4 Rental. ⊠ *Bushtrackers Africa* ☎ *011/465–2559* ⊕ *www.bushtrackers.com.*

from the San rock paintings and sites found here; the camp is in a secluded valley. Watch for white rhinos, elephants, and buffalo. Check in at Berg-en-Dal.

Metsi Metsi Trail. The permanent water of the nearby N'waswitsontso River makes this one of the best trails for winter game-viewing. Midway between Skukuza and Satara, the trail camp is in the lee of a mountain in an area of gorges, cliffs, and rolling savanna. Check in at Skukuza.

Napi Trail. White rhino sightings are common on this trail, which runs through mixed bushveld between Pretoriuskop and Skukuza. Other possibilities are black rhinos, cheetahs, leopards, elephants, and if you're lucky, nomadic wild dogs. The camp is tucked into dense riverine forest at the confluence of the Napi and Biyamiti rivers. Check in at Pretoriuskop.

Nyalaland Trail. In the far north, this trail camp sits among ancient baobab trees near the Luvuvhu River and has the best birding in the park. Walk at the foot of huge rocky gorges and in dense forest. Hippos, crocs, elephants, buffalo, and the nyala antelope are almost a sure thing. Check in at Punda Maria.

Olifants Trail. This spectacularly sited camp sits on a high bluff overlooking the Olifants River and affords regular sightings of elephants, lions, buffalo, and hippos. The landscape varies from riverine forest to the rocky foothills of the Lebombo Mountains. Check in at Letaba.

Sweni Trail. East of Satara, this trail camp overlooks the Sweni Spruit and savanna. The area attracts large herds of zebras, wildebeests, and buffalo with their attendant predators: lions, spotted hyenas, and wild dogs. Check in at Satara.

Wolhuter Trail. You just might come face-to-face with a white rhino on this trail through undulating bushveld, interspersed with rocky kopjes, midway between Berg-en-Dal and Pretoriuskop.

Elephants, buffalo, and lions are also likely. Check in at Berg-en-Dal.

BACKPACK TRAILS

You'll need to bring all of your own supplies (and take out your own trash) for these four-night primitive trails. Guests are expected to provide their own camping equipment, gas stoves, and food. Fires are set up each night, but only for social and safety reasons, not cooking. The cost is about R3475 per person per trail.

Lonely Bull Trail. This is the most iconic and booked-up trail, which winds its way through Big Five country. Check in at Mopani.

Olifants River Trail. As the name implies, this route sticks to the productive shores of the "Elephant River." Expect towering riverine forests, fantastic birding, and perhaps even a dip in the rock pools. Check in at Olifants.

Mphongolo Trail. The newest hike in the park travails the more remote north, where Baobab trees signal the way. Check in at Shingwedzi.

Sabi Sands

The Sabi Sand Game Reserve, more commonly referred to as the Sabi Sands, is a grouping of private game reserves located in 153,000 acres along the border of Kruger National Park, each one featuring private lodges that offer the ultimate safari experience. This is where you'll find the world-famous MalaMala and Londolozi, among scores of other lodges that pamper their guests. Not only will you be treated to luxury accommodations—the kind you see in the glossy travel magazines—your rate includes safaris, chef-produced meals, and lots of personal touches.

As nice as it is to be pampered, you're here to see the wildlife. And Sabi Sands fully deserves its exalted reputation, boasting perhaps the highest game density of any private reserve in southern Africa. With an average of 20 vehicles watching for game and communicating by radio, you're bound to see an enormous amount of game and almost certainly the Big Five; since only three vehicles are allowed at a sighting at a time, you can be assured of a grandstand seat. Sabi Sands is the best area for leopard sightings. It's a memorable experience to see this beautiful, powerful, and often elusive cat padding purposefully through the bush at night, illuminated in your ranger's spotlight. There are many lion prides, and occasionally the increasingly rare wild dogs will migrate from Kruger to den in Sabi Sands. You'll also see white and black rhinos, zebras, giraffes, wildebeests, and most of the antelope species, plus birds galore.

The daily program at each of Sabi Sands' lodges rarely deviates from a pattern, starting with tea, coffee, and muffins or rusks (Boer biscuits) before an early-morning game drive (usually starting at dawn, later in winter). You return to the lodge around 10 am, at which point you dine on an extensive hot breakfast or brunch. You can then choose to go on a bush walk with an armed ranger, where you learn about some of the minutiae of the bush (including the Little Five), although you could also happen on giraffes, antelopes, or any one of the Big Five. But don't worry—you'll be well briefed in advance on what you should do if you come face-to-face with, say, a lion. The rest of the day, until the late-afternoon game drive, is spent at leisure—reading up on the bush in the camp library, snoozing, swimming, or having a spa treatment. A sumptuous afternoon tea is served at 3:30 or 4 before you head back into the bush for your night drive. During the drive, your ranger will find a peaceful spot for sundowners (cocktails), and you can sip the drink of your choice and nibble snacks as you watch one of Africa's spectacular sunsets. As darkness falls, your ranger will switch on the spotlight so you can spy nocturnal animals: lions, leopards, jackals, porcupines, servals (small spotted cats like bonsai leopards), civets, and the enchanting little bush babies. You'll return to the lodge around 7:30, in time to freshen up before a three- or five-course dinner, with at least one dinner in a *boma* (open-air dining area) around a blazing fire. Often the camp staff entertains after dinner with local songs and dances—an unforgettable experience. Children under 12 aren't typically allowed at some of the camps; others have great kids' programs.

GETTING HERE AND AROUND

Kruger Mpumalanga International Airport (KMIA), at Mbombela (Nelspruit), Skukuza Airport, and Hoedspruit Airport, close to Kruger's Orpen Gate, serve Sabi Sand Game Reserve. You can also drive yourself to the reserve and park at your lodge. Most lodges offer charter flights to and from Johannesburg.

VISITOR INFORMATION

CONTACTS Sabi Sand Game Reserve. ✉ *Sabi Sand Game Reserve* ☎ *013/735–5102* 🌐 *www.sabisand.co.za.*

Sabi Sand Game Reserve

Hotels

&Beyond Kirkman's Kamp

$$$$ | **RESORT** | **FAMILY** | You'll feel as if you've stepped back in time at this camp because rooms are strategically clustered around the original 1920s homestead, which, with its colonial furniture, historic memorabilia, and wraparound verandah, makes you feel like a family guest the moment you arrive. **Pros:** family-friendly; superb game-viewing; character-filled with unique artifacts. **Cons:** rooms close together (some share a patio with a divider); gets tour groups. [$] *Rooms from: R31700* ✉ *Kirkman's Kamp, Exeter Private Game Reserve* ☎ *011/809–4300*

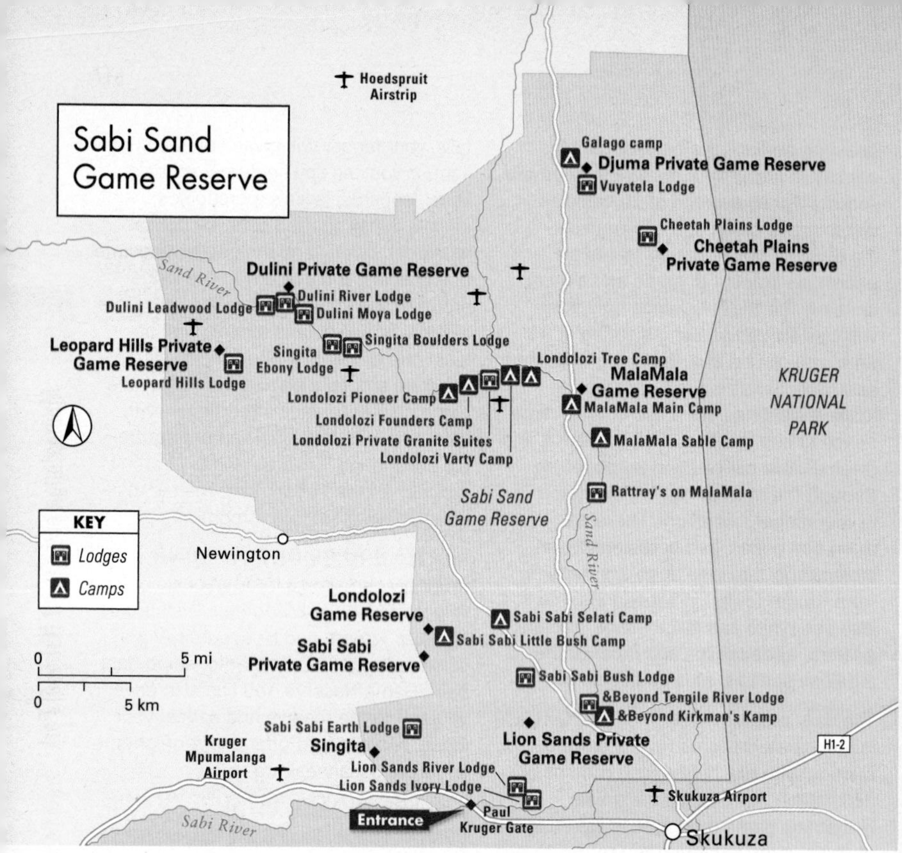
Sabi Sand Game Reserve
Hoedspruit Airstrip
Galago camp
Djuma Private Game Reserve
Vuyatela Lodge
Cheetah Plains Lodge
Cheetah Plains Private Game Reserve
Sand River
Dulini Private Game Reserve
Dulini River Lodge
Dulini Leadwood Lodge
Dulini Moya Lodge
Leopard Hills Private Game Reserve
Leopard Hills Lodge
Singita Boulders Lodge
Singita Ebony Lodge
Londolozi Tree Camp
MalaMala Game Reserve
MalaMala Main Camp
KRUGER NATIONAL PARK
Londolozi Pioneer Camp
Londolozi Founders Camp
Londolozi Private Granite Suites
Londolozi Varty Camp
MalaMala Sable Camp
Rattray's on MalaMala
Sabi Sand Game Reserve
KEY
Lodges
Camps
Newington
Sand River
Londolozi Game Reserve
Sabi Sabi Selati Camp
Sabi Sabi Little Bush Camp
Sabi Sabi Private Game Reserve
0
5 mi
0
5 km
Sabi Sabi Bush Lodge
&Beyond Tengile River Lodge
&Beyond Kirkman's Kamp
Sabi Sabi Earth Lodge
Kruger Mpumalanga Airport
Singita
Lion Sands Private Game Reserve
H1-2
Lion Sands River Lodge
Lion Sands Ivory Lodge
Skukuza Airport
Entrance
Paul Kruger Gate
Sabi River
Skukuza

reservations 🌐 www.andbeyond.com 🛏 12 rooms 🍴 All-Inclusive.

★ **&Beyond Tengile River Lodge**
$$$$ | **ALL-INCLUSIVE** | Set along the predator-dense Sand River, this exceptional lodge takes a refreshing step away from safari stereotypes—in lieu of khaki drapes and colonial heritage, Tengile embraces the riverine shadows and tones for its interior inspiration, prioritizes the luxury of space, and refines attention to detail. **Pros:** palatial riverfront suites; faultless service; complimentary Swarovski binoculars on drives. **Cons:** this will ruin every other safari experience; darker, contemporary interiors might not be to everyone's taste. [$] *Rooms from: R63250* ✉ *Tengile River Lodge* ☎ *011/809–4300* 🌐 *www.andbeyond.com* 🛏 *9 suites* 🍴 *All-Inclusive.*

Djuma Private Game Reserve

504 km (329 miles) from Johannesburg, via N12.

This 17,297-acre reserve sits right up against Kruger within the northeast corner of the world-famous Sabi Sand Game Reserve. Expect classic bushveld terrain—dams, rivers, ancient riverine trees, grassland, and plains. And because no fences separate Kruger from Sabi Sand—and therefore from Djuma as well—game wanders freely back and forth, offering you some of South Africa's best game-viewing. The Big Five are all here, plus hundreds of birds. You'll find none of the formality that sometimes prevails at the larger camps. For example, members of the staff eat all meals with you and join you around the nighttime fire. In fact, Djuma prides itself on its personal service and feeling of intimacy.

GETTING HERE AND AROUND

From Johannesburg it's approximately a seven-hour drive north to Hoedspruit via Dullstroom, Ohrigstad, and through the JG Strydom tunnel. Take the R531 to Klaserie and Acornhoek and follow the signs to Sabi Sand, Gowrie Gate. Djuma is signposted from there. You will drive yourself to the camp, and then go on safari in open game vehicles.

There are daily scheduled flights from Johannesburg to Skukuza Airport and Hoedspruit Airport, and Kruger Mpumalanga International Airport on Airlink (lodge transfers can be arranged), or you can fly in directly to one of the Sabi Sand airstrips by Federal Air charter flight.

Sights

Djuma Private Game Reserve

NATURE PRESERVE | **FAMILY** | Although there's a good chance of seeing the Big Five during the bush walk after breakfast and the twice-daily game drives, Djuma also caters to those with special bushveld interests, such as bird-watching or tree identification. Djuma's rangers and trackers are also adept at finding seldom-seen animals, such as wild dogs, spotted hyenas, and genets. ✉ *Djuma Private Game Reserve* ☎ *076/480-2173 reservations* 🌐 *www.djuma.com.*

Hotels

Galago

$$$$ | **HOUSE** | A delightful and affordable alternative to other upscale lodges, Galago, which means "lesser bush baby" in Shangaan, is a converted U-shaped farmhouse whose five rooms form an arc around a central fireplace. **Pros:** luxurious; exclusive experience. **Cons:** minimum three-night stay. [$] *Rooms from: R21000* ✉ *Djuma Private Game Reserve* ☎ *076/480–2173 reservations* 🌐 *www.djuma.com* 🛏 *3 rooms* 🍴 *No Meals.*

Vuyatela Lodge

$$$$ | **RESORT** | **FAMILY** | Djuma's vibey, most upscale camp mixes contemporary African township culture with modern Shangaan culture, making it very different from most of the other private camps. **Pros:** amazing African art; legendary hosts; ideal for extended family or group of friends. **Cons:** funky township style (corrugated iron, recycled metals, in-your-face glitzy township feel) may not be to everyone's taste. [$] *Rooms from: R28000* ✉ *Djuma Private Game Reserve* ☎ *076/480-2173 reservations* 🌐 *www.djuma.com* 🛏 *5 rooms* 🍴 *No Meals* ☞ *Rate is for entire house.*

Cheetah Plains Private Game Reserve

530 km (329 miles) from Johannesburg, via N12.

Set within the Sabi Sand Game Reserve and sandwiched between Kruger and MalaMala Game Reserve, Cheetah Plains enjoys traversing rights across celebrated Big Five territory, but that's not what makes this region special. Several underrated endangered specials roam the reserve. A safari here may offer a rare glimpse of honey badgers, ground hornbills, African wild dogs, and the namesake cheetah thanks to the varied habitats of grassland, plains, rivers, and established forests.

GETTING HERE AND AROUND

From Johannesburg it's approximately a seven-hour drive north to Hoedspruit via Dullstroom, Ohrigstad. and through the JG Strydom tunnel. Take the R531 to Klaserie and Acornhoek and follow the signs to Sabi Sand, Gowrie Gate. Cheetah Plains is signposted from there. You will drive yourself to the camp, and then go on safari in open game vehicles.

There are daily scheduled flights from Johannesburg to Skukuza Airport and Hoedspruit Airport, and Kruger Mpumalanga International Airport on Airlink (lodge transfers can be arranged), or you can fly in directly to one of the Sabi Sand airstrips by Federal Air charter flight.

 Hotels

★ Cheetah Plains

$$$$ | **ALL-INCLUSIVE** | First opened in 1993, the camp experienced an enormous makeover in 2018, and the property's private villas (each with four rooms) are an exquisite celebration of South African art, food, and nature masterfully marrying eco-friendly innovation with minimalist chic. **Pros:** expert sommelier advice; eco-friendly electric vehicles and off-the-grid lodge complex powered by solar panels; complimentary spa treatments. **Cons:** exclusive-use only; clean and minimal modern aesthetic not for everyone. $ *Rooms from: R130000* ✉ *Cheetah Plains* ☎ *079/694–8430* ⊕ *www.cheetahplains.com* ➦ *3 exclusive-use houses* ⦿ *All-Inclusive.*

Leopard Hills Private Game Reserve

Perched in the western realm of Sabi Sand Game Reserve near Kruger National Park, this private game reserve is, of course, an excellent place to spot its namesake animal, the elusive leopard. But you'll spot plenty of other big game here as well. Leopard Hills Lodge offers elegant accommodations and gourmet dining, though its hilltop perch overlooking a natural water hole is what most guests talk about.

 Hotels

Leopard Hills Lodge

$$$$ | **RESORT** | Renowned for its relaxed and informal atmosphere, Leopard Hills is one of the premier game lodges in the Sabi Sands area. **Pros:** spacious suites; many rangers are expert photographers and offer great shooting tips; very experienced and knowledgeable owners/managers. **Cons:** bit of a steep climb to the top of the hill and the main areas. $ *Rooms from: R39600* ✉ *Leopard Hills Private Game Reserve* ☎ *013/735–5142 lodge, 011/326–0739 reservations* ⊕ *www.leopardhills.com* ➦ *8 suites* ⦿ *All-Inclusive.*

Lion Sands Private Game Reserve

458 km (284 miles) from Johannesburg.

Separated from Kruger National Park by the Sabie River, this reserve has one of the best locations in the Sabi Sand Game Reserve. Purchased in 1933 by the More family as a family retreat, it was opened to the public in 1978 with two lodges and 10,000 acres of undisturbed wildlife that's available only to its guests. The family is so committed to keeping the reserve as close to its original state as possible that they employ a full-time ecologist, the only reserve in the Sabi Sands group to do so. Among its various accommodations are the ultraluxe Ivory Lodge and the relatively more economical River Lodge. There's also the once-in-a-lifetime Chalkleys Treehouse (yes, it really is a bed on a platform in a tree, but it's nothing like the treehouse in your backyard), the once-in-a-lifetime Narina Lodge, the spacious Tinga Lodge, and the Hi'Nkweni Villa, that's perfect for larger groups and comes complete with a personal chef, guide, pool, gym, and wine cellar.

GETTING HERE AND AROUND

If you're coming by car from Hazyview, turn right onto the R536 toward Paul Kruger Gate (Kruger National Park). After 38 km (23 miles), turn left onto a gravel road signposted to Lion Sands, Sabi Sand. At the T-junction, turn right and enter Sabi Sand through Shaw's Gate. Then follow directions to the lodges. There's a vehicle entrance fee of R310 plus R140 per person into the Sabi Sand Reserve, payable on arrival by cash or credit card. The gates close at 10 pm. You can drive yourself to the lodges, but you'll have to park your car and leave it, because while you're at the lodge, you'll be driven around in an open game vehicle.

There are scheduled flights from Johannesburg, Durban, and Cape Town to Skukuza Airport and Kruger Mpumalanga International Airport on Airlink. Lodge transfers can be arranged and all lodges sit within 12 km (7 miles) of Skukuza Airport.

Sights

★ Lion Sands Private Game Reserve

NATURE SIGHT | All of the lodges overlook the river, which is a magnet for all kinds of game. You'll be able to peer into Kruger National Park, on the other side of the river, and watch game meander along the riverbanks among big riverine trees. You may never want to leave your personal deck, or the big viewing decks. But when you do decide to leave your perch, you have all kinds of options for activities, including game drives and walking safaris, spa treatments, and yoga beneath the African sun. ✉ *Lion Sands Private Game Reserve* ☎ *010/109–4900* 🌐 *www.more.co.za/lionsands.*

Hotels

★ Lion Sands Ivory Lodge

$$$$ | **RESORT** | Ivory Lodge offers the ultimate in luxury, privacy, and relaxation. **Pros:** exclusivity; great views; brilliant game-viewing. **Cons:** the temptation of abundant great food—it's so decadent, you might forget to leave. [$] *Rooms from: R67040* ✉ *Lion Sands Private Game Reserve* ☎ *031/735–5000 lodge, 010/109–4900 head office and reservations* 🌐 *www.more.co.za/lionsands/ivory-lodge* 🛏 *9 rooms* 🍴 *All-Inclusive* ☞ *No children under 10 years old.*

Lion Sands River Lodge

$$$$ | **RESORT** | Set on one of the longest and best stretches of river frontage in Sabi Sand, you can watch the passing animal and bird show from your deck or from the huge, tree-shaded, wooden viewing area that juts out over the riverbank facing Kruger National Park. **Pros:** well managed; combinable rooms for families; fabulous river frontage. **Cons:** some chalets quite close together so not much privacy. [$] *Rooms from: R3620* ✉ *Lion Sands Private Game Reserve* ☎ *013/735–5000 lodge, 010/109–4900 head office and reservations* 🌐 *www.more.co.za/lionsands/river-lodge* 🛏 *21 rooms* 🍴 *All-Inclusive* ☞ *No children under 10 years old.*

Londolozi Game Reserve

471 km (292 miles) from Johannesburg.

Established as a family farm and retreat in 1926, Londolozi today is synonymous with South Africa's finest game lodges and game experiences. (*Londolozi* is the Zulu word for "protector of all living things.") Dave and John Varty, grandsons of the original owner, Charles Varty, put the reserve on the map with glamorous marketing and a vision of style and comfort that their grandfather never could never have imagined. Now younger generation, brother-and-sister team Bronwyn and Boyd Varty are carrying on their family's quest to honor the animal kingdom. Game abounds; the Big Five are all here, and the leopards of Londolozi are world-famous. There are five camps, each representing a step in the story of this iconic reserve: Varty Camp (the heart and original stay), Pioneer Camp (a tribute to early intrepid settlers), Founders Camp (a family affair), Tree Camp (looks to the rise of leopards) and Granite Suites (for the elephants and dropped fences that widened their home range into the Kruger National Park). Each is totally private, hidden in dense riverine forest on the banks of the Sand River. The Varty family lives on the property, and their friendliness and personal attention, along with the many staff who have been here for decades, will make you feel part of the family immediately. The central reception, gym, photographic studio and curio shop are at Varty Camp and all camps are within walking distance.

GETTING HERE AND AROUND

Londolozi is an easy six-hour drive from Johannesburg on the NM12 and N4. Turn right onto R536 from Hazyview toward Paul Kruger Gate. After 37.4 km (23 miles) turn left onto a gravel road signposted "Sabi Sand Wildtuin Shaw's Gate."

There are regular scheduled flights from Johannesburg, Durban, and Cape Town to Skukuza Airport and Kruger Mpumalanga International Airport on Airlink (lodge transfers can be arranged), or you can fly in directly to the Londolozi airstrip by Federal Air charter flight.

Sights

★ Londolozi Game Reserve

NATURE PRESERVE | Each of the five camps offers unprecedented access to 34,000 acres of Africa's best Big Five game-viewing, led by renowned rangers and trackers. The camp is most famous for its leopards, with which its rangers and trackers have forged an intimate relationship over the decades. Leopard sightings are frequent. ✉ *Londolozi Reserve* ☎ *010/109–2968 reservations, 013/735–5653 lodge* 🌐 *www.londolozi.com.*

Hotels

Founders Camp

$$$$ | **RESORT** | **FAMILY** | This inviting camp has 10 stone-and-thatch suites in individual chalets set amid thick riverine bush; some chalets are linked by interconnecting skywalks, which is great for families or groups traveling together (children six years and older are welcome). **Pros:** quick, safe access between family rooms; children over four welcome. **Cons:** lodges are in quite close proximity to one another. [$] *Rooms from: R43890* ✉ *Londolozi Reserve* ☎ *010/109-2968 reservations, 013/735–5653 lodge* 🌐 *www.londolozi.com* 🛏 *10 rooms* 🍴 *All-Inclusive.*

Pioneer Camp

$$$$ | **RESORT** | The most secluded of all of Londolozi's camps, Pioneer's three private suites overlook the river and are perfect for getting away from others. **Pros:** most private of all Londolozi lodgings; only three suites; authentic romantic-safari atmosphere. **Cons:** with only three suites it's best if you know all other guests. [$] *Rooms from: R63250* ✉ *Londolozi Reserve* ☎ *010/109–2968 reservations, 013/735–5653 lodge* 🌐 *www.londolozi.com* 🛏 *3 rooms* 🍴 *All-Inclusive* ☞ *No children under 6 years old.*

Private Granite Suites

$$$$ | **RESORT** | Book all three private suites or just hide yourself away from the rest of the world like the celebrities and royals who favor this gorgeous getaway. **Pros:** one of the best locations in Sabi Sands with truly stunning views; the candelit dinner. **Cons:** pricey. $ *Rooms from: R66990* ✉ *Londolozi Reserve* ☎ *010/109–2968 reservations, 013/735–5100 lodge* ⊕ *www.londolozi.com* ➷ *3 rooms* ⦿ *All-Inclusive* ⌒ *No children under 16 years old.*

★ Tree Camp

$$$$ | RESORT | The first Relais & Chateaux game lodge in the world, this gorgeous camp (think leopards, lanterns, leadwoods, and leopard orchids) is tucked into the riverbank overlooking indigenous forest. **Pros:** the viewing deck; state-of-the-art designer interiors. **Cons:** stylishness nudges out coziness. $ *Rooms from: R63250* ✉ *Londolozi Reserve* ☎ *010/109–2968 reservations, 013/735–5653 lodge* ⊕ *www.londolozi.com* ➷ *6 rooms* ⦿ *All-Inclusive* ⌒ *Children under 16 not allowed.*

Varty Camp

$$$$ | RESORT | FAMILY | This camp's fire has been burning for more than nine decades, making Varty Camp the very soul and center of Londolozi. **Pros:** friendly atmosphere; great game; gym, photographic studio and healing house on-site. **Cons:** lots of kids might not be for you. $ *Rooms from: R37290* ✉ *Londolozi Reserve* ☎ *010/109–2968 reservations, 013/735–5653 lodge* ⊕ *www.londolozi. com* ➷ *10 rooms* ⦿ *All-Inclusive.*

MalaMala Game Reserve

455 km (283 miles) from Johannesburg.

This legendary game reserve (designated as such in 1929) is tops in its field. MalaMala constitutes one of the largest privately owned Big Five game areas in South Africa and includes an unfenced 19-km (12-mile) boundary with Kruger National Park, across which game crosses continuously. The first and only community-owned game reserve in Sabi Sands, it is run by a management company in partnership with the N'wandlamharhi Community.

The property includes 21 km (13 miles) of river frontage, providing a lush environment that makes the game viewing perhaps unsurpassed in Africa. The big cat sightings, of lion and leopard in particular, are what makes MalaMala worth every cent.

You'll be delighted with good personal service, tasty food, and discreetly elegant, comfortable accommodations. Rooms are understated from the outside, in traditional African huts, but inside are spacious, contemporary and luxurious. Both the outstanding hospitality and the game-viewing experience keep guests coming back.

GETTING HERE AND AROUND

MalaMala Game Reserve is approximately a six-hour drive from Johannesburg via N12 and N4. From Hazyview, take the R536 toward Skukuza and the Paul Kruger Gate.

After 37½ km (23 miles) turn left onto a dirt road at the MalaMala sign and follow this road for 3 km (1.8 miles).

At the T-junction, turn right and continue for another 4.2 km (2.6 miles) to Shaw's Gate, the entrance to the Sabi Sands Game Reserve, where you will need to pay a reserve entrance fee. From here, follow the signs to the MalaMala camp you are staying at.

There are daily flights on SA Airlink from Cape Town and Johannesburg (and less frequently from Durban) to Skukuza in the Kruger National Park. MalaMala will transfer you to the lodge, about an hour's drive away. This is the best flying option, as it is an easy transfer and is about half the price of a Fedair flight directly to the lodge.

There are also daily scheduled flights from Johannesburg, Durban, and Cape Town to Kruger Mpumalanga International Airport, about 1½ hours on SA Airlink (lodge transfers can be arranged), or you can fly in directly to the MalaMala airstrip by Fedair charter flight.

Sights

★ MalaMala Private Game Reserve

NATURE PRESERVE | MalaMala's animal-viewing statistics are unbelievable: the Big Five are spotted almost every day, along with plenty of other amazing viewings. At one moment your ranger will fascinate you with the description of the sex life of a dung beetle, as you watch the sturdy male battling his way along the road pushing his perfectly round ball of dung with wife-to-be perched perilously on top; at another, your adrenaline will flow as you follow a leopard stalking impala in the gathering gloom. The rangers are top-class and will ensure that your game experience is unforgettable. ✉ *Mala Mala Game Reserve* ☎ *011/442–2267 reservations* 🌐 *www.malamala.com.*

Hotels

★ MalaMala Main Camp

$$$$ | **RESORT** | Stone and thatch air-conditioned rondavels with two bathrooms and an outside shower are decorated in creams and browns and luxuriously furnished with natural finishes like copper and wood, colorful handwoven tapestries and rugs, terra-cotta floors, and original artwork. **Pros:** amazing game-viewing; sweeping wilderness views; authentic. **Cons:** rondavels are a bit old-fashioned, but that goes with the ambience. [$] *Rooms from: R32000* ✉ *Mala Mala Game Reserve* ☎ *011/442–2267 reservations, 013/735–9200 MalaMala Main Camp* 🌐 *www.malamala.com* 🛏 *17 rooms* 🍴 *All-Inclusive.*

★ MalaMala Sable Camp

$$$$ | **ALL-INCLUSIVE** | This exclusive camp with seven ultra-luxurious suites lies at the southern end of Main Camp and overlooks the Sand River and surrounding bushveld. **Pros:** unparalleled game-viewing; privacy guaranteed; small and intimate. **Cons:** you might like it so much you never want to leave. [$] *Rooms from: R37000* ✉ *Mala Mala Game Reserve* ☎ *011/442–2267 reservations, 013/735–9200 MalaMala Sable Camp* 🌐 *www.malamala.com* 🛏 *7 rooms* 🍴 *All-Inclusive.*

★ Rattray's Camp

$$$$ | **RESORT** | The breathtakingly beautiful Rattray's Camp merges original bushveld style with contemporary African luxury. **Pros:** tantalizing views over the river; superb game-viewing; an exclusive feel. **Cons:** though this may be a pro for some, no children under 16; some might find the villas overly opulent. [$] *Rooms from: R43000* ✉ *Mala Mala Game Reserve* ☎ *011/442–2267 reservations, 013/735–3000 Rattray's Camp* 🌐 *www.malamala.com* 🛏 *8 rooms* 🍴 *All-Inclusive.*

Sabi Sabi Private Game Reserve

500 km (310 miles) from Johannesburg.

Founded in 1978 at the southern end of Sabi Sand, the multi-award-winning Sabi Sabi Private Game Reserve was one of the first reserves to offer photo safaris and to link ecotourism, conservation, and community. Superb accommodations and abundant game lure guests back to Sabi Sabi in large numbers. There are four very different lodges, each individually remarkable: Bush Lodge, famous for its friendly hospitality and ever-busy water hole; Little Bush Camp, an intimate, back-to-nature tented camp; Selati, haunt of celebs and royalty, themed on an old Kruger National Park railway line; and the daringly innovative Earth Lodge.

GETTING HERE AND AROUND

Sabi Sabi is an easy six-hour drive from Johannesburg on the N4 and N12. Turn right onto R536 from Hazyview toward Paul Kruger Gate. After 37.4 km (23 miles) turn left onto a gravel road signposted "Sabi Sand Wildtuin Shaw's Gate." There are scheduled flights from

Johannesburg, Durban, and Cape Town to Skukuza Airport and Kruger Mpumalanga International Airport on Airlink (lodge transfers can be arranged), or you can fly in directly to a Sabi Sand airstrip by Federal Air charter flight.

Sights

★ Sabi Sabi Private Game Reserve

NATURE PRESERVE | Daily game drives take place in the early morning and late afternoon. There's a strong emphasis on ecology at Sabi Sabi: guests are encouraged to look beyond the Big Five and to become aware of the birds and smaller mammals of the bush. You can also take a luxury walking safari or a specialist birding or photo safari. There's also the Amani Spa, as well as stargazing in the evenings. ✉ *Sabi Sand Game Reserve* ☎ *011/447–7172 reservations* 🌐 *www.sabisabi.com.*

Hotels

Sabi Sabi Bush Lodge

$$$$ | **RESORT** | **FAMILY** | Bush Lodge overlooks a busy water hole (lions are frequent visitors) and the dry course of the Msuthlu River. **Pros:** always prolific game around the lodge; roomy chalets. **Cons:** big and busy might not be your idea of a relaxing getaway. [$] *Rooms from: R32000* ✉ *Sabi Sand Game Reserve* ☎ *013/735–5656 reservations, 013/110–0134 lodge* 🌐 *www.sabisabi.com* 🛏 *25 rooms* 🍴 *All-Inclusive.*

Sabi Sabi Earth Lodge

$$$$ | **RESORT** | This avant-garde, eco-friendly lodge was the first to break away from the traditional safari style and strive for a contemporary theme. **Pros:** stunning architecture and design. **Cons:** if you favor traditonal safari accommodations, this is not for you. [$] *Rooms from: R48000* ✉ *Sabi Sand Game Reserve* ☎ *013/735–5261 lodge, 011/447–7172 reservations* 🌐 *www.sabisabi.com* 🛏 *13 rooms* 🍴 *All-Inclusive.*

Sabi Sabi Little Bush Camp

$$$$ | **RESORT** | **FAMILY** | Sabi Sabi's delightful little camp is tucked away in the bushveld on the banks of the Msuthlu River and combines spaciousness with a sense of intimacy. **Pros:** solo travellers don't suffer single supplement fees; private viewing deck and heated spa bath; perfect for families. **Cons:** there may be other families. [$] *Rooms from: R34000* ✉ *Sabi Sand Game Reserve* ☎ *011/447–7172 reservations, 013/735–5080 lodge* 🌐 *www.sabisabi.com* 🛏 *6 rooms* 🍴 *All-Inclusive.*

★ Sabi Sabi Selati Camp

$$$$ | **RESORT** | For an *Out of Africa* experience and great game, you can't beat Selati, an intimate, stylish, colonial-style camp that was formerly the private hunting lodge of a famous South African opera singer. **Pros:** unique atmosphere; Ivory Presidential Suite superb value for money; secluded and intimate. **Cons:** some old-timers preferred the camp when it was just lantern-lit with no electricity. [$] *Rooms from: R34000* ✉ *Sabi Sand Game Reserve* ☎ *011/447–7172 reservations, 013/735–5771 lodge* 🌐 *www.sabisabi.com* 🛏 *8 rooms* 🍴 *All-Inclusive.*

Singita

450 km (279 miles) from Johannesburg.

The Bailes family has overseen Singita (Shangaan for "the miracle") since 1926. Located on more than 45,000 acres of private bushland in the greater Kruger area, it has no fences between the parks, so wildlife can stroll freely back and forth as they wish. Although Singita offers much of the same thrilling Sabi Sand bush and game experiences as other camps, superb service really puts it head and shoulders above many of the rest of the herd. Its two lodges, Singita Boulders and Singita Ebony, are modern and stylish, with all the rugged luxury you'll ever need. Among the perks: a resident sommelier (wine can be shipped home), a variety of public spaces (little private dining nooks to a huge viewing deck built round an ancient jackalberry tree), and an attractive poolside bar. In 1998, Singita Sabi Sand established a partnership with the local community, providing support for education and other programs. The group has prioritized wellness and sustainability across the collection.

GETTING HERE AND AROUND
Singita is an easy 6½-hour drive from Johannesburg on the N4 and N12. Turn right onto R536 from Hazyview toward Paul Kruger Gate. After 37.4 km (23 miles), turn left at the sign that reads "Sabi Sand Wildtuin Shaw's Gate" onto a gravel road. Follow the signs for Singita. Singita will arrange scheduled flights or private charters for your trip. All flights land at Singita's airstrip, 10 minutes from the lodge.

Sights

★ Singita Sabi Sand
NATURE PRESERVE | This is the crème de la crème of the Sabi Sands (although you pay for it). At Singita, you'll head out during the day on your choice of game drives, then prepare to be pampered. Whether you fancy a starlit private supper or just chilling alone in your mega-suite, you've only to ask. Forget the usual lodge curio shop and take a ride to the on-site boutique and gallery where objets d'art, handmade jewelry, classy bush gear, and artifacts from all over Africa are clustered together in a series of adjoining rooms that seem more like a curator's home than a shop. ✉ *Singita Sabi Sand* ☎ *021/683–3424 reservations* 🌐 *www.singita.co.za.*

Hotels

Singita Ebony Lodge
$$$$ | **RESORT** | **FAMILY** | If Ernest Hemingway had built his ideal home in the African bush, this would be it. **Pros:** cozy library; children are welcome; the mother lodge of all the Singita properties. **Cons:** the beds are very high off the ground—if you have short legs or creak a bit, ask for a stool. [$] *Rooms from: R69120* ✉ *Singita Sabi Sand* ☎ *021/683–3424 reservations* 🌐 *www.singita.co.za* 🛏 *12 rooms* 🍴 *All-Inclusive.*

★ Singita Boulders Lodge
$$$$ | **RESORT** | Overlooking the beautiful Sand River, Singita Boulders Lodge intermingles the wildness of its setting among boulders with traditional Africa decor at its most luxurious. **Pros:** spacious accommodations; superb food. **Cons:** a bit of a walk from some suites to the main lodge. [$] *Rooms from: R65900* ✉ *Singita Sabi Sand* ☎ *021/683–3424 reservations* 🌐 *www.singita.co.za* 🛏 *12 rooms* 🍴 *All-Inclusive.*

Dulini Private Game Reserve

500 km (310 miles) from Johannesburg.

Established in 1937, Dulini (formerly called Exeter), at 160,600 acres, was an original part of Sabi Sands when it was incorporated in the 1960s.

GETTING HERE AND AROUND
Dulini is about a five- to six-hour drive from Johannesburg. Charter flights from Johannesburg land at the Ulusaba Airstrip, which is near the reserve's lodges. Transfers can also be arranged from other nearby airports with regular flights. The lodges generally arrange your transportation.

Hotels

★ Dulini Leadwood Lodge
$$$$ | ALL-INCLUSIVE | Leadwood is the smallest lodge of the Dulini collection with just four sultry suites generously spaced across the confluence of the Mabrak and Sand Rivers. **Pros:** impressively attentive service; sophisticated and intimate atmosphere; small size. **Cons:** rates exclude spa treatments. [$] *Rooms from: R39900* ✉ *Dulini, Dulini* ☎ *011/792–4927* 🌐 *www.dulini.com* 🛏 *4 suites* 🍴 *All-Inclusive.*

Dulini Moya Lodge
$$$$ | ALL-INCLUSIVE | Previously Dulini Private Game Lodge, the reimagined Dulini Moya Lodge comprises six stone bungalows catering to a maximum of just 12 guests in prime game-viewing territory. **Pros:** likely to spot the Big Five quickly so you'll have time to enjoy the lodge; light, fresh and imaginative meals; rewarding experience even for safari regulars. **Cons:** children are welcome, but the adult elegance is not kid-friendly. [$] *Rooms from: R39900* ✉ *Dulini* ☎ *011/792–4927 reservations* 🌐 *www.dulini.com* 🛏 *6 rooms* 🍴 *All-Inclusive.*

Dulini River Lodge
$$$$ | RESORT | One of Sabi Sand's oldest lodges, Dulini River Lodge scores 10 out of 10 for its gorgeous location—one of the best in the whole reserve—with lush green lawns sweeping down to the Sand River. **Pros:** genuine African-bush ambience and unbeatable setting; seriously spacious suites; on-site gym for fitness plus fresh and healthy cuisine. **Cons:** shares traversing rights with other lodges; situated in a more crowded part of Sabi Sands. [$] *Rooms from: R39900* ✉ *Exeter Private Game Reserve* ☎ *011/792–4927 reservations, 013/735-2000 lodge* 🌐 *www.dulini.com* 🛏 *6 rooms* 🍴 *All-Inclusive.*

West of Kruger

Manyeleti, Timbavati, Thornybush, and Kapama, along with a couple of other smaller game reserves, all lie north of Sabi Sand Game Reserve, but also border Kruger's western boundary. Although the reserves are less well known, they offer much the same game experiences, often at more affordable prices. The best-known ones are Manyeleti and Timbavati with lovely lodges set among typical bushveld, both adjoining Kruger, so you stand a good chance of seeing the Big Five and lots more. A big bonus is that because they are less frequently visited and have fewer lodges than Sabi Sand, there are fewer people and fewer vehicles. Some lodges have no electricity, so no email or Internet, but this will free you from the pressures of everyday life.

Manyeleti Private Game Reserve

502 km (311 miles) from Johannesburg.

North of Sabi Sand, Manyeleti Private Game Reserve ("the place of the stars" in Shangaan) covers 59,280 acres that border Kruger, Sabi Sand, and Timbavati, but it's something of a Cinderella reserve compared with its more famous neighbors; during apartheid, this was the only wildlife reserve where non-whites were welcome. Away from the major tourist areas, Manyeleti is amazingly underused; you'll probably see very few vehicles while you're here. There are only three lodges operating concessions in the reserve (as opposed to the 20 or so in Sabi Sand).

GETTING HERE AND AROUND

Travel north from Johannesburg on the N12 to Ohrigstad and continue toward Hoedspruit via the Abel Erasmus Pass and the JG Strijdom Tunnel. Cross the Blyde River, and turn right at the R531 to the Orpen Gate sign. Turn left here and continue until you see the Manyeleti Reserve sign.

There are daily scheduled flights from Johannesburg to Hoedspruit Airport by SA Express. There are also daily scheduled flights from Johannesburg, Durban, and Cape Town to Skukuza Airport and Kruger Mpumalanga International Airport on SA Airlink (lodge transfers can be arranged).

Sights

Manyeleti Game Reserve
NATURE PRESERVE | The park's grassy plains and mixed woodland attract good-size herds of general game and their attendant predators. This is a provincial reserve (as opposed to a national park) and comprises two sections. The government-operated side is open to self-drivers and offers rustic self-catering camps and the Manyeleti Private Game Reserve operates as a concession with more comfortable and upmarket private lodges. You have a strong chance of seeing the Big Five, but the Manyeleti lodges and tented camps, which are owned and operated by two separate companies (one for the lodge, one for the tented camps), focus more on providing an overall bush experience than simply rushing after big game. You'll learn about trees, birds, and bushveld ecosystems as you go on guided bush walks. ✉ *Manyeleti Game Reserve* ☎ 🌐 *www.manyeleti.com.*

Hotels

Honeyguide Khoka Moya
$$$$ | **RESORT** | **FAMILY** | This delightful, value-priced camp owned and operated by Honeyguide is situated on both sides of a riverbed within Manyeleti Private Game Reserve. **Pros:** excellent value for money; great kids' programs. **Cons:** plain decor; usually lots of kids around so stay away if that's not your thing; no air-conditioning. $ *Rooms from: R11000* ✉ *Manyeleti Game Reserve* ☎ *021/424-3122 reservations, 063/812-2857 lodge* 🌐 *www.honeyguidecamp.com* 🛏 *15 rooms* 🍴 *All-Inclusive.*

Honeyguide Mantobeni Camp
$$$$ | **RESORT** | This tented camp, built on wooden platforms, minimalist but with surprising luxury touches (owned and operated by Honeyguide within Manyeleti Private Game Reserve), gives you the total bush experience at half the price of some of the more upscale lodges. **Pros:** great for solo travellers with minimal supplement fee; superb value for money; complimentary bar and well-stocked wine cellar. **Cons:** very comfortable but far from five-star; Wi-Fi at main area only; canvas structure may not be to everyone's taste. $ *Rooms from: R11000* ✉ *Manyeleti Game Reserve* ☎ *021/424–3122 reservations, 063/812–2857 lodge* 🌐 *www.honeyguidecamp.com* 🛏 *15 rooms* 🍴 *All-Inclusive.*

Tintswalo Safari Lodge
$$$$ | **RESORT** | This gorgeous ultraluxurious lodge, sited under huge jackalberry and fig trees, overlooks a seasonal river, where game (elephants especially) come down to drink and bathe. **Pros:** suites overlook water hole; kids' program on request; drop-dead luxury. **Cons:** potentially over-attentive staff (if there is such a thing). $ *Rooms from: R28500* ✉ *Manyeleti Game Reserve* ☎ *021/773-0900 reservations, 015/15 793 9013 lodge* 🌐 *www.tintswalo.com* 🛏 *9 rooms* 🍴 *All-Inclusive.*

Timbavati Private Game Reserve

515 km (320 miles) from Johannesburg.

The 185,000-acre Timbavati, the northernmost of the private reserves, is a collection of smaller private reserves managed by the Timbavati Association, a nonprofit organization that strives to conserve the biodiversity of the area. The association was established in 1956, and with the removal of fences between the member reserves and Kruger National Park, wild animals roam freely between the reserves. The name, "Timbavati," means "the place where something sacred came down to Earth from the Heavens," referring to the rare white lions that reside here. Ngala ("lion" in Tsonga) and Motswari game reserves have been amalgamated into Timbavati.

A wide selection of lodging options are available, including the popular Ngala Safari Lodge, Ngala Tented Safari Camp, and Tanda Tula Safari Camp.

GETTING HERE AND AROUND

Travel north from Johannesburg on the N12 to Ohrigstad and continue toward Hoedspruit via the Abel Erasmus Pass and the J. G. Strijdom Tunnel. Drive through Hoedspruit and take the R40 to Klaserie. Turn left at the Timbavati/ East Gate signs. Go through the security gate, and drive straight for 17 km (10½ miles), cross the Klaserie River, and enter through the Timbavati Control Gate. Roads can be rough in the reserve, particularly in the rainy season, so a high clearance vehicle is recommended.

There are scheduled flights from Johannesburg to Hoedspruit Airport, and from Johannesburg, Durban, and Cape Town to Skukuza Airport and Kruger Mpumalanga International Airport on Airlink (lodge transfers can be arranged).

Sights

Timbavati Game Reserve

NATURE PRESERVE | Regardless of which lodge you're staying at, you'll be treated to wildlife-rich game drives with wall-to-wall game. You'll most certainly see the King of Beasts, as well as leopards, elephants, buffalo, and spotted hyenas. Rhinos are scarcer, but you might be lucky and see wild dogs, as they migrate regularly to this region from Kruger. The most amazing sighting, however, for which this reserve is famous, is the exceptionally rare white lion. ✉ *Timbavati Game Reserve* 🌐 *www.timbavati.co.za.*

Hotels

Ngala Safari Lodge

$$$$ | **RESORT** | **FAMILY** | Guests return again and again to this classic safari lodge with its timeless *Out of Africa* ambience. **Pros:** superb game and exclusive traversing rights across 36,000 acres; great kids' programs; nostalgic safari feel. **Cons:** kids dine with adults; no riverfront views from the room. [$] *Rooms from: R23800* ☎ *011/809–4300 reservations* 🌐 *andbeyond.com* 🛏 *21 rooms* 🍴 *All-Inclusive.*

★ Ngala Tented Safari Camp

$$$$ | **RESORT** | Marula seeds softly falling on the tents seem to be applauding this gorgeous little camp shaded by a canopy of giant trees. **Pros:** treehouse sleepout experience within easy reach; exclusivity. **Cons:** if you're nervous of too-close game, this is not for you, as hippos (and other game) wander freely around the tents. [$] *Rooms from: R28750* ☎ *011/809–4300 reservations* 🌐 *www.andbeyond.com* 🛏 *9 rooms* 🍴 *All-Inclusive.*

★ Tanda Tula Safari Camp

$$$$ | **RESORT** | Tanda Tula has a well-deserved reputation as one of the best bush camps in Mpumalanga. **Pros:** moonlit bush barbecues; exceptional attention to detail (such as hot chocolate after game drive); emphasis on the whole bush experience, not just the Big Five. **Cons:** no air-conditioning. [$] *Rooms from: R28970* ☎ *015/793–3191* 🌐 *www.tandatula.com* 🛏 *12 rooms* 🍴 *All-Inclusive.*

Thornybush Nature Reserve

504 km (313 miles) from Johannesburg.

Situated within 34,594 acres of pristine wilderness, adjacent to the Greater Kruger National Park in Limpopo, Thornybush Nature Reserve is set among classic bushveld scenery. There are plenty of comfortable, unpretentious lodges offering friendly service, excellent food, and great game, including the original Thornybush Game Lodge. Thornybush was one of the first Lowveld reserves to implement rhino horn treatments (injecting poison that is harmless to the rhinos) as a form of anti-poaching (some disproven but popular traditional Asian medical treatments use rhino horn), and one of the first to introduce elephant contraception as an alternative to culling.

GETTING HERE AND AROUND

Take the R40 from Hazyview to Acornhoek. Turn right after 7.4 km (4.6 miles) and take the Guernsey turnoff. Check in at the security gate, drive approximately 11 km (6.8 miles), and turn left at the T-junction. You'll find the Thornybush Nature Reserve Gate on your right after approximately 4 km (2.5 miles). There are regularly scheduled flights from Johannesburg to Hoedspruit Airport and from Johannesburg, Durban, and Cape Town to Skukuza Airport and Kruger Mpumalanga International Airport on Airlink (lodge transfers can be arranged).

Hotels

★ Saseka Tented Camp

$$$$ | **ALL-INCLUSIVE** | Home to the sexiest tents in the Greater Kruger, this fresh addition to Thornybush delivers unparalleled glamping, for this is no mere tent; it is an ode to the outdoors (but with the comforts of in-room Wi-Fi and air conditioning). **Pros:** unusual and original design; spacious and private suites out of earshot; tracker and guide teams swiftly unearth sightings. **Cons:** thick bush and fallen trees makes off-road driving more difficult; no safari extras, such as a bird book; the lodge still has single-use plastic water bottles. [$] *Rooms from: R39000* ✉ *Kruger National Park* ☎ *011/253–6500* 🌐 *www.thornybush.com* 🛏 *10 suites* 🍴 *All-Inclusive.*

Thornybush Game Lodge

$$$$ | **ALL-INCLUSIVE** | **FAMILY** | Opened in 1961, Thornybush Game Lodge is the oldest and largest in the collection, and despite its size (sleeps 40), the outstanding reputation for refined relaxation and thrilling sightings endures. **Pros:** on-site spa; excellent sightings and off-road game viewing; candle-lit dinners. **Cons:** up to eight people per vehicle; emphasis on (only) ticking off the Big Five; bigger, less intimate lodge. [$] *Rooms from: R24000* ✉ *Kruger National Park* ☎ *011/253–6500* 🌐 *www.thornybush.com* 🛏 *20 suites* 🍴 *All-Inclusive.*

Index

538

Photo Credits

Front Cover: Michal Krakowiak/spooh/GettyImages [Description: Camps Bay near Cape Town, South Africa]. **Back cover, from left to right:** Paco Como/Shutterstock, Alexeys/iStockphoto, Shams/iStockphoto. **Spine:** Richard Cavalleri/Shutterstock. **Interior, from left to right:** Simonhack/Dreamstime.com (1). Ollyy/Shutterstock (2-3). **Chapter 1: Experience South Africa:** Kavram/Shutterstock (6-7). Dereje/Shutterstock (8-9). Giuseppemasci/Dreamstime (9). Franschhoek Wine Tram (9). Frank Kahts / Alamy (10). Michaeljung / istockphoto (10). Fabian von Poser/imageBROKER/Agefotostock (10). Ken C Moore / Shutterstock (10). Shaen Adey/agefotostock (11). Johan Swanepoel / Shutterstock (11). Hel080808/Dreamstime (11). Iwan Baan (11). Claude Huot/Shutterstock (12).South African Tourism (12). Americanspirit/ Dreamstime (12). Matthew de Lange/iStockphoto (12). Tuxone/Dreamstime (13). Timwege/Dreamstime (13). Bennymarty/iStockphoto (14). TCS Photography/Shutterstock (14). South African Tourism (14). South African Tourism (14). South African Tourism (15). Kletr/Shutterstock (18). EcoPrint/Shutterstock (18). Louis Lotter Photography/Shutterstock (18). BrettDurrant/iStockphoto (18). Martin Prochazkacz/Shutterstock (18). Daleen Loest/Shutterstock (19). EcoPic/iStockphoto (19). EcoPic/iStockphoto (19). Bashutskyy/ Shutterstock (19). South African Tourism (19). Turbine Boutique Hotel & Spa (20). Speekhout Tree House (20). Manuel Zublena (20). Kruger Shalati (21). Jodie Bedeker (21). Siamionau pavel/Shutterstock (22). Ezume Images/Shutterstock (23). South African Tourism (24). Giuseppemasci/Dreamstime (24). Chamillewhite/ Dreamstime (24). Da Gama Textiles (24). Solwazi Afi Olusola/Luangisa African Gallery (25). Neilbrad/Dreamstime (32). **Chapter 3: Cape Town:** Hongqi Zhang (aka Michael Zhang)/Dreamstime (61). Kiev Victor/Shutterstock (77). EQRoy/ Shutterstock (79). Leonardospencer/ Dreamstime (86). Philip Massie/iStockphoto (91). Moobatto/Shutterstock (94). Wirestock/Dreamstime (116). Etiennefourie/Dreamstime (124). John Martin Media/Shutterstock (128). **Chapter 4: Cape Peninsula:** Juergen Wallstabe/ Dreamstime (141). Andrea Willmore/Shutterstock (144). LMspencer/Shutterstock (145). Sunshine Seeds/Shutterstock (145). Michael Turner/Dreamstime (146). Frand Gartner (Franky242)/ Dreamstime (155). Kumar Sriskandan / Alamy Stock Photo (157). Kavram/Shutterstock (166). Michaeljung/Shutterstock (169). **Chapter 5: The Western Cape and Winelands:** Hpbfotos/Dreamstime (171). PhotoSky/Shutterstock (174). Hel080808/ Dreamstime (175). Maria- groth/Dreamstime (175). Hel080808/Dreamstime (176). Gerrit Rautenbach/ Dreamstime (177). David Steele/ Dreamstime (187). Fivepointsix/ Shutterstock (216). Roger de la Harpe/Shutterstock (220). A.Emson/Shutterstock (227). René de Klerk/ iStockphoto (229). Grobler du Preez/ Shutterstock (237). Chops_express/Shutterstock (239). Nadine Klose/Shutterstock (241). Wirestock/Dreamstime (243). **Chapter 6: The Northern Cape:** Clint Austin/Shutterstock (247). Vladislav Gajic/Shutterstock (263). Clifford Wort/ Shutterstock (269). EcoPrint/Shutterstock (270). Foto Mous/Shutterstock (280). Aberson/ iStockphoto (285). **Chapter 7: The Garden Route and the Little Karoo:** Dominiquedela- croix/ iStockphoto (289). GroblerduPreez/iStockphoto (298). Domossa/Dreamstime (312). Majonit/Shutterstock (314). Andrea Willmore/ Shutterstock (317). **Chapter 8: The Eastern Cape:** Matt Gorlei/Shutterstock (321). Thula-photography/iStockphoto (339). Gunter Nuyts/ Shutterstock (342). Arnold Petersen/Shutterstock (349). Vanessa Bentley/Shutterstock (351). **Chapter 9: Durban and KwaZulu-Natal:** Kelly Ermis/Shutterstock (363). Shams/Shutterstock (380). Grant Pitcher/Shutterstock (386). Icswart/iStockphoto (407). Lois GoBe/Shutterstock (407). Karel Gallas/Shutterstock (419). PhotoSky/Shutterstock (425). **Chapter 10: Johannesburg:** Rich Townsend Photography/iStockphoto (431). Gil.K/Shutterstock (443). Finn stock/Shutterstock (449). Gil.K/Shutterstock (452). Rich T Photo/Shutterstock (458). Africa Media Online / Alamy Stock Photo (472). Martin Mecnarowski/Shutterstock (477). **Chapter 11: Mpumalanga and Kruger National Park:** Jennifer622/ Dreamstime.com (483). Jens_Bee/Shutterstock (496). Daniele Codegoni//Dreamstime (499). Vaclav Sebek/Shutterstock (500). WitR/Shut- terstock (502). Shams F Amir/Shutterstock (504). **About Our Writers:** All photos are courtesy of the writers except for the following: Keith Bain, courtesy of Craig Pusey; Iga Motylska, courtesy of Nicola Lavin; and Melanie van Zyl, courtesy of Teagan Cunniffe.

*Every effort has been made to trace the copyright holders, and we apologize in advance for any accidental errors. We would be happy to apply the corrections in the following edition of this publication.

Notes

Notes

Notes

Fodor's ESSENTIAL SOUTH AFRICA

Publisher: Stephen Horowitz, *General Manager*

Editorial: Douglas Stallings, *Editorial Director;* Jill Fergus, Amanda Sadlowski, Caroline Trefler, *Senior Editors*; Kayla Becker, Alexis Kelly, *Editors;* Angelique Kennedy-Chavannes, *Assistant Editor*

Design: Tina Malaney, *Director of Design and Production*; Jessica Gonzalez, *Graphic Designer*

Production: Jennifer DePrima, *Editorial Production Manager;* Elyse Rozelle, *Senior Production Editor;* Monica White, *Production Editor*

Maps: Rebecca Baer, *Senior Map Editor;* Mark Stroud (Moon Street Cartography), *Cartographer*

Photography: Viviane Teles, *Senior Photo Editor;* Namrata Aggarwal, Payal Gupta, Ashok Kumar, *Photo Editors;* Eddie Aldrete, *Photo Production Intern*

Business and Operations: Chuck Hoover, *Chief Marketing Officer;* Robert Ames, *Group General Manager;* Devin Duckworth, *Director of Print Publishing*

Public Relations and Marketing: Joe Ewaskiw, *Senior Director of Communications and Public Relations*

Fodors.com: Jeremy Tarr, *Editorial Director;* Rachael Levitt, *Managing Editor*

Technology: Jon Atkinson, *Director of Technology;* Rudresh Teotia, *Lead Developer;* Jacob Ashpis, *Content Operations Manager*

Writers: Keith Bain, Lucy Corne, Mary Fawzy, Barbara Noe Kennedy, Iga Motylska, Kate Turkington, Tara Turkington, Melanie van Zyl

Editors: Alexis Kelly (lead editor), Laura M. Kidder, Mark Sullivan

Production Editor: Elyse Rozelle

Copyright © 2022 by Fodor's Travel, a division of MH Sub I, LLC, dba Internet Brands.

Fodor's is a registered trademark of Internet Brands, Inc. All rights reserved. Published in the United States by Fodor's Travel, a division of Internet Brands, Inc. No maps, illustrations, or other portions of this book may be reproduced in any form without written permission from the publisher.

2nd Edition

ISBN 978-1-64097-356-5

ISSN 2574-3546

All details in this book are based on information supplied to us at press time. Always confirm information when it matters, especially if you're making a detour to visit a specific place. Fodor's expressly disclaims any liability, loss, or risk, personal or otherwise, that is incurred as a consequence of the use of any of the contents of this book.

SPECIAL SALES

This book is available at special discounts for bulk purchases for sales promotions or premiums. For more information, e-mail SpecialMarkets@fodors.com.

PRINTED IN THE UNITED STATES OF AMERICA

10 9 8 7 6 5 4 3 2 1

About Our Writers

 A Cape Town-based journalist and travel writer, **Keith Bain** is the editor of *Getaway,* South Africa's longest-running travel magazine. He got his start in writing as an author of guidebooks to India, South Africa, Italy, Eastern Europe, Ireland, and East Africa, all of which involved long periods on the road, a prospect he loves. During his earlier life in academia, he taught theater and filmmaking to university students. He updated the Northern Cape and Eastern Cape chapters for this book.

 Lucy Corne is a freelance writer focusing on travel, food, and beer. Originally from the UK, she fell in love with Cape Town at the end of a long overland trip through Africa and moved to South Africa in 2010. She's written for an array of guide books, magazines, and newspapers and is the editor of South Africa's only beer magazine. You can find her on Twitter @LucyCorne. She updated the Western Cape and Winelands chapter of this guide.

 Mary Fawzy is a freelance food and culture writer. She updated the Cape Town and Cape Peninsula chapters. You can find her on Instagram @purple_turnips.

 Barbara Noe Kennedy left her longtime position as senior editor with NatGeo Travel Publishing in 2015 to go freelance full-time. She writes about travel for Fodor's Travel, Lonely Planet, BBC Travel, and the *Washington Post*, among others. She resides in Arlington, Virginia, but her heart is in Africa, where she volunteers at an orphanage in Zambia and spends as much time as she can exploring southern Africa. She updated the Experience and Travel Smart chapters.

 Johannesburg-based journalist and photographer **Iga Motylska** has collected passport stamps from over 40 countries in search of World Heritage Sites, culinary delights, and cultural experiences. Her adventures have seen her travel India by rail, hunt (and eat) scorpions in Laos, trace dinosaur tracks in Bolivia, scuba dive with turtles in Reunion, and write about it all for over 50 publications. At the end of the day, it's always good to return home to Mzansi. You can follow her adventures at her website ⊕ *www.eagerjourneys.com,* on Instagram @igamotylska, and on TikTok @eagerjourneys. She updated the Johannesburg chapter.

 Kate Turkington is one of South Africa's best-known broadcasters and travel writers. Like Shakespeare's Puck, she has girdled the world but her heart remains in Africa. She's been there, done that in African countries from Ghana to Lesotho, from Uganda to Morocco, from Burkino Faso to Ethiopia. But South Africa is home where she shares her travels with her four children, nine grandchildren, and assorted rescue dogs. Visit her website ⊕ *www.kateturkington.com* to follow along. She updated the Garden Route and Little Karoo chapter for this edition.

About Our Writers

Tara Turkington is an experienced travel writer and photographer. A qualified tour guide, she has lived in four of South Africa's nine provinces and has been writing for Fodor's since the mid-1990s. Aside from her passion for travel, she runs an award-winning communications company with her sister, Tiffany, called Flow Communications. Nothing makes her happier than being in the African bushveld. She updated the MalaMala Game Reserve and Madikwe Game Reserve content for this edition.

A qualified field guide, diver, and budding birder, **Melanie van Zyl** is a sucker for the wilderness and the creatures that inhabit it, and she greatly admires the people living on its peripheries. She's got a soft spot for responsible travel, impactful design, and sustainably sharing the environment with the natural world. Her stories aim to respectfully uplift the voices of Africa—humanity's home. You can follow her on Instagram @melaniejanevz, on Twitter @melanie_vanzyl, and at ⊕ *www.melanievanzyl. com*. She updated the Durban and KwaZulu-Natal and Mpumalanga and Kruger National Park chapters.